PRACTICAL HOMICIDE INVESTIGATION

TACTICS, PROCEDURES, AND FORENSIC TECHNIQUES

THIRD EDITION

CRC SERIES IN
**PRACTICAL ASPECTS OF CRIMINAL
AND FORENSIC INVESTIGATIONS**

VERNON J. GEBERTH, M.S., M.P.S., B.B.A., FBINA *Series Editor*

PRACTICAL HOMICIDE INVESTIGATION

TACTICS, PROCEDURES, AND FORENSIC TECHNIQUES

T H I R D   E D I T I O N

VERNON J. GEBERTH, M.S., M.P.S., B.B.A., FBINA

Lieutenant Commander (Retired)
New York City Police Department

CRC Press
Boca Raton Boston London New York Washington, D.C.

Joel Claypool:	Publisher
Felicia Shapiro:	Associate Editor
Paul Gottehrer:	Assistant Managing Editor, EDP
Shayna Murry:	Cover Designer
William J. Boone, Jr.:	Marketing Manager, Direct Marketing
Greg Daurelle:	Director, Marketing Management
Gary Bennett, Kevin Luong, Carlos Esser, Greg Cuciak:	Pre-Press
Sheri Schwartz:	Manufacturing Assistant

Library of Congress Cataloging-in-Publication Data

Geberth, Vernon J.
  Practical homicide investigation : tactics, procedures, and forensic techniques / Vernon J. Geberth.
  --3rd ed.
        p.   cm.
  Includes bibliographical references and index.
  ISBN 0-8493-8156-8 (alk. paper)
    1. Homicide investigation--United States. I. Title.
  HV8079.H6G4 1996
  363.2′59523—dc20   96-14023
                                                                                    CIP

No claim to original U.S. Government works
International Standard Book Number 0-8493-8156-8
Library of Congress Card Number 96-14023
Printed in the United States of America   3 4 5 6 7 8 9 0
Printed on acid-free paper

This book is dedicated to
the men and women entrusted with the profound duty
and responsibility of investigating sudden and violent death.

In memory of those *innocent* victims of homicide
and their surviving families, who must find the
strength to go on without their loved ones.

May justice prevail

The Lord God said. . .

𝕿𝖍𝖔𝖚 𝕾𝖍𝖆𝖑𝖙 𝕹𝖔𝖙 𝕶𝖎𝖑𝖑

THE FIFTH COMMANDMENT   Book of Exodus, 20 of THE HOLY BIBLE

THE OATH OF
PRACTICAL HOMICIDE INVESTIGATION

HOMICIDE INVESTIGATION IS A PROFOUND DUTY. AS AN OFFICER ENTRUSTED WITH SUCH A DUTY, IT IS INCUMBENT UPON YOU TO DEVELOP AN UNDERSTANDING OF THE DYNAMICS AND PRINCIPLES OF PROFESSIONAL HOMICIDE INVESTIGATION.

PRACTICAL HOMICIDE INVESTIGATION SUGGESTS THAT "THINGS BE DONE RIGHT THE FIRST TIME", AND "KNOWLEDGE IS POWER". KNOWLEDGE WHICH HAS BEEN ENHANCED WITH EXPERIENCE, FLEXIBILITY AND COMMON SENSE.

PRACTITIONERS MUST BE PREPARED TO USE TACTICS, PROCEDURES, AND FORENSIC TECHNIQUES IN THEIR PURSUIT OF THE TRUTH: AND THEN FOLLOW THE COURSE OF EVENTS AND THE FACTS AS THEY ARE DEVELOPED TO THEIR ULTIMATE CONCLUSION.

DEATH INVESTIGATION CONSTITUTES A HEAVY RESPONSIBILITY, AND AS SUCH, LET NO PERSON DETER YOU FROM THE TRUTH AND YOUR OWN PERSONAL COMMITMENT TO SEE THAT JUSTICE IS DONE. NOT ONLY FOR THE DECEASED, BUT FOR THE SURVIVING FAMILY AS WELL.
      AND REMEMBER; "YOU'RE WORKING FOR GOD."

Lt. Cmdr. (Ret.) VERNON J. GEBERTH
NEW YORK CITY POLICE DEPARTMENT
FORMER COMMANDING OFFICER
BRONX HOMICIDE TASK FORCE

© Vernon J. Geberth, 1988

Contents

Editor's Note

This textbook is part of a series entitled "Practical Aspects of Criminal and Forensic Investigation". This series was created by Vernon J. Geberth, a retired New York City Police Department Lieutenant Commander, who is an author, educator, and consultant on homicide and forensic investigations.

This series has been designed to provide contemporary, comprehensive, and pragmatic information to the practitioner involved in criminal and forensic investigations by authors who are nationally recognized experts in their respective fields.

Foreword

"Investigating a homicide is both an art and a science, a blend of the practical and the scientific. Without that realization, and that blend which includes a coordinated effort by a team of specialists, the chance of a successful case solution is greatly diminished."

I remember having a discussion with a group of homicide detectives in England about the difference between a detective and an investigator. It went something like this, All detectives might be called investigators, but not all investigators can be called detectives. Investigators need a trail of investigative factors which might eventually lead to a successful conclusion of their inquiry. If there are no investigative factors to pursue then they are finished. That is where the detective comes in; a person who can paint a landscape he or she has never seen from inside a darkened room, which is actually the crime scene. That's the difference between the craft and the art."

P.R.B.

Vernon Geberth, a former New York City homicide commander and a personal friend of mine for many years, is not only an experienced and knowledgeable violent crimes investigator, he is a very talented writer and lecturer on the subject. The first edition of this book, *Practical Homicide Investigation: Tactics, Procedures, and Forensic Techniques,* was proclaimed "The Bible" of homicide investigations, and his many articles on the investigation of violent crime and criminal behavior continue to be read by police officers throughout the country.

This Third Edition has been expanded to the level of an encyclopedia of death investigation and should be considered as an integral text for anyone involved in the criminal justice system. The text is not only essential to the criminal justice student and the police academy trainee, but should also be on the reading list for uniformed officers who are invariably first to arrive on scene, as well as all newly assigned detectives.

Experienced homicide investigators will find this text book to be an indispensable and valuable resource as well as reminder that regardless of how many crime scenes we process, we never stop learning. I am also quite sure that members of the court and bar will have occasion to use the book as a reference and to judge the quality and integrity of procedures and techniques used by the police in a major case investigation.

The text is exceptionally well organized. Chapters 1 through 8 chronologically define all aspects of the initial investigation on scene. Chapters 9 through 22 focus on special procedures and techniques that must always be considered in a major crime investigation. Vernon has added additional new chapters on Suicide Investigation, which has been greatly expanded as well as Narcotics-Related Homicides and Homosexual Homicide Investigation. I congratulate him on his chapter regarding Death Notifications. Vernon and I both share a deep commitment to the the surviving family, who are the secondary victims of homicide. This very important function is oftentimes glanced over and/ or neglected in police texts. The death notification protocol in this book should be followed by any officer charged with the responsibility of making notifications to surviving families.

The revised chapters on The Homicide Crime Scene which focuses on "Staged Crime Scenes; Sex-Related Homicides; Investigative Assessment; and Identification of Suspects are highly informative and will alert even the most experienced investigator of the mind—set pitfalls that can occur in the investigation of equivocal deaths.

Good crime scene photos are the next best to being on scene. Many photographs used in this edition are presented for the first time. Perhaps not for the faint hearted, each photo presents one or more lessons in the importance of "detail observation" while processing a crime scene. Comments made in the chapter on management and supervision of a criminal investigation are long overdue. Vernon identifies traditional problems and suggests practical solutions. Additionally, information to consider in establishing written policy and procedures is included.

Vernon, whose experience with DNA cases fully qualifies him to present information related to this particular process of identification from the viewpoint of the police homicide investigator, has revised and updated the DNA section. His case study examples of genetic fingerprint comparison and his "Preservation Sample and Minimum

Amounts" checklist provide important information for those involved in the investigation of violent crime.

This book leaves no question that now, more than ever, a homicide investigation must be based on a mix of the practical and the scientific. In fact, the new chapters and revised materials along with the descriptive photos in this text combined with the procedures and techniques outlined in Vernon's Second Edition will place this edition in the category of a police text classic, an authoritative standard on the subject and make this book the most complete homicide textbook available on the market today.

Pierce R. Brooks
Captain, L.A.P.D. (Ret.)

Preface

This Third Edition of *Practical Homicide Investigation: Tactics, Procedures, and Forensic Techniques* provides the most practical and conventional information available to detectives responsible for conducting intelligent investigations into violent and sudden death.

This revised text is based on my 31 years of law enforcement experience. Formerly a New York City detective, detective supervisor, homicide commander, and now a nationwide consultant, I have integrated this knowledge with my associations with experts in the sphere of forensic science and criminal investigation. I include personal interviews from other homicide authorities, and present an extensive search of forensic literature offering as many actual case histories as possible. *My intention is to provide a comprehensive and practical resource text that will serve as an investigation guide to the homicide professional.*

Professional Homicide Investigation: A Personal Perspective

Homicide investigation is a profound duty with awesome responsibilities. It requires the professional homicide detective to develop an understanding of the dynamics of human behavior as well as the essential details of professional investigation.

The world of the homicide detective is permeated with human tragedies which involve a variety of sudden and violent death scenarios. Many of these events, which are seemingly beyond the comprehension of the average person, reveal motivations and patterns of repetition which are recognized by the experienced homicide detective. Professional homicide investigators become keenly aware of the reality of death and the impact it has on both society and the surviving family.

In fact, we in homicide have a *mission*. Our mission is to bring justice to the deceased and their surviving family. We do this by conducting a professional and intelligent investigation which results in the identification and apprehension of the killer and the successful prosecution of the case.

In order to conduct an efficient and effective investigation, the detective first concentrates on the mechanical aspects of the death, i.e., motives and methods, wound structures, crime scene reconstruction, the cause, manner and time of death, as well as other factors that provide clues to the dynamics of the event.

The professional homicide investigator must learn to deal with death in a clinical manner. Detectives should afford themselves with an emotional insulation by not projecting a personality into the body. *Personally speaking, if you begin to look upon that body as your wife, daughter, son, mother, or father you are going to lose that professional objectivity which is so necessary in the murder inquiry.* My way of dealing with the reality of sudden and violent death is a strong belief in God and a belief in a higher order of things in our existence. My theology informs me that there is an afterlife and I believe that the soul of the murder victim has left the body.

In order to function effectively, it is imperative that the detectives have strong ego defense mechanisms which allow them to engage in isolation of affect through intellectualization. This is not meant to suggest that homicide practitioners can avoid personal feelings about the tragedy. Instead, it allows a professional investigator to focus and concentrate on the dynamics of the event and not become emotionally involved in the crime.

Teamwork and Communication

Another component in homicide investigations are the human behavior factors with present themselves during the course of the inquiry. The interpersonal relationships among and between professionals involved in death investigations are varied. The professional homicide detective must be willing to work as a team player who engenders cooperation by his or her own conduct and behavior. The ability to communicate with different types of personalities and effectively interview and interrogate murder suspects is paramount to a professional homicide investigation.

A professional homicide investigator is someone who is a "Truth Seeker." Someone who is not opinionated, tainted with prejudice, or prone to prejudgment. There is a need for patience and flexibility in homicide investigation. Part of the inquiry is directed towards the elimination of suspects as well as the inclusion.

A professional homicide practitioner cannot be an individual with a "lock-and-load" mentality. The true professional must possess a flexible type of personality that is open to new suggestions, ideas, and concepts that arise in these fluid types of investigations. The detective looks for consistencies as well as inconsistencies and must be prepared to change the focus of the investigation as new information is developed.

The bottom line is that we in homicide are an information-seeking body. Physical evidence such as hairs, fibers, blood stains, and other materials that are gathered are useless unless you have established a base population of suspects to compare it to.

As we prepare to enter the 21st century with advanced forensic and technological changes within the law enforcement community, we should be cognizant of an important prerequisite. In my professional opinion, "The investigation of homicide and the initial actions taken by the police at the homicide crime scene will and/or may eventually determine whether or not the crime is ever solved or the guilty person brought to justice."

Computerized law enforcement data-based systems, which include N.C.I.C., VI-CAP, R.I.S.S., HITS, and other intelligence networks, have provided state-of-the-art electronic technology to the criminal investigator.

The scientific community has developed forensic techniques that put criminal investigation on the cutting edge of science. Over the last few years we have witnessed the potential of DNA technology, which promises to be the future of forensic law enforcement operations.

It should be noted, however, that these advanced technologies will never replace the homicide detective.

The basic criminal investigative techniques stressed in *Practical Homicide Investigation: Tactics, Procedures, and Forensic Techniques,* Third Edition are essential for effective inquiry into sudden and violent death.

The homicide detective, in order to be successful, must have an eye for details and the ability to recognize and evaluate evidence. He or she must have an above-average intelligence in order to absorb the many details that arise. And, most importantly, he or she must be able to effectively interview and interrogate the many different persons with whom he or she will come into contact.

In my opinion, the ingredients of an effective homicide investigation are *flexibility* and *common sense.*

The investigation of murder necessitates a certain tenacity and perseverance that transcends the ordinary investigative pursuit. Homicides are usually solved because the detective cares. The homicide detective becomes the advocate for the victim and the surviving family. That explains how a case three, five, and fifteen years old is eventually solved.

Solving homicides, especially those without witnesses are extremely more difficult to solve because your main witness, the deceased, is dead. One must develop the ability to "absorb" the crime scene, and be able to read the uncollectible nuances of the event. This would include the psychodynamics, which are the underlying motivations and human emotions, as well as indications of the deliberate "staging" of the scene in order to mislead or redirect the investigation.

Homicide investigation is an aggressive business. Not everyone is qualified for the mission-oriented commitment of death investigation. *Your* homicide case is *yours* forever. It may stay with you throughout your career and sometimes your life. I know this because I have been there.

You must be prepared to use tactics and strategies for any given situation. Skilled interrogation is paramount to the successful investigation of murder. "Good-guy and bad-guy" scenarios never grow old. Any number of tactics might be employed in seeking the truth, and the limit is only set by your imagination, initiative, and the boundaries of the law.

A homicide investigator is street-smart and book-wise. The knowledge that he or she develops must then be further enhanced with experience, flexibility, and common sense.

Many factors complicate effective investigation, such as interpersonal conflicts, politics, or the classic scenario of bureaucracy, hypocrisy, and utter incompetence of certain persons in public agencies. Additionally, it could be the apathy and indifference of society or the ludicrous over-concern regarding the defendant's rights by the courts. In any event, the homicide detective must be able to overcome these obstacles and concentrate on what results he or she can obtain from the scene, and pursue the case with dedication and perseverance.

This text begins with a comprehensive discussion of the homicide crime scene, and evolves chronologically from the initial notification to police that a homicide has occured, to how the police should react to this notification, and to what procedural steps are necessary in order to conduct an intelligent homicide investigation.

The early chapters act as an instructional guide to the patrol officer, including *A Patrol Officer's Checklist*. The text then proceeds into the details of criminal investigation at the scene. I have added a revised *Investigator's Homicide Checklist* that helps officers review their own actions at the scene and refreshes their respective memories.

The book then delves into the more technical aspects of homicide investigation, augmented by additional pictures and illustrations with pertinent case histories, which graphically portray exactly what to look for and what to do at the crime scene.

I have added four new chapters to this Third Edition and have revised each of the original chapters from the First Edition. I have revised all of the current chapters from the Second Edition and added an entirely new updated section on DNA technology. I have added additional wound structure and injury photographs to aid the practitioner in properly assessing the mode of death and there are a number of new photographs and case histories to assist the investigator in understanding the dynamics of homicide investigation.

One of the additional chapters deal with Death Notifications and the surviving families of homicide victims. In fact, it should be noted that the homicide detective, in addition to pursuing the case, becomes the advocate for both the deceased and the surviving family throughout the entire process. An entire chapter on Suicide Investigation was added because of the dynamics of suicide and the many additional considerations that these type cases entail. In addition, new chapters on Narcotics-related homicides and Homosexual Homicide Investigations were added to this Third Edition.

The Sex-Related Homicide Investigation chapter has been greatly expanded along with The Investigative Assessment Through Criminal Profiling chapter, which has been revised and expanded in the Third Edition, to enable the investigator to recognize the different classifications of sex-related death and enable the detective to make an early assessment of possible suspects based on the psychodynamics of the event.

The chapter on Management has been restructured to provide guidance to police administrators on the make-up and mission of the investigative unit that handles the homicide investigation including a section on formulating an Apprehension Team to effect the arrest of homicide fugitives.

There is a *Supervisor's Homicide Checklist* to help field supervisors to properly coordinate and direct activities at the crime scene.

I also include a complete *Police-Related Shooting Checklist* that provides the police manager with recommendations on effective documentation of crucial information later used in departmental review. The procedure defined in this checklist is absolutely essential in the event of any subsequent civil action against the agency.

A new and expanded Glossary of Terms has been added to aid the reader with the many medical, anatomical, scientific, technical, and psychological terminology within the text along with street terms and subcultural references as they relate to behavior.

This revised edition stresses the basics, indicates the practicalities of certain investigative techniques, and provides the reader with patterns upon which to build a solid foundation for a prosecutable case. There is deliberate repetition throughout the text: I have strategically placed these cues throughout because certain investigative principles can never be stressed enough.

In real life, you get only one shot at the homicide crime scene and a limited opportunity to question the suspect. Therefore, I recommend that the reader follow the *investigative checklists* and *basic principles* in this text. Remember, things are not always as they appear to be; and do it right the first time, you only get one chance.

Death investigation constitutes a heavy responsibility, and as such, no person, system, nor circumstance should deter you from the truth and your own personal commitment to see that justice is done; not only for the deceased, but for the surviving family as well. That is why my personal philosophy as a murder cop is, *Remember; "We work for God."*

Vernon J. Geberth

Acknowledgments

I wish to personally acknowledge and thank the many people and agencies who have contributed to the *Third Edition* of *Practical Homicide Investigation: Tactics, Procedures, and Forensic Techniques.* Their professional expertise, suggestions, photos, case histories, and reviews encouraged me to successfully complete this third edition, which has been considerably expanded beyond the second edition of my textbook.

I have listed these persons in alphabetical order. I sincerely apologize to anyone I may have inadvertantly ommitted.

Milton Agay, Lieutenant, Benton Harbor Police Department, Benton Harbor, Michigan. Richard Agnoletto, Technician, Bronx District Attorney's Office Video Unit. Greg Allman, Investigator, Morris County Prosecutor's Office, Morris County, New Jersey. James Alsup, Director, Public Agency Training Council. Anthony Ambrose, Sergeant, Former Homicide Detective Newark, N.J. Police Department. Jack Annon, Ph.D., Psychologist. Ellen Arker, Marketing, Manager of National Accounts, CRC Press, Boca Raton, Florida. Kathryn Artingstall, Detective, Orlando, Florida Police Department. Mary Ellen Beekman, F.B.I. Agent, Federal Bureau of Investigation, New York Office. Joseph Beffa, Det. Sgt., City of St. Louis Police Department, Homicide Division. Bergen County Prosecutor's Office, Bergen County, New Jersey. Tom Bevel, Captain, Oklahoma City Police Department, Ray Biondi, Lieutenant(Ret.), Homicide Bureau; Sacramento County California, Sheriff's Department. Robert Bisbee, Retired Detective, N.Y.P.D. Robert Bittle, Det. Sgt. (Ret.), Judicial Investigator; 12th Prosecutorial District State of North Carolina. Retired from the Cumberland County Sheriff's Department. Fayetteville, N.C. Mike Blakely, Sheriff, Limestone County Sheriff's Office, Athens, Alabama. Frank Bolz, Captain (Ret.), Founder of Hostage Negotiations, New York City Police Department. Gary M. Borman, Det. Sgt., Squad Commander — Detective Bureau, New York City Police Department. Sam Bowerman, Detective, Baltimore County, Homicide Criminal Profiler. Robert M. Boyd, (late) Retired Commander Homicide Squad, Metropolitan Police Department, Washington, D.C. William Brinkhous, Investigator, Office of the Chief Medical Examiner, Chapel Hill, North Carolina. Charles S. Brofman, Attorney, Former Bureau Chief and Prosecutor, Bronx District Attorney's Office. Pierce Brooks, Captain (Ret.), Los Angeles, California Police Department and National Homicide Consultant. Larry C. Brubaker, FBI, Supervisory Special Agent, Minneapolis, Minnesota Office. Bureau of Alcohol, Tobacco, And Firearms — U.S. Treasury. Bruce Cameron, Editorial Director *Law & Order Magazine*, Wilmette, Illinois. Homer, Campbell, D.D.S., Secretary, American Board of Forensic Odontologist, Odontology. Donald Casey, Detective, New York City Transit Police. Robert Cates, Detective, Cooper City, Florida Police Department. Thomas C. Childrey, S.B.I., Assistant Supervisor, North Carolina State Bureau of Investigation. Victor Cipullo, Detective, Bronx District Attorney's Office, New York City Police Department. City of New York Police Department's Detective Bureau. Dennis Clay, Detective, Grand Prairie, Texas Police Department. Joel Claypool, Publisher, CRC Press, Boca Raton, Florida. Richard Collins, Detective (Ret.), New York City Police Department. Criminal Investigations Division (C.I.D.) U.S. Army. Matthew T. Coyne, C.P.A., Certified Public Accountant, friend, and financial advisor. Thomas Cronin, Captain, Chicago Police Department. John T. Croston, Homicide Detective Retired. Bronx Homicide Task Force, New York City Police Department. Victor Cruz, Det. Sgt. (Ret.), Homicide — Bronx Detective Area, Squad Commander 42 PDU. Clint Daniels, Retired Detective, Morgue Division — New York City Police Department. Jerry Dargan, Captain, Hudson County Prosecutor's Office, Homicide Unit. Edward Deacy, Detective (Ret.), New York City Police Department, Vocalist — National Anthem. John B. Dean, Lieutenant, Waterford Township Police Department, Waterford, Michigan. Delaware State Police Homicide Unit. Frank Del Prete, Lieutenant (Ret.), Bergen County Prosecutor's Office, Bergen County, New Jersey. John Delventhal, Consultant, Former Inspector General NYC EMS. Edward Denning, Captain, Bergen County Prosecutor's Office, Bergen County, New Jersey. Detectives of the Former 7th Homicide Zone, South Bronx Squad, New York City Police Department's Detective Division. Gary A. Dias, Captain, Scientific Investigation Section, Honolulu, Hawaii Police Department. Jose A. Diaz,

Detective, Bronx District Attorney's Office, New York City Police Department. Park Elliot Dietz, M.D., Forensic Psychiatrist and Attorney, Threat Assessment Group. Orly DiLullo, Chief of Police, Liberty Police Department, Youngstown, Ohio. Dominick J. DiMaio, M.D., Pathologist, Former Chief Medical Examiner, City of New York. Vincent J. DiMaio, M.D., Pathologist, Chief Medical Examiner, Bexar County, Texas. David Dionne, Editor, Former Marketing Manager and Acquisitions Editor. Jim Dooley, Investigator(Ret.), Fairfax County Police Department, Fairfax, Virginia. John Dotson, Chief, Sparks, Nevada Police Department, (Former Homicide Commander, Wichita, Kansas). Paul Dotson, Lieutenant, Wichita Police Department — Homicide Bureau, Wichita, Kansas. Edwin T. Dreher, Retired Deputy Chief, Office of the Chief of Detectives, New York City Police Department. Drug Enforcement Administration — Quantico, Virginia. Fred Drummond, Laboratory Director, Forensic Science Laboratory, Westchester County Medical Examiner's Office. Joseph Dubinski, M.D., New York City Medical Examiner's Office — Tour Doctor. Elizabeth Duecker—Scovill Detective, St. Louis Police Department, Homicide Division. Stephen Dung, Det. Sgt., Honolulu Police Department, Homicide Detail. Anthony Dwyer, Detective Sergeant, Butler County, Ohio Sheriff's Office, Hamilton, Ohio. William G. Eckert, M.D., Former Medical Examiner Wichita, Kansas, Milton Helpern International Center for the Forensic Sciences. Harvey Eisner, Technician, Bronx District Attorney's Office, Video Unit. Alan Ellingsworth, Colonel, Former Commander Homicide Unit, Delaware State Police, Dover, Delaware. Don English, Lieutenant, Jefferson Parish Sheriff's Office, Metarie, Louisiana. Michael Essig, Detective, McLean County Sheriff's Office, Bloomington, Illinois. Terry M. Fail, Postal Inspector, United States Postal Inspections Service — California. Federal Aviation Administration — Washington, D.C. Federal Bureau of Investigation. James Ferrier, Captain, Milwaukee Police Department, C.O. Identification Section. Hal Fillinger, M.D., Forensic Pathologist. Florida Department of Law Enforcement — F.D.L.E. Thomas Fitzgerald, Detective (Ret.), New York City Police Department, 47 Precinct Detective Squad. Dale Foote, Detective (Ret.), Bellevue, Washington Police Department, Crimes Against Persons Section. Wade Ford, Sergeant, Texas Department of Public Safety. Robert W. Fox, Chief of Police, Sevierville Police Department, Sevierville, Tennessee. William F. Franks, Lieutenant, Stony Point, N.Y. Police Department. Kevin Freely, Homicide Detective, Bronx Detective Area — N.Y.P.D. Retired. Michael D. Gambrill, Chief, Former Homicide Commander, Baltimore County Police Department. James Gannon, Sergeant, Morris County Prosecutor's Office, Morris County, New Jersey.

Betty Pat. Gatliff, Forensic Sculpture. Beth Gilmer-Jones, Investigator, Geary County Sheriff's Department, Kansas. Keith Gill, Trooper, Indiana State Police. Arthur D. Goldman, D.D.S., Forensic Odontologist, Vice-President American Academy of Forensic Sciences. Thomas P. Gorden, Colonel, Chief — Department of Public Safety New Castle County, Delaware. Paul Gottehrer, Assistant Managing Editor, EDP, CRC Press, Inc. who edited this book. Edward Grant, Lieutenant, Criminal Profiler — New York State Police. Billy G. Green, Training Supervisor, North Carolina State Bureau of Investigation. Raliegh, North Carolina. Frank Griffen, Lieutenant, Homicide Investigator Connecticut State Police. Frank Guidice, Lieutenant, Homicide Commander — Nassau County Police Department. James J. Hackett, Lieutenant Colonel, Chief of Detectives, St. Louis, Missouri Police Department. George O. Haggerty, Det. Capt. (Ret.), New Castle County Department of Public Safety, New Castle County, Delaware. William Hagmaier, FBI, Supervisory Special Agent, Behavioral Science Unit, NCAVC, FBI Academy, Quantico, Virginia. Oscar Hale, Retired, Senior Police Administrative Aid — Bronx Detective Area, N.Y.C. Police Deparment, Bronx. Robert M. Harris, Homicide Detective, First Grade Detective (Ret.) — Bronx, Homicide, New York City Police Department. Robert R. Hazelwood, FBI, Supervisory Special Agent, Behavioral Science Unit, NCAVC, FBI Academy, Quantico, Virginia. Robert J. Hazen, FBI, Supervising Fingerprint Specialist, FBI Academy, Quantico, Virginia. James Hedrick, Detective, New Castle County Police Department, New Castle County, Delaware. Jack Henander, Investigator, Larimer County Sheriff's Department, Fort Collins, Colorado. Frank Henry, Detective (Ret.), New York City Police Department, Detective Division. Perry Hollowell, Lieutenant, Indiana Law Enforcement Academy. D'arcy Honer, Inspector, Peel Regional Police Force, Brampton, Ontario, Canada. Joseph Horgas, Detective, Arlington County Police Department, Arlington, Virginia. Millard Hyland, Chief Medical Examiner, County of Westchester, N.Y. Former Deputy Chief Medical Examiner, New York City. Harvey Jackson, Sergeant, Homicide Investigator, Salt Lake City, Utah Police Department. Ken Jako, Detective Sergeant, Kalamazoo County Sheriff's Department, Criminal Division. Sam Johnson, Police Officer (Ret.), Program Coordinator, Public Agency Training Council. Mike Johnson, Detective, Peoria, Illinois Police Department. Thomas, N. Jordan, Investigator, Bureau of Police Services, State College, Pennsylvania. Mary Jumbellic, M.D., Forensic Pathologist. Kansas Bureau of Investigation — Kansas. Kansas Law Enforcement Training Center — K.L.E.T.C. Nick T. Kaylor, Postal Inspector, United States Postal Inspections Service — California. Michael Kelty, Detective, T.A.R.U. Chief of Detective's Office New York City Police Department. Robert D. Kepple, Ph.D., Chief Criminal Investigator, Office of the Attorney General, State of Washington. Sherry Kiyler, Lieutenant, Phoenix, Arizona Police Department. Raymond F. Krolak, Det. Lt. (Ret.), Commander — Investigative Division, Colonie Police Department, Colonie, New York. Johnny Kulhman, Lieutenant, Oklahoma City, Oklahoma Police Department. Bruce LaBrie, Laboratory Specialist, Kalamazoo Police Department, Michigan. Jim Lander, Chief Deputy, Limestone County Sheriff's Office. Mel Lapidus, President, Rose Trunk Company, Brooklyn, N.Y. Henry, Lee, Dr. Ph.D., Chief, Forensic Science Laboratory, Connecticut State Police, Meriden, Connecticut. Andrew J. Leffew, Region 10 Detective Unit — Manistee, Detective Lieutenant, Manistee, Michigan. Lowell J. Levine, D.D.S., Forensic Odontologist, President American Academy of Forensic Sciences. Little, Steven Detective, Columbus, Ohio Police Department, Homicide Division. Robert Lloyd, Detective, Former Detroit Police Department Crime Scene Detective — Crime Scene Specialist, Thornton Police Department, Thorton, Colorado. Christopher Longueira, Chief Video Technician, Bronx District Attorney's Office, Video Unit. Andrew Lugo, Detective First Grade (Ret.), Bronx Homicide, City of New York Police Department's Detective Division, Formerly Assigned To 7th Homicide Zone. Leslie, I. Lukash, M.D., Forensic Pathologist, Chief Medical Examiner, Nassau County, New York. Frank MacAloon, Editor Emeritus, *Law and Order Magazine.* Anthony Magnetto, Sergeant, Troy, New York Police Department. Roz Malloy, Finest and Bravest Equipment. Maryland State Police, St. Mary's and Prince Georges County, Trooper Investigators. John Marzulli, Investigative Reporter, New York Daily News, New York City, New York. Richard Mask, Major, Nichol Hills, Oklahoma Police Department. Timothy McAuliffe, Captain, New York State Police. Thomas McCarren, Homicide Detective, Retired — New York City Police Department Detective Bureau. Earl McKee, Detective, University of Utah Police Department. Edward McNelley, Captain, Commanding Officer, Homicide Squad, Boston, Massachusetts Police Department. Bob Mehl, Detective, Quincy, Illinois Police Department. Mike Metcalf, Inspector, Peel Regional Police Force, Brampton, Ontario, Canada. John Miller, Commissioner (Ret.), Deputy Commissioner Press Information, New York City Police Department. Murray S. Miron, Dr. Ph.D., Syracuse University. Rick Morrarty, Captain, City of Killeen, Texas Police Captain Department. Morris County, New Jersey Prosecutor's Office — Detectives. Thomas J. Mullane, Homicide Detective, Detective, Frist Grade – Bronx Homicide, N.Y.P.D. Christopher D. Munger, FBI (Ret.), Special Agent, Training Coordinator, New York

Office of The FBI. Richard Munsey, Det. Lieutenant, Bath Township, Ohio Police Department. Naval Criminal Investigative Service. New Mexico State Police — Investigations Division. New York City Police Department — Officers and Members. New York State Police Bureau of Criminal Investigation. Frank Nicholosi, Detective (Ret.), Ballistics Expert Westchester County, Valhalla, New York, formerly N.Y.P.D. John Nolan, Lieutenant, Commanding Officer, Homicide, Nassau County Police Department. North Carolina State Bureau of Investigation. George Novotny, Acquisitions Editor, CRC Press, Inc. Thomas Nye, Captain, Director, NELEOA, Warwick, Rhode Island Police Department. Ocean County, New Jersey Prosecutor's Office. John P. O'Malley, Homicide Detective, Bronx Homicide Task Force, N.Y.P.D. Mike O'Malley, Detective, Cleveland, Ohio Police Department, Homicide Unit. Karlis Osis, Dr. Ph.D., Director, American Society of Psychical Research. Alan Patton, Detective, Grand Prairie, Texas Police Department. Pennsylvania State Police — Trooper Investigators. Sam Pennica, Investigator, North Carolina State Bureau of Investigation, Raliegh, North Carolina. James C. Peppard, Homicide Det. (Ret.), Apprehension Unit — Bronx Homicide Task Force — N.Y.P.D. Larry Petersen, Detective, King County, Washington Police Department. Michael Phillips, Evidence Technician, Arlington Police Department, Arlington, Texas. Raymond Pierce, Detective, Criminal Profiling Unit, New York City Police Department. Raymond Pietranico, Captain, New York City Police. Rod A. Piukkala, Inspector, Peel Regional Police Force, Brampton, Ontario, Canada. Vincent Pizzo, Deputy Chief (Ret.), New York City Housing Police Chief of Detectives. John W. Plansker, Inspector (Ret.), Former Homicide Zone Commander, Detective Commander Daos—Manhatten. Polaroid Corporation. James C. Power, Inspector, Commanding Officer, Manhatten North Detectives, New York City Police Department, Former Commander of Manhatten Homicide. Rueben Puente, Sergeant, Arlington, Texas Police Department Crime Scene Unit. Mark Prach, Lieutenant, Morris County Prosecutor's Office, Morristown, New Jersey. Mary Ann Pulchinski, Homicide Detective, New York City Police Department. John A. Reeder, Chief of Police, Chief of Police, Logan Township, Altoona, Pennsylvania. Martin Reiser, Dr. Ed.D., Hypnotist, Director of Behavioral Science Services, Los Angeles Police Department, Los Angeles, California. Ms. Noreen Renier, Psychic, Consultant to the FBI. Robert K. Ressler, FBI (Ret.), Supervisory Special Agent, Behavioral Science Unit, NCAVC, FBI Academy, Quantico, Virginia. Jack D. Reyes, Homicide Detective, New Castle County Department of Public Safety, New Castle County, Delaware. Yong Myun Rho, Dr. M.D., Pathologist, Deputy Chief Medical Examiner, City of New York. Peter Robbins, Deputy Chief, Former Commanding Officer, Detective Division, Greenwich, Connecticut Police Department. Richard Rogers, Lieutenant, Town of Haverstraw, N.Y. Police Department. John Roland, Reporter, Fox 5 News, New York City. Arnold Roussine, Detective First Grade, Police Department (Retired), Crime Scene Unit, City of New York. Nancy Ruhe-Munch, Director, Parents of Murdered Children. Thomas Salmon, Sgt. Tpr., Polygraph, New York State Police. Vincent Scalice, Detective (Ret.), Crime Scene Unit — New York City Police Department. Michael P. Scallin, Inspector, Criminal Investigation Division, Newport, Rhode Island Police Department. James Scaringe, Det. Sgt. (Ret.), Crime Scene Unit, City of New York Police Department. Harvey Schlossberg, Ph.D., Psychologist, Former New York City Police Department. Phillip Schnelwar, Judge, Former Homicide Bureau Chief — Bronx, District Attorney's Office. Ms. Monique Scofield, Psychic — Consultant. George Scroope, Homicide Detective, Retired Homicide Detective, 7th Homicide Zone, New York City Police Department. Stephen G. Scurti, Chief of Police, Retired. Stony Point, N.Y. Police Department. Joseph Scurto, Technician, Bronx District Attorney's Office Video Unit. James Sharkey, Detective Sergeant, New Castle County Department of Public Safety, New Castle County, Delaware. Robert Shaler, Ph.D., Director of Serology — City of New York Medical Examiner's Office. Former Director of Forensic Science Lifecodes Corporation, Valhalla, N.Y. National Expert on DNA technology. Harry L. Shapiro, Dr. Ph.D., Forensic Anthropologist, American Museum of Natural History. Robert Simmons, Detective, Portsmouth, Virginia Police Department. Marvin Skeen, Detective, Bellevue, Washington Police Department Crimes Against Persons Section. Robert J. Sklenarik, Det. Sgt. (Ret.), Squad Commander, New York City Police Department's Detective Division. Janice "JJ" Skinner, Senior P.A.A., My Gal "Friday" in the N.Y.P.D., New York City Police Department. Candice Skrapec, Psychologist, Fresno State University. Spencer R. Smith, Detective, Jackson County Coroner, Medford, Oregon, Chief Deputy Medical Examiner. Charles Snyder, Detective, Homicide Division, Akron, Ohio Police Department. Louis N. Sorkin, Forensic Entomologist, American Museum of Natural History. Richard T. Spooner, Major (Ret.), U.S. Marine Corps, Quantico, Virginia. Don Stephens, Lieutenant, Commanding Officer, Crime Scene Unit, New York City Police Department. Michael Strulick, Investigator, Edmonton Police Service, Alberta, Canada. Suffolk County, N.Y. Police Department's Homicide Squad. Suffolk County, N.Y. Prosecutor's Office — Homicide Bureau. James K. Sullivan, Lt. Colonel, Prince William County Police, Manassas, Virginia. Don Swanz,

Evidence Technician, Grand Prairie, Texas Police Department. James
V. Taylor, Ph.D., Forensic Anthropologist, Lehman College, Bronx,
N.Y. Department of Anthropology. Patty A. Tedesco, Composite Artist,
City of Aurora Police Department, Aurora, Colorado. Raymond M.
Theis, Homicide Detective, Bronx Homicide Task Force, New York
City Police Department. Nicholas Theodos, Trooper-Investigator, New
Jersey State Police — Major Case. Virginia E. Thomas, Author,
Technicourse, Inc. Laren Thorsen, Coordinator, Public Security Train-
ing, Northwestern Michigan College. John T. Tierney, Homicide De-
tective, Apprehension Unit — Bronx Homicide Task Force, N.Y.P.D.
(Retired). Elmer Toro, Sergeant (Ret.), New York City Police Depart-
ment Terrorist Task Force. John M. Tracy, Homicide Detective, Retired
— Detective First Grade, Bronx Homicide Task Force — N.Y.P.D.
Pamela Tully, Special Agent, North Carolina State Bureau of Investigation — S.B.I. Frank Turchi, State Trooper, Indiana State Police. Ronald
Turco, M.D., Psychiatrist And Detective, Criminal Profiler. United
States Coast Guard Intelligence Division. United States Postal Inspec-
tions Service. Leslie Van Buskirk, Detective, Indianapolis, Indiana Po-
lice Department, Homicide Division. Frank Viggiano, Detective Ser-
geant, New York City Police Department Former Squad Commander
47 Pct. Det. Squad, Chief Investigator Bronx, DAO. Robin Wagg, Chief
Criminal Investigator, Douglas County Sheriff, Washington. Rick
Walther, Detective, Kenner, Louisiana Police Department. Robert L.
Waters, Homicide Detective, Bronx Homicide Task Force, New York
City Police Department. Dennis Watkins, Chief Prosecutor, Trumbull
County Prosecutor's Office, Trumbull County, Ohio. Mark W. Weaver,
Federal Aviation Administration. Lawrence Welch, Esq., FBI (Ret.),
Director Kansas Bureau of Investigation, Former Director of The Kan-
sas Law Enforcement Training Center (K.L.E.T.C.), University of Kan-
sas. Roy West, Det. Sgt., Homicide Division. Indianapolis, Indiana
Police Department. Tom Witten, Chief of Police, Sugarcreek Town-
ship, Ohio Police Department. Bob Wilbanks, Sergeant, Grand Prairie,
Texas Police Department. John Wisniewski, Inspector, U.S. Postal In-
spections Service, Washington, D.C. Headquarters Division. Wichita,
Kansas Police Department — Investigative Division. James "Skip"
Wright, Jefferson Parish Sheriff's Office, Metarie, Louisiana. Jay B.
Wright, Ph.D., Executive Director, New York Fair Trial/Free Press
Conference, Syracuse University, New York. James Yoghourtjiam, De-
tective, Racinde, Wisconsin Police Department Crime Scene Investiga-
tor. Thomas T., Zugibe, M.D., Rockland County, New York Medical
Forensic Pathologist, Examiner.

A special word of thanks is extended to Pierce Brooks, an internationally recognized authority on the subject of homicide investigation, who graciously provided the forward, Paul Gottehrer, the Desk Editor on this project, who painstakingly assured that every possible editorial detail was accomplished, George Novotny, Acquisitions Editor at CRC Press, Inc., who assisted me with both the Second and Third Editions of my text and Mr. Joel Claypool, Publisher, CRC Press, Inc. who encouraged me to revise this text and assisted by making significant editorial and design contributions.

Special Acknowledgment

To my wife and family,
I wish to extend a very special acknowledgment.
To my children,
Vernon Anthony, B.A., a Detective in the Robbery Division in
The New York City Police Department,
Robert Joseph, B.A., a Trooper, with the New York State Police,
Christopher James, a C.P.A. with Arthur Andersen, LLP.
And Laura Marie, B.S.W., my very special daughter.
And of course, my wife Laura, M.S.W., C.S.W. who assisted me
with her support and encouragement in this endeavor.

The Author

Vernon J. Geberth, M.S., M.P.S., B.B.A., FBINA is a retired Lieutenant Commander of the New York City Police Department with over 30 years of law enforcement experience. He retired as the Commanding Officer of the Bronx Homicide Task Force, which handled over 400 murder investigations a year. During his career he was a Detective, a Precinct Detective Squad Commander, Temporary Commander of the 7th Homicide Zone in the South Bronx, and Commander of Bronx Homicide. He has personally investigated, supervised, assessed, and consulted on over 8000 death investigations. In addition, Commander Geberth has been the recipient of more than 60 awards for bravery and exceptional police work and is a member of the Honor Legion of the City of New York Police Department.

Commander Geberth, has a Master of Science Degree in Psychology (M.S.), California Coast University, Santa Ana, California; a Master of Professional Studies (M.P.S.) C.W. Post College, Long Island University, and a Bachelor of Business Administration (B.B.A.) Iona College in New Rochelle, New York. He is also a graduate of the FBI National Academy in Quantico, Virginia 119th Session, (1979).

Mr. Geberth has served on the New York State Governor's Commission on Domestic Violence Fatalities. He has served as an Adjunct Professor of Criminal Justice at both Mercy College, Dobbs Ferry, New York and John Jay College of Criminal Justice in New York City. He was affiliated with the University of Delaware's Continuing Education Program, as an Associate Professor and was a member of the Faculty of Northwestern University Traffic Institute as a Homicide

Instructor. Commander Geberth also served as a Homicide Instructor for The New York City Housing Police, The New York City Transit and the Police Training Division of the New York Office of the FBI. He continues to serve as Special Guest Lecturer for the New York City Police Department's Detective Bureau's Homicide School, The New Jersey State Police Homicide School and the New York State Police Colonel Henry F. William's Homicide Seminar. Vernon Geberth is a Senior Staff Member and Homicide Instructor for Public Agency Training Council, a National Criminal Justice and Public Safety training firm which provides Academy Quality Module Training throughout the United States. In addition, Commander Geberth has appeared in numerous television productions on the subject of homicide and death investigation and has been referenced as a media consultant on a myriad of national major cases across the United States.

Lieutenant Commander Geberth is the author of *Practical Homicide Investigation: Tactics, Procedures, and Forensic Techniques*, Third Edition, which is recognized in the law enforcement field as "The Bible of Homicide Investigation"; and the *Practical Homicide Investigation Checklist and Field Guide*, which is considered by professionals as an essential prerequisite in conducting proficient death inquiries.

He also has published extensively on topics relating to criminal investigation and forensic techniques and applied criminal psychology. His comprehensive study of serial killers in the United States, which he co-authored with a forensic psychiatrist was published in the *Journal of Forensic Sciences* in January, 1997 and his published works are cited in numerous professional publications throughout the United States, Canada and Europe. In addition, he serves as the Series Editor of "Practical Aspects of Criminal and Forensic Investigations" for CRC Press LLC in Boca Raton, Florida.

Commander Geberth is President of P.H.I. Investigative Consultants, Inc., a New York-based corporation which provides state-of-the-art instruction as well as consultation in homicide and forensic case investigations for a number of law enforcement agencies throughout the United States and Canada. Over 30,000 members from over 3900 law enforcement agencies have attended Geberth's PRACTICAL HOMICIDE INVESTIGAITON® seminars.

Geberth is a nationally renowned lecturer, author, educator, consultant, and expert witness on the subject of death investigations.

The Homicide Crime Scene

1

The homicide crime scene is, without a doubt, the most important crime scene a police officer or investigator will be called upon to respond to. Because of the nature of the crime (death by violence or unnatural causes), the answer to "What has occurred?" can only be determined after a careful and intelligent examination of the crime scene and after the professional and medical evaluation of the various bits and pieces of evidence gathered by the criminal investigator. These bits and pieces may be in the form of trace evidence found at the scene, statements taken from suspects, direct eyewitness accounts, or autopsy results.

Homicide investigation is a highly professional and specialized undertaking, which requires years of practical experience coupled with a process of continual education and training. However, homicide investigation is not the exclusive purview of the investigator, nor are all homicides solved because detectives are "smarter" than patrol officers. In fact, successful homicide investigation often depends on the initial actions taken by patrol officers responding to any given scene. Technically speaking, all police officers have a responsibility to actively and skillfully contribute to the crime solving process.

Whether it be the operator, who initially takes the call and obtains a crucial piece of information, or the officer in a patrol car, who responds to a "homicide run" and detains a key witness or suspect, the fact is that practical homicide investigation is based on the cooperation of patrol officers and detectives working together toward the common goal of solving the homicide.

The three basic principles involved in the initiation of an effective homicide investigation are as follows.

1. Rapid response to the homicide crime scene by patrol officers. This is imperative in order to protect evidentiary materials before they are destroyed, altered, or lost.
2. Anything and everything should be considered as evidence. Whether this evidence is physical or testimonial, it must be preserved, noted, and brought to the attention of the investigators. The *only* evidence collected at this point of the investigation is eyewitness accounts or spontaneous statements of a suspect at the scene.
3. After the scene is secured, immediate and appropriate notification must be made to the homicide investigators.

The importance of preserving the homicide crime scene and conducting an intelligent examination at the scene cannot be overemphasized. If a murder case ends in failure or an officer is embarrassed in court, the primary reason may very well be an inadequate examination of the homicide scene or a failure to implement good basic crime scene procedures as outlined in this text.

The Crime Scene

The investigation of homicide usually starts at the point where the body is originally found. This location is referred to as the *primary crime scene.*

It should be noted, however, that there may be two or more crime scenes in addition to the location where the body is found. These additional crime scenes may include:

Where the body was moved from

Where the actual assault leading to death took place

Where any physical or trace evidence connected with the crime is discovered (this may include parts of the body)

A vehicle used to transport the body to where it is eventually found

Still other areas related to the primary crime scene include the point of forced entry, the route of escape, the suspect (clothing, hands, and body), and the suspect's residence.

It is important that responding police officers be aware of this multiple-crime scene possibility. Therefore, during the initial receipt of information by the police concerning a possible homicide, the officer should attempt to ascertain the exact location of the situation requiring police investigation and possible additional locations that may need coverage.

At the Crime Scene

Any item *can* and *may* constitute physical evidence; therefore, it is imperative that nothing be touched or moved at the scene before the arrival of the investigators. If the need arises that something at the scene be immediately secured or removed before it is destroyed or lost, the officer handling the evidence must document its location, appearance, condition, and any other feature that might affect the investigation. The officer must be sure to inform the homicide detective of the item's original position so that it does not lose its evidentiary value.

The crime scene, especially in homicide cases, is proof that a crime has been committed. It often contains many or all of the elements of the *corpus delicti,* and provides an abundance of physical evidence that may connect a suspect or suspects to the crime.

> Remember, once an item of evidence has been moved or altered,
> it is impossible to restore it to its original position or condition.

Therefore, with malice aforethought, I once again stress the importance of protecting and preserving the crime scene.

The Homicide Investigation Starts at the Crime Scene

The reason why the homicide investigation starts at the crime scene is twofold: (1) The police are usually called to this location by the person who discovers the body, a witness to the crime, or, in some instances, the victim. (2) In homicide cases, the location where the body is discovered yields an abundance of physical evidence and serves as a base of inquiry.

From an investigative point of view, the body and its surroundings (including associative evidence and other factors unique to any specific crime) provide the professional homicide detective with significant information on which to base an investigation. For example, an intelligent examination of the scene may reveal the identity of the victim, the approximate time of death, and important evidence and/or clues to the circumstances of the death.

There is a principle in homicide investigation that refers to a theoretical exchange between two objects that have been in contact with one another. This theory of *transfer* or *exchange* is based on the following facts.

1. The perpetrator will take away traces of the victim and the scene.
2. The victim will retain traces of the perpetrator and may leave traces of himself on the perpetrator.
3. The perpetrator will leave behind traces of himself at the scene.

It is important to repeat that anything and everything may eventually become evidence. The list of items that may constitute physical and/or testimonial evidence is as extensive as the number, type, and causes of homicide itself. Whether it be the *res gestae* utterances of the suspect murderer at the scene or an important piece of trace evidence, the fact remains that the homicide crime scene is the logical and proper point to start the murder investigation.

Determining the Dimensions of the Homicide Crime Scene

The cardinal rule in homicide cases is to *protect* and *preserve* the crime scene. However, before a crime scene can be protected it must be identified as such. In order for the officer to make an intelligent evaluation of the crime scene, he must have an idea of what constitutes physical evidence and where the boundaries of the scene should be established in order to protect the evidence.

Some examples of physical evidence which may be found at the crime scene are listed below. Although the list does not include all types of evidence, these are the three types most frequently found at the homicide crime scene.

The patrol officer, who has the duty of responding to the scene as quickly as possible, begins the investigation by securing the immediate area. Upon confirming that the victim is dead, an assessment is then made by this officer to determine boundaries.

Objects	Body materials	Impressions
Weapons	Blood	Fingerprints
Tools	Semen	Tire tracks
Firearms	Hair	Footprints
Displaced furniture	Tissue	Palm prints
Notes, letters, or papers	Spittle	Tool marks
Bullets	Urine	Bullet holes
Vehicles	Feces	Newly damaged areas
Cigarette/cigar butts	Vomit	Dents and breaks

Figure 1.1.   **CRIME SCENE — BASIC DEATH INVESTIGATION.** Observe the partially clad body of a female. It is important to note that in the early stages of a death investigation you cannot be sure of anything. This apparent case of a sex slaying is actually a natural death due to a ruptured aneurysm. The deceased had been in bed with her boyfriend when she suddenly passed out. He tried to dress her and had placed her on the floor to attempt resuscitation.

Figure 1.2.   **FIRE SCENE.** Observe a victim who has died in a fire. Apparently, the victim was lying in his bed when he was overcome. Notice the deep charring and splitting of the skin. Although this is a typical fire death scene, the cause of death should not be assumed until the pathologist has made a careful examination of the deceased. In fact, this was a typical fire death case. Many times arson is used to cover-up a homicide; therefore, the immediate concern of the investigator at such cases should be the scene examination.

Figure 1.3. **CRIME SCENE.** The victim was stabbed and beaten. There is evidence of a struggle: the apartment is in disarray with various broken objects strewn about the room, and blood has been splattered around the room. (Courtesy Det. Morris Hill, Warren, Ohio Police Department.)

Technically speaking, the homicide crime scene begins at the point where the suspect changed intent into action. It continues through the escape route and includes any location where physical or trace evidence may be located.

Practically speaking, at this stage of the investigation it is next to impossible to know the exact boundaries of the scene. The best course of action for the officer is as follows.

1. Clear the largest area possible. The scene can always be narrowed later.
2. Make a quick and objective evaluation of the scene based on:
   a. location of the body
   b. presence of any physical evidence
   c. eyewitness statements
   d. presence of natural boundaries (a room, a house, hallway, an enclosed park, etc.)
3. Keep in mind the possibility of a multiple series of crime scenes.

Figure 1.4. CRIME SCENE CARDS.
These cards can be used to indicate that a
particular area is restricted to authorized
personnel only.

If the crime scene is indoors, the job of making this determination and securing the area is relatively easy to accomplish. If the scene is outdoors, the determination will have to be based on the type of location, pedestrian and vehicular traffic, crowds, paths of entry and exit, weather conditions, and many other factors peculiar to that specific location.

In any event, the first officer should not examine the contents of the scene. He should, however, stabilize the scene by isolating the body and immediate area, including any visible evidence, from all other persons.

Protecting the Crime Scene

The homicide crime scene must be protected from entry by unnecessary or unauthorized persons so that physical evidence will not be altered, moved, destroyed, lost, or contaminated. Other police officers, including supervisory personnel, who do not have a specific or valid reason for being at the crime scene, should be regarded as *unauthorized persons.*

Probably no other aspect of homicide investigation is more open to error than the preservation and protection of the crime scene. The first official acts taken at the scene will either help to bring the investigation to a successful conclusion or will negatively affect both the entire investigation and eventual prosecution of the case.

Therefore, it is incumbent upon the first officer arriving at the scene to perform this first and necessary aspect of the investigation: *Safeguard the location as quickly and as effectively as possible.* (See Chapter 2, "First Officer's Duties on Arrival at the Scene.")

The first police official to arrive at the crime scene is usually the patrol officer, the agency's primary crime-fighting tool, who is expected to respond immediately to any incident where there is a report of a crime or an opportunity to apprehend a criminal. The patrol officer is also the department's representative, responsible for conducting the preliminary investigation, which begins when the officer arrives at the scene.

In homicide cases, the responding officer's duties in the preliminary investigation may simply be to arrive at the scene, observe enough to know that assistance from investigators is required, and protect the scene so that evidence is not destroyed or changed.

Scene protection may be as simple as closing a door to the room where the body is discovered, or as complex as roping off an area of several blocks. There is no definite method or rule for establishing the boundaries of all crime scenes at first glance. As information becomes available at the scene, various other locations may also have to be secured in order to retrieve important physical and trace evidence.

Many times I have been at the scene of a homicide in one location and (as a result of information developed from witnesses or evidence located at the primary scene) had to immediately secure a second and third location, a vehicle, and even a building's fire escape and alleyway, used as an escape route by the perpetrator. Obviously, the best places for obtaining physical evidence are nearest to where the critical act occurred, such as in the immediate vicinity of the victim. However, other areas related to this primary crime scene should not be overlooked. For example,

The point of forced entry
The route of escape
The suspect himself (i.e., clothing, hands, body, etc.)
The location of the weapon or other physical evidence
A vehicle, which was used in the crime
The suspect's residence
The location where the assault leading to death took place
The location where the body was moved

Figure 1.5.   **HOMICIDE: ASPHYXIA BY DROWNING.** Although rare, drowning can be employed as a means of homicide. Observe the body of a victim immersed in the water of a bathtub. The deceased's hands have been bound and the body lies face down in the water. (The water has been discolored by the victim's blood.) This slaying took place after a "crew" decided to rip-off the victim. (A crew is best defined as a loosely knit association of street kids, whose sole occupation is criminal behavior.) The victim had been set up by a couple of street girls, who promised the victim sex. They kept him busy while the male members of the crew broke into the victim's apartment. The victim was then tortured by the crew members who, after ransacking the apartment, eventually drowned him.

The list of locations that may need protection from contamination are as extensive as the crime is complex.

The scene should be secured by the use of *ropes, barricades, autos, additional officers,* and even *volunteers from the crowd* if necessary. The use of *crime scene cards* and reflective ribbon can be effective scene indicators. However, the presence of a uniformed officer is essential in order to reinforce scene protection during this phase of the investigation.

Once all injured persons and the deceased have been attended to and all emergency conditions cleared up (such as extinguishing fires, removing hostages in barricade situations, clearing any crowds, taking the suspect into custody, etc.), the officers who have secured the scene should review their actions and make adjustments to provide for the safeguarding of any additional evidence that may have been overlooked during those first critical moments.

The police officer or criminal investigator endeavoring to *protect* and *preserve* the homicide crime scene will find that he or she faces a number of obstacles. It is impossible to list all the conceivable events that may occur at any given scene. However, there are five basic factors or "scene contaminators" that seem to crop up at almost every crime scene. These factors can either by themselves or in combination with other events create problems and do irreparable damage to the scene.

Weather. This factor, especially if the scene is outdoors, can create serious problems in that much of the physical evidence — for example, the body, blood, other body fluids, and residues — is subject to change and/or erasure by rain, snow, wind, direct sunlight, and extreme temperature.

Relatives and friends of the victim. They may be so sickened by the sight of the scene that they begin to cleanup and put things back where they "belong." They are also capable of destroying and secreting any notes or evidence of suicide in order to "protect" the family name.

Suspects or associates. They may attempt to destroy or remove incriminating evidence. It is important to note that if a suspect is taken into custody a short distance away from the scene, he should NOT be returned to the actual crime scene. He may contaminate the scene either by adding something to it, or more importantly, negate the value of any trace evidence originally imparted by him or to him from the scene.

Curious onlookers, souvenir collectors, ordinary thieves. This group encompasses those at the scene either out of curiosity or a desire to steal or to take something as a souvenir. They can introduce confusing fingerprints, alter the condition of the scene, add to crowd control problems, and in many instances steal pieces of evidence.(During my homicide assignment in the South Bronx, we often used to joke of how a murder weapon could never be heard to hit the ground in the Bronx, because so many would-be felons were on hand to catch it.)

Other members of police agencies and high-ranking officials. They usually are not assigned to the case, but come along to "help." In my opinion this is the biggest problem encountered in protection of the crime scene.

1. They usually contaminate or destroy valuable trace evidence, either because they don't know what they are doing or because they get in the way.

Figure 1.6.   **HOMICIDE CRIME SCENE — GUNSHOT VICTIM.** This victim was gunned down by robbers and died instantly at the scene. Notice the profuse bleeding from the head wound.

2. Police officers are naturally curious. However, this curiosity can prove very disadvantageous at the homicide crime scene. Sometimes, for no other reason than "to get a better look at the body," inquisitive officers will unnecessarily walk into the secured area to render their "unofficial diagnoses of death." From my point of view there is no reason for 10 or 15 additional *police* medical opinions. Many times items of trace evidence, thought to be valuable physical evidence, turn out to be something left by police officers who were present at the scene and were smoking, running water, etc.

3. The mere presence of additional police officers just standing around or leaning against a doorway may grind valuable trace evidence into the ground or carpet, or may smear a print.

4. Last but certainly not least in the "hit parade" of scene contaminators is the high ranking police official. It is important to note that *rank does not preclude scene contamination.* Even though

Figure 1.7. **BASIC DEATH INVESTIGATION — OUTDOOR SCENE.** Investigators must be cautious each time they are presented with a death investigation. No one can be sure at the start if the deceased is the victim of a homicide or the death is due to other causes. In some instances, preliminary examination of the body and scene will indicate conclusive evidence of murder. However, in a case like the one shown, all you know for sure is that you have a dead body in the woods.

some of these misguided officials think they are able to "walk on water," the fact is that they are just as capable of messing up the scene as the lowest ranking police officer who unintentionally walks on through. Many times, especially if the case is sensational or noteworthy, high ranking officials such as the mayor, the chief of police, fire chiefs, judges, and even the chief prosecutor may appear on the scene. They are usually there to "assist" in operations, but their "assistance" and overall contribution to scene preservation is usually less than helpful. If you are lucky, you may be able to divert them to an area outside the crime scene or to the command post. Or you may gain their cooperation by asking them, in the interests of protecting the scene, that they keep everyone out. In any event, tact will definitely be required in these situations.

Figure 1.8.   OUTDOOR SCENE — NATURAL DEATH. This case turned out to be a natural death due to exposure. The deceased, an outpatient from a mental institution, had apparently been drinking in the woods and fell asleep. The elements eventually took effect. She expired. An empty whiskey bottle was found underneath the body, and there was no evidence of assault. This death was determined to be of natural causes after autopsy. However, the scene examination is vitally important to the pathologist so that the findings can be compared with evidence found at the scene.

I remember one particularly obnoxious chief, who epitomized the "Peter Principle" of bureaucracy, hypocrisy, and incompetence. He had never been a detective and didn't have any experience in murder investigations. However, he actually believed that his position and rank in the organization provided him with knowledge and intelligence far superior to any of his subordinates. In order to demonstrate his proficiency and unrivaled detective skills, he would race the detectives to the crime scene in order to be there first. He traipsed through crime scenes like a large blue elephant, contaminating and destroying any evidence in his path. In fact, whenever any good latent print evidence was found at the scene it usually belonged to the chief. Detectives found his footprints in blood which indicated that he had walked through the blood before the scene could be safeguarded, his palm print at a rape murder, and his fingerprints on guns at two separate incidents, one involving the murder of a police officer. We were finally able to "get a leash" on this guy by convincing the District Attorney to threaten him with a subpoena. This and the Homicide Crime Scene *Sign-In* Sheet (see Crime Scene Sign-in Sheet) proved to be an effective tactic in securing the preservation of the crime scene.

The primary objective in this phase of the investigation is to preserve the body and immediate surrounding area exactly as they were when the body was discovered.

Remember, although the protection of the crime scene is the responsibility of the first officer, all officers responding to and arriving at the scene have an equal responsibility in this duty.

Realistically speaking, various units and additional personnel respond to homicide crime scenes. The toughest job confronting the *first officers* is the effective safeguarding of the crime scene from these additional police officers, emergency services people, and other officials. Obviously, certain personnel must enter the crime scene in connection with their official duties. The first officers, who are safeguarding the crime

Figure 1.9. **BASIC DEATH INVESTIGATION — CRIME SCENE.** Here you can see the body of a male, pants apparently pulled down to the knees and bruises on the face and arms. The body is in a position which suggests that it was "dumped" at the location. Ironically, this is not a homicide; in fact, the deceased is actually the "bad-guy" in the scenario. Investigation revealed that the deceased, who was accompanied by another, was a rip-off artist; they "worked" the local lover's lane, which was under a major suspension bridge. Their particular M.O. was as follows. After couples parked their cars, these two characters would suddenly appear on each side of the car and, at gunpoint, order the occupants out and rob them. The night before the body was found, these two characters had robbed at least two couples. On their last rip-off they selected a foursome. Not satisfied with just robbing them, they decided to bully the two males. However, the two would-be victims wrested the guns from the "bad-guys" and gave chase in the darkened park. The deceased and his partner made it to the bridge and began running against traffic to the other side. About midway, the decedent decided to jump to what he believed was a walkway. Instead of a walkway, he found air and fell about 200 feet down to where the body was discovered. The two couples who were robbed, unaware of this event, reported the robbery attempt to the police and submitted the guns they had taken. Later on, police questioned the dead man's partner, who showed up at a local hospital with a bullet wound he had received during the abortive robbery, and all the pieces began to fall together.

scene, should identify and document the presence of these officials by maintaining a *Crime-Scene Sign-In* procedure to assure crime-scene integrity and prevent unauthorized personnel from engaging in what I refer to as "crime scene sightseeing." During my 23 years of active police service, I have come to realize that, "If anything can go wrong, it will go wrong at the crime scene."

This is especially true at incidents that receive an inordinate amount of media attention. It seems as if every official and his/her brother and/ or sister feel the need to "show their presence" at the scene.

My solution to this oftentimes impossible situation is quite simple. I suggest that the officers establish *two* crime scenes.

1. The *first* or *primary* crime scene is the location where the actual event occurred, or the area where you expect to recover physical evidence. *This is the real crime scene.*
2. The *second* or *secure area* crime scene is an area set aside from the general public. This allows for all those special dignitaries and high ranking guests who arrive an opportunity to violate at least one police line in order to establish their importance. It will also serve to keep them within an area where they will be "out-of-the-way" of actual crime-scene operations and preclude any further contamination by official presence. *This can be called a "Security zone."*

Figure 1.10. **OUTDOOR SCENE.** Here you see the body of a female who has been "dumped" in the woods. A preliminary examination of the victim indicated that she had been shot in the head and body.

Figure 1.11. CRIME SCENE SIGN-IN SHEET.

The Staged Crime Scene

Introduction

The purpose of this section is to alert investigators to the phenomena of the staged crime scene. "Staging" a scene occurs when the perpetrator purposely alters the crime scene to mislead the authorities and/or redirect the investigation. *Staging is a conscious criminal action on the part of an offender to thwart an investigation.* The term "staging" should not be used to describe the actions of surviving family members who cover or redress a loved one, who is found nude or has died in an embarrassing situation. These activities are certainly understandable considering the shock experienced by a relative who encounters the sudden and violent death of a loved one. In my experience investigating suspicious deaths I have oftentimes had a "gut" feeling that something was amiss. Actually, that "gut" feeling is your subconscious reaction to the presentation, which should alert you to the possibility that, "Things are not always what they appear to be." This position is consistent with equivocal death investigations.

Equivocal Death Investigations

Equivocal death investigations are those inquiries that are open to interpretation. There may be two or more meanings and the case may present as either a homicide or a suicide depending upon the circumstances. The facts are purposefully vague or misleading as in the case of a "*staged crime scene.*" Or, the death is suspicious or questionable based upon what is presented to the authorities. The deaths may resemble homicides or suicides; accidents or naturals. They are open to interpretation pending further information of the facts, the victimology, and the circumstances of the event.

In "staged crime scenes," however, the presentation of the homicide victim and the manipulation of the crime scene by a clever offender could make the death appear to be a suicide. I have personally investigated many such cases and the truth of the matter is that initially, the cases *did* look like suicides.

Types of Crime Scene Staging

1. The most common type of "staging" occurs when the perpetrator changes elements of the scene to make the death appear to be a suicide or accident in order to cover up a murder. (Case Histories Numbers 1 and 2).

2. The second most common type of staging is when the perpetrator attempts to redirect the investigation by making the crime appear to be a sex-related homicide. (Case Histories Numbers 3 and 4).
3. Arson represents another type of staging. The offender purposely torches the crime scene to destroy evidence or make the death appear to the result of an accidental fire. (Case History Number 5).

Examples of Homicides Made to Appear to be a Suicide or Accident

CASE HISTORY NUMBER 1

I acted as a consultant in a wrongful death suit brought against an insurance company by surviving relatives of a male who allegedly had committed suicide. The insurance company had refused to pay the beneficiaries based on the police determination of suicide. My review of the crime scene photographs and circumstances of the death of this young man indicated that the young man had, in fact, not committed suicide.

A

Figure 1.12. **STAGED CRIME SCENE.** Murder made to appear to be a suicide. (A) The victim was discovered lying on his back across his bed with a .308 rifle between his legs, suggesting that he had shot himself in the head with the weapon. His head is pointing towards the South with his feet to the North. (B) The hallway of the victim's residence. You can observe his feet hanging off the bed in the bedroom. His brain is found lying by the back door which is Northeast of his position. In order for the brain to have arrived at the place of discovery it would have to have traveled in the opposite direction of the suggested direction of velocity, made a right turn down the hallway, and land by the back door. This situation is obviously forensically impossible.

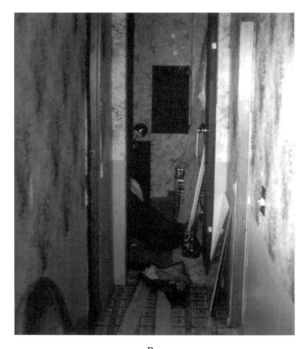

B

Figure 1.12. (continued)

The authorities had been misled into believing the case was a suicide because the scene had been staged.

The victim was discovered lying on his back across his bed with a .308 rifle between his legs, suggesting that he had shot himself in the head with the weapon. There was a large amount of blood and brain matter found in the room where the deceased was discovered. His entire head was blown away. The victim's brain was found down the hallway from the room. The gun belonged to the deceased. There was ammunition for the gun found in the premises. There were two bullet holes in the roof of the victim's trailer, suggesting two shots having been fired, and the police recovered two spent shell casings in the room. The police classified the death as suicide.

A review of the police investigation revealed a perfunctory inquiry totaling a mere eight (8) pages of police reports. The police did not attempt to locate the fired rounds; they did not test or examine the firearm; there were no ballistics reports prepared; and there were no gunshot residue testings (GSR) done on the victim to ascertain whether or not he had fired the weapon; and there was no attempt to reconstruct the event. The police did not process the crime scene for fingerprints nor did they ever conduct a background check or victimology. The autopsy was conducted by a hospital pathologist instead of a forensic pathologist, who couldn't even determine the location of the entrance wound.

However, these observations, without further police investigation into the facts surrounding the death and a reconstruction of the crime scene could be misleading. The investigative reality is that each factor must be brought to its ultimate conclusion. I believe that the authorities made the mistake of assuming that the death of the young man was suicide based on their preliminary observations of the crime scene and as a result subsequently failed to take each factor to its ultimate conclusion.

Analysis

My analysis of the facts indicated that the deceased had made both short- and long-term plans, which is not consistent with a person intending to commit suicide. During the week preceding his death, he had gone out with friends, had attended a birthday party for his sister, and purchased groceries for the upcoming week. On Monday of the week he was killed, he was at work. According to his supervisor, he was in good spirits. In addition, he had even paid his union dues three months in advance. He was expecting a visit from a girl friend and was refurbishing his mobile home. He had built a new deck on the back, purchased paint and wallpaper, and had arranged with a neighbor to borrow tools to fix his kitchen cabinets. His long-term plans included an application for a loan and a trip to Alabama to clear some property in the Fall. Interviews of the friends and relatives of the deceased were conducted which disclosed that certain property and money were missing from the deceased's trailer when he was discovered dead.

A number of persons stated that the deceased was known to keep at least $1000.00 cash in his mobile home. According to the police report there was only $2.50 found in the deceased's pockets. Also, according to another relative who had reconciled the deceased's accounts after the funeral, the victim had made a withdrawal of $200.00 cash from an ATM machine which was unaccounted for and missing from the trailer. A neighbor stopped by the trailer because of his suspicion "that something wasn't right." He observed that the deceased's car doors were unlocked and the keys were in the ignition. This was unusual behavior for the deceased. Later police would recover the deceased's empty wallet from the floor of the car.

The door to the trailer was unlocked and the stereo was blasting. The thermostat was set up as high as it could go. The deceased reportedly never had the thermostat above 65°. According to family members, the victim's radar detector which the deceased always kept on the

A

Figure 1.13. **STAGED CRIME SCENE.** Murder made to appear to be an accidental shooting. (A) Victim's original position when police arrived. (B) Close-up of victim's face showing entrance wound. (C) Close-up of victim's hands with gun in right hand. (Courtesy Det. Michael J. O'Malley, Homicide Unit, Cleveland Police Department.)

sun visor in his car was missing, as were a pouch of tools from the rear seat. In addition, a gold calculator with the deceased's initials inscribed, which the victim had gotten as a gift for participating in a wedding, was missing from the trailer.

All of this information was provided to authorities. However, there was apparently no follow-up by the police into these important observations and suggestions of foul play.

B

C

Figure 1.13. (continued)

In my professional opinion as an expert in homicide and death investigations, the inquiry into the death of the deceased was perfunctory and inadequate according to the recognized standards of professional death investigation. It was readily apparent that this particular crime scene had been staged and it was a reasonable assumption based upon the above facts that the deceased had not committed suicide.

CASE HISTORY NUMBER 2

Police were summoned to a home of a woman, who reported that there had been a shooting. The victim, a white male, 26 years of age was a friend of the woman. He had been watching the woman's children while she went out drinking with a couple of other males. When the police arrived, they observed the victim, sitting on the living room couch, with a gun cradled in his right hand. The victim's right thumb was inside the trigger guard. He had suffered a bullet wound to the left side of his nose and the exit wound was in the upper part of the back of the head. The magazine for the gun had been removed and the ejected shell casing was approximately 6 feet away from where the victim sat. An examination of the wound structure indicated that there was no stippling or soot on the wound; nor was there any evidence of blow-back in the barrel of the gun.

The police were informed by the two males that the deceased had b ˙n "playing" with the gun, which belonged to one of the reporting ˍs, and had accidentally shot himself in the face.

A uniform Lieutenant, who was in charge of the scene, decided that there wasn't any need for detective response. His decision was based on an administrative policy which discouraged overtime. Rather then authorize overtime response for investigators, he had the case classified as an accidental shooting.

The next day, the homicide detectives reviewed the case and examined the crime scene photographs. Their opinion was that the circumstances as described by the reporting officer and witnesses were not consistent with the elements of the crime scene. They initiated an investigation and tested the suspected weapon, which revealed that the gun had to have been fired at least 42 inches away from the deceased's face. The discharged rounds did not eject, but had to be manually removed from the breech. Removing the magazine required both hands. Gunshot Residue Testing (GSR) of the deceased's hands proved negative.

The investigators re-interviewed the woman and the reporting witnesses. The males were confronted with the facts of the case as well as their inconsistent statements. It was learned that all of the parties had been drinking. A gun was pulled out by one of the males, who stated that the gun had accidentally discharged hitting the victim in the face. They had panicked and decided to make it appear that the deceased had shot himself. After they "staged" the scene, they called the police and the ambulance. Both subjects were charged with murder. They were indicted for Involuntary Manslaughter. The male, who had done the shooting pled guilty to Manslaughter and Weapon Possession; the other male pled guilty to Tampering with Evidence.

A

Figure 1.14.   **STAGED CRIME SCENE.** Murder made to appear sex-related. The location where the victim was found is actually a disposal site and not the location of the assault leading to her death. The type of injuries that she received would have caused extensive bleeding not as depicted in Photo C. The body of the victim was posed to suggest a sex crime. The actual injuries however point to an interpersonal motivation. (A) Body of victim is found in an alleyway, nude except for bra and placed in a position suggesting a sexual crime. (B) Breasts have been manipulated to expose areola. (C) Shows blood found beneath victim's head. (D) Wound structure photograph indicating severe head wounds. (Courtesy of Lt. Milton Agay, Benton Harbor Police Department, Benton Harbor, Michigan.)

Example of a Homicide Made to Appear to be Sex-Related

CASE HISTORY NUMBER 3

Police were summoned to a home by a frantic male who reported that he had been attacked by a man with a knife, who had killed his wife. When police arrived they were led into the house by the man, who showed them his wife's body in the basement. He indicated that he had also been injured and showed the officers some superficial cuts and puncture wounds on his body. The man was transferred to the Emergency Room of the local hospital for treatment. The crime scene ex-

B

C

Figure 1.14. (continued)

tended from outside the house to the basement. The female victim, who had received multiple stab wounds was found lying on her back. Her pants had been ripped open and her panties had been pulled down to reveal her pubic area. Her sanitary napkin was pulled away and between her legs the crime scene officers retrieved an unused condom. The male

D

Figure 1.14. (continued)

had stated that he had surprised the intruder, when he had come home from jogging. The male showed the officers evidence of a "burglary." The burglary consisted of items being tossed on the floor and perfume bottles being turned over on the dresser in the master bedroom. However, there wasn't anything missing.

Although the presentation of the female body in the crime scene suggested a sexual attack, the circumstances of the event as well as the inconsistent statements of the husband indicated this murder to be based on an interpersonal oriented dispute and assault scenario.

The husband was charged with his wife's murder based on the police investigation as well as the blood evidence and DNA testing.

CASE HISTORY NUMBER 4

The police were summoned to an apartment, when friends of the deceased recounted that she had failed to report for work. Police entered the apartment and discovered the nude body of the 27-year-old victim lying on the bedroom floor. Her pants and panties had been pulled down and her blouse was in disarray. A hair brush had been inserted into her vagina. She had been beaten and strangled to death with a ligature, which was not present in the scene. A review of the crime scene indicated that someone had gone through the dresser drawers and closets suggesting a burglary. The victim's clothes were found scattered across the floor and

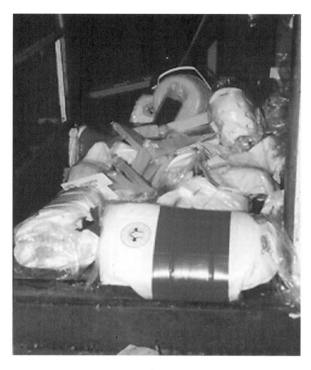

A

Figure 1.15. **STAGED CRIME SCENE.** Murder made to appear as a burglary and sex-related homicide committed by a stranger. (A) Shows objects thrown onto floor indicating a "burglary". (B) The victim has been multiply stabbed and slashed with a number of stab wounds into the chest. The body has been moved and positioned to suggest a sexual assault. (C) The subject has torn the victim's pants and has exposed her pubic area to make the crime appear to be a sexual assault. In addition, he has placed an unused condom between her legs to mislead police into believing that the attack was sex related. (D) Shows the intensity of the attack to the female victim's head. (E) Indicates the insignificant wounds "suffered" by the husband who allegedly was fighting off his attacker, the same assailant who inflicted the devastating wounds to the female victim. (F) An incised injury to the right finger of the suspect who cut himself during the vicious attack on his wife. In fact, he left his blood on the victim's right leg while he was "staging the scene". (G) This location shows where the victim had been multiply stabbed. Note the blood stain pattern indicating arterial blood splatter. (Courtesy of Investigator Jack Henander, Larimer County, Colorado Sheriff's Department.)

the contents of the drawers were spilled out on the bed. There wasn't any forced entry, suggesting the victim had allowed the person into her apartment. A check into the victimology indicated that the young woman was a divorcee who had left an abusive marriage. She had enrolled in a nursing program and had recently received her nurse certification. She had been dating since her divorce but did not have a steady boyfriend. The police investigation indicated that the crime scene had been staged to suggest a burglary. However, nothing of value was missing. There

B

C

Figure 1.15. (continued)

D

E

Figure 1.15. (continued)

F

G

Figure 1.15. (continued)

A   B

Figure 1.16.   **STAGED CRIME SCENE; SEX-RELATED HOMICIDE-INTERPERSONAL VIOLENCE.** (A) At first impression, the hair brush might be considered an item to sexually abuse the victim or a form of penis substitution. In fact, the hair brush had been jammed into the vagina after the victim was strangled to death. (B) The case was actually an interpersonal dispute between the victim and her former husband, who jammed the hair brush into his ex-wife's vagina in a fit of rage. He then staged the crime scene to make it appear to be a burglary and sex-related murder.

wasn't any sexual assault. However, the insertion of the hair brush into her vagina certainly indicated an anger and rage consistent with an interpersonal-oriented dispute and assault. The former husband emerged as the most promising suspect after the detectives were able to break his alibi. He had convinced his current girlfriend to provide him with an alibi. He had gone to his former wife's apartment in an attempt to reconcile with her. When she refused his entreaty, he killed her in anger. He left the apartment and returned 24 hours later. At that time he placed the hair brush into her vagina and staged the crime scene to make it appear that a burglar had entered the location, sexually attacked the young woman, and then ransacked the apartment.

CASE HISTORY NUMBER 5

I remember reviewing a case which originally was reported as a motor vehicle accident involving a vehicle that had apparently crashed and burned in a rural region of Oregon in 1977. The deceased was discovered lying face down inside the cab of his pick-up truck which had

A

B

Figure 1.17.   **MURDER STAGED AS MOTOR VEHICLE ACCIDENT STAGED CRIME SCENE.** Murder made to appear to be an accidental death due to drunk driving. (A) Shows "skid marks" on road allegedly from the truck that careened off road in 1977. (B) Shows the deceased's truck which is upside down from the alleged "crash and burn". (C) Shows the badly burned deceased. His blood alcohol was reportedly 0.41% and the medical examiner ruled the death to be intoxication by ethanol and carbon monoxide with terminal aspiration of gastric contents. (D) X-ray taken during second autopsy in 1993 which shows the shotgun pellets in the region of the deceased's neck. (Courtesy of Detective Spencer R. Smith, Chief Medical Examiner, Jackson County, Oregon.)

C

D

Figure 1.17. (continued)

left the road and flipped over. The body was badly burned and the truck was totaled. The Medical Examiner at the time performed an autopsy and had ruled the death accidental due to intoxication by ethanol and carbon monoxide with terminal aspiration of gastric contents. In 1993, a subject came forward to authorities with information which revealed that the deceased had actually been killed. According to the witness the victim and another had been arguing when the deceased was shot in the neck with a .410 shotgun. After he was shot, the offender poured alcohol down his throat. The deceased was then wrapped in a carpet and driven to the location of the crash site. He was propped-up behind the steering wheel of the truck and doused with gasoline. They then set the cab of the pick-up truck on fire and pushed it over the embankment to stage the scene as an accident. The body was exhumed 16 years later, and examined by another medical examiner, who performed a full radiographic survey of the remains which revealed numerous shotgun pellets still lodged in the neck area of the deceased. The case was ruled a homicide and the subject was charged.

Conclusion

The death investigator needs to be cognizant of the possibility that a crime scene may in fact be "staged" to mislead the authorities and/or redirect the investigation. In the author's experience and travels as a homicide and forensic consultant, he has encountered a number of these incidents in various jurisdictions across the United States. These events seem to be on the increase as people learn more about the process of death investigation through the media, true crime books, television mystery shows, and movies.

Investigative Strategies

Take each factor to its ultimate conclusion.

1. Assess the victimology of the deceased.
2. Evaluate the type of injuries and wounds of the victim in connection with the type of weapon employed.
3. Conduct the necessary forensic examinations to establish and ascertain the facts of the case.
4. Conduct an examination of the weapon(s) for latent evidence as well as ballistics and testing of firearms.
5. Evaluate the behavior(s) of the victim and suspects.
6. Establish a profile of the victim through interviews of friends and relatives.
7. Reconstruct and evaluate the event.
8. Compare investigative findings with the medicolegal autopsy and confer with the medical examiner.
9. Corroborate statements with evidential facts.
10. Conduct and process all death investigations as if they were homicide cases.

Selected Readings

Geberth, Vernon J., *Practical Homicide Investigation: Tactics, Procedures, and Forensic Techniques.* Second Edition. CRC Press, Inc., Florida, 1993.

Geberth, Vernon J., "The Staged Crime Scene. *Law and Order Magazine."* Vol 44 No. 2. Illinois, February, 1996.

Geberth, Vernon J., "Supervision and Magagement of a Homicide Investigation". *Law and Order Magazine,* Vol. 37, No. 11, Illinois, November, 1989.

First Officer's Duties: General

2

This chapter will concentrate on the following events which initiate a homicide investigation.

1. The actions that should be taken by police officers and police personnel who first receive a report of a possible homicide.
2. The actions that should be taken by a police officer when a witness or passerby reports a possible homicide in person.
3. The actions that should be taken by first officers on arrival at the homicide crime scene.
4. The preliminary investigation that should be initiated by the first officer.

Notification of a Possible Homicide: The Official Notification to the Police

The first notification to the police department of an actual or suspected homicide, or an incident that may develop into one, is usually received by telephone. This first call may simply be a request for assistance for an injured person, a call stating that there were "shots fired", or a report of a screaming man or woman. This first call to the police does not always provide sufficient data to enable the officer to assess the true nature and extent of the incident. Under circumstances where the information received suggests the possibility of a homicide, the person receiving the information should do the following.

1. Obtain and record the following information.
   a. The exact time the call was received.

b. The exact location(s) of occurrence.
c. Whether the perpetrator(s), suspicious person(s), or vehicle(s) are still at the scene. Try to get any descriptive information and direction of flight for the immediate transmission of alarms and/or notification to other patrol units.
d. Where the person calling the police is located, and whether that person will remain. If not, where he or she can be contacted.
e. The *name, address, and phone number* of the person reporting the incident.

2. Request the caller's assistance.
   a. Where practical, if the person making the report seems of suitable age and discretion (calm, etc.), request his or her assistance in safeguarding the location of occurrence. This request should be put into specific terms; for example,
      1. that no one be admitted other than law enforcement personnel or medical people,
      2. that nothing be disturbed.

3. When dispatching officers and units to the scene.
   a. The dispatcher should be aware of the multitude of first officer duties that may be required and should dispatch sufficient personnel and equipment to handle the situation based on the data obtained from the first notification.
   b. Make appropriate notifications to supervisors and to the homicide/detective unit.

4. Switchboard operators and communications personnel receiving emergency calls to police.
   a. Switchboard operators and other police personnel should be aware that in many cases the person making the call to the police is actually the perpetrator, who may not identify himself or herself as such. Should the caller indicate that he or she has just killed someone, the necessary information should be obtained in an ordinary and *detached* manner, the radio cars dispatched, and the operator should attempt to keep the caller on the line in the expectation that the call will still be in progress when the dispatched officers arrive. These officers can then verify that call with the switchboard operator, thereby preparing the basis for a later courtroom presentation.
   b. Even if the operator cannot keep the caller on the line until the arrival of the responding police, the operator should be alert to any identifying characteristics of the caller for later voice identification.

The first officer or person receiving notification should, as soon as possible, reduce to writing the word-for-word content of the call or conversation.

Remember, the individual who first reported the incident may later become a suspect and the exact words he or she used become critical to the case.

Most departments today, especially in major cities, record all incoming calls as a matter of official procedure. In departments that either cannot afford this type of operation or do not wish to record all calls, there is still the option to invest in an inexpensive tape recorder with a telephone "pick-up". This equipment can then be activated manually by the switchboard operator to record any calls of importance, with specific instructions to record incoming calls relating to homicide or any other serious crime.

Recording of the initial call, especially if the call is made by the perpetrator, can be of invaluable importance later on in the investigation. I recall one case in particular where the common-law husband of the deceased called the police and reported that he had found his wife wandering around the neighborhood in a dazed and beaten condition. This call, which was received through our central 911 system, was automatically taped before the "job" was given to the unit concerned. The patrol unit was given the assignment, responded to the address, and found the woman DOA. They interviewed the complainant, who had mistakenly changed his original story. The complainant did not realize his original call to the police had been recorded. The officers, realizing the discrepancy, notified the homicide division and went along with the husband's story. Upon our arrival, we examined the body, listened to the husband's account of what had happened, and interviewed the first officers, who clued us in to the discrepancies they had observed. It was soon obvious that the common-law husband of the deceased was our suspect. His original call to "central" about finding his wife wandering around in a dazed and beaten condition was apparently forgotten as he became thoroughly enmeshed in a much more involved "fairy tale". He was now claiming that his wife had been a victim of rape and burglary, because he had found her in a nude and beaten condition when he arrived home. He was promptly advised of his constitutional rights, and we allowed him to give a full statement relative to the supposed rape and burglary. He steadfastly denied that he had beaten his wife and continued to embellish his story in an attempt to explain the inconsistencies that we inquired about. However, when I requested the Communications Division to rerun the original taped call, there was our suspect telling a completely different story on tape. Needless to say, upon being confronted with this verbal piece of evidence, and hearing from his own mouth his original "fairy tale", he changed his mind and gave us a complete confession. His story was that she had returned to the apartment after being out drinking with her friends. He had been home drinking and brooding about her "running around". When she returned, they had an argument, and he proceeded to beat her. And in his drunken rage, he killed her. He couldn't get rid of the body, because there were still people on the front stoop of his building and in the streets. So he undressed her, attempted to cleanup some of the blood (he didn't do a very good job), waited for a while, and then called the police to say that he had found her outside. While he was waiting for the police he came up with the rape and burglary idea.

It is, therefore, very important that the first officer responding to the homicide crime scene *note the time of the call* and/or any initial information, especially if informed of the crime by a passerby or witness. The initial *time* and the officer's *observations* are crucial to the investigation of homicide. Even while responding to the scene and departing from the patrol vehicle, the officer should remain observant and alert to any unusual activity or actions by persons at the scene.

First Notification of Homicide Received in Person by Patrol Officer

If the first notification is received in person by an officer on patrol, he should immediately note the time and the exact information. The person reporting it should be requested to accompany the officer, and this person should be returned to the vicinity of the crime scene and detained for the investigators.

It is important to note that valuable information is often irrevocably lost because the person who reported the homicide to the police officer is allowed to wander off in the confusion at the scene or is not detained for the homicide detective.

If for some reason the officer cannot detain this person, he should at least obtain sufficient identification and other personal information so that the follow-up investigator can interview this important witness at a later date.

> Remember, when returning this reporting person to the possible homicide location, never allow him or her to enter the actual crime scene itself. You may contaminate this scene either by

adding something to it, or by negating the value of trace evidence which will be found later on and may point to the possible perpetrator.

There is always the possibility that the person reporting the crime is actually the killer. I remember one incident where my partner and I were on investigative patrol in Harlem in an unmarked detective auto. I should point out that these unmarked autos are about as nondescript as a fire engine to the knowing eyes of a criminal. In any event, we had just entered West 117th Street off Lenox Avenue when we observed a male running out of an alley. At about the same time, this male spotted us. He came running up to us and excitedly stated, "There's a man getting killed in the alley". At first impulse, we were about to go charging into the alley; however, being street-wise and suspicious of this sudden show of good citizenship, we grabbed him by the arm and brought him along with us into the alley. There had been a homicide all right. Apparently, our "good citizen" had killed a fellow addict over a bag of "junk". Two addicts who were making a futile attempt to revive the deceased quickly identified our "guest" as the killer. He still had the bloody knife in his pocket and there was blood on his shirt and pants. Maybe if we had not been in a high-crime area, or suspicious of our "good citizen's" intentions, we might have gone charging into the alley, only to discover that we had allowed the perpetrator to walk away. It wouldn't be the first time a suspect had pulled this off. Keep in mind that the next person who comes running up to you yelling murder may be the killer.

Remember, do not go running off without detaining this reporting witness or at least obtaining sufficient identity for follow-up investigators.

First Officer's Duties on Arrival at the Scene

In almost all instances, the first officer to arrive at any homicide crime scene is the uniformed patrol officer. Rarely is the patrol officer a witness to the actual homicide. He usually arrives a short time after in response to a radio transmission or emergency call made by some citizen who has either witnessed the crime or has stumbled upon the homicide scene.

There is no doubt in my mind that the initial actions taken by the first officer may determine whether or not there will be a successful homicide investigation.

On arrival at the homicide crime scene, the situation confronting the first officer can fall anywhere between these two extremes:

1. He might be met by one individual, calm and composed, who directs him to a body which manifests obvious, conclusive signs of death, in a location which is easily secured and/or safeguarded; or
2. The scene might be filled with people milling about, shouting and/or weeping, the perpetrator may still be at the scene or just escaping, the victim may still be alive, and in need of immediate medical assistance, and the scene itself may be a public or quasi-public place which is difficult to safeguard.

Whatever the situation at the scene, the first officer has three primary duties.

1. Determining whether the victim is alive or dead and the necessary actions to be taken.
2. Apprehending of the perpetrator, if still present, or giving the appropriate notifications if he is escaping or has escaped.
3. Safeguarding the scene and detaining witnesses or suspects.

Protection of Life

Each case, of course, will require a different pattern of responses, but the major principle which should guide the first officer is the *protection of life*. The protection of life includes not only that of the victim, where there is a possibility of saving him; but also others on the scene including the suspect and the officer himself. Situations such as barricaded felons exchanging fire with responding police units as a victim lies on the line of fire, possible hostages, and the ever-increasing instances of terrorist acts, obviously will require additional police responses, including requests for specialized units.

However, under ordinary circumstances, wherever there is any doubt as to death, the officer should presume that there is life and proceed accordingly. First officers should, therefore, be aware of the signs of death.

Breath stoppage. This is best determined by observation of the upper part of the abdomen, just below the point where the lowest rib meets the breastbone. Any *up* and *down* motion here, however slight, is indicative of breath and life. Where there is no motion, breathing may have either stopped or be too shallow to be observed. However, death must not be presumed from the cessation of breathing alone.

Figure 2.1. **BREATH STOPPAGE.** The cessation of breathing is best determined by observation of the abdomen just below the point where the lowest rib meets the breast bone (see arrow).

Cessation of pulse. In most cases the heart continues to beat after the cessation of breathing for a short period of time, anywhere from a few seconds to a few minutes. Pulse can be detected by placing the tips of the fingers on the undersurface of the radial bone (at the base of the thumb) and firmly pressing inward. The absence of *pulse,* coupled with the cessation of breathing, generates a high probability of death.

Eye reflexes. During life, the pupils of the eyes are round and equal in size, and the eyeball is extremely sensitive. At death, the muscles which control the pupils relax, causing them to lose their symmetrical appearance. They may differ in size. The eyelids become flabby in death, and if they are opened by someone, they will remain open. Finally, whereas in life touching the eyeball will cause some reactive movement of the eyeball or eyelid, no such reaction occurs in death. The absence of eye reflexes, coupled with the cessation of pulse and breath, is a conclusive sign of death.

Of course, there are other conclusive signs of death which are somewhat obvious and require little or no examination, such as *rigor mortis, lividity,* and *putrefaction.* These will be discussed in greater detail in Chapter 9.

It should be noted, however, that the officer is not expected to perform the functions of a physician. If there is the slightest doubt

Figure 2.2.   **PULSE.** A pulse can be detected by placing the tips of one's fingers on the undersurface of the radial bone. In addition, the pulse can also be detected by placing one's fingertips on the temple or flat portion of the side of the victim's forehead.

whether or not the victim is dead, it should be resolved in favor of the presumption of life.

Safeguarding the Scene and Detaining Witnesses or Suspects

The first officer at the scene of a homicide is immediately confronted with a multitude of problems which he must quickly analyze so as to take the necessary steps. Quickness, however, does not imply haste. The first officer's actions must be deliberate and controlled. When the assignment information, communicated to him by radio, passerby, or telephone suggests an incident which is or may become a homicide, the officer, as he approaches the given location, must become *scene conscious*. He must be alert to important details which are transient in nature and which may be subject to chemical change. Changes may occur by dissipation, or simply by being moved by persons on or arriving at the scene. These may include, but are not limited to:

1. The condition of doors and windows, whether closed or ajar, locked or unlocked. Whether shades are drawn or open, the position of shutters or blinds, etc.

2. Odors, such as perfume, after-shave lotion, gas, marijuana, cigar or cigarette smoke, gunpowder, chemicals, putrefaction, etc.
3. Evidence which may be obliterated or damaged on the approach to the central scene, such as tire marks on the roadway, stains such as blood or other body fluids, fibers, shell casings either on the floor or in high grass or soil. In addition there may be discarded cigarettes or cigars, matchsticks, a weapon, fingerprints, and even personal property of the perpetrator left behind in his haste to get away.
4. Whether lights and light switches are *on* or *off*. Condition of electrical appliances — on or off, warm or cold.
5. Original position of furniture or articles which may have been moved in order to get to the victim to render first aid, to make a determination of death, etc. (If ambulance personnel arrived before patrol units, patrol officer should get their identification and determine what, if anything, was moved or touched.)

In most instances the first officer will face an emergency condition at the homicide crime scene. However, he must maintain a professional image which will enable him to perform effectively during this preliminary response stage. The first officer should direct his attention to isolating the body and immediate surroundings from all other persons. This procedure alone will usually call for a great deal of tact in dealing with members of the family who may be present, sympathetic neighbors, and the curious, whether strangers or other police officers who have responded.

In this phase of preservation of the scene and removal of unauthorized persons, the first officer in his diligence to remove unnecessary persons should be careful not to chase off possible witnesses or others who have important information. Do not overlook the possibility that one of the people you might chase off could be the perpetrator. I remember spending an entire nightwatch tour trying to locate a suspect who had literally been chased from the area by uniform officers while they were attempting to secure a homicide crime scene which occurred at a street location. The suspect, who was intoxicated and generally abusive, claimed to be a friend of the victim and had been pushing his way to the front of the crowd to get a better look and "see if the man was really dead". He had been admonished several times to remain behind police lines; however, he wasn't complying. One of the officers, probably out of sheer frustration, grabbed him by his coat collar and the back of his belt and literally tossed him out onto the street. The officer followed this up with an appropriate description of what he would do to the suspect if the suspect returned. Needless to say, the suspect took the officer's friendly advice and "got into the wind;" he disappeared. When the investigators arrived, they began questioning persons in the area and soon learned that the suspect and the deceased had been seen together earlier in the evening drinking and quarreling over a debt the deceased refused to pay. A witness to the murder was located as were various pieces of evidence that linked the suspect to the crime. Only one problem remained; the suspect couldn't be found because the officers had scared him away.

The first officer may even have to guard against his own overzealousness or desire to impress superiors by being the first to discover some piece of evidence, and inadvertently destroy its value by picking it up. He may also have to overcome sheer curiosity, or walking onto the scene "just to get a better look".

In addition, it is important to keep in mind that all personal habits of the officers at the scene must be carefully controlled. These include, but are not limited to, cigarette or cigar smoking, use of the toilet in the crime scene, discarding any foreign substance at the scene, using the telephone, etc.

> **Remember, at this stage of the investigation, the only evidence that should be collected by the patrol officer is eyewitness or testimonial in nature such as *res gestae* or spontaneous utterances of a suspect.**

The First Officer Initiates the Homicide Investigation

The first officer who is confronted by the homicide crime scene has a very involved responsibility. Although the formal investigation will be conducted by detectives or the criminal investigator, it is the *first officer* who has the responsibility of initiating the investigation. I have provided ten practical rules of procedure which may be used as a guide in initiating a professional homicide investigation.

1. Arrest the perpetrator if you can determine by direct inquiry or observation that he or she is the suspect. (As a general rule, do not question him or her at this stage.)
2. Detain all persons present at the scene.
3. Attempt to assess and determine the entire area of the *crime scene* including paths of entry and exit and any areas that may include evidence.

Figure 2.3. **CHALK LINES AROUND BODY AT CRIME SCENE.** You are *not* to draw lines around the body at a crime scene unless the body is to be removed. This photo shows evidence that the crime scene had been visited by a "chalk fairy". "Chalk fairy" is a term used to describe mysterious police officers who feel the need to draw lines around the body and then disappear when investigators attempt to find out who contaminated the scene.

4. Isolate the area and *protect the scene*. Seek assistance if necessary. Notifications must be made to superiors, investigators, and specialized units. (Use crime scene cards; see page 8, Figure 1.4.)

5. Refrain from entering the scene and/or disturbing, touching, or using any item found therein. *Never use the crime scene as a command post or the telephone as a communications center.* In communicating with the station house or headquarters, the first officer should *not*, unless absolutely necessary, use a telephone instrument at the scene. This necessity *should* be determined by common sense and priorities. The first officers should instead establish a temporary command post outside the central crime scene, preferably where there are at least two phones available, one for incoming and one for outgoing calls. In the early stages of the investigation, there is a definite need for rapid communication between the various centers of investigation.

6. Identify and, if possible, retain for questioning the person who first notified the police.

7. Separate the witnesses so as to obtain independent statements.

8. Exclude all unauthorized persons from entering the crime scene until the arrival of the investigators. This, of course, includes police officers not directly involved in the crime scene investigation. The detective supervisor and the investigator assigned are, of course, allowed entry into the scene for evaluation purposes.

Other unavoidable exceptions may include the medical examiner, or a doctor or clergymen. In any event, establish a pathway in and out so as to avoid unnecessary disturbance.

9. Keep a *chronological log* containing the name, shield number, command, and title of any police official who enters; the name, serial number, and hospital of any medical personnel, ambulance driver, or technician; and the names and addresses of any civilians entering the crime scene.

10. Take notes.

Although this list may seem very simplistic and basic, I can assure you from experience that in the confusion that permeates the homicide crime scene, it is inevitable that such a fundamental principle as not touching or using the phone is invariably forgotten as the need for communications overwhelms good technique. Many times I have responded to a homicide in an apartment, only to find that the telephone was now being used as a communications line and one of the rooms as an office or command post. Needless to say, valuable trace evidence is irrevocably lost because of this careless procedure.

Remember, never use the crime scene as a Command Post or the telephone as a communications center.

Dealing with Emergencies at the Scene

It should be noted that rules and procedures are only a guide to assist the first officer in performing his or her functions at the homicide crime scene. The true test, however, in any given crisis is *common sense*. Often he or she does not have the luxury of "clinical textbook conditions" to direct his or her performance. Practically speaking, it is usually the street-wise officer who manages to come up with the appropriate solution in an emergency that occurs in an otherwise routine job, because he or she possesses flexibility and common sense — the two ingredients necessary in an emergency.

Sometimes the first officer is faced with hysterical or violent persons, who may include the perpetrator and/or his hostile family and friends, or the family and friends of the deceased either bent on revenge or so overcome with grief that they become irrational. In addition, especially within inner-city enclaves, hostility may result from a general distrust of the police, or any number of factors ranging from misunderstanding of the police function to the real or imagined grievances of the

Figure 2.4. **TELEPHONE IN CRIME SCENE.** In this close-up photo of a telephone in a typical homicide crime scene, it is obvious that the phone has been handled by someone who has been bleeding. (This may include the perpetrator as well as the victim.) It is imperative that this valuable evidence is not touched or disturbed before a forensic examination is made. Telephone instruments often contain latent prints. The first officer should be aware of the existence of "trace evidence" on the telephone instruments and not use the telephone to communicate with the police station or other police units until it has been processed for evidence. Although this particular telephone obviously contains trace evidence, it should be noted that any object at the scene may contain latent prints or other evidence and should be treated accordingly.

citizens involved, neither of which is amenable to correction by the first officers responding to the crime scene.

In situations like these, the first officer would be foolhardy *not* to pick up any weapons connected with the crime scene, in order to preclude their use by those present against either the officer or another person. Protection of life would in that case take precedence over the general rule of not picking up or disturbing any evidence at the scene. However, the officer should continue to remain scene conscious, disturbing only that which is necessary and being careful to note the location, position, and condition of each item before it is moved or changed.

I remember one crime scene in a South Bronx social club that resembled *The Shoot-out at the O.K. Corral.* There were two bodies lying on the floor, a number of guns strewn about, and a large angry group of combatants who had been temporarily "neutralized" by the responding police. The first officers had instinctively retrieved the guns to prevent further bloodshed. Common sense would dictate removing the weapons before you have an increased body count or you lose the evidence to the local gun collectors.

In extreme cases, it may even be necessary to move the body and abandon the scene. However, *this is a last resort*, only undertaken when police officials at the scene either cannot maintain police lines or are forced by conditions that indicate there will be a further loss of life to innocent bystanders or injury to police officers at the scene.

Such a situation could occur when a militant or radical group has just lost its leader through an assassination, or any incident which may trigger a large-scale civil disturbance. In these cases, if the officers have access to the body, they should, consistent with their own safety, attempt to remove the body from the crowd. While doing so, they should attempt to note the original position, any new blood flow, any rigor or lividity if present, and any other information which may assist in the investigation by the pathologist and detectives later on.

In such situations, there will usually be a number of news media representatives, including still and movie photographers. Police officials at the scene should enlist the assistance of these cameramen and photographers in getting as many photos as possible, with an accent on the persons present at the scene. In addition, there is usually ample time to arrange for police photographers to be present to take intelligence films. If conditions allow, it may even be possible to have these police photographers take the necessary crime scene shots before you move the body, taking special note of the crowd. These photos and newsfilms can later be reviewed for evidence and information.

I recall one such episode which occurred in New York City during a "Unity Day" rally in the early seventies. A major member of organized crime, who had arranged for a rally against alleged "police and FBI harassment", was about to address a large assemblage when suddenly he was shot. Although there were uniformed police officers only a few feet away, they were completely helpless in the chaos that followed. In addition to this attempted "hit", there were literally dozens of guns drawn by both the personal bodyguards of the victim and by members of the opposite faction. The bewildered police officers also drew their guns, but couldn't tell the "good guys" from the "bad guys"; they withheld their fire. However, there were several shots fired. A supposed suspect was killed, no one knew by whom, there were guns strewn all over the place, and there were several ongoing struggles within the crowd. The police were at a complete disadvantage in maintaining any type of original crime scene. However, a later review of the film coverage taken by the major networks and the intelligence photos taken by police and FBI photographers were invaluable in re-creating the original scene and identifying possible perpetrators as well as suspected members of organized crime who were present during the shooting.

Conclusion

In conclusion, the police officer who is responding to or confronted by the homicide crime scene should prepare to take *five basic steps* upon arrival. If he executes them carefully, he will have initiated a proper professional investigation.

The homicide crime scene is not an everyday occurrence for most officers. Usual police activities are either emergencies, requiring automatic reaction, or routine handling of called-for-services. The officer who confronts the homicide crime scene, however, finds himself somewhere between these two extremes. He must therefore force himself to adapt to the situation. I offer the acronym ADAPT as a basic, five-step approach.

A Arrest the perpetrator, if possible.
D Detain and identify witnesses and/or suspects for follow-up investigators.
A Assess the crime scene.
P Protect the crime scene.
T Take notes.

It should be noted that the arrest in A by the responding police officer is actually an apprehension. However, since any seizure of a person is legally an arrest, I have used the term arrest. I recommend that the actual arrest for homicide should be made by the detective or investigator assigned to the case. The police officer should get full credit for the apprehension but the formal arrest is a function of the investigative division of the police agency.

I make this point because the formal arrest is based on the original probable cause resulting in the apprehension of the suspect coupled with all of the investigative information developed during the subsequent inquiry by the detective.

The arrest is only the beginning of a long legal process. There will be additional interviews of witnesses, preliminary hearings, possible grand jury appearance in certain jurisdictions, and a number of court appearances leading up to trial. For the purposes of effective prosecution, it is imperative that the police representative be the arresting officer as well as the case officer. This is an important legal strategy for any subsequent defense tactic to challenge the initial arrest.

The apprehending officer will only be testifying to his or her observations and initial probable cause. The detective will carry the weight of the prosecution's case by providing the investigative details and evidence which supports the charge of homicide.

Selected Readings

Geberth, Vernon J., *Practical Homicide Investigation: Tactics, Procedures, and Forensic Techniques.* Second Edition. CRC Press, Inc., Florida, 1993.

Geberth, Vernon J., "Practical Homicide Investigation: First Officer's Duties", *Law and Order Magazine,* Vol. 28, No. 11 Illinois, November, 1980.

Geberth, Vernon J., "The Homicide Crime Scene", *Law and Order Magazine,* Vol. 28, No. 10, Illinois, October, 1980.

Geberth, Vernon J., "Supervision and Management of a Homicide Investigation". *Law and Order Magazine,* Vol. 37, No. 11, Illinois, November, 1989.

First Officer's Duties: Specific

Chapter 2 concerned the general responsibilities of the first officer who confronts the homicide crime scene. This chapter will treat related situations that call for a *specific* response on the part of the first officer. These specific duties concern the following:

The suspect in custody
Transporting the suspect
Examination of the suspect for evidence
The dying declaration
The victim removed to the hospital
The victim pronounced dead at the hospital
The officer's duties at the hospital
The victim confirmed dead at the scene
Handling witnesses at the scene
Additional officers at the scene
Handling news media personnel at the scene
The documentation of events by the first officer

In addition, I have included in this chapter, a patrol officer's checklist, which the officer at the scene can use to refresh his memory about what vital information must be obtained and duties accomplished in the initial investigation of homicide. Some of the information in this chapter may seem repetitive. It is meant to be. Based on my experience, some elements of investigatory procedure need to be reinforced by repetition.

The Suspect in Custody

If the first officer takes a suspect into custody based on the officer's observations, information, or probable cause developed at the scene, he should *not* as a general rule interrogate him. The interrogation should be conducted by the investigator later on.

Figure 3.1. **SUSPECT IN CUSTODY — DECEASED CONFIRMED DEAD AT SCENE.** The deceased, a 16-year old female, was accidentally shot by her boyfriend while he was practicing his quick-draw with a shotgun, which he wore in a sling under his arm. The boyfriend, a suspect in some local armed robberies (with a shotgun), had been showing-off when the gun discharged. Hearing the blast and screams, neighbors called the police. Three patrol units arrived within minutes of the "shots fired" call. They disarmed the boyfriend at gunpoint, detained the group involved, and notified the detectives. In such situations, the perpetrator is obvious. The patrol officers should take the suspect into immediate custody, based on their observations at the scene. It is better, however, if the suspect is questioned later-on by the investigators and not interrogated by the patrol officers. If the suspect is talkative and wants to make a statement to the patrol officers, then by all means the statement should be taken. Make sure, however, that the suspect has been properly advised of his or her Miranda rights.

MIRANDA WARNING

1. You have the right to remain silent.
2. Anything you say can and will be used against you in a court of law.
3. You have the right to talk to a lawyer and have him present with you while you are being questioned.
4. If you cannot afford to hire a lawyer, one will be appointed to represent you before any questioning, if you wish one.

WAIVER

After the warning and in order to secure a waiver, the following questions should be asked and an affirmative reply secured to each question.
1. Do you understand each of these rights I have explained to you?
2. Having these rights in mind, do you wish to talk to us now?

Figure 3.2. **MIRANDA WARNINGS CARD.**

Practically speaking, however, there are certain types of homicide cases that readily indicate the culpability of the suspect. In addition, there are instances when the suspect is quite talkative and insists on confessing or telling "his side of the story" to the officer. Under these circumstances, the officer should immediately advise the suspect of his constitutional rights under the Miranda ruling, make sure the suspect understands these rights, obtain an intelligent waiver from the suspect, and then allow him or her to make a statement.

I recommend that the officer advise the suspect of his rights using an official form, or a "Miranda Warnings" card, issued by most departments to their officers. This will insure that the rights have been given in a proper manner, and the card can later be presented in court upon the challenge of the defense attorney that his client wasn't properly advised by the officer.

Under the Miranda ruling the suspect must be told the following.

1. You have the right to remain silent and refuse to answer any questions. Do you understand?
2. Anything you say can and may be used against you in a court of law. Do you understand?
3. You have the right to consult an attorney before speaking and to have an attorney present during any questioning. Do you understand?
4. If you cannot afford an attorney, one will be provided for you without cost. Do you understand?
5. Now that I have advised you of your rights, are you willing to answer questions without an attorney present?

If the defendant understands his rights and answers in the affirmative to each of the above questions, an intelligent waiver has been obtained. It should be noted that there are specific rules for non-English speaking suspects and juveniles.

Transporting the Suspect

Sometimes a patrol officer will be requested to transport a suspect to the station house while investigators remain at the scene. If the suspect is to be transported to the police station by patrol officers, these officers should be instructed *not* to interrogate him or her. If the suspect insists on volunteering information, or talking about the case, the officers should listen, remember, and later make notes of any statements made. It is important to note that an interrogation by officers who are not familiar with the facts of the homicide investigation may do more harm than good, and perhaps completely damage the case.

From a practical point of view, it is usually better if the suspect is interrogated by the investigator who is assigned to the case. The homicide investigators are in the best position to question the suspect based on their firsthand knowledge of the investigation, which includes examination of the crime scene, interviews with the first officers, and questioning of witnesses or any others who may have information relative to the case. Obviously, the investigator will be able to determine whether or not the suspect's statements are consistent with the facts of the homicide investigation.

Examination of the Suspect for Evidence

The examination of the suspect for evidence should be performed by the investigator or homicide detective assigned to the case, or another investigator familiar with the investigation. However, in the event that the patrol officer has effected the arrest, or has taken the suspect into custody, he should be aware that there may be physical or trace evidence on the suspect, his clothing, and/or his shoes. My advice is that the officer examine the suspect for any evidence, and preserve the clothes and shoes which can be vouchered as evidence in connection with the investigation. (See Chapter 8.)

The Dying Declaration

If the victim is still alive, the officer must be alert to the possibility of obtaining a *dying declaration*. This can be performed while waiting for the ambulance or en route to the hospital. Officers should be knowledgeable in the requirements of a valid dying declaration. I would recommend that the department issue a checklist or card to patrol officers which will assist them in obtaining a legally admissible statement, which may later prove invaluable in firmly establishing whether or not a crime has occurred and investigating the circumstances surrounding that crime. However, it may be used in a criminal trial only for the death of the declarant. (See Chapter 5, "Obtaining a Dying Declaration.")

The statement can be either oral or written. In any event, the officer should reduce the statement to writing and have the declarant either sign it or make his mark. It is recommended that there be a witness present. However, neither the absence of a witness nor the inability of the declarant to write this statement affects its admissibility.

The Victim Removed to the Hospital

Upon arrival of the ambulance, the officer should guide the intern and/ or ambulance attendants to and through the central crime scene via a preselected route so that there is no destruction or unnecessary damage to any physical or trace evidence. Whatever they touch or move must be observed by the officers on the scene and reported to the investigators when they arrive. An officer should ride in the rear of the ambulance with the victim and remain with him at the hospital, making sure not to interfere in any way with required medical treatment. If the prognosis is that the victim is likely to die, the officer's presence is necessary should the victim make some statement or recall some important fact not previously disclosed.

The officer at the hospital should attempt to have the victim's clothing removed intact. If cutting is necessary, however, it should not be done through any holes, cuts, or tears caused by bullets, knives, or other weapons and instruments. To facilitate this procedure, it is recommended that hospital emergency room personnel be contacted in advance to secure their future cooperation when and if such a situation arises. I would suggest that the investigative supervisor contact the hospital administrator and discuss matters of mutual concern. This liaison between homicide commanders and representatives of the hospital can be advantageous to both parties in getting the job done.

The Victim Pronounced DOA at the Hospital

If the victim is pronounced DOA (dead on arrival) or dies at the hospital, the officer should obtain the necessary information consisting of name of attending physician, cause of death, time of death, and any

Figure 3.3. **VICTIM STILL ALIVE.** Here you see a homicide crime scene where the body has been removed. The victim was still alive when the police arrived. He was rushed to the hospital in a patrol unit, while other officers secured the scene for the investigators. The chalk outline indicates the position of the body when police arrived. This is good procedure. However, if the victim is obviously dead and the body is not going to be removed *do not* draw any chalk lines around the deceased. In this case, first officers at the scene detained witnesses to the slaying. The officers in the patrol unit, which rushed the victim to the hospital, were able to learn the nick-name of the assailant from the victim before he died. When the victim was pronounced dead at the hospital, the officers notified the patrol units at the scene and the homicide squad was dispatched. As a result of the professional and thorough handling of this incident by the patrol units, the detectives were able to effect an arrest within 24 hours.

other factors which may pertain to the investigation. The officer should then immediately communicate with the detective or detective supervisor at the scene, relay this information, and then be guided by any further instructions he may receive.

The Officer's Duties at the Hospital

At the first opportunity, the officer at the hospital should communicate with the investigators at the crime scene in order to keep them advised of any developments at the hospital. In turn, the officer will receive such information as is necessary in order to be able to talk intelligently to the victim should he or she regain consciousness, or should the opportunity arise to obtain a dying declaration.

The Victim Confirmed DOA at the Scene

If the first officer arriving at the scene finds a body showing conclusive signs of death, the body should not be disturbed. Sometimes, inexperienced officers feel a need to "do something," particularly in the presence of family or friends of the deceased. They may feel compelled to cut down a body which has been suspended in a hanging, or otherwise disturb it, even when there are such obvious signs of death as rigor, lividity, and incipient putrefaction. In some instances, officers feel that they should immediately search the decedent so as to quickly identify him or her, or obtain "all the information" for the desk officer when they call in their report. Once again, I emphatically state that the body should not be searched or disturbed until all other investigative processes have been completed and the medical examiner has completed his on-the-scene examination.

I would strongly suggest, based on past experience, that the search and inventory of the deceased be conducted in the presence of a supervising officer, and if possible a member of the family or other civilian, in order to minimize a later charge of theft from the body, which unfortunately arises from time to time in dead-body cases. If the officer does cut down a hanging body because there are no conclusive signs of death, he must be careful first to observe the position of the knot when the body is suspended, and then to leave the knot intact.

Handling Witnesses at the Scene

All witnesses present at the scene upon the officer's arrival must be detained for the investigators. The officer should also be alert to the possibility that one of the witnesses who "discovered" the body may in fact be the perpetrator. If the suspect is taken into custody at the scene, he should ordinarily be detained for the investigators or removed as soon as additional assistance arrives to protect the scene. Keep in mind scene contamination.

Keep witnesses and/or suspects separate from one another, or where circumstances make this situation impossible, at least attempt to prevent discussion of the incident either in the hearing of or between these persons. At the same time, officers should be alert to any declarations which may be admissible under the *res gestae* rule. As soon as the circumstances and number of officers present permit, the witnesses should be moved outside the crime scene area, or at the very least away from the central crime scene. Witnesses should not ordinarily be moved to the station house until the investigators arrive, to permit them to obtain the details basic to the investigation and crime scene search.

The first officer should report all conversations with the witnesses to the investigators when they arrive, and, at the first opportunity, make careful written notes of such conversations.

At times, the person who discovers the body, the witnesses, or perhaps members of the immediate family may be so distraught that some well-meaning person or physician may suggest that they be given a sedative. Officers present should attempt to delay this medication until the arrival of the investigators. Persons who are sedated are often unable to be spoken to for several hours or even until the next day. This could become particularly critical when the sedated individual emerges as a possible suspect or perpetrator of the crime. As always, this situation will require tact and discretion.

Additional Officers at the Scene

As other officers arrive, care must be taken that they conduct themselves in an appropriate manner. Too often, officers who have not seen each other for a while meet at crime scenes and drift into irrelevant conversation during the lulls that occur while waiting for the investigators, the crime scene technicians, the morgue wagon, and so on. At times this banter produces snickers or outright laughter which can be heard by members of the family or friends of the victim. The image of the officers, the department, and police in general may thus be downgraded or even ruined in the eyes of that family, the neighborhood, or even the entire community. This is one of the reasons that I recommend that officers, especially additional reinforcements, arriving at homicides, be directed to report to the command post, which should be away from the central crime scene area. There they can await assignments and be supervised without their conversations being overheard.

Handling News Media Personnel at the Scene

If newspaper or television people arrive on the scene, they should *not* be permitted access and *no* information should be given to them at this time. In addition, if there are any witnesses or suspects being detained, it is imperative that they be kept away from the media. The first officers can best accomplish this task by firmly insisting that *no unauthorized persons* are allowed to interview or ask questions of anyone present in the interests of justice.

First officers should tactfully explain that all information about the case will come from the chief investigator or the detective supervisor in charge at the scene. It can be explained that it would be unfair to make some information available, piecemeal, to some members of the press, which would not be equally available to all others, and that such information will be made uniformly available as soon as possible. This approach must be taken by all members of the department, whether at the scene, the hospital, the morgue, the station house, or still on patrol.

Such an *interests of justice* or *cooperation* appeal will usually be sufficient to handle preliminary inquiries by the press. Most press personalities and news reporters who have dealt with the police before can appreciate the emergency nature of this phase of the investigation and know that any information must come from a ranking official or detective supervisor. However, the first officers may encounter an overzealous or pushy character who insists that the police have no right interfering with the freedom of the press. In these instances, merely exercise good police procedure and courteously remove him or her from the crime scene, just as you would remove any other unauthorized or unnecessary person. (See Chapter 19 "The News Media in Homicide Investigations.")

The Documentation of Events by the First Officer

The first officer (and indeed all officers taking part in the investigation) must be *time-conscious*. He must, as soon as circumstances permit, record the time he was dispatched, the time he arrived on the scene, the time he requested assistance, and so on. Time may become an important factor in terms of the suspect's alibi. Accurate recording of time also makes for a more precise investigation and contributes to a more professional report. In addition, accuracy as to time will create a more favorable impression in court.

The first officer, as well as other officers who arrive on the scene prior to investigators, should realize that they will have to enumerate all their activities at the scene to the investigators when they arrive. The officers should be mindful that they too may be subpoenaed to court later on and their notes subject to review.

The investigators must be informed of *everything* that was touched, moved, or altered in any way, either by the officers or by others who were at the scene when the officers arrived. Officers must not smoke, flush toilets, run tap water, use the bathroom facilities, or anything else at or near the crime scene *unless absolutely necessary*.

As soon as the first officers have performed their immediate duties, they should take advantage of any lulls or waiting time to record times, details, conversations they have had, names and addresses of witnesses or persons known to have been on the scene, and any other information pertinent to the investigation.

When the investigators arrive, the officers should immediately fill them in, out of the hearing of the family, witnesses, suspects, and any others present, on all that has transpired up to that point. The investigators will now assume responsibility, at whatever point that they cut into the investigation, for the conduct of the investigation from that point on.

The Changing Sequence of Command

All officers should be aware of the changing sequence of command at homicide crime scenes. The first officer on the scene is in command until a uniformed officer of higher rank, or an investigator arrives on the scene. The ranking uniformed man will be in charge until the arrival of his superiors or an investigator. As soon as the investigator arrives, he will assume command from that point forward. He in turn will be superseded by an investigator of superior rank. Department regulations should provide for such shifts of command in these situations so as to avoid conflict and maintain a professional investigation.

Patrol Officer's Checklist

As a practical matter the first officer's responsibilities in the preliminary investigation of homicide are divided into three specific duties:

1. Preserve life
2. Arrest the suspect
3. Protect the scene

The officer should record all homicide information in his memo book or notebook as soon as possible, preferably as it is obtained. This book should be retained for later court purposes and shown to the investigator when he arrives at the scene. All dead-body calls should be handled as homicides in this preliminary stage.

I have provided the following checklist of first-officer duties in order to assist the officer at the scene in refreshing his memory as to what vital information he should secure.

Initial Call/Receipt of Information

☐ Record exact time and type of call patrol unit received. (In systems using modern computerized and recorded radio transmissions, unit can check with Communications.)

☐ If first notification is received in person: detain this person for investigators. If unable to detain for some reason, obtain sufficient identification and information for follow-up investigator.

Arrival at the Homicide Crime Scene

☐ Record the exact time of your arrival and/or notify Communications that you are on the scene.

☐ Enter the immediate crime scene area to view victim. (Only one officer should enter scene unless the call is an emergency call and the offender may still be on the scene. Use only one path of entry and exit.

☐ Determine if victim is alive or dead.

☐ Arrest the perpetrator if present.

☐ If there is a possibility of life, summon ambulance and apply appropriate first-aid procedures.

☐ If circumstances indicate the victim is near death or dying, attempt to obtain a dying declaration.

☐ If ambulance crew is present before your arrival, determine if the crew or anyone else moved the body or any items within the crime scene. If there were any items moved, record the following:

    ☐ What alterations were made.

    ☐ When the alterations were made.

    ☐ Purpose of the movement.

    ☐ Person who made the alteration.

☐ Record the names, serial numbers, and hospital of ambulance crew present at the scene.

☐ If the victim is dead, record the official time of pronouncement by ambulance attendant.

☐ *If suspect has just fled the scene, initiate a wanted alarm.*

☐ Record any alterations to the crime scene that were made as a matter of investigative necessity. For example,

    ☐ Lights turned on or off.

☐ Door opened, closed, locked, or unlocked.
☐ Body moved or cut down.
☐ Windows opened, closed, locked, or unlocked.
☐ Furniture moved; anything touched.
☐ Gas turned off, appliances turned off, motor of vehicle on or off.

Protection of the Crime Scene

☐ Attempt to assess the entire crime scene, including paths of entry and exit, and any areas that may include evidence. (*Remember the possibility of a multiple crime scene.*)
☐ Establish a perimeter, secure and protect the scene by isolation and physical barriers such as ropes, cones, and other equipment as necessary.
☐ Record names, addresses, dates of birth, and telephone numbers, etc. of all persons present at the crime scene.
☐ Remove all persons from the immediate area. (*Be careful not to chase off witnesses or the perpetrator, who may still be present.*)
☐ If victim is removed from scene by ambulance, an officer should accompany victim to hospital riding in rear with victim (for possible dying declaration).
☐ An officer should remain at scene in order to provide for its security.
☐ If the victim's clothes are removed at hospital, an officer should maintain control (victim's clothes are evidence).
☐ Request additional units as needed to protect the scene.
☐ If it is necessary that a clergyman or doctor enter the scene, have an officer accompany him through the designated path of entry and caution this person about contamination and/or alteration.

Notifications

☐ Make notifications by telephone if possible (police radios are often monitored by the press).
☐ *Never*, unless absolutely necessary, use a telephone inside the crime scene. Such necessity would involve a life-or-death situation, the need for immediate transmission of alarms, etc.
☐ Notify the investigators or homicide division.
☐ Record time of notification and who was notified.

☐ Establish a temporary headquarters out of central crime scene (preferably a location with two phones, one for incoming, one for outgoing).

☐ Broadcast any alarms for suspects or descriptions of perpetrators from command post to guarantee uniformity and possibility of verification.

☐ Notify Communications of the telephone numbers of the command post to facilitate communications between the various units.

Preliminary Investigation

☐ Initiate and maintain a chronological log recording the names, shield numbers, and commands of any police officers entering the crime scene. In addition, record the names, addresses, etc. of any civilians who may have to enter as well as names, titles, and serial numbers of any ambulance personnel. This log should reflect the entry and exit of any person who enters the crime scene.

☐ Isolate and separate witnesses or suspects. Do *not* permit any conversations relative to the crime. Hold witnesses and suspects for the investigators.

☐ Establish a path of entry and exit based on observation of scene.

☐ For any civilian at the scene, record identifying information and their knowledge of the crime.

☐ Do not touch, move, or alter anything in the scene. If you do, record it.

☐ Do *not* smoke in the crime scene.

☐ Do not flush toilets or run tap water in sinks or bathtubs. If it has been done, record it.

☐ Refer all newspaper and media inquiries to the investigators.

☐ Stand by for investigators and assist them as required.

☐ Advise and inform investigators of all that has transpired since arrival of first officer.

Suspect in Custody

☐ Determine if the suspect is armed (search for weapons). If weapon is recovered, record description and location. Maintain custody pending arrival of investigators who will instruct as to vouchering and disposition.

☐ Handcuff suspect and isolate him/her from any witnesses and/ or associates. (Use rear handcuff method.)

☐ If suspect is arrested outside crime scene, *do not return him/her to scene.*

☐ If suspect is arrested inside crime scene, *remove him/her immediately.* (*Remember scene contamination.*)

☐ Note and preserve any evidence found on suspect, advise investigators.

☐ Do *not* permit suspect to wash hands or use toilet (you may lose evidence).

☐ Do not permit any conversation between suspect and any other parties.

☐ Do not initiate any interrogation (wait for the investigators). However, in certain types of homicides the first officer will take statements. *Make sure, however, that suspect has been warned of his rights* before taking any statement. As a general rule, no interrogation.

☐ Carefully record all spontaneous statements (*Res gestae* rule).

☐ Observe and record behavior of suspect (e.g., nervous, erratic, emotional unemotional, drunk, under influence of drugs, any unusual behavior, etc.).

Suicide and Accidental Deaths

☐ If death appears to be suicidal or accidental, handle as homicide, pending arrival of investigators.

    ☐ Secure immediate scene, detain witnesses.

    ☐ Preserve all evidence, e.g., notes, weapons, pills, vials, drugs, etc. in their original position.

    ☐ Notify investigators.

    ☐ If vehicles are involved, do not allow removal until photos have been taken by crime-scene technicians.

    ☐ If suicide is by hanging and death is evident, *do not cut body down.*

    ☐ If body is cut down because death is not evident, *make cut above the knot.*

    ☐ If relatives are present, get any background information which may assist investigators.

The Preliminary Investigation at the Scene: The Detectives

4

The purpose of this chapter is to provide the homicide investigator/ detective with flexible guidelines to follow in the preliminary investigation of death. The principles set forth in this section are intended to help the detective and chief investigator at the homicide crime scene to systematically check and review all the facts applicable to the investigation.

This chapter will cover the sequence of events starting with the initial notification to the detectives that a homicide has occurred, and then proceed chronologically through the investigative duties and direction of activities at the scene, including direction of uniformed personnel, interview of first officers, handling curious onlookers and witnesses at the scene, interview of ambulance personnel, the canvass, and the preliminary medical examination. Subsequent chapters will address the specific investigative methods employed at the scene. However, this preliminary phase of homicide investigation is the most critical and deserves special attention because this phase sets the tone for the entire investigation.

Initial Receipt of Information

Homicide investigation is probably the most exacting task confronting the criminal investigator. It begins with the initial notification that a homicide has occurred.

Investigators are rarely the first officers at the scene of a homicide. The body is usually discovered by friends, relatives, or citizens who in turn notify the police or call for an ambulance. The notification to detectives or investigators is usually made through department channels.

The response of the homicide investigator and detective supervisor must be methodical. In order not to overlook the obvious, the most basic details should be recorded. I personally recommend that the investigator start a separate steno pad or notebook for use in each homicide investigation.

The first entry should be the receipt of information that a homicide has occurred, including:

Date and time of notification

Method of transmission, e.g., telephone, radio, or in person

Name, rank, shield number, and other data identifying the person who is reporting the information to detectives

Complete details of the information and event

Many times, either from a false sense of urgency and/or a desire to take immediate action, investigators will get caught up in the excitement or confusion that often permeates the homicide crime scene. Subsequently, they may lose the "cool, calm, and detached" projection necessary to assume control and initiate the investigation. A good thing to keep in mind is the fact that the deceased isn't going anywhere; and, more important, that the patrol officers are already at the scene taking preliminary action.

Prior to leaving for the scene, the investigator should instruct the person notifying him or her that patrol officers at the scene should:

Preserve the crime scene

Hold all witnesses and/or suspects

Avoid using telephones located within the crime scene

Initiate a *personnel log* accounting for all activities at the scene, including identification of all persons who have had access to the scene

Record the license numbers and vehicle information of all autos in the area of the crime scene (if applicable)

Arrival at the Scene

When the investigator arrives at the scene, he should not the following:

Time of arrival

The exact address of the scene

Persons present (officers, ambulance or medical people, relatives, friends, etc.)

The condition and position of the body (personally verify death; see Chapter 2 "First Officer's Duties on Arrival at the Scene")

Information concerning death

Weather conditions

Outside lighting conditions in nighttime situations

Points of observation (locations where persons such as the local busybody could have observed what happened)

In addition, the investigator should stop and observe the area as a whole, noting everything possible before entering the actual crime scene for the detailed examination. Only the investigator and detective supervisor should enter the homicide crime scene, of course, with the exception of the first officers, and even then only to confirm death and observe scene conditions.

Homicide investigators must be certain to record the time and place of events and any measurable evidence. It only takes a few moments of the investigator's time to record this information, which may prove vital to the investigation. Basically, there are three reasons for this emphasis on preliminary note-taking.

1. The question of *time* is frequently the first subject covered in a cross-examination. If the investigator cannot be sure of the time of events, he may lose credibility on the rest of the testimony.
2. The subject of *time* may very well be the basis of an alibi.
3. Note-taking forces the investigator to slow down. It thereby sets a calmer tone for subsequent events at the scene, and also causes the investigator to pay attention to details in order to record them in the notebook.

A procedure I have found effective is to photograph the crime scene upon arrival. This can be done either with a Polaroid camera, available at the homicide office and maintained for crime scene use, or with an Instamatic camera, which can be carried in your pocket for ready use at any time. I find the Instamatic with built-in flash device good because of its convenience and simplicity. A photo taken at this point is a priceless record of how the crime scene appeared when the first detectives arrived.

The Crime Scene Unit or police photographer will take any number of photographs of the homicide crime scene, which will be submitted into evidence for the prosecution. However, those first pictures taken before the arrival of additional personnel and supervisors usually prove to be quite valuable.

Figure 4.1. **PROPERLY PREPARED CRIME SCENE: VICTIM DEAD.** This photo was taken immediately on arrival of the investigators at the scene; you can see that uniformed officers have cordoned-off the area to preserve the scene. The emergency medical people have covered the body with a sheet after pronouncing the victim dead. It is a good procedure to obtain pictures of the people in the crowd. Often, witnesses to the event including possible suspects will be watching the police activities at the scene. If their pictures have been taken, you may be able to identify or locate these persons later on in the investigation.

Describing the Scene

A complete description of the dead body and the surrounding area, covering the following items, should be entered in the notebook of the investigator upon arrival. (Although some of the points I have listed may seem quite obvious, I can assure you from my own experience that the obvious is sometimes overlooked, especially during this initial phase, as you attempt to "cover all the bases".)

1. Sex, appearance, age, build, color of hair of the deceased and a description of the deceased's clothing.
2. Evidence of injury and apparent cause of death.
3. Are the bloodstains wet or dry?
4. What is the condition of the body (lividity, rigor, etc.)?
5. Describe the color of the blood (bright red or brown).

6. Note any tears in clothing and evidence of gunshot or stab wounds.
7. Careful examination of the hands. Are there any wounds or a weapon?
8. Note whether or not there is any jewelry (rings, watches, gold chains, etc.). If there is no jewelry, make a negative notation. The defense has been known to resort to dirty tactics during trials. If they can make you appear like a thief to discredit your testimony, *they'll do it.*
9. Describe the immediate surroundings. (See Chapter 7.)

    a. Position of body in relation to articles in the room.

    b. Note doors, windows, furniture, etc.
10. If a weapon is nearby, take detailed notes. Do not handle.
11. Look for bullet holes or fired shells. Note: do not collect at this stage of the investigation. (See Chapter 8.)
12. In poison and drug-overdose cases, note presence of drugs, bottles, or glasses.

Implementing Crime Scene Procedures

The first thing the investigator should do after confirming death is to take charge of the crime scene. In the absence of the detective supervisor, the homicide detective is responsible for the professional investigation, of which the preliminary investigation at the crime scene is the most important and sensitive aspect. Therefore, extreme care must be exercised to preserve and protect the scene, because even the smallest detail can suddenly assume vital importance in the case. Failure to implement proper crime scene techniques may irreparably damage the investigation. I have found that the best course of action is to treat each dead-body call like a criminal homicide until the facts prove differently.

If the crime scene is outdoors, a wide area surrounding the body should be cordoned off for later systematic examination. The patrol officers should be directed to isolate the body and secure the immediate surroundings from all persons.

If the crime scene is indoors, the job of securing the location is relatively easy to accomplish. It may be as simple as closing the door. The biggest problem is removing unauthorized persons from the scene. The investigation should begin with the walkway and front entrance to the structure. These areas and the location where the body lies should be considered part of the scene and appropriately secured.

The homicide detective should determine what areas are to be included or excluded from the crime scene and decide whether or not the homicide involves multiple scenes. (See Chapters 1 and 2.)

I remember responding to a particularly vicious incident in which the victim, a young newspaper delivery girl, was repeatedly stabbed and assaulted during a sex attack on a roof landing. Upon arrival, I was informed by the patrol supervisor that the crime had taken place on the roof landing and that an officer had been assigned to safeguard the scene. I conducted a preliminary survey of the scene and surrounding and discovered at least five additional locations involved in this original crime scene. These included the roof, an adjoining roof landing, an elevator, and two interior staircases, none of which had been secured and all of which contained various bits of trace evidence. Additional personnel were requested and these areas were cordoned off for the later crime scene search and process (multiple crime scene theory).

Direction of Uniformed Personnel at the Scene

The detective supervisor and homicide detective assigned to the case are in complete command at the scene of the homicide. They have the authority to exclude everyone — including other police officers, the news media, and any other unauthorized persons — except the medical examiner or coroner. Often, follow-up investigations of crime scenes have disclosed that valuable evidence was destroyed by the mere presence of police personnel.

Actions such as standing or walking in the scene or leaning against doorways or walls may alter or destroy valuable trace evidence such as latent prints, blood, hair, or skin specimens. If the crime scene can be adequately controlled, the chances of contamination will be minimized. The homicide people should explain these facts to the patrol supervisor and uniformed officers and request their cooperation in keeping *all* unauthorized and unnecessary personnel away from the crime scene.

Sometimes, high-ranking police personnel may inadvertently destroy valuable evidence. Although rank does not preclude scene contamination, I wouldn't advise an officer to tell some high-ranking officer that he has just "screwed-up" the crime scene. Instead, the homicide supervisor should be apprised, who then might be able to gain some cooperation from the ranking official by requesting assistance in preserving the scene and keeping everyone out. Tact will be required in this type of situation.

Sometimes a patrol officer will have taken evidence into custody before the arrival of the investigators. There are many situations where officers will be forced to retrieve evidence or secure firearms either because of safety or the possibility of destruction. They should be directed to properly safeguard this evidence, as they now are involved in the "chain of custody," and to make proper notations in their official reports so that this evidence can later be submitted into evidence. (See Chapter 17.) Likewise, if an officer effects an arrest at the scene based on his personal observations, the officer should be placed under the supervision of the homicide investigator by the detective supervisor. This procedure will assure that the officer is properly guided during the subsequent homicide investigation. In some instances, it may be necessary to "detail" a patrol officer to the Homicide Division during the investigation.

Uniformed personnel at the scene should remain at their posts until relieved by the investigator, although they may be used to transport witnesses or suspects for the investigators at the scene. (See Chapter 3.)

The Teamwork Approach

The detective supervisor and homicide investigator are faced with a crime of the utmost gravity, one which is fraught with a complexity of possible motives and methods and a variety of physical evidence. Therefore, *teamwork* is required for a successful homicide investigation, and it is the detective supervisor and homicide investigators who must set the tone for this teamwork approach as they coordinate the different people involved in the responsibility of the inquiry into death, for example:

The patrol service or uniform division
The detective division and other homicide detectives
The medical examiner or coroner
The crime scene technicians or fingerprint experts
The District Attorney
Medical and ambulance personnel
Other agencies such as the FBI if the homicide involves a federal
    employee

Directing the Investigation at the Scene

Homicide investigators should attempt to obtain all pertinent information from the first officer — out of the hearing of any witnesses, the press, or the public — before taking charge of the investigation. As mentioned earlier, the detective should confirm the fact of death for himself. The investigator must also see that the duties of the first officer have been accomplished.

Duties of the Detective Supervisor on Arrival at the Scene

The detective supervisor or chief investigator, upon arrival, will assume the responsibility for conducting the homicide investigation and will replace the initial investigator as the ranking officer in charge of the case.

It is extremely important that the detective supervisor and the homicide investigator not permit themselves to fall into a fixed routine. Previous experience is invaluable but can become a hindrance when allowance is not made for new possibilities.

> Remember, each homicide case is distinct and unique and may require a fresh approach or perspective. Keep an open mind.

Practically speaking, no one at this stage of the investigation has all the answers, nor can anyone know for sure exactly what direction the case will take. However, the investigators should be guided by certain basic procedures at the scene.

1. Ascertain that there is an investigator at the scene, and that the crime scene is amply protected. Confer with the investigator and be brought up to date on the status of the investigation. Solicit any opinions or theories and objectively evaluate these with your independent observations. Determine any investigative needs and make assignments as necessary.
2. Confer with the ranking uniformed officer at the scene, and interview the first officer so that proper instructions can be given to responding investigators.
3. Priority should be given to the removal of the suspect and/or witnesses to the police station. Each witness should be transported separately. However, before they are transported, the witnesses should be briefly interviewed by the investigators at the scene so that they may have the advantage of the witnesses' observations to guide their investigation at the scene. Written statements can be obtained later on at the police station and the information transmitted back to the detective supervisor at the scene.

4. Use an assignment sheet to indicate assignments as given. This sheet should contain the identification of officers assigned, the location of the assignment, the duties assigned, and the time the assignment was given. Later on it can be used as a control device to assure that official reports are obtained from the investigators assigned. In addition to fixing responsibility for certain investigative duties, the assignment sheet will eliminate duplication of effort as additional assignments are made and put on the sheet.

5. If a suitable communications center or command post has not been established by the patrol officers, the investigator or supervisor should take immediate steps to arrange for one. The station house, Communications Division, and the detective command should be apprised of the telephone numbers of the command post to facilitate rapid communication to and from the scene.

6. Designate an officer to keep a running timetable of events, including arrivals and departures at the scene. When the scene is released, the timetable should be turned over to the detective supervisor.

7. If the victim has been removed to the hospital, insure that proper action is being taken at the hospital regarding any dying declarations, clothing, evidence, etc. (See Chapter 3.) It is advisable to have a detective contact the hospital and confer with the patrol officer and/or doctor. It may even be necessary to assign a detective to assist the officer in these procedures.

8. If the suspect has fled the scene, the investigator and detective supervisor must ascertain exactly what alarms have been transmitted, if any, and the exact information contained therein. Upon verification and the development of any new information, these alarms should be retransmitted.

9. Provide for the dissemination of information to all units involved in the homicide investigation. Ideally, all investigators should be aware of all aspects of the case. It is up to the detective supervisor to coordinate and disseminate this information to the "troops." Properly informed officers can better perform their own assigned functions and contribute more intelligently to the overall effort. This is especially true for those officers assigned to conduct canvasses. (See Chapter 4, "The Canvass.") Uniformed officers assisting at the scene must also be made to feel that they are part of the team.

10. On occasion, too many officers respond to the homicide crime scene. The detective supervisor should not hesitate to direct these officers to return to their original assignments if they are not needed.

Preliminary Interview of the First Officer

The detective must ascertain that the scene is *intact* — that nothing has been added or removed since the arrival of the responding police. To determine this he goes directly to the first officer. A preliminary interview with the first officer can provide an up-to-date appraisal of the crime scene as well as an assessment of what has transpired since the discovery of the body.

The homicide investigators should obtain a detailed account of what the officer or officers have seen and done. Usually, the officers will offer an opinion as to cause, manner, and circumstances of death. Investigators should receive these opinions objectively and graciously. However, they should not allow themselves to be influenced prior to making their own observations. Often the first officers' opinions provide a valuable lead in the investigation. *In keeping with the teamwork principle, give credit where credit is due.* If a patrol officer's performance at the scene is outstanding or proves instrumental in solving the investigation, I personally recommend that an official report be forwarded to the officer's commander. This report should be initiated by the detective supervisor at the scene and sent through channels so that this officer will receive proper recognition.

> Remember, in order to effect a successful homicide investigation, everyone involved must work together — homicide investigation is a team effort and not a one man show.

When interviewing first officers, emphasis should be placed on their activities in the immediate area of the crime scene — for example, how they gained entry into the scene, the position of the body on arrival, things they may have touched or moved, condition of the doors and windows, odors, whether the lights were on or off, etc. (See Chapters 2 and 3.) It may prove valuable to have first officers document their activities and observations on official reports. In addition, I recommend that the investigator assigned to interview the first officers prepare an official report for review by the patrol officer to assure that it is correct, and then have the officer sign the investigator's report which will become part of the homicide investigation.

I have found that it is a good idea to keep the first officers at the scene to answer any questions about the appearance of certain objects when they arrived. In addition, they can report any observations of persons who were in the area when they arrived or who expressed some interest in the activities of the police. I recall one case in which the police had been called to the scene by the fire department after firemen discovered a body on fire in a basement of a South Bronx tenement. Two patrol officers in the vicinity responded immediately and arrived as firemen were still extinguishing the fire. The fire officer in charge advised the two police officers that an individual at the scene had been quite helpful and had directed firemen through the unlit basement to the source of the fire. These two police officers, taking note of the fact that inhabitants of the area were often less than civic-minded, detained this "good citizen" pending arrival of myself and other detectives from the 7th Homicide Zone. They advised us of his actions and detained him as a witness. Needless to say, it wasn't long before we were able to reconstruct what had occurred. Our "witness" had been staying with the deceased in a rear room of the basement. They were both from Jamaica and belonged to the Rastafarians sect (a Jamaican subculture that often deals in marijuana and other illegal activities) and apparently had a falling-out over business resulting in a shooting that left the deceased with a bullet in his head. Why our good citizen just didn't take off, I'll never know, but he stayed with the cadaver all night. The next day he bought kerosene at the corner hardware store, dragged the body to the front of the basement, poured the liquid over it, and lit it up. However, he didn't expect the initial burst of flame and smoke. His immediate problem was keeping the flames down. The people on the first floor, spotting the smoke emanating from the basement, called the fire department. A fire company returning to its station, and still in the area from a previous alarm, responded and arrived in less than a minute. The suspect, finding himself trapped between the body and the firemen, decided to play the part of a good citizen. The two street-wise police officers, however, didn't buy his act, and he was detained. After gathering some trace evidence and interrogating our "witness," an arrest was made and our good citizen charged with murder.

The interesting thing to note in this particular case is the actions of the first officers. They took the initiative and detained this person based on their initial observations and "gut feeling". As a result, homicide detectives were provided with a suspect and were able to successfully conclude the investigation.

A

Figure 4.2. **PROPERLY PREPARED CRIME SCENE: VICTIM ALIVE.** Observe how a crime scene can change prior to the arrival of the investigators. In this case the deceased was still alive when the uniform officers and emergency medical technicians arrived. The body was obviously moved, and the scene changed while first aid measures were given to save the man's life. It is important to obtain the identity of the ambulance personnel and to note their initial observations and recollections of events at the scene when they first arrived. (A) The man has just been pronounced dead after emergency treatment. (B) Emergency medical equipment has been removed from the victim.

Interview of Ambulance Personnel

Frequently an ambulance crew represents the first official agency to arrive at the scene of a homicide. Sometimes these ambulance attendants can render invaluable assistance to the investigator. Since their obligation is to view the body and give medical assistance if the victim is still alive, one or more members of the crew have probably been on the scene and close to the body. Often the perpetrator will still be on the scene and may even engage the ambulance crew in conversation or make an admission. In addition, the deceased may utter a name or description of the assailant. Furthermore, many people who were present when the assault took place will not leave when the ambulance arrives, but instead will stand around to "watch the show." When the police units begin to arrive, these persons suddenly make themselves scarce.

B

Figure 4.2. (continued)

It is up to the homicide investigators to find out exactly what took place before the arrival of police. The investigators must interview each member of the ambulance crew who was present at the scene. Ambulance crew members are not trained criminal investigators and may inadvertently have altered the crime scene in some small but highly significant way. Obtain their names, serial numbers, unit numbers, hospital affiliation, and times of arrival and pronouncement of death. Every detail of their actions should be known, for example, how they gained entry if the scene is indoors, the path of entry if outdoors, things they may have touched or moved in order to get to the body, movement of the body, what areas they were present in, and their observations. They should answer such questions as: Who was present? Did the deceased say anything? Were they smoking? If so, did they discard their cigarettes and where did they discard them? etc.

Handling Curious Onlookers

Using courtesy and a calm professionalism in dealing with civilian crowds can be to your advantage. You may be able, for example, to gain the crowd's cooperation in maintaining police lines pending arrival of additional personnel, or to persuade an onlooker to come forward with some valuable information. This is especially important in areas known for their distrust of and hostility to the police. In some areas, especially in inner cities, the mood of the crowd may turn ugly depending on how the police maintain lines and direct the crowds.

Do not engage in any verbal rhetoric with the *"village idiot."* You may rest assured that in every crowd there is the drunk, the clown, the self-elected spokesman of silliness, the troublemaker, the junkie, or the fool. Your refusal to get involved with such a character may very well be the key to getting the crowd on your side, and through nothing more than plain old-fashioned peer pressure, this person will be neutralized. Furthermore, when the crowd begins to empathize with your function, additional information may be provided by witnesses who were at first reluctant to come forward.

As an investigator you can usually assume a different role than that of the uniformed patrol officer. Persons who have been directed by patrol officers to stand back will instinctively resent the authority, yet may still have a desire to give information to the police. My advice is to take advantage of this and actively solicit their cooperation. People will usually tell a homicide detective things they wouldn't tell another officer.

Furthermore, when dealing with curious onlookers in a crowd, you never know who has information and who will come forward with it. I recommend that you get some of your people, who do not look like detectives, into the crowd. I remember an incident in the South Bronx that the 7th Homicide Zone had responded to. It was a street scene, and the deceased was lying on the sidewalk surrounded by a large crowd of onlookers, most of whom were conversing in Spanish. One of the homicide detectives, who was Puerto Rican, began to mingle with the crowd and ask questions in Spanish. A man he was speaking with suddenly turned to another person in the crowd and said in Spanish, "Hey, look over there, that guy has some nerve. First he kills the 'dude', and then he comes back with all these cops standing around just to look at the body." Needless to say, the detective in the crowd alerted his counterparts but remained in the group to watch and listen. When the other detectives suddenly broke into the crowd and grabbed the suspect, the persons who had been discussing the incident were overheard to say: "Wow, those detectives are really smart. How did they know he killed that man?"

The detective who had infiltrated the crowd not only identified the suspect but came up with two additional witnesses who were brought into headquarters for formal statements.

Handling Witnesses at the Scene

Although the homicide crime scene offers an abundance of informational and evidentiary material, the identity of the perpetrator will usually be uncovered through the intelligent interviewing of witnesses.

The homicide detective should determine the identity of all witnesses who have been at the scene. Valid identification, including names, date of birth, residence and business addresses (with zip codes and telephone numbers) should be obtained in the event that later contact is necessary. It is imperative that the witnesses be separated, and each one should be interviewed individually as soon as possible after the event. The best procedure is to assign homicide detectives to take an informal statement immediately upon arrival while the case officer (the investigator assigned to the case) goes over the crime scene and establishes some basic information about the crime. This procedure assures that a candid statement is obtained before any deterioration of memory takes place either because of a time lapse or a desire "not to get involved."

Usually, a person who tells a detective one story won't suddenly change it later on when a formal statement is taken. These initial interview results should immediately be made known to the homicide supervisor and the case officer to assure sensible direction of activities at the scene. The location for the subsequent formal interview of witnesses should be an office or other place where there is privacy and the necessary recording equipment available. I recommend that witnesses be transported to the station house for formal statements immediately after the initial information has been obtained at the scene. If patrol officers provide the transportation, they should be reminded to keep parties separated both en route and at the police station.

The formal statement should be taken and each witness evaluated by the homicide detectives assigned to the investigation. Needless to say, the homicide supervisor and the investigator who originally took the preliminary statement should confer in this evaluation. This phase becomes crucial when dealing with persons who do not speak English and require an interpreter. The interviewing officer should make sure that the interpreter is phrasing the question properly so that there is no misunderstanding of the meaning of the question, and that the exact response — and not the interpreter's assumption of what the interviewee meant — is recorded. If possible, have an officer who speaks the language conduct the interview with the case officer. Together they can formulate the questions and evaluate the responses.

Obviously, the eyewitness to the fatal act is the most valuable. However, other witnesses may have important information which places the suspect at the homicide crime scene or supplies the motive for the crime, or they may be able to provide personal information about the suspect.

Remember, it is important to keep the witnesses separated from one another.

Witnesses who have conferred with each other may change their stories, not from a desire to mislead the police, but from a very basic factor in human behavior. One or more persons in a group may force their dominant personality on the group, and the other witnesses will compromise their stories so as not to disagree or offend the stronger personalities, or to seem "stupid" by having seen something no one else saw.

In other instances, however, — especially when dealing with criminals or persons sympathetic to criminal enterprise — there may be a conscious effort to mislead and thwart police inquiry into the crime.

The detective should realize these possibilities when questioning prospective witnesses and must be thorough and patient. He must get the witnesses to relax and talk about themselves. He should encourage them to tell the story in their own words. Of course, when dealing with the criminal sympathizer or "bad-guy" type, questioning will have to be more along the lines of authority, and you will look for any weaknesses or fears you can perceive. Usually these types are not too anxious to have the police probing into their life style and may be willing to cooperate either for a price or just to "get the cops off their back." Sometimes you may be lucky enough to have something on them, such as a lesser crime, which can be traded off for information on the homicide. In reality, as I look back on my career, especially in some of the areas where we conducted homicide investigations, *many* of our witnesses were brought in in handcuffs. Often the only good thing you could say about the deceased was that he was *dead*; today's deceased was usually yesterday's perpetrator.

Dealing with these criminal types is always frustrating and dangerous. You never know for sure which side of the fence they are on, nor

WITNESSES

Name _____ Address _____

M ____ F ____ Race _____ D.O.B. _____ Age _____ Tele. # _____

Height _____ Weight _____ Build _____ Complexion _____

Welfare # _____ Social Security # _____

Drivers License # _____ Auto Driven and Reg. # _____

Wife or Husbands Name _____ Address _____

Welfare # _____ Social Security # _____ Tele. # _____

D.O.B. _____ Age _____ Social Status _____

Girlfriend or Boyfriends Name _____ Tele. # _____

Last Known Address _____ D.O.B. _____ Age _____

Welfare # _____ Social Security # _____

Number of Children _____ Names and Ages _____

School Attending _____
Address _____
Mother's Maiden Name (or Family Name) _____
Address _____ Tele. # _____
Business Address _____ Tele. # _____

```
+--------------------------------+
|                                |
|                                |
|            Photo               |
|                                |
|                                |
+--------------------------------+
```

Area Frequents _____ Place of Birth _____

Miscellaneous Information _____

_____

Witness Knows Perpetrator Personally? _____ (Yes/No)   How? _____

Did Witness I.D. Perpetrator _____ (Yes/No)   How? _____

Case # _____ Officer Assigned _____ Homicide # _____

Date of Interview _____ Interviewing Officer _____

Figure 4.3. **WITNESS FORM.** This form can be employed to assure that investigators obtain as much information as possible for later contact. In certain cases it may be advisable to obtain a Polaroid photograph of your witness.

can you be sure of their motivation, or when they will turn on you. Your best defense, of course, is the proper documentation of their activities. Make sure that you confer with your supervisors or commanders. In certain instances, the Office of the District Attorney must be consulted, especially if part of the "deal" concerns court consideration or lack of prosecution in return for testimony against a suspect in the homicide.

Effective interviewing is an art that requires constant improvement. It is a very time-consuming procedure, but often invaluable for the discovery of information. In this interviewing phase, team effort is especially important. There is an enormous work load generated in a very short time at a homicide crime scene. This work load is further compounded by the element of time. There just isn't enough time for one or two homicide investigators to perform all the necessary duties and conduct careful interviews. The detective supervisor should assign enough investigators to conduct these preliminary interviews and be kept up to date with the results. This information should be made available to the other investigators involved so that they can proceed intelligently with their duties.

The Canvass

A *canvass* is a door-to-door, road block inquiry or brief interview with persons on the street by which detectives attempt to gain information about a specific incident. It is an important investigative tool and a vital part of the preliminary investigation at the homicide crime scene.

The detective supervisor should assign investigators to conduct a preliminary canvass of the surrounding area including the approach and escape routes from the crime scene, while the case officer performs his functions at the scene. As the detectives conduct the canvass, their primary purpose should not be to conduct in-depth interviews, but to locate possible witnesses or persons who may have information about the crime. Canvassers should obtain the name and address of each person spoken to, whether the person provides information or not. Where no one is at home or there are additional residents who should be interviewed, this should be noted so that the parties can be reached during a recanvass. Likewise, locations that are negative should be recorded for the follow-up investigation. Because of the vast amount of information generated in a short period of time at the homicide crime scene, I recommend that everyone involved in the investigation possess a notebook. Each apartment, place, or person canvassed should be recorded in the investigator's notes for later official reports or a recanvass, as the case may warrant.

CANVASS QUESTIONNAIRE

(Identify Yourself and Purpose of Canvass)

Name: (last) (first) (middle) Date of Birth:

Address: Phone:

Employment (company name—type of work): Address: Phone:

Other Residents of This Address: (names and ages)

Did you know of the offense? ☐ Yes ☐ No

How did you first learn of it? (when?)

Did you know the victim? ☐ Yes ☐ No

What was your relationship with the victim? (if knew, date, time, and location last seen or talked to)

Were you on the crime scene at anytime? (explain)

What knowledge do you have of the crime?

Typed statement taken from this witness? ☐ Yes ☐ No

Reporting officer (name) (unit) (date) (time)

Figure 4.4. CANVASS QUESTIONNAIRE.

CANVASS QUESTIONNAIRE

Street, Avenue, Road, etc. _____

Number (or name if no number) _____

If Apartment or Office Building (name) _____

	Questionnaire
Occupants (full name and age)	Completed

1. _____   Yes — No

2. _____   Yes — No

3. _____   Yes — No

4. _____   Yes — No

5. _____   Yes — No

6. _____   Yes — No

Officer Recording _____

Time _____   Date _____

Figure 4.5.   CANVASS QUESTIONNAIRE.

At times it may be necessary to recanvass or extend the canvass to include additional areas. The thoroughness of the procedure is the determining factor of success. On the recanvass, a witness who was reluctant to talk the first time or someone who was inadvertently missed will be located. Also consider the physical location of the crime scene in relation to the area canvassed; that is, don't miss the back of the building. I remember one case where an extensive canvass was conducted in a number of buildings that faced the front of a location where a vicious burglary homicide had taken place. The canvass proved negative until someone realized that no one had canvassed the buildings which faced the rear. These buildings were on another street around the corner from the murder site. This particular canvass resulted in locating a witness

Figure 4.6.   **THE CANVASS.** When doing a canvass it is imperative that the investigators consider the buildings and locations which overlook the rear of the crime scene as well as the front of the location. In this particular case, the canvass of apartments which overlooked the rear of the subject building and the building's fire escapes provided police with the description and eventually the identity of the murderer.

who had observed two males climbing up a fire escape toward the victim's apartment. This witness was able to make a positive identification of the suspects in the case. The ironic part of the story is that the witness had not made any connection between this event and the murder and would never have come forward if not located and interviewed by the investigators on the subsequent canvass.

Also consider whether an immediate canvass is necessary. The type of crime or the hour of day or night may determine this. For instance, in an organized crime hit in an area frequented by persons friendly to criminal enterprise, it will probably be necessary to come back at a later time and talk to people out of the hearing or observation of criminal sympathizers and neighbors. A common mistake is to attempt a canvass in the middle of the night. You'll make a lot more enemies than friends if you start ringing doorbells at 3:00 A.M. Wait until a reasonable hour and then do the canvass.

Many homicides have been solved because a good canvass performed by a determined group of canvassers uncovered some vital information, including a motive, or even an eyewitness. These canvassers were detectives who didn't just go through the motions, but took the time to effectively elicit information from the people canvassed. It is extremely important to keep in mind when instituting a canvass not to assign officers arbitrarily just because you are supposed to do a canvass. Usually at the homicide crime scene there will be numerous personnel — sometimes more than can be effectively utilized. A common error committed by some supervisors is to indiscriminately assign these people to do a canvass, a practice that can do more harm than good. This is not to say that the supervisor shouldn't "shotgun" a number of investigators into an initial canvass, but the personnel selected should be either good at this investigative technique or have an interest in the particular investigation. The extra personnel can then be used for some of the other jobs that become necessary during the course of events at the scene.

The assigned detective or member of the team conducting the homicide investigation should conduct formal interviews with anyone located by the canvassers. Likewise, the detective supervisor should be kept up to date with any information uncovered by the canvassers. In this way both the supervisor and the team will be aware of all developments in the case and be better able to put this information into proper perspective.

The correctly done canvass is an invaluable investigative technique that can provide:

An actual eyewitness to the crime
Information about the circumstances of the crime
An approximate time of occurrence and/or estimate of time of death
Information about the deceased — identity, habits, friends, etc.
A motive for the crime

The Preliminary Medical Examination at the Scene

In homicide cases a medical examiner or coroner is responsible for performing an investigation to determine the cause, manner, and mode of death. (See Chapter 18.) The medical examiner's or coroner's office is responsible for conducting an autopsy later on. Ideally, the investigation at the scene should be carried out by the same pathologist who will later perform the autopsy. However, in jurisdictions that lack a medical examiner system or have a large number of homicides, this is not always possible. In most cases, the medical examiner or coroner must rely on the information provided by the medical examiner or medical investigator at the scene, and from the detectives investigating the homicide.

Since the physical aspects of the scene and the cadaver can never be replaced in quite the same manner after a body has been moved, the body, under ordinary circumstances, should not be moved before an examination by the medical examiner or coroner.

The preliminary medical examination should not, however, be undertaken until the crime scene has been photographed and sketched in its original condition. (See Chapters 6 and 7.) If the medical examiner arrives before the crime scene technicians or police photographer, he or she should be requested to delay the examination until after the scene documentation has been accomplished.

The medical examiner should be brought up to date on all aspects of the case as soon as he or she arrives. This includes any determinations or observations made by the investigators at the scene or in the course of the preliminary investigation.

Remember, the teamwork aspect can never be overemphasized, especially in this preliminary medical examination at the scene.

The scene investigation by the medical examiner or coroner includes identification of the deceased, examination of the body, evaluation of the circumstances of death, and removal of evidence from the body. Therefore, it is important that these medical experts obtain as much information as possible about the facts surrounding death so that later autopsy findings can be properly evaluated. For example, an ambulance may have responded and the attendants attempted resuscitation. This information could become important in evaluating rib fractures, facial trauma, or other internal injuries that could have been caused during the resuscitation attempts.

The medical investigation at the scene may indicate the following:

1. The apparent cause of death, by correlating the injuries with the manner in which they occurred. In homicide deaths which are the result of stabbing or shooting, the determination of cause of death may be made at the scene. In some suspicious deaths, the medical examiner may observe *petechial hemorrhages* in the lining of the eyes and eyelids, alerting the police to asphyxial death.
2. Whether injuries are antemortem or postmortem.
3. Whether the deceased, after the initial injury, fell or struck other objects at the scene, thereby causing further injury.
4. Whether the body came to rest upon an object which, due to pressure, produced a postmortem injury (*artefact*) which could be erroneously interpreted as contributory or responsible for death.

5. The approximate time of death (indicated by such signs as loss of body heat, rigor mortis, lividity, etc.) (See Chapter 9).

The best advice I can give to homicide detectives at the scene is to take the medical examiner or coroner into your confidence, tell him about your theories, and ask questions. If you don't understand some obscure terminology, get clarification (in other words, ask the medical examiner to translate it into English or layman's terms). These medical practitioners can give advice concerning medical aspects of the case and later provide information derived from the postmortem examination and the results of any toxicological analysis. The detective supervisor and homicide investigator should seek their advice. Such conferences and exchanges of information often result in a modification of an investigator's approach to a case or a particular aspect of it.

Historically, medical examiners and coroners have enjoyed a good working relationship with homicide investigators, based on expertise and professional cooperation, which tends to complement the investigation. I have been at many homicide crime scenes where the medical examiner has been more than helpful to the investigator by answering the many questions that arise during this preliminary inquiry.

Doctors who specialize in forensic medicine usually have an ardent interest in homicide cases. Often they can be helpful in reconstructing the scene and formulating the sequence of events. Since their inquiry is directed toward the circumstances that led to death, the manner in which death occurred, and whether or not the condition of the body is consistent with the cause of death, what they determine is essential to the investigation. Each professional is aware of the other's duty and capability, and by working together and exchanging information, they can usually arrive at a final determination of what actually occurred.

Specific Investigative Duties at the Scene

5

The purpose of this chapter is to provide practical information and guidelines for the homicide investigator to follow when confronted with additional responsibilities and specific duties at the scene. A section on handling buried-body cases has been included which may prove useful as a general guide for the investigation of this unique type of scene. The following subjects will be dealt with in this chapter:

The suspect in custody
Interrogation of the suspect at the scene
Examination of a suspect for evidence
Evaluation of the suspect's demeanor and mental capacity
Obtaining a dying declaration
Handling buried-body cases

The chapter concludes with an investigative checklist which can be used by the homicide investigator and detective supervisor to systematically check and review his or her actions at the scene.

The Suspect in Custody

When the suspect has been taken into custody by patrol officers, the immediate responsibility of the detectives or homicide investigators should be the following.

1. Insure that the suspect has been removed from, or is not allowed to enter, the primary crime scene. The isolation of the suspect is

necessary in order to prevent scene contamination or destruction of evidence.

2. Interview the arresting officer(s), out of the hearing of the suspect, in order to determine the scope of their initial investigation, the location of any physical evidence, and the probable cause for the arrest of the suspect including any statements made by the suspect or witnesses.

3. Instruct these officers, upon completion of this preliminary interview, to document in writing their observations and activities at the scene, including any overhears or statements made by the suspect, as well as any information provided by witnesses or informants.

4. Ascertain whether or not the suspect has been given his or her Miranda warnings by the patrol officers, to assure the admissibility of any culpable statements made to these officers.

Interview and Interrogation of the Suspect in Custody

The investigators, upon their arrival, take charge of the investigation and are responsible for the interrogation of the suspect. Prior to any interview or interrogation, the detective must again advise the suspect of the Constitutional Rights as specified under the Miranda ruling. The detective should make note of this Miranda warning to the suspect in his or her notebook, indicating the time, date, location, and presence of any witnesses including counsel.

It may be advantageous to conduct a preliminary interrogation of the suspect while he or she is still at the scene. This questioning is usually directed toward the recovery of any weapons or other evidence and is used to gauge the scope of the search. The actual formal interrogation, however, should take place later at the police station, where conditions are more favorable. Furthermore, the investigator will have been able by then to complete the preliminary investigation and will have the advantage of information and observations from the scene.

In some instances, the suspect may insist on confessing or telling his or her story immediately. If the suspect is quite talkative or wishes to make a statement to investigators at the scene, do not delay the interview.

Practically speaking, any statement from a suspect is crucial to the investigation. Although the initial statement may be self-serving, a little less than truthful, or even a complete falsehood, this declaration by the suspect is a valuable piece of evidence which may later be presented in court. If the investigator delays or postpones taking an official statement until he or she gathers "all the facts," the suspect may change his or her mind about making a statement, or request an attorney, and this valuable evidence will be lost forever.

Under circumstances where the suspect wishes to make a statement, the investigator should

Immediately advise the suspect of his or her Constitutional rights under the Miranda ruling, utilizing a "rights card" or Miranda form

Make sure that the suspect understands his or her rights by requesting a response

Obtain an intelligent waiver of these rights from the suspect (preferably a signature of the suspect on the Miranda form)

Allow the suspect to make a complete statement

Take notes, reduce the statement to writing, and have the suspect sign it

The importance of documentation, especially in custodial interrogation situations, cannot be overemphasized. This is the reason why I strongly recommend that the Miranda Warnings be given from a rights card and that the particular card utilized be preserved as evidence. In addition, persons who are given Miranda warnings should be requested to put their signatures on a Miranda form in order to assure the admissibility of any statements in court.

A favorite trick of defense counsel is to distort any custodial interrogation by innuendo, suggesting that there was some impropriety on the part of the police in obtaining statements from a defendant. If the investigator has taken proper notes of the procedures utilized in obtaining any statements, along with notes of the responses of the suspect to these warnings, he or she will have eliminated a possible source of embarrassment in future court proceedings.

When dealing with minors, the Miranda warnings must be given to the parent(s) as well as the underage suspect. Both the parent(s) and the minor must intelligently waive their rights before an interrogation can proceed.

Examination of a Suspect for Evidence

The examination of the suspect for evidence should be performed by the investigator assigned to the case or an experienced detective assigned to the investigation. The ability to recognize and recover trace evidence from a suspect or his or her clothing is a prerequisite to successful search of suspects. During this preliminary phase of the homicide investigation, especially when the suspect is still at the scene, it is not practical to conduct an extensive examination for trace evidence. However, officers should be aware of the possible evidentiary value of the clothing and shoes worn by the suspect as well as any bruises, cuts, or injuries on the hands, face, or other parts of the suspect's body. When the suspect is brought to the police station, a more thorough examination can be undertaken. (See Chapter 8, "Physical Examination of a Suspect in Custody.")

When the suspect is transported to the police station by patrol officers for further examination, the officers transporting the suspect should be advised to preserve the suspect's clothing and shoes for evidence of trace materials and cautioned not to allow the suspect to wash his or her hands or to engage in any activity that may alter or destroy any trace evidence. These instructions should be communicated to all personnel who will be responsible for the custody of the suspect prior to an extensive examination and search by the investigators. I remember reading about a police matron who had been assigned to guard a female murder suspect. The matron allowed the suspect to wash the victim's blood off her blouse while she was in police custody. During the trial the matron was asked by the prosecutor why she had allowed the suspect to wash off the blood. The matron claimed she wasn't advised by the detectives to preserve the clothing of the suspect and that the detectives "hadn't told her anything." Needless to say, her ignorance of the forensic value of the victim's blood on the blouse was compounded by the failure of the investigators to properly instruct and advise her.

Evaluation of the Suspect's Demeanor and Mental Capacity

When a suspect has been taken into custody, the investigator should make an evaluation of the suspect's demeanor and mental capacity based on observations from the time of his or her arrest to the subsequent arraignment. This observation and documentation is necessary to prepare against a possible diminished-capacity defense, which is usually based on the contention that the defendant, at the time the offense was committed, was not able to determine right or wrong because of his or her mental state. Or the defendant may attempt to claim insanity based on mental incapacity. The defense of diminished capacity is a popular one because the police often fail to take proper precautions during the initial investigation. The following are some important observations that should be recorded in the investigator's notebook.

1. Does the suspect speak rationally or irrationally?
2. Does he or she answer in a straightforward or evasive manner?
3. Is the response to questioning intelligent or confused?
4. Does the suspect have control over his or her actions?
5. What is the suspect's emotional condition?
6. Is there any evidence of intoxication, or does the suspect appear to be under the influence of any drugs?
7. Does the suspect give any reasons for his or her actions?

When investigators interview witnesses, they should attempt to obtain as much information as possible regarding the actions of the suspect prior to the crime, during the crime, and immediately after the crime. Any indications of the suspect's demeanor and mental capacity should be recorded. The witnesses should be asked the following questions.

1. What was the suspect's appearance at the time of the crime?
2. How did the suspect act?
3. Could the witness determine the suspect's demeanor or mental state?
4. Did the suspect act rationally or irrationally?
5. Was the act a cold-blooded or unemotional thing?
6. Did the suspect scream or yell?
7. How did the suspect commit the act?
8. Was the suspect under the influence of alcohol or drugs?
9. Did the suspect say or do anything during or after the crime?
10. Did the suspect attempt to flee or cover up the crime?

Often investigators neglect to obtain witnesses' opinions of the suspect during the initial inquiry because they have been trained to gather only "facts." However, independent observations of and opinions about a person's behavior can be vitally important in establishing the existence or nonexistence of diminished capacity in court. From an investigative point of view, these witnesses' observations and opinions should be documented by the detective in preparation for the later prosecution.

Obtaining a Dying Declaration

If the victim is still alive when investigators arrive at the scene, they should attempt to obtain a statement. Likewise, if a victim has been removed to the hospital, detectives should immediately be dispatched so that they may interview him or her. In cases where the victim is seriously injured and death will undoubtedly occur, investigators must be alert to the possibility of obtaining a dying declaration. This can be obtained while waiting for the ambulance, en route to the hospital, or while the victim is in the hospital. As long as investigators do not interfere with life-sustaining measures, nor hinder medical personnel by their presence, there should be no problems.

The dying declaration may prove invaluable in firmly establishing whether or not a crime has occurred, and, more importantly, who was responsible. In order to obtain a legally admissible declaration, however, certain conditions must exist. They are as follows.

1. The victim must believe that he or she is going to die.
2. The victim must have no hope of recovery.
3. The declaration or statement must refer to
   a. The manner and circumstances which brought about the victim's condition and ultimate death.
   b. The identity of the person responsible.
4. The declarant must die.
5. The declarant must have been otherwise competent and rational.

The dying declaration can be used in a criminal trial only for the death of the declarant. If the victim survives, he or she must testify later on in court.

Questions to be Asked in a Dying Declaration

There are no set guidelines for the exact sequence of questions one should ask when attempting to obtain a dying declaration. Basically, you will want to establish through your questions that the witness is competent, lucid, and does believe that he or she is about to die. Here are some questions that the investigator may find helpful.

1. What is your name?
2. Where do you live?
3. Do you now believe that you are about to die?
4. Have you any hope of recovery?

5. Are you willing to make a true statement of how and why you were injured?

Documentation of the Dying Declaration

The statement can either be oral or, if feasible, written by the declarant. Ideally, the investigator will have a cassette recorder available during this event. In any case, the officer should reduce the statement to writing and have the declarant either sign it or make his or her mark. It is recommended that there be a civilian witness present; however, the fact that there was no witness available or that the declarant was unable to write or sign the statement does not effect the admissibility of the declaration in court.

Handling Buried-Body Cases[1]

Conducting crime scene searches involving the discovery and excavation of buried bodies requires special techniques and planning. Certain procedures, which must be followed in order to locate and recover pieces of physical evidence, involve the need for assistance and cooperation between law enforcement and forensic science. The necessary equipment should be available, as should the forensic experts in case their services are needed. An example of some of the experts who can assist the investigator in this procedure are the medical examiner or forensic pathologist, the forensic archeologist, the forensic odontologist, the forensic entomologist, and the botanist. I recommend that the homicide investigator contact these experts prior to their actual need at the scene of a buried-body case. I have found that these experts are usually happy to cooperate as long as they are acting as part of a team. If provided with an undisturbed crime scene, they can contribute to the overall success of an investigation.

The Discovery of the Buried Body

Buried-body cases usually come to the attention of the police as a result of an accidental find, or, more rarely, from information provided by an informant or in the course of a confession. Accidental finds may be made by a passerby, a hunter, or a construction worker involved in

---

[1]The information on handling buried-body cases is based on an article written by Robert M. Boyd, former Commander, Homicide Squad, Metropolitan Police Department, Washington, D.C. This article appeared in the *FBI Law Enforcement Bulletin*, February 1979.

some type of excavation, who then notifies the police. The police respond to the site to verify the discovery and then notify the investigators. As with any crime scene, the basic principles of scene protection and isolation should immediately be instituted. (See Chapter 2, "First Officer's Duties on Arrival at the Scene.")

The investigators should not allow themselves to be rushed into an immediate excavation of the remains. Instead, if the body has not already been removed from the burial site, they should request the services of an archeologist when they notify crime scene technicians and the medical examiner.

From an investigative point of view, there is generally no need to immediately excavate the body at this stage of the investigation. I recommend the following procedures (all of which will be discussed fully in Chapters 6, 7, and 8).

1. Photographs should be taken of the entire area including the site and any item of evidentiary value (tire tracks, weapons, tools, articles of clothing, etc.).
2. Photographs should be taken in black-and-white and color; photographs of any items located in the scene should be taken with and without markers.
3. The area should be mapped out and a crime scene sketch prepared.
4. The path used by the person discovering the body should be marked off and this route should be followed by all investigators and personnel at the scene.
5. A systematic search of the surrounding area should be instituted using metal detectors and any other aids that might be applicable. If any evidence is discovered, it should be photographed separately and included on the crime scene sketch.
6. If daylight hours are limited, postpone the search and excavation until morning.
7. If the weather poses a problem, wait for proper conditions. The area of the grave can usually be protected by the erection of a tent over the site.

The Excavation

The term *site* refers to the entire area of excavation or disturbance and includes not only the grave, but the immediate area contiguous to the grave. The excavation should be conducted under the direction of a forensic archeologist and should begin with the clearing of the ground

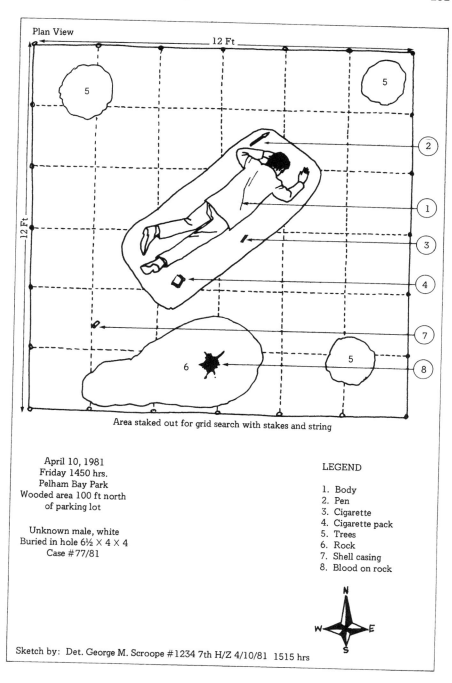

Plan View

12 Ft

12 Ft

Area staked out for grid search with stakes and string

April 10, 1981
Friday 1450 hrs.
Pelham Bay Park
Wooded area 100 ft north
of parking lot

Unknown male, white
Buried in hole 6½ × 4 × 4
Case #77/81

LEGEND

1. Body
2. Pen
3. Cigarette
4. Cigarette pack
5. Trees
6. Rock
7. Shell casing
8. Blood on rock

Sketch by: Det. George M. Scroope #1234 7th H/Z 4/10/81 1515 hrs

Figure 5.1. EXCAVATION OF BURIED BODY, PLAN VIEW SKETCH.

Elevation View

LEGEND

1. Body
2. Pen
3. Cigarette
4. Cigarette pack
5. Trees

April 10, 1981
Friday 1450 hrs
Pelhan Bay Park
Wooded area 100 ft. north
of parking lot

Unknown male, white
Buried in hole 6½ × 4 × 4 ft
Homicide case #77/81

Sketch by:
Det. George M. Scroope #1234 7th H/Z 4/10/81 1540 hrs

Figure 5.2.   EXCAVATION OF BURIED BODY, ELEVATION VIEW SKETCH.

around the actual burial site. This is done to locate the dimensions of
the hole. At this point measurements should be taken and the site
rephotographed. In addition, two sketches should be drawn to show
both plan and elevation views of the grave.

A. Too deep, vapors missed

B. Shallow enough to catch vapors
   but not directly over body

C. Strongest vapors
   directly over body

Figure 5.3.   **VAPOR DETECTOR.**

When a grave is dug, excavated soil is placed on the surface. As a result, the surface vegetation is usually compressed or broken off. When the grave is refilled, some of this surface vegetation is probably placed in the hole. Furthermore, if the body has been buried for some time, roots of trees or bushes may grow through the remains. This is where the botanist comes into play. The botanist can provide you with estimations of how long the vegetation has been damaged or the length of time necessary for the root structures in the remains to have reached their present stage of development. If any dead insects, insect larvae, or maggots are located at the site, they should be collected for examination by a forensic entomologist. (See Chapter 9.)

This is the reason why the excavation must proceed at an orderly and systematic pace. The soil should be removed in somewhat even layers, about 4 to 6 inches deep, and sifted through screens. As items are located and recovered, they should be photographed and plotted on the elevation and plan view drawings to indicate their actual locations. In addition, samples of the soil should be taken as each item is recovered.

The Body

When the body is uncovered, it should immediately be photographed in the condition of discovery before any disturbance. If the medical examiner is there, and the body has soft tissue present, there should be a preliminary scene examination by the pathologist. The body should then be placed on a clean sheet to preserve any additional evidence which may not be readily observable at the scene. The body and sheet should then be removed to a morgue for further examination and autopsy.

After the body has been removed, the grave should again be photographed, and the area which was under the body carefully searched and excavated several more inches. The use of a metal detector at this stage may prove valuable, especially if bullets were fired into the body as it lay in the grave.

The identification of the remains, especially in cases where the body is badly decomposed, will call for the expertise of the forensic anthropologist and the forensic odontologist working along with the medical examiner or coroner. The various methods and techniques are presented in Chapter 10.

Search for a Buried Body

In cases where an informant or confession reveals the existence of a buried body, the immediate problem facing the investigator is locating the site. Unless the exact location is given, the information may be so vague that it involves an area of several acres. Good planning will be necessary to locate and isolate the scene. Practically speaking, the more that is known about the circumstances of the crime, the better your chances are of locating the site. For example, where was the victim killed? If the victim was killed elsewhere, the location of the site may be close to a road or path. If the killing took place at the site, then the victim may have been forced to walk some distance.

The element of time will have a bearing on the condition of any vegetation or the grave itself. The grave may have sunk or there may still be surplus dirt on the mound.

The following methods may be used to locate the burial site:

1. Search by aircraft. Prior to a foot search, this method can be used to cover a wide area and locate visually a sign of soil or vegetation disturbance. In addition, the use of thermal infrared photography, which can detect the heat of a decomposing body, can sometimes be utilized depending on the length of time the body has been buried. Aerial photographs should be taken of the suspected area both before, and, if the search is successful, after.
2. Search by foot. Mechanical aids are a must in this type of search. (See Chapter 8, "Methods of Crime Scene Search.")
3. Probing. This is the most practical method of ground search. It is done with a steel rod which is about 4 to 5 feet long with a "tee" handle on one end and a sharp point at the other. The probe is inserted into the suspected area. If the ground is soft it is left in place, all probing is halted, and a vapor detector is brought into play. The probing should follow a systematic pattern so as not to miss any locations.
4. The vapor detector. This instrument can detect the presence of body gases formed as a result of decomposition. It can be used to locate a cadaver prior to any excavation. Its value is quite evident when several suspected areas must be checked. It can also be used under concrete (roadways, patios, floors) after a small hole is bored through the concrete.

The Investigative Checklist

The homicide detective faces a monumental task at the crime scene. There are a multitude of duties to perform, and each event needs to be documented according to a routine procedure. This routine procedure is necessary so that valuable information or observations are not overlooked. Although each homicide is distinctive and unique, there are certain basic steps to be pursued at all crime scenes. This Investigative Checklist is designed to be utilized by detectives involved in the investigation of sudden and violent death. Although extensive, it is not all-inclusive. The investigator is advised to simply utilize this Checklist as a guide to refresh the memory.

Remember, the fundamental rule in homicide investigation is the documentation of events in the investigator's notebook.

Documentation of the Initial Report

Initial Receipt of Information

- ☐ Date and time of initial report.
- ☐ Method of transmission — report received by.
- ☐ Reporting party — officer, dispatcher, etc.
- ☐ Complete details.

Arrival at the Homicide — Death Scene

- ☐ Record exact time of arrival.
- ☐ Record the exact address of the crime scene.
- ☐ Record outside weather/temperature conditions.
- ☐ Record outside lighting conditions.
- ☐ Interview the first officer and other police personnel at the scene to determine the sequence of events since their arrival.
- ☐ Crime discovered by — date and time of initial call. Complete details of initial police report.
- ☐ Determine the scope of the patrol officer's initial investigation at the scene.
  - ☐ Protection of the crime scene.
  - ☐ Notifications-alarms-teletypes.
  - ☐ Preliminary investigative results.
- ☐ Record persons present at the scene.
  - ☐ Police officers and law enforcement personnel.
  - ☐ Ambulance and/or emergency personnel.
  - ☐ Family and/or relatives and friends of victim.
  - ☐ Witnesses — including persons detained by patrol.
    - ☐ Keep witnesses separated.
    - ☐ Provide for witness security and availability.

Preliminary Inspection of the Body at the Crime Scene

- ☐ Victim pedigree — name and address if known (includes the following: sex, race, and age).
- ☐ Location of the victim: description of body and scene.

☐ Have the patrol officer personally escort you through the scene to the body using same path used by responding police.

☐ Personally determine and verify death.

☐ Note condition of the body.

☐ Ascertain whether or not there are any suspects in custody. (See suspect in Custody Procedure.)

☐ Are there any additional victims?

  ☐ Is this a multiple murder? (If YES establish separate case numbers and provide for the additional documentation.)

☐ Officially assign investigator to case.

☐ If identity of victim(s) is known, get a background check.

Implement Crime Scene Control Procedures

☐ Determine the scope of the general crime scene — assessment.

☐ Make determination of police legal status in crime scene.

☐ Take preliminary photographs with Instamatic or Polaroid camera to "freeze" the crime scene and provide for review by additional investigators as they arrive at the scene. (Polaroid photos are preferred for immediate viewing.)

☐ Stabilize the scene by identifying and establishing perimeters.

  ☐ If crime scene was not established by patrol, secure and protect the scene by isolation — ropes, barriers, etc.

  ☐ Establish outside and inside perimeters — only authorized personnel allowed within respective perimeters.

  ☐ Remember, the two crime scene theory — the *general area* for police and other official personnel at the scene and the *forensic area* where the body as well as any other evidence may be located.

☐ Assign patrol officers as needed to effectively safeguard scene.

☐ Update and expand crime scene protection as necessary. Is this a *multiple scene*? Are there additional areas to protect?

☐ Establish a single path of entry and exit to the crime scene.

☐ Implement procedures to safeguard all evidence found at scene.

Initiate a Crime Scene Log

☐ Assign an officer to obtain the names of all police and emergency personnel who responded to the original call.

- [ ] Assign an officer to record the names of all personnel and civilians involved in the investigation at the crime scene.
- [ ] Allow no entry to the crime scene except to authorized personnel involved in the official investigation.
- [ ] Record arrival/departure times of all officials. This includes the M.E. or Coroner, State's Attorney, Crime Scene Technicians, etc.
- [ ] This crime scene log should be delivered to detectives upon release of the crime scene.

Establish a Policy for Crime Scene Integrity

- [ ] Make a determination relative to obtaining a search warrant prior to any process of the crime scene.
- [ ] Coordinate activities at the scene and direct investigators by fixing responsibility for the performance of certain duties.
- [ ] Do not touch, move, or alter anything at the scene until full documentation has been completed (observe, describe, record).
- [ ] Record any alterations to the crime scene that were made as a matter of investigative necessity or emergency police response.
  - [ ] Lights turned on or off?
  - [ ] Doors opened, closed, locked, or unlocked?
  - [ ] Body moved, or body cut down?
  - [ ] Windows opened, closed, locked, or unlocked?
  - [ ] Names of all parties who moved the body prior to and during police presence at the scene.
  - [ ] Any furniture moved or anything touched?
  - [ ] Gas turned on or off. Appliances turned on or off?
  - [ ] If vehicle involved, is engine off or on? Is the motor cold, cool, warm, or hot?
- [ ] Do not use any telephone(s) located inside the crime scene.
  - [ ] Does the telephone have an answer machine or message capability? — *check messages*. Check the last number redial/listen to messages. Make recording/seal original tape.
  - [ ] Does the deceased have a beeper? — *check messages*. Check the last number redial/listen to messages. Make recording/seal any original recordings.
  - [ ] Does the deceased have voice mail? — *check messages*. Check the last number and listen to any messages or check the answering service. Take recordings/seal original tapes and document.

☐ Is there a computer at the crime scene? — check system. Last date of use; documents; disks; hard drive.

    ☐ Check computer for answering machine-message modem — *check messages,* e-mail, etc.

☐ Is there a camera at the crime scene? — process and check film. Search for photographs — deceased, friends, activities, etc.

☐ Is there a VCR? Check all tapes — check tape in machine. Note rentals, personal tapes, etc. — secure for review.

☐ Implement procedures to protect the evidence from damage by weather or exposure, and the presence of police personnel.

☐ Do not allow smoking by anyone in the crime scene.

☐ Do not turn water on or off, do not flush toilets, do not use any facility in the scene.

☐ Record condition of lights, lamps, and electric appliances such as televisions, radios, clocks, etc.

Establish a Command Post or Temporary Headquarters

☐ Select a location out of the central crime scene, preferably a location with two phones, one for outgoing and one for incoming telephone calls.

☐ Notify communications and/or the station house of the telephone numbers of the command post to facilitate communications between the various units concerned.

☐ Make notifications as necessary from this location.

    ☐ Crime scene technicians.

    ☐ Medical examiner/coroner or representatives.

    ☐ Additional investigators or police personnel.

    ☐ Prosecutor/district attorney/solicitor's office.

Emergency Medical Service (EMS) and Ambulance Personnel

☐ If ambulance or EMS personnel were present in scene before the investigator's arrival, determine if the crew or anyone else moved the body or any other items within the crime scene. If yes, record the following:

    ☐ When were the alterations made?

    ☐ Purpose of the movement.

    ☐ Persons who made the alterations.

☐ The time of death as pronounced by the ambulance or para-medic crew.

☐ Consider taking fingerprints of "crew" if items in the crime scene were touched or handled by crew.

☐ Interview the EMS or ambulance crew for details of any action taken as well as observations.

Initiate a Canvass

☐ Initiate a canvass of the immediate area by assigning sufficient personnel to locate any witnesses or persons who may have information about the homicide or death.

☐ Assign a supervisor or coordinator to organize the canvass.

    ☐ Utilize canvass control sheets.

☐ Assure that canvassers are provided with all information from the investigation and scene so that they may properly solicit information from prospective witnesses. (This includes photos of the deceased taken in life, if available.)

☐ Have investigators check vehicles and record registration numbers of autos in the immediate area.

☐ Require official reports from canvassers indicating:

    ☐ Negative locations (locations with no results).

    ☐ Locations that have been canvassed, indicating number of persons residing therein.

    ☐ Positive locations for possible follow-up and reinterview.

    ☐ Information relating to the event being canvassed.

    ☐ Utilize the canvass questionnaire forms.

Note ☐ Attempt to conduct further canvasses on the same day of the week as the incident, at approximately the same time of the incident, in order to cover the behavioral patterns of persons to be canvassed.

Weapons

☐ If a weapon is discovered, do the following:

    ☐ Firearms — do not attempt to unload.

    ☐ Record where the weapon is located.

    ☐ Safeguard the weapon for forensic examination (this includes not only ballistics, but operability as well).

☐ Have the weapon photographed before further examination.

☐ If weapon was firearm, consider an examination of the suspect's hands for residue analysis (GSR) testing.

☐ Determine the origin of the weapon. (Does it come from the premises? Does it belong to the deceased, etc.)

☐ Determine if there is any blood or any other trace evidence on the weapon.

The Suspect in Custody

☐ Remember that the suspect is part of the crime scene. "Theory of Transfer and Exchange".

☐ If the suspect is arrested and present at the scene, make sure that he or she is immediately removed from the crime scene and not returned to the scene unless the clothing of the suspect is secured. This procedure is necessary to prevent crime scene contamination.

☐ Safeguard all evidence found on the suspect, including blood, weapons, debris, soil, proceeds of crime, etc.

☐ Ensure that the suspect does not wash his or her hands, nor engage in any conduct which may alter or destroy evidence.

☐ Note any injuries to the suspect and record same with black and white film with rule of measure included as well as color photographs indicating these injuries or marks with appropriate anatomical reference photographs.

☐ Record any spontaneous statements made by the suspect(s).

☐ Do not permit any conversation between the suspect and any parties present.

☐ Guard your investigative conversations in the presence of the suspect(s).

Suspect in Custody: Interrogation at the Scene

If the suspect is in custody at the scene, and circumstances indicate that immediate interrogation of the subject would be beneficial to the investigation, the following steps should be taken:

☐ Advise the suspect of his or her rights under the Miranda ruling prior to any custodial interrogation (this should be done from a Miranda Rights card or Miranda form).

- [ ] Determine of the suspect fully understands his or her rights.
- [ ] Obtain an intelligent waiver of these rights from the suspect prior to any questioning.
- [ ] Document this procedure in the investigative notebook.
- [ ] Allow the suspect to make a full statement.
- [ ] Reduce this statement to writing and have the suspect sign it.
- [ ] Keep the suspect isolated at all times from other suspects, witnesses, prisoners, and any personnel not connected with the investigation.
- [ ] Advise any officers transporting the suspect not to engage the suspect in any conversation or questioning. However, if during transport the suspect makes any statement, the officers should document this information.
- [ ] If the suspect is brought to the police station, he or she should be placed in a separate holding cell.
- [ ] Alibi statements should be documented and recorded in the investigator's notebook.
- [ ] Any self-serving statements should also be recorded and documented, in the event the suspect later changes his or her story.

A.D.A.P.T.

- [ ] Before beginning process make an assessment, re: search warrant requirements.
- [ ] The crime scene search should not be undertaken until all photographs, sketches, measurements, dusting for prints, and written documentation have been completed except for emergency situations.

Crime Scene Photographs

The following photographs should be taken:

- [ ] Photos of the entire location where the homicide took place.
- [ ] Photos of contiguous areas and sites.
- [ ] Photographs of the crowd or any bystanders — surreptitiously.
- [ ] Photos of suspect(s) and/or witnesses, if applicable.
  - [ ] Photos of suspect's clothing and shoes.
  - [ ] Photos of any injuries (body, face, hands, etc.).

☐ Do not add any chalk marks or markers prior to taking the original crime scene photographs. Markers can be added later on for close-up shots.

☐ Take photos from the general to the specific.

Documentation of Crime Scene Photographs

☐ Date and time photos are taken.

☐ Exact location of photographs.

☐ Description of item photographed.

☐ Compass direction (north, south, east, or west).

☐ Focus distance.

☐ Type of film and camera utilized.

☐ Lights and weather conditions.

☐ Number of exposures.

☐ Identification of photographer.

☐ Eliminate extraneous objects including any police equipment.

☐ Show the relationship of the scene to its surroundings.

    ☐ Outdoor scenes — fixed objects as they relate to the scene from eye level.

    ☐ Indoor scenes — objects in the room such as doors, windows etc. to "fix" the body to the crime scene.

Recommended Crime Scene Photographs

☐ Front entrance of building.

☐ Entrance to the room or apartment where the deceased is found.

☐ Two (2) full-body views.

☐ A general view of the body and crime scene.

☐ A close-up shot of the body.

☐ Photos of any visible wounds.

☐ If the body has been removed, photos should be taken of the body's original location.

☐ Photos of possible entrance or escape routes used.

☐ Areas where any force was used for entry or exit.

☐ Area and close-up views of any physical evidence such as bloodstains, weapons, shell casings, hairs, fibers, etc.

☐ Fingerprints (plastic, bloodstained, and latents) — as well as any "lifts" — should be photographed before removal.

☐ After body has been moved, additional photos should be taken.

  ☐ Areas beneath the body.

  ☐ Any additional evidence found beneath the body.

The Crime Scene Sketch

☐ Make a simple line drawing of the crime scene, either in the investigative notebook or on a separate sheet of paper.

☐ The following information should be included.

  ☐ Measurements and distance.

  ☐ A title block consisting of:

    ☐ Name and title of sketcher.

    ☐ Date and time the sketch was made.

    ☐ Classification of crime.

    ☐ Identification of victim(s).

    ☐ Agency's case number(s).

    ☐ Names of any persons assisting in taking measurements.

    ☐ Precise address of the location sketched and compass north.

  ☐ A legend, to identify any object or articles in scene.

  ☐ A scale, to depict measurements used.

The Crime Scene Search

☐ Establish the perimeters of the crime scene and document this location by crime scene photographs and sketches, including written documentation.

☐ Reconstruct aspects of the crime in formulating the search.

☐ Ascertain the legal basis for the search prior to any seizure of evidence.

☐ Visibly locate any physical evidence and determine which evidence should be gathered before any destruction or any alteration takes place.

☐ Establish the method of search based on your investigative theory, size of the area to be searched, and any other factors that arise while conducting this phase of the inquiry.

☐ Areas that should be processed:

- ☐ The point of entry.
- ☐ The escape route.
- ☐ The suspect and his or her clothing, including injuries.
- ☐ The location where any physical evidence or weapons may be located.
- ☐ A vehicle used in the crime.
- ☐ The suspect's residence.
- ☐ The location where the actual assault leading to death took place.
- ☐ Location where the body was moved from.

Dust for Fingerprints

The following areas should be processed for "latent prints":

- ☐ Areas of entry and exit.
- ☐ Weapons or objects which were apparently handled.
- ☐ Door handles.
- ☐ Telephone instruments.
- ☐ Windows.
- ☐ Glasses.
- ☐ Light switches.
- ☐ Newly damaged areas.
- ☐ Objects that may have caused death.
- ☐ Objects missing from their original location.

Note that some areas to be processed may require the use of chemical reagents such as luminol, ninhydrin, cynoacrylate, etc. in order to obtain latent print evidence. Consider these options before dusting.

Description of the Deceased

A complete description of the body should be documented in the investigator's notes, including the following information:

- ☐ The position of the body.
- ☐ Sex.
- ☐ Race.
- ☐ Appearance.
- ☐ Age.

- ☐ Build.
- ☐ Color of hair.
- ☐ Description of clothing.
- ☐ Presence or absence of any jewelry.
- ☐ Evidence of any injuries (bruises, bite marks, wounds, etc.).
- ☐ Condition of the body.
  - ☐ Livor mortis.
  - ☐ Rigor mortis.
  - ☐ Decomposition (describe in detail).
  - ☐ Blood wet or dry.
  - ☐ Insect activity.
  - ☐ Putrefaction.
- ☐ Is the condition of the body consistent with known facts?
- ☐ Note and record the condition of the victim's hands for signs of evidence (defense marks, hairs, fibers, etc.).
- ☐ Note and record any creases and folds on victim's clothing.
- ☐ What is the condition of the victim's pockets?
- ☐ Examine the immediate area surrounding the body for evidence.
- ☐ Record the direction and size of any bloodstains.
- ☐ Check the clothing and shoes for any trace evidence.

Preliminary Medical Examination at the Scene

- ☐ Record the time of arrival of the coroner/medical examiner.
- ☐ Obtain a preliminary estimate on the time of death.
- ☐ Document the apparent cause of death after conferring with the medical examiner/coroner.
- ☐ Are injuries consistent with the suspected weapon involved?
- ☐ Release of the body.
  - ☐ Use a new or laundered sheet to wrap body before removal.
  - ☐ Bag the hands of the victim with paper bags (not plastic) to preserve any trace evidence under fingernails.

Victim — Hospital Information

- ☐ If victim was removed to hospital, dispatch investigators, if available, or patrol unit to obtain the following information:
  - ☐ Name, address, and phone number of the hospital.
  - ☐ Attending doctor — name, address, and phone.

☐ Name of officer interviewing doctor.
☐ Doctor's diagnosis.
☐ If pronounced dead — get time and date. If admitted at hospital — get time and date.
☐ Was the victim interviewed — yes or no?
  ☐ Name of officer conducting interview.
  ☐ Dying declaration?
    ☐ Obtain witnesses, preferably doctor or nurse.
☐ Obtain names, addresses, phone numbers of all emergency room and hospital personnel involved in treatment.
☐ Obtain names, addresses, phone numbers of all ambulance or paramedic personnel involved in emergency and transport.
☐ Names, addresses, phone numbers of anyone who accompanied victim to hospital.
☐ Evidence obtained and/or impounded at hospital.
  ☐ Establish chain of custody — identity of person at hospital who impounded any evidence.
  ☐ Obtain any clothing worn by the deceased for forensic examination.
☐ Obtain names of all police personnel at hospital.

Evidence Process and Control Procedures:

☐ Ensure that all evidence is properly marked and packaged.
☐ Establish a "Chain of Custody".
☐ Designate a "searching officer" to take charge of all evidence.
☐ Record the name and unit designation of all persons participating in the homicide crime scene search.
☐ Photograph all evidence in its original position (*in situ*).
☐ Record the position and location of all evidence on the crime scene sketch and the investigative notebook.
☐ Record the name of any officer or person discovering any physical evidence and the location where it was recovered.
☐ Measure the location of any evidence found from two (2) separate fixed points of reference.
☐ Weapons.
  ☐ Are there any shell casings present?
  ☐ Any bullet holes or spent rounds?
  ☐ Determine how many shots were fired.

☐ Position of bullets in revolver (record by diagram).
☐ Safety on or off?
☐ Is firearm loaded or unloaded? Bullet in chamber?
☐ Are wounds consistent with the weapon suspected?
☐ Is there any trace evidence on the weapon?

Release of the Homicide Crime Scene

Critical decision — authorities should hold onto the crime scene as long as possible in the event that further process, investigation or review becomes necessary as additional information becomes available.

☐ Do not release the scene prior to the completion of the canvass and any interviews of witnesses or interrogation of suspect(s).

☐ Have the deceased's mailbox searched and note the date of any mail found therein. Check with post office for undelivered mail and record all information.

☐ Note the telephone numbers of any phones at the scene.

☐ If the scene is to be abandoned temporarily during certain investigative procedures, provide for the continued crime scene protection during the absence of investigators. The assignment of patrol officers to assist detectives at the crime scene is highly recommended.

☐ Before leaving the crime scene, look over the entire area from the perspective of the defense counsel to make sure you have "covered all the bases".

☐ Gather all materials used in the crime scene processing, such as film packs, film containers, Polaroid negatives, notes, tape, evidence containers, etc.

    ☐ Cause these materials to be removed from the scene for destruction and disposal at another location.

    ☐ Utilize large plastic garbage bags at the crime scene for disposal of materials generated during the search.

It is important to note that the extent of the crime scene search can be ascertained by the examination of these type of materials if they are left behind at the crime scene by the authorities.

SUICIDE INVESTIGATION — INVESTIGATIVE CONSIDERATIONS

Important note: Most suicides occur as a result of depression. Therefore, the investigator should concentrate part of the inquiry into the clinical component of the event. However, keep in mind that some suicides are conscious decisions on the part of the victim and the particular motive for the event may never be ascertained.

Evaluation of the Wounds

☐ Could the deceased have caused the injuries and death?
☐ Was the person physically able to accomplish the act?
☐ Are the wounds within reach of the deceased?
☐ Are the wounds grouped together?
☐ Is there more than one (1) cause of death?
☐ Describe that nature and position of the injuries.
☐ Are there any hesitation marks?

Psychological State of the Victim

☐ Obtain a background of the victim from family and friends.
  ☐ This includes medical as well as social information.
☐ Were there any warning signs indicated by the victim? (See listing of these under Psychological Autopsy.)
☐ Were there any recent deaths in the family?
☐ Is there any indication of a recent upset or stress?
☐ Did the victim leave any notes?
  ☐ Request a sample of the victim's handwriting for a comparison analysis with any note found at scene.
  ☐ Request a sample of the victim's handwriting for an analysis in case a note is later discovered.
☐ Did the deceased have any close personal relationships, any close friends, etc.?
  ☐ Interview these persons as soon as possible.
  ☐ Conduct an immediate search of deceased's home and/or place of business for investigative data.

Any Prior Mental Disease or Defect

☐ Has the deceased been under any professional treatment?
☐ Had the deceased ever attempted suicide in the past?
☐ Has anyone in the family ever committed suicide?
☐ Was the deceased a heavy drinker?

☐ Was the deceased on any medication?

☐ Was there a history of drug abuse?

Recognized Warning Signs and Extreme Danger Signs in Suicides Warning Signs

☐ A change in sleeping habits — sleeping more than usual or staying up much later — followed by sadness.

☐ A change in eating habits — weight loss or lack of appetite.

☐ A lack of interest in sex — a loss of the sex drive.

☐ A sudden drop in grades or school attendance — young people.

☐ A loss of work interest — adults.

☐ Loss of interest in favorite activities, hobbies, or sports.

☐ Loss of interest in friends, family, etc. — isolation.

☐ A preoccupation with death, or an unusual interest in art or music dealing with death. Teenagers — "heavy metal," rock, etc. Adults — preoccupation with death and afterlife.

☐ Loss of interest in personal hygiene and appearance.

☐ Involvement with drugs, including an abuse of alcohol.

Extreme Danger Signs

☐ Suddenly becoming cheerful or calm after a depression. A sudden euphoria or burst of activity. This could mean that the person has resolved the inner conflict by deciding to take his or her own life. The decision has been made.

☐ Giving away prized possessions.

☐ Speaking of life in the past tense — for example, saying, "I've loved you," or "You've been a good mother."

AUTOEROTIC FATALITIES (ACCIDENTAL ASPHYXIA): INVESTIGATIVE CONSIDERATIONS

Deaths which result during solo sex-related activities.

☐ Is the victim nude or sexually exposed?

☐ If the victim is a male, is he dressed in feminine attire?

☐ Is there evidence of masturbatory activity?

☐ Are sexually stimulating paraphernalia present? (Vibrators, dildos, other sexual fantasy aids, or pornography, etc.)

- ☐ Is bondage present? (Ropes, chains, blindfolds, gags, etc.)
- ☐ Are the restrains interconnected?
- ☐ Is there protective padding between the ligature and neck?
- ☐ Is there evidence of infibulation?
- ☐ Is there evidence of fantasy? (Erotic literature, diaries, fantasy drawings, etc.) or fetishism?
- ☐ Are there any mirrors or other reflective devices present?
- ☐ Is the suspension point within the reach of the victim?
- ☐ Is there evidence of prior such activities? (Abrasions or rope burns on the suspension point, photographs, etc.)
- ☐ Is there a positioned camera?
- ☐ Does the victim possess literature dealing with bondage, escapology, or knots?
- ☐ Is there any indication of suicidal intent?

INVESTIGATING FATAL FIRES
The Investigative Considerations

- ☐ Was the fire intentional or accidental?
- ☐ Was the victim alive or dead before the fire?
  - ☐ Many times arson is used to conceal a homicide, disguise a crime scene, or destroy evidence.

The Fire Incident

- ☐ Identify the fire officer in charge of fire operations.
  - ☐ Obtain the name, rank, assignment, and unit responsibility of all fire personnel involved in the operation.
  - ☐ Obtain copy of chief's report describing the firematic operations taken to extinguish the fire: This includes:
    - ☐ Determination origin/cause — suspicious or other.
    - ☐ Was the fire incendiary? — what accelerant was used?

Suspicious Designation: General Determination Factors

- ☐ Rate of burning not consistent with type of combustibles present in the location at the time of fire.
- ☐ A person died as a result of the fire.
- ☐ Questionable or multiple points of origin of the fire.

☐ Firefighter(s) noticed odor of gasoline or other accelerant.

☐ Cause not readily determined.

Maintenance of the Fire Crime Scene

☐ Determine the condition of the scene based upon firematic operations. (Body moved, debris removed, building collapse, etc.)

Investigation at the Scene

☐ Interview survivors as soon as possible.

☐ Interview people with an interest in the fire, who may still be present at the scene while firefighters are working.

☐ Interview firefighters who have first-hand knowledge of the conditions within the building.

☐ Obtain information on all injured, evacuated, and relocated persons for interview.

☐ Interview any ambulance, paramedic, or other emergency crews including red cross personnel who assisted with operations.

☐ Initiate an investigative canvass (see canvass technique).

☐ Assign a fire investigator or arson expert to begin an origin/ cause investigation at the scene to make an official determination of the fire incident.

☐ Record the crime scene — conduct the crime scene search.

☐ Examination of the body.

  ☐ Investigative considerations in arson cases.

    ☐ Identity of the victim.

    ☐ Was victim dead or alive?

    ☐ Is victim face up or face down (usually when one collapses, they fall face forward).

    ☐ Does the body evince "pugilistic attitude" (a boxing pose or fetal position caused by the effect of heat upon the muscles).

    ☐ Postmortem lividity (should be pink to cherry red due to the inhalation of carbon monoxide if the person was alive and breathing during fire).

    ☐ Blistering (blisters surrounded by pink ring can be considered as having occurred before death). However, the medical examiner makes final call.

Determination of Arson

☐ The determination of arson must be based upon expert opinion. This opinion is established after a careful review of the facts as well as the ability of the expert to "read the fire" which provides the investigator with the necessary legal basis for an arson determination and subsequent prosecution.

SUDDEN INFANT DEATH SYNDROME (SIDS): INVESTIGATIVE CHECKLIST

Note: Investigators should be aware that some deaths which appear to be SIDS deaths may in fact turn out to be homicides. These homicides may be due to smothering or MSBP cases. Or, in other cases the injuries may be internal and an external examination of the child fails to reveal any trauma.

☐ Infant's pedigree.
    ☐ Age, date of birth, sex, race, birth weight.
☐ Date and time that the death was discovered.
    ☐ Who was the last person to see the child alive? Date and time.
    ☐ Who discovered the dead infant? Date and time.
☐ What was the place of death?
    ☐ Child's crib, bed, parent's bed, other location. Describe.
☐ Position of the infant/child when found dead?
    ☐ Was this original position changed? By whom? And why?
☐ Was resuscitation attempted?
    ☐ Name of person who attempted resuscitation.
    ☐ Method of resuscitation.
☐ Has the infant/child been sick lately?
    ☐ Cold or sniffles?
    ☐ Other minor or major illnesses?
☐ Any medical treatment? What treatment prescribed?
    ☐ Seeing a doctor? Treating physician?
    ☐ Any medication? What type? Name and dosage?
☐ Was the infant/child breast fed? Or bottle fed?
    ☐ When was the time of last feeding?
    ☐ What was fed to the infant/child?

☐ Have the parents noticed any difference in the infant/child's appearance or behavior in the last few days?

☐ When was the baby last examined by a physician? Why and by whom?

☐ Was the baby exposed to any illnesses recently?

☐ Had there been illness in the family recently?

☐ Have there been any other SIDS deaths in the family?

    ☐ If yes, take a complete history.

☐ Was someone other than parent caring for infant/child?

    ☐ Identification name and address, etc.

    ☐ Ascertain whether any other infants/children have died under their care.

Note: The investigator should approach the parents in a sensitive and nonaccusatory manner and conduct the interview to obtain the above information. If the death does appear to be a SIDS death, convey to the parents that they are not to blame and that there wasn't anything they could have done to prevent the death.

MUNCHAUSEN SYNDROME BY PROXY WARNING SIGNS (MSBP)

☐ Illness which is unexplained, prolonged and so extraordinary that experienced doctors state they have never seen anything like it before.

☐ Repeat hospitalizations and extensive medical tests without achieving a diagnosis.

☐ Symptoms and signs that do not make medical sense.

☐ Persistent failure of the victim to respond to therapy.

☐ Signs and symptoms that dissipate when the victim is removed from the suspected offender.

☐ Mothers who do not seem worried about their children's illnesses and are constantly at the child's side while in the hospital.

☐ Mothers who have an unusually close relationship with the medical staff.

☐ Families that have other children labeled as SIDS children.

☐ Mothers with previous medical or nursing experience that often give a history of the same type of illness as the child.

☐ A parent that welcomes medical test of the child, even if painful.

☐ Attempts to convince the staff that the child is still ill, when advised that the child will be released from the hospital.

☐ A "model family" that normally would be above suspicion.

☐ A caretaker with a previous history of Munchausen Syndrome.

☐ A caretaker that adamantly refuses to accept the suggestion that the diagnosis is non-medical.

Source: Adapted from Meadow (1982), Guandolo (1985), and Ophoven (1991).

Selected Reading

Deickman, Edward A. *Practical Homicide Investigation.* Springfield, Illinois: Charles C Thomas, 1961.

Geberth, Vernon J. "Munchausen Syndrome By Proxy (MSBP) — An Investigative Perspective." *Law and Order Magazine,* Vol. 42, No. 8, Illinois, August, 1994.

Geberth, Vernon J. "Sexual Asphyxia — The Phenomenon of Autoerotic Fatalities." *Law and Order Magazine,* Vol. 37 No. 8, Illinois, August, 1989.

Geberth, Vernon J. "Investigating a Suicide." *Law and Order Magazine,* Vol. 36, No. 12, Illinois, December, 1988.

Harris, Raymond I. *Outline of Death Investigation.* Springfield, Illinois: Charles C Thomas, 1962.

Hendrix, Robert C. *Investigation of Sudden and Violent Death.* Springfield, Illinois: Charles C Thomas, 1972.

Hughes, Daniel J. *Homicide Investigative Techniques.* Springfield, Illinois: Charles C Thomas, 1974.

International Association of Chiefs of Police. *Criminal Investigations,* 2nd ed. Gaithersburg, Maryland, 1970.

O'Hara, Charles E. *Fundamentals of Criminal Investigation,* 5th ed. Springfield, Illinois: Charles C Thomas, 1980.

Synder, LeMoyne. *Homicide Investigation,* 3rd ed. Springfield, Illinois: Charles C Thomas, 1977.

Soderman, H. and O'Connell, J. J. *Modern Criminal Investigation,* 5th ed. New York: Funk & Wagnalls, 1962.

Spitz, Werner U. and Fisher, Russell S. *Medicolegal Investigation of Death.* Springfield, Illinois: Charles C Thomas, 1973.

Svensson, Arne, Wendel, Otto, and Fisher, Barry A. J. *Techniques of Crime Scene Investigation,* 3rd ed. New York: Elsevier North Holland, Inc., 1981.

Westen, Paul B. and Wells, Kenneth, M. *Criminal Investigation — Basic Perspectives,* 2nd ed. Englewood Cliffs, New Jersey: Prentice-Hall, Inc., 1974.

The Crime Scene Photographs

6

Crime scene photographs are permanent and comprehensive pieces of evidence which may be presented in a court of law to prove or disprove a fact in question. During the preliminary stage of homicide investigation it is impossible to determine all of the things which may become relevant or important later on. Therefore, it is imperative that photos be taken of the entire area and location where the crime took place, including any sites contiguous with the original crime.

> Remember, you only get one shot at the homicide crime scene,
> so obtain as much information and documentation as possible.

The Value of Crime Scene Photographs

The old adage, "One picture is worth a thousand words," is certainly appropriate when considering the value of crime scene photography. Although an investigator can verbally describe the homicide crime scene, photographs are able to present the same facts in a more accurate and easily understood manner. In addition, photography enables the investigator to stop the clock at any given instant and obtain a durable record which remains long after other more fragile evidence has dissipated. From an investigative point of view, crime scene photographs are practical and valuable tools which can:

1. Pictorially re-create the original crime scene.
2. Refresh the investigator's memory and recall significant details which may have been overlooked or forgotten.

127

3. Review particular aspects of the case.
4. Provide a new slant on the case.
5. Refresh the memory of witnesses.
6. Illustrate details of a scene and the relationship of objects to the crime.
7. Provide proof of injury or wound.
8. Make comparisons.
9. Brief newly assigned investigators.
10. Convey the crime scene and circumstances of the crime to a jury and serve as a *visible* piece of evidence.

Crime Scene Photography and the Investigator

The investigator should have a basic understanding of photography and be able to operate some of the more simple photographic equipment available today. An easy-to-use camera should be provided for use by the investigators at the homicide crime scene. Such cameras as the Instamatic and many of the Polaroid models are simple to operate and ideal for obtaining a record of the crime scene before any changes occur.

The type of camera that is recommended for crime scene photography is one which provides a large negative. A camera such as the 4 × 5 or the 120 model is preferred because the larger negatives provide better clarity and resolution upon enlargement. The 35 mm camera, because of its versatility and relative simplicity, is an excellent substitute for the large-negative types if they are not available. Investigators can be trained to operate the 35 mm camera in a short time.

Although investigators may be able to operate the 35 mm camera or the Instamatics and Polaroids, they should enlist the assistance of a professional with sophisticated equipment for the proper documentation of the homicide crime scene. Most departments maintain police photographers or specialized personnel to photograph crime scenes. In the absence of police personnel, civilian professionals can be employed. However, they should be advised of the legal requirements involved. The primary duty of the investigator will be to maintain the homicide crime scene in a condition that assures the integrity of the photos.

Admissibility of Photographic Evidence

The homicide investigator should have an understanding of the techniques and legal requirements necessary to insure that the crime scene photos will be admissible in court. The basic premise involved in crime scene photography is that the photographs are a true representation of

Figure 6.1. **THE CHALK FAIRY.** Here you see the deceased lying in the position in which he was found. This crime scene photo may possibly be "inadmissible." While the first officers were securing the scene, a "chalk fairy" suddenly had the irresistible impulse to draw chalk lines around the body.

the homicide crime scene as it was at the time the incident was reported. Therefore, before a detailed examination of the crime scene is undertaken, and before any items are moved or even touched, the crime scene must be photographed.

> **Remember, do not draw any chalk lines nor place markers in the crime scene until an original photograph can be obtained depicting the scene as it was when the police first arrive.**

The photographer should show the relationship of one object to another by moving from the general to the specific. Several photos of the general view should be taken at eye level in a clockwise direction or from each point of the compass (north, south, east, and west). The photographer should start at the outside perimeter of the scene and work toward the central scene. In addition, the photos of the body should indicate its position in relation to some landmark or permanent point of reference. The entire roll of film should be exposed in each investigation. Never leave partially exposed film in the camera for another investigation, or the evidentiary value of the crime scene photographs may be jeopardized.

Do not add any chalk marks or markers to the scene before a long shot and close-up detail shot are obtained. Defense counsel can argue that the crime scene photographs are not an accurate representation of the scene as it was upon discovery of the crime because the police have added markers or chalk lines. If chalk lines or markers are needed to pinpoint the location of a small item, such as bloodstains, hair, or similar articles, photos should first be taken without the markers and then additional photos taken with the markers.

The number of photos taken is usually determined by the case. There is no limit on the number that can be taken. Practically speaking, it is always better to overshoot a scene than to miss some vital shots.

As each photo is taken, an accurate record should be made in the investigator's notebook. In addition, an entry should be made on an official photo log. Some agencies maintain logs or preprinted forms for use at crime scenes in order to assure the proper documentation of crime scene photographs. In any event, the following information should be recorded.

 1. The date and time.
 2. The exact location.
 3. A brief description of the detail being photographed.
 4. The compass direction (north, south, east, or west).
 5. The focus distance.
 6. The type of film and camera utilized.
 7. Any special equipment utilized.
 8. Light and weather conditions.
 9. The number of exposures.
10. The identity of the photographer.

The photographer should keep possession of the exposed film for deliver to the laboratory for processing. After these photos are developed, the above information should be entered either on the back of each photo or on an appropriate form indicating each photo by number.

The comprehensive log is necessary to assure the admissibility of the crime scene photos in court. The log includes the ten points mentioned above, as well as the chain of custody from exposure to final disposition and storage of the film and negatives.

In addition, the police laboratory should keep an evidence log containing the following information.

1. The identity of the individual delivering the film for process (name, rank, serial number, etc.).
2. Date and time the film was received for processing.
3. Results of development.
4. Number of prints requested.
5. Location of original negatives.
6. Identity of the person receiving developed prints and/or negatives if there is no central storage.

In the event that a commercial laboratory is used to process the film, the management should be requested to cooperate in adhering to the rules of evidence handling. This should include limiting the number of personnel handling the evidence film, as well as guaranteeing the security of the film and negatives. Needless to say, the commercial firm utilized to process any evidentiary material should be a reputable establishment.

Photographing the Homicide Crime Scene

Recording the homicide crime scene is a major facet of the investigation. It is extremely important that this be accomplished before anything is touched or moved at the scene. Also, it is important while photographing the scene to eliminate persons or items — including officers and police equipment — that do not belong in the scene.

As mentioned earlier in the chapter, the photographer should attempt to show the relationships of objects to each other by shooting from the general to the specific, should take several photos of the general view, and should start at the perimeter and work toward the body. This is followed by close-up shots of the body and any significant pieces of physical or trace evidence. Important items of evidence, such as weapons, should be photographed as they appear at the scene.

Remember, no chalk marks or markers before you get a long shot and a close-up shot of the body and any other evidence.

Outdoor Locations

Outdoor locations should be photographed showing the central scene and the surrounding area in order to show the relationship of the scene to its surroundings and give the viewer a point of reference. These photos should be taken at eye level to show exactly how the scene appeared to the investigators or witnesses. If the homicide takes place in a large area, or the surrounding street locations become significant, aerial photos are often helpful in providing a better perspective.

Indoor Locations

Indoor locations are more restricted than outdoor ones; however, the same principles apply. The photographer takes several overall shots in order to relate the scene to its surroundings. He then photographs the body, showing its position and relationship to objects in the room. Indoor locations may include several rooms in a house, an entire apartment or an individual room, the interior of a closet, an office, a hallway, a fire escape, a cellar, etc. The extent of the indoor photos depends on the facts of the case. The position of any windows and doors should be photographed, and exterior photos should be taken of locations — backyards, entranceways, neighboring residences, etc. — that show the premises from the outside.

The Body

Photos of the body should include a general and close-up view and at least two full-body shots, one from each side. The photos must be taken *in situ* before the body is moved and should show any significant aspects of the crime as well as the body's position in the scene. Any defense wounds on the body should be photographed at the scene and later on at autopsy.

It is recommended that additional identification photos of the deceased be taken at the morgue, prior to autopsy and after the body has been cleaned of any blood or grime. Sometimes the facial features will be so distorted that it is impossible to get an identification photo. In these cases, pictures should be taken of any scars or other markings, including tattoos, for later identification purposes. Photographs should also be taken of any wounds or injuries that caused death or are significant to the investigation. These photos should be taken before and after the body has been cleaned in order to show the specific extent of injury and the character of each wound in exact detail. Photographs of any wounds should include a standard or metric ruler along with an I.D. label indicating case numbers and other pertinent information. In

Figure 6.2.   **THE CU-5 POLAROID CAMERA.**

Figure 6.3.   **PHOTOGRAPH OF BITE-MARK WOUND.** (Courtesy Dr. Arthur D. Goldman, DDS, Forensic Odontologist.)

homicide cases where the victim has received wounds from bite marks, it is recommended that the photographs be taken with a 1 × 1 *fingerprint* camera such as the one produced by Polaroid. These fingerprint cameras will provide the necessary detail needed for comparison and examination of the wound later on. Remember to use a ruler or scale to obtain an accurate measurement. (See Chapter 20, "Bite-Mark Identification".)

Figure 6.4. **NEW POLAROID MICROCAM SLR** produces instant photomicrographs with push button ease. The Polaroid MicroCam SLR, a new instant camera that fits most optical microscopes, combines low cost with a remarkably sophisticated exposure and filtration control system to make photographic recording a possibility for all light microscopists. The new camera offers single-lens-reflex viewing along with automatic exposure and filtration control to ensure perfectly framed, focused, and exposed photographs of microscope specimens. The fully automatic MicroCam SLR produces high-quality Polaroid AutoFilm instant black-and-white and color prints with the press of a button.

Suspects

It is important to note that crime scene photographs are not limited to places, objects, or dead bodies. Many times a suspect's appearance will indicate that he or she has been in some sort of altercation. Suspects may have blood on their hands or body, and there may be blood on their clothes. They may have scratches or cuts on their hands, or there may be some superficial wounds on their face or body. In addition, there may be some visible material on the suspect that links him or her to the crime scene. Crime scene photographs must be taken before this valuable and important evidence is lost. However, in order to assure admissible crime scene photos, the suspect must be in custody, be under arrest, or agree to *pose* after having been advised of his constitutional rights.

Figure 6.5.   **HANDS OF THE SUSPECT.** Both hands of this suspect, who has been charged with homicide, show evidence of a violent struggle, as indicated by the arrows, and are actually part of the crime scene. These photos should be taken in black-and-white and color, with a marker.

Type of Film

I recommend that crime scene photographs be taken in color and black-and-white. Often an issue of color may arise that cannot be resolved by black-and-white photos. I recall an investigation involving a homicide in a rooming house where the suspect had allegedly brought a blue sweatshirt into the room of the deceased. He had changed the shirt because blood from the victim was splattered all over it. The suspect then threw the shirt on a pile of rags after wiping up some of the blood and left the shirt behind. Later on a witness was located who had observed the suspect wearing a blue sweatshirt before the crime was committed. The witness attempted to locate the sweatshirt in the black-and-white crime scene photos but failed to make an identification. Had we been using color film as well as black-and-white, we would have been able to point out the sweatshirt as a piece of evidence.

Photos taken in color give a much more realistic portrayal of the crime scene, which graphically depicts the events to the viewer. However, in certain instances, defense counsel has effectively precluded the submission of color prints into evidence because color was "too inflammatory." There are other occasions where details shot in color are not clear enough for comparison purposes, e.g., latent fingerprint evidence. In any event, if the crime scene photographs are taken in both black-and-white and color, the investigator can choose between the two.

Figure 6.6.   **BLOOD SPLATTER PHOTOGRAPH.** Bloodspatter analysis can be of immense help in the reconstruction of a homicide scene. This particular bloodstain pattern contained more than the usual amount of information. "Jake" was later convicted of this murder. (Courtesy of Yonkers, New York Police Department Crime Scene Unit, Det./Lt. Peter Pizzola, Commanding Officer.)

Recommended Crime Scene Photographs

There is no limit on the number or types of photos one may decide to take at any given crime scene. However, there are certain photographs which should be taken in all homicide investigations. I recommend that the following crime scene photographs be obtained as a matter of routine.

1. The front entrance or walkway to the building or dwelling where the homicide took place; or the external perimeter of an outdoor crime scene wherein the body lies.
2. The entrance to the apartment or room where the deceased is discovered.
3. Two full-body views (one from each side). If the body has been removed, the original location where the body was discovered should be photographed.

Figure 6.7. **PATTERN INJURY IN FIREARM CASE.** (Left) Contact gunshot wound to skin demonstrating muzzle/magazine/front sight imprinting. (Right) Firearm responsible. (Courtesy of Westchester County Medical Examiner's Office. Photograph by W. Reid Lindsay, Westchester County Forensic Science Laboratory.)

Figure 6.8. **PATTERN INJURY IN FIREARM CASE.** (Left) Contact gunshot wound to skin demonstrating muzzle/slide/slide guide rod imprinting. (Right) Firearm responsible. (Courtesy of Westchester County Medical Examiner's Office. Photograph by W. Reid Lindsay.)

Figure 6.9.   **PHOTOGRAPHIC RECONSTRUCTION.** Bullet trajectory reconstruction of shots into mattress using wooden dowels. Note similar angles for three shots and very different angle of fourth slot indicating two different firing positions during this homicide. (Courtesy of Frederick C. Drummond, Westchester County Forensic Science Laboratory.)

Figure 6.10.   **EVIDENCE *IN SITU*.** This knife was left behind by the killers after it had been used to torture and slay the victim, who was also shot as well as stabbed. The knife had been thrust deep into the deceased's chest, to where the bloodmark appears on the blade.

4. Two photographs relating the body location to its general surroundings, from opposite and/or diagonal sides.
5. Possible entrance and/or escape routes of the perpetrator or perpetrators to and from the crime scene.
6. Areas where force was used for entry or exit.
7. Area and close-up view of evidence *in situ*. In addition to the body, this would include bloodstains, weapons, shell casings, hairs, fibers, or any other physical or trace evidence.
8. If a large outdoor area is involved, take aerial photographs to relate scene to surroundings.
9. Photographs of suspect, if in custody, with attention to any new wounds or injuries or presence of physical or trace evidence.

Figure 6.11. **BLOODSTAINS.** The suspect's underwear reveals bloodstains and other evidence from a rape-homicide. The suspect, who raped and killed a homeless woman staying in an abandoned building, was apprehended shortly after the crime. This photograph should also be accompanied by a "stand-up" photo identifying the suspect by face as well as additional photos of the individual evidence.

10. Photographs of witnesses either surreptitiously or as a matter of record, depending on the circumstances of the case.

On completion of these preliminary crime scene photographs, the homicide supervisor should make it a standard practice to keep the photographer at the scene in the event the crime scene search uncovers additional items or details which should be photographed. Many times, after a body has been moved, additional evidence is discovered underneath, such as shell casings, spent rounds, a weapon, etc. These items should be photographed *in situ* before collection, with a reference in the investigator's notebook as to the original location and the discovery.

Practical Application of Crime Scene Photography

In addition to the general application of crime scene photography to the overall investigative process, there are instances when the camera can perform what the investigator cannot. For instance, in street homicides, especially in cities, there is always the possibility that the suspect

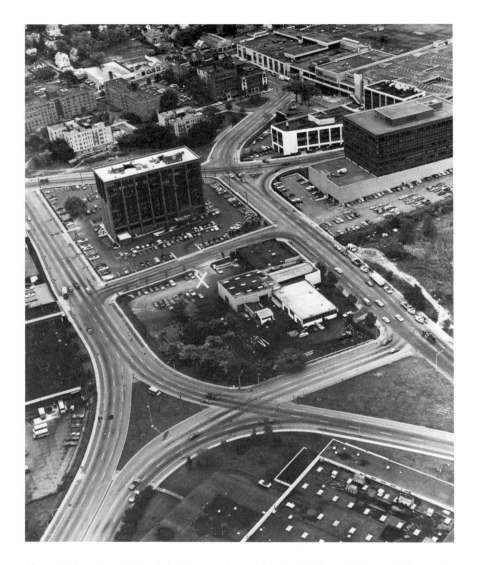

Figure 6.12.   **AERIAL SHOT.** It is a good procedure to obtain aerial views of the murder scene in certain cases.

or a witness to the fatal act may still be in the crowd of onlookers. I personally recommend that pictures be taken of these people either surreptitiously while photographing the scene, or directly before anyone in the crowd realizes that their presence is being documented. In addition, if you have videotape capability, tape the crowd and their reactions. It usually proves to be quite interesting, and may help you to locate persons later on for questioning.

I remember two incidents where the crime scene photos helped us to break a case. On one occasion, while on investigative patrol, we heard a radio broadcast of a possible homicide and a request for detectives to respond. Since we were close by, we arrived as the crowd was still being directed behind hastily erected barriers. As the detective who was with me approached the scene, I stood back and began to take pictures of the surrounding crowd with my Instamatic camera. Later on we discovered that there was a witness to the shooting in the crowd. This witness never would have come forward had we not "captured" his presence on film.

In another case, we were at the scene of a street homicide when we received information that one of the perpetrators was in the crowd. We could not verify this information, nor make an arrest, because the source had made himself scarce and we did not have enough probable cause to make an arrest. I instructed the crime scene photographer to surreptitiously photograph the crowd while taking the crime scene photos. Later on when we showed these blown-up crowd shots to our witness, he positively identified the suspect as one of the participants.

Videotaping

The use of videotape is becoming increasingly popular and has been employed with excellent results in the investigation of homicide. The technical expertise involved is certainly within the ability of the homicide investigator or crime scene technician and should be considered a viable adjunct to other methods employed in the recording of crime scenes.

Advantages of Videotaping

Videotaping has the following advantages:

1. It provides a more realistic and graphic portrayal of the homicide crime scene.
2. It tends to capture the atmosphere of the scene, especially when the homicide detective is narrating the events as they are being depicted on film.
3. It can be used to record suspects' statements. This is especially beneficial if suspects later on change their story or deny having made a confession to police. It should be noted that defendants must be given their Miranda rights on the video prior to videotaping their statements. In addition, a clock which is visible in the background should be employed to record the total time of interview.

4. It can be utilized to record a dying declaration. Often a victim under treatment in a hospital may be diagnosed as critically injured and likely to die. If the victim is coherent, the investigator should attempt to elicit a dying declaration. The use of videotape enhances and permanently documents this legal procedure.

5. It can be used to record a line-up. This recording can be utilized to depict to the jury the exact position of the defendant and can be shown to additional witnesses in an attempt to identify suspects.

6. A video camcorder records 30 frames of video tape per second. This compliments the human eyes' persistence of vision, constantly keeping the viewer informed as to direction, and perspective even though the lens may be moving and its field of view is continually recording differing angles of view. An entire crime scene can be scanned and will be captured in great detail. In addition, items that may have been missed originally will still be preserved on tape.

Purpose of Videotaping the Crime Scene

1. Preserving the entire event for future review of the scene by investigators, medical examiners, serologists, and others for:

   Identification of evidence.
   Conditions at the time of discovery.
   Any subsequent questions regarding the scene.
   Refresh investigator's and witnesses' memory.
   Comparison with other unsolved crimes.
   Blood stains, direction of fall, location, etc.
   Location of windows, doors, rooms, rugs, furniture, etc.
   Lighting conditions (night and day) (interior and exterior).
   Vegetation, outdoor landmarks, trees, lakes, etc.
   Weather conditions.
   Outdoor crime scenes, showing crowds for identification.

2. Presentation of entire or edited relevant portions for presentations to grand jury, judge, juries, etc.:

   Corroborate a confession.
   Contradict an exculpatory statement or defense witness.
   Depict the reality of death.
   Prove lines of sight, lighting, spacing, passage.

There are different methods of videotaping a crime scene. Some agencies utilize a team method whereby one investigator acts as the technician while the other describes or narrates the events as they are being filmed. However, personnel at the scene should be cautioned to remain quiet during this taping, as such conversation may prove distracting or embarrassing. I recall a case that was being videotaped that involved a brutal sex act and murder. The suspect was found lying on top of the deceased female by an employee of the building. The suspect had been sodomizing the dead woman when he was "interrupted." The condition of the victim and the act that had been perpetrated were so heinous that officers at the scene were quite descriptive in their opinions of what should be done to the "perp" (perpetrator). The suspect eventually pleaded guilty and the videotape was never presented. Needless to say, however, if the tape had ever been played in court, the defense counsel would have had a field day depicting the police as crude and vindictive, not to mention unprofessional.

It has been my experience that audio and crime scene narration during the initial taping can become problematic since your initial observations and comments may be erroneous (these are discoverable). Furthermore, incidents such as the one cited above are all too common. An open microphone may pick up idle talk and conjecture not to mention some of the unacceptable commentary that takes place at crime scenes. I recommend that only a beginning and ending statement containing the technician's name, the time, date, and location be recorded for evidential purposes.

Recommended Procedure

The best method is to have one technician with a closed microphone shoot the scene at a normal angle as would be seen with the human eye. The distances portrayed in the scene are then the same as if you were standing where the camera was located. Videotaping of crime scenes should ideally be accomplished before any forensic work and changes to the crime scene have been made by police, detectives, and crime scene technicians.

In order to provide the reader with the most effective and efficient manner of videotaping crime scenes, I consulted with Mr. Chris Longueira, who is the Chief Technician of the Bronx District Attorney's Video Unit. I had the pleasure of working very closely with him when I was a supervisor in homicide. I was impressed with his expertise and the value of videotaping and encouraged its use whenever I had the opportunity. Mr. Longueira, who has been videotaping crime scenes as well as defendant statements since 1978, is considered an expert on the use of video tape within the criminal justice system.

According to Mr. Longueira, "The technician should attempt to keep video continuity so that the viewer will always know where they are in the scene and from what perspective they are viewing the subject in the scene by utilizing consistent reference points."

Mr. Longueira states, "Whenever the recordist must change position which is frequently unavoidable, he/she should make a note of the last frame of video tape recorded and use that as a reference even though the angle and distance may have changed somewhat. Be sure to start recording and hold until the viewer can comprehend where the recordist has moved to. You must always try to avoid the 180 degree jump cut."

The videotaping should begin at the perimeter of the scene or outside the location and progress toward the central scene and the body. Long shots as well as close-ups should be taken in a slow and systematic manner. This is accomplished by first "panning" the entire area and then focusing or "zooming" in on the central scene and corpse. In order to document the location or position of the body, the technician should photograph any landmarks or permanent structures as points of reference to give a perspective on the position of the body.

The same principle used in crime scene photographs applies to videotaping. In order for the videotape to be admitted into evidence the scene must be "intact" and not have been changed. The scene should first be filmed without any markers or scales and then filmed with the necessary visual aids. In addition, the videotape must be in original condition without any erasures or editing in order to be admissible as evidence. The following recommended protocol was designed and provided by Mr. Longueira.

Videotape Protocol

Arrival at Scene

☐ Obtain the preliminary information from the first personnel on the scene regarding the occurrence. Any observations by witnesses, who have entered the crime scene, any EMS activities, etc. Check with the investigators, medical examiners, etc. regarding what they think.

☐ The technician, at this point, should quickly take a look at the scene for such things as:

A. Location
  1. Layout of the apartment.
  2. The room the body is in and other rooms where evidence was found.
  3. Areas you should be careful not to disturb such as blood on the floors or walls, small pieces of evidence that could easily be kicked or stepped on. *Use your elbows to open doors instead of imparting your finger or hand prints in the crime scene.*
B. Body
  1. Size of the room it was found in.
  2. Whether face up or down and is it accessible from what angles.
  3. The wounds: how many, where, and what kind.

Conduct a quick review of these areas after you have obtained the information from the scene investigators. Ask about possible entry and exit ways, windows, whether or not they were forced or let in. Ascertain what evidence has been recovered or located, such as prints whether they appear to be hand or foot and the location of any blood splatterings on walls or floors possibly indicating where the victim was standing or facing when he/she was murdered. Ask about adjoining rooms or areas that are pertinent to the crime. Is there another apartment that this final scene originated from? (More likely in urban settings.) Once you have taken this preliminary information you are ready to start taping. Keep a mental list of all this information and pertinent locations as you proceed to tape the scene. The best method, according to Mr. Longueira, is to let your shots run as long as possible. You can be redundant as long as each frame is continually depicting new information to the viewer. However, being over redundant could make the viewer uneasy. Try to walk through the entire scene in one take. This allows persons who view the tape an uninterrupted orientation.

Taping Protocol

- ☐ Begin taping by putting an introduction on the tape: technician's name, date, time, and location.
- ☐ Turn off the audio. You do not want to have an ongoing commentary regarding the scene. Opinions and perspectives change.

Remember: the tape is subject to discovery. You do not want to pick up stray comments or information on the open microphone. Later on in court the witness can narrate.

- [ ] Begin taping from a logical beginning point; i.e. front door or nearest identifiable landmark or street sign if outdoors.
- [ ] Orientate your camera work so that viewers will know where you are at a given point; e.g., pan the room or hallway before being specific. Go slowly and use long steady shots.
- [ ] Shoot the scene from a normal angle as the eye would perceive it without wide angle or telescopic distortion.

Note: Normal angle. The rule for 35 mm photography is that the diagonal measurement of a 35 mm aspect ratio is 50 mm or a 50 mm lens. (This is why most 35 mm cameras are sold with a 40 to 50 mm lens as standard.) The recordist wants to capture the scene as he would with the naked eye.

- [ ] When you do zoom in, zoom back out to the same spot. This will provide the viewer continuity and perspective and allow editing of zoom portions. *Never zoom without purpose.* The single most over used and abused feature of the novice recordist is the zoom.
- [ ] When zooming in; sharpen focus and hold.
- [ ] Do *not* do each item on a separate zoom (e.g., in and out on each bullet wound). A much more effective tape will be procured when you zoom to a series of small items or wounds and pan across them slowly and then zoom out very slowly.
- [ ] Shoot several angles of the body, room, etc. Try to shoot the body from adjoining rooms if possible or down long hallways. This provides the possible lines of sight that still photos can't depict.
- [ ] Do all doors, locks, windows, closets, kitchen, dining facilities, medicine cabinets, etc.
- [ ] Shoot all lines of sight at location, e.g., top of stairs to downstairs front door and in reverse.
- [ ] Do the body at the end of the scene documentation. After the body has been turned over, reshoot those areas which were hidden from view to document any further wounds or findings.

☐ Shoot hands, feet, eyes, clothes, jewelry, tattoos, gold teeth, scars, etc.

☐ *Option*: shoot the recovery and collection of evidence.

☐ Shoot all bloodstains, weapons, shell casings, hair, fibers, and trace evidence.

☐ Upon completion of the taping, close with your name and time.

☐ Label and number tape and log as evidence; include weather conditions, lighting, etc.

Remember: Videotaping does not replace good crime scene photographs. It should be used in conjunction with the photos.

Videotaping Suspect Statements

When videotaping suspect statements it is important to record the suspect's demeanor during the interview. Frequently a suspect will involuntarily demonstrate some sort of body language that will indicate nervousness or uneasiness at certain questions. This tape can later be played back for evaluation and analysis by the investigator.

A review of the tape and the suspect's reactions may form the basis for a different approach or a concentration on certain points of the interrogation.

It should be noted that there is a difference of opinion on whether or not suspects' statements should be videotaped. Certain experts feel that the implementation of such a system may create additional problems in the prosecution if all statements are not taped, by providing the defense counsel with ammunition to challenge those statements. For example, if a confession or statement is not videotaped, for any number of legitimate reasons, does this mean the agency was attempting to hide something? Because of this, the decision to video tape statements must be given careful consideration.

Conclusion

In conclusion, the application of photography to the documentation of the homicide crime scene is certainly within the capability of the average investigator. Photography is an important element of professional law enforcement that provides an objective, comprehensive, and impartial re-creation of the crime scene as it was upon discovery. It is up to the investigators to provide this vital ingredient, either by taking the photos themselves or by preserving the scene until the arrival of police photographers.

The use of video tape to enhance this documentation is an excellent medium because many people who have VCRs and camcorders in their home are aware of videos and videotaping and therefore can relate to this documentation process.

Selected Reading

Geberth, Vernon J., *Practical Homicide Investigation: Tactics, Procedures, and Forensic Techniques.* Second Edition, CRC Press, Inc. Florida, 1993.

Geberth, Vernon J. "The Use of Videotape in Homicide Investigations." *Law and Order,* Vol. 44, No. 3, 1996.

O'Hara, Charles E. *Fundamentals of Criminal Investigation,* 5th ed. Springfield, Illinois: Charles C Thomas, 1980.

Scott, James D. *Investigative Methods.* Reston, Virginia: Reston Publishing Company, Inc., 1978.

Ward, Richard H. *Introduction to Criminal Investigation.* Reading, Massachusetts: Addison-Wesley Publishing Co., 1975.

The Crime Scene Sketch 7

The *crime scene sketch* is a simple line drawing that indicates the position of the body in relation to *fixed* and *significant* objects in the scene. It supplements both the written reports and the crime scene photographs. Photographs, because of camera perspective and distortion, do not always depict the exact location in which objects are situated or the relation of one object to another. The crime scene sketch is an excellent visual aid which allows for the removal of unnecessary details and the inclusion of significant material. Practically speaking, the homicide crime scene sketch can become one of the most useful tools of the homicide investigator.

The Sketch

A drawing of the crime scene is the simplest and most effective way to present measurements and to identify those items that the investigator deems significant, including the location of the victim's body, the location of any physical or trace evidence, the position of the weapon, and objects which may be significant to the overall scene. In addition, the drawing permits the deletion of irrelevant or distracting items which appear in photographs. In addition to creating a diagram which is specific and selective, the crime scene sketch can be used to:

1. Refresh the memory of the investigator.
2. Refresh the memory of the witness(es).
3. Refresh the memory of the cooperative suspect to assist in detailing his or her actions at the scene.

4. Develop a clearer understanding of what happened and determine the relative likelihood of various possibilities. For instance, persons may be requested to trace their particular movements on copies of the original sketch.
5. Explain to a jury or witness the specifics of a case that may otherwise be too complex or confusing. The value of the crime scene sketch is that its clarity and simplicity motivate understanding.

The crime scene sketch should show the position of doors, windows, staircases, as well as other objects of significance, including blood, weapons, stains, and any other trace evidence identified.

The *rough sketch* should be prepared by the investigator at the scene. He may either use graph paper, which is excellent because it provides lines, or draw the sketch in his notebook. The most important element of the rough sketch is careful attention to measurements and distance. The ability of the investigator to draw is a definite asset; however, the rough homicide crime scene sketch need not be a Rembrandt production.

The rough sketch should contain a *legend*. The legend will explain any numbers or symbols used, and give identification numbers assigned to the case, the identity of the sketcher and person taking the measurements, and a reference to compass direction North.

Many municipalities have a city engineer or graphic arts section with personnel who may, under the direction of the homicide investigator, prepare a professional *smooth* or *finished crime scene sketch*.

In some cases, an existing map or blueprint may be utilized to graphically portray the crime scene. I remember directing investigations involving homicides or shootings on New York City Housing Authority property. The Housing Authority, because it is a city agency, maintained blueprints of all properties under its jurisdiction. While at the scene, we obtained the blueprint of the particular project involved and used the blueprint as our crime scene sketch. Since a blueprint or map will already bear the scales and landmarks of the area, all the investigator need do is add the significant objects in the instant case to the finished blueprint, being careful to measure distances and follow the scale provided in the finished plan.

It should be noted that the original sketch is evidence and, as such, must never be altered, changed, or otherwise tampered with after the investigator has completed his drawing at the scene. In addition, the investigator must assure that this original sketch is properly safeguarded even after a smooth or finished sketch is prepared by an expert

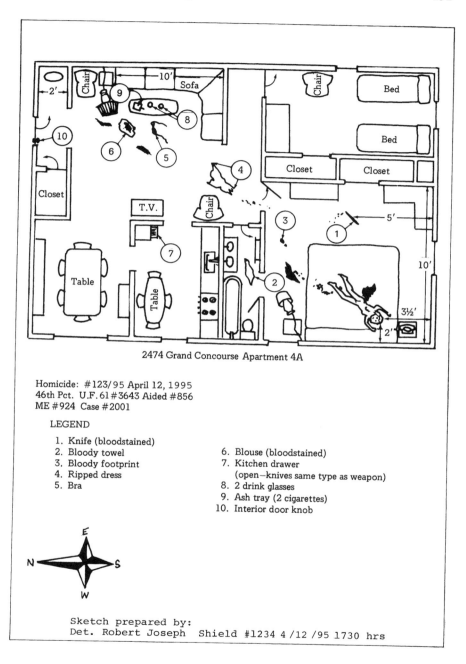

2474 Grand Concourse Apartment 4A

Homicide: #123/95 April 12, 1995
46th Pct. U.F.61 #3643 Aided #856
ME #924 Case #2001

LEGEND

1. Knife (bloodstained)
2. Bloody towel
3. Bloody footprint
4. Ripped dress
5. Bra
6. Blouse (bloodstained)
7. Kitchen drawer
   (open—knives same type as weapon)
8. 2 drink glasses
9. Ash tray (2 cigarettes)
10. Interior door knob

Sketch prepared by:
Det. Robert Joseph   Shield #1234 4/12/95 1730 hrs

Figure 7.1.   **FINISHED CRIME SCENE SKETCH.** Includes case numbers, date and times, the identity of the drawer, and a legend.

Figure 7.2. **ROUGH SKETCH.** This sketch was made in the investigator's notebook, while at the scene. It is nothing more than a simple line drawing, which indicates the position of objects and gives measurements.

HOMICIDE WINDOWS

WINDOW   WINDOW

CHAIR

REFRIG-
ERATOR

COUCH

COUCH

COUCH

CABINET

CABINET

STOVE

TUB

SINK

WASH-
ER SINK

CRIB

BED

BED

BED

7'

6'

② (by cabinet)

① (body)

CHAIRS

LEGEND
1. BODY
2. BLOOD ON DOOR JAMB

E
N ——— S
W

FLOOR PLAN
HOMICIDE CRIME SCENE
123 FRONT ST.
APT. 1B BRONX, N.Y.
4/12/95 1100 hrs.
HOMICIDE CASE #2102
JANET WHITE F/W 29
METHOD: STRANGULATION

APARTMENT
ENTRANCE

SKETCH BY: DET. JAMES V. CARDILLO #1234 1200 hrs.

Figure 7.3. **ROUGH SKETCH.** The floor plan of the entire apartment of the preceding sketch. Any number of sketches can be prepared in any case.

draftsman. The original crime scene sketch *must not* be mutilated or destroyed. Often, especially in cases where the smooth or finished sketch is prepared for court presentation, the defense counsel will attempt to prevent its introduction or to diminish its value by demanding to examine the original rough sketch. Defense counsel will then compare the rough sketch to the finished product and attempt to discover some inconsistencies or discrepancies.

Preparing the Crime Scene Sketch

Obviously, a determination must be made regarding what is to be sketched. If you are dealing with a single room, a line drawing or projection-type sketch may be employed. If the crime scene involves two or more rooms, you should utilize a simple line drawing which follows a floor-pattern technique.

In order to assist the investigator in preparing the crime scene sketch I have provided some practical examples and guidelines.

1. Necessary items:
   a. Notebook, paper ($8^1/_2$" × 11") or graph paper with $^1/_2$" squares, which can be used to scale feet. (Remember to leave an ample margin for the legend.)
   b. Soft lead pencil with eraser.
   c. Straight edge or ruler.
   d. Steel tape (preferably 100' length).
2. Measurements:
   a. All measurements must be taken from *fixed* points, for example, doors, windows, walls, chimney, stairs, etc.
   b. Measurements should be exact, and should be taken with a steel tape or ruler.
   c. One investigator should sketch while another officer takes the measurements.
   d. In drawing the sketch, the investigator can estimate the relative distances or positions of items, since this rough sketch is not a scale drawing and art work and technical detail do not have to be perfect. However, there should be an accurate measurement taken and recorded in the sketch.
   e. If distances are measured by pacing off, this should be indicated by the number of paces. (This procedure is *not* recommended, but may be used in the absence of proper measuring devices.)

Figure 7.4. **CROSS-PROJECTION SKETCH.** All objects are drawn as if seen from above, but the walls are folded down and the items are drawn as if the room was a cardboard box with its sides flattened.

Figure 7.5.   BASE LINE SKETCH. The base line method of sketching can be used when there is a scene without a convenient straight line or boundaries such as a warehouse or large outdoor area. In this sketch the cartons are moveable and the inside area large. By drawing a base line through the scene you create a point of reference. Each end of the baseline should be identified and there should be a starting point or zero end.

3. Methods of obtaining measurements:
   a. *Straightline.* Two measurements are made, one from each side of the object, to a fixed point in the diagram. This method is usually employed to mark positions of furniture or evidence along a wall.
   b. *Rectangular coordinates* or *perpendicular distance method.* Two measurements are taken at right angles of an item to the nearest two permanent objects, usually the walls. This is the most practical method for marking the location of the body and other evidence. There are more accurate methods; however, I find this to be the simplest and most useful at the scene.
   c. *Polar coordinates* or *triangulation.* By utilizing a compass and a protractor the investigator locates two fixed points and transfers this information to the sketch. Measurements are then taken from these two fixed points to the object, forming a triangle. Where the two points intersect is the exact location of the object.
   d. *Base line.* This method is used for a scene that does not have convenient straight perimeter boundaries, e.g., a large wooded area or the interior of an expansive warehouse. A straight line is drawn through the scene, and each end is located and measured. A starting point is designated and the line is then used as a point of reference for all other measurements. The line can follow a seam or some other naturally existing line.
   e. *Two fixed points.* This is a simple method whereby the investigator takes *two* straight-line measurements to *two* fixed points within the scene. There is no need for a right angle, but the two points used should not be close together.
4. The title block:
   a. The professional and legally correct crime scene sketch must contain the following official documentation and information:
      1. The name and title of the investigator who drew the sketch.
      2. The date and time that the sketch was made.
      3. The classification of the crime (homicide, assault, etc.).
      4. The identification of the victim.
      5. The agency's case number.

6. The names of any persons assisting in taking measurements.

7. The precise address of the location sketched.

8. Reference points used during the sketching, including compass direction North, with appropriate indications.

9. The legend. The purpose of the legend is to identify every article or object by either number or letter and explain the significance of these characters on the crime scene sketch. The legend also includes the scale used and a reference to any notes taken and measurements recorded in connection with the investigation.

10. Any other pertinent information which is practical to the investigation at the scene (for example: the season, the ground condition — muddy, dry; traffic or lack of traffic; slope of the ground; site — abandoned building, public place, transportation facility; the position of the camera in any crime scene photographs; etc.).

It is important to note that any number of crime scene sketches may be employed during the investigation at the scene, especially in multiple-crime scene situations. Therefore, it is imperative that any sketch used be properly documented in the investigator's notebook along with descriptions and other pertinent information.

The "Total Station" Crime Scene Reconstruction Program

The author conferred with Mr. Robert Bonaker, Operations Manager for GEO-LINE Instrument and Supply Company in Bellevue, Washington, whose company produces the Total Station unit and Detective-Sergeant Nicholas Theodos, New Jersey State Police, who prepared an in-depth report on its applicability to law enforcement.

Definition

What is a "Total Station" system? A "Total Station" is an electronic measuring instrument, also referred to as an electronic distance meter (EDM) which records distance, slope, and horizontal and vertical angles to a given point. It is an instrument developed for use by surveyors and has been used by them for many years.

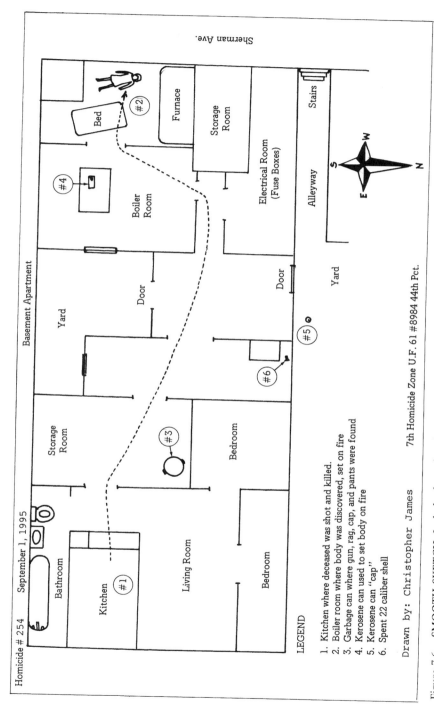

Figure 7.6. **SMOOTH SKETCH.** Includes legend and objects, with a dotted line showing the path the killer took through the scene when he disposed of the body.

Figure 7.7. **STREET LOCATION SKETCH.** This type of sketch is useful when dealing with several locations and pinpointing the movement of various persons. Symbols and letters can be used to show the movements of the persons involved. For example, V is the victim, A and B are the perpetrators, P represents the police, and W is the civilian witness. X is the crime scene.

Figure 7.8. **TOTAL STATION.** The "Station" looks similar to a surveyor's transom, however, it is much more sophisticated. The instrument contains several internal components which perform various functions, and an external hand-held prism on a rod; the prism is placed at the location of the object to be measured. (Courtesy of Mr. Robert Bonaker, Operations Manager, GEO-LINE Instrument & Supply Co., Inc., Bellevue, WA.)

Operation

The "Station" looks similar to a surveyor's transom; however, it is much more sophisticated (see photographs of a "Station"). The instrument contains several internal components which perform various functions,

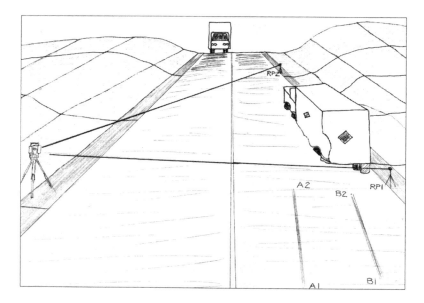

Figure 7.9.   **THE TOTAL STATION CALCULATES 3-DIMENSIONAL COORDINATES.**
The "total station" system is a new modern sophisticated way of using electronic equipment
to take crime scene measurements. (Courtesy of Mr. Robert Bonaker, Operations Manager,
GEO-LINE Instrument & Supply Co., Inc., Bellevue, WA.)

and an external hand-held prism on a rod; the prism is placed at the
location of the object to be measured.

The slope and distance are measured by an electronic distance
meter (EDM). The EDM uses infrared light which it emits in a beam.
The beam of light pulses at a given frequency toward the prism. Once
it reaches the prism, the light returns to the instrument. When the light
returns from the prism, the "pulse" frequency has been changed slightly
based on the distance travelled. The difference in the "pulse" frequency
is calculated and converted into a distance measurement.

The horizontal and vertical angles are measured by an electronic
theodolite, which by definition is a surveyor's device for measuring
horizontal and vertical angles with a small telescope that can move in
horizontal and vertical planes. The horizontal angle is measured either
to the right or left relative to an established "zero" direction (called
backsite or baseline). The vertical angle (or zenith angle) is measured
relative to being level, with straight up being a "zero" angle and level
being a 90° angle.

When the information is gathered, by taking readings from the
electronic station to the prism, it is recorded on a magnetic card by

point number, along with a code describing what the point measured is, i.e., the head of a body, a gun, a knife, the right front tire of a car, etc.

The information can be recorded in several formats: "raw" data, which is the two angles and the distance; "coordinate" data, which is called northing (the difference in latitude between two positions as a result of movement to the north), easting (the difference in longitudinal distance from an eastern meridian), and zenith (zenith being the elevation); a combination of "raw" and "coordinate" data; and "tilt" or "offset" data. A code describing each point is entered and encoded by the operator. The code can describe an individual point or object, or it can describe the start of a line, skidmark, etc.; the number and type is only limited by the imagination of the operator.

Why is the system called "Total Station"? What makes the system complete, and the reason it is called "Total Station" is that once the data is collected at the scene and imprinted onto a magnetic card, it can be downloaded into a computer. The addition of the computer element is what makes this system complete, hence the name "Total Station."

Once the information is downloaded from the magnetic card into a computer, via a card reader, several things can be done with the data. For example, the program that comes with the system can be used to complete a crime scene diagram to scale for reconstruction or courtroom purposes.

Once the data is in the computer several things can be done with it. First, and probably the most important thing, the data is stored in a "read-only file" which cannot be altered in any way. This is an important legal issue. The data can be retrieved at any time and worked with and refined, however it will be stored in a different file never overwriting the original data file. Once the raw data is copied into a working file, from the original file, it calculates northing, easting, and zenith coordinates for each point and processes the codes as defined by the operator and generates a "plot" file of what is measured.

Once the plot file is generated several things can be done with it. The file will be created with a .DXF file extension, which will allow it to be used in conjunction with various "CAD" (Computer-Aided Design) programs, such as AutoCAD, EasyCAD, EdCAD, etc. in two- or three-dimensional files, and/or certain computer animation files. The advantage to this is that the information can be outputted directly to a monitor (screen), outputted to a plotter for a hard-copy, or a disk file can be created for outputting at a later time.

Practical Application

The "Total Station" system is a new modern sophisticated way of using electronic equipment to take crime scene measurements. No longer are the familiar steel tapes and measuring wheels needed. Perhaps more importantly, no longer is it necessary to close down a roadway in order to take crime scene measurements.

Today, using the "Total Station" an investigator sets up the instrument in a position off the roadway where all the necessary points can be observed. The first measurement that the investigator takes after setting up and calibrating the "Total Station" is the end of a certified 100 foot steel tape. This is done as the first and last measurement to insure the instrument is accurate for court purposes.

The investigators, working in tandem, then take the necessary measurements by having one person work the "Total Station" and the other holding the prism-rod. Research has shown that this methodology saves countless hours not only at the scene, but also later producing the necessary crime scene diagrams.

Once the measurements are taken and entered into the computer, an investigator can produce as many diagrams as needed to whatever scale is desired, with just the push of a button. Manual labor hours of producing a diagram are eliminated. Colored diagrams and color transparencies can also be produced by the computer. With the utilization of AutoCAD, three-dimensional and animated reconstructions can be performed.

The Washington State Patrol recently had a case where a woman's body was found on the side of a cliff. Preliminary investigation had led investigators to believe the victim had committed suicide. However, by using the "Total Station" system in conjunction with the crime scene measurements it recorded, investigators were able to prove the incident was a murder because the body had to be thrown off the hill onto the side of the cliff for it to be in the position the body was found. Without the "Total Station" a murderer would have gone free and a family would have unnecessarily suffered the stigma of a suicide, not to mention the loss of insurance monies.

For further information about this crime scene documentation technique, the author refers the reader to:

GEO-LINE (206) 454-0141
Instrument and Supply Co., Inc.
1555 132nd Avenue N.E.
Bellevue, Washington 98005

Selected Reading

Geberth, Vernon J. *Practical Homicide Investigation: Tactics, Procedures, and Forensic Techniques.* Second Edition. Boca Raton, Florida: CRC Press, Inc., 1993.

O'Hara, Charles E. *Fundamentals of Criminal Investigation,* 5th ed., Springfield, Illinois: Charles C Thomas, 1980.

Scott, James D. *Investigative Methods.* Reston, Virginia: Reston Publishing Company, Inc., 1978.

Ward, Richard H. *Introduction to Criminal Investigation.* Reading, Mass.: Addison-Wesley Publishing Co., 1975.

The Homicide
Crime Scene Search

8

The search of the homicide crime scene is the most important phase of the investigation conducted at the scene. Decisions of the courts restricting admissibility of testimonial evidence have significantly increased the value of physical evidence in homicide investigations. Therefore, law enforcement personnel involved in the crime scene search must arrange for the proper and effective collection of evidence at the scene.

Physical evidence, which has been referred to as the "unimpeachable witness," cannot be clouded by a faulty memory, prejudice, poor eyesight, or a desire "not to get involved."

However, before physical evidence can be effectively examined by a forensic laboratory, it must be recognized as evidence. Practically speaking *anything* and *everything* should be considered as evidence until proven differently. I cannot recall how many times I found myself and my detectives returning to a crime scene in connection with additional information which revealed some innocuous item to be important evidence. That is why it is imperative to "hold onto" the crime scene as long as possible. Some item which didn't seem significant on the first day of the investigation may suddenly take on the intrinsic value of gold.

Legal Considerations

Once an item is recognized as evidence it must be properly collected and preserved for laboratory examination. However, in order for physical evidence to be admissible, it must have been legally obtained. The courts have severely restricted the right of the police to search certain

| SUPERVISION OF THE CRIME SCENE SEARCH IS AIMED AT THE PRESERVATION AND DOCUMENTATION OF THE EVENT |

A SEARCH WARRANT SHOULD BE SECURED BEFORE ANY CRIME SEARCH IS UNDERTAKEN. HOWEVER, THE PROFESSIONAL HOMICIDE DETECTIVE AND SUPERVISOR SHOULD BE AWARE OF THE SEARCH WARRANT EXCEPTIONS:

| EMERGENCY | PLAIN VIEW |
| AFTER ARREST | CONSENT |

Figure 8.1.   SEARCH WARRANT EXCEPTIONS.

homicide crime scenes without a warrant. For example, the United States Supreme Court's decision Mincey v. Arizona requires police to obtain a search warrant to search a premises where the suspect and the deceased share a possessory right to the premises. Homicides involving common-law relationships, husbands and wives, or family disputes may necessitate that the detective secure a warrant before a premises can be searched. The professional homicide detective must be aware of the legal requirements for a warrant dependent upon both Supreme Court decisions as well as state law and case law within their own jurisdictional purview. An additional consideration is the dynamics of the event which may present legitimate search warrant exceptions. The courts have recognized certain circumstances which allow for exceptions to the requirement of a search warrant. These exceptions are *emergency or exigent circumstances, evidence in plain view, postarrest search of an individual for weapons and contraband,* and *consent* (see Figure 8.1).

The ruling in the O.J. Simpson Hearings that the authorities properly entered the compound of Mr. Simpson based upon exigent circumstances is an example of a search warrant exception. In addition, blood evidence on the subject's Ford Bronco and in the driveway of his residence which was in plain view of authorities was also allowed into evidence.

Practically speaking, if there is any possibility that evidence you are about to seize for use in a homicide prosecution requires a search warrant, *get the warrant.* You'll save yourself a lot of headaches later on.

Physical Evidence

Physical evidence refers to any tangible article, small or large, which tends to prove or disprove a point in question. It may be used to reconstruct the crime, identify participants, or confirm or discredit an alibi.

Homicide crime scenes usually contain an abundance of physical or trace evidence. The systematic search, collection, and preservation of physical evidence is the goal of the homicide crime scene search. Therefore, the detective supervisor should organize the crime scene search so as to collect as much physical evidence as possible. In addition, the search *must* be based on constitutionally legal grounds, and the evidence collected must be properly documented and handled so that it may be presented in court later on. It is imperative that each piece of physical evidence be treated separately and carefully to avoid cross contamination.

The Concept of Linkage

Dr. Henry Lee, a forensic scientist who is the Director of the Connecticut State Crime Lab, developed the concept of linkage as the basis for any crime scene examination. Figure 8.2 is a visible representation of this concept. The goal is to establish a link between the various facets of the crime scene, the victim, physical evidence, and the suspect. All of these components must be connected for the successful resolution of the case. The basis of conducting such a four-way linkage rests on the principle of the *Theory of Transfer and Exchange*" (see Chapter 1, "The Homicide Investigation, at the Crime Scene").

An excellent example of the four-way linkage concept was presented by the prosecution during the O.J. Simpson case. The "Trail of Blood" theory based on the DNA analysis indicated that blood drops at the scene of the double murder of Nicole Brown Simpson and Ron Goldman, as well as blood in O.J. Simpson's Ford Bronco and his residence positively identified O.J. Simpson as the suspect. The DNA analysis of three stains on the console of Simpson's Ford Bronco indicated that droplets were a mixture of blood from Mr. Simpson, the blood of his ex-wife Nicole Brown, and the blood of Mr. Ron Goldman.

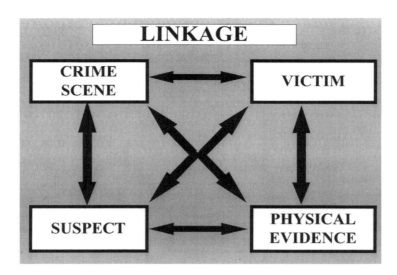

Figure 8.2.   **LINKAGE CONCEPT.** (Reprinted with permission of Dr. Henry Lee, Ph.D., *Crime Scene Investigation,* Central Police University Press, Taiwan, China, 1994, page 80.)

The famous "bloody gloves" that were presented as evidence provided the crucial linkage. One glove was found at Bundy Drive, the scene of the double homicide. The matching right hand glove was found at O.J. Simpson's estate. DNA testing of the glove found at O.J. Simpson's estate indicated that blood matching Simpson and the two murder victims "linked" him to the murders. DNA testing of the blood on the glove at Bundy Drive matched O.J. Simpson. The ski cap found near Ron Goldman's body had fibers like those from the carpet in Simpson's Ford Bronco. Goldman's shirt contained a head hair which matched O.J. Simpson. The socks found in O.J. Simpson's bedroom bore traces of blood from O.J. Simpson and his ex-wife Nicole, who was one of the murder victims. Dr. Cotton, from the DNA testing firm Cellmark, stated that the odds that the blood found at the crime scene belonged to anybody except O.J. Simpson were 1 in 170 million (*New York Daily News,* Friday, May 12, 1995, p. 3).

Dr. Cotton also stated that no one on the face of the earth except for Nicole Brown could have blood matching the stain found on O.J. Simpson's sock in the bedroom of Simpson's home (Ibid). A second DNA expert, Gary Simms informed the court that the odds that the blood on O.J. Simpson's sock came from someone other than his slain ex-wife were a whopping 7.7 billion to one. (*New York Post,* Friday, May 19, 1995 p. 8). (Sources: *USA Today,* January 23, 1995 p.3A; *New York Daily News,* January 25, 1995, p.2,3; *New York Daily News,* Friday, May 12, 1995, p. 3; *New York Daily News,* Wednesday, May 17, 1995, p. 8;

New York Daily News, Thursday, May 18, 1995, p. 4; *New York Daily News,* Friday, May 12, 1995, p. 3.)

From my perspective as a homicide and law enforcement consultant, this evidence represented the ultimate forensic evidence case. In fact, I would prefer to have this type of "unimpeachable evidence" which positively links a suspect to the crime as opposed to relying on eyewitness testimony.

On October 3, 1995, however, the jurors in the O.J. Simpson case totally rejected the State's evidence and voted to acquit Mr. Simpson of the murders of his ex-wife Nicole and Ronald Goldman.

This extremely controversial verdict was rendered in less than 4 hours after 9 months of trial testimony. Early on, the defense team introduced race into the trial and played upon the emotions of the predominantly black jury. The sad truth of the matter is that the "Mark Fuhrman Tapes" actually validated the defense position that their client was a victim of a police frame-up. The murder trial was turned into a race trial. Despite the overwhelming physical and forensic evidence linking Mr. O.J. Simpson to the murders, the jury rejected good solid physical and forensic evidence and rendered a "Not Guilty" finding. The DNA analysis of the evidence in this case overwhelming inculpated Mr. Simpson, so much so that in response to Mr. Simpson's vow to catch the "real killers," "A somber District Attorney Gil Garcetti bitterly dismissed Simpson's promise, insisting that the evidence still overwhelmingly proved O.J. was a cold-blooded killer. And he declared the investigations into the murders closed." (*New York Post,* October 4, 1995, pg. 2.) In addition, the Los Angeles Police Department announced that they would not reopen the case since their investigation indicated that Mr. Simpson had committed the murders. In a *USA Today* report published in the *Rockland Journal News* "Los Angeles Police Chief Willie Williams said he had no plans to reopen the probe" (*Rockland Journal News,* page 1, October 4, 1995).

The goal in the Linkage Concept is to establish a link between the various facets of the crime scene, the victim, physical evidence, and the suspect. Despite the verdict in the above cited case, the linkage concept clearly established these facets of the event.

Methods of Crime Scene Search

The method selected for search of the crime scene is usually determined by the size, location, and complexity of the scene. There are many criminal-investigation textbooks which describe various types of crime scene search. However, there are actually only five basic methods which

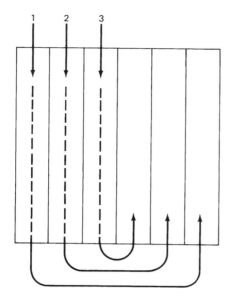

Figure 8.3.   **STRIP METHOD.** This method can be used effectively if the area to be covered is large and open. It is relatively quick and simple to implement and may even be performed by a single investigator in a limited area such as a room.

are universally accepted. These are: (1) the *strip* method, (2) the *spiral* method, (3) the *wheel* method, (4) the *grid* method, and (5) the *zone* method. Practically speaking, it doesn't really matter which method you select, as long as the search is both systematic and complete.

Formulating the Search

The search for evidence begins with the isolation and protection of the scene. The searcher must ascertain that the scene is intact and then proceed to reconstruct the events that have transpired since his arrival.

Obviously, the best places for obtaining physical evidence are nearest to where the critical act occurred, such as in the immediate vicinity of the homicide victim. However, other areas related to the primary crime scene must not be overlooked; for example,

The point of forced entry.
The route of escape.
The suspect (clothing, hands, body, hair, etc.).
The location where the weapon is or may be located.
A vehicle that was used in the crime.
The suspect's residence.
The location where the assault leading to death took place.
The location where the body was moved from.

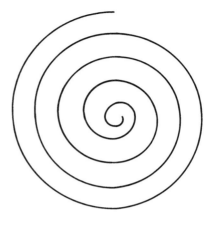

Figure 8.4. **SPIRAL METHOD.** This method sometimes called the circle method is effective in a small area. However, as the circle widens, evidence can be overlooked. The searcher begins either at the center or the perimeter and moves in a circular path.

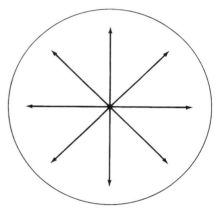

Figure 8.5. **WHEEL METHOD.** The searchers gather at the center of the scene and move out in spokelike directions. The obvious drawbacks in this method are the possibility of ruining evidence when gathering at the center and the ever-increasing distance between searchers as the investigators move outward.

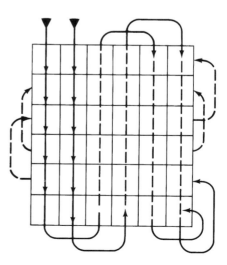

Figure 8.6. **GRID METHOD.** This is the best procedure to cover a large area. The searchers move parallel to one another and cover the same area twice. There are a number of variations of this method. The grid method is considered the most thorough system for covering large areas with a number of searchers.

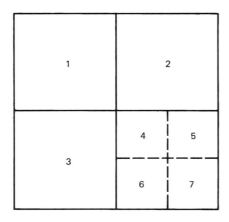

Figure 8.7. **ZONE METHOD.** The area to be searched is divided into squares or sectors. An officer is assigned to each zone or set of squares if the zones are further divided. This method is effective for indoor locations.

Before entering the crime scene, the detective supervisor and the homicide investigator must determine its boundaries, decide how to approach it, and determine if there is any fragile evidence present that requires immediate attention. The crime scene should then be photographed and sketched. (See Chapters 6 and 7.)

The scope of the search is usually determined by a theory or hypothesis agreed on by the investigators, based on their initial observations of the scene. The theory emerges from a set of simple assumptions of *how* and *why* the homicide occurred and the sequence of events that followed. This theory is utilized to guide the investigator in discovering physical evidence. However, remember that *anything* and *everything* may be evidence and become significant later on. Therefore, every item at the scene must be handled as evidence until determined otherwise.

The investigators must keep in mind that their theory is provisional. If new evidence emerges that suggests a different sequence of events, they must be willing to reassess and modify their theory as the new facts dictate. I have been at many different homicide scenes over the years and have seen initial theories change over and over again. The key to success in this phase of the investigation is *flexibility*. Practically speaking, use your common sense in this process. Don't get bogged down in theory and hypothetical speculation. Many times the answer you are looking for is right in front of your nose. The problem is that with all the events going on at the scene, it is sometimes easy to miss a simple observation. Your instincts should not be discounted. They can bring you back to reality or direct you to a situation that would otherwise have slipped by.

Crimes of violence such as homicide usually involve some sort of struggle — a break, use of weapons, use of physical force — or other

Figure 8.8. **DETECTIVES MEASURING THE POSITION OF THE BODY.** (Courtesy of Lt. Daniel Guiney, New York City Police Department.)

contact between the perpetrator and the deceased. Therefore, there is a good possibility that trace evidence will be found and recovered. Remember the basic theory of transfer and exchange. (See Chapter 1, "The Homicide Investigation, at the Crime Scene.")

In formulating the search plan there may be some critical areas that you will want to cover immediately, or there may be some question as to what is or is not evidence. Don't be influenced by the original report, the police call, or any initial statements. Note this initial information and then make your own determination based on the total information available. Ask yourself the following questions.

1. Is the death caused by:
   a. Homicide?
   b. Suicide?
   c. Accident?
   d. Natural causes?
2. Do the facts, the scene, the statements, and physical evidence support this explanation?

3. If the death is homicide,
    a. What was the means or agency of death?
    b. Is the homicide excusable or justifiable?
    c. Does it appear that any effort was made to purposely mislead the police? For example:
        1. A simulated burglary.
        2. Arson.
        3. Murder made to look like suicide.
        4. Suicide made to look like murder. (Insurance case?)
    d. Is there more than one possible cause of death?
    e. Are the witness statements consistent with the facts?
    f. Is the time element consistent with the condition of the scene?
        1. Are the bloodstains wet or dry?
        2. What is the condition of the body (rigor, lividity, etc.)? (See Chapter 9.)
    g. Is there a weapon involved?
        1. Was there more than one weapon used? What does this suggest?
        2. Are the wounds consistent with the weapon suspected?
        3. Is the weapon from the premises?
        4. If the weapon was a firearm,
            a. Are there any shell casings present?
            b. Are there any bullet holes or spent rounds present on the ground, the walls, the ceiling?
        5. Is there a weapon under the body?
        6. Was the deceased armed?

During this self-cross-examination do not make any final evaluation, since you are merely forming a theory to assist you in planning the search. However, you should estimate as closely as possible the time and place of the homicide. In addition, you should have a general idea of how much evidence you plan to collect. During this stage you will be depending on hard work, common sense, and keeping an open mind.

The Homicide Kit

If the search is to be successful, certain equipment and logistical support must be available to the homicide investigators. Many departments maintain a forensic or crime scene unit that responds to major crimes with sophisticated equipment necessary to conduct an extensive crime scene search.

I recommend that homicide units maintain a portable homicide kit with the equipment necessary to provide for the collection and documentation of evidence from the scene. A practical kit can be assembled at nominal cost and will usually prove to be invaluable to the investigator at the scene. Although any number of items may be included, a good homicide kit should contain the following:

Crime scene cards

Plain paper

Graph paper ($8^1/_2$" × 11")

Pencils and marking pens

Straight-edge ruler

Steno pads

Clipboard

Measuring tape (100' steel)

Eraser

Box of envelopes

Adhesive tale

Scotch tape

Surgical gloves

Cotton gloves

Rope (100')

Swivel mirror with 12" handle

Magnifying glass

Magnet extension rod

Saline solution

Cotton cloth

Safety pins

1 box of cotton swabs (Q-tips)

Tongue depressors (50)

Specimen bottles (6 bottles, 3 to 4 oz. size)

Forceps tweezers

Tape steel (12')

Evidence tags

School compass

Paper bags

Plastic bags with zip lock

Tape recorder with microphone

Flashlight (2-cell or 9-volt)

Cassette recorder with extra batteries

Blank tape cassettes

Simple camera (Polaroid or Instamatic)

Extra film

Telephone pick-up

AC/DC hook-up

Thermometer

Spotlight (12-volt, 50' extension)

Light socket extension cord

Electric extension cord

Screwdriver (multiple-head)

Pliers

Hammer with nails

Box of chalk

Lumber crayons

Ball of twine

Razor blades

Knife (multipurpose)

Vise grips

Wire cutters

Crowbar or pry bar (2')

Paper towels   Collapsible shovel
Antiputrefaction masks   Saw (keyhole type)
Pill boxes   Putty knife
1 scissors (8")   Coveralls
Street directory   Fingerprint kit

The Search

The most practical search method is to begin at the point where the body is first discovered and work in an outward direction until the entire room or location has been covered.

> Remember, do not smoke or dispose of any cigars, cigarettes, matches, gum wrappers, or any other item that may be confused with evidence at the scene.

Once the search method has been determined, it is up to the detective supervisor to coordinate the efforts of the investigators in order to provide for location of physical or trace evidence, systematized search techniques, a chain of custody, and the recording of evidence.

The search should begin with an examination for latent fingerprints — before any item is touched or moved, the crime scene technician should "dust" for prints. The supervisor should direct this phase by indicating what areas he wants examined. If possible, an attempt is made to determine points of entry and exit for latent impressions. In addition, any weapons or objects that were apparently handled by the suspect, as well as all door handles, telephones, windows, glasses, light switches, etc., should be dusted. Special attention should be given to objects which may have caused death, newly damaged areas, or items apparently missing from their original location. It is important to note that a good latent print will place the suspect at the scene.

> Remember, it's your case. You only get one shot at the crime scene, so make sure you do it right.

Direct the fingerprint people. If you do not direct that certain areas be dusted, they may not be. Tell the crime scene people or technicians what you want, and then make sure that you get it. All visible details should be observed and described before dusting anything, in the event that something might have to be moved. Note the location of any stains, weapons, etc.

Figure 8.9. **DUSTING.** (A) A crime scene detective is evaluating a latent print, which has been brought-up after "dusting". (B) The detective is preparing to lift the latent print using lifting tape.

During the initial search, each possible item of evidence should be measured from a fixed location (see Chapter 7, "Preparing the Crime Scene Sketch"). The measurements along with a complete description should be entered in the investigator's notebook. This information should also be recorded on the crime scene sketch.

Any latent prints located during this preliminary dusting should first be photographed and then "lifted". The photo should be taken with an identifying label in order to document the lift, in case the lift fails. The photo can then still be used for identification and comparison.

Examination of the Body at the Scene

The actual examination of the body should not begin until all photographs and sketches are completed. In addition, a complete description of the body as well as any clothing must be obtained, including:

Sex
Race
Appearance
Age
Build
Color of hair
Evidence of injury and apparent cause of death
Condition of the body (rigor mortis, lividity, etc.)
Color of blood (wet or dry?)
Position of body relative to objects of significance at the location.

The investigator should then concentrate on recording a complete description of the clothing as follows:

Position of clothes
Condition of clothes (buttoned, unbuttoned, twisted sideways or
    pulled down, inside out, zippered or unzippered)
Damage to clothes (rips, tears, cuts, holes, etc.)
Stains: blood, saliva, vomit, semen, phlegm, urine, or feces. Where
    are they? What are they? Is there any direction of flow?

After a complete description of the clothing and any significant position, condition, damage, or stains have been noted, the investigator begins a careful examination of the body starting with the head and working down to the legs. This description will necessitate moving the body to look for any wounds or evidence of further injuries that are not visible in the origin position.

1. The head:
    a. Are the eyes open or closed?
    b. Is the mouth open or closed?
    c. What is the position of the head in relation to the body?
    d. What is the color of the skin (lividity, etc.)?
    e. Is there any blood present? (Describe.)
    f. Are there any visible wounds? (Describe.)
    g. Is there any foreign material on the head (soil, mud, etc.)?
    h. What is the condition of the deceased's hair (neat or messy)?
    i. Any phlegm, saliva, or vomit present?
2. The trunk:
    a. The position of the trunk (twisted or bent over, on side or back, etc.).
    b. Any injuries. (Describe.)
    c. Presence of any stains (blood, semen, vomit, etc.).
    d. Presence of any hairs or fibers.
    e. Presence of any foreign substances on the trunk (soil, mud, grease, tar, paint, etc.).
3. Arms and legs:
    a. Position of each arm and leg.
    b. Presence of any injuries.
    c. Presence of any stains.
    d. Any foreign matter on the legs or arms?
    e. Are there any defense wounds on the hands, arms, legs, or feet?

Remember, note the presence or absence of any jewelry — rings, watches, etc. — on the body, including any mark on the body indicating that such objects have been worn.

In most cases, it is good to bag the hands of the deceased with paper bags. This will preserve any trace evidence which may be found under the fingernails later on during autopsy. A paper bag is used because plastic tends to accelerate putrefaction, especially if there is any blood on the hands. In addition, plastic does not allow the skin to "breathe" and may even change the chemical composition of certain trace evidence.

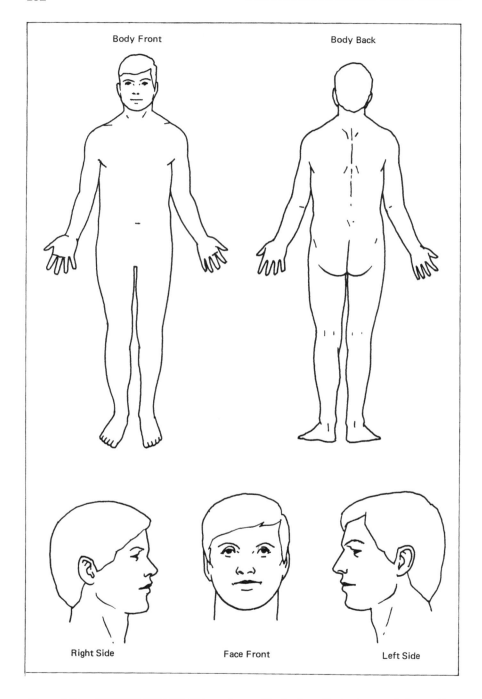

Figure 8.10.   **WOUND CHART.** This can be used by the investigator to record observations of injuries to the deceased.

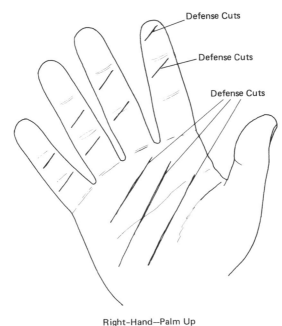

Right-Hand—Palm Up

Figure 8.11.   SKETCH OF DEFENSE WOUNDS ON HAND.

Figure 8.12. **PRESERVING TRACE EVIDENCE.** Following examination at the scene, the hands have been bagged to preserve any trace evi-dence, which may be found under the fingernails. It is recommended that the investigator use paper bags.

A

Figure 8.13.   **APPLICATION OF LUMINAL.** These photos were taken of a murder scene in which a 30-year-old woman was stabbed to death in her bedroom. The suspect transported her body to a dump site, returned to the residence, and cleaned the house of all obvious traces of blood. The Honolulu detectives requested The Scientific Investigation Section to process the scene. Luminal was applied and produced evidence indicating those locations where blood had been prior to the clean-up attempt by the perpetrator. (A) Picture of the hallway leading to the victim's bedroom showing no trace of blood. (B) A view of the floor in the victim's bedroom. (C) The same view after application of Luminal; clearly the impression of a footprint. (Courtesy of The Honolulu Police Department's Scientific Investigation Section, Captain Gary A. Dias.)

The area under the body must be carefully examined, bearing in mind that extensive bleeding may create pooling which conceals bullets, cartridge casings, or other small items of evidence. If the body has been lying on soft earth, bullets may be embedded in the soil. If any such items are found, they should be photographed in the position in which found before being collected and marked.

Remember, appropriate notation should be made on the crime scene sketch and in the investigator's notebook.

B

C

Figure 8.13. (continued)

While this procedure is particularly important in cases of apparent death from gunshot wounds, it should be followed as a matter of routine in all cases.

Release of the Body

The body should not be moved until completion of the preliminary investigation at the scene. The medical examiner or coroner, if responding, should have the opportunity to view the body in its original position. This can be very helpful to these officials in carrying out their responsibilities. After the homicide investigator and medical examiners have completed their work at the scene and details noted, the question arises as to when the body can and should be released.

This decision is critical. Because the consequences of the decision are irrevocable, removal should only be undertaken after due consideration of several factors.

1. Before the body is removed, it should be wrapped in a clean sheet to preserve any evidence or residue for later analysis.
2. If the medical examiner is not going to conduct an immediate autopsy and the body will be lying in the morgue until the following day, there should be no rush to remove the body, particularly in cases of apparent homicide where there are no witnesses and no named perpetrator or arrests. If the body is not in a public place, the location can easily be secured. The reason for this procedure is that information may come to light during the canvass or while talking to witnesses at the station house that may require some additional photos or other police procedure with respect to the body. If the body has been removed hastily, this opportunity will be lost.
3. If an immediate autopsy is to be conducted by the medical examiner, then the removal should be directed only after conferring with the investigators doing the canvass and the interviewing teams at the station house, to determine if there is any new information which may require additional things to be done with the body.
4. If the body is in a public place and the medical examiner has completed his scene examination, and the crime scene work has been accomplished, the detective supervisor can release the body, usually after checking with his detectives at the station house and with the officers doing the canvass.
5. If the body is in a public place and the medical examiner is not responding, the chief investigator will authorize the removal after the crime scene work has been completed.
6. As previously discussed under conditions of violent crowds or public disorders, etc., the body may have to be removed immediately. (See Chapter 1, "Dealing with Emergencies at the Scene".)

The Scene

A technique which I have found useful is to have someone who is thoroughly familiar with the scene go over it with you, bit by bit, first visually and then physically, being careful not to touch any items. This

A

Figure 8.14. (A) Evidence that the perpetrator cleaned-up in the crime scene. These areas should be thoroughly processed for trace evidence. The sinks, sink traps, drains, and garbage cans oftentimes contain valuable evidence. (B) Evidence that the perpetrator was in the refrigerator. The murderer may have fixed something to eat or may have taken something from the refrigerator. It is good police procedure to check the refrigerator and its contents. (C) Latent print evidence from the refrigerator. This case involved a rape and lust murder. The perpetrator had multiply stabbed his victim. Upon completing his assault, he went into the refrigerator to get a cold beer. He had to move the wine box to get to the beer. His bloody hands left a perfect set of latent prints on the wine box which placed him at the crime scene. (Figures A, B, and C courtesy of Detective Alan Patton, Grand Prairie, Texas Police Department. Photo by Evidence Technician, Don Swantz.) (D) Search of garbage revealed a torn letter written in Portuguese by the offender, who had killed his American wife. Detectives, who had searched the garbage discovered this incriminating piece of evidence which was used as evidence against the murder. (Courtesy of Investigator Jack Henander, Larimer County, Colorado Sheriff's Department.)

person can identify the usual positions of objects in the scene. You can then get a complete inventory on the spot. Instruct them to take their time, and ask if they recognize any inconsistencies or "foreign" material present. Have them point out the usual position of drapes, curtains, blinds, pictures, statues, ashtrays, etc. Obtain a detailed report. You may even want them to examine the scene along with an investigator so that they may point out new stains, signs of disorder, or any factor inconsistent with the life style of the deceased.

B

C

Figure 8.14. (continued)

The ideal situation in any crime scene search is to have one officer designated the "searching officer," whose responsibility is to search and take the evidence into custody. Other homicide detectives can assist by taking notes of locations where objects are found and even participating in follow-up searches. However, these officers assisting the searching officer should *not* handle any evidence. Instead, they can alert the

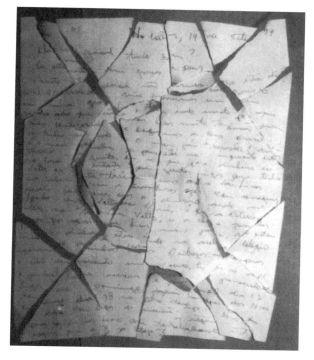

D

Figure 8.14. (continued)

searching officer, who will take significant evidence into custody. This procedure limits the chain of custody and makes the recording of evidence more uniform and professional.

Since items tend to fall to the ground, especially in a violent struggle or confrontation, the floor is the best place to begin the search after examining the body. As the search progresses, the investigators may move from the floor or ground to waist height, and from waist height to ceiling. The areas to be searched depend on the type of homicide. If the homicide is the result of a robbery or burglary, you will want to check the entire apartment or house for locations where the intruder "searched" for valuables. If the homicide was the result of a shooting, you will want to check the walls and ceiling for any bullet holes or spent rounds; any carpeting or rugs should also be rolled back or lifted up for examination.

If the murderer "cleaned up" after the crime, you must examine such additional locations as sinks and sink traps or garbage areas. If there are narcotics involved, you might have to locate a "stash" or secret hiding place. The murderer may have fixed something to eat, or may have taken something from a refrigerator. Did the killer turn the light

Figure 8.15.   **DUSTING FOR LATENT PRINTS.** A robbery-homicide of a cab driver has taken place. The stolen taxicab was abandoned a short distance from the scene of the shooting. The mortally wounded driver was pulled from the driver's seat and left lying in the street. The taxicab, which was safeguarded and secured by patrol officers, was towed to an indoor police facility. It is imperative that nothing inside the cab be touched or moved until "dusted." These photos show a detective dusting the critical areas for latent print evidence. Evidence was recovered from the door and rearview mirror, which the perpetrator had adjusted as he drove from the scene.

off or on? Does the scene give an appearance of being ransacked? Was the door unlocked or locked? Are the windows open or closed? Where is the point of entry? These are all questions you should ask yourself.

Remember the theory of exchange and transfer.

Locations where any physical or trace evidence may be found depend on the individual crime and the actions of the suspect or suspects at the scene, and will vary from scene to scene. However, certain areas and objects should always be given attention:

Under rugs or carpets	Elevator shaft
Under chair cushions	Tops of cabinets or furniture
Doorjambs	Chimney
Light fixtures	Refrigerators
Behind drapes or curtains	Statues
Garbage pails or bags	Behind pictures or clocks
Wastebaskets	Sewers
Hampers or soiled clothes	Drainpipes
Ashtrays	Ventilation ducts
Ceilings	Behind desks set against walls
Suspended ceilings	Closets
Walls	Backs and bottoms of drawers
Under chairs	Inside ovens
Under beds	Inside cabinets
Mirrors	Kitchen or bathroom towels
Telephones	Sinks, toilets, or tubs
Signs of a party	Counter tops
Glasses	Windows
Stairs	Any newly damaged area
Passages	Garments
Back yards	Mailboxes
Behind boxes or cartons	

The ability to recognize and discover evidence at the crime scene is a prerequisite of successful search. The acquired expertise of the homicide investigator and the detective supervisor will probably determine what trace evidence is found.

It is in this search phase that one can see the need for close cooperation between the investigators and the forensic scientist. It is imperative that the officers performing the search have a working knowledge of handling physical evidence. (See Chapter 17.) Most major departments maintain a forensic or crime scene unit with trained personnel to assist in the search of major crime scenes. These officers have the expertise and equipment necessary to work under the detective supervisor for the proper retrieval of physical evidence.

Information sources such as papers, personal effects, address books, etc., and any other property which may aid in the investigation should be taken by the homicide detectives for later perusal and disposition. The patrol or uniformed division should be responsible for the administrative search and safekeeping of any valuables or property of the deceased. These items can be vouchered and safeguarded at headquarters for later disposition to the property clerk, medical examiner, coroner, or family of the deceased.

Any photos of the deceased taken in life should be collected to use in the canvass to clearly identify the victim to persons interviewed, as well as personal acquaintances or associates of the victim. If photos are not available at the scene, they should be obtained from the victim's family, friends, or employer, or from yearbooks or a driver's license. Photos should have a good likeness of the deceased just prior to death so as not to confuse the person they are shown to.

Examining the Outdoor Scene

The general techniques of crime scene search apply to all homicide crime scenes; however, the outdoor scene poses additional problems for the investigator. For example,

1. The scene usually does not have easily defined borders.
2. The "floor" of the scene is usually rough and irregular and may be composed of hills, valleys, bodies of water, swamps, sand, or other natural contours.
3. The investigation is vulnerable to weather conditions. Rain or snow may have washed much trace evidence away, or the threat of a storm may force immediate procedures to collect evidence in a manner that precludes efficient collection of all evidence.
4. The investigator does not have the luxury of electricity, running water, telephones, or other common conveniences found indoors.
5. Daylight is limited; be prepared to return to the scene the following day.

Figure 8.16. OUTDOOR CRIME SCENE — DUMP JOB. This body has been transported from the place of occurrence to an outdoor dump site. Apparent is that the killers used bed clothing, probably from the scene to carry the body.

The investigator's actions at outdoor scenes are usually determined by the weather and the time of day. I have provided some practical procedures to follow. However, they are presented only as a guide. Each individual case will dictate how an investigator will retrieve evidence.

1. Rope off the largest area possible and secure the scene.
2. Establish a path of entry and exit, usually the original path taken by the person who discovered the body. It should be examined for any possible trace evidence and then staked off or marked. All persons approaching the area should be cautioned to use this route and not deviate from the established path.
3. The body and immediate surrounding area should be systematically examined before any weather or lighting conditions change. One of the recommended methods of crime scene search should be used. Get additional people to the scene to implement this procedure.
4. If the weather is obviously contributing to or about to destroy trace evidence, collect the evidence as soon as possible even though some additional evidence may be missed, lost, or destroyed.

Figure 8.17.   **TIRE MARKS.** Here you see the tire impression of the murderer's automobile. The killer had used the auto to transport the victim's body to the place of discovery. Investigators at the scene discovered this tire mark during the crime scene search. This evidence should be preserved through photography and casting.

Remember, some evidence is better than no evidence.

Examples of Evidence Found Outdoors

1. Pollen, vegetation, soil, or seeds may be found on the suspect or the victim. The investigator should collect any foreign matter found on either the suspect or the body for later comparison. However, each individual item must be separately packaged and labeled in order to assure proper examination and admissibility in court later on.
2. *Foot and tire impressions* may appear on the soil. In addition to gathering samples for laboratory analysis, these impressions must be sketched, photographed, and properly casted for later comparison purposes. When gathering this type of evidence, several control samples should be secured for later analysis.
3. *Trees, shrubbery,* and *fencing* should be examined for any trace evidence that may have been transferred during sudden contact.

Fibers, hair, threads, and other material may be affixed to these objects and should be collected and preserved for later comparison with either the victim or the suspect.

4. *Bloodstains, seminal fluid, saliva or phlegm, brain matter, hair, feces,* or *any other biological evidence* are not only subject to rapid change and destruction, but are almost impossible to locate in heavily vegetated terrain. Likewise, these pieces of trace evidence are subject to insect activity and are likely to be washed away if it rains on the scene.

5. *Bullets* and *casings* may be located if the investigator closely examines any foliage or newly broken parts of shrubbery. In some instances the bullet may have lodged in a tree, causing telltale damage to the bark, or there may be pieces of twigs or branches that are lying on the ground in the line of trajectory. The area immediately surrounding the body should be examined for any shell casings and bullets embedded in the ground under the body.

6. *Oil or gasoline traces.* When vehicles are driven through tall grass or weeds there is a transfer of this material from the underside of the vehicle to the vegetation. This residue should be collected for later comparison.

7. *Crankcase traces.* If a vehicle has been driven through an area of heavy foliage or rocky terrain, there will be traces of this material on the crankcase that can be compared.

8. *Any foreign material at the scene.* Many times, a suspect unwittingly will leave traces of himself at the scene that may be gathered and compared later on, e.g., cigarettes or cigars, toothpicks, etc. In addition, there may be some sort of struggle resulting in a lost item of clothing such as a button or piece of jewelry that can link the suspect to the scene.

9. *Foreign material found on the body.* Sometimes the body may reveal traces of evidence that come from a distinctive location. For instance, the body and clothing may indicate that the deceased was a mechanic or cement worker, or there may be traces of sawdust or coal dust on the corpse.

In the event that the body has to be moved before an extensive examination is conducted at the scene, I recommend that it be wrapped in a clean sheet so that any trace evidence remaining on the clothing will be preserved for later inspection.

Examining an Outdoor Scene at Night

Under ordinary circumstances, the examination of the outdoor crime scene should not be undertaken at night. However, there are certain procedures that should be immediately performed: (1) the area should be effectively secured and safeguarded; (2) the body should be photographed; and, (3) the body should be safeguarded against any additional damage due to exposure to the elements. In addition, any changes that occur since discovery should be noted in the investigator's notebook.

The reason for postponing the search until daylight is that it is utterly impossible to detect minute traces of evidence under nighttime conditions. If some larger pieces of evidence are discovered that are not subject to dissolution, they should be covered or secured pending daylight, since their significance can be better realized in connection with the overall scene. However, if you are faced with a sudden change in the weather, delaying the search until daylight may prove disastrous to the investigation. Obviously, there can be no set procedure to cover all possibilities, so — as in all other aspects of homicide investigation — be flexible and use your common sense.

Physical Examination of a Suspect in Custody

The suspect and his or her clothing should be considered part of the homicide crime scene search. If the suspect is in custody at the scene, he or she should be immediately removed. If the suspect is apprehended a short distance away, he or she should not be allowed to return to the central crime scene. Instead, the suspect should be isolated for a preliminary examination for evidence.

> Remember, if a suspect is allowed access to the crime scene, you will negate the value of any evidence found on the suspect which came from the scene, or destroy the value of any evidence imparted by the suspect to the scene.

The examination of the suspect for evidence should be performed by the investigator assigned to the case or by an experienced detective assigned to the crime scene search. The examination must be conducted in a manner that precludes any possible destruction or loss of evidence. In addition, the search for evidence on the person of a suspect requires that the investigator be able to recognize certain materials and marks as related to the actual crime. This ability to recognize and recover trace evidence is a prerequisite to successful search of suspects.

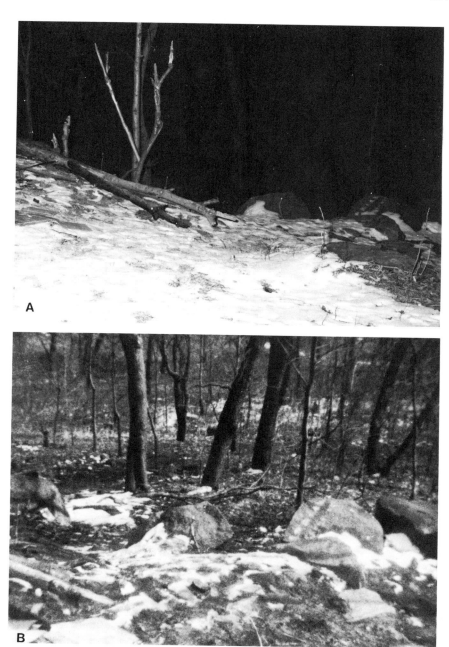

Figure 8.18. **OUTDOOR CRIME SCENE AT NIGHT AND IN THE DAYTIME.** These two photos show the same scene. (A) Taken at night. (B) Taken during the daytime. It is obvious that the investigator has a much better chance of locating evidence under daytime conditions.

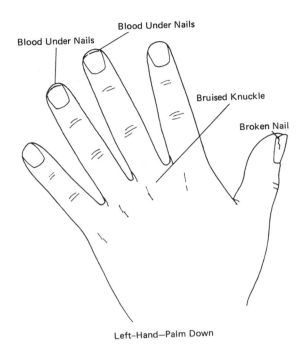

Blood Under Nails

Blood Under Nails

Bruised Knuckle

Broken Nail

Left–Hand—Palm Down

Figure 8.19.   **NEW INJURIES.** The suspect's hands indicate new injuries, which he had received during the struggle with the deceased. A simple sketch can be prepared by the investigator either by tracing his own hand or the suspect's hand and then drawing in the locations of injury. This is usually done in connection with a photograph of the suspect's hands.

The suspect's clothing and shoes should be closely examined for any trace material from the scene or evidence of the crime. These items should be seized and vouchered as evidence. If the suspect has any visible injuries or marks that might link him or her to the crime, such as bruises, bite marks, scratches, cuts, or injuries on the hands, face, or other parts of the body, photographs should be taken in black-and-white and color, using a scale or marker.

Many homicides involve a struggle where both participants receive injuries. Color photographs of these injuries, both to the suspect and deceased, are valuable pieces of evidence which can be presented in court.

It is important to note that once a person is under arrest, he or she has no reasonable expectation of privacy. Suspects under arrest can be subjected to a thorough examination and body search. Under certain conditions, if the case warrants, the investigator should have the suspect undress over a clean sheet or large paper to prevent the loss or destruction of any physical evidence on the clothing, and examine the suspect for any injury. Of course, female suspects subjected to body searches should be processed by female officers, and male suspects processed by male officers, in order to avoid any criticism or objection later on.

If patrol officers have been assigned to transport a suspect to the police station, or are assisting in the examination of the suspect for evidence, they should be cautioned to use extreme care and to preserve the suspect's clothing and shoes for examination for trace evidence. Furthermore, they should be instructed not to allow the suspect to wash his or hands nor engage in any activity that may alter or destroy any evidence. I have seen instances where suspects have "cleaned" themselves with urine and spittle to remove blood from their hands or bodies.

When evidence is located on the suspect, the same procedures utilized in other crime scene searches must be applied.

1. Photographs of the evidence *in situ*, and close-ups of the evidence.
2. The evidence should be described and documented in the investigator's notebook.
3. A sketch should be prepared of the area where evidence is found and the location noted on the sketch. This procedure is quite simple. If the evidence is found on the hands, for example, merely trace your own hand (right or left, depending on which hand of the suspect evidence is found) and indicate on the sketch where this evidence is located. The same procedure, without tracing, can be employed for the face and other parts of the body. Use a simple line drawing of the body part concerned, with appropriate notations.
4. The material should be collected in a manner that preserves its value.

Residue Testing

If the homicide involves a shooting, and the suspect is apprehended within a short time or is in custody at the scene, the investigator may want to consider subjecting the suspect to residue testing. Trace Metal Detection Test (TMDT) was an examination which determined whether or not a person had been in contact with metal. However, its practicality is questionable, since the touching of any metal may give positive results or may show no results whatsoever and TMDT has since been replaced by more specific type testings.

One such test is the *Neutron Activation Analysis* test. The discharge of a firearm may contaminate the shooter's hand with significantly larger amounts of the elements antimony and barium than normally found on an individual who has not fired a weapon. (The contamination results from a "blow-back" of primer residues from the cartridge.) See Figure 12.6 on page 288. These microscopic residues can be removed for analysis by swabbing the back of the index finger, thumb, and connecting web area of the hand with a moistened cotton swab containing a 5% nitric acid solution. It is recommended that two separate swabs be used and that both hands be treated. The swabs should then be placed in separate sealable containers. In addition, a control sample of two moistened swabs not used on the subject should be submitted along with the other swabs to the laboratory for comparison purposes.

The most effective test, however, for GSR is the S.E.M. Test (*Scanning Electron Microscope*) which involves the collection of tiny particles from your subjects and the testing of these particles to determine if they contain lead, barium, and antimony. A positive test shows that a subject was in the vicinity of a gunshot, as long as they were not cross-contaminated. You are advised not to test a victim of a gunshot, in an attempt to show that they did not fire the weapon, because they may have this residue on them. Testing consists of the use of an approved S.E.M. kit, which consists of a small device which is covered with an adhesive substance, which is dabbed around the thumb and index finger area of the hand, sealed and then sent to the lab. It is then tested for the above stated elements. The advantages to this test are the ease of collection, and lower cost. The disadvantages are the ease of cross-contamination, particles can be removed through hand washing and/or two hours of normal activity, and some .22 Cal. Ammo. doesn't contain barium and antimony.

In order for the examiner to properly interpret this data from the swabs submitted for analysis, the following information should be provided to the laboratory:

1. A brief resume of the case.
2. The time and date of the shooting.
3. The time and date the hands were swabbed.
4. Location of shooting, i.e., indoors, outdoors.
5. Treatment afforded the suspect, i.e., if wounded, were the hands washed or contaminated in any way during medical treatment?
6. Activity of the subject from arrest until specimens were obtained, i.e., washing of hands, fingerprinting, etc.
7. Description of the firearm used: caliber, type, manufacturer.
8. Brand of ammunition used.
9. Subject right- or left-handed.
10. Subject's occupation.

Practically speaking, these tests may have no forensic value at all to your investigation. Although antimony and barium are components customarily found in most primer mixtures, they are also commonly found in nature and may have come from some other source. The problem from an investigative point of view is that most testings are inconclusive in that the examiner cannot positively state that the quantity found is sufficient for determining that a gun was definitely fired by the suspect.

You may want to administer this test, however, in order to preclude any attempt by defense counsel to make an issue of why his or her client was not given this examination. Nevertheless, even if you do subject the suspect to this type of examination and the results are positive, the defense counsel could bring in another forensic expert who could dispute the results and challenge your findings based on a different interpretation.

The decision to test or not to test must be determined by the facts of the particular investigation. The investigator should always be aware that residue testing, because of its ambiguous results, can be a two-edged sword that could possibly damage the later prosecution.

Release of the Scene

The decision to release the scene should be carefully considered. Obviously, the problem with releasing the scene prematurely is that soon thereafter information may come forth which would have required different photos or search for and collection of other items. The scene should never be released before the initial canvass is completed, all the known witnesses interviewed, and the suspect in custody questioned fully. In some cases, it may be necessary to secure the scene and post a guard pending interview of witnesses who cannot be immediately located, or in other instances to hold the scene until completion of the autopsy. This may not always be practical, but it is a recommended procedure in case additional examinations or searches are necessary as a result of information obtained during autopsy. Of course, if the autopsy is being conducted while the investigators are still at the scene, any such additional information can be immediately communicated to the chief investigator at the scene. Autopsy findings should always be made available to the homicide investigators as soon as possible to help them in their investigation and in questioning witnesses.

Before releasing the scene, the chief investigator should remember that any good defense attorney will visit the crime scene at his first opportunity. From this inspection he will be able to gauge the nature, character, and extent of the investigation at the scene. He will be alert to things which may have been overlooked; to areas which have been dusted and not dusted; to the shape, pattern, and location of blood and other stains; to flash bulbs, film packs, and other debris which the investigators may have carelessly left at the scene. During police activities at the scene, the chief investigator should see that all waste materials from the lab work and photography are deposited in one container in a location which will not interfere with other activities, and that this container is removed before the scene is released.

The detective supervisor or chief investigator would do well to check over the whole crime scene from the point of view of the defense

Figure 8.20. **WILLSON SAFETY PRODUCTS — PUTREFACTION MASK.** (Courtesy of WILLSON® Safety Products in Reading, Pennsylvania.)

attorney before releasing it. Before abandoning the scene and securing it against re-entry, make sure that you have all your equipment and notes, including any portable radios (which seem to have a way of disappearing at crime scenes). It would be embarrassing if you had to break into the recently secured crime scene to retrieve something that was left behind.

Anti-Putrefaction Masks

The overwhelming odor of a body undergoing putrefaction is a problem that many crime scene investigators and detectives encounter in their duties while investigating sudden and violent death. In the 1970s, Dr. Frederick Zugibe, Chief Medical Examiner for Rockland County in New York State, devised a light-weight nose and mouth mask which protected the wearer against the undesireable odors of cadaverine, butyl mercaptide, and other mercaptides as well as hydrogen sulfide and other sulfides.

The author highly recommends the use of anti-putrefaction masks to prevent exposure to these noxious gases and allow the detectives to go about the job of processing the crime scene with a minumum amount of discomfort. Anti-putrefaction masks are available today through various manufacturers, such as WILLSON® Safety Products in Reading, Pennsylvania 19601, telephone number (800) 345-4112, and SIRCHIE® Finger Print Laboratories, Inc., in Raliegh, North Carolina 27613, telephone number (800) 356-7311.

Figure 8.21 **PHOTO SHOWING MASK USE.** (Courtesy of WILLSON® Safety Products in Reading, Pennsylvania.)

Crime Scene Protocol for the Protection from Airborne Pathogens and other Biohazards[1]

Communicable Diseases

Required Precautions

Investigators should adhere to the following procedures at any crime scene where blood or body fluids are encountered. Since it is difficult to predetermine who may have a communicable disease, all crime scene investigations should be treated with the following precautions:

1. Wear approved disposable gloves while in the crime scene and remain aware that blood and other body fluids may carry diseases.
2. Consider wearing a disposable mask while in crime scenes where airborne communicable diseases such as meningitis or tuberculosis might exist.

---

[1]The above information was provided to the author from Sgt. Ruben Puente, Supervisor and Crime Scene Investigator Michael Phillips, Arlington, Texas Police Department's Crime Scene Unit.

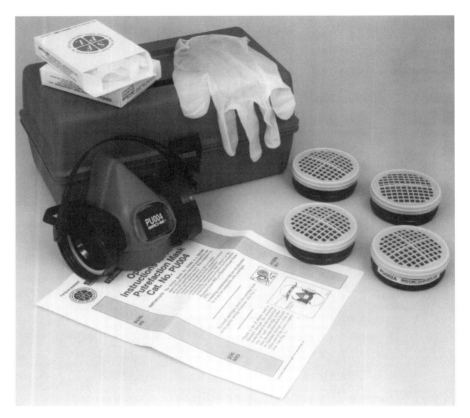

Figure 8.22. **SIRCHIE® PUTREFACTION KIT.** (Courtesy of SIRCHIE® Fingerprint Laboratories, Inc., Raleigh, North Carolina.)

3. Wear eye protective and disposable infectious disease gown to protect clothing when exposed to large amounts of blood or other body fluids.

4. After the investigation is complete, dispose of gloves, masks, and gowns contaminated by *blood* or *body fluids* in a biohazard bag and wash hands thoroughly with an antiseptic hand rinse, i.e., Cida rinse.

5. Before returning to the station, wash hands again with water and a bacterial liquid hand wash, i.e., Bacti-Stat.

6. Restrict the number of investigators on the scene who may come in contact with the scene of the potential infection exposure.

7. Advise any investigators on the scene who may come in contact with the scene of the potential infection exposure.

8. Decontaminate all equipment used prior to your return to the station.

Figure 8.23. **HOMICIDE VICTIM WITH KAPOSI'S SARCOMA**, a disease of the skin usually associated with persons aflicted with AIDS.

9. Change clothing contaminated with blood or other body fluids immediately and decontaminate.

10. Dispose of contaminated supplies as recommended in this protocol.

11. Skin provides a very effective barrier for the prevention of infectious diseases. Wash all contact areas as soon as possible after exposure to help prevent contamination. Wounds such as cuts, sores, and breaks in the skin, regardless of the size, provide an entrance for infection into the body and should be properly bandaged.

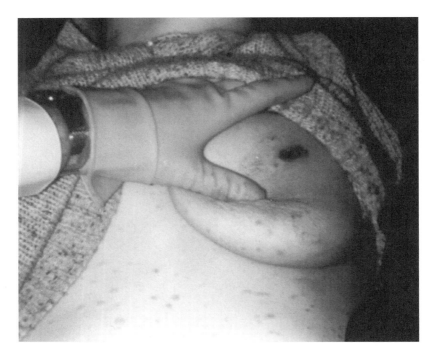

Figure 8.24.   CRIME SCENE DETECTIVE WEARING PROTECTIVE RUBBER GLOVES
when examining the above victim to prevent any possible contact with infectious disease.

12. Report all significant exposures to blood or *other* body fluids
within 24 hours of exposure.

Decontamination of Equipment

Investigators should decontaminate any equipment which was exposed
to blood or other body fluids which could have been transferred to
equipment at the crime scene.

1. Clean equipment such as boots, rulers, cameras, carrying cases,
etc. with a mixture of household bleach and water in a 1:10
dilution.
2. Wipe clean radios and other delicate equipment with a disinfectant solution, i.e., TOR.

Decontamination of Clothing

Investigators should immediately decontaminate clothing that has been
contaminated with blood, vomitus, or other body fluids from the crime
scene as follows:

1. Change contaminated clothing as soon as possible.
2. Use disposable gloves when cleaning possibly contaminated clothing or equipment.
3. Pre-wash contaminated clothing separately in a disinfectant detergent solution and hot water and launder in a normal manner.
4. Use plastic bags to transport contaminated articles before cleaning.

Precautions

Investigators should adhere to the following simple precautions which will provide protection from most communicable diseases:

1. Avoid unnecessary contact with the blood or other body fluids.
2. Always wear gloves when contacting persons who are bleeding or when handling other body fluids.
3. Wash hands thoroughly after each contact.
4. Clean equipment soiled with blood or other body fluids after each call.

The following information is provided as a quick reference guide to the common communicable diseases that investigators may encounter. A communicable disease should be suspected when fever, skin rash and/or weeping lesions, jaundice, diarrhea, or cough are present.

Communicable Diseases

Disease	Transmission
AIDS (Acquired Immune Deficiency Syndrome)	Blood or body fluids, needle sticks, sexual contact
Hepatitis	Contaminated water or food
Hepatitis B	Blood or body fluids
Meningitis	Droplet spread
Tuberculosis	Droplet spread

Exposure Guide

Exposure	Action Necessary
Contact limited to merely being in the presence of a person suspected of having a communicable disease.	No action required except when airborne disease is involved. If airborne disease exposure occurs, seek medical review.
Contamination of clothing or equipment by person's body fluid.	Decontamination of clothing and equipment.
Exposure of skin/mucous membranes to person's body fluid. Also includes needle punctures and human bites.	Emergency medical treatment and necessary precaution.

Prevention

Investigators who are required to respond to crime scene calls should obtain preventative immunization for any disease for which immunization is possible and to which investigators may be exposed in performing their official duties. Immunizations should be offered periodically as needed, based on recommendations from infection control specialists.

Exposure of First Responders

Exposure of a first responders to the AIDS virus requires very specific conditions. The virus must be directly introduced into the person's body. In the first responder environment, this means infected person's blood or body fluids must be introduced through the skin (percutaneous event) or by contact through the eye, mouth, or nose (mucocutaneous event).

It is important to note that acquisition of the Hepatitis B virus and other blood-borne infectious agents occur via these same percutaneous and mucocutaneous events.

A percutaneous event occurs when blood or body fluid is introduced through the skin. This can occur by a needle stick, by sustaining a cut from metal, glass, or other sharp objects contaminated with blood, or by having blood contaminate an existing open wound, sore, broken cuticle, or chapped skin.

A mucocutaneous event occurs when blood or body fluids come in contact with a mucous membrane. This means blood or body fluid is splashed into the eyes, mouth, or nose.

Exposure to Blood-Borne Diseases

Risk of infection from blood-borne diseases varies according to the type of exposure. The list below was published by the Centers for Disease Control and Prevention to help evaluate risk levels (risk level increases from top to bottom).

Blood/body fluid contact to intact skin.
Blood-body fluid contact to the mucous membrane surface of the eyes, nose, or mouth.
Cuts with sharp objects covered with blood/body fluid.
Contaminated needle stick injury.

Infection Control Techniques

Universal Precautions

Universal precautions are based on the concept that blood and certain body fluids of *all* contacts should be considered potentially infectious for HIV, HBV, and other blood-borne pathogens.

Specific body fluids (in addition to blood) to which universal precautions apply include: any body fluids containing visible blood, semen, vaginal secretions, tissues, cerebrospinal fluid (CSF), synovial fluid, pleural fluid, peritoneal fluid, pericardial fluid, and amniotic fluid.

Body Substance Isolation

Body substance isolation goes a step beyond universal precautions and considers *all body substances* potentially infectious. Thus, the following body fluids/substances are considered potentially infectious: feces, nasal secretions, sputum, sweat, tears, urine, and vomitus.

Such an approach is obviously wiser in the crime scene where medical histories are not usually known. In effect, investigators must treat each crime scene as a potential infectious disease exposure.

To achieve body substance isolation, investigators should use the barrier technique, the use of personal protective equipment (gloves, masks, protective eye wear, gowns, etc.) to prevent personal contact with blood or other potentially infectious material.

Exposure Treatment

In the event of an exposure and/or injury in the field:

1. For percutaneous (through the skin) exposure, wash with soap and water if available. If not, wipe off blood and apply alcohol to the wound.
2. For mucocutaneous (in the eyes, nose, or mouth) exposure, flush eyes thoroughly or rinse mouth with water.
3. If the wound is serious, arrange for treatment. All injuries should be documented.

Conclusion

The homicide detective and detective supervisor have the responsibility of locating physical and trace evidence and assuring that this evidence is gathered in proper fashion for delivery to the police laboratory. It is up to them to interpret and evaluate the lab results with all the other information developed during the investigation. Hopefully, the total results obtained from the homicide investigation will do what the deceased cannot do, point the finger at the murderer.

Practically speaking, all murders are distinctively different and unique. However, there is one solid base on which to build the case — the determinations you have made from your study of the crime scene and how you apply that knowledge. Keeping in mind the theory of transfer and exchange, you can be sure the minute a killer "does his thing," whether it's a carefully premeditated crime or a spur-of-the-moment impulse, he must go places, handle objects, and move things. The murderer will do this without thinking, either on purpose or by accident. This is the rationale behind a good crime scene search.

Remember, you only have one shot, so do it right the first time.

Selected Reading

Geberth, Vernon J. "The Use of Videotape in Homicide Investigations." *Law and Order Magazine,* in press, 1996.

Geberth, Vernon J. "The Staged Crime Scene." *Law and Order Magazine,* Vol. 44 No. 2, Illinois, February, 1996.

Gebreth, Vernon, J. *Practical Homicide Investigation: Tactics, Procedures, and Forensic Techniques.* Second Edition. CRC Press, Inc., Florida, 1993.

Geberth, Vernon J. "Supervision and Management of a Homicide Investigation." *Law and Order Magazine,* Vol. 37, No. 11, Illinois, November, 1989.

Hughes, D. J. *Homicide Investigative Techniques.* Springfield, Illinois: Charles C Thomas, 1974.

Kirk, Paul L. *Crime Investigation.* New York: John Wiley and Sons, 1974.

Lee, Henry C. and Gaensslen, R. E. *Advances in Fingerprint Technology.* CRC Press, Inc., Florida, 1993.

Lee, Henry C. *Crime Scene Investigation.* Central Police University Press, Taiwan, China, 1994.

O'Hara, Charles E. *Fundamentals of Criminal Investigation.* 5th ed. Springfield, Illinois, Illinois: Charles C Thomas, 1980.

Scott, James D. *Investigative Methods.* Reston, Virginia: Reston Publishing Company, Inc., 1978.

Svensson, Arne, Wendel, Otto, and Fisher, Barry A. J. *Techniques of Crime Scene Investigation,* 5th ed. New York: Elsevier Science Publishing Co., Inc., 1992.

Ward, Richard, H. *Introduction to Criminal Investigations.* Reading, Massachusetts: Addison-Wesley Publishing Co., 1975.

Estimating Time of Death

9

If the circumstances surrounding death indicate the possibility of homicide, then both the body and immediate surrounding area become crucial in estimating *time of death*. Time is one of the most important factors of consideration in a murder case. It may very well convict a murderer, break an alibi, or eliminate a suspect. Estimating the time of death, especially in cases where there are no witnesses, is critical to the investigation. A good homicide man is going to want to know the time of death in order to establish a foundation for further inquiry.

Time may focus attention on various suspects. For example, the deceased may have had an appointment with someone at a specific time. Or, in cases of "exclusive opportunity" (where only certain persons are present during a specific time, e.g., husband and wife during the evening) if one of those persons is found in nightclothes the following afternoon dead from a beating, and the estimation of time of death places the incident in the range of 3 to 6 A.M., the spouse is sure to be the suspect.

A definite time of death (given by witnesses who noted time) can corroborate or disprove a suspect's alibi.

In civil matters, time may be the factor that determines whether or not an insurance policy was in effect or was void. Most insurance companies include "suicide clauses" in their policies whereby they are released from contract to pay if the insured commits suicide within a specific time, usually within one year after becoming insured. Furthermore, in probating a will, it can be crucial to learn whether the husband or wife died first, since the estate usually goes to the one who expired last.

Figure 9.1.   **PUTREFACTION AND INSECT ACTIVITY.** These photographs depict the body of a man in a bathtub, fully clothed and lying in the water. The cause of death was electrocution. A hair dryer was found in the tub. This event occurred indoors during the summer time. The body is in an advanced state of decomposition due to the extensive maggot activity.

Throughout the years, forensic scientists and pathologists have searched for a definitive method of determining time of death, yet at present there is no single reliable method. Moreover, it is impossible to fix the exact time of death; hence, we refer to an estimated time. Based on an appreciation of a large number of variables, an experienced pathologist can arrive at a reasonable estimation of time of death; usually placing it within a range of hours. The process is subject to error, especially if some crucial piece of information is omitted. It should be noted, however, that this estimation certainly represents more than just an educated guess. It is a scientifically derived opinion based on a totality of specific factors distinctive to each particular case compared with ordinary time factors attributed to the pathological changes that occur in a human body.

Although the homicide investigator is not expected to have the knowledge of a forensic pathologist, he would certainly do well to have some basic understanding of the postmortem changes that occur in the human body and the effect of time and atmosphere on the cadaver, on

Figure 9.1. (continued)

blood pools, and on stains, so that he can make intelligent observations at the scene.

I have found that it is good procedure to take notes of the appearance of the deceased and any blood at the scene so that you can relate to the medical examiner exactly what you observed. The investigator should also interview the first officer for his observations of the scene along with the exact time of his arrival. These observations will be helpful in the analysis of approximate time of death when coupled with the results of the medical examination and autopsy. Generally speaking, the sooner after death a body is found, the more accurate and precise the estimation of time of death. A "fresh" body gives a better time-frame than one which is in advanced putrefaction. However, it is utterly impossible to fix the exact hour and minute that life ceased unless you were there at the moment of death.

The Process of Dying

To understand what takes place in the body after death, one must first have some basic knowledge of the processes that occur in the living body. During life, the systems of the human body have the capacity to maintain themselves by providing oxygen to all the body tissues. In addition, the system provides for the removal of waste products that result from body functions. This is accomplished by the circulation of blood through the arteries and veins. The heart keeps the supply of oxygen continually flowing by its pumping action. As the blood deposits oxygen to the tissues, it picks up the waste products and returns to the lungs where a new supply of oxygen is obtained. During this process, the body is able to defend itself from bacteria and germs within the body. Upon death, however, these bacteria grow at will and begin to release enzymes which dissolve the internal body components. The changes that occur in the dead body are recognized as *postmortem decomposition*.

The body begins to decompose from the time of death, in a manner dependent on any number of variables such as temperature, time, location of the body (outdoors, indoors, in soil, in water, in the desert, etc.), humidity, air currents, physical condition, clothing, etc. Externally, insects and animal life may attack the remains so as to further disfigure the body. These changes in the human body result from the same process one observes in an unrefrigerated piece of meat when it rots.

Figure 9.2.   **PUTREFACTION AND INSECT ACTIVITY.** Identification was made through forensic odontology.

Dying is a process, and estimating the time of death depends on those factors that occur during that process. Death can be said to occur in stages, and a "smart" medical examiner will want to see the scene before he attempts to make any determination about the time of death.

Body Changes After Death

Color. Upon death the heart ceases to function. As a result, the blood and its life-giving properties cease to circulate through the body. As the blood settles into the dependent capillaries of the lower portions of the body, it gives the upper surfaces of the skin a waxy or translucent look. The lips and nails lose their normal pinkish or life-like color.

The blood, which has ceased to circulate, changes from a bright red to a deep purplish color as it loses oxygen. This is apparent even in persons with darker skin. This is the beginning of *lividity*, the process whereby the blood settles into dependent capillaries and eventually "fixes" in certain areas of the body.

Eyes. The eyes, which are the most sensitive area of the human body, do not react to light, touch, or pressure in death. The cornea or clear part of the eye becomes slightly milky or cloudy within eight to ten

Figure 9.3.   **POSTMORTEM CHANGES IN THE BODY.** Notice the lack of postmortem changes over pressure areas (Courtesy of Dr. Dominick J. DiMaio, Former Chief Medical Examiner, City of New York.)

hours after death. In fact, to the experienced observer, the eyes alone will indicate that death has occurred.

Loss of body heat. During life the body maintains an approximate temperature of 98.6° F. After death, the body gives off heat until it becomes the same temperature as the surrounding medium. The rate of cooling can be an important measurement in the estimation of time of death. Body temperature can be taken by rectum with a thermometer to obtain an accurate reading. The environmental temperature should be taken at the same time if the body temperature is to have any meaning. Never take the temperature by inserting a thermometer into a wound; the body, when the wound was received, was probably standing or sitting, not lying face down or in a supine position. If a thermometer or probe is carelessly inserted into the wound, it will probably cause additional damage to the organs or tissues beneath the wound entrance or destroy or distort the *wound track*. In addition, in gunshot cases it may destroy or obscure the ballistics value of a spent round lodged within the *wound track*. From a practical viewpoint, there are "just too damn many" variables that affect the rate of cooling, such as size and amount of fat on the body, clothing, the position of the body (bent upon itself or lying flat on surface), age of the victim, drafts, environmental humidity, etc. — that it is almost impossible to calculate them all. 1 recommend to investigators who want to get a rough idea of just how long the body has been dead that they place the palm of their hands on a protected surface of the body, such as under the arms. *If the body is warm, death occurred a few hours ago; if the body is cold and clammy, death occurred anywhere between 18 and 24 hours ago.*

Rigor mortis. The process of rigor mortis is the result of a stiffening or contraction of the body muscles related to chemical changes occurring within the muscles after death. As a general rule, rigor mortis begins 2 to 4 hours after death. Contrary to popular belief, rigor mortis starts at the same time throughout the entire body; however, it is first observed in the jaws and neck. It then seems to progress in a head-to-foot direction and is complete in 8 to 12 hours after death. At this stage, the jaws, neck, torso, and upper and lower extremities are literally "stiff as a board" and, in this marked state of stiffening, resist any change in position. Rigor "fixes" the body in the position assumed at death. I had one particular case where the body of a young boy who had been brutally murdered and sodomized became literally "frozen" in the position of assault. A body seated in a chair at death will remain in that position, with arms and legs fixed in the position of a seated individual, even after removal.

Figure 9.4.   **RIGOR MORTIS.** This young boy was found literally "frozen" in the position of assault. He had been brutally sodomized and stabbed to death. Rigor mortis has resulted in "fixing" the body in the position in which it was lying at the time of death.

This complete rigor begins to disappear about 18 to 36 hours after death and, in the average body, is completely gone within 48 to 60 hours.

A word of caution: this factor is the poorest of the gauges used in estimating time of death because of the many variables involved. The various theories on rigor mortis are loaded with contradiction and misinterpretation. For example, obese people do not always develop rigor, skinny people develop it fast; heat speeds up the process of rigor, while cold retains it; a fight or body shock usually accelerates it; no two bodies even under similar circumstances develop it at the same time, etc.

Practically speaking, if the underarms are warm to touch and the body is without rigor, death probably occurred less than 3 hours earlier.

Cadaveric spasm. Under certain conditions the stiffening of the hands or arms may take place immediately at the time of death. This is known as *cadaveric spasm* and is often confused with rigor mortis. It is not uncommon for persons who had a firearm or a knife in their hand at the time of death to clutch it tightly in their hands after death. Also, suicides have been known to have the weapon clutched tightly in their

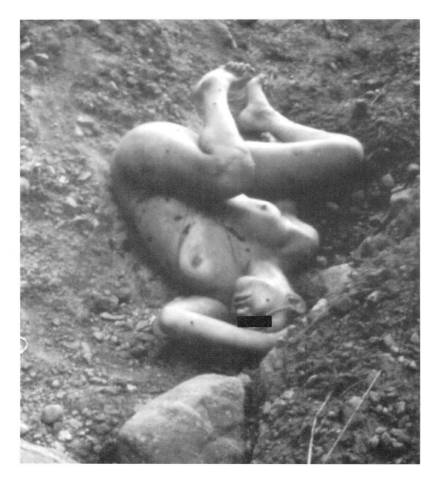

Figure 9.5. **RIGOR MORTIS.** Victim of homicide found rigored in this position. The body had been dumped down a ravine where it came to rest after tumbling down the incline. (Courtesy of Lt. Mark Prach, Morris County Prosecutor's Office, Morris County, New Jersey.)

hands after death. It is important from the investigator's point of view to note such clutching of weapons, since you can be sure that the person held this weapon at the time of his or her death. It is impossible to "duplicate" this spasm. For example, a person attempting to place the weapon in the deceased's hand after death cannot get the same type of tight grasp. Cadaveric spasm remains until putrefaction.

Postmortem lividity. Also known as *livor mortis*, this is caused by the pooling and settling of blood within the blood vessels from the effect of gravity. It appears as a purple discoloration of the skin. During life, the

Figure 9.6. **RIGOR MORTIS.** Body recovered on the shore of the Hudson River evincing rigor mortis. Note the position of the victim's arm indicating rigor mortis. (Courtesy of Dr. Frederick Zugibe, Chief Medical Examiner, Rockland County, N.Y.)

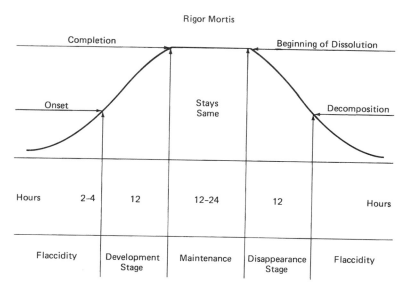

Figure 9.7. The general time elements involved in rigor mortis.

Figure 9.8. **CADAVERIC SPASM.** The deceased's hand tightly clutches the weapon in cadaveric spasm, which is instantaneous rigor mortis.

Figure 9.9. **POSTMORTEM LIVIDITY.** Note how the blood has settled towards the back of the decedent's body suggesting that the body has lain upon its back after death.

pumping action of the heart maintains a constant flow of blood through the numerous vessels of the body. Upon death, this pumping action ceases, and the blood pools within the dependent portions of the body. The location of livor mortis is determined by the position of the body after death. If the body is lying face down, livor will develop on the front of the body rather than on the back. The observation of lividity is important for two reasons: (1) it gives the investigator a general idea how long the body has been dead; (2) it tells you definitely whether or not the body was moved after death. For example, if lividity is observed on the back of the body found lying face down, you can be sure that the body had originally been on its back. Lividity begins about 30 minutes after death and becomes "fixed" in 8 to 10 hours. *Fixed* means that the livor has settled in one position for more than 8 hours and can no longer be significantly shifted by changing the position of the body. However, parts of the body that remain in direct contact with an object, such as the floor, a piece of pipe or wood, or even the weapon, will remain white, as the pressure will not allow the blood to settle into the dependent capillaries.

If when lividity first develops, the investigator presses his finger firmly against the discolored skin, the pressure will cause "blanching." When pressure is released, the discoloration returns. After 4 or 5 hours the discoloration becomes clotted and pressure will not cause blanching.

The investigator should know that the discoloration will not be the same for all types of death. For instance, a person whose death was caused by inhalation of carbon monoxide will have a livor mortis which is cherry-red in color. If a person lost a great deal of blood, there will be little or no discoloration; or in cases where death was caused due to heart failure or asphyxia, there will be a deep purple color. These observations should be recorded and the coloration of the lividity evaluated with the later toxicological examination performed at autopsy.

Suppose you have a body that is cool to the touch, rigor has set in in the neck and jaws, and when you press against the lividity it does not blanch. Under ordinary conditions, you can assume that the body has been dead about six to eight hours. Notice I said *ordinary* conditions, and watch the word *assume*.

> **Remember, you are dealing with tricky circumstances, and even the experienced pathologist will have to weigh all the facts before he attempts an estimate.**

Gastrointestinal tract contents. Although commonly referred to as stomach contents, this also includes digested and undigested matter within the entire body. The presence of food particles in the stomach and upper small intestine provides still another source of information to the pathologist regarding time of death. From an investigator's point of view, the presence of food on the table may offer some assistance if the victim maintained a routine eating time. When and what the deceased ate for his last meal is important information for the pathologist who will do the autopsy.

Various ingested food materials remain within the stomach for variable periods of time, depending on the nature and size of the meal. It has been determined through extensive research that under ordinary circumstances the stomach empties its contents four to 6 hours after a meal. If the stomach, at autopsy, is found to be filled with food, and digestion of the contents not extensive, it is reasonable to assume that death followed shortly after the meal. If the stomach is entirely empty, death probably took place at least 4 to 6 hours after the last meal. If the small intestine is also empty, the probability is that death took place at least 12 or more hours after the last meal. In certain cases the medical examiner will be able to determine the type of food which still remains in the stomach, if matched with the last known meal. This can help establish a time period.

Of course this determination will be made by the medical examiner conducting the autopsy. I have been present at many autopsies where the stomach contents were examined and it was quite discernible what foodstuffs were ingested by the deceased prior to his death. In certain cases it is a good procedure to obtain a control sample of the food products found at the crime scene, which were apparently eaten by the deceased, for comparison with the stomach contents, especially in cases which involve the possibility of murder by poison or suicide by ingesting toxins or deadly drugs.

Figure 9.10. **PUTREFACTION INDOORS.** Note the bloated face of the deceased. This victim's body was found indoors during the summertime. He had been dead for only 60 hours when discovered.

Figure 9.11. **POSTMORTEM BIRTH.** Note the dead fetus between the legs of the deceased. The woman, who was 7 months pregnant, died from a heart attack. As the body began to decompose, the putrefactive gases and bloating caused the fetus to descend and the baby was expelled from the mother's womb. (Courtesy of Dr. Dominick J. DiMaio, Former Chief Medical Examiner, City of New York.)

Putrefaction. As soon as death occurs, the bacteria or micro-organisms within the intestinal tract escape from the bowel into the other tissues of the body. As they grow, they begin to produce gases and other properties that distort and discolor the tissues of the body. As a result, the body begins to swell. The rate of decomposition depends on the temperature, ground conditions, amount of clothing, size of the body, etc. For example, a body in a warm climate will not only encourage insect attack from the outside, but will also increase the interior bacteria

Figure 9.12. **MARBLING.** Produced by hemolysis of blood vessels with reaction of hemoglobin and hydrogen sulfide and development of red, purple, or greenish black discoloration along the vessels.

development and subsequent tissue attack from within. As the tissues inside are destroyed and enzymes released, the gases formed emit a foul and sickening smell.

This particular method of determining time of death is very inaccurate because of the variables involved. The putrefactive changes disfigure the facial features making visual identification by relatives impossible. Postmortem changes may also alter the appearance of and may camouflage antemortem injuries. When bloating and darkening occurs it may be difficult to determine the race and color of the deceased.

Since putrefaction, just like rigor mortis, is subject to a great variation, the estimate will have to be based on other sources derived from both the autopsy and the scene. It has been established that even in deaths occurring as a result of the same cause, with identical environmental conditions, one body showed an advanced state of putrefaction while the other showed little change. The general signs of putrefaction are:

1. Greenish discoloration of abdomen and genitals.
2. Veins in skin blue or purplish due to pigment of decomposing blood. (This is referred to as *marbling.*)

Figure 9.13. **ADIPOCERE.**
(Courtesy of Dr. Leslie I. Lukash,
Chief Medical Examiner Nassau
County, New York.)

3. After the body fluid dries, a yellow parchmentlike membrane forms.
4. After several days:
   a. Abdomen sells, body bloats (from gas).
   b. Fluid emits from mouth and nose (the source being the lungs and stomach).
   c. Rectum may empty.
   d. Skin blisters, resembling peeling sunburn.

Adipocere. This is a greasy, soaplike substance which develops on the surface of a body that has been lying in a moist area such as a swamp or in damp soil. It is due to chemical changes that occur in the body fats — hydrogenation of body fats into fatty acids. It develops mostly in warm weather and usually forms in a few weeks. The material is rancid smelling and floats in water. Adipocere usually covers the face and buttocks, but any part of the body can be affected. Where present, the internal organs are usually in good shape, having been dehydrated and mummified in the process.

Mummification. The conditions that produce mummification are the exact opposite of those which cause adipocere. If death occurs in a hot dry place with an adequate and constant circulation of dry air,

Figure 9.14. **MUMMIFICATION.** In this photo we see the effects of mummification upon a body of a man who hanged himself. The mummification was due to the hot and dry climate and circulation of dry air where this death took place. (Courtesy of Det. Jerry Fariss Las Cruces, New Mexico Police Department, Criminal Investigations Division.)

and body fluids are rapidly absorbed, the body tissues become hard and dry instead of decomposing. The mummification process delays putrefaction, and as a result the form of the body may be preserved for years.

Figure 9.15. **POSTMORTEM ANIMAL FEEDING.** Bodies are also subject to animal feeding both indoors and outdoors. This woman's face was eaten by the family dog, which increased putrefactive changes to the internal components of the body. You can also observe skin slippage on the woman's scalp, as her hair separates from the skull.

External Agents of Change

Insects

Various insects may eat the flesh of, or lay eggs on, the body of the deceased. Observation of insect larvae can aid in the estimation of time of death. This is an example of the assistance that an *entomologist* — insect expert — can lend to the investigator. Many insects develop from eggs and then progress through growth stages before emerging as adult insects. The time element involved in this developmental stage is rather constant for any given species. For instance, the adult female housefly deposits eggs upon the remains, usually on the eyes, mouth, nostrils, and wounds. These eggs become maggots which then feed off the body. The usual time span for hatching of the maggot is 24 hours.

Development time varies among the various species of flies. Temperature and humidity play very important roles in this developmental stage, as do other factors. The larvae may even go into a period of suspended animation if conditions do not warrant further development.

The bluebottle or blowfly is the most common type found on remains discovered outdoors. The investigator at the scene and the medical examiner at the autopsy should collect some specimens for examination by an entomologist. The entomologist can identify the specific insect and provide an estimated time frame based on the stage of growth or development of the larvae. In addition, the experienced entomologist can possibly identify the stage of the life cycle and ultimately the season of the year in which death occurred.

In order to assist the entomologist in making an accurate determination, the following procedure for collection and preservation of specimens is recommended:

1. Collect some maggots from the remains and place them in a KAAD solution. (This is a mixture of kerosene and alcohol along with certain other ingredients for preservation.) If this solution is not available, place the sample in hot water first, then in a bottle containing alcohol, and then seal it. The hot water bath will prevent the alcohol from shriveling the sample and maintain the specimen in a condition for examination.
2. Collect some live maggots as a control sample and place them in a separate container.
3. Collect any pupae (hard shell-like casings or cocoons) from around the site, under the body, and from the corpse. Keep the samples separated. The presence of pupae usually provides a minimum time span of approximately 2 weeks. However, there may be several cycles involved, and the determination should be left up to the entomologist.

Note that the type of maggots found on the body may be significant. For example, the presence of larvae from a housefly found on a body outdoors will indicate that the body had previously lain indoors.

In addition to flies and maggots, a body is also subject to insect attack from different types of beetles and ants and even worms that bore their way into the body. The recommended procedure for collecting all insect samples is to place them in alcohol for preservation.

The forensic entomologist has knowledge of many of the habits of insects and other invertebrates most likely encountered on the corpse and/or in the immediate surroundings of the scene. Seemingly insignificant data to the untrained eye such as insects not found on the body, habitat information, and climatological conditions can be observed by the entomologist. This knowledge enables him to form certain determinations and opinions of how long the body has been at the scene.

In keeping with the team concept of homicide investigation, I recommend that an entomologist, if available, be brought to the scene to assist the investigators. The entomologist's expertise will ensure that proper entomological techniques are employed and the collection of specimens conducted as it should be.

Plants

Bodies found lying on the ground are usually in areas that are abundant with plant life. A competent *botanist* can estimate the age of vegetation found under the body in relation to the vegetation found in the immediate surrounding area. Samples of the sod and vegetation found under the body, as well as a control sample from the immediate area, should be collected for examination.

> **Remember, keep the two samples in separate containers to prevent any contamination.**

The botanist can then examine these samples and may be able to determine how long the body has lain in a particular location. Although this information will not provide an estimate of time of death, it can contribute a relevant time factor to the investigation.

Animals

Bodies are also subject to animal feeding, both indoors and outdoors. Animals feed off the remains of a dead human body just as they feed off any other piece of meat.

Household pets as well as rats and other rodents often attack the body in indoor locations. I investigated one scene in which the deceased's dogs had actually begun to devour the body. Outside locations increase the chances of this occurrence, since many wildlife creatures are carnivorous. Bodies that have been mutilated by domestic and wildlife creatures or insect activity may give an appearance of gross injury, which is not necessarily associated with an antemortem attack. In addition, certain portions of the body may have been carried away or are missing from the cadaver due to animal activity. Practically speaking, investigators must be careful not to jump to any false conclusions based on their initial observations at scenes of this type.

Bodies in Water

Similarly, marine life, especially crabs, are known to nibble on "floaters" or bodies in the water. In addition, movements of the currents and/ or contact with marine propellers will further add to disfigurement.

Figure 9.16.   **BLOATED BODY OF A "FLOATER."** This female body had been in water for approximately one week. Notice the effects of submersion and postmortem changes in the tissue.

These types of postmortem injuries require the knowledge and interpretation of the forensic pathologist, so as not to mistake the injury for one that occurred in life.

From an investigative point of view, the body exposed to the air for one week is equivalent to a body submerged in water for a 2-week period. The following are some general time spans associated with bodies in water:

Hands swollen after several days.

Outer layer of skin separated from the body within 5 to 6 days, skin of the hand and fingernails separated from the body in 8 to 10 days.

Seaweed vegetation on body within 8 to 10 days.

Floating — in warm water 8 to 10 days, in cold water 2 to 3 weeks.

Information Derived from the Scene

Even though certain pathological changes in the body after death are subject to measurement, the variables involved require additional supportive information before an estimate of time of death can be made. Data obtained by the investigator relative to events associated with the deceased is of utmost importance. This is where the work of the homicide detective really comes into play.

The date and time the deceased was last seen alive gives the detective a starting point to begin the task of narrowing the time of death. The status of the deceased's home or apartment lends additional information — e.g., are there any current newspapers, milk deliveries, mail in the mailbox, dishes in the sink, food on the table, etc.? Are the electric lights on or off? If the lights are burned out, is the light switch in an *on* or *off* position? Are the shades drawn or open?

The detective will want to reconstruct the deceased's last known movements. These would include who spoke to him or her last and where the deceased was prior to being found (at home, at work, with a friend, etc.). The failure of the deceased to perform a daily routine, such as picking up the newspaper, reporting for work, jogging, calling friends or family, or any other personal habit which was routine in his or her life, will also help narrow the time frame.

Another factor to be considered is the weather. For example, if the deceased is found outdoors covered with snow, and the ground beneath is dry, it is important to know what time the snow started in the area. It would be safe to assume that the body was on the ground before the snow fell.

In cases where there has been a struggle and the deceased has a broken watch, or there is a clock in the room that has been damaged, causing it to stop, the time of death can be pinpointed if the investigator can ascertain if the timepiece was in working order prior to death, and if it kept correct time.

> Remember, the presence of prepared food on the table may offer assistance in determining time of death if the investigator can ascertain that the victim maintained a routine eating time.

Information derived from the scene as well as knowledge of any personal habits of the deceased will play an important part in the final estimate of time of death. These are referred to as associative factors.

Conclusion

The estimate of time of death is complex. Before you lock yourself into a specific time frame, it is imperative that all the information available be examined by competent experts. If the time of death tends to fix responsibility for the death, or becomes the factor that points the finger at a particular suspect, then the estimate must be based on positive facts and interpreted by the experienced pathologist.

The physical manifestations of death discussed in this chapter, as well as the autopsy findings, the deceased's personal habits, the medical opinion regarding *survival interval*, the period between the infliction of injury and death, and the statements of witnesses must be taken into consideration in the final analysis.

Therefore, complete cooperation between the experienced homicide investigator and the medical examiner/coroner is essential if there is to be an intelligent estimate of time of death.

Selected Reading

Deickman, Edward A. *Practical Homicide Investigation.* Springfield, Illinois: Charles C Thomas, 1961.

DiMaio, D. J., M.D. and DiMaio, V. J. *Forensic Pathology.* New York: Elsevier, 1989.

Geberth, Vernon J. *Practical Homicide Investigation: Tactics, Procedures, and Forensic Techniques. Second Edition.* Boca Raton, Florida: CRC Press, Inc., 1993.

Harris, Raymond I. *Outline of Death Investigation.* Springfield, Illinois: Charles C Thomas, 1962.

Hughes, Daniel. *Homicide Investigative Techniques.* Springfield, Illinois: Charles C Thomas, 1974.

Snyder, LeMoyne. *Homicide Investigation,* 3rd ed. Springfield, Illinois: Charles C Thomas, 1977.

Spits, Werner and Fisher, Russel. *Medicolegal Investigation of Death.* Springfield, Illinois: Charles C Thomas, 1993.

Svensson, Arne, Wendel, Otto, and Fisher, Barry A. J. *Techniques of Crime Scene Investigation,* 3rd ed. New York: Elsevier North Holland, Inc., 1981.

The Identity of the Deceased

10

The purpose of this chapter is to provide practical information on identifying deceased persons and to assist the homicide investigator in the difficult and often frustrating task of identifying badly decomposed bodies or skeletal remains.

Most deceased persons are readily recognizable to relatives and friends and can be officially identified for law enforcement purposes. Decomposition and dismemberment pose problems, since ordinary means of identification such as photographs and fingerprints are not effective. The criminal investigator should be aware of the contributions forensic experts, such as forensic anthropologists and odontologists, can lend to the process of identification of human remains.

I recommend that the homicide investigator establish personal contact with these forensic people and include them in the investigative team.

Remember, joint contribution to a team effort is not only professional, but effective as well.

The Identification

The identification of the victim is critical because in order to prove a charge of homicide, it must be established that a named or described person is in fact dead. (This verification of death is usually made by a physician; however, in many jurisdictions an ambulance technician's pronouncement of death is sufficient.) Furthermore, from an investigative point of view, identification provides a starting point and direction for the inquiry.

Practically speaking, most homicide victims are killed by someone they knew. Therefore, the identity of the deceased may provide you with motive and establish a clue to the identity of the killer. In addition, even in "stranger-homicides," the identity of the victim will furnish information about his or her movements, which may establish time of occurrence and other information about the crime. Knowing the identity allows the investigator to find out:

> The family, spouse, and relatives of the deceased.
>
> The friends, lovers, and neighbors of the deceased.
>
> The residence of the deceased (which will provide additional information about the deceased).
>
> His or her business associates.
>
> Whether or not the deceased was involved in criminal enterprise.
>
> Where the deceased socialized and locations frequented.
>
> Habits and routines of the deceased.
>
> The character of the deceased.
>
> Personal information and life style of the deceased, enemies of the deceased (if you know the enemies of the deceased, you can consider one of them — a business competitor, a spouse, a lover, etc. — as a suspect).

Identification at the Scene

Personal Identification

In many cases there are relatives or acquaintances present who will make an identification to the police at the scene. Usually this identification will be sufficient for investigative purposes, pending official identification by some member of the family to the medical examiner or coroner. The investigator, however, should still pursue established practices of identification. The body should be photographed, a complete description of the body and clothing should be obtained, information relative to medical and dental data should be gathered, and a request for blood-typing at autopsy should be made. In addition, all dead bodies, especially in homicide cases, must be fingerprinted.

I recall a case which took place in another jurisdiction, north of New York City. A suspect was shot and killed during a narcotics rip-off by the would-be victims. The police who had responded to the shooting arrested the would-be victims and a female accomplice of the dead man, and seized a gun as well as other evidence. The woman gave the police a fictitious name for the deceased. Although fingerprints were taken during the autopsy, they were mistakenly put in the dead file under the fictitious name. No record check was ever made. However, a separate investigation by New York City police was undertaken because the gun used in the aborted stickup was the same caliber as one used in three New York City homicides during similar rip-offs. An additional set of prints was taken by the City detectives for comparison with latents obtained during the homicide investigations, and a record check was conducted at New York City Bureau of Criminal Identification. The gun was also subjected to ballistics tests in new York City and was positively identified as the same weapon used in the three homicides. The record checks revealed that the dead suspect was not the person named by his accomplice, but was in fact a wanted escapee who had already been identified as a murder suspect along with his female partner. The female accomplice had purposely misled police in an attempt to avoid identification. Her ruse would have worked, had it not been for the second fingerprint record check. Although she gained temporary freedom, she was rearrested in New York and subsequently indicated for murder on the three outstanding homicide cases. The original prints should never have been simply filed before a record check.

Obviously, an oversight such as this can result in a wrong identification, and identity should be positively established before the body is released and the case closed.

Clothing and Possessions

The clothes and possessions — such as driver's license, social security card, and I.D. card — of the deceased are the best sources of tentative identification at the scene. The pockets of the deceased should be searched for any other material documents or photos. This information and a Polaroid picture of the deceased, if the body is in good condition, can be utilized by investigators to attempt to locate family or friends and verify identity. The clothing should be preserved for future identification.

Identification by Photographs

If the body is in good condition, a color photograph should be taken of the face. A full facial shot and a profile as well as detailed pictures of any tattoos, scars, and the ears (which are distinctive) should be obtained. If the body is found indoors and there are photos of the deceased therein, they should be retrieved and duplicated with a 1 × 1 fingerprint camera and distributed to the investigators doing the canvass.

Remember, the body should be photographed before autopsy with and without clothes.

This should be done even in cases where the body is in decomposition. In addition, x-rays should be taken of unidentified bodies since there may be medical records available which can be used to make an identification. I recall a case where the headless and handless bodies of two young women were found in a midtown motel. The murderer had poured a flammable liquid over the bodies and set them on fire in an attempt to prevent identification. Extensive medical and pathological efforts were employed to establish identity. The autopsy revealed a 3-inch surgical scar on the abdomen of one of the victims. This scar eventually provided police with the identity of the victim, a 22-year-old prostitute. The killer was eventually caught after he committed a series of similar mutilation-sex killings in the metropolitan area. However, the key to his involvement in the New York City killings was the identity of the torso. A search warrant was obtained for the suspect's residence, and items belonging to the 22-year-old victim were found in his home.

Description of the Body

A complete description of the body should be obtained, with emphasis on any deformities, markings, abnormalities, and distinctive traits. The ears make a good identifying feature, because even in the event of decomposition and other changes, they remain the same. The following information should be obtained if possible.

1. Name (if papers or documents indicate name — tentative only)
2. Sex
3. Age (date of birth if available or estimated age)
4. Race, color, and nationality
5. Length or height
6. Build (be careful in cases of decomposition)
7. Shape of face (square, round)
8. Neck (thin, large, adam's apple, etc.)
9. Hair (color, length, type — curly or kinky, wavy or straight)
10. Beard or mustaches
11. Forehead (high, protruding, receding hair line, etc.)
12. Eyebrows, eyes, lashes (bushy, thin, fake, etc.)
13. Ears (cauliflower, large, small, deformed, etc.)
14. Nose (small, large, base of nose)

15. Chin, jaw (protruding, receding, square, round, etc.)
16. Mouth, teeth (condition of teeth, missing, spaces, size of lips, etc.)
17. Lips (thin or thick) — note decomposition
18. Hands (small, large, rough or smooth, etc.)
19. Fingers (long or short, marks of any rings, jewelry, etc.)
20. Feet (big, small, shoes, etc.)

Clothing

Clothing should be examined for identification marks. The use of laundry marks and dry-cleaning tags by commercial cleaners can be traced to specific locations. In addition, there are manufacturers' marks and, in some instances, serial numbers for valuable items.

Jewelry and Watches

Most items of jewelry are quite distinctive and may contain inscriptions or jewelers' marks. In addition, there are wear patterns that are distinctive to certain items, and the rare "special piece" that can be identified as belonging to a certain individual.

The more expensive watches can be traced to their source of retail sale, and, if the watch was worked on by a watchmaker or jeweler, the item will usually have some marking which will identify the particular craftsman.

In the absence of fingerprint and/or positive identification, the investigator should attempt to obtain as much information as possible from the clothing, jewelry, body, and material found in the pockets, as well as photographs, with a view toward publication of this information in local papers and on radio and television. Many identifications have been obtained with appeals to the public for information.

I remember one case in which the body of a young woman was found dead in the wooded area of a park. The woman had apparently been shot, "execution style." The body was stripped of all identification except jewelry. One of the pieces of jewelry was quite distinctive. It consisted of a caricature of a devil's head with two diamond eyes and ruby mouth. This item and five or six other pieces of jewelry were carefully described, as was the body and clothing of the deceased. The description was given to the press, with a request for anyone with information to please call the police. Twenty-four hours later we received a call, based on the description of the devil ring. A positive identification was obtained and the case continued.

Fingerprints

The fingerprints of the deceased matched with fingerprint records on file provide positive identification. If the victim does not have fingerprints on file, the comparison and match of the deceased's prints with latent prints taken from the dead person's home or place of employment is sufficient to prove identity. In the absence of identification by immediate family, fingerprint records represent conclusive evidence of identity.

The circumstances of death and the condition of the body usually determine whether or not good fingerprints can be obtained. The methods utilized to obtain prints from dead bodies range from the simple to the complex.

Obtaining Fingerprints from Dead Bodies

A standard fingerprint card, preferably a thin one, can be cut into two strips, one strip for each set of five. The fingers are inked either with a roller or pad. Each inked finger is then placed on the strip in the corresponding box. The strip is held in a curved holder or spoon. The finger is pressed against the strip and an impression is obtained.

If there is rigidity in the fingers, the joints can be bent back and forth several times until they are sufficiently flexible. You may have to take several prints before you get a good impression. Select the best impression and paste this on the respective section of the fingerprint card.

Remember, be careful not to mix up the prints.

In the cases where the skin is dried out or shriveled up, as in mummification, the fingers are amputated and immersed in a softening solution or water for several days until the skin softens. Each finger is placed in a separate bottle and each bottle is numbered 1 through 5 for each hand. It is imperative that these fingers not be mixed up. This procedure should not be undertaken without the permission of the medical examiner, who usually will do the cutting. The examination will be performed by a technician or laboratory.

If the fingers have been immersed in water or the body is that of a "floater," a fingerprint technician or expert is the best person to attempt to obtain prints. There are various procedures employed, depending on the condition of the body. If the fingers are shriveled or wrinkled, but the skin is still intact, a print can be obtained by filling out the finger, injecting water under the skin until the finger's normal contour has been

Figure 10.1. **FILLING OUT A FINGER.** Injection of water into a finger, which has become shriveled or wrinkled, so that the fingerprints can be obtained. It is recommended that the fluid be injected to restore the finger's normal contour and that a string be tied above the needle hole to prevent the water from leaking out.

Figure 10.2. **SKIN SEPARATING FROM THE HAND.** This "floater" was removed from the Hudson River water of New York City. In some instances, the entire outer layer of skin from the hand can be removed intact.

restored. The best instrument for this procedure is a hypodermic syringe with a fine needle so as not to break the skin. It is recommended that a string be tied around the finger directly above the hole after injecting the water to prevent the fluid from leaking out. Also, the point should not be too close to the skin since the pressure may break the skin.

Figure 10.3. **SKIN REMOVED FROM THE HAND.** Here the entire epidermis of the hand has been removed intact from the body of a "floater". A fingerprint technician will be able to effectively obtain prints from this fragile tissue.

Sometimes the skin will be so loose that it will come off the hand like a glove and can be cut away from the fingers. Each tip should be placed in a separate test tube, so as not to mix up the prints. The tubes can then be sealed with water and sent to the FBI Laboratory for examination.

In certain cases, the technician can remove the skin and place it over his own finger (wearing a thin surgical glove), and "roll" the skin as if it was his or her own finger. Another method used to obtain prints is by brushing black fingerprint powder on the fingers and removing the impression by "lifting" the print with transparent fingerprint tape. The tape is then placed on the fingerprint card in the respective box.

Remember, once again, be careful not to mix up the fingers or prints and place the proper lift in the right box.

The Iceman Case

CASE HISTORY

On July 1, 1981, Louis Masgay left his home in Pennsylvania, and headed for Little Ferry, New Jersey. Masgay, who was 50 years old, owned and operated a discount variety store. He had told his wife that he was going to New Jersey to meet a supplier who had agreed to sell him a large quantity of blank video tapes at a very good discount. He was taking the money in cash, nearly a hundred thousand dollars, which he had stashed in a concealed compartment in the driver's side door of his black 1980 Ford Carry Van. The "supplier" he was going to meet was Richard Kuklinski.

Unbeknownst to Masgay, Richard Kuklinski was planning to rob and kill the merchant. Richard Kuklinski was a contract killer, who eventually would admit to over 100 murders. In fact, it would be the murder of Masgay that would ultimately earn Kuklinski the title "The Iceman".

Masgay's black 1980 Ford Carry Van was found abandoned on Route 17 North in Rochelle Park, Bergen County, New Jersey. The family was sure that something terrible had happened. The cab was locked, and the police had to break in to move it. Police found that the primary gas tank was empty, but the secondary tank was full, leading them to suspect that whoever was driving the van did not know how to engage the reserve tank. A hidden compartment in the driver's side door was also discovered, but it was empty.

In September 1983, a body was found in a wooded area off Clauseland Mountain Road in Orangetown, New York, three miles north of the New Jersey border. The body was taken to the Office of the Rockland County Medical Examiner, where the Chief Medical Examiner, Dr. Frederick Zugibe, performed the autopsy.

A

B

Figure 10.4.   Photos A and B depict the condition of the body found in September 1983 in a wooded area off Clauseland Mountain Road in Orangetown, New York. The body was taken to the Office of the Rockland County Medical Examiner, where the Chief Medical Examiner, Dr. Frederick Zugibe, performed the autopsy. (Courtesy of Dr. Frederick Zugibe, Chief Medical Examiner, Rockland County, N.Y.)

Figure 10.5. **MYOCARDIUM SHOWING ICE CRYSTAL ARTIFACTS.** Note the nuclear distortion (black and white arrows) and vacuoles and spaces around the nuclei (arrow heads) and between the fibers (black arrows). (Courtesy of Dr. Frederick Zugibe, Chief Medical Examiner, Rockland County, N.Y.)

The body had been carefully trussed with tape and then wrapped in 15 to 20 plastic garbage bags, a task that must have taken some time and effort, Dr. Zugibe noted. One arm was taped to the body, but the other had apparently come loose during the wrapping. This hand was less protected than the other, and it had dried out. In effect, the hand was mummified.

As the final layer of plastic was removed, Dr. Zugibe saw that decomposition was advanced and that the flesh was greasy. The color of the man's skin was putty beige. There was a single bullet wound in the back of the head.

When he opened up the body, Dr. Zugibe noticed something very peculiar. The body was not distended and the organs were less decomposed than the outside of the body. Decomposition had started from the outside, which is the reverse of the normal process. Checking the heart muscle, he discovered ice crystal artifacts, which supported his immediate suspicion that the body had been frozen, perhaps by a killer whose intention was to disguise the time of death. Had the murderer dumped the body in the early Spring, the time of death might have been completely disguised and Dr. Zugibe probably would have concluded that this was a recent killing.

Dr. Zugibe's Medical Evaluation

During an investigation of illegal dumping, several plastic bags were found along a mountain road in September of 1983. One bundle appeared suspicious because it contained an object suggestive of a body. X-rays of the bundle at the medical examiner's office confirmed the presence of a human body with radiopaque objects noted within the skull. Careful unwrapping revealed that the body was wrapped in about 20 consecutive layers of plastic garbage bags and rope. The inner layers appeared older than the outer layers and each bag was taped with 2-inch wide plastic tape and tied with small segments of clothesline rope in-between each layer of plastic. The body appeared to be markedly decomposed but without any discernible distention or bloating. The body emitted a peculiar, foul odor not representative of the usual odors associated with decomposition. The surface of the body appeared to be very greasy in consistency. In contrast, there was significantly less decomposition internally than externally with no significant distention of the gut and with fair preservation of the viscera. The head region, however, showed a greater degree of decomposition than the rest of the body. A contact-type entrance bullet hole was present in the left occipital-parietal region and a fracture emanated from the bullet hole and extended for a distance of 10.5 cm. into the parietal bone. The brain was liquified. A lead bullet and two large bullet fragments were found in the cranial cavity.

Information for identification purposes was tabulated that included anthropomorphic findings, odontological charting, physical characteristics, unusual characteristics, clothing, shoe size, jewelry, glasses, and fingerprints using a special technique developed by this office for securing fingerprints from mummified bodies (Zugibe and Costello, 1986 in "Selected Reading" section). Dr. Zugibe was able to rehydrate the fingers by using a chelation technique based on an entirely new process. He used disodium ethylenediamine tetracetic acid in a detergent solution adjusted to a pH of 7.5 and obtained the fingerprints that identified the body as that of Louis L. Masgay.

Forensic Evaluation

According to Dr. Zugibe, the peculiar decomposition with the external aspects of the body markedly more decomposed than the visceral aspects and with no intestinal or tissue distention, suggested that the victim may have been frozen for a period of time. Freezing would either kill or alter the growth pattern of enteric flora and the external aspects of the body would be the first to thaw and therefore, be directly exposed to microorganisms from outside of the body. The head region showed more decomposition than the rest of the body because the bullet hole to the head would allow entrance of organisms from the outside. Moreover, if the body had indeed been frozen, the head may have decomposed more rapidly because of rapid thawing due to its small size. Tissue sections were evaluated for the presence of ice crystal artifacts in an attempt to confirm our impression that the body may have been frozen prior to dumping it.

Dr. Zugibe's careful examination of the heart muscle sections revealed features suggestive of ice crystal artifacts. According to Dr. Zugibe, "This preliminary hypothesis was met with skepticism by other law enforcement agencies. However, we pursued our suspicions by carefully laundering all of the clothing of the deceased and meticulously describing each item including color, size, style, brand labels, etc. so that in the event that he was successfully identified, they could be compared with the clothing he was reportedly wearing when he was last seen alive."

The body was subsequently identified as Louis Masgay, Sr. from Forty Fort, Pennsylvania, who was last seen alive about two and one-quarter years prior to his death. A comparison was then made of the clothing found on the victim's body with a description of the clothing that Masgay was wearing when he had left home July 1, 1981 (about two and one-quarter years previously) with a large amount of money to meet a Mr. Richard Kuklinski to buy video tapes. He was never seen again. This appeared to confirm Dr. Zugibe's suspicions that he was frozen for over 2 years prior to dumping the body.

This hypothesis was fully corroborated almost three years later, when The Rockland County Medical Examiner was contacted by the New Jersey Attorney General's Office that they had a suspect named Richard Kuklinski in connection with a series of homicides, which included the Masgay case. Dr. Zugibe stated, "They were greatly impressed by our conclusion that the victim had been frozen because one of their informants, a convicted murderer who was unaware of our findings, in exchange for certain personal requests, provided them with a sworn statement that he had observed a body hanging in a freezer compartment within Richard Kuklinski's North Bergen warehouse. Moreover, a taped conversation of Kukliski by an undercover agent wearing a "wire" reaffirmed that the body had been frozen and afforded the impression that Kuklinski had fooled the authorities. Our case was responsible for Kuklinski being dubbed the "Iceman" although this was the only victim that he purportedly froze."

Advanced decomposition will necessitate special lab techniques, the use of photography with side lighting to emphasize ridge patterns, and more sophisticated procedures that are beyond the capability of the ordinary investigator.

Fingerprint impressions and finger stalls can be sent to the FBI Laboratory for identification by mailing as follows:

Director
Federal Bureau of Investigation
10th and Pennsylvania Avenue, N.W.
Washington, D.C. 20537

Attention: Identification Division, Latent Print Section

The Teeth

Dentition provides an excellent means of identification, especially when antemortem records and x-rays of the deceased are available for comparison. Forensic odontology — the scientific application of dentistry to legal matters — has become a viable asset to the law enforcement community. According to Dr. Levine,[1] a small but growing nucleus of dentists in this country today have been trained to respond to the needs of law enforcement officers, the legal profession, and forensic pathologists.

Forensic odontologists work on problems involving identification, bite marks, and dental and oral injuries. In addition, they are invaluable in the identification of bodies in mass disasters, where the only semblance of human remains may be a jaw fragment, shattered teeth, or broken dentures.

As a result of modern dental procedures involving restoration such as tooth capping and root canal work, dentists have made extensive use of x-rays and molds, both of which are accurate records of oral anatomy. Fillings and caps are highly individual, and jawbone construction provides information based on certain anatomical landmarks that never change in an individual.

Practically speaking, in cases where the remains have been badly mutilated or burned, are in advanced putrefaction, or have been submerged in water for a long period of time, etc., the possibility of obtaining any fingerprints of value is quite remote. This is where the

[1]Dr. Lowell J. Levine is President of the American Academy of Forensic Sciences and Consultant to the New York City and Nassau County Medical Examiner's Office.

forensic odontologist can be of assistance. Using powerful cameras, x-rays, and medical records, he or she can, through examination of the dentition and jawbones of the deceased, provide the investigator with information about the deceased, including age, general facial characteristics, race, socioeconomic group, occupation or habits, positive identification, and bite-mark identification.

Age

The eruption of teeth in the human body is a relatively predictable process during the early years of growth. The forensic odontologist can provide a rather accurate estimate of age of persons under fourteen. The first teeth, referred to as baby teeth or deciduous teeth, make their appearance from 7 months to 2 years. The loss of these baby teeth and the eruption of the first permanent molars begins at approximately 5 years of age and continues into the early teens. After age 14, the forensic odontologist relies on the wear patterns. As a general rule, the older a person becomes, the more his or her teeth show evidence of wear, dental repair, and gum recession. The forensic odontologist, using microscopic and radiological (x-ray) examination of dentition, can estimate the age of an adult within 5 years' accuracy. Estimates of age for the prepubertal child can be calculated within 6 months by examining the stage of development of the permanent tooth buds.

General Facial Characteristics

By comparing certain aspects of the configuration of teeth and jaws, a forensic odontologist can roughly determine the shape of the face. According to certain experts there are three basic shape formations, square, tapering, and ovoid. These computations, however, are not infallible and are subject to different interpretations.

An importance factor used in arriving at facial contour is the positions; the lower front teeth fit inside the upper front teeth and are in direct contact with the upper teeth. The exceptions to this rule can help in identifying facial features. The following are possible conditions:

1. Normal anatomical position.
2. Overbite: in this case, the lower teeth fail to meet the upper front teeth because of a protruding upper jaw. This results in an overprominence of the upper jaw, accompanied by an underprominence of the lower jaw, resulting in a receding chin. This is commonly referred to as the "Andy Gump" look.

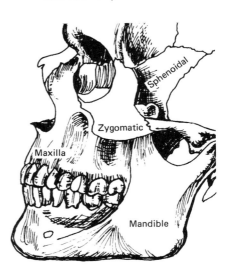

Figure 10.6. **NORMAL ANATOMIC POSITION OF THE TEETH AND JAWS.**

3. Prognathic: in this case, the lower teeth protrude beyond the upper teeth. The lower jaw and chin are excessively prominent. This is referred to as the "Fearless Fosdick" look.

It should be noted that there are now operations whereby these abnormalities can be corrected, resulting in drastic changes in profile. These procedures are known as orthognathic surgery.

Race

The forensic odontologist can sometimes determine the race of the deceased by examination of the jawbones and teeth. There are certain anthropological traits within races which make such a determination possible. However, with mixed races it is extremely difficult. From a practical point of view, the investigator would obtain a more definite determination from the physical anthropologist, who may even have to utilize a computer.

Socioeconomic Group

The socioeconomic group and relative economic status of a person may be estimated by the quality of dental treatment he or she obtained in life. The forensic odontologist bases his determination on the general oral hygiene of the deceased and the manner and type of dental restoration. For instance, missing teeth which have not been replaced, unfilled cavities, and a generally poor dentition would indicate a low economic status. On the contrary, gold inlays, root canal work, and prostheses such as well-made bridgework and dentures indicate that the individual was able to afford good dental treatment. Expensive dental work is readily observable to the odontologist during examination.

Occupation or Habits

In some instances, habits of the deceased which have caused dental change will be noted during a forensic examination. For example, the holding of nails between the teeth, which is a habit of carpenters, or the playing of certain musical instruments, like the trumpet, causes a distinctive type of wear which may provide a clue as to occupation. Furthermore, habits such as holding a pipe between the teeth or longtime cigar smoking will be evidenced by both wear patterns and heavy tar accumulation.

Positive Identification

Practically speaking, this is the most valuable information which can be learned from an examination of the teeth. Forensic odontology is probably the most effective means available to the investigator for arriving at a positive identification in cases where fingerprints are unobtainable or there are no matchable fingerprints of the deceased on file.

Figure 10.7. **ARSON-HOMICIDE VICTIM.** A 6-year old boy was burned beyond recognition. Positive identification was obtained from teeth. (Courtesy of Dr. Arthur D. Goldman, Forensic Odontologist.)

Figure 10.8.   **X-RAYS OF VICTIM'S TEETH.** (A) X-rays are postmortem. (B) X-rays are antemortem. Identification was based on the shapes of crowns and root form. (Courtesy of Dr. Goldman, Forensic Odontologist.)

Figure 10.9.   **ENGRAVED DENTURE.** This denture has been engraved by the dentist. The denture, along with antemortem records, led to the identification of the victim who had been kidnapped and slain. (Courtesy of Dr. Goldman, Forensic Odontologist.)

It should be noted that no two sets of teeth are exactly alike. A full complement of teeth is 32. Each tooth has five surfaces, with various fissures and grooves. The arrangement of the teeth within the jaw is different for each person. In addition, there are individual differences in the arch of the palate and the mode of occlusion (bite). Add to these individual physiological differences the many types of dental operations, such as caps, fillings, root canal work, crowns, dentures, prostheses, and other surgical procedures, and one realizes that the teeth are quite distinctive. In fact, there are literally thousands of identifying characteristics of teeth.

Modern equipment utilized by dentists today, specifically the high-speed, air-driven handpiece, has allowed dentists to undertake many more sophisticated dental treatments and operations. These advanced procedures have created the need for comprehensive dental examinations, involving x-rays and molds of teeth, both of which are highly accurate and individualized. In addition, all dentures have manufacturers' brands that may be traced to a specific dental laboratory in a specific area. In some instances, the dentist will personalize the appliance by engraving the patient's name or social security number on the denture. When attempting to identify an edentulous (toothless) person, the forensic odontologist will take an impression of the palate and upper arch, since the palate's anatomical form and characteristics are distinct. In addition, even an old denture may prove useful in identification procedures. If the investigator can locate this denture, it can be examined by the odontologist. Many people are like "pack rats" and save even the most useless articles; so too do wearers of dentures. Often an investigator who needs to locate an old denture for identification purposes will be surprised to find two or three such appliances.

Military service and private and governmental insurance programs have made dental services available to most of our population. Since comprehensive dental examinations are mandatory prior to treatment, a wealth of dental information on our citizens is now in the hands of the dental profession, insurance companies, and government agencies.

If the investigator can locate the dental records of the deceased, the forensic odontologist can make an absolute and positive identification. It is for this reason that experts in the field of odontology recommend the data banking of dental information by computer. This knowledge would certainly aid in the identification of unknown homicide victims and greatly assist in the tremendous job of identifying bodies in mass disasters.

Bite-Mark Identification

This particular phase of forensic odontology will be discussed in more detail in another section (see Chapter 20, "Bite-Mark Identification"). However, as a practical matter, the investigator who is at the scene of a homicide where teeth either have been used as a weapon, or the body indicates that the murderer may have assaulted the victim by inflicting bite marks, must view these wounds as evidence. Bite marks are specific to the person who has inflicted them. In addition, saliva washings should be obtained for later serological comparison. It is important to note, however, that these washings must take place before the lapse of too much time.

I recommend that the investigator, using a 1 × 1 fingerprint camera, or a 35 mm camera with color film, obtain photos of these marks. Side lighting is sometimes useful to accent the marks. In addition, a scale should be included in the photo to assist the experts in their later examination and comparison of the bite marks and evaluation of any impressions obtained from possible suspects.

Inquiries Relative to Forensic Odontology

There is a national organization of forensic odontologists where investigators may request information or obtain the location of an odontologist within his or her specific geographic area. The address is:

> The American Board of Forensic Odontology, Inc.
> Administrative Office: The Forensic Sciences Foundation
> 11400 Rockville Pike
> Rockville, Maryland 20852

In addition, I have corresponded with Dr. H.R. Campbell, DDS, who is Secretary of the American Board of Forensic Odontology. He processes many requests for listings of current certified diplomats to

Figure 10.10. **SKELETAL REMAINS OF A BODY FOUND OUTDOORS.** (Courtesy of Dr. Leslie I. Lukash, Chief Medical Examiner, Nassau County, New York.)

various law enforcement agencies. He can be reached at the following address:

6800-C Montgomery NE
Albuquerque, N.M. 87109

The Bones

The examination of skeletal remains by a physical anthropologist can provide certain basic classifications which may assist police in determining the identity of the deceased. Depending upon the completeness and condition of these skeletal remains, the forensic examination can supply the age of the deceased at the time of death, as well as his or her sex, race, height, and other individual characteristics such as, right- or left-handedness, overweight or underweight, well or poorly developed musculature, and, prior bone injuries. The examination can also determine the cause of death in certain cases, and ascertain whether the bones are human or animal.

Estimates of age, sex, race, and stature do not provide positive identification of an individual. However, they become an integral part of the identification process when compared with unique characteristics and matchable records of the deceased made in life. An example of such records, which would yield positive identification, are medical records (operations, births, amputations, etc.), dental records, and antemortem x-rays.

The investigator, armed with the information provided by the anthropologist's examination of skeletal remains, now has a general description of the deceased which can be compared with missing persons reports, registered ownership records if there is property involved, and official records.

Age

A trained radiologist and physical anthropologist can provide an estimate of age, based on skeletal remains, which ranges from somewhat unpredictable to considerably accurate depending on the age of the deceased. After age thirty the reliability of the formulas used by scientists to gauge age decreases, and tooth structure gives a better estimate of age than do the gross bones after that age.

Anthropologists use formulas based on the *epiphyses* of bones (the stage of uniting of bones, a condition which varies with age) to make their determinations.

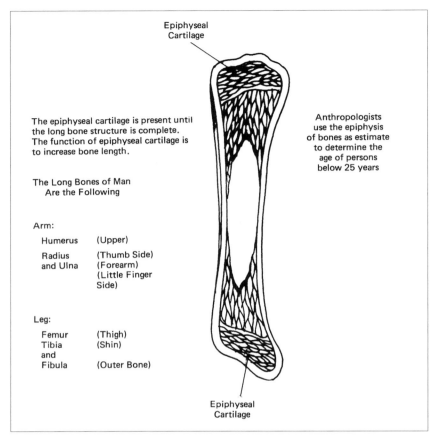

Epiphyseal
Cartilage

The epiphyseal cartilage is present until
the long bone structure is complete.
The function of epiphyseal cartilage is
to increase bone length.

Anthropologists
use the epiphysis
of bones as estimate
to determine the
age of persons
below 25 years

The Long Bones of Man
Are the Following

Arm:

Humerus   (Upper)

Radius   (Thumb Side)
and Ulna   (Forearm)
               (Little Finger
               Side)

Leg:

Femur   (Thigh)
Tibia   (Shin)
and
Fibula   (Outer Bone)

Epiphyseal
Cartilage

Figure 10.11.   **LONG BONE STRUCTURE — EPIPHYSIS OF BONE.**

Basically, science has determined that the bones develop from small areas known as *ossification centers*. These ossification centers produce calcium and other minerals which are deposited to form bone. Many of the ossification centers start their production during the early months of fetal life, while others do not completely finish producing bone until the early twenties. Anthropologists have worked out a series of formulas to estimate age based on the appearance of these different ossification centers. X-ray examination can with considerable accuracy determine age up to twenty-five years.

Another determining factor in estimating age is the skull. The skull is composed of several curved bones joined together along irregular lines called *sutures*. As an individual approaches the early twenties, these sutures begin to fill up with bone and close. This process continues with age and follows a distinct pattern. Anthropological studies of these patterns resulted in the establishment of a formula whereby sci-

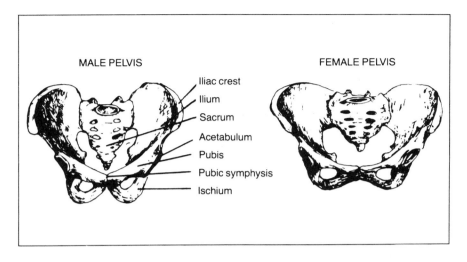

Figure 10.12.   **MALE AND FEMALE PELVIS.** The pelvis bone is the most accurate indicator of sex. If you look closely at the two drawings you may observe the different structure between the male and female pelvis. Of course, to the trained eye of the anthropologist the differences are readably discernible.

entists could determine the age of an individual by examination of the skull. Suture closing, however, is not as reliable as first predicted. Instead, scientists have developed a new scheme, which yields both an estimate of age and an error of estimate. Most estimates of age for remains of persons between 30 and 80 years of age are given in 7-to-10-year brackets.

The pelvic bone can also be used to determine age. There are various changes in the structure of the bone which occur within approximately 5-year intervals.

In addition, there are studies that indicate that calcification begins in the cartilages of the larynx and ribs at about 55 years of age, and that males in the age bracket of 35 to 40 show a presence of arthritic lipping in certain joints, especially in the vertebral column. At present, research is being conducted on calculating age based on spectrographic evaluation of bone particles, a procedure still under evaluation.

Although the criminal investigator need not comprehend the technical aspects of these anthropological computations, he would do well to be aware of their value in the identification process.

Sex

If an anthropologist has the whole skeleton to examine, sex can be determined with 90% accuracy. Male skeletons are larger than female skeletons, and the bone surfaces of the male are rougher than those of the female. The pelvic bone, however, is the most accurate indicator of sex. Since the female pelvis is designed for childbearing, its difference is readily observable to the trained eye of the anthropologist. Scars of parturition on the pelvic bone not only help to determine sex, but can also provide evidence that the deceased has borne one or more children.

In addition, anthropologists now have a variety of metrical techniques, such as the *ischium-pubis index*, to assist them in determining sex.

Race

Through the application of sophisticated statistical procedures to skull dimensions, anthropologists can now determine the race of the skeletal remains. Because of the number of mixed racial heritages in this country, the variables are considerable and a computer is often used to sort out all the information. Determining the race of an individual utilizing the skull is almost without error. However, without the skull the possibility for error drastically increases.

Height and Other Individual Characteristics

In determining height, several different formulas have been devised based on the measurement of the long bones. The most accurate method is based on the measurement of the long bones compared with a simple table. While there is some slight variation in different races, the height can in general, be determined within an inch of accuracy.

The anthropologist can determine whether the person was overweight or emaciated, and, by examining the muscle attachments to the bone, whether the remains are from a muscularly well developed person. In addition, the skeleton reveals whether or not the person was right- or left-handed, since the bones of the dominant arm are slightly longer. Certain characteristics of the *scapula* (shoulder blade) and *clavicle* (collarbone) also help to determine handedness.

The bones will readily indicate whether or not there has been past trauma such as a fracture. If the antemortem x-rays can be obtained, this information will provide positive identification of the deceased.

Determination of Cause of Death

In some instances, the bones will readily reveal the cause of death. For instance, the skull is most likely to yield important evidence of direct violence in gunshot cases or direct blunt force injuries. The penetration

Figure 10.13. **FORENSIC EXAMINATION OF SKELETAL REMAINS.** These cremains were of a victim, who was cremated by her ex-husband in a crematorium. They were placed in anatomical order by the forensic anthropologist, who came to the following conclusions: the bones were those of a white female, approximately 32 years old, weighed approximately 100 pounds and had given birth within the last 5 years. (Courtesy of Major John Dotson formerly with Wichita, Kansas Police Department. Presently Chief of Police Sparks, Nevada.)

of a bullet through the skull will be easily recognizable from its telltale pattern. Likewise, evidence of injuries to the skull or other bones by a hammer, crowbar, or other weapon will be evident upon examination. In addition, if a person died as a result of one of the metallic poisons, the poison can still be extracted from the bones years later.

Determination of whether the Bones are Human or Animal

The first two questions in identifying unknown skeletal remains are: (1) are they human? and (2) is more than one person or animal represented? A complete human skull is readibly identifiable as human. However, the investigator may be confronted with pieces of broken jaw, bone fragments, teeth, or other parts of a skeleton. Practically speaking, law enforcement personnel should consider all pieces of skeleton human until experts determine otherwise. For example, parts of bear paws are misidentified more often as human than any other animal. In addition, many animal skeletons lacking the telltale skull have been thought to be those of a small child. I remember one incident in the South Bronx that confused the hell out of the police. A body of an apparently nude, decapitated male was found lying in the gutter. The body weighed about 300 pounds. The case was reported as a "possible homicide." Although this was not a skeleton, I bring this case to your attention because upon medical examination at the scene it was discovered to be the body of a full-grown skinned gorilla!

Often bones or remains can fool people. Therefore, it is imperative that the investigator suspect each case to be human until proven otherwise.

Examination of the Bones

The examination of the bones should be performed by the forensic experts, particularly the physical anthropologist, the radiologist, and the forensic odontologist. Although this phase is beyond the skill of the criminal investigator, it is the investigator who will set the stage for the successful evaluation of this evidence by following certain preliminary procedures. These include photographing and sketching the remains before moving them, consulting with the medical examiner and anthropologist for any instructions, and, if there is more than one skeleton, keeping the parts separate and assigning them in consecutive numbers.

Facial Reconstruction

Facial reconstruction from the skull is a method sometimes used in forensic anthropology to identify skeletal remains. In fact, according to Dr. Harry L. Shapiro, Curator Emeritus of the Anthropology Department of the American Museum of Natural History, facial reconstruction is a procedure that has been used for years by anthropologists to recreate general physiological features of an individual based on infor-

Figure 10.14.   **FACIAL RECONSTRUCTION.** This restoration technique is employed in forensic anthropology to recreate an identity from a human skull. This particular restoration was created by Ms. Betty Pat. Gatliff, Forensic Sculptor, and her associate, Dr. Clyde C. Snow, Ph.D. Physical Anthropologist. (Reprinted with permission from Ms. Betty Pat. Gatliff Skullpture, Inc., 1026 Leslie Lane, Norma, Oklahoma 73069 and Mr. Mark Weaver, Public Affairs Officer AAC-5, Federal Aviation Administration, P.O. Box 25082, Oklahoma City, Oklahoma 73125.)

mation derived from skeletal remains. Although, the physical anthropologist can arrive at an osteo-biography of an individual based on the examination of the bones, Doctor Shapiro is quick to caution the investigator that determination of individuality based on these findings is subject to error. As he points out in his own reconstruction of a skull called "The Peking Man," the reconstruction is an approximation of what a general or nonspecific Peking Man looked like. Doctor Shapiro contends that arriving at an individual or specific face based on examination of the skull and bones leaves too much margin of error because the soft-tissue features — such as shape of eyelids, mouth width, lip thickness, lower part of the nose, and ears — are not necessarily indicated by the skull's shape. However, there is a relatively new process of facial reconstruction which combines both the science of anthropology and artistic judgment based on anatomical knowledge and experience. It is called forensic sculpture.

Forensic Sculpture

Forensic sculpture — the creation of an identity out of skeletal remains — is a specialty that combines both art and science. Practically speaking, it should be employed only after all other means of identification have proven fruitless.

Figure 10.15.   **FACIAL RECONSTRUCTION.** (Reprinted with permission from Ms. Betty Pat. Gatliff Skullpture, Inc., 1026 Leslie Lane, Norman, Oklahoma 73069 and Mr. Mark Weaver, Public Affairs Officer AAC-5, Federal Aviation Administration, P.O. Box 25082, Oklahoma City, Oklahoma 73125.)

In fact, Ms. Betty Gatliff, a forensic sculptor, and her associate, Dr. Clyde C. Snow, a physical anthropologist, both of whom pioneered work on facial reconstruction, are more than candid in their evaluation and recommendations of their method.[2] They advise that facial reconstruction be employed only as a last-ditch effort by law enforcement

---

[2]These practitioners can be reached through Skullpture, Inc., 1026 Leslie Lane, Norman, Oklahoma 73069.

Figure 10.15. (continued)

authorities. However, by the same token, they report a 70% success rate on the reconstructions they have created.

The forensic sculptor and the physical anthropologist collaborate to construct the facial features of the unknown skeletal remains on the basis of the underlying cranial architecture. First, the anthropologist examines the skull to determine sex, race, and approximate age. This information is important because the depths of the soft tissue of the face are different in males and females and in the three major racial groups; Mongoloid, Caucasoid, and Negroid. The anthropologist looks for evidence of individual anatomical peculiarities, diseases, or injuries that

81-10 HUMAN SKELETON FROM STONE COUNTY, MISSISSIPPI

(Mississippi State Crime Laboratory Case #80-2800)

BACKGROUND

This skeleton was discovered by two hunters in a wooded area near Wiggins, Mississippi, on October 5, 1980. The hands and feet were bound with heavy baling twine. Moderate quantities of dried soft tissues were adherent to the bone. A considerable amount of medium-dark brown, shoulder length hair was recovered. In a dark-green plastic bag found with the remains was a page from the March 3, 1980, issue of the Las Vegas (Nevada) *Mirror*.

TIME OF DEATH

Based upon the degree of soft tissue preservation, the season of discovery and local climatic factors, death is estimated at about *2-6 months* prior to discovery.

AGE AT DEATH

Based on symphyseal morphology, cranial suture closure and other age-related skeletal features, the age at death is estimated at *40 ± 6 years* (**34-46** years). The lack of vertebral osteophytosis makes the lower part of this range (34-40 years) somewhat more likely than the upper part.

SEX

Cranial and sexual morphology is *female*. Discriminant function analysis of the cranium and postcranial skeleton also yield diagnoses of female.

RACE

Cranial morphology is *Caucasoid*. Discriminant function analysis of cranial measurements confirms this diagnosis. Hair is also Caucasoid in color and form.

STATURE

Using the Trotter-Gleser formula for white females, stature estimated from the combined lengths of the femur and tibia is *64 ± 3 inches*.

PHYSIQUE

Muscle attachments areas are well developed, especially in the upper extremities. These findings suggest a rather *muscular, compact physique* characteristic of a woman who was physically active through either occupation or athletics.

Figure 10.16.   **FACIAL RECONSTRUCTION:** description used. (Reprinted with permission from Dr. Clyde C. Snow, Clinical Anthropologist.)

HANDEDNESS

Scapular beveling and length differences in upper extremity bones suggest that this individual was *right-handed.*

PARITY

A very small, poorly developed preauricular sulcus is present on the right innominate; on the left innominate, the sulcus is absent. These borderline findings suggest that this individual was either nulliparous or, possibly, may have given birth to a child many years previously.

OLD DISEASES, INJURIES, ANOMALIES

1. Healed nasal fracture with nasal bridge deviation to the right.
2. Healed fracture of lateral end of right clavicle.
3. Slight porotic hyperostosis suggests at least one episode of chronic iron deficiency anemia.

TRAUMA

There is evidence of postmortem damage to the ribs and some smaller bones of the hands and feet by small carnivoral scavengers. The only evidence of possible circummortem trauma is a linear fracture of the right 7th rib.

CAUSE OF DEATH

Aside from the rib fracture suggestive of *possible* blunt force trauma, there is no evidence of the cause of death.

MANNER OF DEATH

Probable Homicide

SUMMARY

This skeleton is that of a white female who was around 40 ± 6 years of age at the time of her death from unknown causes. Location of the body and binding of the hands and feet indicate homicide as manner of death. The victim was about 5' 4" ± 3" in height and was somewhat more muscular than the average female. She was right-handed and had suffered a fractured nose and broken right collar bone some years prior to her death. Death is estimated to have occurred about 2–6 months prior to the discovery of her skeleton.

date

Clyde Collins Snow, Ph.D.
Forensic Anthropology Consultant

Figure 10.16. (continued)

Figure 10.17. Composite of unidentified deceased homicide victim of the preceding figure created by facial reconstruction by Dr. Snow and Ms. Gatliff. (Courtesy of Trooper T. P. Naylor Mississippi Highway Patrol.)

could influence a person's facial features during life. Depending on the completeness of the skeleton, the anthropologist will be able to determine whether the deceased was fat or thin and if the person was muscular. In addition, both the anthropologist and the sculptor will want to see any clothing or other items which may provide clues as to hair color and style.

Armed with the anthropological information, the sculptor begins the reconstruction by placing small blocks or cylinders which correspond to the average thickness of the soft tissue over certain bony landmarks. These blocks are then glued to the skull. Using the tissue-depth blocks as contour guides, the face is built up in clay as shown in steps A through D. Soft-tissue features which have no necessary correlation with the underlying bone present unique problems. According to Ms. Gatliff, determining the contour and shape of these soft-tissue locations challenges the anatomical knowledge, artistic judgment, and the experience of the artist.

When the facial reconstruction is completed, the sculptor selects a wig based on the color, length, and style of the hair found with the remains. If no hair is found, the sculptor bases the selection on other factors inferred from the bones, clothes, and artifacts found with the body.

The completed facial reconstruction is then photographed and the photos given to the law enforcement agency that requested the service. The agency usually, through the cooperation of the media, distributes these photos and circulates the information so as to reach as many persons as possible, with a request to call the police with any information. Any information as to identity will enable authorities to obtain dental records, antemortem x-rays, and other evidence necessary to provide positive identification.

Although this particular method is relatively new and based on a limited number of cases, both Dr. Snow and Ms. Gatliff are optimistic about improved techniques and research in the field, resulting in additional data on soft-tissue depths.

Practically speaking, the homicide investigator must ask himself the following question: "Will facial reconstruction enable me to identify my homicide victim?" If the answer is yes, this method certainly deserves serious consideration, especially after all else has failed.

Conclusion

The identification of the deceased is obviously critical to the overall success of the homicide investigation. The same principle that applies to estimating time of death, however, applies to determining the identity of the deceased: the "fresher" the body, the better the chances.

The normal methods of identification, such as informational sources found at the scene, photographs, and fingerprints can be performed by the investigator. The more technical aspects of identification involving radiological examination, forensic odontology, and physical anthropology require the assistance of scientists and experts from various fields. The homicide investigator does not have to possess the expertise of these scientists, but he or she should have a working knowledge of their availability and potential for determining the identity of the deceased.

I have had the pleasure of working with two distinguished forensic odontologists, Dr. Lowell J. Levine, President of the American Academy of Forensic Sciences and consultant to the New York State Police; and Dr. Arthur D. Goldman, DDS, Vice President of the American Academy of Forensic Sciences and consultant to the Rockland County Medical Examiner's Office in New York State. Dr. Levine and Dr. Goldman contributed their expertise to this chapter by reviewing the section on "Teeth" and providing me with personal opinions and practical information, which I have included herein.

Dr. Harry L. Shapiro, Curator Emeritus of the Anthropology Department of the American Museum of Natural History in New York City, is a renowned educator and scholar whose work in the field of forensic anthropology is widely known. He very graciously provided me with his personal experiences and practical information relative to the section on bones. Dr. James Taylor, Lehman College, Bronx, New York, is a forensic anthropologist. He personally reviewed the material on bones and contributed his experience with criminal investigations. Dr. Taylor is director of the Metropolitan Forensic Anthropology Team located at Lehman College, C.U.N.Y. The team is composed of a forensic anthropologist, a forensic odontologist, a criminalist, and an archeologist.

I have also had the pleasure of working with Dr. Frederick T. Zugibe, Chief Medical Examiner of Rockland County, New York, who has provided me with his expertise in the identification of human remains through fingerprint analysis. The case history on the Iceman provides excellent insight into the forensic aspects of identification. He has also provided me with his expertise in the area of medicolegal medicine.

In addition, I interviewed Ms. Betty Gatliff, a forensic sculptor, whose expertise in facial reconstruction has gained her recognition in the field of forensic science. Her technique, based on anthropological interpretations and an "artist's eye," is used to create an identity or face from a human skull. This field is relatively new to law enforcement; however, there has been some remarkable success with this method, and further research is being undertaken to improve the technique.

Selected Reading

Angel, J. Lawrence. "Bones Can Fool People." *F.B.I. Law Enforcement Bulletin.* January 1974.

Bruno, Anthony. The ICEMAN: *The True Story of a Cold-Blooded Killer.* New York: Delacourte Press, 1993.

Fisher, Barry A. J., Svensson, Arne, and Wendel, Otte. *Techniques of Crime Scene Investigation,* 5th ed. New York: Elsevier Science Publishing Co., Inc., 1992.

Gatliff, Betty Pat and Snow, Clyde C. "From Skull to Visage," *The Journal of Biocommunication* (1979).

Geberth, Vernon J. *Practical Homicide Investigation: Tactics, Procedures, and Forensic Techniques,* Second Edition, CRC Press, Inc., Florida, 1993.

Kochevar, I. E., Pathak, M. A., and Parrish, J. A., "Photophysics, Photochemistry, and Photobiology," in *Dermatology in General Medicine, Textbook, and Atlas, 3rd edition,* Fitzpatrick, T. B., et al., Eds., 1987, McGraw-Hill Book Co.: New York, pp. 1441–1151.

Krogman, W. M. *The Human Skeleton in Forensic Medicine.* Springfield, Illinois: Charles C Thomas, 1962.

Levine, Lowell J. "Forensic Odontology Today — A New Forensic Science." *F.B.I. Law Enforcement Bulletin,* August 1972.

Levine, Lowell J. et al. "The Use of Dental Characteristics in the Identification of Human Remains," *Oral Surgery, Oral Medicine, Oral Pathology* 35 (1973): 275–281.

Personal interview with Dr. Frederick T. Zugibe, March 15, 1995 and April 8, 1995.

O'Hara, Charles E. *Fundamentals of Criminal Investigation,* 5th ed. Springfield, Illinois: Charles C Thomas, 1980.

Shapiro, Harry L. "Forensic Anthropology." *Annals of New York Academy of Sciences.* Curator Emeritus American Museum of Natural History, New York, N.Y. Personal interviews.

Synder, LcMoyne. *Homicide Investigation,* 3rd ed. Springfield, Illinois: Charles C Thomas, 1977.

Stewart, T. D. *Essential of Forensic Anthropology,* Springfield, Illinois: Charles C Thomas, 1979.

"Identification by Skeletal Structures." In *Gradwohl's Legal Medicine,* edited by F. E. Camps. 2nd ed. Baltimore: The Williams & Wilkens Company, 1968, pp. 123–154.

"What the Bones Tell — Today." *F.B.I. Law Enforcement Bulletin,* February 1972.

Stewart, T. D., Ed. "Personal Identification in Mass Disasters." Washington, D.C.: Smithsonian Institution, 1970.

Zugibe, Frederick T. Personal interview, March 15, 1995 and April 8, 1995.

Zugibe, F. T. and Costello, J. T. "The Iceman Murder: One of a Series of Contract Murders." *Journal of Forensic Sciences,* Vol. 38, No. 6, November, 1993, pp. 1404–1408.

Zugibe, F. T. and Costello, J. T. "A New Method for Softening Mummified Fingers." *Journal of Forensic Sciences,* Vol. 31, No. 2, April, 1986, pp. 726–731.

Death Notifications: The Surviving Family as Secondary Victims

11

The purpose of this chapter is to emphasize the professional responsibility of the homicide investigator when making death notifications and focus on the dynamics of dealing with the secondary victims of homicide.

Secondary victims are those persons left behind when a husband, wife, child, or other loved one is prematurely deprived of their life due to a homicide. These persons are the survivors. The homicide detective has a profound duty and awesome responsibility in dealing with the surviving family in the murder investigation process.

1. The homicide detective encounters the reality of sudden and violent death and then must deal with the emotions and dynamics of the surviving family.
2. The homicide detective must personally process this information and then establish a base of inquiry that does not further traumatize the survivors.
3. The homicide detective makes the notification of death to the surviving family and next of kin.
4. The homicide detective assists the family and arranges for the official identification process at the morgue and/or medical facility.
5. The homicide detective provides the family with the information relative to the circumstances of the death and the progress of the investigation.
6. The homicide detective must guide the family through a complicated and confusing criminal justice system that is void of human compassion.

269

In fact, the homicide detective, in addition to pursuing the case, also becomes the advocate for both the deceased and the surviving family throughout the entire process.

Therefore, it is extremely important that the homicide detective understand the psychodynamics of the grief process and recognize the value of professional crisis intervention.

Psychological Reactions to Death

The subject of death and dying is depressing and most people avoid thinking or talking about the subject. In fact, death is considered fearful and frightening. Some persons even avoid going to funerals or wakes in an exercise of denial. The terminally ill are usually sent to hospitals or institutions to die and the general public is seldom exposed to the presence or reality of death.

Yet, most of us have experienced the loss of a loved one due to illness or the aging process and have gone through a period of bereavement. Although death is an inevitable event for each of us, we usually ignore or deny that it can happen to us and we remain basically unprepared for it. When death occurs suddenly and/or is otherwise unexpected, the survivors find themselves in an emotional turmoil and become psychologically disoriented. The first reaction is disbelief, followed by feelings of sadness, grief, despair, and anger. Then there is a natural progression of healing termed the normal grieving process.

The Normal Grieving Process

The normal grief period following the loss of a loved one begins with a period of numbness and shock and the first reaction is usually one of disbelief. This is the *acute phase*. In this acute phase, which follows the initial notification of death, the person will usually grieve quite intensely. There will be crying, screaming, denial, and depression. For several days the feelings may be blunted and the person is in a semi-dazed state punctuated by episodes of irritability or anger.

This initial phase usually ends by the time of the funeral which allows for the release of tears and feelings of despair which may have been bottled up in the grief stricken person.

Thereafter a very intense grief reaction ensues. The mourner weeps copiously, yearns for the lost person, and wishes he or she had been more helpful and considerate when the loved one was still alive. The mourner may also be preoccupied with memories of the dead person.

For a period of days, and perhaps weeks, the mourner remains somewhat depressed and apathetic, expresses a general sense of futility, and becomes socially withdrawn. During this period of despair the person is likely to suffer from insomnia, psychosomatic (psychologically induced) intestinal disorders, loss of appetite, restlessness, and general irritability. A tendency to deny the fact of death may persist for many weeks.

Gradually, mourners go through a psychological reorganization. There is the experience of hours, days, weeks, and even months that they will not consciously think about their loss and there will be no grief. They are able to return to work and resume daily activities after about two or three weeks, but may continue to withdraw from certain types of social affairs.

After a month or two even the most acute symptoms begin to subside but there may still be residual sadness, yearning, and attacks of acute grief during the ensuing months.

However, there will always be something that reminds the mourner of the loss. It might be a birthday, an anniversary, or even a seemingly unrelated event which might bring the thought forward into consciousness. A news story, television program, or discussion might suddenly thrust a person back into grief. But, the intensity of the grieving process becomes shorter in duration and gradually less intense. (Janis et al. pp. 179–80, 1969) from (Coleman, et al. 1988.)

The Stages of Grief

The work of Elizabeth Kubler-Ross and other experts have identified various stages of grief in death and dying. The Kubler-Ross Model identifies the five stages of grief as denial, anger, bargaining, depression, and acceptance (Kubler-Ross, 1969).

According to the National Organization for Victim Assistance (NOVA)the stages of grief for survivors of homicide victims also follows the Kubler-Ross Model and consists of five stages:[1]

1. **Denial:** shock, confusion, avoidance, refusal to participate in acknowledgments, crying, physical pain, weakness, nausea, sleep disturbances, loss of appetite.
2. **Protest or anger:** anger at self, loved one, God, the world, irritability, lack of concentration, frenzied activity, fatigue.

---

[1]Community Crisis Response Team Training Manual. NOVA, 1991.

3. **Despair:** urge to recover what was lost, slower thinking and actions, sorrow, agony, depression, hopelessness, and powerlessness.
4. **Detachment:** apathy, indifference, decreased socialization, disengagement from the world, absent spontaneity, and effect.
5. **Reconstruction of life:** spasms of grief, a loss is forever.

The important point to note is that grief is a natural process that seems to allow survivors to mourn their loss and then free themselves for life without the departed person.

However, an even more important point to note is that the grieving process, despite clinical interpretations and definitions of stages and references to "normal periods" is unique to each individual. People grieve in different ways and process that grief over different lengths of time. In fact, the grieving process is often the entire life span of the griever. There are cultural and religious differentiations as well as individual dynamics. Survivor behaviors vary considerably from one person to another and there is a wide range of normal responses in thinking, feeling, and behavior.

Psychological Reactions to Murder

Homicide creates an intense psychological turmoil due to the sudden and violent nature of the death. The surviving families of murder victims are suddenly thrust into the terrible reality of the permanent loss of a family member under horrifying circumstances. The initial shock is devastating and survivors find themselves totally unprepared for such a tragedy.

The unfairness of the loss is magnified by the knowledge that their loved one will never have the opportunity to experience his or her full potential in life; nor will the surviving family members be able to express to the victim how much they loved him or her. The grieving process under these circumstances is extremely more intense and is commonly accompanied by acute feelings of rage and anger as well as a sense of injustice and helplessness.

Psychological Reactions to Murdered Children

The death of a child under any circumstance is an extremely tragic and sad event. The death evokes strong emotions because it seems to go against the natural order of things. Children usually do not die before their parents and parents usually do not have to bury their children.

When a child is murdered, the parents are totally devastated. It is so unacceptable, inappropriate, and unnatural that parents cannot even begin to comprehend what has happened. The result is extreme psychological stress which is termed *parental bereavement.*

Research has shown that the grief of parents is much more intense than any other kind of grief. The sorrow and depression are long lasting; and the anger and bitterness are extremely difficult to resolve. The death of a child due to murder oftentimes invokes self-blame as the grieving parents begin to convince themselves that they may have prevented the murder or been able to protect the child.

In addition, the family may experience intense interpersonal difficulties which result in marital discord and separation. Detectives should be aware that parental bereavement and unresolved grief may require professional intervention. For further information I recommend contacting **Parents of Murdered Children Inc.** (see listing at the end of the chapter). This organization maintains a directory of local chapters and is an excellent resource for victim support services.

Psychological Reactions to the Murder of Police Officers

The murder of a police officer has a psychological effect on the entire department. Although death and homicide are part of the everyday work of many police officers, when a fellow officer is killed, "in the line of duty," the terrible reality of death suddenly strikes home.

Psychologically speaking, false feelings of invulnerability are suddenly shattered with the realization that "It could have been me." There may be fear and confusion on the part of fellow law enforcement officers as they go through the trauma of losing a co-worker. Families of police officers killed in the line of duty often find themselves isolated or abandoned by the police department after the funeral because they represent the "bad reminder" of law enforcement's ultimate sacrifice. It is very common to hear officers exclaim that "Every time I see that family (the slain officer's family) I see my own family and that gives me the creeps." The most common psychological defense and reaction thus is avoidance. This might work out fine for the co-worker, but what about the surviving police officer's family?

The important point to note here is that men and women in police service are certainly not immune from death and the grief process. Homicide detectives should be aware of the impact upon police survivors and be prepared to assist them through the department's resources as well intervention services.

An excellent national organization which was formed to assist police survivors and provide emotional care for the deceased officer's family is **Concerns of Police Survivors Cops, Inc.** (see listing at the end of the chapter).

Notifications of Death by the Homicide Detective

Homicide detectives become an integral part of the family's grieving process. How detectives make the notification of death, the information they provide to the family regarding the incident, and what assistance and support they offer the family have been identified by experts in the field of grief therapy as crucial to the eventual healing process. Most experts agree that death notifications should not be made by telephone unless there is no other alternative.

The compassionate expression of condolences coupled with dignity and respect are necessary components of a proper notification. This empathic consideration will ultimately assist survivors in coping with their great loss.

Notifications of death are extremely difficult for both survivors and law enforcement personnel. Practically speaking, there isn't really a "good" way to notify survivors that a loved one has been murdered.

I recommend that death notifications in homicide cases should be made by at least two detectives. The case officer can communicate the information while the other detective carefully observes the reactions of the survivors.

Individuals may react to death in a violent manner, or they may suffer physical reactions which require emergency first aid. Needless to say, the second officer can assist as necessary.

There may be circumstances which require detectives to notify two or more survivors separately in order to obtain investigative information; or, there may be an indication that a family member is involved or suspect in the homicide.

In either event, it is crucial that detectives be prepared to obtain and document these significant interviews.

I recommend that detectives have a uniform officer accompany them when making an official death notification. The presence of an officer in uniform can have a calming effect which will prevent confusion and readily identify those making the notification as police officials.

In addition, detectives may wish to consider the assistance of a crisis counselor when making a notification of death. The crisis counselor may often choose to remain behind with the family after the detectives have left and provide support services to the survivors.

Recommendations and Guidelines for Effecting Proper Death Notifications to Surviving Family Members

The following recommendations and guidelines are based upon my personal experience in making death notifications as well as information from *Revised Homicide and Sudden Death Survivor Guidelines* established by the Attorney General of the State of New Jersey, The National Organization for Victim Assistance (NOVA), *Community Crisis Response Team Training Manual,* and research developed by The National Victim Center.

☐ Notification should be made in person by the assigned detective as soon as possible after identity has been established. *Under no circumstances should the media be advised of an identification prior to next of kin.*

☐ Try to assure that the appropriate closest adult relative receives notification first.

☐ Get as much information about the person(s) to be notified as possible. Medical information, i.e., heart condition, etc. of the person to be notified is particularly important, if available.

☐ Identify yourself as the assigned detective and present your credentials. Request permission to enter their home.

☐ Encourage survivors to sit and sit down with them when you talk to them.

☐ Make sure there are no dangerous objects nearby. This includes scissors, knives, heavy objects, etc.

☐ The actual notification of death should be made simply and directly, i.e., "I have some bad news for you. Your son is dead." Tell the surviving family that you are sorry for their loss and express to them your condolences in a professional and empathic manner.

☐ Answer all questions tactfully and honestly *without jeopardizing the criminal investigation.*

☐ Be prepared to explain what happened, when it happened, where it happened, and how it happened. Be prepared to present confirming evidence and the source of positive identification in a clear and convincing fashion in the face of denial.

☐ After the survivors have recovered from the initial shock, explain that you need to ask certain informational questions about the deceased in order to initiate the investigation and that you will try to keep these questions as brief as possible.

☐ The detective should then explain that it will be necessary for a family member to identify the deceased. Allow the family to choose who will make the identification.

☐ Transport or arrange for their transportation to and from the hospital or morgue.

☐ Inform the survivors that a medicolegal autopsy is required to establish the exact cause of death.

☐ Focus on the immediate needs of the survivors. Offer to assist them in notifying and contacting others, i.e., "Is there someone I can call to see if they could come over now?"

☐ Make sure that the survivors are not left alone. Have an officer or crisis worker remain pending the arrival of some designated friend or relative.

☐ Explain that you will be available for any of their questions and provide them with your business card and office telephone number.

☐ Offer information on Crime Victims Services by providing them with the telephone number(s). See listing in article.

☐ If the survivor is at her or his place of employment, the notifying officers should proceed there, contact the survivor's supervisor, and request to speak privately with the survivor so proper notification can be made.

☐ In some instances the survivors of sudden and violent death are not immediately available. In these circumstances the officers should make inquiries of neighbors to ascertain when the family is expected home. Explain that there has been a medical emergency involving the deceased and request the neighbor to contact them if the survivors return home.

☐ The officers should request that the neighbor not provide the next of kin with any information regarding the medical emergency until the officers contact them.

☐ If surviving family members do not reside within the jurisdiction responsible for investigating the death, or within a reasonable distance of that jurisdiction, the detective should contact the appropriate law enforcement agency which covers the residence of the family. That agency should be requested to make an in person notification to the surviving family and provide the family with the investigating officer's name, agency, and telephone number.

Providing Information to the Surviving Family

There is some difference of opinion on what information can and should be released to the surviving family in murder investigations. If there is a possibility that some member of the family is involved in the homicide then obviously any disclosure of investigative information would jeopardize the investigation.

However, in most instances the surviving family members are not suspects and they express a need to know certain details. The most immediate concern of survivors is the physical injury that was inflicted upon the victim and the varying degrees of trauma associated with the murder. "How was the victim killed?", "Did he or she suffer?", "What did the killer do to the victim?", and "Who did it?" (if known). NOVA identifies specific situational factors that affect the survivor's trauma such as the relationship of the survivor to the murder victim and the occurrence of significant events.

In circumstances where survivors have witnessed the event or there was a relationship to the assailant, there is an added grief. Certain types of murder and how the victim was killed invoke greater anguish. For instance, murders accompanied by sexual assault, torture, and/or mutilation can be psychologically overwhelming to survivors as they imagine what degradation and suffering the victim must have endured.

The determination of what information and how much detail is provided to the surviving family is unique to each case.

The homicide investigator is in the best position to make this determination based upon the nature of that case and the ability of the family to process the information.

In the early stages of the inquiry there is a tactical and strategic rationale in withholding certain information known only by the police and the murderer.

The detective should advise the family accordingly so that they understand why the police do not provide them with all the details. Most persons will accept this explanation early on into the investigation.

However, what should be noted is that as the case progresses the family should be provided with as much information as possible. If an arrest is effected the family should be notified immediately before they learn of it through the media. Once an arrest has been effected, the family should be prepared for the court process.

Guiding the Surviving Family Through the Criminal Justice System

The criminal justice system impacts heavily upon the surviving family. Although the law enforcement community is fully aware of the inequities of the criminal justice system, most people are not prepared for a system that punishes the innocent by protecting the guilty.

According to the research conducted by Crime Victims Research and Treatment Center of the Medical University of South Carolina, "six out of ten family members (56%) thought that the criminal justice system treated the defendant better than it treated them, and more than six out of ten (61%) said that they felt mostly or totally helpless while the case was in progress." (*The Impact of Homicide on Surviving Family Members*, August 1, 1990.)

Many survivors experience outrage as the homicide case progresses through a system which bends over backwards to be fair to defendants while completely ignoring the victim. While judges and attorneys ponder endlessly over the technical issues of the case and the rights of the accused, the surviving family is oftentimes left completely out of the process which adds to their feelings of helplessness and frustration.

There may be legal delays and postponements that last for months and even years. The family may be barred from the courtroom so as not to prejudice the jury against the defendant. Or, the victim may be maligned by the defense in order to minimize the significance of the murder.

The responsibility to guide the family through this criminal justice process falls on the shoulders of the homicide detective who must act as an advocate for them.

Detectives should warn the family that the defense may attempt to contact them. Advise them that there is no obligation to speak to any representative of the defense. Provide the family with the telephone number and name of the State's Attorney assigned to their case. Put the family in touch with a victim's rights organization and encourage them to ask questions. I personally recommend *The Stephanie Roper Committee and Foundation*, 14804 Pratt Street #1, Upper Marlboro, Maryland 20772; telephone number (301) 952-0063.

In April, 1982, 22-year-old Stephanie Roper was abducted by two offenders who brutally raped, sodomized, tortured, and murdered her over a period of hours. Her two assailants were arrested, brought to trial, and convicted. However, the murderers received sentences which would have permitted them parole eligibility in less than twelve years. There was a public outcry. The Ropers, who thought that their family would receive justice from the courts expected that the offenders would

Figure 11.1.   The author consoling the family members at the scene of the homicide. Family members who arrive at the scene of the murder oftentimes express a desire to see their loved one. This can be discouraged by advising them that it would be better to remember their loved one as they were in life. The author is consoling and guiding the mother of the victim away from the crime scene as he provides the family with the necessary details of the event that are required in a death notification.

be punished for what they had done to Stephanie. They were devastated to learn that the offenders had more rights then an innocent victim. They decided to do something about the criminal justice system to ensure that the victim's rights and the survivors would be empowered.

The Ropers effectively channeled their grief and dedicated their resources to force the criminal justice system to become more responsive to victims and victim's rights.

Today, *The Stephanie Roper Committee and Foundation* named after their daughter Stephanie, has become one of the nation's most effective voices for victims and citizens.

The Committee and Foundation:

1   Provides support and encouragement to victims of crime during court proceedings.
2   Ensures that the legal rights of victims are maintained.
3   Facilitates healing and resolution for the secondary victims and survivors through support group services.
4   Legislative advocacy.

Conclusion

I included this chapter in the text based upon my strong belief in victim's rights and the rights of the surviving family to see that justice is done. In my professional opinion, as a homicide consultant, investigators should avail themselves of the information within this chapter and be cognizant of their duties and responsibilities to the survivors.

Victim's Assistance Organizations

Changing Lives
The Center for Crime Victims
 and Survivors, Inc.
Post Office Box 6201
Clearwater, Florida 34618   Tel.#(813) 535-1114

Concerns of Police Survivors
C.O.P.S.
9423-A Marlboro Pike   Tel. #(301) 599-0445
Upper Marlboro, Maryland 20772   Fax #(301) 500-0918

Crime Victims Research and
 Treatment Center
Medical University of South Carolina
171 Ashley Avenue   Tel. #(803) 792-2945
Charleston, South Carolina 22425   Fax #(803) 792-3388

Justice for Murder Victims   Tel. #(415) 905-6419

National Victims Center
2111 Wilson Boulevard
Suite 300   Tel. #(703) 276-2880
Arlington, Virginia 22201   Fax #(703) 276-2889

National Organization for Victim
Assistance (N.O.V.A.)
1757 Park Road, N.W.   Tel. #(202) 232-6682
Washington, D.C. 20010   Fax #(202) 462-2255

Parents of Murdered Children
& Other Survivors of Homicide Victims
100 East 8th Street, B-41   Tel. #(513) 727-5683
Cincinnati, Ohio 45202   Fax #(513) 721-5685

The Stephanie Roper Committee, Inc.
14804 Pratt Street #1
Upper Marlboro, Maryland 20772

Tel. #(301) 952-0063
Fax #(301) 952-2319

Selected Reading

American Psychiatric Association. (1987) *Diagnostic and Statistical Manual of Mental Disorders,* 3rd ed., rev. Washington, D.C.

Carson, Robert C., Butcher, James N., Coleman, James C. *Abnormal Psychology and Modern Life.* 8th ed. Illinois: Scott Foresman and Company, 1988, p. 154.

Geberth, Vernon J. "Secondary Victims of Homicide." Illinois: *Law and Order Magazine,* Vol. 40, No. 9, September, 1992.

Geberth, Vernon J. "A Personal Perspective Concerning Homicide Investigation." *International Journal of Offender Therapy and Comparative Criminology.* New York, Vol. 39, No. 1, Spring, 1995.

Harris, Jerry, Ph.D., Sprang, Ginny, and Komsak, Karen. This Could Never Happen to Me: A Handbook for Families of Murder Victims and People Who Assist Them. A Project of the Mental Health Association of Tarrant County. Fort Worth, Texas. 1986.

Kilpatrick, Dean G. et. al. "The Impact of Homicide on Surviving Family Members." Crime Victims Research and Treatment Center, Department of Psychiatry and Behavioral Sciences, Medical University of South Carolina.

Kubler-Ross, Elisabeth. *On Death And Dying New York*: Collier Books. MacMillan Publishing Company, 1969.

NOVA, 5. Death and Dying. Community Crisis Response Team Training Manual. Washington, D.C. National Organization for Victim Assistance, 1991.

NOVA Bulletin, "Survivors of Homicide Victims." Network Information Bulletin. Washington, D.C. National Organization for Victim Assistance. Vol. 2, Number 3, October, 1985.

Rando, Therese A. *Parental Loss of a Child.* Illinois: Research Press Company, 1986.

Redmond, Lula M. Surviving: When Someone You Love Was Murdered. Florida: Psychological Consultation and Education Services, 1989.

Sawyer, Susan F. Support Services to Surviving Families of Line-of-Duty Death, Maryland: Concerns of Police Survivors C.O.P.S., 1990.

Working Group on the Development of Homicide and Sudden Death Survivor Guidelines. (Stephen G. Raymond, Chairperson). Revised — Homicide And Sudden Death Survivor Guidelines. Report to the Attorney General, New Jersey, April 18, 1986.

Modes of Death   12

From an investigative point of view, it is imperative that the detective have a practical understanding of the manner, means, and mode of several kinds of death. (See Chapter 18, "Purpose of the Autopsy.") During the course of basic death investigations, the investigator will be confronted by various situations and types of death. Since this chapter cannot conceivably cover all of the possibilities involved, it will address the more common methods of death:

Gunshot and firearm wounds   Poisons
Cutting wounds   Asphyxia deaths
Stabbing wounds   Autoerotic deaths
Blunt force injuries   Arson and fire deaths

In order to provide only the basic knowledge necessary to conduct an intelligent investigation, I have purposely avoided a technical and in-depth discussion of the pathology of wounds, injuries, and forms of death.

Gunshot Wounds

Gunshot wounds may resemble stab wounds in external appearance. However, there are certain physical characteristics of gunshot wounds that will assist the investigator in differentiating stab wounds from wounds caused by firearms. In addition, certain wounds will provide the investigator with a clue to the circumstances under which they occurred.

Figure 12.1.   **CLOSE SHOT — GREATER DISTANCE.** Unburned powder grains but no smoke deposits in the zone of blackening. (Reprinted from A. Svensson, O. Wendel, and B. A. J. Fisher, *Techniques of Crime Scene Investigation,* 3rd ed., New York: Elsevier North Holland, Inc., 1981.)

In order to appreciate the nature of gunshot wounds, one must first understand what takes place as a bullet is fired from a weapon and what happens to the body as this projectile or bullet strikes it.

Basically, when a firearm is discharged, four things occur:

1. Fire or flame is emitted from the barrel.
2. Smoke then follows this flame.
3. The bullet emerges from the barrel.
4. Additional smoke and grains of both burned and unburned gunpowder follow the bullet out of the barrel.

As this material exits the barrel, it spreads out like a funnel. As the distance from the barrel increases, the density of the pattern decreases, i.e., the flame doesn't go very far, the smoke goes a little further, the powder grains travel different distances depending upon individual factors, and the bullet travels the greatest distance of all.

Depending on the material present on the body or clothing, and the degree of density, it *may* be possible to determine the distance involved. To make this determination, it is necessary to conduct test firings with similar ammunition.

The Projectile Striking the Body

There are two basic types of wounds.

1. The entrance wound
   a. Generally smaller than an exit wound.

Figure 12.2. **ENTRANCE WOUND.** This was taken at the crime scene. Notice the neat round hole with smudging around the wound.

    b. Typically round, neat hole with an abrasion collar, and a gray or black ring around the edges.

    c. Comparatively small amounts of blood.

  2. The exit wound

    a. Generally larger than an entrance wound.

    b. Ragged and torn in appearance, shreds of tissue extruding.

    c. Generally a greater escape of blood than entrance wounds and possible profuse bleeding.

The Nature and Extent of Gunshot Wounds

There are a number of factors that will affect the characteristics of the wound and change its appearance. For example,

The distance	Passage through clothing
Ricocheting	The type of weapon
Type of ammunition used	The part of the body affected
Passage through body	

The homicide investigator should have a working knowledge of the pathology of wounds and the effect of a firearms discharge on the

Figure 12.3. **ENTRANCE WOUND.** Observe the entrance wound of the bullet. Note the smudging and powder of collar around the wound.

Figure 12.4. **EXIT WOUND.** This type of wound is usually larger than the entrance wound. It is jagged and torn in appearance.

human body. Human skin is very elastic and resistant. When a projectile or bullet strikes the skin, it causes an indentation. As the bullet perforates the skin and bores through, it causes a circular perforation and an *abrasion collar*, which is caused by the damage to the skin as a result of the friction between the bullet and the stretched, indented skin. In addition to this perforation and abrasion collar, there will be a blackening effect around the wound's edges caused by the discharge of

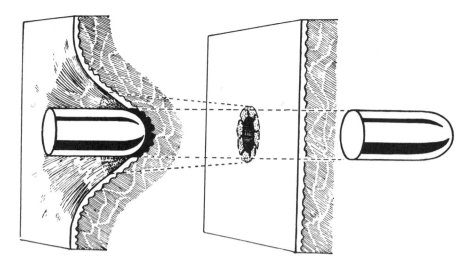

Figure 12.5.   **DIAGRAM OF A BULLET PENETRATING THE SKIN.** The skin is pressed inward, stretched, and perforated in the stretched condition, after which it returns to its original position. The entry opening is smaller than the diameter of the bullet. Immediately around the opening is the contusion ring, since the bullet rubs against this part of the skin and scrapes off the external layer of epithelial cells. (Reprinted from A. Svensson, O. Wendel, and B. A. J. Fisher, *Techniques of Crime Scene Investigation,* 3rd ed., New York: Elsevier North Holland, Inc., 1981.)

lubricants, smoke particles, and grime from the barrel of the weapon onto the bullet. The skin actually wipes this residue off the bullet as the bullet enters the tissue.

The skin which has been stretched by the bullet then returns to its normal or former position. This will make the wound appear smaller than the projectile which has passed through it. The resistance of the skin is evidenced by the fact that many times a bullet will go clear through the body only to be stopped by the skin on the opposite side.

A bullet usually travels in a straight line as it passes through the soft tissue of the body. However, if the bullet hits bones, its direction is unpredictable and will be determined by the velocity of the bullet, the size and shape of the bone, and the angle at which it strikes the bone. In some instances the bone may be shattered, creating additional projectiles of bone fragments which cause even further tissue destruction. The exit wound will be both large and ragged as this impacted tissue and bullet push their way through.

As mentioned above, a bullet hitting a bone may deflect. Often a bullet fired into the chest cavity or skull will be deflected because of angle, and, instead of entering straight into the body, may travel under the skin, sometimes encircling the entire chest or head of the victim.

Figure 12.6. **EXAMPLE OF GUNSHOT RESIDUE DISTRIBUTION.** This revolver discharge demonstrates how gunshot residue particles fall on a shooter's hand during firing. The crime lab can perform analysis on these particles if collected in an appropriate fashion by the aware investigator. Also note the cloud of discharge materials following the bullet from the muzzle. This soot and particles can be detected on clothing and/or skin and muzzle/bullet impact site distance can be estimated from the spread of these materials. (Photograph courtesy of the Federal Bureau of Investigation.)

Smudging or Smoke

a. Smoke and soot deposited around the wound.
b. Dirty and grimy appearance.
c. Is easily wiped off the skin.
d. Indicates that the gun was held close to the victim, but was not in actual contact.
e. Clothes should be held for examination.

Searing

A yellow singeing effect due to the discharge of flame from the muzzle.

Tattooing or Stippling

a. Pinpoint hemorrhages due to the discharge of burned powder.
b. Unburned powder or pieces of metal of the bullet from the blast are driven into the skin.
c. Unlike "smudging," cannot be wiped off the skin.

Figure 12.7. **RECOVERY OF A BULLET DURING AN AUTOPSY.** Observe the pathologist, recovering the bullet that has come to rest subcutaneously in the victim's back. The bullet entered the chest area, traveled through the ribs, heart, and lungs; it was stopped by the skin on the opposite side.

Figure 12.8. **TATTOOING OR STIPPLING.** The bullet entrance wound is surrounded by pinpoint hemorrhages due to the discharge of burned powder and fragments, which have been driven into the skin. This is a result of a "close shot". (Courtesy of William K. Brinkhous, Investigator, North Carolina Office of the Chief Medical Examiner, Chapel Hill, North Carolina.)

Figure 12.9.   TATTOOING AND NEAR CONTACT WOUND. A near-contact type wound with a clustered tattooing around the entrance wound (results from the gun's muzzle pressed directly to the victim's chest). The wound is a perforating type with the bullet exiting the victim's back. The muzzle blast caused the tattooing.

Reentry

If the bullet has already passed through another part of the body and reenters, an irregular wound will result which may appear as an exit perforation.

Ricocheting

Similarly, if a bullet has struck another object before entering the body, the entry wound will be irregular.

Shotgun Wounds

The shotgun, specifically the 12-gauge, is the most common weapon confronting law enforcement, and it is the most deadly.

Figure 12.10. **EFFECT OF HIGH VELOCITY AMMUNITION.** This woman was hit in the face at close range with a bullet from a 30.06 rifle.

1. Massive tissue destruction.
2. Wadding will usually be embedded in the wound if the shotgun is fired within ten feet of the victim.
3. Wadding can provide the investigator with (1) the type of shot, (2) the gauge of the gun, and (3) possible evidence to identify the gun used.

Contact Wounds

1. Muzzle of gun is held directly against the skin at discharge.
2. Shape is result of penetration of bullet and escape of flame and expanding gases.
3. The perforation will be larger than the diameter of the bullet.
4. Wound is dirty looking.
5. Skin edges are ragged and torn.
6. Charring of skin tissue due to tremendous heat from muzzle blast.
7. Particularly large and marked tissue destruction when the contact wound is in the head or over bones. There will be a charac-

Figure 12.11. SHOTGUN ENTRANCE WOUND TO THE CHEST.

Figure 12.12. INTERNAL VIEW OF THE PRECEDING WOUND TO CHEST AREA.

Figure 12.13.   **CONTACT SHOT.** The weapon is pressed against the head or the body; consequently, gases from the explosion expand between the skin and the bone producing a bursting effect and a ragged entrance wound. (Reprinted from A. Svensson, O. Wendel, and B. A. J. Fisher, *Techniques of Crime Scene Investigation,* 3rd ed., New York: Elsevier North Holland, Inc., 1981.)

Figure 12.14.   **CONTACT WOUND TO THE SIDE OF THE HEAD.**

teristic cross-shaped or star-shaped wound, sometimes referred to as stellate. Due to the force of the explosion and the gases against the skull there is an expansion under the scalp, producing a ragged and torn wound that is much larger than an exit wound.

Figure 12.15. **MUZZLE STAMP.** Contact gunshot wound to neck under chin demonstrating muzzle/slide/slide guide rod impression. (Courtesy of Westchester County Medical Examiner's Office.)

It should be noted that the contact wound is the exception to the general configuration of entrance and exit wounds.

In some instances, the muzzle of the gun may be in contact with the skin and the underlying organs allow for the expansion of gases. The result will be a *muzzle stamp* or *brand* whereby the muzzle of the gun causes an abrasion on the body outlining the muzzle of the barrel and front sight. In this situation the wound will not be ragged but clean and round, because the charring and destruction takes place under the skin. This is the exception in contact wounds.

Bullet Track

The *bullet track* is the path of the bullet or projectile as it passes through the body. In certain instances the on-scene examination may readily indicate the direction of fire if the classic entrance/exit wounds are present. The bullet track is usually straight but may be bent, changed, or erratic, depending on any number of factors. The most common

Figure 12.16. **INTERNAL VIEW OF THE SKULL SHOWING THREE BULLETS.** Two bullets had become lodged in the barrel of the revolver. When the third bullet was fired, all three projectiles entered the skull producing a single entrance wound with three bullets. (Courtesy of Detective James M. Yoghourtjiam, Crime Scene Investigator, Racine, Wisconsin Police Department.)

Figure 12.17. **RECOVERED PROJECTILES.** Photo of the three recovered projectiles (labeled). (Courtesy of Detective James M. Yoghourtjiam, Crime Scene Investigator, Racine, Wisconsin Police Department.)

cause for change of track is when the bullet or projectile has hit or been deflected by bone. However, keep in mind that outer garments may deflect the path of the bullet, or the wounded person may have fallen and been hit again. Other factors that may affect bullet tracks are:

1. The velocity of the bullet (high or low), which will determine the direction of track.

A

B

Figure 12.18.   **BULLET TRACK.** Observe the skull cavity. (A) Two separate probes inserted into the entrance wounds of the projectile. (B) The direction of the bullet through the brain. Both (A) and (B) indicate the bullet track of the projectile. The pathologist will be able to make a determination of the direction and travel based on this procedure.

Figure 12.19. **LOCATING A LODGED BULLET.** This x-ray shows the bullet lodged in the chest cavity of the male victim.

2. The type of bullet (lead or copper jacket), which will determine how far the projectile traveled.
3. The ricochet factor — increasing size and number of projectiles — which can give a wrong impression as to size and number of wounds.

Remember to note your observations, but be prepared to reevaluate your thinking in light of additional information.

The bullet track is important in ascertaining the direction of fire. However, this determination must be made by the forensic pathologist, who can properly evaluate entrance and exit wounds through both microscopic and physiological methods conducted during the autopsy.

Cutting Wounds

An incision or cut-type wound is caused by a sharp instrument or weapon and is generally longer than it is deep. The cut or incised wound is deepest where the weapon was first applied to the skin. If the cutting

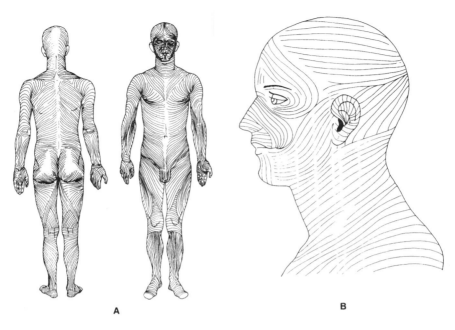

A   **B**

Figure 12.20.   **LINES OF CLEAVAGE.** (A) Body. (B) Head.

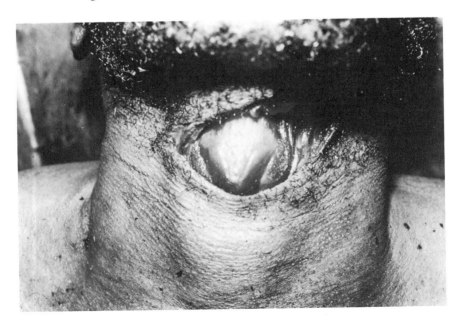

Figure 12.21.   **INCISED WOUND: NECK.** (Courtesy of Dr. Dominick J. DiMaio, Former Chief Medical Examiner, City of New York.)

Figure 12.22. **SLASHING OF THE THROAT IN SEXUAL ASSAULT.** The victim's throat was cut by her assailant during a sexual assault destroying her larynx preventing her from crying out for help. (Courtesy of Detective Alan Patton, Grand Prairie, Texas Police Department.)

is done parallel to the lines of cleavage, the edges of the wound will remain together. If the cutting is across the lines of cleavage, the wound will be gaping or open.

The incised wound usually involves the skin and underlying tissue, but may be deep enough to slice bones or organs. It is difficult to determine whether or not cutting wounds are antemortem or postmortem; therefore, only the pathologist should attempt to make this determination.

Characteristics of cutting wounds are:

Clean and sharp edges
Minimum bruising
Longer than deep
No bridging of skin
Bleeds freely

It should be noted that it is extremely difficult to make any determination of the type of instrument or weapon used.

Figure 12.23.   **STABBING WOUNDS.** The victim's back shows a series of deep stabbing wounds received during a street fight.

Stabbing Wounds

Stabbing wounds are piercing wounds which may extend through the tissue and bone into the vital organs. They are caused by relatively sharp pointed instruments such as knives, screwdrivers, ice picks, daggers, scissors, or pieces of glass.

Stab wounds vary according to the type of weapon employed and how it was used in the attack, (thrust, pulled out, twisted, etc.) The principle involving lines of cleavage is also applicable to stab wounds. The shape of the stab wound *may* indicate what type of weapon or blade was used. However, like a bullet wound, the stab wound will be smaller than the blade which caused it due to the elasticity of the skin. The type of wound is, therefore, determined by estimates of minimum and maximum size. Sometimes the knife hilt may bruise the skin and leave an identifiable mark.

Characteristics of stabbing wounds are:

Deeper than wide
Possible damage to vital organs beneath skin and bone
Internal bleeding with little or no external blood

Figure 12.24. **DEFENSE WOUNDS TO THE HAND.** (Courtesy of Dr. Dominick J. DiMaio, Former Chief Medical Examiner, City of New York.)

May indicate type of weapon used

The pathologist will examine the wound track and can determine the position of the deceased when he or she was stabbed. In addition, if the victim fought with the assailant, there will be evidence of *defense wounds* on the hands and arms and between the fingers. Many times, the victim will have grabbed the knife only to have it pulled away by the assailant. This will leave a deep gash in the palm or on the undersurface of the fingers.

The type of weapon, the direction of injury, and the position of the victim are all factors which can be ascertained by a careful examination of the stab wound. The clothing of the victim should always be obtained for later inspection to determine the position of the deceased during the attack and to correlate injuries to the body with tears or rips in the clothing.

Blunt Force Injuries

Blunt force injuries are evident by outward signs such as lacerations and bruising. However, lack of external injuries does not mean that blunt

Figure 12.25.   **LACERATION OF SCALP FROM BLADED INSTRUMENT.** (Courtesy of
Detective Larry Petersen, King County Washington Police Department.)

force was not applied. In many instances, internal damage to organs
occurs without any external sign of violence.

Lacerations

A laceration is a tear in the tissue which may be external (on the skin)
or internal (such as a torn spleen). The torn edges of the skin will be
ragged and bruised, and bridges of connective tissue may be stretched
across the gap.

Chopping Wounds

These wounds are caused by a heavy object which has an edge, e.g., an axe.
A wound produced by an axe will not only cut into the skin, but will also
cause contusions and structural damage to the body parts beneath. There
will be a deep gaping wound, with contusions and structural damage.

Blunt force injuries are usually directed at the head of the victim.
The evidence of injury to the head is evident in the lacerations of the
scalp or the blackening of the eyes. However, a severe injury to the head

Figure 12.26. **DEPRESSED SKULL WITH MULTIPLE CONTUSIONS — CHOPPING-TYPE WOUND.** The weapon here was an axe. (Courtesy of Dr. Dominick J. DiMaio, Former Chief Medical Examiner, City of New York.)

need not be accompanied by evidence of laceration or eye trauma. A person may receive a blow to the head and appear to be all right, only to die later as a result of an internal hemorrhage.

Injuries to the brain in the back of the head are more likely to be fatal than injuries to the brain in the front part of the skull. This information must be well known in the underworld, since in many execution-type murders the victim is found face down and shot through the back of the head.

Blunt force injuries to abdominopelvic cavity, which contains many organs, can cause severe internal bleeding and death. The most common injury within this area is a torn spleen. However, damage to the liver, intestines, and bladder is relatively easy to cause when blunt force is directed to the body.

Bone injuries also result from the use of blunt force. In a fractured skull, the direction of the cracks or fractures may make it possible to determine the direction of force.

Poisons

Practically speaking, murder by poisoning is extremely rare. Investigators are usually confronted with cases in which the victim has commit-

Figure 12.27. **PATTERN INJURY.** A blunt force injury to the head. Notice how the pattern of the weapon matches that of the wound. (Courtesy of Dr. Dominick J. DiMaio, Former Chief Medical Examiner, City of New York.)

ted suicide by taking an overdose of pills or ingesting something dangerous in order to cause death. Other cases of poisoning are usually accidental and involve narcotic overdoses or the inadvertent taking of the wrong medication.

The examination at the scene and the intelligent questioning of witnesses, members of the family, and others is of paramount importance in determining whether the mode of death was a homicide, suicide, or accident.

Figure 12.28. **THE INTERNAL EFFECT OF A BLUNT FORCE INJURY TO THE SKULL.** (Courtesy of Dr. Dominick J. DiMaio, Former Chief Medical Examiner, City of New York.)

Figure 12.29. **OVERDOSE — SECONAL STAINS ON THE LIPS.** (Courtesy of Dr. Dominick J. DiMaio, Former Chief Medical Examiner, City of New York.)

Many times, the initial investigation at the scene will reveal the presence of a suspected material or fluid. This material should be retrieved by the detective for later toxicological analysis. Any glasses, cups, or other containers which the deceased may have been drinking from, as well as a sample of the fluid or material believed to have been ingested by the deceased, must also be obtained. Any liquid evidence should be placed in a sterile container, sealed, and delivered to the medical examiner/coroner. Any residue or solid material should be placed in a clean paper bag for similar disposition.

In certain cases, it will be obvious to the police that the death was due to the introduction of some poisonous substance. Drug overdoses are the most common. Any drug paraphernalia or residue found at the scene, including hypodermic needles or syringes, should be collected and forwarded to the pathologist. It is important to secure any needles in order to prevent injury or infection by cutting oneself. A cork placed on the end of the needle will be sufficient to prevent the needle point from scratching or cutting anyone during transportation.

In some instances, a corrosion or burning around the mouth may be present. This usually indicates the consumption of some sort of caustic substance. If a person is desperate, as are most suicides, he or she may ingest a corrosive chemical such as lye or one of the common household cleaners. However, any number of chemicals or substances can be introduced into the human body to cause death. The investigator must be alert to the presence of any material found near the body.

The most important fact to keep in mind is that the scene examination and investigation into the events leading to the death must be thorough and complete. The medicolegal autopsy will determine the type and quantity of the poisonous substance involved. However, determination of the mode of death will be based on the police investigation at the scene.

Deaths by Asphyxia

Death by asphyxia can occur through any number of circumstances. The most common, however, are:

Strangulation (manual or ligature)
Hanging
Drowning
Inhalation of poison gases
Suffocation

Figure 12.30. **ASPHYXIATION: STRANGULATION.** Observe the marks on the throat of the victim, which were caused by the fingernails of the assailant as he choked her.

Figure 12.31. **HEMORRHAGE IN EYES FROM MANUAL STRANGULATION.** (Courtesy of Dr. Dominick J. DiMaio, Former Chief Medical Examiner, City of New York.)

In fact, any death in which air is cut off from the victim is considered to be asphyxial in nature. This would also include those which have been classified as *sexual asphyxia* and *autoerotic deaths*, which are discussed later in this chapter.

Strangulation

Direct strangulation involves the choking of a person, either manually (by the hands) or mechanically (using a ligature). However, strangulation can also occur through such means as Judo moves, use of forearms or legs, as in yoking, and use of instruments employed in combat to restrict air flow or to render an assailant unconscious by cutting off the supply of oxygen to the body.

In ligature-type homicides, any number of instruments can be employed, such as ropes, wires, pieces of clothing, etc. Any type of material or action which causes a person to stop breathing is considered to be asphyxial.

A cord, wire, or similar instrument will leave an obvious groove on the victim's throat which resembles the mark on a hanging victim. The pathologist can often tell the investigator whether or not the marks left on the throat by the assailant's fingernails during the attack took place from the rear or the front of the victim.

Strangulation homicides will cause damage to the interior structures of the neck, throat, and larynx, which will be evident to the forensic pathologist who performs the autopsy.

The investigator can make certain observations at the scene which may enable him or her to determine the manner of death. For example:

1. The presence of new abrasions, bruises, or fingernail marks on the throat of the victim may indicate a strangulation.
2. The presence of *petechial hemorrhages* (minute blood clots which appear as small red dots) in the *conjunctivae* (the mucous membrane lining the inner surface of the eyelids) are presumptive evidence of strangulation.
3. Evidence of trauma to the tongue. Many times persons who are asphyxiated will bite their tongue.

Hanging

Incidents of hanging are usually suicidal or accidental, as in autoerotic deaths. However, the investigator must be alert to incidents in which a hanging may have been purposely staged in order to cover up another crime, thereby making a homicide appear to be suicide.

Figure 12.32.   **HANGING CASE.** Clothesline ligature used. Notice the marks of ligature on the neck of the victim. (Courtesy of Dr. Dominick J. DiMaio, Former Chief Medical Examiner, City of New York.)

Figure 12.33.   **SUICIDE BY HANGING.** Notice the groove mark on the neck. (Courtesy of Dr. Dominick J. DiMaio, Former Chief Medical Examiner, City of New York.)

A   **B**

Figure 12.34.   **REMOVING A NOOSE FROM THE NECK OF A BODY.** The knots should not be disturbed or loosened. (A) A fixed noose should be cut off and the ends immediately bound together. (B) With a running, the position of the knot on the standard part is fixed, after which the noose is cut off. If the noose consists of a number of parts, they should be cut and the ends bound together. (Reprinted from A. Svensson, O. Wendel, and B. A. J. Fisher, *Techniques of Crime Scene Investigation,* 3rd ed., New York: Elsevier North Holland, Inc., 1981.)

Hanging deaths must be thoroughly investigated by both the detective and the medical examiner/coroner. Practically speaking, the homicide investigator should be aware of certain characteristics of hanging deaths:

1. A body need not be completely suspended in order to suffer asphyxia. If a suicide has fastened a rope, noose, or other type of material around the neck and attached the other end to a door-knob, towel rack, or other hook-type object, and then allowed his or her throat to be contracted; asphyxia will take place, whether or not other portions of the body are in contact with the floor. A majority of the body weight supported by the ligature will effect the required result.

2. If the material used is small or ropelike, there will be a deep groove across the neck, usually high up.

3. Minute areas of bleeding due to the rupture of small blood vessels in the skin will cause small black-and-blue marks to appear within the area of the groove line. This type of rupture indicates that the person was alive when the hanging took place.

4. Persons who have died as a result of asphyxia may expel urine or feces.

Figure 12.35. **ASPHYXIA DUE TO DROWNING.** The white frothy fluid in the mouth and nostrils of the deceased, hemorrhagic edema fluid, is common in drowning victims.

5. Postmortem lividity will be pronounced in the head, above the ligature, and in the arms and lower legs due to gravity.

It should be noted that if the body is obviously dead, and there is no need for immediate lifesaving methods to be employed, nothing should be touched, handled, or otherwise disturbed until the body and scene have been photographed. If the material around the neck must be removed, the knot or tie should not be touched. Instead, the material should be cut in an area which does not disturb the knot. When the noose is cut, the ends should be tied together with string to show the original position.

Actually, this procedure is usually performed by the pathologist who performs the autopsy. There is no need to remove the noose from the dead person at the scene unless there is the possibility that the victim is still alive.

Drowning

This type of asphyxia is the direct result of liquid entering the breathing passages, preventing air from going to the lungs. Practically speaking, a person need not be submerged to drown. As long as the mouth and nose are submerged in any type of liquid, drowning will occur.

I remember one case in which a *crew* (violent urban youth gang) had forced their way into the victim's apartment. They proceeded to torture the man and then tied his hands and feet together. He was then carried

Figure 12.36.   "FLOATERS." (Top) Bloated body of a floater, which shows the effect of submersion and drowning asphyxia. (Bottom) Close-up of the same floater's face. (Courtesy of Dr. Leslie I. Lukash, Chief Medical Examiner, Nassau County, New York.)

to the bathroom, where one of the youths had filled the tub. The victim was placed facedown into the half-filled tub. They held his face under the water until he stopped squirming. The cause of death was drowning.

The most indicative characteristic of drowning is the white foam which forms as a result of the mucus in the body mixing with water. The presence of this white lathery foam in the mouth and windpipe prevents air from entering and contributes to the asphyxia. Bodies which have been in the water for long periods of time are subject to additional damage or injury which is unrelated to the actual drowning. (See Chapter 9, "External Agents of Change.") Most bodies will sink upon drowning only to rise later when the gases from putrefaction begin to inflate the body, causing it to rise to the surface. The amount of time before this occurs depends upon water temperature, the condition of the body (fat or thin), and other variables such as currents. The victim of a drowning will often be found grasping objects such as mud, grass, or other material found in the water.

Inhalation of Poison Gases

The most common type of asphyxia results from the breathing in of certain chemicals, such as carbon monoxide. These deaths are best determined after toxicological testings are made of the blood. At the scene, examinations sometimes will indicate the possibility of carbon monoxide poisoning if the lividity is cherry red. However, this is only a rough gauge, and before attributing the death to carbon monoxide, the investigator should await the results of the autopsy.

Suffocation

Suffocation or smothering occurs when the passage of air through the mouth and nose is blocked. The mechanisms necessary to accomplish this suffocation vary. If the smothering is homicidal, hands may be placed over the mouth and nose, or a pillow forcibly compressed over the face, or a plastic bag, gag, or other obstruction forced into the mouth. When the suffocation is done with the hands, there may be evidence of scratches on the face.

I remember reading about one particularly brutal suffocation in which two teenage boys forced pebbles down the throat of a youngster to prevent him from telling his parents that they had stolen his bike.

Other types of death which are not homicidal but are attributed to suffocation are those which occur in accidents such as industrial cave-ins, or where a person has dirt, sand, or other powdery material blocking the mouth, nose, and airway.

Arson and Deaths by Fire

It should be noted that acts of arson to commit homicide and to cover up homicides have become very common. Therefore, homicide investigators should have some basic knowledge of arson-type fires and be familiar with the effects of fire on the human body, in order to properly interpret events at the scene.

Practically speaking, the average investigator lacks the expertise to thoroughly investigate crimes of arson. However, most arson-related homicides are very amateurish, and it will be obvious to the investigator that there is something wrong. The presence of flammable liquids, several points of origin of the fire, and intensity of the blaze are examples of clues which may indicate arson. Meaningful interpretations of these clues, however, must be left to the experts, since arson investigation is highly technical and complex. Therefore, death investigations in which arson is the cause of the death, or has been employed by the killer to cover up the crime, require that the homicide detective team up with the arson investigator.

The discovery of a body or bodies in a burned-out building or vehicle presents additional investigative problems. The mode of death could be natural, suicidal, accidental, or homicidal. The body may be too badly burned even to recognize whether it is male or female, or there may be evidence of gross injury and dismemberment. The investigators will have to rely on the pathologist to interpret these injuries and make determinations of the cause of death at the autopsy.

Deaths caused by fire generally result from the inhalation of noxious gases and fumes created by the fire. The victim is usually dead prior to any burning or charring of the flesh. The pathologist will be able to determine the critical question of whether or not the victim was alive at the time of the fire. In addition, the pathologist will be able to make certain determinations regarding cause of death. The examination at autopsy will reveal the wounds or injuries which actually caused the death despite the tissue damage done by the fire. Most incidents of arson are perpetrated to destroy evidence or conceal the crime by destroying the body. However, the body does not burn as easily as most people believe. Instead, the body resists the destructive forces of the fire with amazing durability, allowing the pathologist to make determinations from the remains. If the body was alive at the time of the fire, it will evidence (1) smoke stains around the nostrils, in the nose, and air passages, (2) carbon monoxide in the blood, and (3) blistering and marginal reddening of the skin. Burned bodies usually assume a distorted position referred to as the *pugilistic* attitude or position, caused

Figure 12.37. **BURNED BODY.** (Above) The classic pugilistic attitude is assumed by a body as a result of the coagulation of the muscles due to heat. The deceased doused himself with gasoline and ran until he collapsed. The gasoline burned the clothing off the body. (Left) Note the severe burning and positions of the arms on the body after it has been turned over. Self-immolation is extremely rare.

Figure 12.38.   **SCALDING BURNS.** This woman was scalded to death in her shower. A defective water heater had heated the water to a temperature of approximately 200°F.

by the contraction of muscles due to the heat of the fire, and not as some persons believe because the victim was alive at the time of the fire. All bodies will react in this manner. The skin will crack, giving the impression of wounds, and bones may break, or the heat will cause the cranium to crack or shatter. All these factors will be properly interpreted by the pathologist.

Sexual Asphyxia: The Phenomenon of Autoerotic Fatalities

Autoerotic deaths, or deaths attributed to solo sex-related activities, are not common. Nonetheless, as cases have been recorded by police and medical examiner/coroners in various jurisdictions, the homicide detective should be aware of them. The cause of death may be asphyxia, but the mode of death, based on first observation, may be classified as either suicide or homicide, when in fact it is actually an accident that occurred during a dangerous autoerotic act.

Most of the literature on the subject of autoeroticism analyzes the involvement of teenage boys and older men, who through certain ritu-

Figure 12.39. **AUTOEROTIC DEATH INVOLVING BONDAGE FANTASY.** A 35-year-old male expired during an autoerotic act. His fantasy involved bondage. He has a black garbage bag over his head. His body is bound in several areas, with his feet tied together. His arms are bound behind his back with belts, which are attached to a metal hook. All of the bindings are interconnected and join a metal clasp that is attached to a rope with a loop knot, which is connected to a hook in the ceiling. As bizarre as this appears, the deceased was able to tie himself up in this fashion and reportedly had done this a number of times without injury. (Courtesy of Sgt. David Vanderploeg, Village of Glenview Police Department, Glenview, Illinois.)

Figure 12.39. (continued)

alistic activities obtain some sort of sexual gratification. The bodies usually have been discovered nude, attired in female clothing, or in normal attire. It should be noted, however, that there are documented cases of female participants. The investigator confronted with a female victim found under these circumstances is cautioned to assess carefully

Figure 12.40. **AUTOEROTIC DEATH: FEMALE.** Notice the material around the ligature to prevent any marking of the neck. (Courtesy of Special Agent Robert R. Hazelwood, Behavioral Science Unit, FBI Academy, Quantico, Virginia.)

all of the information available before jumping to any conclusions. In some cases there is evidence of infibulation and other autosadistic acts. Contraptions or ligatures with padding, to prevent visible marks of this activity, are often used to cause the hypoxia, which is oxygen deprivation.

Doctor H. L. P. Resnick, an author and researcher in this field states that, "A disruption of the arterial blood supply resulting in a diminished oxygenation of the brain… will heighten sensations through diminished ego controls that will be subjectively perceived as giddiness, light-headedness, and exhilaration. This reinforces masturbatory sensations."[1]

A combination of ritualistic behavior, oxygen deprivation, danger, and fantasy appears to bring about sexual gratification for these people. According to Robert R. Hazelwood, Supervisory Special Agent, "Death during such activity may result from: (1) a failure with the physiological mechanism; (2) a failure in the self-rescue device; (3) a failure on the part of the victim's judgment and ability to control a self-endangering fantasy scenario."[2]

This author cites the results of some 150 cases, which were the basis for an in-depth study and subsequent textbook, *Autoerotic Fatalities* (D.C. Heath and Company, 1983)[3] by Supervisory Special Agent Robert

Figure 12.41. **AUTOEROTIC DEATH: ASPHYXIATION/HANGING.** Notice the bondage. (Courtesy of Special Agent Robert R. Hazelwood, Behavioral Science Unit, FBI Academy, Quantico, Virginia.)

R. Hazelwood, Dr. Park Elliot Dietz, M.D., M. P. H., Professor of Law, Behavioral Medicine and Psychiatry at the University of Virginia, and Ann Wolbert Burgess, R.N., D.N.Sc., Associate Director of Nursing Research, Department of Health and Hospitals, Boston, Massachusetts. In my opinion, their text is the most thorough and comprehensive study to date on the subject of autoerotic fatalities.

According to their text, approximately 500 to 1000 people die from autoerotic asphyxiation each year in the United States. Many times this type of case has either been misclassified or gone unrecognized due to lack of knowledge, misinformation, or misguided efforts on the part of the surviving family to "cover-up" what is perceived to be an embarrassing situation.

I have personally investigated and assessed over 100 of these investigations. Oftentimes, during a class presentation on the subject of autoerotic deaths, one of the participants will remark how his department had a case like the ones being presented and that the death had been classified as either a suicide or homicide.

I became involved in one case after reading a *New York Daily News* article that described the suicidal death of a 17-year-old. Based upon my professional experience in the investigation of this type of death, I immediately recognized the possibility of an accidental autoerotic fatality. The following day I called the Detective Commander of the local jurisdiction with whom I had grown up and I felt would be open to my speculations. He filled me in on the details of his investigation, which further assured me that this alleged suicide was in fact a tragic accident. In this incident, the crime scene had been changed. The brother of the deceased had discovered the body, removed the ligature from his brother's neck, and re-dressed him out of embarrassment. I learned that the detective supervisor had never heard of autoerotic fatalities. After I provided him with the necessary information, the case was properly reclassified. More importantly, the surviving family was made aware of the actual circumstances of their son's death. The family, who had been blaming themselves, could not understand why their son would commit suicide. We enlisted the services of a family priest to assist in explaining what had happened to their son. Although at first they were astonished and embarrassed (a typical response in this type of case), they were greatly relieved to learn that their son had not taken his own life due to some unknown personal or family problem, but had died accidentally. In fact, this family actually wanted to go public to warn other parents of this phenomenon. I counseled them against going public, but advised them they could work anonymously to accomplish the same objective without exposing their family to any further trauma.

Periodically, one will read a story in the local newspaper that focuses on one or more deaths believed to be teenage suicides. I remember one particular story in my area that made reference to a "Teenage Suicide Epidemic." The series of stories that followed these initial events was directed toward warning the public about this devastating public health problem. There was a call for a renewed effort in bringing suicide prevention programs into the schools as public health officials sought a solution for what was perceived to be the contagious effect of suicide among teenagers. Parents, teachers, and public health officials were mobilized in an effort to identify a motive for these unexplained deaths. Ironically, it was discovered that half of the reported suicides were actually autoerotic fatalities. However, the focus of attention on this issue, although initially misinterpreted, was instrumental in identifying other potential problems and issues of concern regarding suicide.

Figure 12.42. **BONDAGE FANTASY.** The victim had used the blow-end of a vacuum cleaner to inflate a plastic bag which was inside a canvas bag, which was secured with a rope around his neck. However, when the bag inflated he had no way of letting the air out and he suffocated.

Some syndicated publications have reported on the phenomena of autoerotic fatality quite accurately. Stories with headlines such as, "Answers Sought in Unusual Deaths" or "Six Deaths in Past Year Stir Warning," and "Medical Examiner Concerned about Bizarre Fatal Accidents," actually provide a genuine insight into these types of deaths. Of course, there is always the possibility that publicity about this phenomenon may actually increase incidents. I believe, however, that persons predisposed to this type of behavior will neither be encouraged nor discouraged by the presentation of information on sexual asphyxia. Instead, I believe that certain details need to be made public for the purposes of alerting people to the dangers of this potentially lethal practice. As a result, I agreed to an interview with the Associated Press entitled, "Autoerotic Deaths — Shocking Practice Often Mistaken for Teen Suicide."[4] Parents, who have the responsibility of raising their children, as well as educators and others responsible for the public welfare of society have a right to information and need to be educated about this phenomenon. I have investigated and consulted on a number of autoerotic deaths involving teenage boys. Teenagers, who are going through a period of sexual experimentation, are extremely vulnerable to peer suggestions. Teenagers have traditionally developed their own life-styles, which involve different pleasures, amusements, and pastimes than those of their parents. They have their own slang, music, expressions, dancing, TV programs, movies, etc. Often parents are not even aware of their children's socialization into the teen culture. They are certainly not privy to their children's secret conversations, social groups, and/or risk-taking ventures, which explains their total shock, horror, and disbelief when advised of this phenomenon.

I supervised one investigation where a 16-year-old boy's mother showed him an article about autoerotic deaths in a newspaper so that he would be aware of the dangers. He offhandedly remarked to his mother, "Those kids are stupid. They don't know what they're doing." His mother missed the significance of the remark. her son was engaged in such activities himself and was found dead two weeks later, the victim of an autoerotic fatality.

In most of the cases in which I was involved, the teenage victim was made aware of the practice through "word-of-mouth." There have been cases, especially those involving adult practitioners, where the victim had learned of this activity through pornographic magazines, x-rated movies, underground publications, the media, and even novels.

Preliminary Investigation at the Scene

Every autoerotic fatality is unique because the circumstances surrounding this activity are based upon the person's fantasy and perception of what is considered sexually stimulating. The death scene will vary according to the victim's age, resources, and/or sexual interests. However, there are some common denominators to suggest that the death may be accidental.

There are five criteria for determining death during dangerous autoerotic practices:

1. Evidence of a physiological mechanism for obtaining or enhancing sexual arousal that provides a self-rescue mechanism or allows the victim to voluntarily discontinue its effect.
2. Evidence of solo sexual activity.
3. Evidence of sexual fantasy aids.
4. Evidence of prior dangerous autoerotic practice.
5. No apparent suicidal intent.[5]

The most common method practiced during this type of activity is neck compression or hanging, with some sort of padding between the neck and the ligature to prevent any markings left by the tightening noose or rope. However, more elaborate and exotic methods such as chest compression, airway obstruction, and oxygen exclusion with gas or chemical replacement have been found.

Asphyxial Deaths — The Pathology of Autoerotic Death

Asphyxiation is the end stage of significant interference with the exchange of oxygen and carbon dioxide. According to Drs. Dominick J. DiMaio and Vincent J. DiMaio, both nationally renowned forensic pathologists, "Asphyxial deaths are caused by the failure of the cells to receive and/or utilize oxygen. This deprivation of oxygen may be partial (*hypoxia*) or total (*anoxia*)."[6]

Asphyxial deaths can be grouped into three categories: suffocation, strangulation, and chemical asphyxia. The most common form of asphyxial death in autoerotic fatalities is strangulation, which is characterized by the closure of the blood vessels and air passages of the neck from hanging or ligature. The suspension of the body may be complete or incomplete. In sexual asphyxia cases, the body is usually in touch with the ground. There may be elaborate bindings of the body and hands of the victim. However, an analysis of these bindings will reveal that the victim was capable of binding him or herself.

Suffocation is the second most frequently occurring form of autoerotic death, which may result from covering the mouth and nose with a plastic bag or mask, or in what is described as proximal or positional asphyxia, such as in chest compression.

Chemical asphyxia takes place when oxygen is excluded by inhaling noxious gases. The most common chemical asphyxial deaths involving autoerotic activities are with nitrous oxide.

The practitioners of this activity often are aware of the possibility of death and may even have taken precautions against a fatal act, but die as a result of a miscalculation. It would appear that the victim, who may be intent upon achieving an orgasm, misjudges the existent hypoxia already present and the time required to reach orgasm by masturbation. The victim loses consciousness and succumbs to the fatal cerebral anoxia.

I had the opportunity to review a case in which the victim had set up a video camera to record his autoerotic fantasy. The victim, who was married with children, had selected an isolated area in the family home to create some sort of execution scenario for his fantasy. He had placed a large sheet over the furnishings in the room to create a background for the camera. A hangman's noose was secured by a hook in the ceiling and was tied off to the side. Directly below the hanging noose was a small platform upon which the subject could stand to place the noose over his head and around his neck. The subject was observed walking into the camera's view wearing a pair of women's panties over his head. He looked into the direction of the camera and placed the noose over his head and around his neck. He then stood with his hands behind his back. The hypoxia began to take effect. He suddenly lost his balance and the noose became tightened around his neck. At this point he could have saved himself. However, he was not aware of the impending danger and again placed his hands behind his back and continued with the fantasy. In less than 20 seconds he lost consciousness and went into fatal cerebral anoxia. He attempted to escape, however, it was too late. He had lost muscle coordination and began to convulse. His video production had gone from fantasy to reality in less than 4 minutes. It was an extremely dramatic portrayal of the reality of sexual asphyxia.

Sexual Asphyxia — The Psychosexual Aspects of Autoerotic Activity

The purpose of this section is to acquaint the investigator with some of the clinical terminology used to define bizarre and deviant human sexuality. The psychopathology of this phenomenon is better left to the clinicians and other professionals trained in the fields of medicine and psychiatry. I refer the reader to the *Diagnostic and Statistical Manual of Mental Disorders* (DSM-IV) (American Psychiatric Association, 1994), *Abnormal Psychology and Modern Life* (7th edition by Coleman et al.), and Chapter 5 of *Autoerotic Fatalities* (Hazelwood et al., 1983).

The investigative interpretation of the psychosexual aspects of autoerotic activities can be found in a group of persistent sexual arousal patterns defined in DSM-IV as *paraphilias*.

The essential feature of disorders in this subclass is that unusual or bizarre imagery or acts are necessary for sexual excitement. Such imagery or acts tend to be insistently and involuntarily repetitive and generally involve either: (1) preference for use of a nonhuman object for sexual arousal, (2) repetitive sexual activity with humans involving real or simulated suffering or humiliation, or (3) repetitive sexual activity with nonconsenting partners. In other classifications these disorders are referred to as sexual deviations. The term paraphilia is preferable because it correctly emphasizes that the deviation (para) is in that to which the individual is attracted (philia)…

Since paraphiliac imagery is necessary for erotic arousal, it must be included in masturbatory or coital fantasies, if not actually acted out alone or with a partner and supporting cast or paraphernalia. In the absence of paraphiliac imagery there is no relief from nonerotic tension, and sexual excitement or orgasm is not attained.

The imagery in a paraphiliac fantasy or the object of sexual excitement in a paraphilia is frequently the stimulus for sexual excitement in individuals without a Psychosexual Disorder. For example, women's undergarments and imagery of sexual coercion are sexually exciting for many men; they are paraphiliac only when they become necessary for sexual excitement.[7]

According to DSM-IV there are nine (9) paraphilias. I will list them here with a brief definition. However, for further information I direct the reader to *Diagnostic Manual of Mental Disorders IV and Abnormal Psychology* 7th edition by Coleman, et al.

1. **Exhibitionism (302.4):** Exposing the genitals to an unsuspecting stranger for the purposes of obtaining sexual excitement.
2. **Fetishism (302.81):** Use of nonliving objects for sexual arousal. (Female undergarments, panties, shoes, etc.)
3. **Frotteurism (302.89):** A sexual attraction to rubbing against the genitalia or body of another.
4. **Pedophilia (302.2):** Engaging in sexual activity with prepubertal children.
5. **Sexual masochism (302.83):** Getting pleasure from being humiliated, bound, beaten, or otherwise made to suffer for sexual arousal. (Considered a chronic disorder.)
6. **Sexual sadism (302.84):** The infliction of physical or psychological pain on another person in order to achieve sexual excitement. (Considered a chronic and progressive disorder.)
7. **Transvestic fetishism (302.3):** Cross-dressing by heterosexual male for sexual excitement. (Ranges from solitary wearing of female clothes to extensive involvement in a transvestite subculture.)

8. **Voyeurism (302.82):** Repetitive looking at unsuspecting people, who are either naked, in the act of disrobing, or engaging in sexual activity. (The "Peeping Tom.")

9. **Paraphilia not otherwise specified:** This category is included for coding Paraphilias that do not meet the criteria for any of the specific categories.

Telephone scatolgia: A sexual attraction to making obscene telephone calls. (Lewdness.)

Necrophilia: A sexual attraction to dead bodies; having intercourse with a dead body.

Patialism: An exclusive focus on a part of the human body, a breast, leg, penis, etc.

Zoophilia: Use of animals for sexual arousal. (Includes intercourse with animals as well as training the animal to lick or rub the human partner.)

Coprophilia: A sexual attraction to feces.

Klismaphilia: A sexual attraction to the giving or receiving of enemas.

Urophilia: A sexual attraction to urine.

Mysophilia: A sexual attraction to filth (DSM-IV).[6]

CASE HISTORIES

Hanging. A 40-year-old married salesman was discovered in the basement of his residence totally suspended from a floor joist with a large piece of rope ending in a hangman's noose encircling his head. The body was dressed in a white shirt, a white panty-girdle with nylons, and a pair of women's open-toed shoes. A women's girdle was over the victims' head and his hands were bound by a belt.[10]

Hanging. A white, male in his late forties, never married, living at home with his mother and sister was found hanging in his basement workshop. He was wearing street clothing, which covered woman's undergarments. A bra stuffed with padding, woman's panties, woman's boots, and leather gloves. A mask, which he had apparently been wearing, was found on the floor beneath him. He was hanging by a rope affixed to a hook in the ceiling. There was a Polaroid camera positioned on the workbench and a number of photographs of the deceased participating in this conduct. There were a number of pornographic magazines depicting female bondage, lesbian conduct, and sadomasochistic behavior found in his room. In addition to these commercial products, police discovered sadomasochistic drawings depicting the deceased dressed as a woman. In these drawings, this "woman" is observed with an erect penis threatening and abusing other women. There were also a number of these sexually

A

Figure 12.43. **FANTASY DRAWINGS.** (A) The victim has drawn a woman, which is actually himself, dressed in "LaFemme" undergarments. His fantasy involved cross dressing. (B) Here we see a female victim who has supposedly hanged herself with her own bra. In both drawings the victim has created a fantasy which involves urophilia. There were approximately 20 of these drawings found at the death scene. Additionally, the victim had taken Polaroid photos of himself dressed in female attire acting out similar fantasies.

explicit drawings of nude and seminude women urinating. These "fantasy drawings" were further illustrated with words indicating that the deceased was actually verbalizing his sadomasochistic fantasies. Also discovered were two legal-size sheets of paper listing approximately 200 pieces of woman's apparel and undergarments that the deceased had purchased. The victim had listed these items by number, description, price, and the name of the store from which the item was purchased. He then had a separate column which indicated whether or not he had photographed himself in the item. This individual's total sex life was involved with solo sexual activities. His drawings further suggested

B

Figure 12.43. (continued)

paraphilias of transvestism, sadism, and masochism with fantasies of necrophilia and urophilia.

Chest Compression. The victim was a 49-year-old commercial airline pilot who was married and the father of two small children. On his day off he left his residence, advising his wife that he was going to target practice. A fisherman discovered him a short time later crushed against the left rear fender of his 1968 Volkswagen. The scene was a large turn-around area at the end of a secluded road. The left door was open and the motor was running. The steering wheel was fixed in an extreme left turn position and the automatic transmission was in low gear. Tire tracks indicated that the automobile had been moving in concentric circles. The body was held against the car by a heavy linked chain and was totally nude except for a chain harness. The harness had a moderately tight loop around the neck and was bolted in front. The chain passed down the

Figure 12.44. **AUTOEROTIC DEATH SEQUENCE.** A male has dressed in female attire with a discipline mask over his head. His eyes were covered with duct tape, his mouth stuffed with foam rubber, a small rubber ball was in each ear, and he had a headband around the ears. The victim was wearing pantyhose and female undergarments beneath this outfit. All of the chains and binds were interconnected. A cooper loop of wire had been connected to an electrical apparatus with a timer, which sent intermittent shocks to the victim. The victim was a 66-year-old man. (Courtesy of Det. Lt. Raymond Krolak, Commanding Officer, Investigations Division, Colonie, New York Police Department.)

Figure 12.44. (continued)

sternum and abdomen and around the waist to form a second loop. From the waist loop, strands of chain passed on each side of the testicles and into the gluteal fold and was secured to the waist loop in the small of the back. A 10-foot length of chain was attached from the waist loop to the rear bumper and had become wound around the rear axle five times. It is not known whether he jogged behind the car or was dragged; however, when he tired of the exercise he approached the car intending to turn off the motor. In so doing, the chain became slack and the back tire rolled over it causing the chain to become wound onto the rear axle. The trunk of the car contained his clothing, a zippered bag holding locks, bolts, chains, and wrenches. A lock and key were on the ground beside the body and another lock was found twenty feet from the body.[11]

Suffocation. A white male, 66 years of age, was discovered lying upon his bed by police, who had been called to the man's apartment. The deceased was wearing women's clothing, which consisted of a grey turtle neck sweater with crotch snaps and red panty hose. The upper torso was bound with straps and chains which were interconnected by a series of locks. A rubber mask covered his face and the mask was connected to the bedboard by rope. There was an electrical apparatus attached to a hook in the ceiling, which consisted of a timer and two wires. This equipment was plugged into a wall socket. One of the wires extended down to the crotch area of the victim. A copper wire loop had been fitted beneath the snaps of the turtle neck sweater and this could be connected to the electrical device. In the man's room, police investigators discovered three suitcases full of woman's undergarments, wigs, and "falsies," as well as other sexual paraphernalia consisting of dildos, discipline masks, and pornographic materials. When the body was examined, the victim was found to be wearing women's undergarments. Under the head mask, duct tape covered his eyes, foam rubber was stuffed in his mouth, and a headband held a small rubber ball in each ear. He was totally in the dark and couldn't hear a thing, but all of the bindings and chains were within his grasp.

His escape mechanism was a single lock, which secured all of the chains wrapped around his body. The deceased had held the keys for this lock in his right hand. He had apparently dropped his keys on the floor, where the police discovered them. The duct tape and rubber balls in his ears certainly shut out any possibility of seeing the keys or hearing them drop to the floor. He had been bound to the bed in such a manner that he would not have been able to reach down to the floor even if he had heard the keys drop. The cause of death was suffocation. The police supervisor as well as the detective investigating this case had both been to one of my Practical Homicide Investigation lectures. They immediately recognized the death to be an autoerotic fatality based on the above information. However, when the medical examiner of the jurisdiction arrived at the scene, he told the detectives it appeared to be a homicide related to "biker-gang" activity. He obviously was not familiar with such cases and based his conclusion of homicide on the bizarre binding of the body.

Oxygen Exclusion. A deceased male was discovered lying on a bed in a rental cabin with a plastic bag over his head. This male had rented the

Figure 12.45. **VICTIM OF AN AUTOEROTIC FATALITY.** A metal bolt was inserted into the victim's vagina from the rear. The victim was discovered bent over a tub filled with water. The actual cause of death was drowning. This, at first, was thought to be a sex-related homicide.

summer cabin during the off-season. The proprietor, who was checking on the rental, made the discovery when he entered the premises and noticed the nude body of the deceased on the bed. Police were called to the location and discovered an array of pornographic magazines opened to the centerfolds on the floor next to the bed. Also next to the bed was a canister of nitrous oxide. The investigators learned that the man, who had been involved with this activity in the past, had been sniffing the pure nitrous oxide by releasing the gas into the plastic bag from the tank. He would then write down his sexual fantasies on a pad while viewing the pictures of the nude models in the magazines next to the bed. When he placed the plastic bag over his head, the oxygen which had been excluded resulted in asphyxiating the victim.

Female Victims of Autoerotic Fatality

Although most of the cases of autoerotic death involve males, it is important to realize that this type of practice is not limited to males. For example, what may appear to be a sex slaying, involving the bondage and suffocation of a female victim, may in fact be the accidental death of a female practitioner of autoerotic activities. One such case was reported by retired Special Agent Frank Sass of the FBI. A 35-year-old female divorcee was discovered dead by her 9-year-old daughter. The woman was nude and lying on a small shelved space in the rear of a closet in her bedroom. She was on her stomach and an electric vibrator with a hard rubber massaging head was between her thighs and in contact with her vulva. The vibrator was operating when the victim was discovered. Attached to the nipple of her right breast was a spring-type clothespin, compressing her nipple. Immediately below her left breast another clothespin was found. Around the victim's neck was a handtowel; a nylon stocking went over the towel in loop fashion and was fastened to a shelf bracket above her head. The lower portion of the body was supported by the shelf and the victim's upper body rested on her arms, which were extended downward from her body in a push-up position. The clothespins were used to cause discomfort, the vibrator was used in a masturbatory exercises, and the ligature reduced oxygen flow. She obviously intended to support her upper body weight with her arms, but she lost consciousness and the weight of her body, hanging from the nylon stocking, caused her to strangle.[12]

It should be noted that the female victim of an autoerotic fatality, who has involved herself in binding and some sort of sadomasochistic scenario, presents authorities with circumstances which actually resemble a sex-related homicide.

Hazelwood et al. cite the following case. A 23-year-old black woman was found dead in her bathroom. The victim's upper torso rested on the edge of the bathtub, her face was in the water, and her knees were on the floor. The faucets were turned on, and the water had filled the tub, spilled on the floor, and ran throughout the house. There was vomitus in the tub water. A piece of rope had been doubled and looped around her on the left side of her neck, with the loose ends coming across and over her right shoulder. Her wrists were wrapped together in front of her body and the end of the rope securing them rested in her right hand. The decedent was nude, and a 9 1/2-inch bolt was on the floor beside the body. There was a bruise on the left side of her forehead and drops of blood were found on the edge and side of the tub. Autopsy revealed the cause of death to be aspiration of vomitus.[13]

This case was investigated initially as a suicide, based upon statements by a relative and friend of the victim. It was also investigated as a possible homicide, with the boyfriend, who had discovered the body, as a primary suspect. Actually, this case had enough factors to support both possibilities. In actuality, the case was eventually classified as an autoerotic fatality. According to the authors, "A theory that accounts for all of the facts in this case is that the victim had been drawing a bath while asphyxiating herself with the rope, intending to use the bolt for manual masturbation, or already having done so. Through asphyxiation, she lost consciousness, struck her head on the bathtub, and aspirated vomitus…"[14]

Equivocal Death Investigation

Many times while conducting homicide programs, participants will provide me with cases in order to get my opinion. One such case involved the reported suicide of a 17-year-old black female. The detective, who brought this case to my attention, was concerned that the medical examiner and other detectives had classified this case as suicide. He felt, based on his investigation into the background of the victim and what he observed at the scene, that the death might have been an autoerotic fatality. He was concerned that the family was blaming themselves for the daughter's death. I reviewed his case file and crime scene photos and provided the detective with a full report which included the following information, which he could bring to his superiors and the medical examiner for review.

Crime Scene

The location of the incident was in the basement of a single family home occupied by the deceased and her family. The victim was home alone at the time of the incident. The area that the victim selected was secluded from the rest of the home. There was no evidence of any break or entry. The victim, who was found by her brother, had been hanging from a wire noose, which had been affixed to a rusty metal clothes rod. There was a white towel wrapped around the victim's neck, which would have formed a padding between the wire and her neck. The victim was nude from the waist-up and was wearing a pair of black sweat pants. A white T-shirt was observed approximately 6 feet away and appeared to have been discarded by the deceased. A white five-gallon bucket was observed lying on its side near to the area where the deceased was found. Forensic examination of this bucket revealed latent prints, which were later identified as belonging to the right foot of the deceased. The material on the deceased's hands turned out to be rust from the metal pipe to which the wire had been affixed.

The Victim

The deceased was a healthy and apparently happy 17-year-old young woman. The investigation disclosed that the deceased came from a good family background, where both the mother and stepfather provided parental guidance and support. The family consists of the 17-year-old victim, her 19-year-old brother, the victim's mother, and her stepfather. In addition, the inquiry into the victim's background indicates that the victim maintained good social relationships with peers and was performing well in school. The interview of the deceased's best friend indicated that the victim was popular and well-liked. The victim had two boyfriends and was sexually promiscuous with a young man. *There is no indication in the reports that the deceased was depressed or suicidal. In fact, from all indications (name withheld) was functioning well both physically and socially as any typical 17-year-old teenager.*

Investigative Considerations

A teenage female victim, found partially nude in a secluded area of the house when no one was home. The location that the victim selected afforded her an opportunity to engage in a private fantasy. The most common method practiced in sexual asphyxia is neck compression or hanging with some sort of padding between the neck and ligature to prevent any markings. The suspension point was within the reach of the deceased. This suspension point was within the reach of the deceased (rust on hands) until the plastic bucket was knocked over. It is a known fact that most victims of suicide are not found partially or fully nude. In this case the victim's breasts were exposed.

> **Remember, this is an investigative theory. Don't get bogged down in theory and hypothetical speculation. In death investigations there are no absolutes.**

Opinion

In my professional opinion, (name withheld) died as a result of a tragic accident involving sexual asphyxia. The basis for this conclusion are twofold: (1) the indicators which were present at the scene and enunciated within this report, and (2) the lack of suicidal intent on the part of the victim. This fact is supported by the thorough police investigation into the background of the deceased. I recommend that the authorities confer with the Medical Examiner to reclassify this death as an *autoerotic fatality.*

Results

The detective took this report and conferred with his superiors and the medical examiner. Reportedly, the medical examiner's initial concern about classifying this case as accidental was that the deceased did not fit the stereotypical profile of a practitioner of autoeroticism because she was a black female. However, the professional in-depth investigation undertaken by the detective provided enough factual basis to have this case reclassified. My consultative report simply validated the detective's hypothesis. The important point here is that the detective's dedication to properly classify this case as accidental provided a measure of consolation to the surviving family. The family was advised that their daughter did not commit suicide.

Notification and Advising the Surviving Family of the Mode of Death

Advising surviving family members of the circumstances and nature of this type of death can be quite stressful and difficult. The tragedy is often compounded by survivor reactions, which range from guilt, shame, and humiliation to anger and rage.

As professional investigators, we are entrusted with a profound duty and responsibility — not only to the deceased, but to the surviving family as well. It is imperative that we do all in our power to assist the surviving family by our professionalism. The official explanation of the circumstances of the death is best undertaken with the assistance of clergy or a professional practitioner after considering the family's ability to cope with the facts of the case. However, it is important to note that each case and set of circumstances will dictate the proper course of action. In some instances, I believe investigators, who recognize what has happened, may make a conscious decision to spare the family and allow them to believe the death to be a suicide. Under certain circumstances this action might be an entirely appropriate alternative. I offer this personal advice as a veteran homicide cop. Whatever course of action you decide, "just make sure you do the right thing."

Investigative Considerations

Although each autoerotic death scene may be unique, there are many common factors for the investigator to consider in making his or her determination of the mode of death. I have listed some of these considerations within this section.

Victim Profile. Research has indicated that most victims of this activity are white males ranging from 13 years of age to their late thirties. This group is followed by white females in their early twenties, black males 20 to 40 years of age, and one reported black female in her late twenties. The victims are considered to be basically moral people, successful in their respective occupations. They may be considered shy by friends because they are not sexually or romantically active. However, they may be married or involved with a significant other person. Interviews and investigations do not disclose any indications of depression or suicidal tendencies.

Location. The location selected is usually secluded or isolated and affords the practitioner the opportunity to involve himself or herself in a private fantasy. Some examples are as follows: locked rooms at home, attics, basements, garages or workshops, motel rooms, places of employment during nonbusiness hours, summer houses, or outdoor locations.

Nudity. Most victims of suicide are not found in the nude. Although this is not a conclusive indicator, the discovery of a nude victim should alert the investigator to the possibility of an autoerotic fatality if other indicators, such as those listed below, are present.

Determining the Involvement of Sexual Asphyxia: Autoerotic Checklist

There are certain questions which the investigator should consider in determining whether or not the death is related to autoerotic activity.

1. Is the victim nude, sexually exposed, or — if a male — is he dressed in articles of feminine attire: transvestism, make-up, wigs?
2. Is there evidence of masturbatory activity: tissues, towels, or hanky in hand, or in shorts to catch semen? Seminal fluids?
3. Is there evidence of infibulation: piercing or causing pain to the genitalia, self-torture, masochism, pins in penis, etc.?
4. Are sexually stimulating paraphernalia present: vibrators, dildos, sex aids, pornographic magazines, butt plugs, etc.?
5. Is bondage present: ropes, chains, blindfolds, gags, etc.? Are any constrictive devices present: corset, plastic wrap, belts, ropes, or vacuum cleaner hoses around the body or chest constraints?
6. Is there protective padding between the ligature and the neck: towels, rags, or cloth to prevent rope burns or discomfort?

7. Are the restraints interconnected? Do the ropes and ties come together or are they connected? Are the chains interconnected through one another? Is the victim tied to himself, so that by putting pressure on one of the limbs the restraints are tightened?

8. Are mirrors or other reflective devices present? Are they positioned so that the victim can view his or her activities?

9. Is there evidence of fantasy (diaries, erotic literature, etc.) or fetishism (woman's panties, bras, girdles, leather, rubber, latex, high-heel shoes, etc.)?

10. Is the suspension point within reach of the victim or is there an escape mechanism (keys, lock, slip knot, etc.)?

11. Is there evidence of prior such activities (abrasions or rope burns on suspension point)? Unexplained secretive behavior, or long stays in isolated areas, rope burns on neck, etc.?

12. Does the victim possess literature dealing with bondage, escapology, or knots?

13. Is there a positioned camera? (Check film and/or videotapes. Look for photos and view any videotapes in camera.)

While not all such deaths will involve the above characteristics, their presence will certainly alert the investigator to the possibility of death occurring as the result of sexual misadventure.

Summary

The investigation of sexual asphyxia and the appropriate determination of mode of death require that the investigator conduct a knowledgeable scene examination. This obviously means that the investigator should have an understanding of clues that may be present both at the scene and in the background of the deceased.

The psychological autopsy (see "Suicides", Chapter 13) can be helpful in resolving those cases in which it is not clear whether the motivational intent was suicidal or autoerotic in nature.[15] As further information on this mode of death becomes available through research, the investigator will be afforded additional assistance in making this determination and properly classifying these cases.

References

1. H. L. P. Resnick. "Eroticized Repetitive Hangings — A Form of Self-Destruction." *American Journal of Psychotherapy*, January 1972, p. 10.

2. Robert R. Hazelwood, Ann Wolbert Burgess, and Nicholas Groth. "Death During Dangerous Autoerotic Practice." *Social Science and Medicine.* Elmsford, New York: Pergamon Press, Vol. 15E, pp. 129–133.

3. Robert R. Hazelwood, Park Elliot Dietz, and Ann Wolbert Burgess. *Autoerotic Fatalities.* Lexington, Massachusetts: Lexington Books, D. C. Heath & Company, 1983.

4. Paul Raeburn, "Autoerotic Deaths — Shocking Practice Often Mistaken for Teen Suicide." *Sunday Journal News.* December 2, 1984.

5. Robert R. Hazelwood, Ann Wolbert Burgess, and Nicholas Groth. "Death During Dangerous Autoerotic Practice." *Social Science and Medicine.* Elmsford, New York: Pergamon Press, Vol. 15E: 129–133, p. 2.

6. Dominick J. DiMaio and Vincent J. DiMaio. *Practical Aspects of Forensic Pathology.* New York: Elsevier Science Publishing Co., 1989.

7. American Psychiatric Association. *Diagnostic and Statistical Manual of Mental Disorders,* 3rd ed. Washington D.C.: American Psychiatric Association, 1980, pp. 266–267.

8. Robert R. Hazelwood, Park Elliot Dietz, and Ann Wolbert Burgess. *Autoerotic Fatalities,* Lexington, Massachusetts: Lexington Books, D.C. Heath and Company, p. 100.

9. American Psychiatric Association. *Diagnostic and Statistical Manual of Mental Disorders,* (DSM-3R), 3rd ed. Washington, D.C.: American Psychiatric Association, 1987, p. 275.

10. Robert R. Hazelwood, Ann Wolbert Burgess, and Nicholas Groth. "Death During Dangerous Autoerotic Practice," *Social Science and Medicine.* Elmsford, New York: Pergamon Press, Vol. 15E: 129–133, p. 3.

11. J. Rupp. "The Love Bug." *Journal of Forensic Science* 18:259–262 (1973).

12. Frank Sass. "Sexual Asphyxia in the Female." *Journal of Forensic Science* 20:181–185 (1975); also in *Psychiatric Nursing in the Hospital and the Community,* 3rd ed. Ann Wolbert Burgess (Ed.), Englewood Cliffs, New Jersey: Prentice-Hall, Inc., 1981, pp. 316–319.

13. Robert R. Hazelwood, Park Elliot Dietz, and Ann Wolbert Burgess. *Autoerotic Fatalities,* Lexington, Massachusetts: Lexington Books, D.C. Heath and Company, pp. 136-137.

14. Robert R. Hazelwood, Park Elliot Dietz, and Ann Wolbert Burgess. *Autoerotic Fatalities,* Lexington, Massachusetts: Lexington Books, D.C. Heath and Company, pp. 138.

15. N. Hibbler. "The Psychological Autopsy." *Forensic Science Digest* 5:42(1978).

Selected Reading

Adelson, Lester. *The Pathology of Homicide.* Springfield, Illinois: Charles C Thomas, 1974.

American Psychiatric Association. *Diagnostic and Statistical Manual of Mental Disorders,* 3rd ed. (DSM-III). Washington, D.C.: American Psychiatric Association, 1980.

Burgess, Ann W. *Psychiatric Nursing in the Hospital and the Community,* 3rd ed. Englewood Cliffs, New Jersey: Prentice-Hall, Inc., 1981.

DiMaio, Dominick J., and DiMaio, Vincent J. M. *Forensic Pathology.* New York: Elsevier Science Publishing Company, Inc., 1990.

Geberth Vernon J. "Sexual asphyxia — the phenomenon of autoerotic fatalities." *Law and Order* vol. 37 (1989).

Geberth, Vernon J. *Practical Homicide Investigation: Tactics Procedures, and Forensic Techniques.* Second Edition. CRC Press, Inc., Florida, 1993.

Harris, Raymond I. *Outline of Death Investigation.* Springfield, Illinois: Charles C Thomas, 1962.

Hazelwood, Robert R., Burgess, Ann W., and Groth, Nicholas. "Death During Dangerous Autoerotic Practice," in *Social Science and Medicine.* Elmsford, New York: Pergamon Press, Ltd.

Hazelwood, Robert R., Dietz, Park Elliot, and Burgess, Ann W. *Autoerotic Fatalities.* Lexington, Massachusetts: D. C. Heath & Company, 1983.

Hughes, D. J. *Homicide Investigative Techniques.* Springfield, Illinois: Charles C Thomas, 1974.

O'Hara, Charles E. *Fundamentals of Criminal Investigation,* 5th ed. Springfield, Illinois: Charles C Thomas, 1980.

Raeburn, Paul. "Autoerotic Deaths — Shocking Practice Often Mistaken for Teen Suicide." *New York Sunday Journal News,* December 2, 1984.

Resnick, H. L. P. "Eroticized Repetitive Hangings — A Form of Self-Destruction." *American Journal of Psychotherapy,* January 1972.

Sass, Frank. "Sexual Asphyxia in the Female." *Journal of Forensic Science.* 20:181–185 (1973).

Synder, LeMoyne. *Homicide Investigation,* 3rd ed. Springfield, Illinois: Charles C Thomas, 1977.

Spitz, Werner U., and Fisher, Russell S. *Medicolegal Investigation of Death: Guidelines for the Application of Pathology to Crime Investigation.* Springfield, Illinois: Charles C Thomas, 1973.

Svensson, Arne, Wendel, Otto, and Fisher, Barry A. J. *Techniques of Crime Scene Investigation,* 3rd ed. New York: Elsevier North Holland, Inc., 1981.

Suicide Investigation 13

The rationale behind suicide, which is defined as the intentional taking of one's own life, can be as simple or as complex as life itself. The person who commits suicide may see his or her actions as some sort of solution to a severe physical or psychological dilemma. Oftentimes, a police investigator will find a note indicating that the victim had suffered psychological torment, or was severely depressed. The note might even suggest that he or she believed that suicide was the last resort. Many of the suicide notes I have seen over the years indicate the acute depression of persons who have taken their lives. Depression does not discriminate. It affects the young and old alike. According to Dr. Patrick Cachur of The Centers for Disease Control in Atlanta, Georgia, 30,906 persons committed suicide in 1990. The majority of the cases (approximately 6500) occurred in the age bracket of 25 to 34 years of age. There were 258 suicides among pre-teens ages 10 to 14 years old and there were 6 suicides of children between the ages of 5 and 9 years of age.[1] Ms. Sandy Smith, Public Affairs Officer for The National Center for Health Statistics, Office of Data Processing, recorded 29,760 suicides in 1992 placing suicide as the ninth leading cause of death. Homicide ranked number ten.[2]

There are more suicides occurring in the 1990s according to the experts and the rate of suicide among pre-teens and the elderly has significantly increased. Teenage suicides have been described as epidemic in proportion to their representation within society. Periodically, the nation's newspapers and television networks may cover this phenomenon by reporting a series of events including "Teenage Suicide Pacts." Ironically, the media attention often results in further teenage suicides. The course of action would be to seek out professional assistance and create programs within the school system to deal with this problem.

Depression: A Clinical Perspective

The primary motivation for suicide is depression. Depression is a mood disturbance which is characterized by feelings of sadness, despair, and discouragement resulting from and normally proportionate to some personal loss or tragedy. Depression can become an abnormal emotional state which exaggerates these feelings of sadness, despair, and discouragement out of proportion to reality.

There are four major clusters of depressive symptoms; *emotional, cognitive, motivational,* and *somatic.* Each of these clusters of depressive symptoms impact both dependently and independently upon the depressed individual. In fact, as one set of clusters begins to affect the individual another impacts and reinforces the depressive effect. Eventually, the emotional and cognitive clusters effect the motivational symptoms causing what clinicians refer to as a "paralysis of the will" and/or psychomotor retardation (psychomotor pertaining to or causing voluntary movements usually associated with neural activity). In severe depression the depressed person may actually experience a slowing down of his or her movements. They may even have trouble walking and talking. The depressed individual experiences physical changes which further exacerbate the depressive symptoms. The physical changes which occur are referred to as the somatic symptoms.

Emotional Symptoms

Sadness is the most conspicuous and widespread emotional symptom in depression. Depressed people may even articulate their depression by such statements as "I feel sad." This emotional symptom is felt worse in the morning usually as a result of not having been able to sleep. Feelings of anxiety are also present along with a loss of gratification and loss of interest. The loss of interest may start with work and extend into practically everything the individual does (hobbies, recreational activities, etc.). Finally, even biological functions such as eating and sex lose their appeal.

Cognitive Symptoms

The term cognitive refers to the mental process characterized by knowing, thinking, learning, and judging. It is an intellectual process by

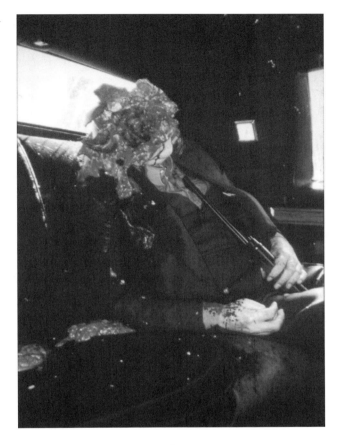

A

Figure 13.1.   **SUICIDE BY RIFLE.** (A) This suicide victim's locale, the interior of a vehicle, shows the effect blast. Note the brain matter on the interior roof as well as the back seat of the car. (B) We see a close-up of the same victim and the extensive damage inflicted by the blast. The victim committed suicide by placing the barrel of a .308 rifle into his mouth and by pulling the trigger. (Courtesy of Det. Lt. Raymond Krolak, Commander, Investigative Division, Colonie, New York Police Department.)

which a person perceives or comprehends. The depressed individual thinks or perceives of himself or herself in a very negative way. Their future is viewed with despair. The individual may feel that they have failed in some way or that they are the cause for their own problems. They believe that they are inferior, inadequate, and incompetent. Their depressed cognitive functioning causes them to have intense feelings of low self esteem. This sows the seeds for eventual hopelessness and pessimism. The depressed individual actually believes that he or she is doomed and there is no way out.

B

Figure 13.1. (continued)

Motivational Symptoms

These particular symptoms are first noticed by those who are close to the depressed person. Depressed persons generally have trouble "getting started." Most of us are able to function by getting up in the morning, going to work, interacting with one another, and engaging in routine activities. The depressed individual is marked by passivity or lack of activity. This passivity and lack of normal response undermines the individual's ability to engage in important life functions and general socialization. In its extreme form there may even be a "paralysis of will" whereby the individual doesn't even feel like doing what is necessary for life such as attending to proper nourishment.

Somatic Symptoms

These are the biological manifestations of depression. They are perhaps the most insidious set of symptoms due to their impact. As depression worsens, every biological and psychological joy that makes life worth living is eroded. Loss of appetite, loss of interest in sex and sexual arousal, weight loss, and sleep disturbances lead to weakness and fa-

Figure 13.2.   **SUICIDE.** Observe the broom handle, which has been placed through the trigger guard. The deceased had apparently placed her feet against the broom handle to put pressure on the trigger, causing the firearm to discharge into her chest.

tigue. Depressed individuals *physically* feel the depression. They are more susceptible to physical illness because the depression, as it becomes more severe, erodes the basic biological drives.

Clinical Scenario

An individual begins to feel sad and sustains a restless sleep. He begins to feel sad in the morning and experiences a lack of interest in work (*emotional symptoms*). He then begins to question his ability to perform at work and starts to feel inadequate. This adds to the individual's anxiety and low self esteem (*cognitive symptoms*). He then discovers that

Figure 13.3. SUICIDE. Same case as the preceding figure. (A) The deceased is lying on her back; the bullet wound is evident in her chest area. (B) With her blouse pulled up, notice the entrance wound directly into the chest cavity. The deceased had used birdshot. If the shot had been of a higher caliber, the wound would have been larger and might have exited from the opposite side.

Figure 13.4. **SUICIDE WHICH APPEARS TO BE HOMICIDE.** Notice the extreme violence to the body. (Courtesy of Dr. Leslie I. Lukash, Chief Medical Examiner, Nassau County, New York.)

he just can't get started in the morning and cannot bring himself to go to work and just loses interest in life (*motivational symptoms*). As the depression deepens, the individual loses his appetite and experiences weight loss which leads to weakness and fatigue. He then slips deeper and deeper into depression and becomes ill (*somatic symptoms*). The cycle of depressive symptoms will continue to evolve and the depression will worsen. At this point the individual is in dire need of assistance. (Source: Rosenhan, David L. and Seligman, Martin. *Abnormal Psychology* Second Edition. New York: W.W. Norton & Co., 1989.)[3]

Other Motives for Suicide

Although depression may be the primary motive for the suicide, other factors frequently play a part. Alcohol, drugs, stress, frustration, fear,

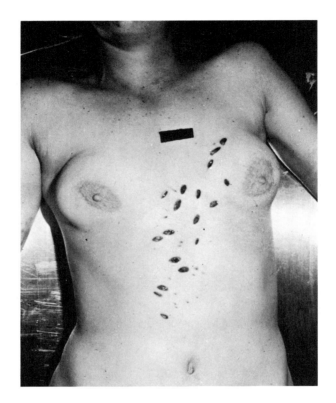

Figure 13.5.   **VICTIM AT THE MORGUE.** Observe the victim of the preceding figure after she was cleaned at the morgue. Notice the number of wounds. (Courtesy of Dr. Leslie I. Lukash, Chief Medical Examiner, Nassau County, New York.)

Figure 13.6.   **WEAPON USED BY THE VICTIM OF THE PRECEDING FIGURE.** (Courtesy of Dr. Leslie I. Lukash, Chief Medical Examiner, Nassau County, New York.)

Figure 13.7. **HESITATION MARKS.** Notice the marks on the throat of the victim. (Courtesy of Dr. Dominick J. DiMaio, Former Chief Medical Examiner, City of New York.)

Figure 13.8. **SUICIDE INVOLVING MULTIPLE SHOTS.** Victim had attempted suicide by shooting himself in the face. When this did not result in his death, he placed the barrel of the rifle into his mouth and fired a second time creating this effect.

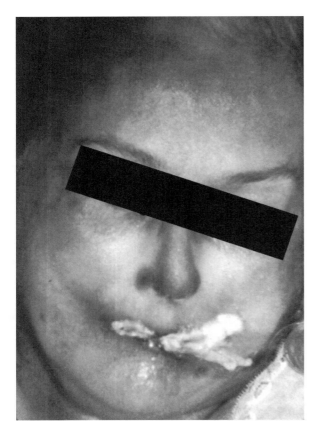

Figure 13.9. **SUICIDE BY OVERDOSE.** This woman had taken an overdose of prescription pills which resulted in her death.

anger, hostility, and guilt may lay the groundwork for suicide. In fact, motivations for suicide may range from the clinical to the bizarre. Some persons may actually take their own life in order to punish the survivors, i.e., their family, co-workers, or even society in general for some conceived wrongdoing.

I recall reading a *Daily News* story and seeing on television a particularly bizarre case in which the victim had planned his death for approximately 7 months. He had promised reporters that his story would be "The Story of the Decade" (*Daily News*, January 24, 1987, p. 6). The victim was a state official, who had been found guilty of bribery earlier in the year. On the day of his death, he called for a news conference ostensibly to resign from public office. As he read his statement, he urged the reporters and camera crews to keep their lenses on him. He then pulled a .357 Magnum handgun from a manila envelope and placed it into his mouth, pointing the barrel of the gun up toward his brain. He fired and effectively blew his brains out for the viewing audience.

In addition, there are persons who feel that they have a right of self determination and take their own lives rather than suffer with an illness or disease. These types of suicides will be discussed later in the section entitled "Final Exit Suicides."

Also, there are persons who wish to end their own lives but don't want to do it themselves. They create a confrontational situation in order to force the police to shoot them. These types of suicides will also be discussed later in the section entitled "Suicide-By-Cop."

The Investigation

Investigatively speaking, all death investigations should be handled as homicide cases until the facts prove differently. The resolution of the mode of death as suicide is based on a series of factors that eliminate homicide, accident, and natural causes of death.

It has been my experience that suicide cases repeatedly cause more problems for the investigator than homicide investigations. There is the possibility that suicide notes may have been taken or destroyed. In addition, the weapon and/or other evidence may have been removed prior to the arrival of the police. Also it is not surprising to encounter misdirected grief and/or anger. The surviving family grieves the loss of a loved one and is faced with the psychological uncertainty of whether or not they could have prevented the act. These relatives frequently suffer a deep sense of guilt about the death, anger at the deceased, and feelings of shame because there is a social stigma attached to a suicide incident.

I remember one case in which an 84-year-old woman was found with a gunshot wound to her head. The police had been notified of the death by a daughter of the deceased. Unbeknownst to the police, the deceased had been suffering from terminal cancer and had been very depressed. Her daughter, who had unsuccessfully attempted to call the mother at home, went to the mother's house.

She opened the door with a key and discovered her mother's body. She saw a .32 caliber handgun, which she immediately recognized as an old family heirloom. The daughter removed the gun from the premises, along with some personal papers and a codicil she found in her mother's dresser drawers. She went home, got rid of the gun, and then called the police to report that she had not been able to get through to her mother. She requested the police to respond to her mother's apartment and she would meet them there.

Needless to say, when we arrived, we were looking at a burglary/homicide case and not a possible suicide. Later that week, we were

A

Figure 13.10. (A) Shows the victim in her original position when police arrived. She has incised wounds to her neck and blood emanating from her mouth and nose. (B) Shows close-up of victim's face. (C) Shows kitchen knife between her legs and a large blood stain on the carpet. (D) Close-up of incised wound to her neck indicating stigma of hesitation. (E) Close-up of victim's chest after blood is removed. Shows that the first two stab wounds hit the sternum. Only one wound was in fact fatal, the wound to the left.

called by the family's priest, who advised us of what had taken place. The case was properly reclassified as a suicide. Many times the surviving family cannot or will not accept the fact that a relative has committed suicide. They have been known to accuse the police of a cover-up, or to petition state and federal agencies to review the local investigation with the belief that they can change the outcome.

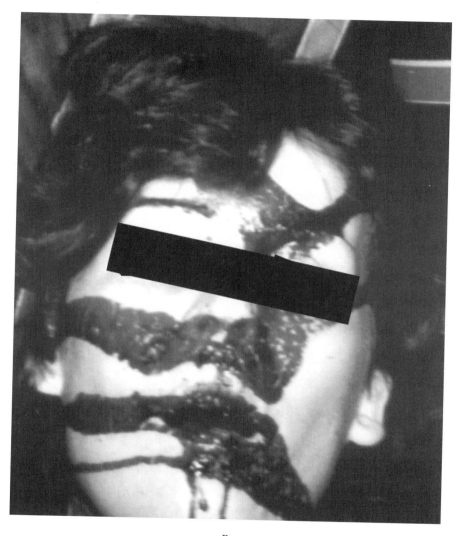

B

Figure 13.10. (continued)

One of the more problematic cases of suicide I investigated involved the suicide death of an attractive 27-year-old woman. She was discovered in her sister's fiance's apartment with a cut throat and three stab wounds to the chest. She had been hiding at the apartment from a boyfriend, who at first was our primary suspect. However, upon a complete and thorough death investigation, it was soon discovered that the circumstances of her death, as well as the evidence

C

Figure 13.10. (continued)

obtained by investigators during the crime scene search, indicated this death to be suicide. The cutting to the throat was superficial with a stigma of hesitation. The stabbing to the chest was self-inflicted. The weapon came from the scene. The premises were locked from inside. Her palm prints were found on the blade of the kitchen knife. A note found at the scene, although not a classic suicide note, did indicate the victim's depression. A handwriting analysis revealed that the deceased had written the note. A background check of the deceased indicated drug and alcohol abuse. Interviews of family and friends were conducted. Additional evidence was discovered that indicated the deceased had first tried to kill herself with a rifle found in the apartment.

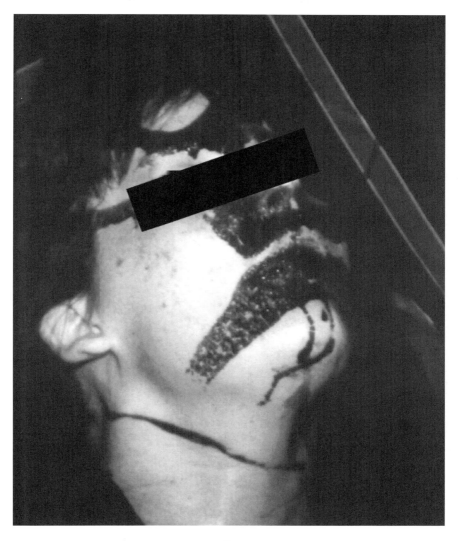

D

Figure 13.10. (continued)

There were no signs of a struggle, nor signs of forced entry into the locked apartment. The medical examiner, who responded to the scene, agreed with the investigative hypothesis and confirmed that the death was suicide.

However, the following day an associate medical examiner, who lacked the expertise of the medical examiner at the scene and the homicide detectives involved in the case, reclassified the case as a homi-

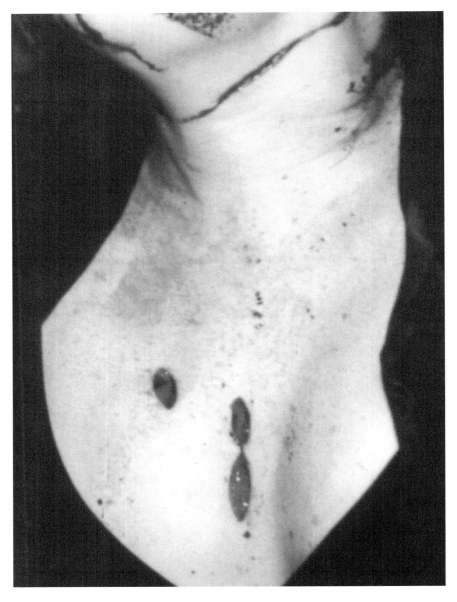

E

Figure 13.10. (continued)

cide. Her rationale was that she had never seen a body with three stab wounds to the chest and a cut throat. She made this determination without consulting the "tour" doctor, who had been at the scene. She disregarded his official notes, refused to discuss the case with me or the detectives, and adamantly insisted that this case was a homicide. As a result of her arrogant incompetence and the family's insistence, this case was subject to review by the State Attorney General's Office, the New York City Department of Investigation, and the NYPD Internal Affairs Division.

I would later have the pleasure of conferring with the Chief Medical Examiner to make an official complaint against her for her inappropriate and unprofessional behavior. The case was properly reclassified as suicide. However, the damage was done; to this day the family of that girl is convinced that their daughter was killed by the boyfriend. It was easier for them to believe that their child was killed than to accept the fact that she killed herself.

> Remember: Suicide cases can cause more problems for detectives than homicide investigations.

In fact, in my present capacity as a homicide and forensic consultant, many of the inquiries I receive concern death investigations that had originally been classified as suicides. Many of these cases raise serious questions about the actual cause of death (*homicide, suicide, accident,* or *natural*). These cases have either been inadequately investigated, or there has been inappropriate interference in the investigative process due to political or other personal considerations beyond the control of the investigator. However, in some situations the police have been too quick to classify a case as suicide based on their initial observations at the scene. The death might have looked like a suicide, however, the presentation of the circumstances was created by a clever offender who "staged the scene" to make it appear to be a suicide. I have personally investigated many such cases and the truth of the matter is that initially, the cases *did* look like suicides.

Staging a Scene

> Staging a scene occurs when the perpetrator purposely alters the crime scene to mislead the authorities and/or redirect the investigation.

The term "staging" should not be used to describe the actions of a surviving family member who covers or redresses a loved one who is found nude or has died in an embarrassing situation.

> Staging is a conscious criminal action on the part of an offender to thwart an investigation.

A

Figure 13.11.   (A) Homicide made to look like a suicide. Victim was discovered hanging from a piece of construction equipment. (B) Close-up of victim. Closer examination indicated that the victim had been "strung-up" after death and the scene staged to look like a suicide.

B

Figure 13.11. (continued)

A STAGED CRIME SCENE — CASE HISTORY

I remember one case I responded to that had been initially reported to the police as a suicide. When I arrived at the scene, I observed the nude body of a young woman lying on the floor next to the tub in the bathroom. The tub was half full of water, and the body was still wet, as though it had been submerged. The husband, who was distraught and crying, stated to the police that he had found his wife submerged in the tub upon returning to the apartment. He had pulled the body from the tub and had attempted mouth-to-mouth resuscitation. He also added that his wife had been despondent and had probably committed suicide by taking an overdose of pills and drowning herself in the tub. Officers at the scene had recovered a prescription bottle next to the victim. The general condition of the scene and the statements of the husband seemed to indicate the possibility of suicide.

I examined the body and noticed a slight bruising in the neck area. The husband explained that upon finding his wife submerged in the tub he had attempted to resuscitate her and had held her by the throat to force air into her lungs. However, when I opened the eyelids of the deceased and examined the conjunctivae, I observed the presence of *petechial hemorrhages*, and was immediately convinced that the death was, in fact, homicidal and not suicidal, as the husband claimed.

Later on, we learned that the husband had been fighting with his wife and he strangled and killed her. In order to cover up his crime, he filled the tub with water, removed his wife's clothing, and placed her in the tub.

A

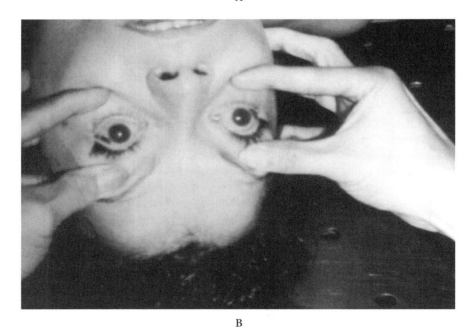

B

Figure 13.12. (A) Position of body when police arrived. The husband had indicated that he had removed his wife's body from the tub and had given her mouth-to-mouth resuscitation. (B) Evidence of petechial hemorrhage. Petechiae as well as an injury are observed in the victim's eyes.

He held her under the water to simulate the drowning and then removed her body and placed it on the floor next to the tub. In fact, he had even placed the half-empty bottle of pills next to her body to show to the responding police. The case was properly classified as homicide

It should be noted that the autopsy would have readily revealed that the death was due to manual strangulation. However, the offender, who was looking to "buy time" certainly would have evoked his right to counsel the next day when confronted with the autopsy results. The observation of petechial hemorrhages at the scene gave the investigators a head start on their murder investigation. They made further inquiries of the facts and circumstances at the scene and gathered additional evidence. When the suspect was eventually confronted with this evidence, he made a full confession to the police.

Investigative Considerations

The investigator should be aware of three basic considerations to establish if a death is suicidal in nature.

1. **The presence of the weapon or means of death at the scene.**
2. **Injuries or wounds that are obviously self-inflicted, or could have been inflicted by the deceased.**
3. **The existence of a motive or intent on the part of the victim to take his or her own life.**

It should be noted that the final determination of suicide is made by the medical examiner/coroner after all the facts are evaluated. However, the investigation at the scene and an inquiry into the background of the deceased may indicate the presence of life-threatening behavior or activities that suggest suicidal intent. Of course, the medical examiner/coroner is supposed to avail him or herself of the input of the investigators, who were present at the scene and conducted the death investigation.

The Weapon

The weapon or means of death should be present in cases of suicide. However, the absence of a weapon does not necessarily indicate that death was due to a homicide. The weapon could have been stolen or otherwise disposed of prior to the arrival of the authorities (as seen in the case of the heirloom handgun). Furthermore, family members have been known to conceal weapons and/or suicide notes in order to collect on an insurance policy. There have been many cases recorded in which the suicide victim has arranged to make his or her death appear to be a homicide for a number of reasons.

If the weapon is observed in the hands of the deceased, the investigator should examine the hand to see if the weapon is clutched tightly, due to *cadaveric spasm* (instantaneous rigor mortis) (see Chapter 9, "Body Changes After Death"). In some instances, the firearm or knife will be tightly clenched in the victim's hand at the time of death due to an intense muscular contraction of the hand. Some victims of suicide have been found tightly grasping their weapon in death. It is important to note such clutching of weapons, as you can be sure that the person held this weapon at the time of his or her death. A person attempting to place a weapon in the deceased's hand after death would *not* be able to recreate the same grasp. This is especially important in cases involving firearms. Usually when a person shoots himself in the head with a handgun, the weapon will fall from the hand of the victim. Long barrel rifles and shotguns may be found cradled in the arms of the suicide victim depending on the original position of the victim when the firearm was discharged.

In all suspected suicidal gunshot wound cases, an examination of the hands should be made for the presence of soot or powder. The weapon should be examined for evidence of discharge and operability. In addition, the weapon should be examined for the presence of any blow-back materials including blood from the victim. A ballistics test should also be conducted. It should be noted that the weapon need not be in the hand of the deceased in order for the death to be a suicide. It is important to note the survival time factor, time between injury and death, which may have enabled the deceased to perform any number of activities, including disposal of the weapon or leaving the original location where he or she first attempted suicide.

Wounds

Injuries and wounds in suicides may be very similar to those observed in homicides. However, certain observations that the wounds found on the body are consistent with homicide or suicide should be made. For example, a person found dead from multiple stab wounds of the back would certainly not be considered a victim of suicide. Likewise, in suicide cases, there appear to be preferences and avoidances for certain parts of the body. If the victim used a knife to commit suicide, the wounds will usually be on the throat or wrists. If the injury is a stab wound, it will generally be through the heart. Most suicidal stab wounds involve the mid and left chest area and are multiple in nature. The investigator should closely examine any slashing-type wounds for evidence of hesitation marks, which appear as parallel slashes alongside the

Figure 13.13. Suicide-gunshot wound to the head. This woman had shot herself in the head. The weapon was found at the scene by her hand. Although generally speaking, women do not usually shoot themselves in the head, it does occur.

mortal wound and are indicative of suicide. The investigator should not jump to any conclusions based on hesitation marks, as an assailant, who is knowledgeable about these factors, might leave similar markings to cover up a homicide.

If the victim uses a handgun, their target will likely be their head, followed by the chest into the heart, followed by the abdomen. Head shots with handguns are usually found in the temple (consistent with the handedness of the victim), followed by the forehead, or directly into the mouth. The wounds will be close-range as opposed to long-range. There should be evidence of powder burns and/or smudging.

In some instances, there may even be evidence of hesitation gun shot wounds or evidence of other shots fired prior to the fatal shot. The investigator should also examine the hands of the deceased for evidence of any blood or tissue splattering. In suicides with rifles and shotguns, the preferred sites are the head, chest, and abdomen (DiMaio, V.J., 1985).[5]

It is important to remember that wounds are never too painful to a person determined to take his or her own life. Deranged persons may inflict several extensive wounds on themselves before they collapse and die. I reviewed one case in which the deceased had attempted to hang

A

B

Figure 13.14.   (A) **SUICIDE VICTIM SITTING IN FIREPLACE.** This victim actually sat in her fireplace to end her life. Remember, do not assume that something have been too painful for the suicide to endure. (B) Same suicide victim when removed from the fireplace. Note pugilistic attitude.

A

Figure 13.15.   (A) Victim's fire-damaged automobile at the edge of the canal. The fire department had responded to a reported brush fire at this location by the St. Jude Canal in Plaquemines Parish. (B) Victim's body was found in the rear of the hatch-back. The fire department discovered the badly burned body of a female victim wrapped in chains in the rear of the auto and notified police. (C) View of the victim's body when removed from the auto. The case was first thought to be a homicide. (D) Evidence of gas containers. Four 5-gallon gas cans were located by investigators approximately 60 feet west of the burned auto. They were band new and had been recently purchased. (Courtesy of Detective James "Skip" Wright and the Jefferson Parish Sheriff's Office, Gretna, Louisiana.)

himself with an electrical cord, but the cord broke under his weight. He then cut open his stomach with an eight-inch knife and systematically removed his intestines, which he cut into pieces using a pair of tin snips. Investigators at the scene recovered an eight-inch knife, a pair of tin snips, scissors, and towels containing blood and intestines.

Just as investigators should not presume homicide based merely on the extent of injury, they should not be fooled by the method. Although suicide by fire is extremely rare, gasoline is readily available and can provide a convenient method of self-immolation. Ironically, I have found more women resorting to death by fire than men. I presume that the reason for this situation is that men are perhaps more likely to obtain firearms.

Equivocal Death Investigations

Equivocal death investigations are those inquiries that are open to interpretation. There may be two or more meanings and the case may

B

Figure 13.15 (continued)

present as either a homicide or a suicide depending upon the circumstances. The facts are purposefully vague or misleading as in the case of a "staged crime scene." Or, the death is suspicious or questionable based upon what is presented to the authorities.

I reviewed one particularly bizarre case in which a psychologically disturbed woman committed suicide under circumstances which made the case appear to be a sex-related homicide.

Investigators were called to the scene of a "possible homicide" in a secluded area near a canal. Upon arrival they observed a vehicle, which had been completely burned at the edge of a canal as if someone had pushed the car towards the water. In the rear hatchback of the auto, the detectives observed the badly burned and charred body of a white female with her pants pulled down to her mid-thigh area. The body was secured to the spare tire wheel well bracket with a steel chain. Investi-

C

D

Figure 13.15 (continued)

gators found four 5-gallon gas containers approximately 60 feet from the vehicle. It appeared that the victim had been sexually assaulted and killed by an offender who then secured the body by chain to the vehicle. The vehicle was doused with gasoline and pushed towards the canal. The car had been stopped from going into the river by a small tree.

However, upon closer examination, it was discovered that the chain was actually loose enough for someone to crawl into. The vehicle was registered to a woman, who had a history of psychological problems and had just been released from a mental institution. Authorities went to her residence where they found documents and letters indicating her intention to take her life along with her Will leaving her possessions to her son. The investigators were able to trace the gas cans to a Wal-Mart, where the deceased had purchased them along with the chain and a cigarette lighter. She had paid with American Express checks. Detectives had retrieved the sales slips and cancelled checks.

In addition, the detectives located the gas station where the deceased had filled her containers. At this gas station there was a 24-hour video. She was observed on the video making the purchase the day of the incident. She also paid for the gas with American Express checks.

Investigative reconstruction indicated that the woman had secured the chain to the spare tire wheel well bracket beforehand. She had left it loose enough to crawl into after she doused herself and her automobile with the 20 gallons of gasoline. After crawling into the chain, she lit the cigarette lighter and caused an explosion. The explosion caused the windows to blow out and the extreme heat caused the auto, which was in gear, to start and move down towards the canal. As she struggled and writhed in pain from the flames and fire, her pants were pulled down to her mid-thighs by the chain which was wrapped around her torso. The case was properly classified as a suicide.

Motives and Intent

The manner of death may be important in determining suicidal intent. For example, people who hang themselves or jump to their deaths from fatal heights have certainly indicated an intention to take their lives. Similarly, deaths that involve a combination of methods (poisoning, shooting, slashing, inhaling gas, etc.) show an extreme desire to die.

There are numerous motives to consider in suicide cases. I have found from my own personal experience, however, that some people's motives never surface; the motive died with the deceased. Some of the more common motivations are as follows:

Depression	Marital or family crisis
Drugs	Severe emotional trauma
Alcohol	Psychological problems
Stress	Physical deterioration
Frustration	Loss of a loved one
Fear	The death of a child
Anger	Financial situations
Hostility	Teenage problems
Guilt	Loss of employment
Terminal illness	Despair
Illness in the family	General inability to cope with life

I remember a case in which the body of the deceased was found at the base of a high drop. There was evidence of some cutting on the wrists and it was apparent that he had jumped or fallen from the ledge approximately 70 feet above. An examination of the body, however, indicated that his wallet was missing. A further examination of the area on the ledge failed to locate the wallet or any type of blade that could have been used to cut the wrists. The deceased had been at work the previous day and seemed to have been fine. Friends and family of the deceased had not noticed any suicidal tendencies. The case was definitely shaping up into a real mystery. Later in the day, we received a call from a neighboring jurisdiction. The police had recovered the wallet belonging to the deceased in a motel room. The room was very bloody and it appeared that there had been an assault in the premises. Further examination, however, disclosed a suicide note, an empty bottle of pills, and a bloody razor blade. Apparently, the deceased had gone to the motel room to take his own life. He had cut both wrists, consumed the contents of the prescription bottle, and bled all over the place. When death did not occur, he left the motel, got into his car, and drove approximately 10 miles back to New York City. He then selected a relatively high building in the area and jumped to his death. The suicide note, which was recovered by police, indicated that the deceased was extremely upset with his life and had planned to kill himself at the motel.

Suicide Notes

Suicide notes are direct communications indicating an intent to commit suicide. Letters and notes addressed to relatives and friends may be left at a death scene, which indicate severe depression and/or anger. The notes are often coherent and legible. The notes may be instructional and/or admonishing. Suicide notes oftentimes have mixed emotional content including "positive" and "negative" feelings. Many notes reveal what are referred to as "suicide ideations." These are the formation and conception of ideas in the mind of a person, which present suicide as a viable option. References to an "after life" or once again being with a loved one, or "looking down" are quite common.

The presence of a suicide note certainly suggests suicide. However, the investigator should conduct a further inquiry to ascertain whether or not the note is genuine. Was it written by the deceased? Was it written voluntarily? The investigator should collect the note in a manner that will preserve any latent fingerprints. In any event, known writings of the deceased (exemplars) should always be collected for comparison. Remember, even when you are sure that the deceased has written the note and you are not anticipating doing a handwriting analysis, you should still collect exemplars. This could become an issue at a later date and you will not have an opportunity to obtain such exemplars.

Excerpts are provided below of a few suicide notes from cases I have investigated and consulted on over the years in order to add some insight into the "thinking" of a person who has chosen suicide as the final solution to a real or imagined problem.

The psychology of suicide becomes an integral part of the professional investigation, and often the note provides the detective with a basis of inquiry into the background of the victim for a later psychological autopsy.

> Dear Mom and Dad, I guess the past ten years escapades have finally paid off — with my Life...I'm sorry I'm letting a lot of people down, who had faith in me, but I no longer had any faith in myself...

This case involved a young man, who had a serious alcohol problem. The actual note was two pages, and contained his telephone number and home address. The note was found in his vehicle, which had been parked on the George Washington Bridge in New York City. The note also contained a drawing that indicated he had jumped into the waters of the Hudson River. His body was found approximately five days later.

> To my family, I just got a little tired. It's not your fault, but I want you to know I love YOU very much... Love always Dad.

This case involved the suicide of a police officer. I knew this man for some 15 years and would never have suspected that he would ever take his own life. I remember interviewing his wife, who told me, "This was not the (Jack) you or I knew. He changed. There was a drastic change during the week. I think it was the medication he was taking." Jack, not his real name, had been prescribed drugs for an infection. The prescription had put him into a deep depression.

> Last will and testament, Everything goes to (Jim) with the exception of the things that belong to (John). I love you all.

This case involved a young woman, who had moved to New York City from the Midwest and had become depressed with her life. Although she had a good job as a nurse in a hyperbaric center, her real goal was to be in fashions. She decided to kill herself in front of her place of work. She probably decided that no one would miss her and she didn't want to die alone, so she took her pet dog with her. She hooked-up a vacuum cleaner hose, which she taped to the exhaust pipe of her car, and ran the hose into her vehicle. She was found by her fellow employees the next morning.

> Now, (Eva) doesn't have to say Oh she a pain now I'm dead. Now everybody is happy. I hope I wasn't a problem to nobody but if I was now I am not... I hope I didn't cause so much trouble. Tell everybody I say goodbye. Have a Happy Thanksgiving .

This was an extremely sad case involving a 12-year-old girl who took her life rather than risk being sexually abused any further by her father. The young girl, who was staying with relatives, believed that her father, who had recently been released from prison, might take her back to live with him. Investigation indicated that she had been abused since she was five years old. She shot herself with an unlicensed .38 caliber handgun after swallowing a number of pills.

> Brother and sister, we didn't have anything else in this world. Please put our bodies in the same coffin... We love you all... Don't be sad about us. Everything is in God's hands...

This was a classic "Lover's suicide pact." The two bodies were found in a motel; both of them had been shot through the head. The male was found with the gun by his hand. They were both lying in bed. The note was found on a lamp table next to a Vietnamese symbol, which meant eternity.

I reviewed an investigation for a detective, who wanted me to analyze the suicide notes left by the victim. The series of notes which the victim left were classic examples of suicide cognition. These notes contained a

A

B

Figure 13.16.   (A) **SUICIDE VICTIM'S AUTO.** Note how the vacuum hose has been taped to the exhaust pipe. The victim had placed the hose inside the front door of the auto. (B) **CLOSE-UP OF THE VICTIM'S FACE.** The victim's face was cherry red which is consistent with the inhalation of carbon monoxide.

A

B

Figure 13.17. (A) **SUICIDE PACT.** Two Vietnamese lovers made a pact to kill each other when their respective families objected to their relationship. They were discovered together in a motel room. Both suffered gunshot wounds to the head. (B) **CHINESE SYMBOL** for eternity. This was found on the night table next to the bed where the two suicide victims ended their lives.

combination of intense feelings. There was anger, rage, and revenge. There were classic suicide ideations of a better after life to be shared with loved ones. There was acceptance, hope, and a plea to God for forgiveness. There were instructions to her best friend on burial arrangements. There was an expression of gratitude to her friend, whom she thought of as family, and there were admonitions. The notes indicated an intense anger and rage towards the victim's granddaughter, whom she accused of stealing her money. The victim blamed her granddaughter for all of her depression. There was even a suggestion of revenge as the deceased wrote,

> "When you receive this letter from me, I will be gone and where you can not *hurt* me anymore."

The note then went on to list all of the money and gifts that the woman had given her granddaughter over the years, including the "power of attorney," to assure her well-being in later life.

> "How could you rob a grandmother, who did all that."..." I hope that you shed as many tears as I did. Any person, that can do what you did to me, is a person lost."...God can see you for what you are"..." Before, I close I want you to know that no matter where you are day or night, I will follow you with my eyes."..." Remember, I am your shadow looking at you until you tell me why you robbed me, mistreated me, and then hated me. You will suffer as I have suffered."

In another note, the deceased asks for forgiveness and expresses her thanks to her best friend.

> "You have been a good friend, a sister, a mother God has sent to me. I love you like a daughter. I can't thank you enough for taking care of me...I will be looking down smiling at you and I hope that I will find peace...I will pray for you and will be at Joe's wedding. You won't see me, but I will be there." (*Classic ideation.*)

> "Dear God forgive me. I can't keep going on anymore. I don't want to live anymore, I want to be with my God. I want to go home and be with my beloved daughter and be with my Lord." (*The daughter had predeceased the victim. Another classic ideation.*) "I know that God will forgive me, because He knows that I have tried. I am so sorry...Christmas coming, just can't do it." I will be with God and my daughter and my husband. *God loves me. Please think kindly* of me and forgive me."

> (*Instructional*) (Name), maybe you should have this (note) copied just so it doesn't get lost in case you may need it.

"I want to keep my little medal of the Blessed Virgin that I have around my neck on me. I want to take the medal with me." (*Ideation of going to heaven.*)

(*Instructional*) "Remember to check and see that I have all the underclothes on me when am layed out. Thank you for every thing and God will repay you some day..."

The deceased, who was elderly was concerned about modesty.

Background Information

It is important to note that the deceased may have indicated an intent to commit suicide through activities and statements prior to death. The investigation should focus on any prior mental disease or defect. Was the deceased under any professional treatment? Consider obtaining this information via subpoena if necessary. The therapist-client relationship is terminated with the death of the client. Has the deceased ever attempted suicide in the past? Research has indicated that persons who have attempted suicide in the past are likely to repeat these behaviors under similar circumstances. Has anyone in the family ever committed suicide? There may be underlying pathological or psychological dynamics to consider. Any diaries, unmailed letters, or similar writings should be examined for information that may explain the death. Many suicide deaths are preceded by verbal threats of self-destruction and other indications of despondence. In some instances these threats are made to people whom the deceased respects or highly regards. In other instances sudden change in behavior is shown by subtle actions, such as increasing life insurance, giving away prized possessions, disregarding doctor's advice, or abuse of alcohol or drugs.

Psychological Autopsy

The psychological autopsy is a collaborative procedure involving law enforcement and mental health experts who attempt to determine the state of mind of a person prior to the fatal act. By examining the victim's life-style and interviewing the victim's friends and relatives, they determine whether the death was accidental or involved suicide.

Warning Signs

1. A change in sleeping habits — sleeping more than usual or staying up much later — followed by sadness
2. A change in eating habits — weight loss or lack of appetite.

3. A lack of interest in sex — loss of sex drive.
4. A sudden drop in grades or school attendance — young people; loss of work interest — adults.
5. Loss of interest in favorite activities, hobbies, or sports.
6. Loss of interest in friends, family, etc. — isolation.

Extreme Danger Signs

1. Suddenly becoming cheerful or calm after a depression — a sudden euphoria or burst of activity. This could mean that the person has resolved the inner conflict by deciding to take his or her life. The decision is made.
2. Giving away prized possessions.
3. Speaking of life in the past tense — e.g., saying, "I've loved you," or "You've been a good mother."

Investigative Considerations

Evaluation of the Wounds

1. Could the deceased have caused the injuries and death?
2. Was the person physically able to accomplish the act?
3. Are the wounds within reach of the deceased?
4. Are the wounds grouped together?
5. Is there more than one cause of death?
6. Describe the nature and position of the injuries.
7. Are there any hesitation marks?

Psychological State of the Victim

1. Obtain a background of the victim from family and friends. This background should include medical as well as social information.
2. Were there any *warning signs* indicated by the victim?
3. Were there any recent deaths in the family?
4. Is there any indication of a recent upset or stress?
5. Did the victim leave any notes? Request a sample of the victim's handwriting for analysis in case a note is later discovered.
6. Any close personal relationships, close friends, etc.? Interview as soon as possible.

Any Prior Mental Disease or Defect

1. Has the deceased been under any professional treatment?
2. Had the deceased ever attempted suicide in the past?

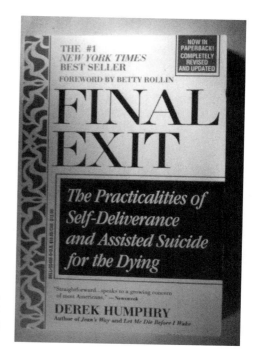

Figure 13.18. The book *Final Exit*. Often found at the scene of a "Final Exit Suicide" with notations or highlighting of pertinent chapters.

3. Has anyone in the family ever committed suicide?
4. Was the deceased a heavy drinker?
5. Was the deceased on any medication?
6. Was there a history of drug abuse?
7. Was there a history of physical or psychological abuse to the deceased?

"Final Exit" Suicide Investigations

Introduction

This section of the chapter addresses the phenomena of victim-facilitated suicide and victim-assisted suicide events in which the individual has followed instructions provided in the book *Final Exit*. In my capacity as a homicide consultant, I have had the opportunity to interact with many investigators from a number of different agencies within the United States and Canada. As a result of an informal survey conducted among attendees at my *Practical Homicide Investigation* programs, I have discovered an increase in these type suicides. I have selected the city of St. Louis for my case illustrations; however, my research indicates that there are a significant number of "*Final Exit*" suicides occurring throughout the country. In an article which appeared in the *New*

York Times, dated November 6, 1993, medical authorities in New York City have reported an increase in the number of suicides since the publication of the book. The article also referred to statistics from the National Center for Health Statistics which reported that plastic bag asphyxiation-type suicides increased 30.8% between 1990 and 1991 (*New York Times,* November 6, 1993, p. A12).[6]

In 1991, Mr Derek Humphrey wrote a very controversial book entitled: *Final Exit: The Practicalities of Self-Deliverance and Assisted Suicide for the Dying* (New York: Dell Publishing).[7] Ironically, this book about suicide and death actually topped the *New York Times* best-seller list in 1991. In 1992 it was published in many languages and made available in a revised and updated paperback version. This book, published as an informational aid to end life, actually provides detailed instruction and guidance to the reader on how an individual can effectively terminate his or her own life.

The initial impassioned debates over whether or not this book should have been published have since diminished. The moral implications of such a treatise rightly remain the subject of theology and personal religious beliefs. However, Mr. Humphrey does make a statement early on in his book, and I quote:

> "If you consider God the master of your fate, then read no further. Seek the best pain management available and arrange for hospice care." (Humphrey, 1991, p.4)[8]

However, once Mr. Humphrey gets that "God" question out of the way, he further states;

> "If you want personal control and choice over your destiny, it will require forethought, planning, documentation, friends, and decisive, courageous action from you. This book will help." (ibid, p.4)[9]

In my professional opinion this book provides someone, who is predisposed to suicide, the wherewithal and step-by-step guide to terminate his or her life. It is not my intention to debate the moral implications of this book, nor to impose my personal theology and belief in God to the reader. Instead, I wish to focus on the investigative considerations that this book presents in suicide investigations. Investigators need to be cognizant of the concept of self-deliverance and the methodologies which are presented in *Final Exit* in order to conduct professional death inquiries, particularly, if the deceased was assisted in the suicide by another person. At the risk of increasing Mr. Derek

Humphrey's book sales, I do recommend that investigators secure a copy of *Final Exit* for their research library as a reference source in the event that they encounter such cases.

Synopsis of Contents

Final Exit is comprised of two major sections, Part 1 is entitled "Self-Deliverance for the Dying Person" and is comprised of twenty-three brief chapters. Each of these sections address substantive issues in the dynamics of suicide and euthanasia. Contents include "The Euthanasia Decision," "Shopping for the 'Right Doctor'," "Beware of the Law," "The Hospice Option," "The Cyanide Enigma," ways to die (presenting a number of options and case scenarios), going together, "Self-Deliverance Via the Plastic Bag," recommendations of medications and how to obtain the drugs, how to avoid the medicolegal autopsy, insurance considerations, what letters need to be written, sample legal forms, documentation, and a Final Exit Checklist. Part 2 is entitled "Euthanasia Involving Doctors and Nurses" and is comprised of five chapters which address the medical profession and the law including a section on Dr. Jack Kevorkian's "Suicide Machine." *Final Exit* includes a Drug Dosage Table (with footnotes to drug dosage) which identifies, by both generic and trade name, the most effective drugs for self-deliverance. In addition, there is a listing of recommended readings, information on the Hemlock Society (a group formed in 1980 to campaign for the right of a terminally ill person to choose voluntary euthanasia), and four appendixes dealing with The Death and Dignity Act, Pain Control, Suicide Hot Lines, and A Living will and Durable Power of Attorney for Health Care.

Investigative Considerations

There are specific instructions within the book *Final Exit* that will indicate that the deceased intended to commit suicide and was guided by the rationale of self-deliverance. The presence of the book at the crime scene as well as the dynamics of the suicide event should be properly documented. In addition, certain items at the scene as well as the circumstances of the death might suggest the possibility of victim assistance.

Letters to be Written

In Chapter 17, Mr. Humphrey explains to the reader the importance of the "suicide note."

"It must clearly state why you are taking your life, that you accept sole responsibility, and that nobody else persuaded you. In the event you are discovered before death has taken place, you must demand that you are not to be disturbed but allowed to die. Using the law of informed consent, you cannot be touched or treated without your permission. If you were revived you could, technically, sue for battery." (Humphrey, 1991, p. 81.)[10]

Mr. Humphrey also states that the person can utilize a tape recorder to make the suicide statement, clearly marking the cassette, "My Final Statement." (ibid, p. 83).[11]

In addition, the reader is advised to attach to the suicide note copies of a Living Will and Durable Power of Attorney for Health Care (the reader is provided with an address and telephone number for information where to obtain these items). The reader is also advised to make two copies, since the police and/or coroner will take a copy.

Case History

On March 24, 1993, St. Louis Police were called to an apartment to "check the well-being" of the occupant. Upon arrival the officers met the concerned friend who had called the police after being unable to make contact. The police were admitted to the secured apartment by the building manager where they discovered the deceased. The victim was discovered nude, face down. There was a syringe and a large amount of prescription drugs at the scene.

Police Investigation

P.O. Daniel Chitwood conducted a preliminary investigation for follow-up by Det. Sgt. Joseph Beffa, St. Louis Homicide. The investigation revealed that the deceased was HIV positive and was terminally ill with the AIDS virus. According to his close friend, the deceased had talked of committing suicide on several occasions. There were three letters found at the crime scene indicating the deceased's suicidal intention as well as a copy of the book *Final Exit*. The case was classified as suicide. The three letters were written according to the recommendations in *Final Exit*, one of which used the "Law of Informed Consent"

"To whom it may concern:
I, (name deleted) have decided to end my life because of my AIDS DISEASE. I have seen too much pain and been through alot! I am tired of trying and no longer wish to continue life as I know it and as I know my body will become...

> This decision is known to no other and has been mine alone in a normal state of mind. No one helped or persuaded me to take my life.
>
> If I am discovered before I stop breathing. I will certainly sue anyone who attemp (sic) to revive me. Do not touch me until I'm dead. (signed by the deceased)

Self-Deliverance via the Plastic Bag

In Chapter 19, Mr. Derek Humphrey makes reference to the use of a plastic bag as an aid in self-deliverance. He states, "If you don't have the help of a physician to aid the dying, then a plastic bag as well as drugs is highly advisable" (Humphrey, 1991, p. 91). Mr. Humphrey states that it is important that the bag be firmly tied around the neck in order to prevent any air from coming through. He also makes reference to the use of an ice-bag to avoid the distress of the breathing of hot air which may create an unpleasant hot and "stuffy" feeling.

The author makes reference to "devoted couples" wanting to handle the process themselves and also instructs the reader on the law relative to assistance in suicide. I quote,

> "The actual helping of the person constitutes the crime by demonstrating intent. Intent is necessary for successful prosecution. So it is preferable if the person wanting deliverance does it alone. There is no legal risk in removing the bag once the person stops breathing. Removal also reduces the chance of police or medical examiners suspecting suicide." (Humphrey, 1991, p. 95)[12]

Mr. Humphrey points out that the two best methods of self-deliverance are from the use of selected prescription drugs, aided by a plastic bag (ibid, p.109).[13] Mr. Humphrey recommends the barbiturate drugs such as secobarbital (Seconal) and pentobarbital (Nembutal) as first choice followed by Valium and Darvon which are nonbarbiturates. He asserts that drinking alcohol will hasten the drug's effect by 50 percent (ibid, p. 110)[14] and states that Vodka is extremely effective (ibid, p.112).[15]

Case History

On November 11, 1992, St. Louis Homicide detectives were dispatched to a call of "suspicious sudden death." Upon arrival at the location, they observed a female victim, lying on her bed with an ice-pack under her neck and a plastic bag covering her head. The detectives also observed eleven (11) bottles of various prescription medication bearing the deceased's name.

Figure 13.19.   **FINAL EXIT SUICIDE VICTIM.** The victim was discovered with a plastic bag over her head and evidence that she had taken an overdose of prescription drugs. (Courtesy of Lieutenant Alfred Adkins and Detective Dave Calloway, City of St. Louis Metropolitan Police Department.)

Police Investigation

Det. Sgt. Alfred Adkins and Det. Dave Calloway conducted the police investigation. Their analysis of the circumstances and facts surrounding this incident revealed that the deceased had numerous medical problems and was seeing a psychiatrist. She had recently been despondent and according to a close friend had stated that she was going to get all of her affairs in order and leave the world. The deceased often spoke about suicide and had bought several books on the subject including *Final Exit*.

The detectives seized the book as evidence. In their police reports they referenced Chapter 19 "Self-Deliverance Via the Plastic Bag" and Chapter 22 "The Final Act" due to the similar circumstances of the decedent's death. The victim had apparently followed the instructions in *Final Exit*. Their investigation indicated that the victim was not assisted in her death and the case was classified as suicide.

In Chapter 22, Derek Humphrey presents the reader with the following "self-deliverance" procedure which I have cited below:

A

Figure 13.20. (A) **FINAL EXIT CASE.** Victim used a canister of carbon monoxide to end his life. *Final Exit* book was found at the scene. (B) Notes found at the scene. Suicide notes and book were found at the scene just as described in *Final Exit*. (Courtesy of Detective Sergeant Joseph Beffa, Homicide Squad, City of St. Louis Metropolitan Police Department.)

B

The Final Act

1. An hour beforehand have an extremely light meal — perhaps tea and a piece of toast — so that the stomach is nearly vacant but not so empty that you would feel nauseous and weak.

2. At the same time take a travel sickness pill such as dramamine which will ward off nausea later.
3. When the hour has elapsed, take about ten of your chosen tablets or capsules with as large a drink of spirits or wine as you are comfortable with. Vodka is extremely effective. If you cannot drink alcohol, use your favorite soda drink.
4. Have the additional powdered tablets already mixed into a pudding and swallow that as fast as is possible.
5. Throughout, keep plenty of alcoholic drink or soda at your side to wash this all down. It will also help dilute the bitter taste.[16]

Case History

May 1, 1993, the body of a 38-year-old male was discovered in a warehouse in St. Louis, Missouri by two members of a rock band that used the building for band practice. The deceased was found lying on his back. There was a cylinder of compressed gas and an empty bottle of vodka lying next to the body. The label on the cylinder indicated that the gas was carbon monoxide. There were several handwritten notes, apparently written by the deceased, found near the victim which indicated his intention to take his life by inhaling the carbon monoxide gas along with instructions of "what to do" to whoever found his body. Also found next to the victim's body was the book, *Final Exit.*

Police Investigation

Det. Sgt. Joseph Beffa and P.O. Daniel Chitwood conducted the death scene investigation. The deceased left four notes. The first note was addressed to "Young Rockers" dated 4/30/93. He instructs them to (1) turn-off the gas and (2) no smoking. He then explains that he got into the "Rock Warehouse" and hid in the corner while the band rehearsed. He states, "I enjoyed it — Thanks." He then adds, "Sorry for the hassal." (Signed his name).

In Chapter 17, Mr. Humphrey states,

"If you are unfortunately obliged to end your life in a hospital or motel. It is gracious to leave a note apologizing for the shock and inconvenience to the staff." (Humphrey, p. 82)[17]

The deceased, although not in a hospital or motel took the advice and left this note apologizing for any inconvenience he caused by taking his life at the warehouse.

There were two suicide notes. One stated, "I have committed suicide" and provided the name of a police official from his home town to contact. The second suicide note was a three-page handwritten letter in which the deceased discussed his rationale for "ending his life."

The fourth note was attached to a gas company receipt. This receipt indicated that the deceased had put a $100.00 deposit down for the carbon monoxide cylinder. In his note he apologizes to the company representative for "tricking" her into providing him with the gas. He then requests that they help his parents get the deposit money back.

On pages 152 and 153 in the *Final Exit* book found at the crime scene, the investigators noticed that the deceased had underlined and circled those passages relative to the use of carbon monoxide gas and had written "How many cubic feet?" on page 153. The authorities seized the book and xeroxed this reference for their file on this case. The death was classified as suicide.

Investigative Checklist for Final Exit Cases

- [ ] Is the book *Final Exit* at the crime scene?
- [ ] Check the book for any entries, highlighting, or writing relative to what is observed in the crime scene and how this relates to what is observed in the crime scene or any evidence of "acts of self-deliverance."
- [ ] Are there any "suicide notes" at the scene?
- [ ] Seize these notes as evidence for fingerprint and handwriting analysis.
- [ ] Obtain a handwriting exemplar (writings of the deceased when she or her was still alive).
- [ ] Compare the contents of the notes with the "Letters to be Written" chapter recommended in the book *Final Exit*.
- [ ] Take "major-case" prints of the deceased. These include not only fingerprints, but palmar (hand) prints as well.
- [ ] Request "major case" prints from all persons present or who are considered close to the deceased.
- [ ] The plastic bag: Presence of a plastic bag at the scene is highly suggestive of *Final Exit* type suicides. The investigator should note and document the following:
  - [ ] Is there a plastic bag over the victim's head or present at the crime scene?

☐ Submit the entire plastic bag for an examination of latent fingerprints. Check the plastic bag for any fingerprints for comparison/elimination with the deceased.
☐ Seize all prescription/drugs medication at the scene for subsequent toxicological examination.
☐ Note trade name, Doctor, Pharmacist, and date.
☐ Compare these with "Drug Dosage Chart" in *Final Exit.*

Remember: There is a presumption of possible victim assistance in these type suicides based upon the information in *Final Exit*.

Recommendations

I recommend that investigators be cognizant of the concept of self-deliverance and the methodologies which are presented in *Final Exit* in order to conduct professional death inquiries. At present there isn't any empirical study of these cases due to the lack of an identifiable population of cases. The informal sampling that I conducted tends to support that hypothesis that these events are occurring with some regularity. Therefore, I recommend that investigators who encounter these events make an appropriate reference to the case as a *Final Exit Suicide.*

Conclusion

Final Exit type suicides are distinctively unique from other suicide cases. They are planned events with the possibility of victim assistance. Law enforcement personnel who investigate sudden and violent deaths have a responsibility to properly document and classify these events.

Staged Crime Scenes Involving Final Exit

Investigators should be aware that a clever perpetrator could mislead the police by committing a homicide and making it appear to be a "Final Exit" suicide. The author reviewed a case in which the scene had been staged as a Final Exit suicide. The victim, who had been on chemotherapy after an operation to remove ovarian and liver cancer, had recently been informed that the cancer tumors had started to grow. She was found in her bed with a gun by her right hand. There was a typed note at the scene stating, "I can't take it anymore, no more, no more." The book *Final Exit* was found next to the victim. The death appeared to be a suicide especially considering the victimology of the deceased. However, the woman's death was in fact a cleverly disguised murder. The son of the victim had purchased the book "*Final Exit*" with the mother's credit card. He had shot her in the head while she was sleeping. He then wiped off the gun and placed it near her hand. He typed the suicide note and placed it on the night table next to the book *Final Exit* and then called police to report that his mother had killed herself. (See "Staged Crime Scenes" in Chapter 1.)

Suicide-By-Cop

Introduction

The term "suicide-by-cop" is a police colloquialism used to describe incidents in which individuals, bent on self-destruction, engage in life-threatening and criminal behavior in order to force the police to kill them.

Example

May 22, 1986, 11:05 P.M. A 27-year old male, identified as Tim Sebastian calls the Butler County Sheriff's Department, in Hamilton, Ohio to report that a man (Tim Sebastian) is prowling around his home and that the man is armed and dangerous. He then cuts his telephone lines so that his wife cannot call back. When the officers arrived, Sebastian approached them despite their instructions for him to remain still. The officers attempted to discourage Sebastian from making any further threatening motions. He then pulled a shiny metallic object from his belt and pointed it at one of the officers. Both officers fired hitting the man in the chest. The object turned out to be a pair of vice grips. A review of the incident indicated that the subject had given a farewell birthday gift to his son before calling police and had made a prior suicide attempt earlier in the month by swallowing rat poison. This is an example of *suicide-by-cop*.

This relatively new phenomenon confronting law enforcement appears to have begun in the mid-1980s. Seemingly, these events are on the increase. However, since they are not classified as *suicide-by-cop* the actual number of these incidents is unknown. To date, there has not been an empirical study of these events. Historically, there have been many justifiable homicide events resulting from the imminent use of deadly physical force against law enforcement officials. Most of these police shootings occur during the commission of a violent crime or in connection with an independent police action resulting in a confrontation between the offender and the police.

However, more recently, there has been a growing number of *justifiable homicides*, in which police officers have shot and killed an apparently armed individual who has threatened the officer or others with the immediate use of deadly physical force. The subsequent homicide investigation, assessment, and review of the circumstances reveal many of these events to be *victim precipitated.*

The dynamics of such victim precipitated homicides is that the police officer is confronting an individual who has a death wish and intends to force the police into a situation where the only alternative is for the police to kill him. The motivations of these people bent on self destruction range from the clinical to the bizarre.

An example of one such bizarre circumstance was played out in Jasper, Arkansas. Keith "FOU" Haigler and his wife Kate took a busload of hostages in order to force a confrontation with the police. They were members of a religious cult called the Foundation of Ubiquity (FOU) also known as the Father of Us. Keith Haigler stated, "I am the spiritual son of the long awaited Messiah." The entire episode was based on a delusional belief that they would be resurrected after the police killed them. The media covered the event, during which Keith Haigler made the following statements. "We are the two witnesses spoken about in the Book of Revelations...We want you (the media) to put this nationwide. The long awaited Messiah is here. The proof is that we are going to be shot by the police officers. We have the consent of my father to have our bodies placed on his land for 3 1/2 days. After the 3 1/2 day period the spirit of life and God enters. They stand on their feet...It's all in the Book of Revelations."

As the police were attempting to negotiate with Haigler, the media advised that they would have to get their film to the local T.V. station in time for the evening news. At this point, Haigler stated, "I want you to get the shooting in." A short time later, Keith and Kate "FOU" Haigler exited the bus with their guns in hand. The police fired at their right shoulders to immobilize and save them from themselves. However, both parties turned the guns on each other in a homicide/suicide ending. *It should be noted that on the third day neither one of them rose from the dead.*

Clinical Interpretations

I interviewed Dr. Harvey Schlossberg, former Director of Psychological Services of the New York City Police Department and presently Chief Consulting Psychologist for the Port Authority of New York and New Jersey.[18] I asked him whether or not he recognized the phenomenon of "suicide-by-cop" scenarios. He stated, "Absolutely. It is crystal clear. These type incidents represent clear-cut suicides in which the offender is inviting the police to kill him." Dr. Schlossberg described an incident involving two police officers. They had responded to a "man with a gun" call and were confronted by an individual who took up a barrier position and pointed his weapon at the police. The police ordered the man to drop his gun. He refused and made actions as if he was about to fire the pistol. The man was shot and killed by the police. His pistol was actually a toy gun. This case is an example of a clear-cut intention to die by police gunfire.

Dr. Schlossberg has testified as an expert witness in many such cases in New York City and across the United States. He states that, "the motivational elements in such incidents illustrate the person's desire oftentimes unconscious, sometimes conscious to commit suicide. Determining the motive is based on the type of weapon which include, unloaded or imitation guns, the threat to shoot, which forces the police to fire and the discovery of an intent on the part of the subject to commit suicide. In other situations, the individual may be seriously psychiatrically disturbed and there will be an extensive psychiatric background."

I asked Dr. Schlossberg, "Why do people select police officers as a vehicle of their own death?" Dr. Schlossberg stated, "It's the most obvious and easiest way to die. Suicide by jumping from a tall building, suicide by running your car into a tree and suicide by blowing your own brains out requires a decision on the part of the person bent on self-destruction. If you can get someone else to do it for you, you are 'writing-off the sin' or avoiding the stigma or social taboos associated with suicide. The police are a good object for this. Police symbolically represent the social conscience. Sometimes, suicidal people feel guilty about something real or imagined. They seek punishment. In other cases they just don't have the guts to end it all."

The Psychopathology of Suicide-By-Cop Scenarios

I interviewed Dr. Ronald Turco, M.D. a psychiatrist and police detective from Beaverton, Oregon, who stated that suicide-by-cop scenarios may take several forms.[19]

1. Individuals simply are depressed to the extent that they wish to die, but do not want to take their own lives. There may be a degree of grandiosity associated with the act of a public display of their difficulty and having the supreme authority figure take their lives.

2. In other instances, and possibly at the root of all such occurrences, is the identification that the individual has with a parent

figure or substitute that has been rejecting and critical. In such an instance, the parent may have harbored an unconscious wish for the destruction of the offspring. It is as if the individual is asking the police officer to kill him or her because this represents the ultimate hostility toward the original parent. It is as if they are saying, "You want me dead. Go ahead kill me. This is what you want. To hell with you."

3. In some cases of terrorists activity, the individual has identified with a "super cause" and desires to die at the hands of the hated enemy in a show of defiance. Usually this type of suicide-by-cop comes at the end of a hostage negotiation that has gone sour or under circumstances in which the member or members of the terrorist group do not wish to capitulate to the 'enemy'; and, therefore choose to be blown-up, shot, etc., and go down "in a blaze of glory."

According to Dr. Turco, "The most commonplace police officer assisted suicide is that of a mentally ill person who is simply depressed, is acting out a rage toward a parent or parent substitute (in psychiatric terms an introjected object), and who has basically cast the police officer in the role of despised parent. Therefore, the individual accomplishes his own destruction; but flaunts it in the face of authority. Police officers in such instances experience various degrees of guilt sometimes necessitating treatment."

Hostage Situations

Many suicide-by-cop scenarios involve hostage taking. This requires that police personnel on the scene be effectively able to diffuse the situation and/or dissuade the hostage taker from harming the hostages or himself. Hostage negotiation skills are of paramount importance in such incidents. Dealing with hostage incidents requires setting up communications, establishing a command post and support personnel for the negotiator, and effective intelligence gathering in order to formulate a negotiating strategy and cooperative team effort with the tactical unit.

I interviewed retired Detective Captain Frank Bolz, Jr.[20] who was one of the founders of the New York City Hostage Negotiation Team and is presently a crisis management consultant. Bolz states, "The perpetrator of a hostage situation has four perceived options: escape, surrender, suicide, or homicide. For two of these options, *suicide and surrender*, there seems to be a ritual that a subject will go through. These are difficult for the police to differentiate."

Some suicide indicators are:

1. The subject sets a deadline for his or her own death.
2. Mentioning names of people who are dead and talking about them as if they are still alive or indicating that he or she will soon be with them.
3. Making verbal statements or arrangements for the disposition of "worldly goods;" giving away "prized possessions", which includes items he or she has at the time of the negotiations; i.e., wrist watch, rings, etc.
4. Subject may create a confrontational face-to-face negotiating posture with the police.
5. Making an announcement or declaration of an intent to die.
6. Making biblical references, specifically as they relate to the Book of Revelations and resurrection.

According to Bolz, who is a recognized authority on hostage negotiations, "The resolve to commit suicide many times fades or is diminished if the person is contained and allowed to articulate and ventilate his or her problems. Many times, in hostage/barricade situations, the tactical people inadvertently contribute to the success of the perpetrator committing suicide by police, because they do not have good cover and are forced to respond with fire power in order to save their own lives. *However, when one sets his or her mind to commit suicide-by-cop, police negotiations and tactics will probably not dissuade their intentions. The Jasper, Arkansas incident in which two religious cult members wanted to die at the hands of the police is an example of such intent.*"

EXAMPLE OF THE PSYCHOLOGY OF A WOULD-BE SUICIDE-BY-COP EXCERPT FROM A STATEMENT GIVEN TO POLICE

The subject had gone to a local restaurant with a fake bomb in a box. He asked to speak to the manager, showed him the "bomb" and told him to have everyone leave. The manager advised the patrons that there was a gas leak and they would have to leave. He then called the police and reported that "There was man in the restaurant with a bomb." Houston Police responded with hostage negotiators, who convinced the suspect to surrender his bomb. The subject gave police a complete confession and explanation of his actions. I have taken an excerpt from the statement to illustrate the subject's thinking:

"...my mom had come by to my apartment and accused me of breaking into my grandmother's house. I have pawned some of my grandmother's things in the past when I was on drugs, but I haven't caused any problems since I have been clean. So when my mom accused me of breaking into my grandmother's house it didn't feel right. It just didn't seem right. It crushed me. So, I thought about killing myself but I didn't want to go to hell. I am religious and I didn't want to go to hell. So, I figured I would just throw a bottle in a box and say it was a bomb and they (police) would have to shoot me. I just figured the police would do it...I figured I would use the fake bomb because I would know that I wouldn't hurt anybody. I knew that if the police were going to shoot me that I would have to be a threat. So, if I had a bomb that would be a threat. I didn't want to use a real bomb or a gun because then I would really be endangering other people's lives. My intentions were not to harm anybody but myself...." (signed by subject)[21]

This particular statement which was taken by the Houston Police is a classic example of the thinking of someone who wants to end his life but doesn't want to do it himself. The subject was charged with making a "terroristic threat" and "possession of a hoax bomb."

CLASSIC CASE HISTORY — INVOLVING A RETIRED POLICE OFFICER

On August 6, 1992, at approximately 6:57 P.M., Richard Raymond Segura entered a retail store in a shopping mall located at 3329 E. Bell Road in Phoenix, Arizona. He approached the clerk and asked her to call the police, stating that there was a man in the parking lot waving a gun around. The clerk called 911 and was asked for a description by the police operator. The clerk went outside and contacted Mr. Segura. When the clerk asked about the man with the gun, Segura told her it was him and showed her a gun. The clerk returned to the store and notified the 911 operator. Phoenix police officers, Gregory Sargis, Dean Flaherty, Ben Leuscher, and James Collins were among the first officers to arrive at the parking lot of the shopping complex. The officers had received a description of the "man with the gun" and his vehicle from the police radio and spotted their suspect on the north side of the parking lot. As officer Collins drove towards the subject's vehicle, he saw the man get out of the car with a gun in his hand. The man held his weapon up for Collins to see and "worked the action." Officer Collins exited his vehicle and drew his service weapon. The man then reached back into his auto and removed a red-colored book. He held his weapon in his right hand and the red book in his left hand and began to move towards Collins. In the meantime, officers Sargis, Flaherty, and Leuscher had positioned themselves behind their police vehicles. Officer Collins yelled to the man to drop his gun, Segura stated, "I can't do that," and kept advancing. Segura then stated, "Shoot me, but don't mess up my face." As the suspect got closer, Collins retreated to the rear of his car. At this point, all four of the officers were yelling to the man to drop his gun, who repeatedly yelled, "Shoot me." During this confrontation, Segura was facing Collins and Flaherty. Officers Sargis and Leuscher were south of the suspect. As Segura made a movement of his right arm towards officer Collins, Officer Sargis fired two shots one of which hit the suspect in the chest. The suspect, Segura died at the hospital. The weapon was a .380 caliber semiautomatic pistol, which was unloaded, but with the hammer cocked.

Richard Raymond Segura, was a 42-year-old male, Hispanic, who had been a deputy with the Pima County Sheriff's Office. He had retired in 1989 due to injuries he had received on the job. Investigation revealed that approximately 2 weeks before this incident, Richard Segura and his wife had become involved in a domestic altercation. Richard Segura was reportedly despondent over the break-up of his marriage and apparently decided to take his own life by forcing the officers to kill him. Among the items that Segura held in his left hand during the confrontation was a handwritten note stating, "I love you my dear wife. To live without you and Krystal is not to live at all." The note had his address and telephone numbers and was signed, "Love Chiquito." At the bottom of the piece of paper Segura had apparently left a message for the police officers who were forced to fire upon him. It stated, "Thanks guys, always trust your own to do the job."

Psychological Ramifications for Police Officers Involved in Suicide-By-Cop Incidents

Suicide-by-cop scenarios psychologically traumatize the officers involved in such incidents. According to psychiatrist, Dr. Ronald Turco, M.D. and psychologist, Dr. Harvey Schlossberg, both forensic experts in the field of police related stress, officers will be depressed and angry upon discovering that they were used for an execution. They need to ventilate and get in touch with their anger. Both recommend intervention strategies.

According to Dr. Harvey Schlossberg, who has treated a number of officers for shooting-related stress, the effects of a "suicide-by-cop" incident can be devastating. It amounts to a psychological assault on the officer. He or she is basically shattered as a result of the incident.

As a general rule, people tend to feel guilty about their actions. It is part of human nature to feel guilty. We are basically governed by guilt. You should do this; you shouldn't do that, etc. The officer finds him or herself second guessing the incident. Maybe I should have held fire until I could get a better look at the gun. Maybe I should have tried to physically disarm him, etc. All of these thoughts are psychologically damaging and parallel Post Traumatic Stress Disorder (PTSD). The officer begins to relive the incident over and over again. Some of the most common symptoms are depression coupled with anxiety, an inability to sleep, hypersensitivity, irritability, nightmares, and flashbacks.

In addition, most probably there will be civil suits filed by lawyers for the family of the deceased against the police and the sympathies will generally be for the surviving family. This seems to reinforce the guilt the officer is already experiencing. According to Dr. Schlossberg, critical incident stress debriefings and intervention are a must. Ironically, the officer finds himself or herself in a moral dilemma based on role conflict. The messages police receive are twofold. Shoot to kill. Defend yourself. You are supposed to shoot the bad guy. The media, T.V., and movies, i.e., Dirty Harry, Out for Justice, Lethal Weapon all support the concept of the police shooting the offender. At the same time the other message being driven home by many police administrators is, "You're not supposed to shoot your gun. Shoot only as a last resort. You will be suspended and placed under investigation, etc." According to Dr. Schlossberg, these dual messages amount to the "double-bind" concept where the individual receives contradictory messages as portrayed by the schizophrenogenic mother who tells the child you have to drink your milk and then adds you're putting on too much weight, don't drink so much milk.

The Racial Component in Police-Related Shooting Incidents

A police-related shooting incident in which a minority subject is killed by police can cause community unrest and in some instances major civil disturbances. The shooting may be justifiable, but many times the potential for civil violence can be exacerbated by certain individuals, who can best be described as racial racketeers. I refer to them as the racial PEP squad; the *provocateurs, entrepreneurs,* and *prevaricators,* who have made a business of racism in this country. In the two cases cited below, there were allegations by some members of the black community that the police shootings were unnecessary. There were demonstrations against the police and a suggestion that the deaths were racially motivated.

CASE HISTORIES — RACIAL INCIDENTS

Incident: St. Louis, Missouri. Wednesday, December 23, 1992. A 17-year-old, male, black is shot and killed by police. A hostile crowd gathers and surrounds the police, who call for assistance. The allegation by some members of the community was that the police shot an unarmed youth for no reason.

Facts: The police officers had attempted to pull the suspect over for a series of traffic violations. There was a pursuit when he failed to comply. The suspect drove onto a front yard. When the police approached the suspect he reached for a gun in the back seat and pointed it at the officers. The officers yelled to the suspect to "drop the gun" twice. The suspect shouted "You'll have to kill me." He then turned toward one of the officers with a gun in his right hand. The officer fired four shots at the suspect. As the suspect was being handcuffed he stated, "Please kill me, please kill me." The gun was unloaded.

Investigation: Revealed that the suspect, who was upset with his girlfriend, had told his grandmother that he was going to kill himself or someone else. Other relatives confirmed that the subject was "acting and talking crazy" and had made statements that he was going to kill himself. He was last seen by a friend, who saw him run out of the house, enter his jeep and speed away.

Incident: Indianapolis, Indiana. Monday, October 8, 1990. A 40-year-old, male, black was shot and killed by an off-duty police officer who was working an overtime shift in full uniform as a security officer for a restaurant. The subject was identified as an ex-convict and prison-rights activist, who had tried to establish a career as a columnist and minister in the black community.

Facts: The man, who was brandishing a handgun, entered the closed restaurant through an open door and surprised two men who were steam cleaning the rugs. The officer, who was seated in the rear saw the man from the back and asked it he could help him. The subject then turned and started towards the officer with the handgun at his side. As the man came closer to the officer, he raised his left hand, which held the gun and began to point it at the officer. The officer drew his weapon and fired hitting the man in the chest. The gun was unloaded.

Investigation: Revealed that the suspect, who had been arrested 19 times since 1967 and had served 10 years for armed robbery, had recently returned to drug use. The weapon was a .32 caliber semi-automatic pistol. The hammer was in a cocked position with the safety lever in fire mode. The magazine and chamber were void of ammunition. According to friends, the subject had stated that if he didn't get out of town, he felt he was going to die in a police action shooting. He told another acquaintance that he was contemplating suicide. The restaurant, where the shooting took place, always has an armed officer in full uniform at the premises. Witnesses had seen the subject peering into the window of the establishment approximately 10 minutes before entering.

Investigative Considerations

Practically speaking, incidents of suicide-by-cop should be investigated as *both a homicide and suicide.* The investigative procedures employed should not only focus on the homicide aspect but also the clinical considerations and dynamics of suicide. The reality of police-related-shootings is that the onus is on the police agency involved to articulate and explain exactly how and why the incident took place. In addition, most police-related shootings will become matters of civil litigation. Therefore, it is imperative that the police agency's investigation take into account not only the legal justification aspects of the shooting, but also indicate whether or not the incident and police actions were consistent and in conformance with that agency's department policy. In cases where the elements and facts indicate victim precipitation, I would recommend a specific reference to the incident as suicide-by-cop, with official reports and witness statements supporting this classification based on the dynamics of the event.

References

1. Cachur, Patrick, Ph.D. The Centers for Disease Control. Atlanta, Georgia. Personal Interview. February 22, 1994.
2. Smith, Sandy. Public Affairs Officer, National Center for Health Statistics, Office of Data Processing. Personal Interview, February 22, 1994.
3. Rosenham, David L. and Seligman, Martin. *Abnormal Psychology*. Second Edition. New York: W.W. Norton & Co., 1989, p.355.
4. *New York Daily News*. January 24, 1987, p.6.
5. DiMaio, Vincent J. *Gunshot Wounds: Practical Aspects of Firearms, Ballistics, and Forensic Techniques.* New York: Elsevier, 1985, p. 296.
6. New York Times, November 6, 1993, p. A 12.
7. Humphry, Derek. *Final Exit: The Practicalities of Self- Deliverance and Assisted Suicide for the Dying.* New York: Dell Publishing Group, Inc., 1991.
8. Ibid., p.4.
9. Ibid., p.4.
10. Ibid., p.81.
11. Ibid., p.83.
12. Ibid., p.91.
13. Ibid., p.109.
14. Ibid., p.110.
15. Ibid., p.112.
16. Ibid., p.111–112.
17. Ibid., p.82.
18. Dr. Harvey Schlossberg. Personal interview. Feb. 20, 1993.
19. Dr. Ronald Turco, M.D. Personal interview. Feb. 19, 1993.
20. Bolz, Frank Capt. (Ret.) NYPD personal interview. 3/13/93.
21. Sgt. J.G. Burmester, Houston Police Dept. January 28, 1994.
22. Lubrano, Alfred. *New York Newsday*. Nov. 24, 1992 p. 44.

Selected Reading

American Psychiatric Association. (1994). Diagnostic and Statistical Manual of Mental Disorders (4th ed.,rev.). Washington, D.C.: American Psychiatric Association.

Coleman, James C., Butcher, James. N. and Carson, Robert C. *Abnormal Psychology and Modern Life,* 7th ed. Texas: Scott, Foresman and Company, 1984

DiMaio, Dominick J., DiMaio, V.J. *Forensic Pathology.* New York: Elsevier, 1989.

DiMaio, Vincent J. *Gunshot Wounds: Practical Aspects of Firearms, Ballistics, and Forensic Techniques.* New York: Elsevier, 1985.

Geberth, Vernon J. "The Racial Component in Suicide-by-Cop Incidents." *Law and Order Magazine* 42:318–19(1994).

Geberth, Vernon J. "Final Exit Suicide Investigations." *Law and Order Magazine* 41:67–70(1993).

Geberth, Vernon J. "Suicide-by-Cop." *Law and Order Magazine* 41:105–109(1993).

Humphry, Derek. *Final Exit: The Practicalities of Self-Deliverance and Assisted Suicide for the Dying.* New York: Dell Publishing Group, Inc., 1991.

Rosenham, David L. and Seligman, Martin. *Abnormal Psychology.* Second Edition. New York: W.W. Norton & Co., 1989.

The Investigation of Sex-Related Homicides 14

Introduction

Sex-related homicides include rape murders, serial murders, killings which involve both anal and oral sodomy and other acts of sexual perversion, as well as sexually oriented interpersonal violence cases.

A homicide is classified as "sex-related" when there is evidence of sexual activity observed in the crime scene or upon the body of the victim. This includes:

1. The type of, or lack of attire on the victim.
2. Evidence of seminal fluid on, near, or in the body.
3. Evidence of sexual injury and/or sexual mutilation.
4. Sexualized positioning of the body.
5. Evidence of substitute sexual activity, i.e. fantasy, ritualism, symbolism, and/or masturbation.
6. Multiple stabbing or cuttings to the body. This includes slicing wounds across the abdomen of the victim, throat slashing, and over-kill type injuries which are considered highly suggestive of a sexual motivation.[1]

The victims of these crimes are usually females and young children, and the killer a male. However, it is important to note that sex-related homicides involve homosexual as well as heterosexual relationships. (See "Homosexual Homicide Investigation," Chapter 15.)

The homicide might have sexual implications even without an overt sex act or observable sexual activity at the crime scene. It is important to note that unlike other murders, the motive or reason for the killing may not always be readily discernable or as "clear-cut" as is presented in a robbery-homicide, a drug-related murder, or an organized crime "hit."

Practically speaking, if the body is that of a female, and it is found nude or partially clothed, the investigator should think "sex crime."

The Crime Scene Investigation

The search of the homicide crime scene is the most important phase of the investigation conducted at the scene. It begins with a two-fold purpose:

1. The complete documentation of events. Photographs (both black and white and color) and/or video tape as well as crime scene sketches should be accomplished prior to any other police procedures at the scene.
2. A careful and complete search conducted for any forensic materials and other evidence, which might provide a clue to the identity of the killer.

Sex-Related Crime Scene Checklist

☐ Physical evidence in the form of seminal fluid must be collected as soon as possible before it is lost or destroyed. Samples can be allowed to air dry naturally or you can use a hair dryer on low speed. Wet samples can be drawn into an eyedropper and should be placed in a sterile test tube. Dry stains will have a stiff "starchy" texture. If on clothing submit entire article, being careful not to break or contaminate the stained area. *Consider DNA testing technique requirements.*

☐ Blood (wet) should be collected using an eyedropper and transfered to a sterile container. The blood can be put into a test tube with EDTA, an anti-coagulant, and refrigerated. Small amounts can be collected using 100% cotton swab, #8 cotton thread, or gauze pad. Allow swab to air dry and place in sterile container. *Consider DNA testing techniques.*

☐ Blood stain, spittle, and hair (including pubic combings) should be obtained at the scene; properly packaged and forward to lab. *Consider DNA testing techniques.*

☐ Trace evidence found on the victim and/or upon victim's clothing should be collected. Search for hair, fibers, and other microscopic evidence. Use forceps, vacuum cleaner fitted with an in-line cannister attachment in the hose, or use tape. Tape and forceps is the best method so as to not contaminate samples.

☐ Bruises and marks on the victim, including the presence of sadistic injuries should be noted and documented in the investigative notes.

☐ Urine or feces may be left at the scene by the assailant. This evidence should be recorded and collected. Urine can be removed by eyedropper or gauze. Place in a sterile test tube or other container. If on clothing, submit entire article. *DNA Testing can be performed on urine.*

☐ Fingernail scrapings should be obtained for an analysis of any blood, skin, or hair from the perpetrator. *Consider DNA testing technique.*

☐ Confer with the Medical Examiner and assure that specimens are taken from the body (e.g., hair from various areas of the body). In addition, vaginal washings, as well as anal, nasal, and oral swabs should be requested for serological evaluation and examination. *Consider DNA testing technique.*

☐ Examine the scene for evidence of a struggle. The presence of torn clothing, missing buttons, ripped textiles, marks on the ground or floor, and blood splatters must all be photographed, documented, and collected as evidence.

☐ Homicides involving mutilation may yield clues such as style of attack, the type of weapon used, the amount and location of mutilation, the position of the body, etc. These items should be recorded. (See Chapter 21, "Investigative Assessment-Criminal Personality Profiling.")

☐ If a suspect has been taken into custody, his or her clothing should be taken and an examination conducted for any physical evidence. Examine for hairs and fibers.

☐ Each piece of evidence should be packaged in a separate container in order to prevent cross contamination.

☐ The suspect's body should be examined for any fingernail scratches, bite marks, or other indications of a violent struggle.

☐ Hair and blood samples should be obtained. (Assure that any such samples are obtained legally.)

☐ The body should be examined for the presence of bite mark evidence. Collect and record:

☐ Saliva washing of the bite-mark area for blood grouping. Use 100% cotton dampened in distilled water. *Important:* Obtain a control sample from another area of the body.

☐ Photograph the bite mark. Obtain black and white and color photos. Use a rule of measure and obtain an anatomical landmark.

☐ Casting (if possible). Use dental materials.

Method for Diagnosing Abrasions, Lacerations, and Other Skin Disruptions in the Perineum and Perianal Areas

According to Dr. Frederick T. Zugibe, Chief Medical Examiner, Rockland County, New York, an excellent procedure in determining sexual assault injuries can be visualized by the application of Toluidine Blue in 0.01% solution and/or Methylene Blue or Azure.

Toluidine stains ground substance or mucopolysaccharides which are found in abrasions as well as other skin injuries. The intact skin will not stain but injured skin will be visualized with the application of Toluidine Blue and/or Methylene Blue or Azure. This test is extremely effective in child sexual abuse cases. It can also be administered by doctors in hospital emergency rooms who treat live victims of sexual assault to document the presence of mucopolysaccharides. A simple color Polaroid taken before and after the application produces excellent documentation of sexual abuse which can be used in trial.

Toluidine Blue is applied with cotton or gauze to the area of suspected trauma. The excess is wiped off with a K-Y jelly or similar substance. The stain will remain in the area of trauma.

For further information on Collection of Evidence and DNA testing see Chapter 17.

In sex-related homicide cases, basic evidence collection procedures acquire an increased importance. Human behavior patterns and psychosexual activities, not generally amenable to ordinary collection techniques become additional factors to consider in determining the reason and motive for the killing. *Practical experience in homicide investigation* coupled with an understanding of human behavior patterns and human sexuality are important prerequisites in analyzing these types of cases.

Human Sexuality and Sexual Deviance

The three components of the human sex drive are biological (instinctive), physiological (functional), and emotional (mental). The

Figure 14.1. **BONDAGE AS FANTASY — CORDOPHILIA.** This bondage scenario shows a person as a willing participant in a sex game.

Figure 14.2. **BONDAGE AS REALITY — SADISTIC MURDER.** In this photo we see the bound victim of a serial killer. While acting out a sadistic fantasy, he would bind and sexually abuse his victims prior to killing them. The killer took this photograph of the victim shortly before her death. Police recovered a number of these types of photos at the killer's residence.

Figure 14.3. **SEXUAL PARAPHERNALIA.** (Courtesy of Dr. Dominick J. DiMaio, Former Chief Medical Examiner, City of New York.)

emotional or mental component is the manifestation of the culmination of our psychosexual development. According to experts, the psychosexual or emotional component is the strongest of the three, accounting for approximately 70% of the human sex drive.

As emotions are controlled by the mind, it follows that "The mind controls the act." The mind determines what is and what is not sexually arousing to an individual.

Essentially, our human sexuality is established during our psychosexual development through conditioning and experience which involves both nature and nurture.

Sexual behaviors are learned behaviors in which the individual develops a perception of what is sexually satisfying and what is socially appropriate within the context of his or her environment.

Clinically speaking, there is a behavioral distinctiveness in human sexuality. This unique aspect of our arousal and response system accounts for why individuals differ in their sexual behaviors and show selectivity in choosing their mates or sexual partners. Human sexuality is no longer simply instinctive but is based upon learned patterns of attraction, activity, and fulfillment. Our sexual arousal and response system is affected by hormones, the brain's capacity to recall pleasurable experiences, fantasies, emotions, various sensory processes, and the level of intimacy between two people. Sex is also a sensory act, involving the five senses of touch, sight, sound, smell, and taste. Each of our five senses are employed to a greater or lessor degree in our sexuality. For example, the sight of a scantily clothed woman might be an arousal factor for a man. Or, the sense of touch as it relates to a tender caress might be the stimulus that serves as an arousal factor for a woman. These are perfectly appropriate responses as they relate to human sexuality because they are viewed as acceptable behaviors. However, persons who are inhibited sexually may develop unconventional forms of sexual expression. The person who becomes aroused looking at the scantily clad woman might become obsessed with this sensory "turn-on." A deviance might then begin to emerge in a sexual behavior that becomes compulsive such as in the paraphilia voyeurism.

Sexual behaviors are classified as either *acceptable* or *unacceptable*. This determination is based upon statistical, cultural, religious, and subjective considerations. The subjective determination of what is sexually pleasing to the individual could be and many times is in conflict with the *acceptable* standards determined by the majority, which is statistical, cultural considerations, or religious influence. This does not prevent the individual from expressing his or her sexual needs. According to Coleman et. al. (1984), "The sex drive is normally sufficiently powerful enough to override all but the most severe social sanctions. Thus we see variant sexual needs frequently erupting into variant sexual behaviors."[2]

These variations are divided into two groupings. The distinction between the categories is based on social effect. Does the activity infringe on the public welfare? Or is the activity a victimless sexual variant?

We in law enforcement are oftentimes called upon to investigate what are described as nuisance violations or sexual deviations. This can be an important consideration when analyzing "*What took place?*" in a sex-related crime scene.

It also is the basis for an important investigative concept, which we in homicide investigation refer to as the "signature aspect" of the offender (see "Signature" in Chapter 21).

According to Dr. John Money (1986) there is a kind of love map depicting an idealized lover, love scene, and a program of erotic activities. These are related to the natural human development of the individual and are influenced by both biological aspects as well as the environment; nature and nurture. Sexual deviation occurs when these "love map" patterns become derailed. Child molesters, rapists, deviant

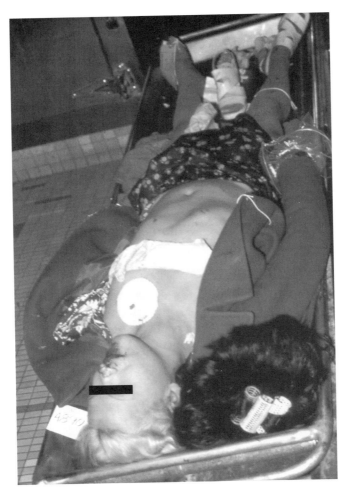

Figure 14.4. **TRANSVESTIC FETISHISM.** This subject who was a transvestite was killed by a "John" who thought he had "picked up" a woman. (Courtesy of Dr. Dominick J. DiMaio, Former Chief Medical Examiner, City of New York.)

murderers, and others with peculiar erotic interests are an example of this phenomenon. The formulation of sexual deviance can usually be traced to aberrant erotic development. For example, strict antisexual upbringing, sexual abuse of a child by the primary care giver between the ages of five and eight, overexposure to sexually stimulating behaviors, and/or inappropriate and pathological family dynamics.

According to Coleman et. al., the *sexual deviations* are described as "Acts which involve nonconsent or assault and those acts which can be described as problematic from the standpoint of the welfare of society." The sexual deviations are:[3]

Figure 14.5. **KLISMAPHILIA.** A sexual attraction to the giving or receiving of enemas.

Voyeurism	Exhibitionism	Pedophilia
Sexual sadism	Incest and rape	Masochism

The term paraphilia (para — deviance) philia (attraction) is an attraction to deviance.[4] "The paraphilias are a group of persistent sexual arousal patterns in which unusual objects, rituals, or situations are required for full sexual satisfaction to occur."[5]

According to DSM-IV there are nine (9) paraphilias. I will list them here with a brief definition. However, for further information I direct the reader to *Diagnostic Manual of Mental Disorders IV and Abnormal Psychology* 7th edition by Coleman, et. al.

Figure 14.6. **SEXUAL MASOCHISM.** This subject engaged in penis infibulation as part of his masochistic inclinations.

1. **Exhibitionism (302.4):** Exposing the genitals to an unsuspecting stranger for the purpose of obtaining sexual excitement.
2. **Fetishism (302.81):** Use of nonliving objects for sexual arousal. (Female undergarments, panties, shoes, etc.)
3. **Frotteurism (302.89):** A sexual attraction to rubbing against the genitalia or body of another.
4. **Pedophilia (302.2):** Engaging in sexual activity with prepubertal children.
5. **Sexual masochism (302.83):** Getting pleasure from being humiliated, bound, beaten, or otherwise made to suffer for sexual arousal. (Considered a chronic disorder.)
6. **Sexual sadism (302.84):** The infliction of physical or psychological pain on another person in order to achieve sexual excitement. (Considered a chronic and progressive disorder.)
7. **Transvestic fetishism (302.3):** Cross-dressing by heterosexual male for sexual excitement. (Ranges from solitary wearing of female clothes to extensive involvement in a transvestite subculture.)
8. **Voyeurism (302.82):** Repetitive looking at unsuspecting people, who are either naked, in the act of disrobing, or engaging in sexual activity. (The Peeping Tom.)
9. **Paraphilia not otherwise specified:** This category is included for coding Paraphilias that do not meet the criteria for any of the specific categories.

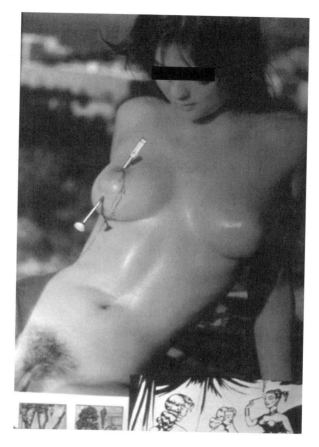

Figure 14.7.   **SEXUAL SADISM AS A FANTASY.** This photo was altered by a subject who fantasized about what he would like to do to a woman. The device was glued onto a photograph complete with blood drippings and shadow.

Telephone scatolgia: A sexual attraction to making obscene telephone calls. (Lewdness.)

Necrophilia: A sexual attraction to dead bodies; having intercourse with a dead body.

Patialism: An exclusive focus on a part of the human body, a breast, leg, penis, etc.

Zoophilia: Use of animals for sexual arousal. (Includes intercourse with animals as well as training the animal to lick or rub the human partner.)

Coprophilia: A sexual attraction to feces.

Klismaphilia: A sexual attraction to the giving or receiving of enemas.

Urophilia: A sexual attraction to urine.

Mysophilia: A sexual attraction to filth. (DSM-IV)[6]

Figure 14.8. **SEXUAL SADISM AS A REALITY.** The perpetrator of this lust murder inserted a safety pin into this victim's breast as part of his sadistic fantasy. (Courtesy of Inspector Rod Piukkala. Photos taken by Peel Regional Police Force, Brampton, Ontario, Canada.)

Determining Motivation

An extremely important aspect of homicide investigation is the determination of the *motive* for the killing. In the sex-related homicide, there are a number of possibilities to consider. Sex-related homicides include rape-murders, serial murders, killings which involve anal and oral sodomy and other acts of sexual perversion, as well as interpersonal violence scenarios.

No one acts without motivation. According to the late Dr. James A. Brussel, M.D., a criminal psychiatrist,

> "...the motivations behind the acts of a madman possess their own logic. The psychotic murderer does not act wholly irrationally. There is a method to his madness: there is a logic, a rationale, hidden behind what he does and how he does it, however wildly bizarre and completely without reason it appears to be..."[7]

The investigative challenge is to discover this perverse or seemingly irrational logic and then apply this information to the case.

Figure 14.9. **CRIME SCENE — SEX-RELATED HOMICIDE.** This is a crime scene photograph of a sex-related homicide. The first question is, "What took place?"

Figure 14.10. **RAPE-MURDER? OR SEXUAL PERVERSION?** This victim of a suicide was sexually assaulted 12 hours after death. At first viewing, one can see how this scenario might be mistaken for a rape-murder. (Courtesy of Detective Early McKee, University of Utah Police Department.)

A careful search should always be conducted at the crime scene and within the surrounding area for evidence of sexual activity. This includes the presence of sexual assault activity as well as substitute and paraphiliac behaviors. This evidence may be seminal fluid in the vagina, mouth, nasal area, or rectum. Or, there may be semen and other

What is the Motive?

PSYCHOPATHIC	PSYCHOTIC
Sadistic	Motiveless
Impulsive	Bizarre
Organized	*Disorganized*

Figure 14.11.   WHAT IS THE MOTIVE?

Figure 14.12.   **DEFEMINIZATION.** A disorganized offender mutilated this female victim and removed her breasts.

evidence discovered outside the body or upon the clothing. There may be pornographic books, videos, magazines, and/or photographs found at the crime scene. The photographs may depict the victim involved in sexual activity. Or, there may be writings or messages left by the offender at the crime scene and/or upon the body of the deceased. In any event, these factors are important in determining what type of sexual activity that may have taken place.

Human behavior, although unpredictable, is oftentimes repetitive. Research has indicated that certain actions engaged in at the homicide crime scene by certain types of personalities will repeat themselves in other homicide investigations. The homicide detective, who has en-

Figure 14.13. **EVISCERATION AND ANTHROPOPHAGY.** Subject engaged in postmortem mutilation of the victim's body. He eviscerated her and removed the ovaries, which he consumed.

hanced his experience with a comprehension of the psychodynamics of human behavior, will be able to develop a base of knowledge which can be applied to the review of similar cases.

Figure 14.14 **SEX-RELATED HOMICIDE INVOLVING BIZARRE ACTIVITIES.** Anthropophagy and post-mortem mutilation of body. These photographs show the partially clad body of an eviscerated female. The victim was hit in the head with a baseball bat. Her throat was cut, and there are multiple cuttings to the breasts and legs of the victim. A soda bottle was placed in the abdominal cavity and there was evidence that the offender had drunk the victim's blood.

There are certain preliminary questions an investigator should ask when examining a crime scene. *"What took place?"*, *Why did it occur?"*, and *"Who could have done it?"*

The reason and motivation for the crime is an extremely important consideration in establishing the investigative direction. "Was the murder the result of a lover's quarrel? Is the case attributed to interpersonal violence? Does it appear the victim was killed during a rape or sodomy attempt? Is the killing sexually oriented? Is there a psychotic motive, which sometimes appears to be motiveless or bizarre? Or, is the homicide the work of a sexual psychopath, with sadistic or impulsive implications? Each of these scenarios suggests a specific course of action.

However, in sex-related homicide investigations the motivation behind the killing may not be immediately ascertained. And, even when you do believe you have determined the motive, my personal experience suggests caution.

I remember reviewing an investigation in which the partially clad body of a 28-year-old college coed had been found on campus of a large university. Her pants and panties had been removed and her legs had been spread apart. Her blouse had been pushed up to reveal her breasts. The cause of death was not readily apparent at the scene. However, it was ascertained that there had been sexual activity at the crime scene and the medical examination confirmed the presence of semen in the girl's vagina. The motive in this case was determined to be a rape-homicide. However, upon further investigation it was discovered that the young woman, who was a pharmaceutical student at the university, had actually committed suicide the evening before. A suicide note was found in her dorm explaining that she had taken an overdose of prescription drugs and was extremely depressed. The medicolegal autopsy confirmed that her death was related to an overdose of drugs. Eventually, the homicide inquiry revealed that the grounds keeper, who had initially reported finding the body, was responsible for the sexual act. He confessed to police that he had come across the body and experienced a "sexual urge." The girl's body which had been lying there for some 12 hours was in rigor. He broke the rigor to loosen her legs and then removed her clothing. He then engaged in an act of necrophilia. What had appeared to be a rape homicide was actually a suicide with an act of sexual deviance committed upon the body after death.[8]

Remember; "Things are not always what they appear to be."

The identification of the victim is a crucial consideration in determining motivation. An intensive investigation into the victim's background, lifestyle, and associations many times will reveal a possible motive. An examination of any relationships, acquaintances, and risk factors may provide a clue to the *"Who could have done it?"* scenario. For example; Who does the victim live with?, Who was with the victim last?, Does it appear that the victim knew his or her assailant?, What is the victim's current social status?, Why was this particular victim selected?, Does the crime appear to be a "stranger-homicide"?, Was the deceased in a high-risk occupation (call girl or prostitute)?, Was the victim a runaway or hitchhiker?, or, Was the victim a late hours worker, e.g., waitress, or service worker, who had to travel alone at night?, What method of transportation did she utilize?, What route did she travel?, etc.

I remember reviewing and critiquing a serial murder case in which an offender had killed ten young women over a period of two years. In the first case, authorities had little or no information except that the deceased was a drug user and prostitute. The second case involved a missing person, who was not found until the killer was apprehended. However, the next two cases which came in about 4 months apart, were strikingly similar. Both young women had been killed in their respective apartments and there weren't any signs of forced entry suggesting they might have known their assailant. In both of these cases the investigators failed to interview friends and co-workers of the two young women. Had the detectives conducted this very basic inquiry, they would have become aware that the two cases were not only related but that both young women had worked at the same fast food restaurant where the offender had made their acquaintance. This failure to conduct basic investigative inquiry proved to be devastating to an entire community as six additional young women were found under similar circumstances over the next year. Ultimately a serial murderer was apprehended, but not before ten (10) young women had become victims in this series of sex-related attacks.[9]

There are any number of questions which can be asked and answered depending upon the circumstances and/or scenario of the crime scene. Consequently, an important factor in the proper formulation of an hypothesis will be the experience and knowledge of the investigator assigned to the case.

Examining a crime scene with the purpose of identifying and interpreting certain items which may serve as clues to the type of personality is an excellent technique. (See Chapter 21 entitled "Investigative Assessment — Criminal Personality Profiling.") There are common denominators between the psychological make-up of the criminal and the psychological clues the crime scene reveals.

Research by the FBI's Behavioral Science Unit into sex-related homicides has disclosed a remarkable consistency in the type of person who commits certain acts. Although there is a wide range of differences among offenders who commit similar offenses, these offenders also share similarities and common traits.

Organized and Disorganized Offenders

The organized and disorganized dichotomy devised by the FBI's Behavioral Science Unit is a description of criminal offender typologies. The information presented herein as it relates to the phenomena of organized and disorganized offenders is based upon the studies and research of the Behavioral Science Unit, personal interviews with retired Supervisory Special Agent Robert K. Ressler, and others involved in the project, interaction with colleagues across the United States who are homicide experts, as well as the personal experience of the author as a homicide practitioner, instructor, consultant, and expert in the field of homicide investigation.

What is the Motive?

Psychotic	Psychopathic
Motiveless	Sadistic
Bizarre	Impulsive
Disorganized	Organized

The Organized Offender

The clinical definition of the elements which comprise an *Organized Offender* are found in *DSM-IV* under the category *Antisocial Personality Disorder.* Antisocial personality is often referred to as *psychopathic* or *sociopathic* behavior.

The organized offender is usually above average in intelligence. He is methodical and cunning. His crime is well thought out and carefully planned. He is likely to own a car which is in good condition. The crime is usually committed out of his area of residence or work. He is mobile and travels many more miles than the average person. Fantasy and ritual are important to the organized type personality. He selects a victim, which he considers the "right" type, someone he can control (either through manipulation or strength), usually a stranger. Most of his victims will share some common traits.

He is considered socially adept. He uses his verbal skills to manipulate his victims and gain control over them until he has them within his "comfort zone." He is fully cognizant of the criminality of his act and takes pride in his ability to thwart the police investigation. He is likely to follow news reports of the event and will oftentimes take a "souvenir" from his victim as a reminder, which is sometimes used to relive the event or continue with the fantasy. (The souvenir is referred to as a "trophy" when describing this particular action by the organized offender.)

He is excited by the cruelty of the act and may engage in torturing the victim. Sexual control of the victim plays an important part in this scenario. He avoids leaving evidence behind and usually brings his own weapon. He is aware of police procedures. The body is often removed from the crime scene. He may do this to "taunt" the police or to prevent its discovery by transporting it to a location where it will be well hidden (see Chapter 21 for a more indepth profile of the Organized Offender).

The Disorganized Offender

The clinical definition of the elements which comprise a *disorganized offender* are found in such diagnoses as the *psychotic disorders*, i.e., the schizophrenias, which are characterized by gross distortions of reality involving delusions and hallucinations and paranoia, which may or may not effect the personality as well as paranoid schizophrenics, who are marked by acute personality fragmentation. In addition, individuals who are not psychotic may experience psychotic episodes. A psychotic episode, which is referred to as *brief psychotic disorder* in the DSM-IV,[10] relates to a temporary condition brought on shortly after or in response to an extreme stressor. The individual will typically experience emotional turmoil or overwhelming confusion.

Under certain conditions an inadequate individual who is experiencing intense sadistic sexual fantasies may suddenly "act out" these fantasies on a victim of opportunity. The crime scene would be disorganized and his actions and behavior could be viewed as psychotic.

The disorganized offender is usually of below average intelligence. He is generally a loner type, who usually is not married, lives either alone, or with a relative in close proximity to the crime scene. He experiences difficulty in negotiating interpersonal relationships and is described as socially inadequate.

He acts impulsively under stress and will usually select a victim from his own geographic area. In most instances this type of offender will not own a vehicle, but will have access to a vehicle. Generally, he will avoid people. He is described as sexually incompetent without any meaningful sexual relationships. He uses a "blitz" style of attack, which catches the victim off guard. This spontaneous action in which the offender suddenly "acts out" his fantasy does not allow for a conscious plan or even a thought of being detected. This is why the crime scene will be disorganized. In homicide investigation we call these events a clustered crime scene. *A clustered crime scene involves a situation where most of the activities take place at one location; the confrontation, the attack, the assault and sexual activity, etc.*

The disorganized offender usually depersonalizes his victim by facial destruction or overkill type of wounds. Any sexually sadistic acts are performed postmortem. Mutilation to the genitalia, rectum, breasts of females, neck, throat, and buttocks are performed because these parts of the body contain a strong sexual significance to him (see Chapter 21 for an indepth profile of the Disorganized Offender).

According to Ressler, et. al. (1986) "...there are significant differences between the organized and disorganized offender. However, there are no situations where the organized and disorganized offenders are mutually exclusive. That is, both types of murderers are capable of all types of behavior".[11]

Classifications

In my professional opinion, as an expert in the sphere of homicide investigation, sex-related homicides can be classified into *four* distinct categories based upon frequency of occurrence.

1. Interpersonal violence-oriented disputes and assaults.
2. Rape- and/or sodomy-oriented assault.
3. Deviant-oriented assault commonly referred to as a lust murder or psychotic killing (in these situations the motive for the murder is not readily discernible).
4. The serial murder.

Interpersonal Violence-Oriented Disputes and Assaults

The most common type of sex-related homicide originates from interpersonal violence. "Sexual domestic disputes" involve husbands and wives, men and women, boyfriends and girlfriends, boyfriends and boyfriends, girlfriends and girlfriends, and even on occasion siblings. They may also involve third party relationships, such as "love triangles," former husbands and/or wives, and jilted lovers.

Figure 14.15. **RAPE-HOMICIDE CRIME SCENE.** This is the victim of a rape-homicide that occurred in an unoccupied apartment within a building in the South Bronx. The victim was raped and sodomized by the killer, who had forced her into this location after confronting her in the building. She was a classic "victim of opportunity" who just happened to be at the wrong place at the wrong time.

Figure 14.16. **RAPE-HOMICIDE CRIME SCENE — DEPERSONALIZATION.** This young woman was raped and murdered by an *organized offender*. The woman, who had been bound for the purposes of sexual assault, was "under the control" of this killer for a number of hours. The covering of the face and/or turning over of the body is referred to as *depersonalization*. (Courtesy of Det. Sgt. (Ret.) Robert L. Bittle, Cumberland County Sheriff's Department, North Carolina.)

Figure 14.17. **RAPE-HOMICIDE CRIME SCENE — PREVENT IDENTIFICATION.** The offender engaged in multiple breast assault by knife and assured the victim's death by cutting her throat. The police investigation indicated that the victim could have identified her assailant. She was killed by the offender to prevent identification. (Courtesy of Det. Sgt. (Ret.) Robert L. Bittle, Cumberland County Sheriff's Department, North Carolina.)

In some instances the death may not appear to be sexually motivated. However, upon an examination into the background and relationships of the victim a new possibility soon presents itself to the authorities.

I remember a case in which a 36-year-old female executive was found shot to death "execution style." She had been shot three times in the head at close range and her body was left in her automobile, which was found parked under the George Washington Bridge. The police investigation revealed that the victim had an ongoing lesbian relationship with a 31-year-old female bartender. Detectives ascertained that the deceased had become embroiled in an argument with her lesbian girlfriend over another woman. The victim had met this woman at an East Side "singles" bar. When the "other woman" arrived the argument began and the three women ended up leaving the bar together. The deceased drove the auto with her "new friend" sitting in the front seat and her lesbian lover sitting in the rear seat. The argument continued as they drove. During the argument, the jealous lover shot her friend in the head from the back seat. The woman passenger fled the scene as the "shooter" exited the vehicle and got behind the wheel of the auto. She then drove the victim's car and body to the location of discovery. The "witness-passenger" eventually came forward and police arrested the jealous lover, who was hiding-out at another woman's Manhattan apartment. Initially, this case did not appear to be a sex-related homicide.[12]

The motive in this category of slayings is most often based upon elements of rage, hate, anger, jealously, or revenge.

The psychological dynamics involved in such violent interpersonal disputes and assaults oftentimes present scenarios which involve violent actions and statements such as, "If I can't have you then nobody will have you." This is most common in sexual domestic dispute cases. The woman petitions the court for an "Order of Protection." The court order directs the man to stay away from the petitioner and refrain from any further harassment. The man becomes enraged with this attempt by the woman to "break the relationship". This oftentimes culminates in a violent homicidal episode in which sexual aggression is evident in the crime scene. An estimated 1432 females were killed by intimates in 1992 according to the *FBI's Crime in the U.S.* Female victims represented 70% of the intimate murder victims.[13] Most of the women who are murdered in the United States are killed by former husbands, lovers, and friends.

> Murder serves as the ultimate form of sexual revenge for certain abusive types of personalities. That is why the author classifies interpersonal violence as the most prevalent form of sex-related murder.

I remember another case in which the nude body of an apparent rape victim was found in a city park. Initially, it was believed that the victim had been raped at an undisclosed location, shot to death, and then transported to the park where the body was "dumped." However, upon identification of the victim, it was ascertained that she had been missing from the day before. Investigation revealed that she had been abducted by her estranged husband. He had kept her captive in his auto where she was repeatedly raped and subsequently killed when she refused to reconcile with him.[14]

In some domestic dispute cases, especially those involving "crack," which is a concentrated form of cocaine, the crime may appear to be based upon some sort of psychotic episode. The body of a nude woman was found in her neatly furnished apartment. She had been stabbed seven times in the back, chest, and neck and there was evidence that she had been sexually assaulted. Investigation revealed that her boyfriend, a 24-year-old ex-marine, had smoked six vials of crack earlier in the day. The suspect, who worked for a Long Island electronics firm, was reportedly a good employee. He did not have any criminal history and according to family members had apparently been happy in his relationship with the woman. Yet, while under the influence of the "crack" he had sexually assaulted her and stabbed her to death with a 9-inch carving knife.[15]

An enraged lover or spouse who is acting under extreme emotional circumstances is capable of anything. I recall a number of cases in which offenders attempted to dispose of their wives and girlfriends through dismemberment. Initially, the police are confronted with a complete mystery and some unidentified body parts. However, once the identity is ascertained, the investigation usually leads to a relative or friend and an interpersonal violence scenario.

There may be an attempt to destroy the victim by depersonalizing the body. Facial destruction, multiple cuttings and stabbing, sexual assault, over-kill, and even postmortem attack may be present.

I remember supervising the investigation of a case which appeared to have been committed by a lust murderer or a psychotic killer. The partially clad body of a 22-year-old black female was discovered in her apartment. She had been savagely beaten on the head with a baseball bat and her throat had been slashed. Next to the body was a blood-stained drinking glass. I observed a lip print in blood upon the rim of the glass, suggesting that the glass had been used to drink blood. On the coffee table in the living room were a number of kitchen knives which had been used to slice the victim's body. All the utensils were lined up on the coffee table like an operating room in a hospital. The victim had been eviscerated and a large soda bottle had been thrust into her abdominal cavity. Her intestines could be observed inside of the clear plastic bottle. There were a number of postmortem slicing to her breasts and chest. In addition, the killer had also carved diagonal wounds into both of the victim's legs. This murder was actually committed in a fit of rage by the victim's live-in boyfriend.[16]

It is important to note that the *motivation* in an interpersonal violence-oriented dispute may be obscured by what was done to the body of the victim, or how the crime scene was staged or changed. Originally, what appeared to be a rape-murder, the work of a sexual psychopath, or a lust murder is oftentimes based on interpersonal violence.

Rape- and/or Sodomy-Oriented Assault

In this category of sex-related homicide, the offender's primary intent is to rape and/or sodomize the victim. The offense may be heterosexual or homosexual depending on the circumstances of the crime. These homicides occur under the following circumstances:

1. The assailant has used excessive force in overcoming the resistance of the victim and/or furthering the sexual assault.
2. The death is intentional because the assailant is known to the victim. The assailant kills to prevent the victim from identifying him.

These cases are extremely brutal, and death usually results from the assailant overcoming the resistance of the victim to the rape, sodomy, or homosexual assault. The victim may be choked or strangled into submission, or the mouth and nose may be held tightly in order to stifle the victim's screams, thereby causing asphyxia.

Blunt force injuries may be present when the killer has attempted to beat the victim into submission. In addition to the brutality of the attack, a victim may also die of shock or other trauma. This is especially evident in young children or older persons.

The "Murder at the Met" case in New York City is a classic rape-homicide. In this case a young violinist, who was performing at the Metropolitan Opera House, was attacked and killed by a stage hand. The young woman was walking through one of the many hallways back stage when she was spotted by a stage hand who had been drinking. He followed her to an elevator, forced her to accompany him into a stairwell and attempted to rape her. He then brought her up to the roof, where he bound and gagged her. He returned a short time later when he heard her making noise as she struggled to break free. He then pushed her from the roof into a ventilating shaft where she was crushed to death in the fall. The offender killed the victim to prevent her from identifying him.

In some cases, the offender may actually attempt to mislead the authorities by staging the crime scene to make it appear to be something other than a sex crime. For instance, I remember a case where the police were requested to respond to a "possible suicide." When they arrived, EMS personnel were attempting to revive a partially clothed female. The EMS personnel advised the officers that when they arrived they observed the unconscious female with a ligature around her neck. Her body was partially suspended by this ligature, which was affixed to some molding. However, upon closer examination of the death scene, the officers noticed signs of a struggle. The officers noticed that the victim's blouse had been ripped open. They also observed some buttons on the floor along with a broken wrist watch which belonged to the deceased. In addition, a closer examination of the victim's neck revealed concentric fingernail marks, which would be consistent with a manual strangulation. The officers immediately initiated basic crime scene procedures and notified detectives. As a result additional evidence was located and a proper crime scene investigation conducted.

Investigative Strategy

The usual intent of the offender in sexual assault is to rape and/or sodomize. The offender in this category generally does not receive any sexual satisfaction from the murder. Therefore, as a practical matter the police are dealing with a rapist who has killed and not a murderer who rapes.

Investigatively speaking, it has been my experience that a rape-murder is usually preceded by other sexual offenses including rapes and/or sodomies where the victim has not been killed. The investigative approach should be to first ascertain whether or not other cases involving a similar modus operandi have taken place in the jurisdiction. This can then be expanded to include other jurisdictions within the immediate area. This avenue of inquiry can then be expanded to research records for similar offenses committed in the past by persons who have since been released.

In the investigation of rape/sodomy-oriented homicides, remember, you are dealing with a sexual offender. Larger and more progressive police departments usually maintain specialized operations, such as Homicide, Robbery, and Sex Crimes Units. The investigators in these specialized units have a unique advantage. They become experts within their respective fields and are able to gain an insight into certain criminal behaviors that the average generalist-detective will not experience. I personally think it is good procedure to assign a member of the Sex Crimes Unit to work with the homicide detectives on sex-related homicide investigations. In fact, on *major case investigations* involving a series of rapes or homicide, I recommend that teams of Sex Crimes and Homicide Detectives work together in a *Task Force* type operation.

I remember a particularly brutal rape-homicide in which the semi-nude body of a 21-year-old victim was found "dumped" in a Bronx lot. The victim was an art therapist who was last seen at a college campus in New Rochelle, New York. Her body was discovered at approximately noontime on Saturday. At the time of the body's discovery, the victim's car was missing as were her wallet and keys. She had been at The New Rochelle Public Library on Friday, the day before and had checked out a few books. An autopsy confirmed that the young woman had been raped and that the cause of death was due to manual strangulation. The day after her body was discovered someone found her wallet in Pelham, New York, which is a town between the Bronx and New Rochelle. Three days after her murder her car was located in a parking lot in New Rochelle. In the victim's auto were four library books she had checked out of The New Rochelle Public Library. There was also a slip of paper from the library upon which she had written the "key numbers" for the books she had borrowed.

It was quite apparent to the New York City Police investigators that the abduction of the deceased had taken place in the Westchester County City of New Rochelle and that in reality this investigation should be focused in New Rochelle and Pelham.

The detectives got their first break when Latent Prints was able to develop a fingerprint off the slip of paper from the library which had been found in the victim's car. However, there weren't any suspects to compare this print with and the investigation began to wind down. Detectives from the Bronx decided to look into all rape and sex crimes within Westchester County during the period of the murder.

They came up with a rape pattern involving a male/black 27 years of age, who had been arrested and convicted for a rape abduction. In fact, he had been apprehended with the victim less than one-half mile from where the Bronx victim's body had been found. Detectives requested a latent print check of the suspect's fingerprints with the slip of paper from the victim's car. The latent print from the murder case matched the suspect, who was incarcerated in The Westchester County Jail. However, when the information was presented to the Bronx District Attorney's Office in 1984, the late Mario Merola, District Attorney for the Bronx declined to prosecute citing lack of evidence.[17]

I ordered this investigation to be reopened in 1985.

The detective, who had originally discovered the rape pattern was assigned to the investigation. However, once again our efforts were thwarted by the failure of the Bronx District Attorney's Office to prosecute.

However, in 1989 approximately nine years after the murder, a detective and detective sergeant decided to try a different tactic. Using DNA information supplied by the author as well as current newspaper articles dealing with this state-of-the-art forensic technique they constructed an interview strategy. The strategy was to allow the suspect to peruse the materials on DNA and then convince the offender through explanation of DNA technology that he had been forensically identified as the rapist. The suspect, who had since been released from prison on the rape charges was invited in for an interview with the New York City detectives.

The suspect, who was "jail-smart" thought that he could invoke the "Statute of Limitations" on the rape charge. He would have been correct if the only charge was rape.

The "Statute of Limitations" on felonies in the state of New York is seven years. However, the authorities in this case were pursuing a *rape-homicide* investigation. *There isn't any statute of limitations on homicide.*

During the interview the suspect made statements implicating himself in the rape and indicated that he had an accomplice who actually did the killing. The original police investigation had never revealed an accomplice in the rape pattern for which the suspect had been convicted. Oftentimes an offender who is providing police with an inculpatory statement will attempt to minimize his participation. The detectives presumed that this suspect was likewise trying to minimize his involvement and allowed the suspect to continue with his statement. Surprisingly, when the detectives conducted a record check for the alleged accomplice, they were able to document the existence of this person as described by their suspect.

This individual was located and invited in for questioning. This suspect came up with the exact same story as the first suspect. The only difference was in *who* did the killing. The second suspect predictably blamed the first suspect. However, both suspects were charged with the rape-murder of the 21-year-old victim.

I personally feel that this case is an excellent example of the principles of practical homicide investigation. Murders are solved because of the tenacity of homicide detectives who care. I was personally involved in the above case as were a number of other detectives. You can imagine our frustration when the district attorney's office refused to prosecute.

However, that did not prevent the detectives from utilizing tactics, procedures, and forensic techniques to continue to pursue this case. Allow me to quote from the *Oath of Practical Homicide Investigation.*

> "...Death investigation constitutes a heavy responsibility, and as such, let no person deter you from the truth and your own personal commitment to see that justice is done, not only for the deceased, but for the surviving family as well".[18]

Categories of Rapists

According to Groth, Burgess, and Holmstrom (1977), there are four categories of rapists. I will list the categories with a brief description. They are (1) power reassurance, (2) power assertive, (3) anger retaliatory, and (4) anger excitation.[19]

1. **POWER REASSURANCE** — This type assaults to assure himself of his masculinity. Lacks the confidence to interact socially and sexually with women.

Indoor type	Victim can negotiate
Victim alone with small children	Takes a souvenir
Local victims	Probably is married
Attacks victims as they are asleep	Weapon only for show
Uses ski mask or pillow (or)	Maintains guilt; may
makes victim turn over	call the victim
Loner type; dominant mother	Will kiss victim; wants
May keep a diary or scrapbook	to please her.
Non-athletic	Underachiever

2. **POWER ASSERTIVE** — This type has no doubts as to his masculinity. Uses rape to express his dominance over women. Uses force.

Same age as victims	Sports minded
Cruises for victims	Flashy vehicle
Resides in area near crime	Body conscious
Selects victim of opportunity	Tears clothing
Short time-span between attacks	Oral assault
Prior institutionalization	Direct approach
Selfish actions	Commits crime outdoors
Poor record if in the Service	Alcohol user

3. **ANGER RETALIATORY** — This type is getting even with women. They use sex as a weapon to punish and degrade. Anger-oriented.

Strikes out at women; may	Selects symbolic victims
select prostitutes or elderly	Tears clothing
Does not spend much time	Uses alcohol
Blitz style of attack	Random times (no pattern)

4. **ANGER EXCITATION** — This type is sexually turned-on by the victim's response to the infliction of physical and/or emotional pain. The sexual acts will be varied and experimental and intended to cause pain.

Might work with an accomplice	Into S & M activities
No mental or health problems	No remorse
Uses auto	Brings weapon
Uses degrading language	Good I.Q.

Decomposed body. Notice the bloating and peeling of skin. (Courtesy of Dr. Dominick J. DiMaio, M.D., Former Chief Medical Examiner, City of New York.)

Putrefaction. Note the bloating and decompositional blisters as well as the greenish discoloration around the area of the abdomen. This is a classic example of autolysis, the breakdown of cells and organs from the aseptic chemical process caused by intracellular enzymes.

Lividity. Notice the deep purplish discoloration as well as the white pressure areas of "blanching" on the victim's back, where the body was in contact with a hard surface. This is a classic example of lividity.

Lividity in a victim of carbon monoxide poisoning. Note the pinkish discoloration of the skin consistent with a person who has ingested carbon monoxide. This cherry-red color is the result of *carboxyhemoglobin*, a compound produced by the exposure of the hemoglobin to carbon monoxide. (Courtesy of Dr. Frederick Zugibe, Chief Medical Examiner, Rockland County, New York.)

Insect infestation. This body has been subject to advanced putrefaction and insect infestation from house flies and maggots. It should be noted that an entomologist can make determinations of estimated time of death based upon a forensic evaluation of the structures and habits of certain necropagous insects collected from the carrion, which provide cycle time frames for the species.

Close-up of a floater's face. This body which was recovered from the waterways is a classic "floater." (Courtesy of Dr. Leslie I. Lukash, Chief Medical Examiner, Nassau County, New York.)

Entrance wound. A classic entrance wound structure. Note the typically round, neat hole with an abrasion collar, and the black ring around the edges. (Courtesy of Detective James M. Yoghourtjiam, Crime Scene Investigator, Racine, Wisconsin Police Department.)

Muzzle stamp impression. Contact gunshot wound to the neck under the chin demonstrating muzzle/slide/slide guide rod impression. Left: contact gunshot wound of the neck. Right: the weapon responsible. (Courtesy of the Westchester County Medical Examiner's Office.)

Evidence of stippling and defensive posture of the victim. Just before this victim was shot by her boyfriend she brought her hands up to her face demonstrating the defensive posture. (Courtesy of Dr. Mary I. Jumbelic, M.D., Forensic Pathologist.)

Classic defense wounds of the hand. This victim tried to defend herself from a knife-wielding assailant. (Courtesy of Detective Alan Patton, Grand Prairie, Texas Police Department. Photo by Evidence Technician Don Swanz.)

Pattern Injuries. Depicts classic circular contusions and laceration due to the round head of a hammer with the weapon held against the scalp injury demonstrating a match. (Courtesy of Dr. Mary I. Jumbelic, M.D., Forensic Pathologist.)

Pattern injuries. Paired injuries on the forehead due to the claw end of a hammer. (Courtesy of Dr. Mary I. Jumbelic, M.D., Forensic Pathologist.)

Soot in the trachea. Indicating that the victim was alive during the fire and breathed in smoke and carbon monoxide. (Courtesy of Dr. Frederick Zugibe, Chief Medical Examiner, Rockland County, New York.)

Evidence *in situ*. Note the trace evidence of black pubic hairs (arrow) discovered intertwined in the light brown pubic hairs of this victim of a rape-murder. (Courtesy of Detective Alan Patton, Grand Prairie, Texas Police Department. Photo by Evidence Technician Don Swanz.)

Self-mutilation. This young man under the influence of "angel dust," peeled his face from his skull with pieces of a mirror and fed the flesh to his pet dogs. He survived due to the large amount of drugs anesthetizing his system. The dogs were removed by police to the animal shelter. The author directed veterinarians at the shelter to pump the dogs' stomachs. This procedure resulted in the recovery of pieces of the man's face, lips, and nose.

Petechial hemorrhage. Minute (pin-like) hemorrhages that occur at points beneath the skin. Usually observed in conjunctivae. (The mucous membrane lining the inner surface of the eyelids and anterior part of the sclera.) (Courtesy of William K. Brinkhous, Investigator, North Carolina Office of the Chief Medical Examiner, Chapel Hill, North Carolina.)

Sexual mutilation — evisceration. This female victim of lust murder has been eviscerated. The killer then engaged in anthropophagy, which is the consumption of human blood and flesh to achieve sexual pleasure and satisfaction. (Courtesy of Retired Lieutenant Ray Biondi, former Commanding Officer Homicide Bureau, Sacramento, California Sheriff's Department.)

Piquerism. This victim of a sex-related murder manifests evidence of "piquerism" on her left shoulder. Piquerism is a sadistic sexual inclination to stab, pierce, or cut. (Courtesy of Detective Marsha Reed, Ft. Collins, Colorado Police Department.)

Male homosexual wound structures. This is a classic wound pattern observed in male homosexual assaults and homicides. The "overkill" type injuries as well as the slashing and cutting to the throat of the victim. (Courtesy of Dr. Dominick J. DiMaio, M.D., Former Chief Medical Examiner, City of New York.)

Homosexual mutilation. This is a photograph of one of Jeffrey Dahmer's victims. Dahmer confessed to drugging, strangling, dismembering, and cannibalizing his victims. Police found photographs of some of the victims in various stages of mutiliation. (Courtesy of the Milwaukee, Wisconsin Police Department.)

Murder scene which has been "cleaned-up." This is a photo of the bedroom floor where a woman has been stabbed to death by an offender, who then disposed of her body. (Courtesy of The Honolulu Police Department's Scientific Investigation Section, Captain Gary A. Dias.)

Example of the application of Luminol at the crime scene. This is the same view as the above photograph after the application of Luminol, showing where the blood had pooled. (Courtesy of The Honolulu Police Department's Scientific Investigation Section, Captain Gary A. Dias.)

The perineum area of a victim of an anal sexual assault. Evidence of injury is not present to the naked eye. (Courtesy of Dr. Frederick Zugibe, Chief Medical Examiner, Rockland County, New York.)

The same area after the application of Toluidine Blue. Note the purplish discoloration in the region of the anal cavity. Toluidine stains ground substance or mucopolysaccharides which are found in abrasions as well as any other skin injuries. Toluidine Blue is applied with cotton or gauze to the area of suspected trauma. The excess is then wiped-off with a K-Y jelly or similar substance. The stain will remain in the area of trauma. This application was positive for abrasive injuries in the perineal area. (Courtesy of Dr. Frederick Zugibe, Chief Medical Examiner, Rockland County, New York.)

I recommend the textbook *Practical Aspects of Rape Investigation: A Multidisciplinary Approach Second Edition,* edited by Robert R. Hazelwood and Ann Wolbert Burgess, CRC Press, Inc. 1994 to the investigator for further information and case studies of these types of offenders.[20]

Deviant-Oriented Assault — The Lust Murder

This type of sex-related homicide is usually committed by someone who is defined as a lust murderer. Lust murders are premeditated in the obsessive fantasies of the offender.

A psychological view of the development and effects of deviant fantasies and behaviors can be found in the psychosexual disorders, specifically the paraphilias.

The lust murderer is oriented towards deviant and sexually sadistic assault and is distinguished from other sex-related homicide offenders by his involvement in mutilation of the victim. Lust murderers can be *organized* or *disorganized*. According to studies conducted by the FBI, most of these offenders are *disorganized* and do not engage in penis penetration of the victim. Instead, they may masturbate upon their victims and engage in postmortem mutilation. There may be displacement of the breasts of females (defeminization), postmortem attack of the genitalia of males and females, evisceration, the insertion of objects into the body cavities of victims, and sometimes anthropophagy, which is the consumption of human flesh and blood. However, in the case of an organized lust murderer, there will be penis assault as well as other varied acts inflicted on the victim. The cutting and overkill type wound structures will be directed towards those parts of the body that the offender finds sexually significant to him.

I remember participating in an investigation in which the nude body of a 26-year-old woman had been discovered on the roof landing of her Bronx building. She had been the victim of a classic lust murder. The young woman's jaw and nose had been broken suggesting a "blitz-style" of attack. She had been manually strangled with a strap from her purse and her panties had been placed over her face (depersonalization). Her body had been placed in a grotesque position (a position which was probably sexually significant to the offender). Her nylon stockings had been loosely tied around her wrists suggesting evidence of symbolic postmortem binding (fantasy and symbolism). The items used to create this postmortem binding came from the victim and included a belt, which was draped across her abdomen representing bondage.

The killer had cut off her nipples and placed them upon the victim's chest. An umbrella and a pen had been inserted into the dead girl's

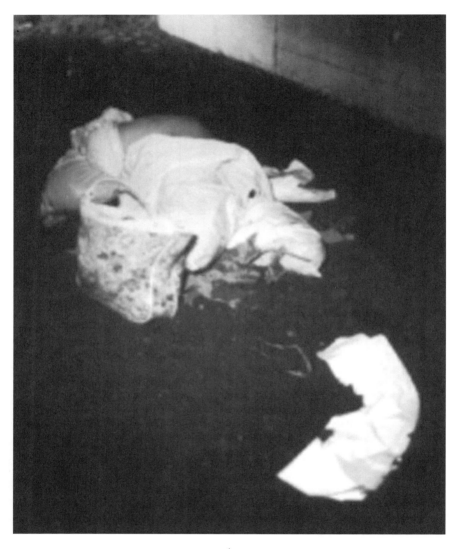

A
Figure 14.18.

vagina (penis substitution), and a comb was placed in her pubic hair. The words, "fuck you" were written upon her abdomen and on the inside of her left thigh the killer had etched in pen, "You can't stop me." In addition, there were postmortem bite marks on the victim's thighs. This offender was classified as disorganized based on the analysis of the crime scene information. The profile which was prepared by the FBI matched one of the suspects developed during the police investigation. This suspect was a patient at a local psychiatric hospital. The suspect

Figure 14.18. (A) **GANG-RAPE AND LUST MURDER.** Victim was discovered under a bridge of a highway within a rural area in McLean County, Illinois. This particular highway served as a truck-route between Chicago and St. Louis. At first, authorities felt they were dealing with a serial killer due to the location of discovery. This location was obviously a disposal site. The body was hog-tied and bound in plastic bags and there were two used condoms found at the location of discovery. An examination of the body indicated that there was a hole in the plastic bags in the area of the perineum of the victim. It appeared that the offender(s) had sexual intercourse with the victim's body after she was bound. (B) **BODY AT AUTOPSY.** There was evidence of multiple stabbing to the chest area which is consistent with sex-related homicides. (C) **BODY AT THE AUTOPSY.** The Medical Examiner observed white plastic in the area of the perineum of the victim. Three plastic bags were removed from the vaginal vault of the victim. These three bags bore latent prints of one of the subjects of this rape-murder. (Courtesy Detective Mike Essig, McLean County Sheriff's Department, Bloomington, Illinois.)

B

Figure 14.18. (continued)

claimed to have been in the hospital on the day of the murder. Although the authorities knew that the suspect had been absent from the institution on the day of the murder, the hospital records did not indicate his absence. This created an additional problem for the police, who were attempting to obtain a court order for teeth impressions of the suspect. When the court order was finally approved, the suspect's teeth impres-

C

Figure 14.18. (continued)

sions were compared to the bite mark evidence. Three forensic dentists agreed that the suspect had inflicted the bite mark wounds on the victim's body.

The suspect was arrested after an exhaustive 13-month police investigation. The bite-mark evidence was crucial in the outcome of the case. The suspect was found guilty and is presently serving 25 years to life in a New York State facility.[21]

Lust murders are primarily heterosexual and intraracial, yet there are recorded instances of homosexual lust murder. I performed a case analysis for a jurisdiction which experienced a vicious lust murder of a young boy. He had been multiply stabbed, sticks and dirt had been forced into his throat, and the body had been sexually mutilated.

The offender usually lives or works in close proximity to the crime scene. This type of killer, who acts on the spur of the moment, is obsessed with some sort of perverse fantasy. In his own mind he has planned the event. However, when the opportunity presents itself, this type of offender does not have a plan for avoiding detection. He either panics or becomes so involved in the fantasy that he is totally oblivious to the fact that he is leaving evidence behind.

I had the opportunity to assess a sex-related homicide for the United States Postal Inspections Service. The case involved the lust

Figure 14.19.   **CLASSIC LUST MURDER — SEX-RELATED HOMICIDE, DISORGANIZED PERSONALITY.** After postmortem mutilation and sexual abuse, the body was positioned in a sexually provocative manner significant to the offender. There is postmortem binding as well as penis substitution into the vaginal canal with foreign objects. (See "Case History".)

murder of a female letter carrier. The crime had originally been classified as an attempted rape. However, upon analysis of the case reports, the crime scene information, the victimology, and the facts of the case, it was soon apparent that the offender in this investigation was a classic disorganized personality. In my opinion this offender would not have been able to sexually perform with a live victim. Any sexual activity that would have taken place would have occurred after death.

The victim was a 30-year-old letter carrier. Her partially nude body had been discovered in the rear seat of her postal vehicle in a church parking lot. This location was approximately one mile from the deceased's assigned route. There was evidence of blunt force trauma to the head and multiple stabbing to the torso. The victim's uniform shirt and bra had been pulled up over her arms exposing the woman's breasts. The obvious lack of blood for such devastating injuries suggested that the victim had been killed elsewhere and the body had been transported to this location.

There was an extensive amount of evidence in and upon the postal vehicle. In fact, police utilized a flat-bed truck to transport the vehicle directly to the lab. The large amount of bloodstained mail suggested that the victim had not gotten too far along her route. The murder weapon was found in the trunk of the car, along with the shoes of the victim and additional bloodstained mail. The mail bore bloody footprints that did not match the victim's shoes as well as bloody fingerprints. On the rear of the trunk was a patent print in blood. Crime scene technicians also located vegetative matter consistent with plant debris, long strands of blond hair (the victim was a brunette), a large leaf from a philodendron plant, small flecks of green and blue paint, and a portion of panty-hose that did not belong to the victim. An inspection of the odometer of the postal auto did not show any significant deviation from the carrier's assigned route except for the distance between the delivery area and the church parking lot. The autopsy revealed the cause of death to be cerebral hemorrhage and stabbing wounds. The victim had eighteen stab wounds from a hunting knife, which was matched to the knife recovered at the scene and had suffered extreme blunt force trauma to the head. The time of death was placed between 12:00 noon and 2:00 P.M. that day.

The victim had last been seen at approximately 11:30 A.M. and only a small portion of her mail had actually been delivered.

It was obvious to seasoned detectives that the actual assault and murder had taken place somewhere along the victim's mail route. However, they couldn't utilize the undelivered mail to ascertain deliveries since the mail that was recovered from the victim's auto contained evidence. Investigators targeted her postal route and conducted a door-to-door canvass in an attempt to locate the crime scene. Tracking dogs were brought in and scented with a leather steering wheel cover. The dogs led investigators back to the victim's route. Detectives located the crime scene and discovered blood on the driveway of the home. In addition, there was a large philodendron plant on the front porch. The vegetative matter found on the victim's body came from a juniper bush in front of the house. The blue and green flecks of paint came from the weathered Christmas bulbs, which were left on the house year round. The paint had flecked and fallen into the cracks in the driveway. When the suspect had dragged the body from the house, the trace evidence had adhered to the woman's body.

Police obtained a search warrant for the premises. Although the interior of the house had been cleaned and scrubbed, additional evidence of the crime was recovered including the matching piece of panty hose found in the auto.

The offender was an 18-year-old youth who had dropped out of high school. A loner type with a drug habit. He was enrolled in a community college but was doing poorly. He was described as weird and argumentative by persons who knew him. At one point he had lived in a tent behind his house for a 6-month period. The long strands of blond hair found at the crime scene came from the family dog. The suspect had been having sex with his dog and was reportedly into solo sex-related activities, which involved sadistic fantasies. The pieces of pantyhose in this particular case were fetish items for the offender. He was found guilty and is presently incarcerated.[22]

However, despite the fact that most of these deviant-oriented homicides and lust murders are committed by *disorganized type* offenders, the investigator must keep in mind that *organized offenders* are just as likely to involve themselves in this type of conduct. The Jerome Henry Brudos case is an excellent example of such a circumstance.

> Jerome Henry Brudos was considered by his neighbors to be a gentle mild mannered man. To his employers, he was considered an expert electrician, the kind of skilled worker you just don't find anymore. To his wife Darcie, Jerry was a good husband and a loving father to their children despite his increasingly bizarre sexual demands on her. To the Oregon police, Jerry Brudos was the most hideously twisted killer they had ever unmasked. (Rule, 1988)

Jerry Brudos killed four young women in a series of lust murders that were predicated on a sadistic and bizarre plan to kidnap and kill women, whom he would force to dress and pose in various sexually provocative positions. In some instances he would continue to dress the bodies after death and interact with the corpse. These series of lust murders began with the killing of an encyclopedia saleswoman who mistakenly went to Jerry Brudos's home. Brudos, who had a number of fetishes for both woman's panties and high heel shoes amputated the woman's foot after killing her. He then placed this foot into various high heel shoes which he had stolen and kept in his workshop. He preserved the foot by keeping it in the freezer in his workshop in his garage.

The second killing took place about 10 months later. He strangled this victim and then took her body to his workshop where he engaged in necrophilia with the corpse. He removed this victim's breast and attempted to make an epoxy mold of it.

The third victim whom he abducted at gunpoint was brought to his garage workshop alive. He had sexual intercourse with the victim and then took pictures of her dressed in various stolen undergarments which he had in his collection. He then strangled her. However, he wasn't finished with his outrages. He performed necrophilia with the corpse and then cut off both her breasts to make plastic molds.

Less then one month later Brudos killed his fourth victim, a 22-year-old college student that he tricked into his car when he displayed a fake police badge and told her she had to accompany him to the police station. He brought her back to his garage, where he strangled her as he was raping her. He then hung her corpse from a hook in the ceiling and undressed the body, which he subjected to electrical charges to see if he could make the body dance. He also engaged in necrophilia with this corpse before disposing of the body.

In each of these cases the victims were brought to his garage workshop, which he had equipped for this purpose and where he acted out his sadistic sexual fantasies. He then effectively disposed of the bodies by depositing them in rivers. He was apprehended after an intensive police investigation in which he was identified on an attempted assault. He finally admitted his killings in a manner that suggested he was proud of his accomplishments. He at no time showed any remorse.[23]

The Serial Murder

The definition of serial murder, according to *Practical Homicide Investigation,* is "two or more separate murders where an individual, acting alone or with another, commits multiple homicides over a period of time, with time breaks between each murder event."

According to the original definition of the FBI, "Serial murder is the killing of three or more separate victims with emotional time breaks between the killings."[24] The FBI has since changed serial murder to conform to the "Practical Homicide Definition."

These breaks or "cooling-off" periods range from days to weeks or months between victims.

In recent years there has been a great deal of public interest generated in the phenomenon of serial murder. A number of books and articles have been published on the subject. There have been television documentaries as well as an NBC mini-series based upon the deviant exploits of Ted Bundy, a convicted serial killer, who was finally executed by the State of Florida in 1989.

In my professional opinion as an expert in homicide investigation, the most complete study and research into the serial killer can be found in *Sexual Homicide: Patterns and Motives* by Robert K. Ressler, et al.[25]

In the case of the psychopathic killer who is a serial murderer, I would suggest based upon the studies of the FBI and my personal experience and research into these type offenders, that he kills because he likes to kill. According to Ressler et. al. (1988), "These men have conscious, detailed plans for murder. Often these plans are improved

A

Figure 14.20. Three photos of serial murder victims of Michael Ross, who killed six young women in Connecticut between 1982 and 1984. This is a classic case of a geographical serial killer whose killings increased along with a decreased "cooling-off" period between the murders. (A) The body of a victim killed in June, 1982 discovered in October, 1982 and left in a wooded area. (B) The body of a victim killed in November, 1983. The body was discovered before the killer could return to the scene. (C) The body of Ross's last victim, a 17-year-old, who was discovered in a wooded area. (Courtesy of Lieutenant Frank Griffen, Connecticut State Police.)

upon with each successive killing; each new experience gives the offender insight into his next murder."[26]

Serial killers have been described as intelligent, charismatic, streetwise, charming, and generally good looking. They are mobile individuals capable of traveling any number of miles in search of the "right" victim. I analyzed one case in which the killer cruised a local strip for three hours and put over 120 miles on his van while searching for a victim. They target a certain type of victim. Someone who is vulnerable and easy to control. Their victims are males and females. They may select children, vagrants, prostitutes, or homosexuals. If the

B

Figure 14.20. (continued)

victim is a female, she may resemble other female victims in some aspect (long hair, brunette, or redhead, coed, nurse, waitress, female executive, etc.).

Serial killers are extremely manipulative. Oftentimes, they are able to talk their victim into what has been described as their "comfort zone." This is a location where they feel comfortable and safe and can control the victim. Many times they use a ruse to gain access to a potential victim. Ted Bundy used a cast on his arm. John Wayne Gacy offered young men jobs in his construction business. Bittaker and Norris as well as others offered hitchhikers a lift, or as in the case of Christopher Wilder, posed as a talent scout, and offered modeling assignments. Bianchi and Bouno as well as others have posed as police officers, etc. They continually perfect their ruse and seem to have an uncanny knack at recognizing potential victims. They are quickly able to gain the victim's confidence with their verbal skills.

C

Figure 14.20. (continued)

Many serial killers have a fascination for police procedure. Some have even worked as police officers, reserve officers, or security guards. They use this experience to avoid detection. They have been known to frequent police hangouts and eavesdrop on police conversations during a case. They may even interject themselves into the investigation or offer to assist authorities in some manner which will avail them an opportunity to monitor the investigation.

In some instances, these types of killers have gone back to the crime scene or location where the body was discovered either to assess the police investigation or to taunt police with additional clues. I remember one case where the killer complained that the police had discovered the body sooner than he had anticipated. He was upset because he hadn't had time to make sure he hadn't left any evidence behind.

The serial killer, despite his outward facade, is a very insecure individual. He is without power unless he is in control. This is reflected in his personal life and in his behavior. He is at his "peak" when he has a victim under his control. They enjoy the publicity of their crimes for the same reason.

They are likely to follow news events of their crimes very closely and gain satisfaction in the knowledge that they have defeated the police. Some serial killers communicate with the press. David Berkowitz, "The Son of Sam" serial killer, in New York City communicated with authorities by sending cryptic messages to a major metropolitan newspaper. Another serial killer, who referred to himself as "BTK" sent messages to the press demanding that they acknowledge his killings by affording him a title like other serial murderers.

My research has indicated that many of these serial killers are aware of police techniques. For example, perpetrators of crimes will change their modus operandi as they become more sophisticated in their criminal activities. Some criminals even read specialized journals to learn about law enforcement techniques. Many of the serial killers within my study followed the police investigation in the newspapers and media. They would adjust their activities and change their modus operandi to thwart the police investigation. In fact, many of these serial murderers were "students" of serial killings and had read about the activities of other serial murderers in the many popular books detailing these cases.[27]

This type of offender engages in purposeful postmortem mutilation of the corpse as opposed to the disorganized offender who engages in sexual or exploratory mutilation. The organized offender will employ mutilation to hinder identification, for shock value, or to allow ease of transport of the body. In one of the New York City serial murders, the offender removed the heads and hands of two prostitutes in order to prevent the identification of the victims. In another case this same offender removed the breasts of one of his victims and left them on the bed board for police to find. The serial killer who displays bodies and body parts does so for the shock value. In the Gainesville, Florida case, in which a serial killer named Danny Rollings terrorized an entire college community, the police were confronted with posed bodies, which had been horribly mutilated. In one particularly grotesque murder scene, Rollings had eviscerated the nude victim and had sliced off both of her nipples. He then decapitated the young woman's head and propped it up on a bookshelf. The first officer who entered the scene would see the head with its eyes open, staring back at him.[28]

Serial killings are considered by a number of experts in the field of psychology and psychiatry to represent the ultimate extension of violence. From a rational standpoint, serial killings are completely senseless acts. However, in the mind of the serial killer, he experiences great pleasure in exerting power and control over his victim including the power of life and death. The sex act is secondary. He is excited by the cruelty of the act and will engage in physical and psychological torture of the victim. His pleasure is derived by watching the victim writhe in pain as she is humiliated and tortured to death.

Richard Ramirez, dubbed the "Night Stalker" terrorized Southern California during 1984 and 1985. He was responsible for the rape, sodomy, mutilation, and murder of thirteen victims. Ramirez perpetrated unspeakable horrors upon his helpless victims which included women, men, and children.

Kenneth Bianchi and Angelo Bouno dubbed "The Hillside Strangler" because authorities were not aware that there were two killers, sexually violated and brutally murdered twelve young women between them. They would tape and gag their victims and proceed to torture and sexually abuse them. Bianchi and Bouno experimented with various techniques of torture, such as injecting them with Windex, smothering them with gas from the stove, subjecting them to electrical shock, and then eventually killing them by strangulation when they tired of their perverse and inhuman entertainment.[29]

The serial killer operates in an emotionally detached manner. It is almost as if he is following a script. The script is usually based upon a sadistic fantasy. Police investigations of serial murderers have revealed intricate and precise planning on the part of the serial killer. In some instances, detectives have seized recorded evidence of the offense, such as audio tape recordings of his victim's screams of pain, writings, photos, and even videotape segments of their sadistic activities. The videotapes depicting the atrocities committed by Leonard Lake and Charles Ng in Calaveras County, California are an example of the depravity of a sadistic serial killer.

Lawrence Bittaker and Roy Norris, however, provide the most graphic example of evil. These two psychopaths, who met in prison, shared a mutual interest in female domination, rape, torture, and murder. They eventually murdered five young women using a combination of methods which included stabbing them through the ears with an ice-pick and strangling them manually and with wire coat hangers, which were tightened around the victim's necks with pliers. They tape recorded two of their torture sessions while they repeatedly raped, sodomized, and tortured the young women.

In one session, a young woman is forced to perform fellatio and then describe her activity into the tape recorder as she is being beaten. The two offenders then proceeded to torture her by striking her on the elbows with a hammer and squeezing her nipples with a pair of pliers. She was ordered to continue to scream until the only sounds on the tape are a series of unintelligible moans. The victim, who was only 16 years old was finally killed with a coat hanger which had been tightened around her neck with a pair of vise grips.[30]

In each of these examples, the conduct displayed by the offenders suggests that the sex act is secondary. Instead, the offender is sexually excited by the cruelty of the acts and engages in physical and psychological torture of the victims. Their pleasure is derived by watching victims writhe in pain as they are humiliated and tortured to death. The murder itself is an expression of power and control. Necrophilia is an extension of their control and sadistic quest for complete and total domination.

Other offenders have used a variety of torture techniques, such as biting, whipping, burning, electricity, and forcing the victim to ingest a caustic cleaning fluid.

Many of these serial killers seemingly maintained a respectable lifestyle and engaged in sexual relations with a primary female in their lives. However, they really don't have any type of satisfactory relationship with anyone. They are into self gratification to a point where nothing else matters.

Most of the serial killers, who were interviewed by the FBI's Behavioral Science Unit or by psychiatrists conducting independent examinations, reported that they had been victims of child abuse, usually at the hands of a female parent or parent figure. Many of the offenders were reportedly under the influence of alcohol or marijuana while committing the crime, which tended to exacerbate their sadistic fantasies.

The serial killer tends to increase his killings. It appears that they have to kill more often to maintain an equilibrium. The fantasy and psychic high that they obtain through their conduct induces bold and more frequent attack sometimes with a complete disregard of risk. Consequently, many of the country's most notorious serial killers were caught either by accident or during some independent police action not related to the murder investigation. New York serial killer Joel Rifkin, who was responsible for the murder of eighteen young women, most of whom were prostitutes, was apprehended by two alert New York State troopers on routine patrol. They observed Mr. Rifkin's vehicle operating without headlights and missing a rear license plate. He attempted to flee. However, when the troopers captured him they found the rotting corpse of one of his victims in the rear of his truck. This routine vehicle and traffic incident uncovered one of New York's most prolific serial killers.

A Clinical Perspective

In clinical terminology a serial killer may be defined as either psychotic or psychopathic depending on the information supplied during the examination and the facts as presented to the clinician. In the experience of the author, serial killers are rarely psychotic. They are more properly defined as *sexual psychopaths* or *psychopathic sexual sadists* depending on the circumstances of the homicide and what was done to the victim. They obviously have a profound personality disorder but are keenly aware of their own criminality and certainly not out of touch with reality. If serial killers were psychotic they probably wouldn't be as successful in eluding the police.

In the case of the *psychotic killer*, one could propose that he kills because his psychosis drives him to kill. An example of this type of serial killer was Joseph Kallinger, whose exploits were detailed in Schreiber's 1983 book, *The Shoemaker.*[31] Kallinger reportedly was acting under orders from God to kill his victims.

In any event, it is not the purpose of this section to present psychiatric information or engage in an indepth psychological analysis of the serial murderer. Instead, I present this information from an investigative perspective with clinical references for the purpose of analyzing the sex-related murder investigation.

I completed an exhaustive study of documented serial murder cases in the United States up to December, 1993. I was able to identify 387 known serial offenders; 248 of these offenders were sexually motivated.

The offenders in this study displayed aggressive and antisocial behaviors during their childhood which escalated and took on elements of sexual sadism in adulthood. There was also a style and pattern to their killings which involved domination, control, humiliation, and sadistic sexual violence. The murders were committed without the least sense of guilt or shame and the killers displayed a total lack of remorse. The victims were chosen at random and the murders carried out in almost an obsessive manner. The behaviors of these subjects can appropriately be described as *psychopathic sexual sadism*.[32]

Conclusion

The criminal investigator confronted with a sex-related homicide investigation should first address the basic crime scene techniques as outlined in this text. He or she should concentrate on the total documentation and preservation of the scene including those factors which suggest the possible psychodynamics of the event.

Remember, there are four classifications of sex-related homicide; (1) interpersonal violence oriented disputes and assaults, (2) rape- and/or sodomy-oriented assault, (3) the deviant-oriented assault — the lust murder, and (4) the serial murder.

I have presented them in the order of their frequency of occurrence. Start your investigation with an eye toward an interpersonal violence scenario and then work your way through the other options. Specific law enforcement strategies can be applied to the investigation upon identification of the motive.

An example would be computer analysis of similar offenses, a request for a criminal personality profile through VI-CAP, utilizing a state-wide or regional information system, or simply a recanvass of the neighborhood wherein the crime took place. Remember, that within each of the categories there exist elements of human behavior, human sexuality, and possible sexual deviance. In any event, there aren't any simple clues, solutions, or explanations which account for the logic of a person who commits a sex-related homicide.

> **Just remember "that things are not always what they appear to be."**

References

1. Vernon J. Geberth. "The Investigation of Sex Related Homicides". *Law and Order Magazine.* July, 1986, p. 40.
2. James C. Coleman, James N. Butcher, and Robert C. Carson. *Abnormal Psychology and Modern Life*, 7th ed., Texas: Scott, Foresman and Company, 1984, p. 457.
3. Ibid., p. 457.

4. American Psychiatric Association. Diagnostic and Statistical Manual of Mental Disorders, (3rd ed.), Washington, D.C.: American Psychiatric Association, 1980, p. 267.

5. Coleman, et. al. op. cit., p. 460.

6. American Psychiatric Association. Diagnostic and Statistical Manual of Mental Disorders, (4th ed., rev.), Washington, D.C.: American Psychiatric Association, 1994, p. 522–532.

7. James A. Brussel, M.D. *Casebook of a Crime Psychiatrist*. New York: Geis Publishing Company, 1968, p. xii.

8. Author's files.

9. Author's files

10. American Psychiatric Association, op. cit., p. 302.

11. Robert K. Ressler, Ann W. Burgess, John E. Douglas, Carol R. Hartman, and Ralph B. D'Agostino. "Sexual Killers and Their Victims". *Journal of Interpersonal Violence*, 1:293 (1986).

12. Author's files.

13. U.S. Department of Justice. Bureau of Justice Statistics Selected Findings."Domestic Violence." November 1994.

14. Author's files.

15. Author's files.

16. Author's files.

17. Author's files

18. Vernon J. Geberth. "The Oath of Practical Homicide Investigation." 1988.

19. Nicholas A. Groth, Ann W. Burgess, and L.L. Holmstrom. "Rape: Power, Anger and Sexuality". *American Journal of Psychiatry*, 134:1239–1243 (1977).

20. Robert R. Hazelwood and Ann W. Burgess. *Practical Aspects of Rape Investigation: A Multidisciplinary Approach*. 2nd ed., Florida: CRC Press, Inc. 1994.

21. Author's files.

22. Inspector T.M. Fail, U.S. Postal Inspections Service. Personal Interview with Agent Fail, January, 1987.

23. Ann Rule. *Lust Killer*. New York: Signet.

24. Robert K. Ressler, Ann W. Burgess, and John E. Douglas. *Sexual Homicides: Patterns and Motives*. Massachusetts: D.C. Heath & Company, 1988, p. 139.

25. Robert K. Ressler, Ann W. Burgess, and John E. Douglas. *Sexual Homicides: Patterns and Motives*. Massachusetts: D.C. Heath & Company, 1988.

26. Ibid., p. 49.

27. Vernon J. Geberth. Antisocial Personality Disorder, Sexual Sadism, and Serial Murder. Thesis in press, 1994.

28. John Philpin and John Donnelly. *Beyond Murder: The Inside Account of the Gainseville Student Murders*. New York: Signet, 1994, p. 72.

29. Darcy O'Brien. *Two of a Kind — The Hillside Stranglers*. New York: Signet, 1985 and 1989.

30. Vernon J. Geberth. "Serial Murder: A Psychology of Evil. *Law and Order Magazine*. May, 1992, p. 109.

31. Flora Rheta Schreiber. *The Shoemaker — The Anatomy of a Psychotic.* New York: Simon and Schuster, 1983.
32. Vernon J. Geberth. Antisocial Personality Disorder, Sexual Sadism, and Serial Murder. Thesis in press, 1994.

Bibliography

American Psychiatric Association. *Diagnostic and Statistical Manual of Mental Disorders,* (DSM-IV), 4th ed. Washington, D.C.: American Psychiatric Association, 1994.

Blackburn, R. (1992). Psychopathy, personality disorder, and aggression: A cognitive-interpersonal analysis. In Proceedings of the Fourth Symposium on Violence and Aggression, Saskatoon, Canada, June 21–24.

Brittain, R. "The Sadistic Murderer." *Medicine, Science, and the Law,* 10:198–207 (1970).

Brooks, P., Devine, M., Green, T., Hart, B., and Moore, M. "Serial Murder — A Criminal Justice Response." *Police Chief,* 54:37–45 (1988).

Brown, J. S. "The psychopathology of serial sexual homicide: A review of the possibilities." *American Journal of Forensic Psychiatry,* 12:13–21(1991).

Burgess, A. W. and Ressler, R. K. (1985). Sexual Homicide Crime Scenes and Patterns of Criminal Behavior Final Report. Boston: Boston City Health and Hospitals Department.

Brussel James A. *Casebook of a Crime Psychiatrist.* New York: Bernard Geis Publishing Company, 1968.

Burgess, A. W. and Ressler, R. K. "Sexual Homicide Crime Scenes and Patterns of Criminal Behavior" Final Report. Boston: Boston City Health and Hospitals, 1985.

Cartel, M. *Disguise of Sanity — Serial Mass Murderers.* North Hollywood, CA: Pepperbox Publishing Co., 1985.

Cleckley, Hervey. *The Mask of Sanity.* 5th ed., Georgia: Emily S. Cleckley, 1988.

Coleman, J. C., Butcher J. N., and Carson R. C. *Abnormal Psychology and Modern Life.* (8th ed.). Texas: Scott, Foresman and Company, 1988.

Crooks, Robert and Baur, Karla. *Our Sexuality.* 4th ed. Redwood City, CA: The Benjamin/Cummings Publishing Co., Inc., 1990.

De River, J. *Crime and the Sexual Psychopath.* Springfield, Illinois: Charles C Thomas & Co., Inc., 1958.

Dietz, P. E. (1986). Mass, serial and sensational homicides. *Bulletin of the New York Academy of Medicine,* 62:477–491(1986).

DiMaio, Dominick J., M.D., and DiMaio, Vincent J. M., M.D. *Forensic Pathology.* Boca Raton, FL: CRC Press, Inc. 1990.

Egger, S. A. "Utility of case study approach to serial murder research." Paper presented at the annual meeting of the American Society of Criminology, Atlanta, GA. 1986.

Egger, S. A. (Ed.). *Serial Murder: An Elusive Phenomenon.* New York: Praeger, 1990.

Fromm, Erich. *The Heart of Man: Its Genius for Good and Evil.* New York: Harper and Row, 1964.

Freud, S. (1916)."Some character types met with in psychoanalytic work." *Standard Edition* 14:309–333. London: Hogarth Press, 1957.

Geberth, V. J. *Practical Homicide Investigation: Tactics, Procedures, and Forensic Techniques* (2nd ed.). New York: Elsevier Science Publishing Company, Inc. 1990.

Geberth, Vernon J. "Mass, Serial and Sensational Homicides: The Investigative Perspective". *Bulletin of The New York Academy of Medicine.* 62:492–496 (1986).

Geberth, Vernon J. "The Investigation of Sex Related Homicides." *Law and Order Magazine* 34:40–47 (1986).

Geberth, Vernon J. "Serial Murder: A Psychology of Evil." *Law and Order Magazine,* 40:107–110 (1992).

Geberth, Vernon J. "Lust Murder: The Psychodynamics of the Killer and the Psychosexual Aspects of the Crime." *Homicide Investigators Journal,* Official Publication of the International Homicide Investigators Association, Spring, 1992.

Geberth, Vernon J. *Antisocial Personality Disorder, Sexual Sadism, and Serial Murder.* Thesis. California Coast University, 1994 (in press).

Geberth, Vernon J. "Serial Killers as Psychopathic Sexual Sadists." *Law and Order Magazine,* 43: (1995).

Hare, R. D. *Without Conscience: The Disturbing World of Psychopaths Among Us.* New York: Pocket Books, 1993.

Hazelwood, Robert R. and Burgess, Ann W. *Practical Aspects of Rape Investigation: A Multidisciplinary Approach.* 2nd ed. Boca Raton, Florida: CRC Press, Inc., 1995.

Hickey, E. *Serial Murderers and Their Victims.* Monterey, CA: Brooks-Cole/Wadsworth, 1991.

Holmes, R. M. and De Burger, J. *Serial Murder.* Beverly Hill, CA: Sage Publications, Inc. 1988.

Holmes, R. M. "Profiles in Terror: The Serial Murderer." *Federal Probation,* 4:29–34 (1985).

Kernberg, O. (1982). An Ego Psychology and Object Relations Approach to Narcissistic Personality. Washington D.C.: American Psychiatric Association Press, *Psychiatry,* Annual Review. 510–523.

Kernberg, O. (1990). Malignant Narcissism Continuing Medical Education Tapes. Tape 1 through 3. California: CME, Inc.

Linedecker. C. *Night Stalker.* New York: St. Martin's Press, 1991.

Lunde, D. T. *Murder and Madness.* New York: W.W. Norton & Company, 1976.

Lunde, D. T. and Morgan, J. *The Die Song: A Journey into the Mind of a Mass Murderer.* New York: W.W. Norton & Company, 1980.

Markman, Ronald, M.D. and Bosco, Dominick. *Alone With the Devil: Famous Cases of a Courtroom Psychiatrist.* New York: Bantam, 1989.

McCord, J. "The Psychopath and Moral Development." In W.S. Laufer and J.M. Day (Eds.), *Personality Theory, Moral Development, and Criminal Behavior.* Lexington, MA: Lexington Books, 1983.

McCord W. and McCord, J. *Psychopathy and Delinquency.* New York: Grune and Stratton, 1956.

Meloy, J. Reid. *The Psychopathic Mind: Origins, Dynamics, and Treatment.* Northvale, NJ: Jason Aronson, Inc., 1992.

Michael, R. T., Gagnon, J., Laumann, E., and Kolata, G. *Sex in America: A Definitive Survey.* New York: Little Brown and Company, 1994.

Monahan, J. *Predicting Violent Behavior: An Assessment of Clinical Techniques.* Beverly Hills, CA: Sage, 1981.

Money, John. *Lovemaps: Clinical Concepts of Sexual/Erotic Health and Pathology, Paraphilia, and Gender Transposition in Childhood, Adolescence, and Maturity.* New York: Irvington Publishers, Inc., 1986.

O'Brien, Darcy. *Two of a Kind — The Hillside Stranglers.* New York: Signet, 1985 and 1989.

Peck, M. Scott, M.D. *People of the Lie: The Hope for Healing Human Evil.* New York: Simon and Schuster, 1983.

Podolsky, E. "The Lust Murder." *Medico-Legal Journal.* 33: 174–178. England: W. Heffer Publishing Ltd., Cambridge Medicolegal Society,1965.

Ressler, Robert K. and Shachtman, Tom. *Whoever Fights Monsters.* New York: St. Martin's Press, 1992.

Ressler, Robert K., Burgess, Ann W., and Douglas, John E. *Sexual Homicide: Patterns and Motives.* Lexington, MA:Lexington Books, 1988.

Ressler, Robert K., Burgess, Ann W., Douglas, John E. et al. "Crime Scene and Profile Characteristics of Organized and Disorganized Murderers." *FBI Law Enforcement Bulletin,* 54:1985.

Ressler, Robert K., Burgess, Ann W., Douglas, J. E., Hartman, Carole R., and D'Agostino, Ralph B. "Sexual Killers and Their Victims: Identifying Patterns Through Crime Scene Analysis." *Journal of Interpersonal Violence,* 1:288–308(1986).

Schreiber, Flora Rheta. *The Shoemaker — Anatomy of a Psychotic.* New York: Simon and Schuster, 1983.

Homosexual Homicides 15

Introduction

Homosexual homicides are relatively common and may involve male victims killed by other males, or female victims, involved in some sort of lesbian relationship, who are killed by another female.

Homosexual-related homicides, like all sex-related homicides, include interpersonal violence-oriented disputes and assaults, killings that involve forced anal and/or oral sodomy, lust murders and other acts of sexual perversion, and serial killings.

Homosexuals, who engage in "cruising" and other high-risk behaviors, drastically increase their potential to become victims of robbery-homicide as well as fatal incidents of "gay-bashing," which present additional considerations for the detective engaged in the investigation of homosexual homicide.

Homosexual Relationships

There are a wide variety of lifestyles among homosexuals who, like heterosexuals, are represented among all social classes, occupations, races, religions, and political persuasions.

Individuals who are in homosexual relationships engage in sexual behaviors similar to those of heterosexual persons with the exception of penile-vaginal intercourse. Touching, kissing, body contact, manual and oral genital stimulation are common sexual expression (Crooks, 1990).[1]

Sex in America: A Definitive Study, which is considered the most extensive research on human sexuality to date, found that only 2.8% of men and 1.4% of women identified themselves as gay or bisexual, far below the one out of ten number popularized by the Kinsey Report study (1994, pp. 175–176).[2] Present research has indicated that there are differences between homosexual men and women regarding the number of sexual partners (Rothblum, 1989 and Michael, et al. 1994).[3] Research also indicates that lesbian couples are more likely to have monogamous relationships than male homosexuals (Thoresen, 1984).[4] However, more importantly, the current research indicates that most homosexuals do not fit the commonly held *effeminate* and *butch* stereotypes.

> **It should be noted that uncomplicated homosexual male and female relationships as well as sexual orientation are not the subject of this section.**

Homosexual Lifestyles — Investigative Considerations

There are some homosexuals, however, whose appearance, dress, and demeanor do fit the exaggerated *effeminate* and *butch* gestures and dress of homosexuals or lesbians. These individuals are highly visible within the general population due to these attributes. The males are often referred to as "fag," "faggot," or "flit." The lesbians, who take on the role of masculinity through clothing, dress, gestures, or hair are referred to as "dykes," "bull dykes," or "diesel dykes." Male and female homosexuals might dress as "bikers" and other macho types or "femme" and "fruit" depending upon what role they assume in their sexual exploits. These lifestyles represent specific subcultures within the subculture of homosexuality.

In addition, there are many male homosexuals who engage in brief casual sex with multiple partners. They participate in what is called "cruising," as they seek out a homosexual pick-up or partner for a brief sexual encounter.

There are a number of "gay bars" which cater to different segments of the homosexual community. For instance, there are lesbian bars, leather bars, business suit bars, drag bars, dancing bars, etc. These locations provide gays, who have a specific orientation, a place where they can be themselves. However, there are other establishments which exist exclusively for cruising opportunities which make multiple sexual encounters convenient and easy. There are back rooms and stalls where patrons can participate in various sexual activities privately with a partner or publicly, while other patrons stand around and watch. It is not uncommon for some of the more active patrons to have several sexual encounters throughout the evening. They engage in furtive eye contact, staring, smiles, bodily moves, and wearing apparel which signal

Table 1. Standard Color Codex for Homosexual Handkerchief Codes

Handkerchief color	Sexual acitivity	Where worn	
		Left	Right
Red	Fisting	Top	Bottom
Dark blue	Anal intercourse	Giver	Receiver
Light blue	Fellatio	Desires	Provides
Robin egg blue	Sixty-nine	Both	Both
Mustard	Penis more than 8″	Has	Desires
Orange	Anything	Top	Bottom
Yellow	Golden shower	Giver	Receiver
Green	Hustler	Seller	Buyer
Olive drab	Into uniforms	Both	Both
White	Masturbation	Desires	Dual
Grey	Bondage	Giver	Desires
Brown	Scat (fecal matter)	Spreads	Receives
Black	Heavy S&M	Top	Bottom
Purple	Genital torture	Piercer	Receiver

an interest in participating in a particular sexual encounter (see Table 1, Color Codex for Homosexual Handkerchief Codes).

In an article written by a freelance writer who specializes in gay issues, the author states: "The number of businesses allowing unsafe sex has grown." (*New York Sunday News*, Nov. 20, 1994, p. 36).[5] Statistics indicate that AIDS is far more common in men with many sexual partners then in the general population (Meredith, 1984). This behavior, despite the fact that it has made AIDS an epidemic among gay men, continues into the 21st century.

In fact, "straight gays" as some homosexuals refer to themselves, speak of the above activities and the types of gays who participate in them as "queer queers" (Hunt, 1987 p. 167).[6] Gays, in general, resent these extreme types and usually avoid social contact with the "queer queers" who they feel cast all homosexuals in a bad light (Hunt, 1987, p. 169).[7]

In order for professional homicide investigators to effectively investigate homosexual murders, they must be able to break through these various subcultures in a nonthreatening and nonjudgmental manner to open up lines of communication.

It should be noted that individuals within the homosexual community devised and regularly use specific slang terms to describe certain activities and lifestyles such as "flaming faggots," "drag queens," "leather queens," "diesel dyke,""rough trade," "chicken hawks," "trash," or "deviant," etc.

Figure 15.1. **HOMOSEXUAL HOMICIDES** involving "lover's quarrels" slashing and cutting to the throats of the victims. Note the increased level of violence and "overkill"-type injuries that are in homosexual homicides. This type of violent wound structures to the throat and chest of victims is attributed to the dynamics of two biologically engineered sexual aggressors involved in an emotional conflict with elements of rage, anger, and revenge. (Courtesy of Dr. Dominick J. DiMaio, M.D., Former Chief Medical Examiner, City of New York.)

In the investigation of homosexual murders, the proper and discreet use of these terms may be necessary to aid in communication and assist the investigator in understanding the dynamics of an event. Therefore, the author has included some of these descriptive terms in the Glossary at the end of the book.

Interpersonal Violence-Oriented Disputes and Assaults

It has been my experience that male homosexual homicides involving interpersonal violence often present patterns of injuries which can best be described as overkill.

These injuries are usually directed to the throat, chest, and abdomen of the victims. It has been suggested, but not empirically proven, that the assault to the throat takes place because of the sexual signifi-

Figure 15.2.   **INTERPERSONAL VIOLENCE — LOVER'S QUARREL.** This man was a victim of a dispute involving his younger male partner. After his lover had killed him, he covered the victim's face with the bloody towel.

cance of the mouth and throat in male homosexual "love-making." There are certain "psychosexual wound structures" present in both homosexual and heterosexual homicides. The cutting of the throat, the stabbing into the chest, attacks to the breasts in females, the slashing of the abdomen, and attacks to the genitalia are indications of the sexual significance of the motive. The psychological significance in an attack to the throat in male homosexual homicides manifests the destruction of this "substitute sex organ," which engulfs the penis. Anal intercourse is often thought to be the most prevalent sexual behavior between homosexual men. However, according to Crook, 1990, the Bell and Weinburg study of 1978 found that fellatio was the most common mode of sexual expression.[8]

Although most of these interpersonal violence-oriented scenarios involve male participants, there are similar cases of extreme sexual violence involving female victims engaged in a lesbian relationship. The author is aware of a brutal sexual torture and mutilation murder of a 12-year-old girl in Indiana.

The victim, whose first name was Shanda, was killed because she had begun a lesbian relationship with a young girl, who had previously dated another lesbian named Melinda. Melinda talked three other teenage girls into helping her kill Shanda. Shanda was taken to a remote

Figure 15.3.   **INTERPERSONAL VIOLENCE — LOVER'S QUARREL.** Note that the wound structures to the neck and throat are consistent with male homosexual violence. (Courtesy of Dr. Dominick J. DiMaio, M.D., Former Chief Medical Examiner, City of New York.)

location where she was stripped. She was physically and sexually assaulted. The pathologist later reported findings which concluded numerous multiple insertions had been made into the victim's anus. She was strangled, stabbed, and hit in the head with a tire iron. Her tormentors then poured gasoline on her and burned her while she was still alive. All four were convicted and currently are serving their sentences in Indiana Women's Prison in Indianapolis, Indiana.

Interpersonal violence-oriented scenarios can also include instances wherein a homosexual male solicits or is solicited by another male to engage in fellatio. Young heterosexual male subjects and others, who are described as "hustlers" will participate in this conduct as long as the nature of the sexual activities allows them to maintain the more masculine role. In other words, the parties will agree to certain "ground

Figure 15.4.   **HOMOSEXUAL HOMICIDE-THROAT CUT.** (Courtesy of Dr. Dominick J. DiMaio, M.D., Former Chief Medical Examiner, City of New York.)

rules." The homosexual male (customer) is allowed to perform fellatio on the subject, but the subject will not reciprocate. The author has investigated and consulted on murder cases where these "ground rules" were broken resulting in an apparent homosexual homicide. These cases usually involve older homosexual males in a sexual liaison with younger males or hustlers. The older male may attempt to carry the activities beyond performing fellatio or demands that the younger male reciprocate. The younger male, who usually denies being a homosexual, suddenly has his masculinity threatened and he responds with violence and viciously attacks the victim. The injuries inflicted upon the victim usually will indicate an extreme rage and sexual violence.

In any event, if presented with the death of a male in a crime scene that suggests sexual activity, and there is cutting or slashing of the throat, consider a homosexually-oriented interpersonal violence motivation. I would suggest that these interpersonal violence-oriented scenarios and "lover's quarrels" between male homosexuals manifest an increased level of violence due to the fact that the parties involved in the emotional conflict are both "biologically engineered" sexual aggressors.

A

Figure 15.5.   **HOMOSEXUAL ROBBERY CASE — BITE MARK EVIDENCE.** (A) Crime
scene. The deceased, who was a Mexican Diplomat, had "picked-up" his assailant at the
Greyhound Bus Terminal. he then took him home for a sexual liaison during which time
he was assaulted, robbed, and killed. The assailant took the victim's credit cards and his
vehicle. (B) Suspect was identified and located in jail in another jurisdiction on an unrelated
matter. During the interview detectives noticed a number of fresh scratches, bruises, and a
bite-mark on the suspect. (C) Detectives secured a search warrant to obtain evidence from
the suspect's body, particularly the bite mark, which was ultimately matched to the dentition
of the victim. (Courtesy of Lt. Col. James J. Hackett, Deputy Chief, Bureau of Investigation,
St. Louis Police Department.)

Murders Involving Forced Anal Rape and/or Sodomy

Homosexual homicides involving forced anal and/or oral sex are to
some extent analogous to the rape-homicide among the heterosexual
population. These can be extremely brutal homicides, where death
occurs from the amount of force used to overcome the victim's resistance, or the victim is killed to prevent identification.

The author is aware of one particularly brutal sexual assault on a
male homosexual, who thought he was going to a party to participate
in a "little S&M." He was almost killed. He was physically and verbally
abused, as his tormentors called him "faggot, scum, and asshole." He
was whipped on his back and buttocks until bloodied. The group then
urinated on him. He was then forced to perform oral sex on the leader

B

C

Figure 15.5. (continued)

Figure 15.6.   HOMOSEXUAL HOMICIDE — VICTIM ANALLY ASSAULTED. Belt used to overcome victim's resistance. These photographs show a homosexual homicide crime scene. Note the belt around the neck of the victim may be a clue, which suggests that the offender may have spent time in a prison or institution.

of the group before he was allowed to leave, with a warning that if he told the cops he would be killed.

In prisons and institutions, many less aggressive males ("punks") and females ("bitches") are sexually dominated by macho male ("gorilla") and female ("bull") offenders.

The more aggressive homosexuals (both male and female) are referred to as "insertors." Examples are the homosexual male who puts his penis in the partner's mouth or anus and the lesbian who performs cunnilingus on her partner. The "insertees" are the homosexual males who receive the partner's penis in his mouth or anus and the lesbian who receives the partner's tongue in her sexual parts.

I remember supervising the investigation of a homicide on a South Bronx rooftop landing. The deceased, who lived in the building, was "discovered" at the location by a male resident of the building. The reporting witness told police that he had gone to the roof to urinate when he came upon the body. He told the officers that he had lit a match and recognized the dead man as a fellow resident. He then reportedly summoned his wife to the roof and she called the police. The victim, was fully clothed but there was a belt around his neck.

Once again, I caution the reader. I do not have any independent empirical data to support this theory. *However, it has been my experience that when you observe a belt, strap, or ligature around the neck of a male victim, you can expect that there has been forced anal sodomy.*

This method of controlling the victim by choking off the air is a "prison trick" employed by the more aggressive male inmates to intimidate and sexually dominate other weaker males.

I immediately recognized the significance of the belt and directed that the male who found the body be brought in for questioning as a "witness." Investigation at the scene indicated this to be a sex-related death. A canvass of the building yielded evidence that the victim and the reporting witness were observed going to the roof together. The "witness" had just been released from prison. Originally, he told his wife that some "faggot" in the building had "hit-on-him" sexually. He then explained to her how he got mad and beat the guy to death. He conveniently forgot to tell his wife that he had anal intercourse with the deceased before strangling him. When the wife was advised of what had actually transpired on the roof landing, she became the state's best witness.

Lust Murders and other Acts of Sexual Perversion

In sadomasochistic sex one partner is the "master" and the other is the "slave." The "master" who is usually a sadistic-type personality, obtains sexual pleasure in tying-up the slave, whom he beats or whips. The "slave," who is usually a masochistic-type personality obtains a sexual thrill from being treated this way. Oftentimes, male-oriented homosexual homicides involve bizarre and sadistic methodologies, such as "S&M" (sadomasochism) or "B&D" (bondage and discipline) scenarios. A male might be chained to a rack to be whipped by a "master," who is dressed in a special leather suit. The slave might wear a leather discipline mask in a display of submission. In some scenarios in these "B&D" sex games, the "slave" is forcibly "raped" (anally sodomized) by the "master" or other more dominant participants.

Other male homosexual activities include the insertion of a live gerbil into the anal cavity and then allowing the rodent to extricate itself from this oriface, as well as "shrimping." Shrimping is a disgusting action in which one homosexual, who has engaged in anal intercourse with another then "sucks out" the ejaculate from the recipient's anal cavity.

In some cases, the slave will be urinated or defecated on by others. In other male homosexual scenarios, the activities include urolangia

Figure 15.7. **SADOMASOCHISTIC PARAPHERNALIA.** S&M paraphernalia that was removed from a sex-related death.

Figure 15.8. **SADOMASOCHISTIC PARAPHERNALIA.**

(the consumption of urine) and coprolangia (the consumption of human feces). The author is aware of a homosexual homicide involving these activities which were videotaped by the participants.

There is an organization of homosexuals who refer to themselves as the "Fist Fuckers of America." (F.F.A.) This loosely knit organization

Figure 15.9. MALE HOMOSEXUAL BONDAGE — WILLING PARTICIPANT. Sadomasochistic activities involving bondage.

made their debut in San Francisco, California in May of 1981 where they held their first conference. They even produced a videotaped "training film" for their members on the proper method of "fisting." In "fisting" the "top-man" inserts his lubricated fist and forearm up to the elbow into the anal cavity of the "bottom-man." These sadistic acts and other sexual perversions, which are considered deviant and abnormal, can result in serious injury and death.

The Rockland County, New York, "Death-Mask" case, which made national headlines, is an example of depraved homosexual violence involving bondage, anal assault, beatings, and torture. This case was a classic example of a sadistic homosexual "snuff" killing.

The victim, who was a Norwegian fashion student, had been at a homosexual club in Manhattan. He was brought to the Rockland home of one of the perpetrators for what he thought was a coke and sex party. While at the house the three men drank wine and did some "coke." He

Figure 15.10. **MALE HOMOSEXUAL HOMICIDE INVOLVING BONDAGE.** The victim was discovered face-down and tied in this sadomasochistic position. The victim was sexually assaulted and robbed by a man he picked-up in a gay bar. (Courtesy of Dr. Dominick J. DiMaio, M.D., Former Chief Medical Examiner, City of New York.)

Figure 15.11. **NECROPHILIA — HOMOSEXUAL ASSAULT.** This male victim was stabbed to death and *then* sexually assaulted anally in an act of necrophilia.

Figure 15.12. **FISTING.** In "fisting" the "top-man" inserts his lubricated fist and forearm up to the elbow into the anal cavity of the "bottom-man."

Figure 15.13. **DISTENDED ANAL CAVITY OF A MALE HOMOSEXUAL.** (Courtesy of Dr. Dominick J. DiMaio, M.D., Former Chief Medical Examiner, City of New York.)

was stripped, handcuffed, sexually abused, and tightly laced into a leather bondage mask. He performed fellatio on one of the offenders, who told the other offender that this would be a good night to kill a "faggot." The victim was brought outside to an area by an old

Figure 15.14. **RUPTURED BOWEL.** These sadistic acts and other sexual perversions, which are considered deviant and abnormal, can result in serious injury and death. (Courtesy of Dr. Dominick J. DiMaio, M.D., Former Chief Medical Examiner, City of New York.)

smokehouse on the property. While one of the offenders was engaged in anal sex with the victim, the other offender shot him twice in the head at point-blank range. After shooting the victim, the offenders cut a hole into his chest cavity. The blood was collected in a cup. Both offenders drank this blood in an oath to keep their evening of sadistic homosexual depravity a secret.

Homosexual Serial Murders

Homosexual serial murders involve sadomasochistic torture, lust murders, thrill killings, and child killings as well as robbery homicides which are homosexually-oriented. Homosexual serial killers can be loosely divided into three groups: (1) the homosexual serial killer who exclusively targets other male homosexual victims, (2) the homosexual-oriented serial killer who attacks heterosexual and homosexual victims, and (3) the male pedophile homosexual serial killer who attacks young males and boys.

Figure 15.15. **HOMOSEXUAL "SNUFF-KILLINGS".** The "death-mask" case. These two photos show the decomposed body of a male victim of a homosexual "snuff-killing". Note the leather mask on the skeleton. Ironically, the face of the victim, which was tightly covered by the mask in an outdoor location during the winter months, was preserved well enough for physical identification of the deceased by family members. (Courtesy of Stephen G. Scurti, Chief of Police, Stony Point, New York Police Department.)

Figure 15.16. **HOMOSEXUAL MUTILATION.** This homosexual male, who had gotten breast implants, was killed by his male lover, who then castrated him for "fooling around" with another male.

It should be noted however, that these three categories presented by the author are not mutually exclusive due to victim opportunity and victim availability. For instance, John Wayne Gacy and Wayne Williams, who were basically homosexual male pedophiles, sexually assaulted and killed children and young adult males who were heterosexuals as well as homosexuals. Jeffrey Dahmer solicited homosexual young men, but he also was charged in the death of heterosexuals as well as a young boy (see Table 2, Homosexual Serial Killers in the U.S.).

The author's research, which appears in Table 2 shows a listing of 37 known and documented homosexual serial killers, which represent 30 cases of homosexual serial murder. These 37 offenders were charged with the deaths of approximately 280 male victims and were actually suspected of murdering approximately 755 victims.

Seven of the offenders worked in teams. Offender William Bonin worked with three other males. Offender Dean Corll worked with two other males, and Kelbach and Kearney each worked with a partner.

The most frequent motivation was sadomasochistic sexual acts followed by male pedophilia. Lust murders and robbery accounted for the balance. Twelve pedophile homosexual serial killers were suspected in the deaths of 126 young males and boys. John Wayne Gacy, for example, killed 33 young men and boys. He was executed in 1994. Dean

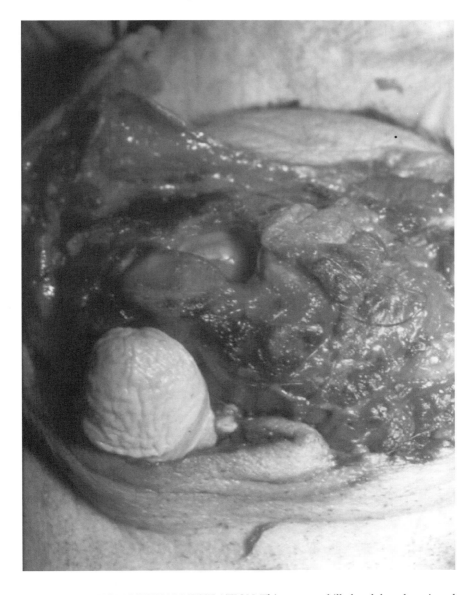

Figure 15.17. **HOMOSEXUAL MUTILATION.** This man was killed and then decapitated and disarticulated. The assailants then placed his penis into the neck structure as some sort of macabre message. (Courtesy of Dr. Dominick J. DiMaio, M.D., Former Chief Medical Examiner, City of New York.)

Corll, with the assistance of Elmer Wayne Henley and David Brooks killed 27 young men and boys.

Cruising or tricking by male homosexuals, who hang out at gay bars, gay baths, rest rooms, bus stations, amusement parks, truck stops,

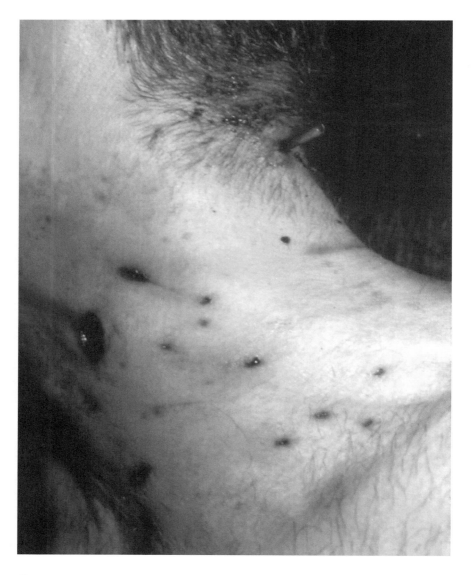

Figure 15.18.   **HOMOSEXUAL PIQUERISM.** Sexual inclinations to stab, pierce, or cut. Obtaining a sexual gratification from the shedding of blood, tearing of flesh, and/or observing such pain and suffering of a victim who is being subjected to this activity. (Courtesy of Dr. Dominick J. DiMaio, M.D., Former Chief Medical Examiner, City of New York.)

and other kinds of public places looking for casual sex represent a high-risk victim group. Serial killers who "work" these locations can operate anonymously among their victims. The impersonal nature of cruising, where participants meet to engage in sexual acts with complete strangers, affords the clever serial murderer with a number of killing fields of

Figure 15.19. **MUTILATED REMAINS.** Part of a body recovered from the Hudson River. This victim had been killed by a serial killer. (Courtesy of Dr. Dominick J. DiMaio, M.D., Former Chief Medical Examiner, City of New York.)

opportunity. Approximately 70 of the victims listed in Table 2 were "cruising" before they got killed. Approximately 80 of the males were victims of thrill killings and were selected *because* they were homosexual.

Jeffrey Dahmer, who engaged in necrophilia, anthropophagy, and other bizarre activities with the bodies of his victims, is recognized as one of America's most notorious male homosexual killers. He had managed to kill 17 young men and boys over a 13-year period before he was apprehended by authorities on July 22, 1991. Police found the body parts of 11 victims in Dahmer's Milwaukee apartment. There were four male torsos stuffed into a metal barrel, two heads in the refrigerator, two heads in a freezer, and seven skulls. There were boxes of bones and severed hands, a man's genitals in a lobster pot, a freezer packed with lungs, intestines, a kidney, a liver, and a human heart that Dahmer told police he was "saving to eat later" (Davis, p. 143). He confessed to drugging, strangling, dismembering, and cannibalizing his victims. Police

Table 2. Homosexual Serial Killers in the U.S.

Name	Race	St	A	Killed	Sus	Dates	Method	Motive	Type
Paul Bateson	W	NY	G	1	6	1977–78	Beat, dismember	Lust murders	Cruising murders
Robert A. Berdella	W	MO	G	6		1982–88	Strangle, torture	S&M	
Arthur Bishop	W	UT	G	5		1979–83	Shot, beat, drown	Pedophile	
William G. Bonin	W	CA	G	14	26	1972–80	Stab, strangle, torture	S&M	Thrill killings
David Owen Brooks	W	TX	G	2	8	1973	Shot, strangle	S&M	Team w/Corll
Eugene Butler	W	ND	G	6		1901–06	Blows to skull	S&M	
Vernon Butts	W	CA	G	6		1972–80	Stab, strangle, torture	S&M	Team w/Bonin
Dean Corll	W	TX	G	27		1970–73	Shot, strangle, torture	S&M	Thrill killings
Juan Corona	H	CA	G	25		1970–71	Machete, head	S&M	
Jeffrey Dahmer	W	WI	I	17		1978–91	Strangle, torture	Lust murders	
Bruce A. Davis	W	IL	I	3	29	1969–71	Shot, stab, poison	Robbery	Cruising murders
Frank Davis	W	IN	G	3		1971–83	Strangle, ax, shot	Pedophile	
Westley Allen Dodd	W	WA	I	3	1	1989	Stab, strangle	Pedophile	
Donald Wm. Dufour	W	FL	I	5		1982	Shot, stab	Robbery	Thrill killings
Larry Eyler	W	IN	I	3	22	1982–84	Stab, dismember	Lust murders	Cruising murders
John Wayne Gacy	W	IL	G	33		1972–78	Strangle, torture	Pedophile	Cruising murders
Arthur Fred Goode	W	FL	I	2	2	1976	Strangle	Pedophile	
Anthony Goodin	W	AL	I	1	4	1984–87	Stab	S&M	Cruising murders

Name									
Waldo Grant	W	NY	G	4		1971–76	Stab, mutilate	Lust murders	
Vaughn O. Greenwood	B	CA	G	8	1	1974–75	Stab	S&M	Thrill killings
William Guatney	W	IL	I	5	15	1979–	Slayed	Pedophile	
Elmer Wayne Henley	W	TX	G	7	19	1973	Shot, strangle	S&M	Team w/Corll
David Hill	W	CA	G	21	11	1977	Dismembered, shot	S&M	Team w/Kearney
John Joubert	W	NE	I	3		1982–83	Stab, torture	Pedophile	
Joseph Kallinger	W	PA	I	3		1974–75	Stab, torture	Pedophile	
Patrick W. Kearney	W	CA	G	21		1977	Dismembered, shot	Lust murders	Thrill killings
Walter Kelbach	W	UT	G	6		1966	Shot, torture	S&M, robbery	Thrill killings
Randy Steven Kraft	W	CA	I	21	39	1972–83	Strangle, stab	S&M	Thrill killings
Myron Lance	W	UT	G	6		1966	Shot, torture	S&M, robbery	Team w/Kelbach
Greg Miley	W	CA	G	2	8	1972–80	Stab, strangle, torture	S&M	Team w/Bonin
Michael Munro	W	CA	G	1	8	1972–80	Stab, strangle, torture	S&M	Team w/Bonin
Gordon Northcott	W	CA	I	3	20	1928	Shot, axed	Pedophile	
William Sarmento	W	RI	G	4		1987	Beat, stab	Pedophile	
Erno Soto	H	NY	G	5		1972–73	Stab, mutilate	Pedophile	
Michael Terry	B	GA	G	5		1985–86	Shot, stab	S&M	Cruising murders
David Villarreal	H	TX	G	7		1974–81	Stab	S&M	
Wayne B. Williams	B	GA	G	2	27	1978–79	Strangle	Pedophile	

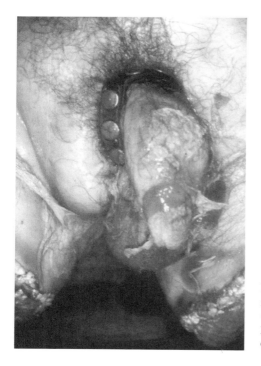

Figure 15.20.   Note the "cock ring" recovered from the mutilated body. (Courtesy of Dr. Dominick J. DiMaio, M.D., Former Chief Medical Examiner, City of New York.)

Figure 15.21.   **DAHMER VICTIM.** Photograph of dead victim taken by Jeffrey Dahmer. (Courtesy of the Milwaukee, Wisconsin Police Department.)

Figure 15.22. **POSING OF DEAD VICTIM'S BODY.** Dahmer would pose his victims after death in various positions and then photograph them as trophies. (Courtesy of the Milwaukee, Wisconsin Police Department.)

Figure 15.23. **POLAROID PICTURE OF BODY PARTS.** Dahmer also photographed the decapitated heads and body parts of his victims which he kept as trophies. (Courtesy of the Milwaukee, Wisconsin Police Department.)

found photographs of some of the victims in various stages of mutilation.

Dahmer had decapitated some of his victims, boiled their skulls to preserve them, and then painted the skulls, which he kept as trophies. Dahmer reportedly had tried to create homosexual love slaves or "zombies," by drilling holes in the victim's skulls and pouring acid into the holes while they were still alive. In addition, he performed sexual acts with some of the bodies of his victims after they were dead, including an act of anal sex with one corpse.

Jeffrey Dahmer was killed in prison by another inmate, who was serving time for murder on November 28, 1994.

Robert Berdella, who killed six male victims, was also interested in creating "sex slaves." Police recovered 357 photographs at his residence which depicted 23 persons in various states of sexual torture. Six of these 23 people were identified as homicide victims. The other persons in the photos had been consensual partners of Berdella who engaged in sadomasochistic activities with his "guests."

Berdella established "Rules of the House" for his sex slaves, who were punished by beatings and electric shock. Berdella, who would put bleach into his victim's eyes and injected different types of drugs and caustics into his "slaves," recorded the effects in a diary. He experimented by injecting his captives with Thorazine, animal tranquilizers, curare, and other unknown type drugs. He also injected "Drano" into their throats. He anally raped his victims and submitted them to the insertion of foreign objects into their anal cavities.

Larry Eyler was responsible for the sadistic murders of 23 young men in Indiana, Illinois, Ohio, and Wisconsin. His killings started in 1982 and ended with his arrest in 1984. In a stunning jailhouse confession, which Larry Eyler made through his attorney on December 4, 1990, law enforcement authorities were provided with a vivid insight into the sadistic murders of young gay men by Eyler and an associate.

Eyler described how a young man named Steven was brutally killed during an evening of sadistic sex orchestrated by an associate who was a college professor. The professor was subsequently acquitted of murder. The author will refer to him as *John* in this case history. Lt. Perry Hollowell, who had originally investigated the homicide in 1982, was provided with this information during an interview with Eyler and his attorney in December, 1990. Lt. Perry Hollowell, now with the Indiana Law Enforcement Academy and Trooper Frank Turchi, Indiana State Police provided the following details, which the author has edited for brevity and legal considerations due to the acquittal of the associate who is referred to as "John."

Figure 15.24.   **PHOTOGRAPH OF A "HOMOSEXUAL LOVE SLAVE."** Robert A. Berdella took photographs of his "slaves." This man's head was found buried in Berdella's back yard. (Courtesy of Special Agent Jon Perry, Virginia State Police. Formerly with the Kansas City, Missouri Police Department.)

CASE HISTORY

According to Larry Eyler, he and *John* were driving around in Eyler's Ford pickup truck in an area frequented by gays. They had decided "to play a scene." *John* liked to play 'director' and create sexual scenes which he photographed. *John* liked everything to follow a sequence. They saw the victim (Steve) who they recognized to be homosexual. Eyler nodded his head at him and he nodded back. They made some small talk with the victim and asked him if he wanted to take a ride. They rode around for a while and talked about doing some sex. *John* said something about

Figure 15.25.   **PHOTOGRAPH OF THE VICTIM BEFORE THE MURDER.** This photo depicts a victim being tortured by Berdella shortly before he was sadistically murdered. (Courtesy of Special Agent Jon Perry, Virginia State Police. Formerly with the Kansas City, Missouri Police Department.)

being horny and he wanted 'get his dick off.' The victim, Steve stated that he was also horny. According to Eyler, they asked Steve if he wanted to fuck around with them and the victim reportedly agreed. They told him that they were looking to get into 'bondage.' Eyler explained that they would tie him up and one of them 'would suck him off.' Steve agreed to participate. *John* told the victim that he would be paid for participating in the sex game. Both offenders then drove off with Steve sitting between them in the front seat of the truck. They made a brief stop so that *John* could pick up a bag. (Author's note: Murder Kit.) The bag had rope, tape, handcuffs, knife, a beige wrap. *John* also brought along his cameras — a Polaroid and a Nikon camera with its own flash. All three ended up at an abandoned farm house. *John* told Steve they were going to tie him up to

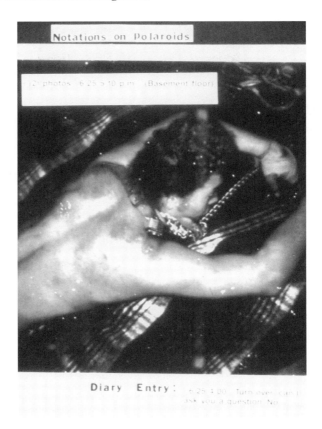

Figure 15.26. **PHOTOGRAPH FROM BERDELLA'S COLLECTION.** Berdella had hundreds of photographs which he would keep as trophies. On some of the photographs he had made notations. (Courtesy of Special Agent Jon Perry, Virginia State Police. Formerly with the Kansas City, Missouri Police Department.)

some beams. Steve agreed and Eyler tied Steve to the beams. Eyler wrapped duct tape around Steve's head four or five times and then placed the Ace bandage around his eyes. According to Eyler, *John* had an erection at this point and he began taking pictures of Eyler removing Steve's clothes. *John* then switched cameras from the instamatic to the Polaroid camera. *John* told Eyler to "Get the knife." John then took pictures of Eyler holding the knife against Steve's stomach. After a few minutes *John* said, "O.K. Kill the motherfucker." Eyler then stabbed Steve in the stomach. *John* took pictures of the stabbing. *John* then took the knife and he also stabbed Steve. According to Eyler, Steve's body went limp. *John* then started to masturbate over it. Eyler then cut the body down with *John*. Eyler stated that he suddenly felt this rage build up so he took a piece of wood and began to beat Steve's dead body. *John* then took pictures of this

Figure 15.27. HOMOSEXUAL SERIAL KILLER VICTIM. The victim was found face-down on farm property by a real estate agent who was showing the property to a prospective client. (Courtesy of Lieutenant Perry Hollowell, Indiana Law Enforcement Academy and Trooper-Investigator Frank L. Turchi, Indiana State Police.)

beating. They then took the body behind the house, where Eyler took out his knife and cut the body open. *John* took pictures of the eviscerated body. Both offenders then "cleaned-up" the crime scene by collecting all of the evidence in plastic bags which they took from the scene. Eyler wore Playtex gloves. Both offenders then went to *John's* house where they cleaned up and washed their clothes. According to Eyler, *John* kept the pictures of the murders in his bedroom closet. *John* would periodically look through these pictures and masturbate to them. Eyler stated that after he was arrested in Indiana the police went to *John's* house to search it for evidence and missed the box with the pictures of the murder victims.[9]

Larry Eyler and his activities were unknown to authorities in Indiana and Illinois, who were investigating a series of homosexual homicides in varying jurisdictions. In fact, during Christmastime, 1982 three different bodies including that of "Steve" were found in Indiana. A Multi-Agency Task Force was formed to investigate these series of murders in Indiana, as the body count continued to rise into the Spring of 1983. Many of the bodies were mutilated and disemboweled and in an advanced state of decomposition. In early June of 1983, a man who was upset with Eyler for taking his male lover, called the task force office and informed authorities that he believed that Larry Eyler was responsible for the recent murders. Authorities began to "look" at Eyler, whose

Figure 15.28. **VICTIM DISEMBOWELED.** The serial killer would disembowel his victims in his homosexual rage, which would greatly enhance the postmortem artifacts and decomposition of the bodies. Most of the remains were skeletonized when they were recovered. This was one of 22 victims of Larry Eyler, homosexual serial killer. (Courtesy of Lieutenant Perry Hollowell, Indiana Law Enforcement Academy and Trooper-Investigator Frank L. Turchi, Indiana State Police.)

name appeared in a number of police reports. However, the evidence was at best circumstantial. The multi-agency task force began surveillance on Eyler and alerted various troop barracks to report any unusual activities of Eyler to the task force. A problem occurred when an Indiana trooper observed Larry Eyler and another male park a truck on the side of an interstate and walk into the woods. The trooper, who went to investigate, asked Eyler for identification. When the trooper called in the information, he was erroneously informed that "Larry Eyler was 'wanted' by the multi-agency task force." At this time, Eyler was placed under arrest and brought into the barracks. The Task Force responded and Eyler was 'unarrested.' However, during the interview of the other male, it was learned that Eyler had made a homosexual proposition to the male. The authorities searched the pick-up truck with Eyler's permission. They seized a pair of boots, surgical tape, rope, and a hunting knife stained with blood.

Unbeknownst to Indiana officials, Larry Eyler was also quite active in Illinois. The body of Ralph Calise was found dumped in a field on August 31, 1983 in Lake County, Illinois. Calise had been bound with clothesline and surgical tape. He was stabbed 17 times and his pants were pulled down to his ankles. Ironically, the Calise homicide appeared to have the same signature of the slayings in Indiana. Authorities finally made the connection. The evidence seized by Indiana authorities was forensically matched to the Calise case. Eyler was charged, but the evidence was excluded and Eyler was acquitted on the Calise case.

On August 21, 1984 Larry Eyler was arrested for the murder of 15-year-old Danny Bridges, a street hustler in Chicago, Illinois. Danny Bridges, whose dismembered body had been wrapped in garbage bags and placed in a dumpster, had been lured by Eyler and an associate to an Eyler's apartment in Chicago. Eyler was convicted and sentenced to death on this case. Larry Eyler died of AIDS while in prison in March of 1994.

Investigative Significance

It should be noted that in each of the three serial murder cases discussed in this section, the behaviors of these offenders can appropriately be described as psychopathic sexual sadism.

There was a style and pattern to their killings which involved domination, control, humiliation, and sadistic sexual violence. The murders were committed without the least sense of guilt or shame and the killers displayed a total lack of remorse.

The victims were chosen at random and the murders carried out in almost an obsessive manner.

Sexual sadists rely heavily on fantasy and ritual to obtain sexual satisfaction. There is an element of compulsivity as well as an obsession on the part of the sexual sadist to keep trophies and recordings of the event. Photographs of the victims played a significant part in their rituals as well as their ability to recall their sadistic acts.

Therefore, the author recommends that any search warrant applications in these type cases should certainly reference photographs as well as any records, scripts, letters, maps, diaries, drawings, audio tapes, video tapes, and newspaper reports of the crimes as possible evidence to be seized.

Psychological Considerations

Serial killers attempt to satisfy psychological desires. That is to say, they seek sensual gratification. These desires are aggressive libidinal wishes that are not expressed in their daily lives and are a product of their developmental arrests and unresolved needs. Following the outburst of lust murder, behavior returns to "normal" (Podolsky, 1965 and Liebert, 1986) until the next outburst of murder. The victim in homosexual serial murders becomes the target of the "badness" displaced from the mother. This fusion of the destructive impulses results from disorganized developmental experiences and faulty object relations (Kernberg, 1982) along with the incapacity for empathic bonding both typically found in the antisocial personality disorder individual. This dynamic is consistent with their superficial adaptation and noninvolvement in any socially integrative manner.

In the homosexual serial murderers the mechanism of projection is utilized to displace the "badness" to the same sexed victim. The destructive elements of the early mother-child relationship are "introjected" and "split" and then projected with a recycling of this badness through projection and displacement. The male victim becomes dehumanized from the point of view of the killer. The role of the father as a passive "object" in the lives of the homosexual perpetrator also plays a role in the displacement of the aggression to another male. The victim becomes the "object" of the "badness" that the perpetrator perceives about himself. The perpetrator can thus unconsciously identify with the victim yet destroy him, thus preserving himself.

Robbery/Homicide of Homosexuals

Male homosexuals, who engage in "cruising" and other high-risk behaviors, drastically increase their potential for harm. If they cruise gay establishments looking for a partner, they may inadvertently "pick-up" an offender who frequents these locations with the intention of "setting-up" and robbing homosexual victims. Or, in some instances, peer delinquent prostitutes, who work alone or in groups, use homosexual prostitution as a vehicle for assault and robbery. They will solicit a "gay" customer who is willing to pay to perform fellatio on them. They then rob and physically assault the victim in a display of masculinity. These offenders are known within the criminal element as "fag workers."

Four of the homosexual serial killers listed in Table 2 accounted for the robbery homicide of 43 males. Two of the killers, Donald Dufour and Bruce A. Davis, were suspects in the murders of 37 homosexual male victims who were sexually assaulted as well as robbed. Walter Kelbach and Myron Lance were two aggressive homosexuals who enjoyed inflicting pain on their victims. Their victims, who were not homosexual, were anally raped by the offenders, who were sadistic thrill killers.

I remember working a robbery/homicide of a known homosexual who was found tied up in his ransacked apartment. What made this case

Figure 15.29. **HOMOSEXUAL ROBBERY-HOMICIDE.** This victim met his assailant, who pretended to be gay, at a homosexual bar. He brought the man back to his apartment for a sexual liaison. During the sexual activity the offender killed the victim and robbed the apartment.

interesting was the fact that we had investigated this man's attempted murder about four years earlier. It was during the attempted murder investigation that we learned that the victim, who was gay, had gone cruising at a popular gay bar in Manhattan. He had picked-up a young man, who pretended to be gay and brought him back to his apartment for a sexual liaison. The victim had a double-key-type lock on his apartment door. In order to enter or exit, a key had to be inserted into the lock. The man had installed this lock because some of his former "guests" had ripped him off while he was sleeping. While at the apartment, after engaging in some sexual activity, the young man suddenly turned on his guest with a knife. He told the victim that he was going to rob him and began stabbing the man in the chest and shoulder. The victim, who was seriously injured, traded his key for his life and the assailant ran from the apartment with the victim's jewelry and wallet. The police were summoned and the victim was brought to the hospital in serious condition. In fact, we were handling this case as an attempted murder and robbery due to the medical condition of the victim. As the victim began to recover he was interviewed by my detectives regarding his life style and his activities the evening of the assault. He directed us to the club where he had met the offender and provided us with a description. After an extensive investigation, we were able to obtain an identification of the offender and ready to proceed with a prosecution. However, as soon as the victim had made a complete recovery, he informed us that he was dropping the charges. He moved away and was unavailable for the prosecution.

It was four years later when I received a call from a Detective Sergeant, who requested my response to the location. I remember standing in the crime scene and remarking how the apartment looked familiar. I soon learned why. The deceased was our former complainant in the attempted murder and robbery case. I told the sergeant to pull the notes from the original case and sure enough, the deceased had gone back to the same location and had picked-up another "trick" from the same crew.

Homophobic Assault and "Gay-Bashing" Incidents

There are instances of homosexual homicides in which the victim is killed by a person described as homophobic. Homophobia is defined by Martin Weinberg (1973) as irrational fears of homosexuality in others, the fear of homosexual feelings within oneself, or self-loathing because of one's homosexuality (Crooks, 1990, p. 324).[10] The term "gay-bashing" is the politically correct version of what street people refer to as "fag-bashing."

I remember a case that took place in Greenwich Village in New York City. The homophobic son of a minister was apparently distressed over his own homosexual tendencies and went on a shooting rampage with an automatic rifle and "sprayed" street corners outside The Ramrod, a popular hangout where homosexual men would congregate. Two males were killed and six others were wounded.

In New York City, a corrections officer was arrested and charged with a series of killings. He reportedly would cruise a certain area in his vehicle looking for gay men whom he would proposition. He then would bring them to a secluded location and kill them with his newly issued off-duty revolver. Three murders were linked to this individual.

In another incident, a Vietnam war veteran who was gay was attacked as he walked along the deserted Arthur Kill Beach in Staten Island, New York. This victim was purposely hunted down and killed by two assailants because he was homosexual. The killers removed the victim's trousers and boots and took his house keys to burglarize his home. The victim's body bore numerous stab wounds to the chest and his throat was slashed (*New York Times*, Jan. 25, 1990, p. B1).[11]

According to one of the suspects, who was apprehended, the victim was killed because "he was a queer." In fact, one of the suspects had a previous arrest for kidnapping and assaulting another gay man. Both suspects could appropriately be described as homophobic.

Conclusion

The investigation of homosexual homicides presents law enforcement with additional and unique considerations. The mere fact that the death is classified as homosexual-related might prove to be problematic due to factors beyond the control of the police. Social agendas and personal issues relating to gay rights as well as the politics of special interest groups can possibly impact on the police murder inquiry.

If authorities appear to be indifferent to the sensitivities of the homosexual community or critical of homosexuals in general, the inquiry may be seriously hampered.

The law enforcement community needs to stress the fact that the murder and not the homosexual community or life-style is under scrutiny.

Homicides involving interpersonal violence, killings that involve forced anal and/or oral sodomy, lust murders, and other acts of sexual perversion, robbery-homicide, and "gay-bashing," as well as the prolific killings of victims by homosexual serial murderers is cause for concern by everyone in society.

The circumstances and dynamics involved in homosexual homicides require detectives to be able to effectively communicate with the homosexual community. They must be able to break through various subcultures in a nonthreatening and nonjudgmental manner in order to open up critical lines of communication in pursuit of the necessary information relating to the murder investigation.

References

1. Crooks, R. and Baur, K. (1990). *Our Sexuality*. 4th ed. California: Benjamin/Cummings Publishing Co., Inc., p. 332–333.
2. Michael, R. T., Gagnon, J, Laumann, E. and Kolata, G. (1994). *Sex in America: A Definitive Survey*. New York: Little Brown & Company, p. 175–176.
3. Crooks, p. 333 and Michael, p. 209.
4. Thoresen, J. (Apr. 1984). Lesbians and gay men: Complements and Contrasts. Paper presented at the Society for the Scientific Study of Sex Conference, Philadelphia.
5. *New York Sunday News*, Nov. 20, 1994, p. 36.
6. Hunt, 1987 p. 167.
7. Hunt, 1987, p. 169.
8. Crooks, p. 340.
9. Author's files.
10. Crooks, 1990, p. 324.
11. *New York Times*, Jan. 25, 1990, p. B1.

Selected Reading

American Psychiatric Association. (1994). Diagnostic and Statistical Manual of Mental Disorders (4th ed., rev.). Washington, D.C.: American Psychiatric Association.

Author's files.

Bell, A. and Weinberg, M. (1978). *Homosexualities: A Study of Diversity among Men and Women.* New York: Simon & Schuster.

Crooks, R and Baur, K. (1990). *Our Sexuality.* 4th ed. California: Benjamin/Cummings Publishing Co., Inc.

Davis, D. (1991) *The Milwaukee Murders: Nightmare in Apartment 213: The True Story.* New York: St. Martin's Press.

France, D. (1992). *Bag of Toys: Sex, Scandal, and the Death Mask Murder.* New York: Warner Books, Inc.

Geberth, V. (1995). *Homosexual Serial Killers and Their Victims.* Illinois: Law and Order Magazine, Vol. 43 No. 6.

Hunt, M. (1987). *Gay: What Teenagers Should Know About Homosexuality and the AIDS Crisis.* New York: Michael Di Capua Books.

Jones, A. (1994). *Cruel Sacrifice.* New York: Windsor Publishing.

Kernberg, O. (1982). An Ego Psychology and Object Relations Approach to Narcissistic Personality. Washington D.C.: Amercan Psychiatric Association Press, *Psychiatry, Annual Review.* 510–523.

Kernberg, O. (1990). Malignant Narcissism Continuing Medical Education Tapes. Tape 1 through 3. California: CME, Inc.

Liebert, J. (1986). Contributions of Psychiatric Consultation in the Investigation of Serial Murder. *International Journal of Offender Therapy and Comparative Criminology.* New York: Guilford Press. 187–188.

Linedecker. C. (1980). *The Man Who Killed Boys.* New York: St. Martin's Press.

Meredith, N. (1984). "The Gay Dilemma. " *Psychology Today*, January 1984.

Michael, R. T., Gagnon, J., Laumann, E., and Kolata, G. (1994). *Sex in America: A Definitive Survey.* New York: Little Brown & Company.

Money, J. (1988). *Gay, Straight, and In-Between.* New York: Oxford University Press.

New York Daily News, November 20, 1994, p. 39.

New York Daily News, February 6, 1995, p. 27.

New York Times, January 25, 1990, p. B1.

Personal Interview, March 12, 1991 with Tpr. Investigator Frank Turchi, Indiana State Police, re: Larry Eyler case.

Personal Interview, March 19, 1992 with Lt. Perry Hollowell, Indiana Law Enforcement Academy, re: Larry Eyler case.

Personal Interview, April 26, 1993 with Lt. Richard Munsey, Bath Township Police, re: Jeffrey Dahmer case.

Personal Interview, July 19, 1994 with Lt. Bill Franks, Stony Point, New York Police, re: Eigel Vesti case.

Podolsky, E. (1965). The Lust Murder. *Medico-Legal Journal.* 33: 174–178. England: W. Heffer Publishing Ltd., Cambridge Medicolegal Society.

Thoresen, J. (Apr. 1984). Lesbians and gay men: Complements and Contrasts. Paper presented at the Society for the Scientific Study of Sex Conference, Philadelphia.

Warren. C. (1974). *Identity and Community in the Gay World.* New York: John Wiley & Sons.

Wilson, C. and Seaman D. (1990). *The Serial Killers: A Study in the Psychology of Violence.* New York: Carol Publishing Group.

Narcotic-Related Homicides

16

Introduction

The purpose of this chapter is to provide an effective and practical investigative strategy for the investigation of drug-related homicides. Drug-related homicides are defined as those murders which occur as a direct result of the use, sale, and distribution of narcotics and other illegal drugs.

In my professional opinion as an expert in homicide investigation, the classification of drug-related homicides can be further divided into four specific categories. These subdivisions include drug hits, which represent the largest percentage of drug-related homicide and take into account the killing of undercover police officers involved in narcotics enforcement; interpersonal violence drug disputes; the murder of innocent bystanders; and drug assassinations. Although each of these categories involve violence and criminal enterprise, the cause, reason, and intentions for the murderer present authorities with additional investigative options and considerations. These categories are listed numerically based on their frequency of occurrence.

Classifications

1. **DRUG HITS** — These are premeditated murders intended to eliminate competition or enforce control over the members of the cartel or drug group. Or, the victim might have been murdered because he or she provided information to authorities or may have been a potential witness in a drug prosecution and was

considered a risk to the drug group. Murders which occur during "drug rip-offs" are also considered drug hits.

2. **INTERPERSONAL DRUG DISPUTES** — These are homicides that occur spontaneously, usually without any premeditation. These murders take place during drug-related disputes and interpersonal violence scenarios among and between persons who are under the influence of drugs and/or are involved in illicit drug activity.

3. **KILLING OF INNOCENT BYSTANDERS IN DRUG-RELATED HOMICIDES** — Drug-related homicides also include the murder of innocent civilians and bystanders who are caught in a crossfire or hit by random shots fired between rival gangs or participants during drug-related disputes. The number of civilian casualties, especially within the inner cities, has drastically increased with the proliferation of drugs and the high-powered weaponry utilized by drug dealers.

4. **DRUG ASSASSINATIONS** — These are premeditated murders which are directed towards government officials, law enforcement personnel, and civilians. The attacks are actually a form of terrorism and are intended to discourage active drug enforcement policies and/or create the impression that the drug groups or cartels are as powerful as authorities. Drug assassinations rarely occur in the United States. However, American authorities and government officials operating and traveling within countries which operate as home bases for some of the major drug cartels are certainly potential targets of an assassination as the United States continues to put pressure on these drug producing countries in the "war on drugs."

On February 26, 1988, New York City Police Officer Edward Byrne was literally assassinated by members of a drug cartel while guarding the home of a drug witness. The subsequent homicide investigation in the Byrne case revealed that the police officer was killed on the orders of a jailed drug lord. The offender ordered the murder because he wanted revenge on the police. The drug dealer had been previously prosecuted and incarcerated on another unrelated narcotics case.

The Drug-Related Murder: The Investigative Dilemma

Drug-related homicides are difficult homicides to solve because of the nature of the incident. In most instances, the murder is a premeditated act. The actual motive for the killing is not readily apparent except that

Figure 16.1. **DRUG "HIT" AND RANSACK.** This man was killed and his stash house ransacked by a rival drug gang.

criminal enterprise or drugs may be involved. The exception to the above scenario is sudden and violent confrontations between persons involved with drugs and/or the murder of innocent civilians. Therefore, the police investigation actually becomes a two-pronged inquiry. The police must first investigate the homicide case and then concentrate their investigative efforts on the narcotics aspects of the case. Actually, these types of cases create at least twice the workload of a routine murder investigation and may further be complicated by interjuris-dictional considerations. In addition, drug-related homicide incidents within the United States have drastically increased which further de-pletes law enforcement resources.

In some jurisdictions drug-related murders account for 50 to 60% of the homicide investigations. Jurisdictions that police large urban areas have traditionally encountered high levels of violence and drug-related criminal activity. The clearance rate for murder within these jurisdictions has been appalling due to the overwhelming work load, lack of personnel, and the absence of an effective strategy for dealing with drug-related murder investigations.

Figure 16.2. **DUMP JOB.** This member of an organized crime gang was executed and dumped in a trunk at an isolated location.

The Drug-Related Murder and the Investigative Reality

Investigatively speaking, most drug-related homicides are eventually solved through intelligence and/or informant information. Witnesses in homicide investigations are generally reluctant to get involved. In my professional opinion, this reluctance turns into active resistance during drug-related murder investigations. The only exception is in the murder of police officers and innocent civilians.

Therefore, the police must concentrate their efforts on obtaining information from gathering criminal intelligence. Intelligence information is

Figure 16.3.   Drug dispute. This crack addict was shot and killed during an argument with another drug dealer.

Figure 16.4.   **DRUG KILLING.** This victim, who went to this location for a drug meeting, was executed by his own people.

Figure 16.5.   **DRUG "HIT" AND DUMP.** This individual was tortured at one location and then dumped. He had stolen "product" from his organization.

Figure 16.6.   **EXECUTION SHOT.** This victim was shot in the head at this location and left as a "message" to anyone else in the organization who had similar ideas.

A

B

Figure 16.7. (A) Dump job upper torso. Drug execution; the body was mutilated to prevent identification. (B) Same case. Legs found at another location.

Figure 16.8. **DRUG KIDNAPPING AND RANSOM CASE.** The victim was kidnapped and
held for ransom. He was then executed. Note the wound structure which suggests an overkill
pattern. The killer was homosexual.

usually developed through an independent police narcotics operation which may evolve within the police department or through outside agencies, such as the DEA, ATF, U.S. Customs, or the FBI.

This intelligence may be in the form of court-approved wiretaps or electronic eavesdropping warrants employed during a narcotics investigation, the execution of search warrants, or through routine debriefings of informants and/or persons arrested for drug violations. Informant information is the most valuable source of inside knowledge about any criminal enterprise. It may be motivated by any number of factors including financial reward, fear, revenge, or court consideration in a pending criminal action.

The Three-Phase Strategy

Practically speaking, authorities should implement an enforcement strategy which addresses three distinct phases of the drug-related murder investigation.

> PHASE 1 — The application of procedural and forensic techniques as well as investigative resources to the homicide crime scene and murder investigation.
>
> PHASE 2 — The evaluation of intelligence resources with the objective of cultivating reliable sources, whose information can be effectively corroborated with the information developed at the homicide crime scene.
>
> PHASE 3 — The implementation of crime clearance procedures which enable authorities to successfully clear a case without an arrest utilizing exceptional means.

The rationale of a *three-phase* strategy is based upon the premise that most drug-related homicides are the direct result of an on-going criminal enterprise. The solvability of each case depends upon the factual information which can be developed at the time of the event coupled with current informational intelligence relative to the specific drug operation involved in the murder event.

The ability of authorities to develop and maintain current intelligence sources and reliable informants is prerequisite to the successful investigation and/or resolution of drug-related murders.

Phase 1 — The Homicide Crime Scene

The process of the homicide crime scene is without a doubt the most important phase of any murder investigation. However, in drug-related homicide investigations the crime scene process takes on an additional significance. In this phase of the investigation it is absolutely imperative to effectively document each and every aspect of the event with the objective of establishing a basis for future corroboration. The police authorities must first attempt to establish the investigative facts of the case based upon the dynamics of the event as well as the circumstances under which the person was killed. The investigation usually starts at the point where the body is originally found. This is the primary crime scene. This presents authorities with two possibilities. Was the deceased killed at the location of discovery? Or was the body dumped at the location?

This is an important consideration because it will focus the investigation and determine the scope of the crime scene process. If the homicide is a "dump-job" there may be two or more crime scenes; i.e., the location where the actual assault and murder took place and a possible vehicle used to transport the body. Obviously, authorities will not have access to these areas during the initial inquiry. However, as the investigation unfolds additional scenes may be discovered. These scenes and areas should be processed as soon as possible in order to obtain additional evidence and information. If the person is killed at the location of discovery, either in the street or in an apartment, then the crime scene process may result in the retrieval of additional evidence as well as additional informational sources. Personal papers, personal effects, telephone records, correspondence, address books, etc., and any property which may aid in the murder investigation should be seized by detectives for later perusal and disposition. This information will assist in any interviews of family members and friends and may reveal a possible motive. The identification and victimology of the deceased becomes an extremely important starting point for the subsequent police investigation. If the murder took place at the point of discovery, the identification of the victim is usually established early on either due to witness identification or personal papers and information sources at the crime scene. If the homicide was a "dump-job," then the identification may be delayed pending fingerprint analysis or subsequent notification through missing persons reports.

During **Phase 1** of the investigation, authorities should also attempt to ascertain the motive and specific category of the murder, drug-hit, interpersonal drug dispute, murder of innocent bystander, or drug assassination. Each category will suggest an investigative option.

In either event, the crime scene process should focus on body position, wound structures, ballistics, blood, clothing trace evidence,

Table 1.

Category	Investigative options
Drug hit	Intelligence information
	Narcotics buy operation
	Buy and bust operation
	Informant information
Interpersonal drug disputes	Buy and bust operation
	Informant information
	Narcotics buy operation
Murder of innocent bystanders	Reward money
	Crime stoppers program
	Use of news media and press
	Community activists
	Buy and bust operation
	Informant information
Drug assassinations	Intelligence operations
	Electronic eavesdropping
	Narcotics buy operations
	Reward money — crime stoppers
	Use of news media and press

and informational resources which represent the tangibles and collectables in drug-related homicides. It should be noted that any subsequent prosecution under state or federal conspiracy laws and/or implementation of exceptional clearance procedures will require the independent corroborative information developed during the Phase 1 operations.

Phase 2 — The Application of Drug Intelligence

In this phase of the murder investigation, authorities should direct their resources towards developing intelligence information as it relates to the murder. The objective is to establish the identity of the members and structure of the drug cartel or operation so as to focus on motivations and possible suspects involved. Drug operations and "key players" within criminal organizations may change. Arrests, prosecutions, murders, and any number of factors may impact on specific individuals or groups; however, the illegal activity remains the same.

Criminal enterprise maintains its continuity through adjusting operations and recruiting new members to engage in criminal conduct on an on-going basis. This generates a tremendous amount of strategic and tactical intelligence information. This intelligence information, which is utilized by narcotics officers, to identify, target, and penetrate drug operations and arrest offenders, can also be utilized by the homicide investigator to investigate his or her murder inquiry.

In my professional opinion as an expert in homicide investigation, each drug-related homicide should be analyzed and assessed in conjunction with available drug intelligence information for the purposes of identifying and targeting specific offenders involved in the homicide investigation. In fact, in jurisdictions that experience a high percentage of drug-related murders, the author recommends that the homicide division maintain within the command an intelligence operation team. We maintained a "special homicide-narcotics team" within the 7th Homicide Zone of the New York City Police Department. We had been experiencing an inordinate amount of drug-related homicides within our zone. We attributed this increase to a series of drug wars involving different ethnic groups; 65 to 70% of the 200 homicides which occurred in this zone were drug related. This Zone encompassed an area of approximately two square miles in the South Bronx. Our clearance rates were down to 40% and the body count was steadily increasing. As a direct result of implementing our "special homicide-narcotics team" our drug intelligence network expanded and our arrest clearance rate was increased to 75%.

The author recommends that the team should include narcotics officers, who are familiar with drug operations, as well as homicide detectives, who have experience with career criminals. There should be a sufficient number of personnel to effectively engage in both reactive and proactive operations. The mission of this team is to develop pertinent information on drug-related homicides through investigation, analysis, and assessment. This is accomplished through independent "street-level" enforcement action, debriefings of confidential informants, and the exchange of intelligence information with other law enforcement agencies. It requires establishing intelligence liaison with narcotics enforcement units as well as outside agencies involved in the investigation of narcotics violations with the objective of establishing an effective intelligence network. Many offenders, who are arrested, are willing to make deals. They elect to cooperate with authorities to avoid extended jail time. This presents the homicide detective with an effective strategy for developing criminal informants for the drug-related homicide investigation.

1. Specific offenders, who have been identified as witnesses in the drug slaying, can be targeted for a "Narcotics Buy Operation" in order to force their cooperation in the murder case. Or,
2. A particular neighborhood can be targeted with a "Buy and Bust" operation with the objective of snaring potential witnesses to the drug slaying. In some instances, authorities at the homicide crime

scene may be provided with "bonus information" in the form of elaborate records of drug deals. I have been involved in a number of drug-related homicide investigations in which the records and ledgers we seized contained code names of other dealers and customers, dates and quantities of drugs sold, and financial transactions of specific drug operations. This information can be provided to narcotics officers to assist in their operations as well as target potential witnesses in the drug-related homicide investigation. It is important to note that the intelligence aspects of the drug-related homicide investigation requires mutual law enforcement cooperation between and among the different units and agencies involved in narcotics investigations.

Phase 3 — Crime Clearance Procedures

Homicides are usually considered solved or closed when the offender has been arrested and charged with the murder. However, homicides can also be effectively cleared utilizing Exceptional Clearance. Exceptional Clearance procedures enable authorities to successfully clear a case without an actual arrest. This method of crime clearance requires an agency to document the following information.

1. The identity of the offender is known, and
2. The exact location of the offender is known, and
3. There is sufficient information to support an arrest and prosecution, but
4. There is some reason beyond police control that prevents the offender from being arrested.

The specific reasons which explain "beyond police control" must be documented within the report closing the case by Exceptional Means. An example of "beyond police control" in a homicide case would be the verified death of the perpetrator either through an unrelated homicide or by official state execution. I was involved in a number of drug-related homicide investigations during my 23 years in the New York City Police Department. Oftentimes, during a homicide investigation we were able to identify a specific suspect and establish sufficient probable cause for arrest only to have this suspect himself become a victim of another drug-related murder. By utilizing Exceptional Means to close cases our agency was able to sustain sufficient homicide clearance. Ironically, drug-related homicides, which are difficult cases to solve, are particularly amenable to Exceptional Means clearance due to the continuity and violent nature of drug criminal enterprise. However, in order to effectively utilize this method of crime clearance, the agency must invest the necessary time and resources into Phase 1 and Phase 2 of the drug-related homicide investigation.

Conclusion

The analytical process of classifying each drug-related homicide into one of four categories and then applying the Three-Phase Enforcement Strategy to the investigation enables the detective to establish priorities and maximize his or her investigative efforts. Upon the completion of Phase 1 operations, the homicide investigation can either be inactivated or pursued depending on whether or not further information can be developed in Phase 2 operations. This strategy allows investigators to concentrate their efforts on the cases which are most amenable to clearance. However, in order for this strategy to be effective, police agencies must implement a persistent and aggressive law enforcement policy as it relates to narcotics violations. The strategic and tactical intelligence generated through this continuous narcotics enforcement will provide the informational basis for the successful investigation of drug-related homicides.

Selected Reading

Geberth, Vernon J. "Investigation of Drug-Related Homicides." *Law and Order Magazine*, Vol. 38, No. 11, Illinois, November, 1990.

Collection of Evidence 17

Physical evidence is any tangible article, small or large, which tends to prove or disprove a point in question. It may be used to:

1. Reconstruct the crime.
2. Identify the participants.
3. Confirm or discredit an alibi.

The proper collection and disposition of physical or trace evidence from the crime scene and the body of the deceased is of utmost importance to the investigation and eventual court presentation. The evidence must have been obtained legally in order for it to be admissible. Therefore, it is imperative that both the legal authority to collect the evidence and the proper collection techniques be considered prior to the actual collection of the evidence.[1]

Procedures for Collection of Evidence

In order to be introduced as physical evidence in a trial, an article must:

Be properly identified
Show a proper chain of custody

---

[1] The techniques of collection presented in this chapter are based on the recommendations and procedures of Dr. Robert C. Shaler, Ph.D. Doctor Shaler, who holds a M.S. and Ph.D. in Biochemistry from Pennsylvania State University, is the Director of Serology for the New York City Medical Examiners Office. Doctor Shaler has lectured at various universities and forensic symposia and has published several articles related to the forensic sciences.

Be material and relevant

Meet all legal requirements

The crime scene technician or crime scene investigator who is summoned to the scene should have operational supervision over gathering, collection, and marking of evidence for identification. However, the investigator assigned to the case is still in charge of the investigation and should be consulted prior to any evidence gathering or crime scene processing.

The proper collection and disposition of evidence will be accomplished if the following guidelines are adhered to:

1. Each piece of evidence should be marked (on the container or item as applicable) to show its original position and location. This information should also be recorded in the investigator's notebook.
2. Each article should be marked distinctively by the searching officer to identify the person who found the particular piece of evidence. In cases of small or fluid specimens this marking is done on the container.
3. Each item should be described exactly and completely with the corresponding case numbers affixed and the date and time of collection indicated.
4. Each item should be packaged in a separate, clean, and proper-sized container to prevent cross-contamination or damage.
5. Each package should be sealed to retain evidence and prevent any unauthorized handling.
6. Each piece of evidence should show proper disposition:
   a. Police department laboratory
   b. Property clerk's office
   c. FBI Laboratory
7. Proper records should be kept regarding each piece of evidence showing chain of custody. These records should reflect any movement of the evidence from the point of origin to its final disposition.

Remember, each item should be photographed before it is collected as evidence. These photographs should include a long-range view to show the relationship of the object to its surroundings and a close-range view to show the actual item being collected. (See Chapter 6.)

Collection of Specific Types of Evidence

The homicide investigator is usually confronted with the same general type of evidence in most murder investigations, such as blood, bullets, and fingerprints. The evidence ordinarily falls within three distinct categories: *body materials, objects,* and *impressions.*

This text will focus on the practical methods for collection of those types of evidence commonly found at the scene of a homicide. The more advanced and detailed methodologies have been purposefully omitted from this section because they are usually beyond the capability of the average investigator and are best performed by crime scene technicians and other experts who have been specially trained in forensic science techniques.[2]

Body Materials

Blood (Wet)

1. Large amounts or pools:
   a. Use an eyedropper or hypodermic syringe to collect the fluid and transfer to a sterile container (5 cc is sufficient for testing purposes).
   b. Transfer immediately to laboratory or refrigerate specimen. However, *do not freeze blood.*
   c. In some instances, depending on the jurisdiction regulations, a chemical preservative such as Sodium Azide or EDTA can be used to prevent blood spoilage.
2. Small amounts of wet blood:
   a. Use a 100% cotton swab, #8 cotton thread, or gauze pad to collect specimen.
   b. Allow swab or gauze pad to air dry.
   c. Place in sterile test tube or other clean container.

Blood Stains (Dry)

1. Nonporous surface:

---

[2] These advanced methodologies are covered in several comprehensive works on the subject. If the reader wishes a more in-depth knowledge of evidence collection, he or she is advised to consult the more technical textbooks on forensic science. See for example, Paul Kirk, *Crime Investigation,* 2nd ed., New York: John Wiley & Sons, Inc., 1974 or *Crime Scene Investigation* by Dr. Henry Lee, Ph.D. Central Police University Press, Taiwan, Republic of China, 1994.

Figure 17.1. Sequential evidence such as this barefooted bloodstain trail and blood drip pattern can inform the investigator about events and movement through the scene, aiding in the reconstruction of the crime scene. (Courtesy of the Westchester County Medical Examiner's Office.)

  a. If there is sufficient amount of dry blood, it can be scraped from the surface with a clean razor blade or sterile scalpel. These scrapings should be shaved into a sterile container.
2. Porous surface (fabric, unfinished wood, etc.):
  a. Collect and submit the article containing the stain to the laboratory as found.
  b. Wrap in separate and sterile container. If the article is too large or inappropriate to transport, remove a portion of the material containing an adequate amount of the stain for transport to the laboratory for analysis.
3. Traces or smears which cannot be scraped into container:
  a. Moisten a 100% cotton swab or gauze pad with distilled water. Also obtain a control sample which should be forwarded to the lab for analysis with the specimen.
  b. Stain will soften and soak into swab or gauze pad.
  c. Allow to air dry.
  d. Place into a sterile test tube or container for laboratory.

Figure 17.2. **PHOTOGRAPH OF CLEAN-UP ATTEMPT.** A clean-up attempt at this homicide scene is evident by the swirling patterns which obliterated most footwear impressions at this scene. A remaining impression is partially visible under the victim's knee and another is visible in the center of the photo. Large bloodstains, drying at the surface only, were disturbed during the clean-up as can be noted at the lower right of the photo. This drying gave investigators a rough time estimate between the homicide and the clean-up. (Courtesy of the Yonkers, New York Police Department Crime Scene Unit, Det./Lt. Peter Pizzola, Commanding Officer.)

> **Remember, do not use a swab or other instrument to collect blood from more than one stain. Use separate swabs, razors, scalpels, or other instruments for each separate stain to be sampled. This is to prevent contamination of samples.**

It is possible that the assailant's blood may also be present. If the same instrument is used to collect all samples, the evidence will be tainted. Furthermore, you should be careful not to touch the surface which has contacted the blood sample because your own secretions may contaminate the collected sample (see "DNA Testing").

Semen

Next to blood, semen is the physiological fluid most commonly discovered at homicide crime scenes. If a sexual assault is suspected, the investigator should carefully examine the body and clothing of the

Figure 17.3. **DRIED SEMEN EVIDENCE.** This close-up shot of the vaginal area of a rape-homicide victim discloses the traces of dried semen. (See arrow.) Notice the "starchy" appearance. This trace should be gathered using 100% cotton moistened with distilled water, allowed to air-dry, and then placed in a sterile container for delivery to the laboratory.

deceased prior to moving the body. If any stains are observed, procedures to collect this evidence should be performed at the scene. Later at autopsy, the medical examiner or coroner will take a vaginal swab or vaginal aspirant to obtain any semen traces from within the vaginal canal. In addition, oral and anal swabs may be taken, if sodomy is also suspected, and air dried immediately.

The following techniques should be employed at the scene.

1. Wet stain:
   a. Swab or wash (by medical examiner if possible).
   b. Draw the fluid into an eyedropper or hypodermic syringe.
   c. Place in sterile test tube.
   d. Use swab or cotton gauze pad for samples of smaller quantities which are still moist.
   e. Allow to air dry immediately and place in sterile container.
2. Dry stain:
   a. Dry stain will have a stiff "starchy" texture.
   b. If it is on clothing, submit the entire article, being careful not to break or contaminate the stained area.

Figure 17.4. **TRACE EVIDENCE — DOCUMENTATION.** With the use of macro photography, we see the various pieces of trace evidence that have been transferred from the victim to the site of recovery. This forensic evidence consists of the victim's blood, a long strand of hair, as well as vegetative matter from the primary crime scene which was approximately one mile from this location.

> c. On body, using 100% cotton gauze pad moistened with distilled water, gently remove stain and place in sterile test tube or container after allowing to air dry.

Sometimes an ultraviolet light can be utilized to locate seminal stains. However, in many instances a false reading will be obtained due to the "brighteners" used in certain laundry detergents (see "DNA Testing").

Urine

1. Remove by eyedropper or gauze pad.
2. Place in sterile test tube or other container.
3. If on clothing, the entire article should be submitted.

Spittle or Saliva

1. Remove with eyedropper or 100% cotton gauze pad.
2. Place in sterile test tube or other clean container after drying.

Feces

1. Large amount:
   a. Remove with a small clean shovel. Allow to air dry.
   b. Place in sterile container.
2. Small amount:
   a. Remove with 100% cotton swab or gauze pad moistened with distilled water, then air dry or scrape into container.
   b. Place in sterile test tube.

Vomit

1. Remove with eyedropper or small shovel depending on amount.
2. Place into sterile container.

It should be noted that any physiological fluid found at the scene, such as urine, saliva, feces, perspiration, ear wax, nasal mucus, etc., can be typed into the same grouping as blood providing the material comes from an individual who is a secretor. Secretors make up approximately 80% of the general population. Physiological fluids of these secretors can be blood-typed by the serologist. Other genetic factors sometimes can also be identified regardless of secretor status.

Tissue

1. Remove with tweezers.
2. Place in a glass container or sterile test tube.
3. Forward to the medical examiner.

Hair

During crimes of violence, specifically against persons, certain trace materials such as hair or fibers will be transferred between the victim and the perpetrator. These traces may also be left at the scene. Hairs are considered a *class characteristic* — although they cannot be identified as being absolutely identical to a given suspect's hair, they can be classified as similar to a known sample. In addition, they can be used to exclude a suspect. However, from an investigative point of view, hairs and/or fibers can:

1. Help determine the extent of the crime scene.
2. Place the perpetrator at the scene of the crime.
3. Connect the suspect to the weapon.

Figure 17.5.   **HAIR EVIDENCE.** Detective recovering hair from a woolen cap; evidence in a homicide case. (Courtesy of Lt. Daniel Guiney, Commanding Officer, Crime Scene Unit, New York City Police Department.)

4. Corroborate statements of witnesses.
5. Determine the route to and from the crime scene.
6. Be located in any number of areas involved in the homicide:
   a. The victim
   b. The crime scene
   c. The weapon
   d. A tool
   e. A vehicle
   f. An article of clothing
   g. The suspect

Determinations from Hair

1. Species — human or animal.
2. Race — Caucasoid, Negroid, or Mongoloid. (In certain instances, the determination of a combination of racial characteristics can be ascertained.)
3. Location of growth — body area from where the particular hair originated (head, thorax, chest, pubis, etc.)
4. Treatment — dyed, bleached, straightened, etc.
5. How it was removed — pulled, fell out, cut, etc.
6. Disease and/or damage.

Figure 17.6.   **EXAMINATION FOR HAIR EVIDENCE.** Forensic scientist Elayne Schwartz examines an article of evidence from a homicide case for hairs, fibers, and other trace evidence. (Courtesy of the Westchester County Forensic Laboratory. Photograph by Joseph Rue.)

Figure 17.7.   **HAIR EVIDENCE.** Hair evidence can be identified and compared by structure or morphology. Recent advances in molecular biology give the homicide investigator a new tool: DNA (deoxyribonucleic acid analysis). This hair root (enlarged 400 times) contains a "tag" of cells from the owner's follicle and DNA analysis of this material can be highly probative to the case. (Courtesy of Robert A. Adamo. Photograph by W. Reid Lindsay, Westchester County Forensic Science Laboratory.)

7. Genetic information:
    a. Blood type, from shaft of hair
    b. Other genetic markers, from roots of pulled hair
    c. Sex, from roots of pulled hair

It is recommended that a sample of hair from various parts of the body be obtained in all homicide cases. Even though hair evidence may not be crucial or known to exist in the early stages of the investigation, it may be discovered later even after the body has been buried or destroyed through cremation. Samples should always be taken from various parts by pulling or plucking so as to obtain a piece of the root. If pulling or plucking absolutely cannot be undertaken for some reason, cutting the hair close to the scalp will suffice. An ordinary sampling will comprise approximately 24 to 48 pieces of hair. Hair removed from the head should be taken as follows: front, back, left side, right side, and top. The sample roots should then be air dried.

Collection of Hairs from the Scene

Using oblique lighting, scan the surfaces of the crime scene.

1. If hairs or fibers are located, gather by tweezers, being careful not to bend or break.
2. Masking or Scotch tape can be used to gather small fibers or hairs.
3. Place in sterile container and seal. (Folded paper or envelopes may also be used.)

Conclusions from Hair Samples

1. Hair did not come from unknown hair source.
2. Hair could have come from known hair source.
3. Hair sampling too limited for meaningful comparison.
4. No conclusion.

Objects

Bullets

When a bullet is fired from a weapon, certain distinctive characteristics are imparted to the bullet by the gun. These markings can be examined through internal ballistics and provide the investigator with certain general information regarding the type of weapon used. In addition, ballistics evidence is highly individualistic, and a fired bullet recovered from the scene can be positively matched with the suspect weapon.

Figure 17.8. **MARKING OF BALLISTICS EVIDENCE ON THE BASE AND NOSE OF THE PROJECTILE.** Recommended procedure.

Figure 17.9. **COMPARISON MICROSCOPE.** Comparison microscope (split screen) image of two fired cartridge case primers. The left side is the evidence casing. The right side is the test fired casing. Note matching impressed striations on the primer faces caused by irregularities (toolmarks) in firearm's breech face. Firing causes rearward travel of the casing as the bullet moves forward down the barrel. Three-dimensional imprintings are made when the soft primer metal is pressed against hard metal of the breech face. (Courtesy of Frank M. Nicolosi, Ballistics Unit, Westchester County Police Department.)

Figure 17.10.   **COMPARISON MICROSCOPE.** Comparison microscope (split screen) image of two fired bullets. The left side is the evidence bullet. The right side is the test-fired bullet. Note matching impressed striations in the soft metal of both bullets caused by irregularities (toolmarks, rust, etc.) in the firearm's hard metal barrel (bore). Even sequentially produced barrels from a manufacturer's assembly line have slightly differing individualizing (unique) characteristics caused by microscopic damage to the cutting edges of the tools used to cut the rifling into the bore. (Courtesy of Frank M. Nicolosi, Ballistics Unit, Westchester County Police Department.)

1. Bullets should be collected without damaging or marking the *rifling*, the series of grooves or lines on the interior surface of the barrel which cause the bullet to spin and travel forward through the barrel with accuracy. These grooves and lines are transferred to the bullet as it is fired and are used by the ballistics expert to make comparisons.
2. Bullets embedded in doors, trees, walls, etc. should be removed by taking out a portion of the object in which the bullet has become lodged rather than by probing or digging. Digging for the bullet may cause additional marks which may destroy the ballistics value of the evidence.
3. Recovered bullets should be examined for blood or other materials before packaging.
4. Bullets should be marked on the base or nose.
5. Each bullet should be packaged separately in an appropriate container, preferably one which will prevent any cross-contamination or accidental abrasion of the rifling marks.

6. Package should be marked to show identification and location of discovery.

Discharged Casings or Cartridges

The recovery of discharged shells may indicate the direction and location of the attack as well as how many shots were fired. In addition, certain class characteristics such as make and caliber can be ascertained. Furthermore, if an automatic weapon was used, certain ejector or clip markings may be present.

1. Recovered casings should be marked on the inside wall of the shell by the mouth end, or, if this is not possible, as near to the opening as possible.
2. Never mark the recovered casing on or near the end which contains the primer cap, because examination of weapon markings may be destroyed.
3. Always consider the possibility of fingerprints on the sides of these casings and take appropriate methods to preserve them.
4. Package in separate containers with proper documentation.

Shotgun Shells

1. Plastic or paper shotgun shells should be handled in the same manner as other discharged casings.
2. These items can be marked on the metal side part of the casing.
3. *Never mark on base of shell casing.*

Live Cartridges or Rounds of Ammunition

1. Examine for fingerprint evidence prior to marking.
2. Mark on side of casing.
3. Package, indicating the location of recovered rounds.

Shotgun Wadding

1. Recover and submit for laboratory examination.
2. Place in a separate container.

Weapons

1. Photograph and examine for fingerprints.
2. Examine for any serology or other trace evidence.

3. Place in special container according to size to protect evidence and prevent handling.
4. Forward to serology or crime lab for further analysis.

Firearms

1. Photograph in original position.
2. Examine for fingerprints.
3. Examine for any serology (e.g., blow-back of close-range firing may result in blood, hair, or tissue being transferred to weapon or in barrel of weapon).
4. Upon completion of preliminary examination for above, unload weapon and render safe before transporting.
5. Package individually in an appropriate container. (In circumstances in which the firearm must be transported for further examination at a proper facility, use a cardboard box. Draw a string through the trigger guard and attach this string at either end of the box, leaving the gun in a suspended position. For larger firearms like rifles or shotguns, cut a notch in each end of the box and lay weapon across container.)
6. Indicate the brand name, model designation, serial numbers, caliber, and number of shots the weapon is capable of firing, e.g., 5- or 6-shot revolver, etc. in reports and on evidence containers. Also indicate the type of finish — nickel plate, etc.
7. All weapons recovered should be marked for identification as soon as possible in the following manner:
   a. Revolvers — mark on frame, barrel, and cylinder.
   b. Rifles and shotguns — mark on receiver, bolt, and barrel.
   c. Semiautomatic weapons — receiver (frame), the slide, barrel, and any clips.

Fibers

Fibers, like hairs, may be transferred between the victim and perpetrator, and provide the investigator with an additional piece of class evidence which can be subjected to microscopic and microchemical testing. Items such as fibers, rope, string, or twine should be collected for examination.

1. Examination of fibers will indicate origin as follows:
   a. Vegetable — cotton and hemp

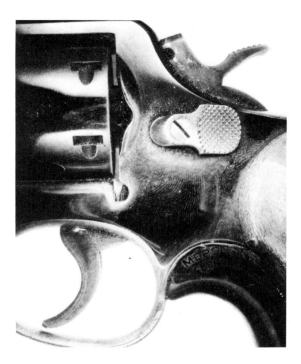

Figure 17.11.   **LATENT PRINT.** The print on this revolver is photographed in order to preserve the evidence. The camera used for this particular latent impression is the Polaroid CU-5. (Courtesy of the Polaroid Corporation, Cambridge, Massachusetts.)

    b. Animal — wool and mink

    c. Mineral — glass wool and asbestos

    d. Synthetic — nylon and orlon

2. Examination of fiber evidence will determine if the fiber is similar to the control sample.

3. Collect fibers as follows:

    a. Forceps

    b. Tape

    c. Vacuum sweeping (it should be noted that this is the least desirable method because too many contaminants are also collected)

4. Collecting samples by using sticky side of tape is considered the most practical method.

5. Place samples in individual containers from each area gathered, mark appropriately, and forward to laboratory for examination.

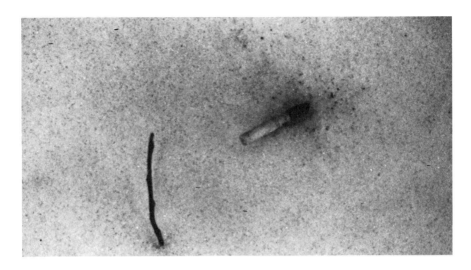

Figure 17.12. **OUTDOOR CRIME SCENE SEARCH.** Here you can see a partially smoked cigarette butt lying in the snow. The cigarette butt contains lipstick and has apparently burned out in the snow. This piece of evidence was discovered by investigators who were searching the area where a body was found. In fact, the cigarette's condition was consistent with the time element of how long the body had been lying at the location. It is important to note that saliva will be transferred to the cigarette and can be typed in certain instances to reveal the blood type of the person who smoked it.

Fabric

1. Pieces of fabric found at the scene can be examined in a manner similar to fibers to determine:
   a. Color
   b. Type of cloth and fiber
   c. Thread count
   d. Direction of fiber twist
   e. Dye
2. Class as well as individual characteristics can be obtained from fragments of fabric when matched by physically fitting the evidence pieces into its source.

Cigarette/Cigar Butts

Cigarette or cigar butts found at the crime scene, especially those with filter tips, can be examined by serologists for the determination of blood type and sometimes other genetic factors (e.g., sex) of individuals who are secretors (also see page 536, "DNA Analysis").

1. Collect with forceps or tweezers and insure dryness.
2. Place into separate containers to prevent contamination.
3. Containers should be appropriately marked.
4. Forward to serology.

Displaced Furniture

1. Examine for any fingerprints or serology.
2. Useful in crime reconstruction.

Soil

1. Soil on shoes, clothing, tools, weapons, and other objects may be useful in placing a suspect at the scene and providing the investigator with additional evidence. Also microbiological comparisons in addition to mineral comparisons can be made.
   a. Color of soil may be distinctive.
   b. Minerals can be distinctive.
   c. Bacterial profiles can be distinctive.
   d. Vegetation (fungal spores, etc.) can be distinctive.
2. Collection of soil samples:
   a. Collect several samples at the scene from various locations since mineral and organic contents vary within short distances.
   b. Gather at least a cupful or handful from each location.
   c. Insure dryness.
   d. Package in separate containers.
   e. Mark properly for identification and location.

Tools

Tools which are suspected of being used in the crime should be examined as follows:

1. Examine for serology or fingerprints.
2. If the tool contains any serological evidence, it must be carefully packaged to preserve this evidence.
3. If tool contains traces of certain materials that are to be matched up with known samples, care must be taken so that this material is not rubbed off.
4. Portion of tool to be matched must be protected.

5. Broken tools and/or knives can be fracture-matched to provide positive identification.
6. *Never try to fit tool into tool mark or match broken pieces together.*

Vehicles

1. Photograph and examine for serology.
2. Process for fingerprints.
3. Examine for other items of evidence.
4. Search for weapons.

Clothing

Each item of clothing collected as evidence should be individually wrapped in order to prevent cross contamination. If the clothing to be collected is wet, it should be air dried before it is packaged. Clothing may provide the investigator with additional evidence:

1. Stains on clothing may match stains from the scene, the victim, or the suspect.
2. A suspect's clothing may contain blood similar to the victim's.
3. The victim's clothing may contain saliva and/or seminal fluid from the perpetrator.
4. Hairs or fibers may be present on clothing that match similar hairs or fibers from a particular scene or location or from the victim.
5. Tears or cuts in clothing made by the weapon can be matched to show the position of the victim at the time of the assault.
6. The deposit of gunshot residues on clothing can be analyzed to determine the approximate distance from which the gun was fired.

Documents (Letters, Notes, Papers)

These items may be examined to ascertain authenticity, locate finger-prints, or determine authorship in suicide cases, or for more advanced techniques such as psycholinguistic examination. (See Chapter 20, "Psycholinguistics.")

1. The primary consideration in handling this type of evidence is the preservation of any fingerprints which may be on the item.
2. Evidence should be collected by using tweezers or forceps to gently pick up the paper.

3. Each item should be placed in a separate package. A package which is clear or see-through is best since it will allow the investigator to examine contents without contaminating the document with additional fingerprints.
4. If see-through packages are not available, the object can be photocopied using forceps to place the object on the machine and later to transfer it to the evidence envelope. (This will allow for reading and other examination of content without disturbing evidence value of the original document.)
5. Marking this type of evidence depends on the type of examination to be conducted. In some instances, a mark can be placed on a back corner of the paper. In other instances just the package in which the document is placed will be marked.
6. Documents should not be folded.
7. Examine for latent prints.
8. Saliva on envelopes can be blood-typed and sometimes analyzed for sex origin.

Examination of Documents

The examination for latent prints on papers, documents, and other porous materials such as wood proceeds in a series of steps.

First step: Iodine fuming — reacts with oil or fatty fluids in latent print.

Second step: Ninhydrin — penetrates material and reacts with amino acids in perspiration. Heat should be applied and print will emerge.

Third step: Silver nitrate — reacts to salt in the perspiration. The document is then exposed to strong light.

Glass

Examinations can be conducted on glass and glass fragments using a *refractive index*, which proves that the known sample and the evidence glass may have come from a similar source. In addition, in certain cases the fragments can be physically matched. Furthermore, the direction and sequence of bullet holes through glass can be determined by examination of radial and concentric fractures and may prove important in reconstructing the crime. Glass should be collected as follows:

Figure 17.13. **VISIBLE PRINT** (also referred to as a patent print). This actual fingerprint was left in blood at the crime scene. This is a visible or patent print. The offender's blood-drenched hands and fingers transferred this fingerprint to the glossy surface of an automobile.

Figure 17.14. **DUSTING FOR LATENT FINGERPRINTS.** (Courtesy of the Polaroid Corporation, Cambridge, Massachusetts.)

1. Small pieces should be placed in a vial or pillbox.
2. Large pieces should be placed in a sturdy cardboard box with proper padding or protection to prevent further breakage during transport.

Impressions

Fingerprint Examination

The most valuable evidence that an investigator can obtain from the homicide crime scene are the fingerprints of the suspect. From an investigative point of view, any crime scene search should include a detailed examination for visible, plastic, and latent prints. It is important to note that the officer(s) performing this function should preserve all developed prints. Even partial prints which may seem insignificant may become valuable later when compared to prints taken from a suspect. It should be noted that fingerprint powders *do not* interfere with serological analyses. However, ninhydrin sprays and other chemical means to make prints visible may interfere with serology tests.

Types of Fingerprints

Fingerprints are divided into three separate categories: plastic prints, visible prints, and latent prints.

1. **Plastic prints.** These impressions occur when the finger touches or presses against a soft pliable surface such as putty, gum, a newly painted area, the glue on a stamp or envelope, wax, flour, thick dust, soap, grease, tar, resin, clay, etc. A negative impression of the friction ridge pattern is produced, resulting in a *plastic print*.
2. **Visible prints.** These prints occur when the fingers, palms, or feet which have been contaminated with a foreign substance come into contact with a clean surface and are pressed onto the surface, leaving a print. The most common type is the dust print. However, substances such as ink, blood, soot, paint, grease, face powders, oils, etc. contaminate the friction ridges of the fingers, when they are pressed against another surface, an image is transferred.
3. **Latent prints.** These prints occur from the natural skin secretions such as perspiration. When grease or dirt is mixed with the natural secretions, a stable print may be deposited on the surface. Latent prints, which are not visible, are usually found on

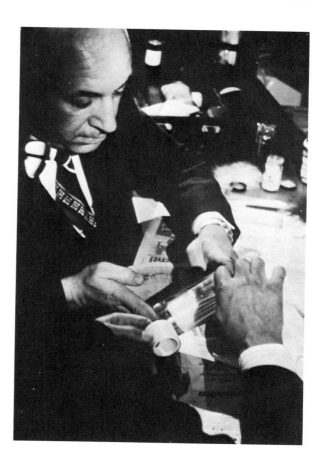

Figure 17.15. Detective lifting a latent print.

objects with smooth or polished surfaces or on paper. The latent print is developed by dusting or chemical process. In some instances these latent prints can be developed on rougher surfaces by using certain chemical processes.

Development of Fingerprints

The most common and practical method of developing prints at crime scenes is through the "dusting" technique. This is done by dusting or spreading fingerprint powder with a brush over the surface of the object suspected of bearing prints. The choice of the color of the powder to be used depends on the background of the object to be dusted. If the object is dark or black, a light powder is used, and conversely, if the object is light or white, a dark or black powder is used. The most common color powders are black, silver, grey, and white. However, fingerprint pow-

Figure 17.16. **PLACING THE LIFT ON A CARD.** (Courtesy of Lt. Daniel Guiney, Commanding Officer, Crime Scene Unit, New York City Police Department.)

ders come in many other colors which can be used to contrast with any background. The brushes available are composed of camel's hair, feather dusters, fiberglass, or nylon.

1. A small amount of powder is poured onto a clean piece of paper.
2. The brush is drawn across the powder and then tapped with the finger to remove excess material.
3. The surface of object to be searched is then lightly brushed by the investigator who uses curved strokes to locate prints.

The fingerprint powder adheres to the material and forms the latent print. This latent print will first appear as a smudge and will require further treatment before it becomes a distinct print. This is done by brushing the powder parallel to the ridge structure of the print, being careful not to rub the print too hard. After the print is developed it should be photographed first and then lifted.

Another method of dusting is done with magnetic powders. The Magna-Brush is dipped into the magnetic powder which then adheres to the magnet in the brush. When the powder, which is actually fine iron fillings, is evenly distributed on the end of the brush, the investigator uses the applicator like any other fingerprint brush. The advan-

Figure 17.17. Polaroid's
CU-5 camera.

tage of this method is that there is no mess or excess powder left on the object. The disadvantage is that the Magna-Brush method cannot be used on ferrous metals and is very expensive. The prints that are located are lifted in the same manner as those obtained with the regular fingerprint powder.

Preservation of Fingerprints

Prints found at the scene of a homicide should be immediately recorded by photography before any attempt is made to "lift" the print. This procedure is recommended in the event lifting is not successful or the print is damaged during attempts to remove it from the item on which it is found.

In addition, photography also makes it easier to introduce the fingerprint evidence into court, since parts of the object that contained the print can be seen in the picture. The method of photography used will vary with the expertise of the technician. I recommend that the investigator use the 1 × 1 or "fingerprint" camera. Polaroid produces a fixed-focus camera called the CU-5 which is ideal for this type of work.

Figure 17.18.   **FIREARMS.** Latent print developed after the gun has been processed for prints, using dusting powders. The developed print is then photographed with the CU-5 camera. It is recommended procedure to photograph any latent prints before attempting the lift. In the event that the lift fails, the photograph can still be used to evaluate and compare the latent print. (Courtesy of the Polaroid Corporation, Cambridge, Massachusetts.)

It should be noted that in addition to latent fingerprints, *palmar* (palm, wrist) or *plantar* (foot, toe) skin designs may also be found at the scene.

> Remember, these impressions or prints can also be used to positively identify suspects and should be preserved accordingly.

Chemical Processes

In addition to the powders, there are a series of chemical procedures which can be employed to develop latent prints. These are: iodine fuming, ninhydrin, and silver nitrate. Furthermore, there have been some remarkable results in developing latent prints by use of the laser. Practically speaking, the average investigator will not be employing these procedures. However, one should be aware of the availability of these methods in the event that further examination of evidence is necessary in order to discover and develop latent print evidence.

Tire Tracks and Footprints

These impressions may be left in various types of material. The foot-print is the most common impression left at or near the scene of a

Figure 17.19. **LATENT PRINT.** Fingerprints such as this coupled with the new computerized automated fingerprint identification systems (AFSI) can be a rapid and precise way for the homicide investigator to place individuals at the crime scene or tie two or more events to one perpetrator. (Courtesy of Westchester County Forensic Laboratory. Photograph by W. Reid Lindsay.)

crime. A *footprint* is formed when the foot or sole and heel of a shoe becomes contaminated with some foreign substance, such as blood, paint, or dust. A *foot impression* is formed like a tire track, when the foot or tire treads are pressed into some type of moldable material such as dirt, clay, or snow. Any such impression should be preserved and used for comparison with suspects or vehicles. Impressions may be identifiable by wear, damage, characteristic properties, or repair marks. Impressions should be collected in the following manner.

1. Photograph: Prior to photography, the impression should be cleaned of all foreign matter. Lighting should be employed so as to enhance the details. A scale of measure should be included in the photo. Then a long-range view and a close-up should be taken.
2. Casting: A casting kit should be available for use at the crime scene which contains the following materials:
   a. Plaster of paris (5 pounds).
   b. Mixing container (flexible for reuse).

Figure 17.20.   **BLOODSTAINED SNEAKERS.** These are the bloodstained sneakers of an offender who was apprehended while standing in a crowd of on-lookers at a homicide scene. The offender had gotten the blood on his sneakers during an assault. He had stabbed the victim multiple times during a dispute in a hallway. He then fled from the scene, but had to walk through the blood thereby leaving sneaker prints in blood at the crime scene. The sneaker prints matched the impressions and the blood on the sneakers matched the blood type of the deceased.

     c. Stirring stick.

     d. Reinforcement material (sticks, wire, etc. to hold form).

     e. Shellac or plastic spray (to form soft earth or dust).

     f. Oil spray (to serve as release agent).

  3. Preparation for casting:

     a. Clean out the loose material without disturbing impression.

     b. Plastic spray to fix soil prior to plaster.

     c. Build a form around impression to avoid run-off.

     d. Gently pour plaster of paris over impression.

     e. Add reinforcement sticks as form builds.

  4. Preservation of dust prints:

     a. Photograph first.

     b. Use a special lifter (black rubber with a sticky surface) placed sticky-side down over impression. Press on the impression and then remove lifter.

Figure 17.21. Evidence photograph depicting a bloody sneaker print. Note the rule of measure. (Courtesy of Dr. Robert C. Shaler, Chief of Serology, New York City Medical Examiner's Office.)

Figure 17.22. **IMPRESSION EVIDENCE.** Impression evidence such as these tire impressions can prove extremely valuable for the homicide investigator. (Courtesy of Karen Vallaro. Photograph by W. Reid Lindsay, Westchester County Forensic Science Laboratory.)

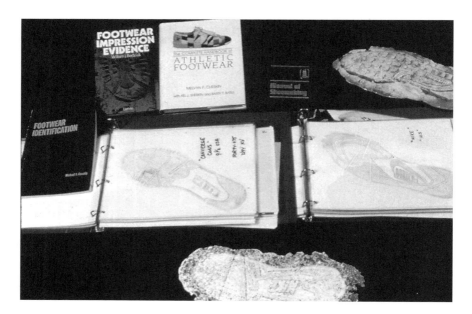

Figure 17.23.   **FOOTWEAR IMPRESSION.** The proliferation of footwear styles and sole designs make footwear impressions more important than ever for the investigator. Most crime labs keep impressions or photo files of footwear outsole designs. (Courtesy of Karen Vallaro. Photograph by W. Reid Lindsay, Westchester County Forensic Science Laboratory.)

> **Remember, do not overlook soil evidence which may later be found on suspect's shoes.**

In addition to obtaining castings, the investigator should collect soil samples from the location.

Tool Marks

Tool marks, like footprints and tire tracks, may contain minute imperfections which are unique and can sometimes be microscopically compared to the tool or object in question. It is better if the investigator can remove the object which bears the tool mark. This can be done by removing the surface for submission to the laboratory. In instances where this would be impractical, the tool mark can be cast with a silicone rubber material. To collect tool marks:

1. Photograph (long-shot and close-up with 1 × 1 camera).
2. Cast with a silicone rubber casting after spraying surface with silicone release agent.

Figure 17.24. Boot impression in soil using an oblique source for contrast. Note the position of the camera 90° to the impression and the use of a ruler to allow a photographic enlargement to 1:1 (life size) image. General (class) characteristics (size, design) as well as unique (identifying) features (random nicks, cuts) can be discerned from such scene documentation and compared to the footwear of a suspect. (Courtesy of Frederick C. Drummond. Photograph by W. Reid Lindsay, Westchester County Forensic Science Laboratory.)

Bite Marks

Practically speaking, bite marks may be considered as tool marks and are valuable physical evidence. (See Chapter 15, "Bite Mark Identification".)

Bullet Holes

1. In walls or furniture, first photograph and then examine trajectory.
2. In garments:
   a. Photograph.
   b. Safeguard for examination for powder residue.
   c. Wrap (do not fold) and place in proper container. Direction of fire can be ascertained by using a color test to determine presence of lead (the Harrison Test).

A

B

Figure 17.25. Presenting impression evidence. (A) Section of plate glass broken during burglary. Note the footwear impressions in the center of the photograph (after fingerprinting dusting, the dirty side was cleaned before the photo was taken). (B) Court display of the sole design of the suspect's sneakers. (C) Court display of the plate glass impression of the perpetrator's footwear showing placement of 14 unique (individualizing) random damage (nicks, cuts, etc.). (D) Court display of the impression of the suspect's left sneaker sole showing corresponding unique damage. Footwear impression evidence can be almost as good as a fingerprint placing a suspect at a crime scene. (Courtesy of Frederick C. Drummond. Photograph by W. Reid Lindsay, Westchester County Forensic Science Laboratory.)

C

D

Figure 17.25. (continued)

Newly Damaged Areas

The presence of damaged furniture, objects, and any other newly damaged areas are indicative of some sort of violence or struggle.

1. Photograph.
2. Examine for any serology.
3. Process for fingerprints.

Application of DNA Technology

Introduction

Biological evidence retrieved from a victim or crime scene can now be examined at its most fundamental level — the deoxyribonucleic acid (DNA) molecule.

The purpose of this section is to acquaint the reader with the application of DNA and Genetic Identification techniques in criminal investigation. There are several private corporations which perform forensic DNA analysis, as well as the FBI laboratory. The private corporations include: Lifecodes Corporation in Connecticut; Forensic Science Associates in California; Cellmark Diagnostics in Maryland; Genetic Design and Roche Biomedical Labs in North Carolina; Gene Screen in Texas; and ACTG, Inc. in Colorado.

The author served as an investigative consultant for The Lifecodes Corporation under the supervision of Dr. Robert Shaler, Ph.D. Dr. Shaler was the Forensic Director of Lifecodes Corporation and now is the Director of the Department of Forensic Biology which houses two laboratories; the Forensic Biochemistry and Hematology and the Forensic Molecular Biology for the New York Medical Examiner's Office and is a nationally recognized authority on forensic DNA applications.

The information within this section is based on the research and experience, as well as personal interviews with Dr. Shaler.

The Lifecodes Corporation is a DNA-based genetic diagnostic research laboratory in Stamford, CT which developed the first available DNA profiling testing system in the United States known as the DNA-PRINT Identification Test, which has enabled forensic scientists to examine the specific genetic code of a biological specimen for individual characteristics. The specimens may be blood, tissue, semen, hair, urine, or any evidence containing or exhibiting traces of the genetic code, DNA.

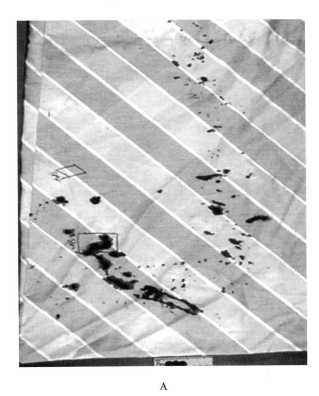

A

Figure 17.26.   (A) **BLOODSTAINS.** Pillowcase with bloodstains in a stabbing homicide case. Note the curved-line bloody impression at the lower center of the photo. (B) **BLOODSTAIN CLOSE-UP.** Close-up photo of the above impression. This is an outline of the knife used by the perpetrator. Lines can be extrapolated to give an estimation of the blade shape and length. Note four heavily stained dots in bloodstain to the left of the blade outline. These are knuckle imprints of a hand surrounding the knife handle. (Courtesy of Frederick C. Drummond. Photograph by W. Reid Lindsay, Westchester County Forensic Science Laboratory.)

Deoxyribonucleic Acid — DNA

DNA or deoxyribonucleic acid is housed in every nucleated cell in the body. These DNA molecules are often described as the body's blueprints since they carry the genetic codes that govern the structure and function of every component of the body. DNA has been described as the fundamental natural material which determines the genetic characteristics of all life forms. Although there are portions of our DNA that are relatively conserved through the evolutionary process, as humans we share a human form that is basically human specific, while other

B

Figure 17.26. (continued)

classes of organisms share a DNA composition unique to that particular species, i.e., an elephant, fish, or mouse.

In fact, the DNA molecule carries the genetic information that establishes each person as separate and distinct. We as humans create progeny through the transfer of this DNA to our children.

According to the genetic experts, the DNA molecule's configuration does not vary from cell to cell. Therefore, the billions of cells that comprise each person contain the same molecules of DNA carrying the same codes in precisely the same sequence.

The Cell

The cell is the basic unit of all living organisms including humans, animals, insects, and plants. The human body has more than ten trillion cells.

The cell is composed of two parts: the nucleus, which contains two structures; the chromosomes and the nucleoli; and the cytoplasm, which is all of the material inside the cell membrane outside of the nucleus.

The Nucleus

The nucleus contains the cell's genetic program, a sort of master plan that controls everything the cell does. The chromosomes within the nucleus are composed mainly of DNA and associated proteins. The chromosome stores and transmits genetic information.

Figure 17.27. **DNA TESTING.** Deoxyribonucleic acid (DNA) analysis is one of the newest tools in the crime lab. Some types of DNA testing allows forensic scientists to replicate genetic material and obtain information from tiny blood and body fluid stains that was only dreamed about just a few years ago. The astute homicide investigator will use these new advances in scientific law enforcement to eliminate or include suspects during the investigation and add to the body of evidence for a subsequent trial. (Courtesy of W. Reid Lindsay, Westchester County Forensic Science Laboratory.)

Figure 17.28. Forensic DNA specialist, Ted Pool, examines a DNA autoradiograph. The odds against any two unrelated individuals sharing identical genetic information for a series of DNA "probes" can exceed 1 billion to 1. (Courtesy of Westchester County Forensic Science Laboratory. Photograph by Joseph Rue.)

Figure 17.29. **A DNA AUTORADIO-GRAPH ("AUTORAD").** The vertical banding patterns (looking much like bar codes in a supermarket) help identify individuals by comparing the placement of these bands to known standards or "ladders." The four "ladders" can be seen as the multi-banded patterns equally placed on this "autorad." (Courtesy of Ted Pool. Photograph by W. Reid Lindsay, Westchester County Forensic Science Laboratory.)

Figure 17.30. **AUTORAD.** An additional DNA autoradiograph of DNA probe D17S79. Several matching (2-banded) patterns are seen in the photograph. (Courtesy of Ted Pool. Photograph by W. Reid Lindsay, Westchester County Forensic Science Laboratory.)

Figure 17.31. The DNA-Print™ process. (Courtesy of Lifecodes Corporation, Valhalla, New York.)

Figure 17.32.   In this autoradiograph (autorad), we know the match between a serial murder suspect and the autorad of two of his victims. Lanes 1 and 2 show suspect evidence and whole blood of the suspect, and lanes 3 and 4 show the victim.

The DNA molecule is tightly coiled within the nucleus of a cell similar to a ball of yarn. When unraveled, a molecule of DNA is approximately six (6) feet in length. This molecule is recognized by the scientists as a double-stranded helix.

The Structure of the DNA Molecule

According to the 1953 studies of Watson and Crick, each chromosome consists of a double spiral of deoxyribonucleic acid in the shape of a twisted ladder, hence the term double stranded helix. The sides or backbone of the ladder are composed of alternating sugar (deoxyribose) and phosphoric acid (phosphate) molecules. The "rungs" of the ladder are composed of "pairs" of purine and pyrimidine bases.

DNA is built up of units or building blocks called nucleotides composed of a sugar, a phosphate group, and a base. Millions of these nucleotides form a single strand. However, there are only four bases: two (2) purines; (A) adenine and (G) guanine; two (2) pyrimidines; (T) thymine and (C) cytosine.

Figure 17.33.   Note this interior view of the crematorium. (Top) The crematorium is operating in normal fashion. (Bottom) Malfunctioning of the crematorium is evident with only one jet operating. The killer was unaware of the second burner malfunction. (Courtesy of Major John Dotson, Wichita, Kansas Police Department.)

The purine and pyrimidine bases interact with each other through hydrogen bonding and form predictable associations. Adenine (A) always binds to or associates with (T) thymine and (G) guanine always binds to or associates with (C) cytosine. These are the only possible

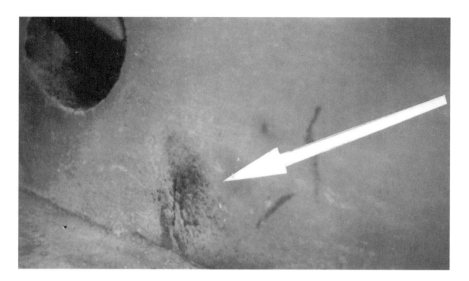

Figure 17.34. An arrow points to the dried blood of the victim on the inside wall of the crematorium. This blood was collected by authorities and submitted to The Lifecodes Corporation, which provided positive identification of the deceased after comparing evidence to the whole blood samples of the victim's parents. (Courtesy of Major John Dotson, Wichita, Kansas Police Department.)

Figure 17.35. **DNA-PRINT AUTORAD.** This autoradiograph (autorad) shows the DNA of two Richmond victims indicating a positive match. This autorad establishes that the semen at each of the crime scenes was from the same source. Later in the investigation, the blood sample taken from the suspect was also submitted for DNA analysis and indicated him to be the donor.

Figure 17.36. Autorad indicating match of suspect to Arlington victim. In lane 1 we see the DNA of suspect Spencer. Lane 2 is a marker. Lane 3 is the sleeping bag of the victim upon which the sperm was retrieved. Lane 4 is the DNA of the victim's blood. Lane 5 is the nightgown of the victim, which also contained semen evidence. Lane 6 is the DNA of the suspect Spencer. Note the DNA match between Spencer and the semen evidence from the crime scenes. (Courtesy of The Lifecodes Corporation, Valhalla, New York.)

combinations which form the "rungs" of the ladder and are referred to as complimentary base pairs. Thus we have a T-A, A-T, C-G, and G-C formulation within the helix.

It is important to note that these base sequences are fairly fixed and that these genetic base sequences determine the protein and enzyme make-up of our human cells.

Research and Development

Since the early 1970s a number of remarkable discoveries have been made in DNA by a new breed of molecular biologists known as genetic engineers. These scientists have learned to "edit" the language of the DNA molecule using a technology referred to as recombinant DNA (rDNA).

Through this research, scientists have learned to synthesize or clone these molecules and have generally engineered certain structural changes within organisms.

A modern day application of this research is found in genetic diagnostics. Scientists have been able to isolate and produce individual fragments of DNA that carry the code for specific inherited disorders. These DNA fragments, known as gene probes, are applied to a test specimen of DNA where they act as genetic sleuths seeking out and binding to areas of DNA carrying defective gene codes.

In their study of specific diseases, molecular biologists came across small areas of the DNA molecule that showed marked variations in base sequence from one individual to the next. They called these naturally occurring variations polymorphisms.

As human beings we all share a common species of DNA. Long stretches of DNA remain the same from person to person. For instance, we all have a head, a heart, lungs, legs, arms, etc. However, within the polymorphic areas the DNA can vary quite dramatically from one individual to another.

The scientists referred to some of these highly polymorphic regions as anonymous sequence or "Junk DNA" since their function is not clearly understood. These polymorphic DNA regions are known to repeat themselves over and over again like a stutter and are called Variable Number of Tandem Repeats or VNTRs which are unique to the individual. The terminology for these polymorphisms can be confusing and were originally referred to as minisatellites. The original VNTRs identified contained fairly large repeat units with allele sizes begin thousands of base pairs long. Additional research identified smaller VNTRs which were referred, and were only a few base pairs long. For example, one such was identified by the probe pMCT118 or its locus D1S80, has 16 base pair repeat units with allele sizes as much as approximately 1000 base pairs.

Another class of VNTRs, called microsatellites or STRs, Short Tandem Repeats, have two to five repeat units per tandem repeat. The sizes of STR alleles is in the hundreds of base pairs depending on the STR. The STR polymorphisms have been found interspersed within gene introns and have been associated with certain diseases and their severity.

Using minisatellites, the chances of any two individuals, except identical twins, having the same polymorphisms in these segments of the DNA molecule was quite remote. These highly variable polymorphic regions, or sequences of DNA provided the basis for DNA fingerprinting.

Forensic investigators reasoned that a technique that enabled them to identify the polymorphisms in the DNA of one individual and compare them with the polymorphisms in the DNA of another individual could serve as a means of genetic identification.

Initially, to find these polymorphisms they needed a gene probe similar to the one used in diagnostic medicine. However, instead of seeking out the codes of disease, they utilized DNA technology to create a probe that would seek out and label the genetic polymorphisms peculiar to the DNA of each individual.

Initially, there were two types of probes utilized in forensic DNA identification. The Multi locus probe, which was first developed by Jeffreys (1985) and who coined the term *DNA Fingerprinting* to identify specific fingerprints of human DNA. This probe focused on multiple points on multiple chromosomes. The single locus probe, on the other hand, focused on one region within one chromosome. The law enforcement community has chosen the single locus probe, originally used by Lifecodes Corporation and endorsed by the FBI for analysis of forensic evidence in criminal investigations. Since then, all private and public laboratories performing DNA profiling use single locus probes. A second technological breakthrough occurred in 1985 with the publication of a technique called the Polymerase Chain Reaction or PCR. This technique, for which the Nobel Prize was awarded to its discoverer, Kerry Mullis, in 1992, has become the newest forensic DNA tool and will someday become the standard in DNA testing, replacing the original RFLP test.

As long as one knows the region that is to be amplified, the PCR for amplification of multiplication of DNA will be present in a sample. One application of the test has been in continuous use in forensic DNA testing since 1986, the HLA-DQA1 test. A new PCR-based test which is just being introduced into forensic casework and, like the HLA-DQA1 test, is available in kit form, the AmpliType® PM DNA Amplification and Typing Kit, allows for the identification of five separate polymorphic loci, e.g., LDLR, GYPH A, HBGG, and GC. The HLA-DQA1 locus has been combined with the kit.

The PCR has also been used extensively for identifying VNTR loci. In this regard, it identifies polymorphisms categorized as Amplified Fragment Length Polymorphisms or AmpFlps. Common loci in this category are D1S80, YNZ22, and 3′ Apo B. The STR class of polymorphisms has also been analyzed by the PCR and adapted to automated fluorescence analysis where up to four can be analyzed at the same time. It has been speculated that if twelve or thirteen of these could be analyzed simultaneously, the discrimination potential would equal that of the original RFLP test. The advantage of the STR system is that the alleles are small allowing for the analysis of degraded DNA and the turn-around-time is short, theoretically being capable of being done in a day or two.

Scientific Techniques Employed in DNA Profiling

DNA Purified

All DNA tests require that the DNA be purified before the test is run. To accomplish this, the DNA must first be extracted from the nucleus of the cells of the biological specimen. The goal is to remove protein bound to the DNA so that it can be exposed to reagents needed to perform the test. For RFLP testing this means that the DNA is free to be reacted upon by restriction enzymes and other manipulation of DNA is not inhibited. For PCR testing this means that the DNA is sufficiently free to allow the enzyme TAQ polymerase to work with it.

Another goal is to isolate the DNA in as close to native form as possible. Native DNA, called high molecular weight or intact DNA is easily isolated from fresh biological specimens, i.e., whole blood. However, DNA present in forensic specimens, i.e., vaginal swabs, blood stains, etc., may not be intact. Therefore, the extraction procedure should be gentle and allow DNA with as high a molecular weight as possible to be isolated.

There are currently three techniques used by forensic scientists. These include the organic extraction procedure, the nonorganic extraction, and the chelex extraction procedure. Of these, only the chelex procedure is unsuitable for use with the RFLP test. Each has its advantages and disadvantages and each has specific applications depending on the type of DNA, i.e., RFLP, PCR, or sequencing, test being performed and evidence specimen, i.e., tissues, blood stains, semen, and saliva, being analyzed.

The RFLP Test

Step #1: DNA is Cleaved into Fragments

Restriction endonucleases and restriction enzymes work like a pair of molecular scissors. These molecular scissors are actually cutting enzymes designed to cleave the DNA at specific base sequences. The history of which enzyme to use for forensic work has varied with the history of the different laboratories using the technique. Since there is not a single enzyme which can be used to obtain DNA profiles, it is not surprising that different companies and public laboratories used different enzymes. For example, initially Lifecodes Corporation used a cutting enzyme designated Pst 1. It is obtained from bacteria and is designed to cleave the DNA molecule whenever it recognizes the base sequence CTGCAG. It cuts the DNA molecule at this specific "A-G" point along the entire helix where the CTGCAG occurs. It is known as

A

Figure 17.37. (A) Bloodstains on the pillowcase in a stabbing homicide case. Note the design of the bloody impression in the center and upper right of the photograph. (B) Close-up photo of the bloody impression from the above pillowcase. Note the straight lines of bloodstains indicating a fold in the pillowcase when the impression was left. The item has since been unfolded. (C) Close-up photo of the bloody impression with the pillowcase refolded almost to its original position. Note that the impression is now identifiable as a bloody handprint. Parallel lines to the lower left is the imprint of a cuff of the garment worn by the perpetrator. This is a left hand palm print since the thumb is pointing to the right and the fingertip impression is visible above. This perpetrator was leaning on his left hand for balance during the attack indicating right handedness. If this was a right hand back impression, the knuckle impressions should show. This assailant plunged the knife through the back of his own left hand during the vicious assault leaving behind his blood and impressions. A check of nearby hospitals disclosed a patient with a hand injury. Blood DNA analysis matching the suspect to the scene completed the case. (Courtesy of Frederick C. Drummond. Photograph by W. Reid Lindsay, Westchester County Forensic Science Laboratory.)

a six base cutter because it recognizes a sequence of six bases, the sequence of purine and pyrimidine bases in the order of (C) Cytosine, (T) Thymine, (G) Guanine, (C) Cytosine, (A) Adenine, and (G) Guanine — CTGCAG. Whenever Pst-1 sees this CTGCAG sequence it cuts the DNA fragment.

The FBI uses HAE III, a four base cutter, as a cutting enzyme which recognizes the sequence GGCC. Whenever the enzyme recognizes this particular base sequence it cuts the DNA at this point.

B

Figure 17.37. (continued)

Currently, all private and public laboratories in the United States performing the RFLP test in forensic casework have adopted the FBI's procedure and incorporate the HAE III restriction enzyme protocol.

The enzyme action results in millions of DNA fragments. In the areas of the helix that are highly variable or polymorphic, there are differences in the length, the amount of DNA present at the VNTR, due to the VNTR's or the varying number of base pairs that lie between the cutting points that the enzyme selects. These varying number of base pairs are referred to as "Variable Number of Tandem Repeats" or "VNTRs." Since the fragments can be created by the actions of the restriction enzymes and since these fragments are polymorphic (mean-

C

Figure 17.37. (continued)

ing many forms), they are termed "Restriction Fragment Length Poly-morphisms," or "RFLPs."

It is important to understand that a VNTR does not have to be an RFLP and that an RFLP does not have to contain a VNTR.

The above process is used in the RFLP technology, which means Restriction Fragment Length Polymorphisms. The fragments of DNA are cut with a restriction enzyme and the lengths of the polymorphisms differ for each individual. Under RFLP technology, DNA can be ex-tracted and analyzed at the molecular level and then compared with DNA from a known biological specimen for identification purposes.

Step #2: Fragments are Size Separated

The DNA fragments which have been digested into RFLPs are separated in an agarose gel medium using an electrical charge in a process known as electrophoresis. This is a technique for arranging the biological particles on an agarose gel through exposure to electricity. The distance each fragment travels depends on its length. The longer the fragment the slower its rate of migration. Positively charged particles will migrate towards the negative pole and negatively charged particles, such as DNA, will migrate towards the positive electrode of the electrophoretic field. All DNA carries a negative charge and will migrate towards the positive pole. At the conclusion of the electrophoresis, the fragments represent a continuous smear of DNA fragments, size separated, in the gel.

However, because the gel is extremely fragile, it is necessary to render the separated DNA fragments in a more stable arrangement. The technique in which this happens is known as Southern Blotting.

Step #3: Southern Blotting

This is a process by which the DNA fragments separated during electro-phoresis are transferred from the wobbly and fragile agarose gel onto a sheet of nylon membrane. Once blotted, the pattern is ready for the gene probe. During this process, capillary action moves the DNA frag-ments out of the agarose gel onto the nylon membrane. The DNA fragments are then fixed onto the membrane using ultraviolet radia-tion, heat, or air drying.

Step #4: Hybridization

The specific regions of the DNA which are being analyzed are recog-nized using DNA probes which are applied to the nylon membrane in a solution and allowed to incubate at a high temperature for several hours. Normally four probes, one at a time, are used per DNA profile meaning that four different regions of the DNA will have been analyzed at the conclusion of the test.

The probes are usually tagged with a radioactive marker but are sometimes bound with enzymes. The probes are designed to "seek out" a predetermined chromosomal locus, a location on the DNA contain-ing a polymorphic region of interest.

A probe is a segment of Recombinant DNA (rDNA) or synthetic DNA that is designed to go to a particular predetermined locus on a particular chromosome. Lifecodes Corporation originally used four probes, D2S44, D14S1, D17S79, and DXYS14 in this test. Since then, many different probes are in use by the major DNA-typing laboratories in the United States and the probes commonly used by American forensic laboratories embody the group used by the FBI.

The probe nomenclature is simple where the "D" stands for DNA; the numbers, i.e., 2, 14, 17, XY, etc., indicate the chromosome recognized; "S" refers to the region as being polymorphic; and last the number is the number of loci mapped on the chromosome to the time of the application to the Human Gene Mapping Convention.

Upon finding a DNA fragment that carries all or part of its complimentary base sequence, the probe "binds" to or hybridizes to that fragment.

Once the probe binds to the nylon membrane, it is invisible to the naked eye and must be visualized. Most commonly this is accomplished using a technique called autoradiography.

The Autoradiograph

The autoradiograph or AUTORAD is most commonly the final product. First, the excess probe is washed away from the nylon membrane. Then, the nylon membrane is placed against a piece of x-ray film and exposed for 1 to 10 days. When the film is processed, gray to black bands appear where the radioactive probes stuck to the fragments that it recognizes. Single locus probes normally will each produce one or two dark bands on a white column in each individual.

A relatively recent innovation is the use of chemiluminescence instead of radioactivity. In this scenario, probes are labeled with an enzyme which, during development, causes the production of light. The light exposes the x-ray film causing black bands to appear wherever the probe has bound. The visual result is the same. However, the process is much faster requiring only a few hours of development time instead of from 1 day to 2 weeks.

Interpretation of the Results

The pattern of bands can be unique for each individual, except for identical twins. When comparing the two DNA fragment patterns, the forensic investigator simply looks to see where the probe landed on the two patterns. If the specimens are from the same person, the investigator can expect to find the probe on fragments of identical length, and consequently, in identical positions on the two patterns.

However, the statistical rarity of each pattern is based on population genetics taking into account specific allele frequencies and other considerations which may require additional experiments, techniques, and controls in arriving at a justifiable scientific conclusion.

It has been reported in some forensic journals that the probability that an identification is positive has been calculated to be some 30 billion to one that two unrelated individuals will have the same genetic make-up.

Sometimes the patterns derived are fairly common being only a few million to one. In casework, it is not uncommon to find that only one or two probes have been successful in giving a readable autorad. When this happens, the frequency of the DNA pattern is diminished and may be only one in a couple of hundred.

In recent years a controversy has required that statistical data be reported according to a conference held by the National Research Council (NRC). Their report in 1992 specified that an interim ceiling principle be applied to all calculations. This meant that, if the population database showed that the true frequency of the upper confidence limit of any band at a given locus was less than 10%, the only reportable value allowable is 10%. This effectively reduces the true power of the technology but supposedly eliminates any substructuring in populations which might be unfairly biased against defendants.

Because of a scientific controversy about the meaning and reliability of the interim ceiling principle calculations, a second NRC meeting has been convened to resolve the dispute.

The Polymerase Chain Reaction (PCR)

The future of forensic DNA testing lies with tests based on the use of the Polymerase Chain Reaction. The basis of PCR is that it mimics the cell's ability to replicate DNA. That is, by using this tool, forensic scientists have the ability to take a small sample of DNA and make more, essentially copying it, a millionfold.

The PCR has discrete steps which are basically the same but specific parameters for different loci may be different. All PCR procedures have basic steps: DNA extraction, amplification, and detection.

DNA Extraction

The section above about DNA extraction is essentially the same for PCR as it is for RFLP.

Amplification

The amplification is the heart of the PCR process and is a three step process: denaturation, annealing, and extension. The amplification process takes place in a machine, a thermal cycler, which automatically, according to a preprogrammed set of instructions, raises, lowers, and holds temperatures.

Denaturation

Before DNA can be duplicated, the DNA must be split apart, i.e., denaturation. This process is accomplished by heating the DNA sample above 94°C for a prescribed period of time. If the DNA is not heated long enough or hot enough, incorrect results can be obtained because the DNA may not split apart properly. This would account for the loss of a signal during the detection step.

Annealing

The second step requires a lower temperature during which small segments of DNA called primers bind specifically to the DNA which borders the polymorphic region of interest. The primers become starting points for the DNA duplication process. They prime the pump so to speak.

Extension

The temperature is raised slightly, often to 72°C, which causes the enzyme, a DNA polymerase — TAQ Polymerase — to extend the primers and in essence copy the two separated strands of DNA. The TAQ Polymerase utilizes nucleotides, the building blocks of DNA, inserting them opposite the appropriate base, thus insuring the integrity of DNA's base pair complementarity.

Once the primers have been extended and the DNA copied, the cycle is begun again. As many as 30 or more cycles will permit in excess of a million copies of DNA to be synthesized.

Detection

Detection of the amplification products can be done in different ways depending on the type of polymorphism being detected. For VNTR polymorphisms, they are first separated by electrophoresis which is followed by a visualization; usually fluorescent detection or silver staining.

Sequence polymorphisms, such as for HLA-DQA1, the common detection method is to use a reverse dot blot procedure where colored, the amplification products are labeled with a chemical called biotin. After the amplification products bind to a strip containing allele- or sequence-specific probes, a reaction using horseradish peroxidase and a colored dye causes blue dots to appear. The pattern of blue dots denotes which alleles are present.

DNA Identification Tests

Human Cells

In each human cell there are forty-six (46) chromosomes arranged in pairs of twenty-two (22) plus two (2) sex chromosomes. Twenty-three (23) are contributed by the father's sperm and twenty-three (23) are contributed by the mother's egg. Practically speaking, we are part of our mother and part of our father in that we each inherit part of our parent's DNA.

DNA technology can be utilized in paternity testing in order to establish a child's rightful parentage. The private DNA typing laboratories have performed literally hundreds of thousands of DNA paternity tests since 1987.

These tests allow investigators to compare DNA patterns and establish positive identification. DNA identifications can also be used in forensic paternity, immigration disputes, missing persons cases, unidentified body cases, etc.

Applications in Forensic Medicine

Victim Identification

DNA profiling has been successfully used in a number of criminal investigations to positively identify the deceased. In one particular case, Lifecodes' scientists were able to confirm that the brain matter found in a missing woman's vehicle belonged to the victim, who was identified through her DNA and the DNA of her parents. Skeletonized remains (bone marrow), body parts, and other materials which contain nucleated cells can be analyzed for DNA and provide authorities with an identification.

CASE HISTORY

The following case history is based upon a personal interview with Chief John Dotson, Sparks Police Department, Nevada formerly a Major with the Wichita, Kansas Police Department.

In December of 1987, Wichita homicide detectives encountered a bizarre crime. The suspect in this case had allegedly killed his wife by putting her into a crematorium. Police were alerted to this possible crime by a civilian complainant, who was suspicious of a bucket which had been left in her garage. The police recovered burnt remains consisting of a number of small fragments of bone and burned flesh which the medical examiner, Dr. William Eckert, had determined to be human. A forensic anthropologist was also brought in to assist the police and medical examiner's office in establishing an identity.

The homicide investigation revealed that the offender thought he had planned the perfect murder. His reasoning according to witnesses was "No body — no crime". Police learned that he had lured his former wife to a shopping mall on the pretense of shopping together for Christmas presents for their child. At the time, he had been involved in a bitter custody battle over this child with his ex-wife.

Somehow, he managed to get his wife to the funeral home, where he was employed as an usher. And somehow, no one knows for sure whether she was dead or alive, he managed to place her body into the crematorium and activated the furnace.

The crematorium could reach temperatures of 1500°F and it would take approximately $2^1/_2$ hours to reduce the body to ashes. However, the suspect didn't know that one of the burners wasn't working properly. He realized that he was running out of time. He wasn't even authorized to operate the crematorium. The suspect then decided to get the evidence of the burning out of the crematorium and out of the building before his employer found out. He tried to clean up but was left with a bucket full of cremains. This bucket of cremains was subsequently seized by Wichita police which resulted in the suspect's arrest. The cremains provided circumstantial evidence of this brutal slaying. In addition, a unique piece of jewelry, which the deceased wore, was found in the catch basket of the crematorium. However, prosecutors wanted more.

The District Attorney's office decided on establishing the victim's identity, beyond the jewelry and anthropological evidence.

In February, 1988, the following evidence was sent to Lifecodes Corporation. A partial femur bone, as well as tissue from the pelvis and blood scrapings from the crematorium were forwarded along with whole blood samples of the victim's parents. Lifecodes extracted DNA from the blood scrapings from the crematorium, which they were able to compare with the DNA from the whole blood samples of the victim's parents. Identification of the remains was positively established through the DNA-PRINT identification test, which was in actuality a paternity-type testing.

Assailant Identification

Forcible Rape

DNA offers the criminal justice system an unprecedented opportunity to obtain the strongest possible evidence from semen specimens. Prior to DNA technology, the best that forensics scientists could provide was an exclusion or suggestion of inclusion based on specimens which were analyzed for blood type and protein polymorphic enzymes. Semen would be mixed with the vaginal fluids, which also contain proteins.

This would make determining identity by protein analysis difficult. In other cases, where there were multiple assailants, several semen samples would become intermingled making any determination of identity by protein analysis almost impossible.

DNA profiling, however, can provide close to positive individual identification. Because it is possible to physically separate sperm cells from vaginal epithelial cells and since each contains its own DNA, mixtures can be sorted out and interference by bacteria is eliminated. It is also applicable to old stains. It's like the criminal leaving his name, address, and social security number at the scene of the crime.

Investigation of a Series of Crimes

DNA profiling is useful in investigations of a series of similar crimes. If several rapes have been committed in the same general area, forensic experts can test the semen specimens from the victims and know whether they should be looking for one suspect or multiple suspects. Forensic scientists in public and private DNA laboratories have provided forensic evidence in a number of serial rape cases and provided prosecutors with crucial evidence in a significant serial-murder case.

CASE HISTORY

On September 19, 1987, the body of a 35-year-old woman was found dead in the bedroom of her first floor apartment in Richmond, Virginia. Her body was discovered by a police officer who went to her apartment after her car, which had been abandoned and running, was found a few blocks away. She had been strangled and there was evidence of sexual activity at the scene.

On October 3, 1987, 2 weeks later, a 32-year-old female physician was found dead in a second floor bedroom closet in her home in Richmond, Virginia. Her body was discovered by her husband, who had returned home from school in Washington. She also had been strangled, and there was also evidence of sexual activity at the scene.

Police investigation indicated that in both cases the murderer had entered the homes of the women by cutting a screen and climbing through an open window. In the first murder scene, police recovered semen samples from the bedding of the victim. In the second murder scene, the killer left semen on the victim's slip. Medicolegal examination revealed that the first victim has been raped and strangled to death with a sock which had been tightened around her neck with a pipe from a vacuum cleaner. According to the Medical Examiner, the second victim had been raped, sodomized, and then strangled to death with a belt. Both women had been bound with their hands tied behind their backs and both women had been strangled with ligature. The police investigation immediately focused on the similar modus operandi of the two murders. However, the only evidence that the police had recovered in these two cases was biological. At the time this forensic evidence seemed insignificant in comparison to any solid "leads" in the case.

A special task force operation, which involved uniform as well as plainclothes officers, was initiated within the two neighborhoods where the killings had taken place. Community apprehension over these two murders was at a peak as police attempted to identify a possible serial killer, whom the media called Richmond's "South Side Strangler."

As the police intensified their presence within the areas of the murders, the community began to regain composure. However, 51 days later, in an adjoining county, another vicious sex-related homicide had occurred. This time, the victim was a teenager.

On November 22, 1987 a 15-year-old young woman was found dead in her parent's apartment in Chesterfield County, which is just south of Richmond city limits. The killer had entered her bedroom through a window as the family was asleep. The victim had been strangled, her hands were tied behind her back, and once again there was evidence of sexual activity at the crime scene.

Police authorities from Richmond and Chesterfield Counties met to compare notes on what was apparently the work of the Richmond's "South Side Strangler."

Nine days later and over 100 miles away in Northern Virginia another rape-homicide was being investigated by the Arlington County Police. On December 1, 1987 a 44-year-old woman was found dead on her bed on the second floor of her two-story home in Arlington County in Northern Virginia. She had been strangled and there was evidence that she had been raped. Police recovered semen from the victim's nightgown and a sleeping bag at the crime scene.

Det. Joseph Horgas was in charge of this seemingly unrelated homicide in Arlington. The first thing Detective Horgas looked for was if any similar cases had occurred within the jurisdiction. A 1984 rape-homicide seemed to fit the M.O. but there had been an arrest and the suspect was still in jail. As Det. Horgas began the tedious job of searching through old files he came upon a series of rapes in 1983 in which the victims had not been killed. The detective would later forward this evidence from the 1983 rape case to Lifecodes for a DNA analysis. This 1983 evidence matched the DNA of the evidence from the 1987 rape-murder in Arlington. Meanwhile, Det. Horgas began to develop information on a male/black, named Timothy Spencer, who had lived in the Arlington area before going to jail on an unrelated charged.

He discovered that Spencer had recently been released and was living in the Richmond area in a half-way house. A check of parole records indicated that this very same suspect had been given a 4-day furlough to visit his family in the Arlington area for Thanksgiving. This put Spencer in the immediate area at the time of the rape-murder in Arlington. After conferring with authorities in Richmond, Horgas was sure that his suspect, Timothy Spencer, was the "South Side Strangler."

In fact, Detective Horgas believed that Timothy Spencer had perpetrated the rape-homicide in 1984 and that the suspect who had been jailed was innocent. Ultimately the evidence developed by Det. Horgas proved this man to be innocent and he was released after being pardoned by the Governor of the State of Virginia.

On January 20, 1988, Detective Joseph Horgas traveled to Richmond where he arrested Timothy Wilson Spencer for the homicide in Arlington. Spencer, who had been released from prison to a half-way house in Richmond, was finally exposed as "The South Side Strangler." In fact, all four murders had occurred within 3 months of Spencer's release.

The most important evidence in this series of rapes and murders was the biological fluids recovered from the crime scenes. In fact, three of the rape-murders had been connected forensically through the DNA analysis of the semen.

Lifecodes Corporation, which did the analysis of the evidence from the two Richmond cases as well as the Arlington murder, was provided with blood samples from the suspect, Timothy Wilson Spencer. The evidence from the Chesterfield murder was forwarded to Forensic Science & Associates by Lifecodes for DNA amplification due to the limited amount of genetic material.

The DNA-Print™ Identification Test indicated that the DNA patterns in Spencer's blood were identical to the DNA patterns from the semen left at the murder scenes.

Spencer went to trial as his attorneys tried to exclude genetic fingerprint evidence from being introduced. However, prosecutors were able to convince the court that DNA evidence should be presented in each of the murder trials.

Lifecodes Corporation was allowed to testify to their DNA-PRINT™ analysis which showed a match between Spencer's blood and semen found at each of the murder scenes.

The DNA analysis also enabled prosecutors to pass the legal test for "signature crimes," meaning enough similarities exist to believe that the crimes were committed by the same person. This "signature-crime" tactic was used in the Chesterfield County case as well as the subsequent penalty phase hearings on each of the convictions.

Timothy Wilson Spencer was ultimately convicted of all four rape-murders. DNA evidence was also utilized in the penalty phase of the trials and Spencer has been sentenced to death on each one of the murders. In September of 1989 the convictions and sentences on two of the rape-murders were upheld on appeal before the Virginia Supreme Court. This case was significant because it is the nation's first murder conviction based on the use of DNA fingerprinting. In 1994, Mr. Timothy Wilson Spencer was executed by the State of Virginia.

Reopening Unsolved Cases

Since DNA maintains its integrity in dried specimens for prolonged periods, DNA profiling can be utilized on old evidence. In my capacity as an investigative consultant I have reopened a number of cases for DNA analysis. I conferred with the detectives in a case which was approximately 12 years old to consider this forensic technique. The authorities in that jurisdiction now have forensic evidence linking a serial killer to crimes a dozen years old.

DNA patterns from old evidence can also be compared with DNA patterns of recently apprehended suspects. Or, cases from the past in which evidence was inconclusive can now be tested using DNA technology.

Admissibility Criterion

In determining the admissibility of any evidence into trial there must be method validation and laboratory validation. The scientific acceptance of this technology is the basis for the legal acceptance in a court of law. The medical research, Nobel Prize awards, peer level publications, as well as general acceptance by the scientific community is the basis for legal argument.

In the early 1900s a Nobel Prize was awarded for the discovery of DNA as the Genetic Basis For Life. In 1953 Dr. James Watson and Francis Crick were awarded a Nobel Prize in connection with defining the structure of DNA. Their elucidation of the double helix structure of DNA revolutionized the field of molecular biology and genetics.

In the 1970s further genetic research produced the restriction enzymes. Genetic engineering through gene splicing and cloning were soon accepted procedures within the scientific community. In the early 1980s scientists discovered RFLP technology, which was the basis for determining individual identity.

The ASCLD Lab Inc., the American Society of Crime Laboratory Director's private corporation for accreditation of crime laboratories have included DNA laboratories under their accreditation umbrella. Additionally a group of scientists from crime laboratories both private and public, academia, and industry have formed a group called TWGDAM, the Technical Working Group on DNA Analysis Methods, which is sponsored by the FBI, has formulated guidelines for quality assurance in DNA laboratories. These guidelines have become the standard by which forensic DNA laboratories are judged in court.

Dr. Richard J. Roberts, formerly the Assistant Director for Research at the Cold Spring Harbor Laboratory on Long Island in New York is

Deputy to the Director of said laboratory. The Director is Dr. James Watson — the very same James Watson, who in 1953, together with Francis Crick received a Nobel Prize for their elucidation of the double helix structure.

Dr. Roberts, in his testimony during a Frye hearing in New York, People v. Wesley, County of Albany, 1988., stated that the protocols used by Lifecodes Corporation, "... were not only acceptable by the scientific community, and deemed reliable therein, but were among the most detailed and specific laboratory protocols for the procedures involved that he had ever seen..."

The availability of appropriate controls and procedures to assure reliability of DNA laboratory results promises favorable judicial reviews for the admissibility of DNA evidence in trial courts.

The Legal Standard of Admissibility

A majority of jurisdictions follow the Frye Rule for determining admissibility of evidence. This is based on the Supreme Court ruling in Frye v. United States, F. 1013 at 1014 (D.C. Cir. 1923). The court in this case held:

> Just when a scientific principle or discovery crosses the line between the experimental and demonstrable stages is difficult to define. Somewhere in this twilight zone the evidential force of the principle must be recognized, and while courts will go a long way in admitting expert testimony deduced from a well recognized scientific principle or discovery, the thing from which the deduction is made must be sufficiently established to have gained general acceptance in the particular field in which it belongs.

Practically speaking, the Frye Rule requires that the evidence to be introduced has gained general acceptance in the scientific community. It has been established in a number of courts that DNA identification is capable of producing reliable results and that there is general scientific acceptance of the theories underlying DNA identification.

The courts have also concluded that DNA forensic identification tests to determine inclusions are reliable and meet the Frye standard of admissibility.

Conclusion

DNA and genetic fingerprinting represent the most important breakthrough in crime detection since the discovery of the fingerprint.

DNA-Print Test Preservation of Sample and Minimum Amounts

Blood (White Cells)	
Liquid	1–100 µL
	Size of a quarter
	One drop
Preservation	EDTA (Purple Cap) refrigeration
Dried	Approximately size of a dime
Preservation	Dried — keep dry — refrigerate/ freeze

Semen	
Liquid	1–20 µL
	Approximately dime size
Preservation	Add EDTA and refrigerate
Dried	Requires an appropriate amount of sperm
Preservation	Keep dry — refrigerate or freeze
	Laboratory — separate sperm

Urine	
Cellular material	10,000 cells (approximately 60 ml)
	60–100 cc (approximately 2 oz)
Liquid	Isolate cellular material
	Freeze (−70°C)
Dried	Keep dry — freeze

Saliva	
Buccal cells	10,000 cells (one drop)
Liquid	Separate buccal cells, dry/freeze
Dried	Keep dry, refrigerate or freeze

Tissues (bones)	
Minimum amount	100–500 mg (1 in.)
Fresh	Freeze (−70°C)
Dried	Keep dry — freeze

DNA profiling can be utilized to: (1) Establish the link between evidential DNA with that of the possible suspect's DNA; and (2) Identify whether the DNA in question is human or nonhuman and establish sex.

DNA technology represents the future of forensic medicine and the experts have only begun to scratch the surface with this technology. It is a powerful tool which protects the innocent just as surely as it pinpoints the guilty. Genetic identification takes the "gamesmanship" out of the trial — it either is the defendant who committed the crime, or it is not.

Bibliography

Balazs, I., Wexler, K., Nicholas, L., Guisti, A., Baird, M., Rubinstein, P., Allen, F.H., and Sussman, L. "The use of restriction length polymorphisms for the determination of paternity." Toronto, Canada. Presented to the American Society of Human Genetics. November, 1984.

Blake, E.T., and Sensabaugh, G.F. "Genetic markers in human semen: A review." *Journal of Forensic Sciences,* Vol. 21 No. 4., pp. 784–796, 1976.

Geberth, V.J. "The Application of DNA in Criminal Investigations." *Law and Order Magazine* Vol. 36. No. 7., July, 1988.

Gill, P., Jeffreys, A.J., and Werret, D.J. "Forensic Application of DNA Fingerprints." *Nature.* Vol. 318, pp. 577–579., 1985.

Guisti, A., Baird, M., Pasquale, S., Balazs, I., and Glassberg, J. "Application of DNA polymorphisms to the analysis of DNA recovered from sperm." *Journal of Forensic Sciences.* Vol. 31 No. 2, pp. 409–417, 1986.

Harris, J. J.S.C. Frye Ruling. People v. Wesley, 140 Misc. 2nd 306 Supreme Court, County of Albany, July 15, 1988.

Jeffreys, A.J., Wilson, V., and Thein, S.L. "Individual — Specific Fingerprints of Human DNA." *Nature.* Vol. 316, pp. 76–79, 1985.

Kanter, E., Baird, M., Shaler, R., and Balazs, I. "Analysis of restriction fragment length polymorphisms in DNA recovered from dried bloodstains." *Journal of Forensic Sciences.* Vol. 31 No. 2., pp. 403–408., 1986.

McNally, L., Shaler, R., Giusti, A., Baird, M., Balazs, I., DeForest, P., and Kobilinski, L. "The Effects of Environment and Substrata on DNA: The Use of Case Work Samples from New York City." *Journal of Forensic Sciences.* Vol. 34. No. 5., September, 1989.

McNally, L., Shaler, R., Guisti, A., Baird, M., Balzas, I., DeForrest, P., and Koblinski, L. "Evaluation of Deoxyribonucleic Acid (DNA) Isolated from Human Bloodstains Exposed to Ultraviolet Light, Heat, Humidity, and Soil contamination." *Journal of Forensic Sciences.* Vol. 34 No. 5., September, 1989.

Mones, P. *Stalking Justice.* New York: Pocket Books, 1995.

Rabson, A. B. and Rabson, A. S. "Recombinant DNA technology and laboratory medicine." *Archives of Pathology and Laboratory Medicine.* Vol. 107. pp. 505–509, 1983.

Shaler, R.C. Ph.D. Personal Interview and communication. February, 1995.

Sheindlin G. J.S.C. "Decision on the Admissibility of DNA Identification Tests." People v. Castro. Supreme Court, County of the Bronx, August 14, 1989.

The Bureau of National Affairs. "Virginia Upholds Admission of Results of 'DNA Fingerprint' Analysis." The Criminal Law Reporter. Vol. 46. No. 2., pp. 1026–1027. Washington, D.C. The Bureau of National Affairs, Inc., October 11, 1989.

The Autopsy

18

A *medicolegal autopsy*, an examination of a body after death, is always required in homicide cases. In this chapter we will look at the purpose of the autopsy and describe the examination. I have also included a brief section on human anatomy to acquaint the investigator with some basic terminology used by the medical profession.

The Medical Examiner/Coroner

The medical examiner's or coroner's office is primarily concerned with the investigation of violent, sudden, unexpected, and suspicious deaths. The procedures used in the official medicolegal investigation of death fall under the supervision of the chief medical examiner or coroner, who is responsible for the evaluation and interpretation of the results of this inquiry. It should be noted that the terms pathologist, coroner, and medical examiner may be but are not always synonymous. In some jurisdictions the coroner is not a physician, but an elected or appointed official responsible for taking legal charge of the body. In other jurisdictions, medical examiners are not pathologists, and pathologists are not necessarily medical examiners. The recommended standards for a medical examiner system are that the chief medicolegal officer — whether referred to as medical examiner or coroner — be a qualified doctor of medicine who is also a certified pathologist skilled in forensic pathology. In those jurisdictions lacking a forensic pathologist, the author recommends that the investigator seek out the services of a pathologist, preferably one with some experience in forensic medicine, and refer

Figure 18.1. **MODERN MEDICOLEGAL FACILITIES: STORAGE.** (Courtesy of Dr. Leslie I. Lukash, Chief Medical Examiner, Nassau County, New York.)

this pathologist to the procedures recommended by the National Association of Medical Examiners.[1]

For purposes of this chapter the term medical examiner or coroner will be synonymous with forensic pathologist and will refer to the medicolegal authority responsible for conducting the investigation.

The certified pathologist has received advanced training in recognizing and interpreting diseases and injuries in the human body. It is this knowledge that enables the medical examiner/coroner to make significant contributions to the homicide investigation. Practically speaking, forensic experts play an active part in the homicide investigation and should be considered an important part of the investigative team. If the investigation is to be successful, the homicide detective and the forensic pathologist must work together.

Investigation of Death

An autopsy is always required in homicide cases. However, the chief medical examiner or coroner has the authority to investigate and certify any death which falls in the following categories:

---

[1] Leslie I. Lukash (Chairman) et al. *Standards for Inspection and Accreditation of a Modern Medicolegal Investigative System.* National Association of Medical Examiners, Wilmington, Delaware, 1974.

Figure 18.2.   **MODERN MEDICOLEGAL FACILITIES: AUTOPSY ROOM.** (Courtesy of Dr. Leslie I. Lukash, Chief Medical Examiner, Nassau County, New York.)

Figure 18.3.   **MODERN MEDICOLEGAL FACILITIES: AUTOPSY TABLE.** (Courtesy of Dr. Leslie I. Lukash, Chief Medical Examiner, Nassau County, New York.)

OFFICE OF CHIEF MEDICAL EXAMINER
OF THE CITY OF NEW YORK

IDENTIFICATION OF BODY

STATE OF NEW YORK
CITY AND COUNTY OF NEW YORK, ss.:
BOROUGH OF

....age................., residing at

....in the ....

being duly sworn, deposes and says: That   he is a..

of the person whose body was found at.., 19 ......,

and subsequently sent to the Office of Chief Medical Examiner; that deponent has seen the............................

of said deceased, and has every reason to believe that the body now recorded at the Office of Chief Medical

Examiner as...

is..who was last seen or heard from by deponent on

...., 19 ......

     Deponent therefore prays that   identification of said deceased person be accepted by the Chief

Medical Examiner of The City of New York.

Age :............................ Sex :............................ Color :............................

Marital Status : ....

Occupation : ....

Residence : ....

Sworn to before me this

    day of..............................19 .....   X...

Identified to :...Death Ctf. issued by :...................................Date :.................

ME-21 (1/79)

Figure 18.4.   FAMILY IDENTIFICATION FORM.

2010A-20M-315055(76) 346

Compartment No. ....

**OFFICE OF CHIEF MEDICAL EXAMINER
CITY OF NEW YORK**

Police Identification of Body

STATE OF NEW YORK
CITY AND COUNTY OF NEW YORK, ss
BOROUGH OF ....

PATROLMAN .... SHIELD .... PCT. ....

1. That he was the Patrolman who first saw the body of deceased:

....
Name of Deceased   M. E. Case No.

at ....
Place of Death   Date of Death

2. PLACE of OCCURRENCE (State exact location, streets, apt. etc.):

....

....
Time   Date

THAT HE OBTAINED THE FOLLOWING INFORMATION AS TO THE CIRCUMSTANCES
OF THE OCCURRENCE:

....

....

....

THAT HE IDENTIFIED THE BODY OF THE DECEASED AT THE OFFICE OF THE
CHIEF MEDICAL EXAMINER, IN THE PRESENCE OF OR TO:

DRS. ....

....

....

Sworn to before me this ....

day of .... 19 ......

Time ....

....
Signature of Patrolman

Figure 18.5. **POLICE IDENTIFICATION FORM.**

Criminal violence
Suicide
Accident
Suddenly when in apparent good health
Deaths under unusual or suspicious circumstances
Abortion (legal and criminal)
Prisoner and inmate deaths or any death while in legal custody
Deaths where the deceased was unattended by a physician
Poisoning
Unclaimed bodies
Diseases constituting a threat to public health
Disease, injury, or toxic agent resulting from employment
Death associated with diagnostic or therapeutic procedures
When a body is to be cremated, dissected, or buried at sea
When a dead body is brought into a new medicolegal jurisdiction
    without proper medical certification

The medical examiner takes charge of the body upon notification of death. The medical examiner/coroner or a duly authorized representative should respond to the scene of the homicide to conduct an investigation into the circumstances of death. In order to conduct the investigation properly, he or she must obtain as much information as possible from the homicide investigator at the scene. An investigator fully apprised of all developments of the case should be present later at the autopsy.

In some jurisdictions, only the first officer is required to attend the autopsy, and only then to identify the body for the chain of custody. From an investigative point of view, I recommend that the investigator who is familiar with the facts of the case be present to brief the pathologist. Many times, during the autopsy, questions will arise that only someone who was present at the scene can answer. The investigator who was present at the crime scene can provide the pathologist with a detailed account of all that transpired from the discovery of the body to the preliminary investigation at the scene and thereby assure that both parties will have the benefit of all available information. In addition, sometimes certain changes take place in the body during transportation and storage. These changes may be misinterpreted if someone who was present at the scene and observed the body in its original condition is not present at the autopsy to point out these changes. I recall one case in which the deceased's face was flattened, giving the impression that

Figure 18.6. **BODY BEING WEIGHED AND MEASURED PRIOR TO AUTOPSY.** (Courtesy of Dr. Leslie I. Lukash, Chief Medical Examiner, Nassau County, New York.)

the body had been face down, when in fact the body was on its back when discovered. A heavy piece of furniture placed on the deceased's face by the killer had created this postmortem artifact. The pathologist who performed the autopsy was at first confused by this apparent contradiction. However, since I had been at the scene and observed the body in its original position with the piece of furniture on the face, I was able to explain.

Purpose of the Autopsy

The purpose of the medicolegal autopsy is to establish the cause of death and make a medical determination of all the other factors which may be involved in the death. The autopsy provides the forensic pathologist with an opportunity to examine the body externally and internally to determine what wounds and injuries were sustained and to determine the cause of death.

Cause, Manner, and Mode of Death

From an investigative point of view, we can consider the *cause of death* as the pathological condition which produced the death; the *manner of death* as the instrument or physical agent which was used; and the *mode*

Figure 18.7. **BODY BEING X-RAYED PRIOR TO AUTOPSY.** (Courtesy of Dr. Leslie I. Lukash, Chief Medical Examiner, Nassau County, New York.)

of death as the intent (or lack of intent) when the instrumentality was employed, and by whom. Four modes are possible: natural, accidental, suicidal, or homicidal. For example, the cause of death may be a subdural hemorrhage; the manner of death may be an injury to the skull by blunt force; and the mode of death may be homicidal. In other types of cases the death may be natural as in a myocardial infarct (cardiac arrest), which may be caused by arteriosclerosis (hardening of the arteries).

There may be instances where the cause of death cannot be determined, but because of the condition of the body and the circumstances surrounding its discovery, the medical examiner will determine that the death should be considered a homicide.

The findings of the autopsy will usually determine whether or not death is the result of a homicide. This is important since some conditions which are in fact natural may sometimes suggest homicidal violence. Such cases can present serious problems for the homicide detective. For example, a person suffering a cerebral hemorrhage may become convulsive, compelling the police to subdue him or her. Actually, the victim may have suffered a subarachnoid hemorrhage due to a spontaneous rupture of a small aneurysm (dilatation of the wall of an artery) in the brain. The spontaneous nature of this condition is unaffected by the fact that the deceased may have been slapped, punched, or otherwise subjected to physical abuse during any minor argument or restraining activity. The hemorrhage may be either rapid or slow. If it is slow, the victim usually remains conscious, but may become disturbed or assaultive and may cause a commotion. In certain instances, these persons may expire while police are attempting to subdue them, prompting the erroneous assumption that the use of force by the police caused the death. The pathologist's findings during the autopsy will determine that the death was caused by the ruptured aneurysm and not by any physical restraint. Likewise, death from lobar pneumonia is sometimes preceded by delirium or excitement which may require that police be summoned. This situation may also produce minor injuries which are totally unrelated to the death.

The death of an alcoholic may at times cause investigators to believe that the death is suspicious or possibly homicidal, based on the general condition of the body. It should be noted that alcoholics may physically deteriorate to a point where they continually fall or cut themselves, resulting in numerous cuts, abrasions, and contusions which may be fresh or in various stages of healing. Furthermore, such persons are generally untidy and during their delirium may upset furniture, drop things, throw things around, and generally create an appearance of some sort of violent assault which did not in fact occur.

Investigators should also be aware of the various postmortem changes, as well as the possibility of the presence of postmortem artifacts which can appear to be wounds or additional injuries on the body. Examples of postmortem artifacts are insect and animal activity and decomposition. Discolorations in the skin may resemble bruises or injuries and may mislead the investigator. All observations at the scene should be recorded in the investigative notes and brought to the attention of the pathologist to assure that he or she can separate antemortem from postmortem conditions.

Conversely, investigators should realize that fatal violence may be inflicted without any external signs of trauma. Poisoning is probably the most obvious type of homicide in which no external wound is present. However, in any number of circumstances an injury may not be readily observed, such as a torn spleen from a kick or other trauma to the abdomen, or an asphyxiation where the victim has had a pillow held over the nose and mouth. I remember reading about a series of senior citizen deaths, all of which were thought to have been natural. There wasn't any evidence of a crime, and preliminary medical examination did not reveal any trauma. However, later on a suspect was developed after evidence of asphyxia was discovered in a similar case. A review of the other cases both by the medical examiner, who ordered the exhumation of certain bodies, and the police, who reopened their investigation, indicated that these "natural" deaths were in fact homicides. It was later learned that the suspect would enter the bedrooms of the victims and hold a pillow over their faces as they lay in bed, causing suffocation. The suspect would then steal the TV and other small items of value without disturbing the general condition of the scene. In most instances, the bodies had begun to decompose before discovery. Police later located a witness who had observed the suspect leaving the apartment of one of the victims with a TV. Although evidence of this type of trauma could have been identified earlier, the procedures involved in cases of apparent natural death where no suspicion was involved were not sufficient to address this possibility. The jurisdiction involved subsequently changed its policy.

Determining mode of death obviously requires the expertise of the forensic pathologist. The detective should be constantly aware that things are not always as they appear to be. He or she should keep an open mind, conduct a thorough investigation, and remember that teamwork is essential. Then the two will be able to pool their knowledge to reach a successful conclusion.

Investigative Information Provided by the Autopsy

In addition to supplying the homicide investigator with an official cause of death, the forensic pathologist conducting the autopsy can assist the investigation by answering such questions as:

1. What type of weapon was involved in the death? (A hammer or screwdriver might leave impression-type wounds, for example.)
2. Are the wounds consistent with investigative evidence?
3. Which wound was the fatal wound? (Where there are numerous gunshot or stab wounds this determination frequently cannot be made.)
4. Approximately how long could the deceased have lived after the assault? (Survival time.)
5. How far could the deceased have walked or run?
6. Was the body dragged or dumped?

Figure 18.8.   Laceration of the scalp caused by a blunt force injury.

Figure 18.9.   Pattern impression of a hammer head in the skull from the above homicide case. Careful measurements and photographs would allow for calculations of shape and dimensions of a tool used as a weapon. (Courtesy of Frederick C. Drummond. Photograph by W. Reid Lindsay, Westchester County Forensic Science Laboratory.)

Figure 18.10.   **NECK COMPRESSION INJURY.** (Courtesy of Dr. Dominick J. DiMaio, Former Chief Medical Examiner, City of New York.)

7. From what direction was the force applied?
8. What was the position of the deceased at the time of injury (sitting, standing, lying down, etc.)?
9. Are the injuries antemortem or postmortem?
10. Is there any evidence of sexual assault (rape or sodomy)?
11. Was the deceased under the influence of drugs?
12. Was the deceased under the influence of alcohol?
13. Are there any foreign objects in the cadaver (bullets, broken blades, fibers, etc.)?
14. Is there any evidence of a struggle (defense wounds, etc.)?
15. What is the estimated time of death?

It is important to note that most initial injuries do not cause immediate death. There is often a "survival interval" during which the person may engage in considerable activity before collapsing and dying. In fact,

Figure 18.11.   **PATTERN IMPRESSION OF A SNEAKER COMPARED TO THE INJURY.** (Courtesy of Dr. Dominick J. DiMaio, Former Chief Medical Examiner, City of New York.)

Figure 18.12.   Gunshot residue deposit surrounds the bullet hole on the under-garment. Traces of red fibers from the outer garment are present around the bullet hole as carried through by the bullet. This is a "contact" shot with the firearm's muzzle pushed against the victim. (Courtesy of Frederick C. Drummond. Photograph by W. Reid Lindsay, Westchester County Forensic Science Laboratory.)

instances have been documented in which persons who have been severely injured, or who have suffered multiple gunshot wounds, have performed unusual physical accomplishments. This type of activity before death will be readily observable to the trained pathologist, who will be able to reasonably determine the survival time by noting the condition of internal organs and the forms of hemorrhage in the body cavities or stomach of the deceased. For example, hemorrhage into the chest and heart cavities following a penetrating wound usually indicates that the individual survived for only a short time, while bleeding into the stomach or lower abdominal tract indicates a longer survival time.

The presence of a wound on a body does not necessarily mean that someone else inflicted the wound. Suicide must always be considered. It is a common error to believe that certain wounds would have been too painful to be self-inflicted.

> **Remember, there is no such thing as a wound which is too painful if the person is determined to take his or her own life.**

The pathologist considers the location, size, shape, character, and type of wound before the death is determined a homicide. For wounds to be self-inflicted, the locations must be accessible to the deceased. In most suicides, the instrument of death will be nearby. (However, the absence of a weapon is not conclusive evidence that the death is a homicide.)

The number, type, and location of wounds may also provide information to the investigator. Unusual types of wounds — such as mutilation of the body, removal of private parts, or eyes put out — may offer clues. Secondary wounds or "overkill" injuries may indicate extreme emotion.

The pathologist can ascertain how recent a wound is and which wound caused the death. The pathologist can also distinguish between wounds produced before and after death. Furthermore, in cases where the body has been out of doors or in water, there will be evidence of feeding by wild animals or postmortem injuries due to marine life or boat propellers, which the investigator might mistakenly interpret as being related to the cause of death. The pathologist also looks for defense wounds; these are usually found on the arms and legs of the victim, particularly between and on the inside of the fingers.

In some instances, the autopsy examination will reveal a specific type of weapon. When the barrel of a gun is pressed close to the skin of a victim, it will leave a mark of the barrel.

The investigator can assist the medical examiner by keeping the crime scene under police control until after the autopsy has been completed. This procedure allows for further search in case additional information is discovered during the autopsy, and assures admissibility of any additional evidence.

The Medicolegal Autopsy

The complete *medicolegal autopsy* or *postmortem examination* involves the following steps:

Examination of the crime scene
Identification of the body
External examination of the body
Internal examination of the body
Toxicological examination of body fluids and organs

The medicolegal autopsy is ordered by the medical examiner or coroner for the purposes of:

1. Determining the cause, manner, mode, and time of death.
2. Recovering, identifying, and preserving evidentiary material.
3. Providing interpretation and correlation of facts and circumstances related to death.
4. Providing a factual, objective medical report for prosecution and defense.
5. Separating natural death from unnatural death for protection of the innocent in suspicious deaths.

It is important to note that an autopsy must be complete if it is to be accurate. The basic principle of homicide investigation is "do it right the first time; you only get one chance." Theoretically a body can be exhumed for further examination. However, exhumation is costly and usually unnecessary if the examination was complete the first time. There is no excuse for haphazard or short-cut methods to be taken in this crucial investigative step. Once a body has been embalmed and buried, many forms of evidence — especially toxicological and pathological — will be lost forever. Therefore, a systematic routine must be followed in postmortem examinations.

The medicolegal autopsy is much more involved than a general autopsy, which is performed in a hospital. It involves special training, skill, and cooperation between independent organizations including the police, the prosecutor's office, and specialized personnel such as serologists, toxicologists, anthropologists, and odontologists. Usually when the autopsy is performed by the pathologist it is impossible to foresee the questions which may arise hours, weeks, or years later. Therefore, if an autopsy is to be done professionally, it must be done completely and all possible information obtained.

> Remember, the purpose of the medicolegal autopsy is more than just to establish cause of death. It involves the determination of all other factors which may or may not be involved.

In order to acquaint the investigator with the requirements of the medicolegal autopsy, I have provided the following guidelines based on the National Association of Medical Examiners' *Standards for Inspection and Accreditation of a Modern Medicolegal Investigative System.*

Examination of the Crime Scene

In many jurisdictions a medical investigator, medical examiner, or coroner will respond to the crime scene to ascertain the essential facts concerning the circumstances of death and make a preliminary examination of the body. Once the body has been identified, the examiner looks for and evaluates any external evidence of trauma. Then a more complete examination of such factors as body heat, lividity, rigor mortis, decomposition, etc. is made to determine the approximate time of death. Often a determination of cause of death will hinge on facts or circumstances derived from an examination of the scene. However, although cause of death can frequently be determined during the scene investigation, particularly in gunshot or stab wound cases, the exact number of bullet or stab wounds cannot usually be ascertained until the autopsy. This is particularly true in cases where the body is clothed or has been covered with blood or dirt. The medical examiner or coroner takes charge of the body, any clothing on the body, and any article on or near the body that may assist the pathologist in determining cause and manner of death.

The crime scene examination does not end at the location of death. If the medical examiner who was present at the scene will not be performing the autopsy, the information from the crime scene investigation must be conveyed to the pathologist who will conduct the autopsy. The homicide detective who conducted the preliminary police investigation and was present at the crime scene should attend the autopsy and provide the medical examiner or coroner with the following:

1. Description of the circumstances of death.
2. Description of the scene of death. (Complete notes taken at the scene include a description of the deceased, color of any blood, injuries and wounds observed, etc.)
3. Condition of the body when first discovered (rigor mortis, lividity, temperature, putrefaction, decomposition, maggots or other insect activity, etc.).
4. Statements taken from witnesses and/or suspects.
5. Police photographs taken at scene. (Polaroid photos can be taken in addition to the usual police photos since they are ready for viewing immediately and can be available at autopsy.)

6. Diagrams and sketches of the crime scene.
7. Any weapons or articles found at the scene which relate to the death (knives, guns, other weapons, notes, paper, drugs, etc.).
8. Any questions formulated during the initial phase of the investigation. These may be evaluated in light of the medical evidence found by the pathologist.

Identification of the Body

The body must be properly identified to the medical examiner. The legal identification of the body is one of the requirements in the chain of custody and is vital to the homicide investigation. In criminal cases both a personal and a police identification must be made directly to the medical examiner. These identifications are made on official affidavits, sworn to in the presence of witnesses, with the time and date affixed, and signed by the person or official making the identification.

The police identification is made by an officer who observed the body at the scene, saw where it was found, or saw where the crime was committed. A personal identification is made by a relative or someone who knew the deceased.

The medical examiner assumes responsibility for the proper identification of the dead body. In homicide cases, all available means of identification should be employed to ascertain the identity of the deceased. The various methods of identification are as follows.

Personal identification (next of kin, relatives, friends, etc.)

Fingerprints

Teeth

Scars and/or surgical procedures (medical records)

Tattoos

Body build

Congenital malformations

Comparison x-rays

Identification of clothing on the body and its contents

Photographs

If the body is badly decomposed or skeletonized, an additional function of the autopsy will be to identify the remains. The pathologist is in the best position to know what additional experts — odontologists, anthropologists, etc. — may be needed.

External Examination of the Body

The date, time, and place of autopsy should be recorded, where and by whom it was performed, and the identity of any witnesses and/or participants. This recording can either be done by a stenographer or by use of mechanical recording equipment.

Preliminary Procedure

1. The body is examined before the clothing is removed to determine the condition of the clothing and to correlate any tears or other defects with obvious injuries to the body. These observations are then recorded.
2. The clothing, body, and hands of the deceased should be protected from possible contamination prior to the examination. (Hands should have been covered with paper bags at scene before body was transported.)
3. Clothing should then be carefully removed by unbuttoning, unzippering, or unhooking without tearing or cutting. This should be done systematically, and the condition of the clothing as well as any torn buttons, unsnapped garments, etc., should be recorded so the cutting is not confused with any tearing or cutting from the weapon or incident which caused death.
4. Clothing should then be laid out on a table so that a relationship can be established between the wounds on the body and the damages to the clothing. This procedure enables the pathologist to determine the position of the body at the time the wounds were inflicted, and to know where to look for external and internal damage.
5. Each item of clothing should be properly marked for identification. (If clothing is wet or bloody, it should be hung to air dry in order to prevent any putrefaction.)

The External Examination

1. The body is identified for the record and a complete physical description is taken as follows.
   a. Age
   b. Height
   c. Weight
   d. Sex
   e. Color of hair and eyes

   f. State of nutrition

   g. Muscular development

   h. Scars

   i. Tattoos

   j. Detailed description of teeth (number and general condition)

   k. Any abnormalities or deformities

   l. Evidence of any fractures

2. The body should then be carefully washed to remove any dried blood and/or dirt from the surface. (In gunshot cases, the pathologist should record the presence of any smoke or powder residue prior to this washing.)

3. A detailed description of the injuries should then be recorded, noting the number and characteristics such as size, shape, pattern, and location in relation to anatomic landmarks.

4. Photographs should then be taken of the body for identification and to record specific injuries.

   a. Photographs of injuries should include a scale and an identification number.

   b. If police have recovered a weapon, this weapon can be photographed alongside the wound. However, the weapon should be held away from the body in order to prevent any contamination of evidence, such as blood or hair being transferred between the body and the weapon.

5. The presence of any bite marks should be noted and these wounds or marks photographed with a 1 × 1 (fingerprint) camera, using a scale and measure along with an identifier label. (If these bite marks were observed prior to the body washing, a saliva swabbing should have been obtained for a possible blood grouping.)

6. X-ray and fluoroscope examination should then be undertaken to:

   a. Locate bullets, broken blades, or other radio-opaque objects.

   b. Document any old or new fractures, anatomic deformities, postsurgical materials such as metal plates, screws, nails, etc.

   c. Identify remains where there is no personal identification. (These x-rays can then be held pending the comparison of any antemortem records when and if located.) (*Note:* In all decomposition and child-abuse cases, the remains are x-rayed to document past trauma.)

7. During this external examination a record is made of any post-mortem artifacts, such as:
   a. Artifacts of decomposition.
   b. Third-party artifacts, e.g., animal or insect activity, emergency medical treatment, deliberate mutilation, or any dismemberment.
   c. Artifacts of storage and/or transportation prior to autopsy.
8. Examination of the hands, wrists, and arms for evidence of defense wounds. In addition in certain types of homicides, the pathologist will clip the fingernails to obtain trace evidence from the deceased's fingers, which may include tissue and blood specimens from suspects. Hands may also be examined for powder residue by neutron activation analysis.
9. In sex homicides, samples of scalp and pubic hair should be obtained from the body of the deceased. All hair should be plucked to secure the entire hair including the root. The pubic area should first be combed to secure any foreign or loose hairs which may be compared with the suspect's hair. Other samples should be obtained which represent different parts of the body. In addition, oral, nasal, vaginal, and anal swabs should be taken for further examination.

Internal Examination of the Body

An internal examination of the head, neck, cervical spine, thorax, abdomen, and genitalia is then performed by the pathologist. The examination records the course of wounds through the various structures and any evidentiary items such as bullets, pieces of weapons, pellets, and foreign material are preserved. Their particular point of recovery is noted for the record, and each item is labeled for proper identification. The internal examination generally proceeds as follows.

The Head

1. The exterior of the scalp is first examined for any injuries which may be hidden by the hair.
2. The eyes and eyelids are then examined for any petechiae in the conjunctivae. (This is a pathological condition caused by asphyxia. Tiny hemorrhages in the form of specks are seen on the mucous membrane lining the inner surface of the eyelids.)
3. The ear canals are then examined for evidence of hemorrhage.
4. The interior of the mouth, lips, and cheeks are examined for evidence of trauma.

Figure 18.13.   **GUNSHOT WOUND OF VICTIM'S LEFT CHEEK.** Note the crescent of the gunshot residue opening away from the ear. This shot came from close range, but gunshot residue should appear round, oval, or fan shaped — not crescent shaped. An intervening object was indicated. (Courtesy of Frederick C. Drummond. Photograph by W. Reid Lindsay, Westchester County Forensic Science Laboratory.)

Figure 18.14.   Gunshot injury to victim's left hand ring finger near the fingernail.

5. The teeth are then examined for any injury or breakage. The pathologist can use a dental chart to identify each tooth, its condition, location of fillings, evidence of injury, etc.
6. A *coronal mastoid incision* is then made across the head. The scalp is pulled back exposing the cranium. The interior of the scalp is examined for any evidence of trauma, and the cranium is examined for fractures. The calvarium is then removed, exposing the dura and the brain.
7. The brain is removed and examined for any injury or disease.
8. The brain is weighed.
9. A slice of brain tissue is taken for later examination.
10. The dura is then stripped from the cranial cavity and the interior of the skull is examined for any fractures or injury.

The Chest

1. An incision is then made across the chest of the subject. This incision is called the *thoracoabdominal incision*, more commonly referred to as the "Y" or primary incision.

Figure 18.15. **POSITIONING OF A RING FINGER INJURY.** Showing the origin of a crescent shape of gunshot residue pattern on the cheek. The victim must have observed the gun and lifted his hand by reflex to try to ward off the shot. (Courtesy of Frederick C. Drummond. Photograph by W. Reid Lindsay, Westchester County Forensic Science Laboratory.)

Figure 18.16.   **CORONAL MASTOID INCISION — HEAD INCISION.** (Courtesy of Dr. Leslie I. Lukash, Chief Medical Examiner, Nassau County, New York.)

Figure 18.17.   **HEAD INCISION.** (Courtesy of Dr. Leslie I. Lukash, Chief Medical Examiner, Nassau County, New York.)

Figure 18.18. **HEAD INCISION.** (Courtesy of Dr. Leslie I. Lukash, Chief Medical Examiner, Nassau County, New York.)

Figure 18.19. **HEAD INCISION.** (Courtesy of Dr. Leslie I. Lukash, Chief Medical Examiner, Nassau County, New York.)

Figure 18.20.   Scalp brought forward to expose the cranium. (Courtesy of Dr. Leslie I. Lukash, Chief Medical Examiner, Nassau County, New York.)

Figure 18.21.   Opening of the skull cavity. (Courtesy of Dr. Leslie I. Lukash, Chief Medical Examiner, Nassau County, New York.)

Figure 18.22. Opening of the skull cavity. (Courtesy of Dr. Leslie I. Lukash, Chief Medical Examiner, Nassau County, New York.)

Figure 18.23. Opening of the skull cavity. (Courtesy of Dr. Leslie I. Lukash, Chief Medical Examiner, Nassau County, New York.)

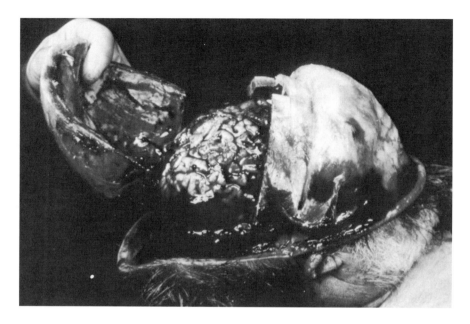

Figure 18.24.   Calvarium or top of the skull removed exposing a hemorrhaged brain. (Courtesy of Dr. Leslie I. Lukash, Chief Medical Examiner, Nassau County, New York.)

Figure 18.25.   Brain being removed from skull. (Courtesy of Dr. Leslie I. Lukash, Chief Medical Examiner, Nassau County, New York.)

Figure 18.26. Brain being removed from skull. (Courtesy of Dr. Leslie I. Lukash, Chief Medical Examiner, Nassau County, New York.)

Figure 18.27. Skull cavity after brain removed. (Courtesy of Dr. Leslie I. Lukash, Chief Medical Examiner, Nassau County, New York.)

2. The chest is then examined for any fractures of ribs, noting their specific anatomic location. In cases where an ambulance crew has attempted resuscitation, there may be additional injuries to the body which will not be properly evaluated if the medical examiner is not given this information. I cannot overemphasize that an investigator assigned to the case should be present during the autopsy so the pathologist can be briefed about what transpired at the scene.

3. The breast plate is then removed by cutting through the ribs, exposing the heart and lungs for examination.

4. A sample of blood is then taken directly from the heart, after opening the pericardial sac, for determining blood type and later toxicological examination.

5. The heart and lungs are then removed, weighed, and examined and a slice of tissue taken for later examination.

6. The quantity of fluids in the pericardial and pleural cavities is measured and recorded.

7. The chest flap is then pulled upward to chin level to examine structures of the neck muscles and organs. Any hemorrhage is noted, and the organs of the neck and throat are removed including the tongue for further examination.

8. Signs of asphyxia are noted within these structures, the upper chest, and in the pericardium and pleurae.

9. The tongue is then examined by lateral dissection for any evidence of trauma. (In many instances the deceased will bite his or her tongue during strangulation.)

10. The interior of the chest is then examined for any trauma or other injuries along the cervical and thoracic spine.

The Abdomen

1. The abdomen is examined, noting the positions and condition of the organs.

2. The course of injuries is traced and recorded before any organs are removed.

3. All fluids in this cavity are measured and recorded.

4. Each separate organ is weighed and dissected for later toxicological examination after it has been examined for any projectiles. In addition, a section of the intestines is kept for testing.

5. Stomach contents are measured and recorded and a sample kept for toxicology.

6. The fluid in the gall bladder is kept intact for testing.

Figure 18.28. Preparing to open the chest cavity. (Courtesy of Dr. Leslie I. Lukash, Chief Medical Examiner, Nassau County, New York.)

Figure 18.29. The thoracoabdominal or "Y" incision. (Courtesy of Dr. Leslie I. Lukash, Chief Medical Examiner, Nassau County, New York.)

Figure 18.30.   The thoracoabdominal or "Y" incision. (Courtesy of Dr. Leslie I. Lukash, Chief Medical Examiner, Nassau County, New York.)

Figure 18.31.   The thoracoabdominal or "Y" incision. (Courtesy of Dr. Leslie I. Lukash, Chief Medical Examiner, Nassau County, New York.)

Figure 18.32. Chest and ribs exposed. (Courtesy of Dr. Leslie I. Lukash, Chief Medical Examiner, Nassau County, New York.)

Figure 18.33. Removal of the chest plate. (Courtesy of Dr. Leslie I. Lukash, Chief Medical Examiner, Nassau County, New York.)

Figure 18.34.   Breast plate being removed. (Courtesy of Dr. Leslie I. Lukash, Chief Medical Examiner, Nassau County, New York.)

The Pelvic Cavity

1. The external and internal genitalia are examined for evidence of foreign matter and injury.
2. In sex homicides, vaginal and anal swabs are taken (oral swabs should also be obtained).
3. The urinary bladder is removed and the fluid measured and kept for toxicological examination.

The Protocol

The *protocol* is the official report of the autopsy by the medical examiner or coroner. It may be dictated to a stenographer or recorded into a mechanical recorder for later transcription. The preparation of this report is the responsibility of the chief medical examiner or coroner. The protocol or autopsy report reflects the entire examination, both negative and positive, and gives the official cause of death expressed in acceptable terminology. It contains the following information:

1. External examination
   a. Description of the clothing
   b. Description of the body

Figure 18.35. Internal organs of the chest exposed for autopsy. (Courtesy of Dr. Leslie I. Lukash, Chief Medical Examiner, Nassau County, New York.)

2. Evidence of injury
   a. External
   b. Internal
3. Central nervous system (head and brain)
4. Internal examination — cardiovascular system, pulmonary system, GI (gastrointestinal) system, stomach, small and large intestines, etc.
5. Anatomical findings
6. Toxicological findings
7. Opinion

The medical examiner at the end of this protocol then reports the official diagnosis of the cause of death. Today, many pathologists use a

Figure 18.36. Containers of physiologic fluids and organs to be sent for further toxicologic examination. (Courtesy of Dr. Leslie I. Lukash, Chief Medical Examiner, Nassau County, New York.)

prepared autopsy form that not only guides the procedure but assures the completion of the autopsy. If death is determined to be the result of homicide, the pathologist will indicate this by placing the word "homicidal" on the protocol. The opinion will then be expressed in simple, understandable English, avoiding medical terminology, indicating the nature of the injury which caused death and any major complicating factors. For example: "It is my opinion that John Smith, a 30-year-old male, died as a result of a gunshot wound to the chest. The bullet, a 38-caliber which was recovered from the body, passed through the right lung and heart causing massive internal hemorrhage. No other injuries or significant natural disease process was found at the time of autopsy."

The value of the diagnosis and protocol from an investigative point of view is that it provides a factual and medical opinion of the death. This can then be used to determine if the facts and evidence gathered during the homicide investigation are consistent with the cause of death as determined by the medical examiner.

Summary

The success of the medical examination and the homicide investigation is assured when there exists a mutual cooperation between the pathologist and the homicide investigator. Teamwork is essential in this phase of the investigation, just as it is in other phases. It requires an appreciation and understanding of each other's duties and responsibilities so that all parties can benefit from one another's contributions and expertise in the professional investigation of homicide.

Human Anatomy

In order to provide the reader with some basic reference material and understanding of the terminology used in medicolegal investigations, I have included this section on human anatomy.[2] Investigators are not expected to have the medical knowledge of a forensic pathologist. However, they should have a working knowledge of anatomical terminology in order to communicate intelligently with the pathologist and comprehend the final autopsy report. Furthermore, an understanding of the fundamental structures of the human body and the location of vital organs and bones can enable the investigator to make intelligent observations at the scene.

The word *anatomy* is derived from two Greek words which mean literally, "to cut apart." Through usage, it has come to mean the study of the structure of the body, describing the size, shape, composition, and relative positions of the organs and various parts of the body. In order to describe the structures within the body, medical terminology employs a number of "points of reference," which assist in visualizing each organ's position within the human body. For example, to describe the heart's position it is necessary to detail what is above, below, to the right and left, and in front and back of it, and where all these positions are located in reference to easily identified points on the outside of the body. In order for these points of reference to be meaningful, there must be a set position of the body known as *anatomical position*.

All terminology used in describing the body and its parts is based on this anatomical position, which is that of the body standing erect, arms at the sides, with the palms facing forward and the thumbs to the outside.

Therefore, when studying anatomical plates, like the figures presented in this section, the right side of the body will be on the left side of the drawing, and the left side of the body will be on the right side of the drawing, as when looking at a person facing you.

---

[2] The material in this section is based on *Gray's Anatomy* and *Life Sciences for Nursing and Health Technologies* by Virginia E. Thomas.

Figure 18.37.   **ANATOMICAL POSITION.** (Courtesy of Virginia E. Thomas, Technicourse, Long Beach, California.)

Directional Terms

These are the terms used in anatomy to describe the position of a particular organ in relation to other organs.

1. *Superior:* Indicates direction toward the head end or upper part of the body. Hence, the lungs are *superior* to the liver.
2. *Inferior:* Indicates direction further away from the head end of the body or toward the lower part of the body. Hence, the intestines are *inferior* to the stomach.
3. *Anterior (ventral):* Indicates the front or belly side of the body. Hence, the toes are *anterior* or *ventral.*

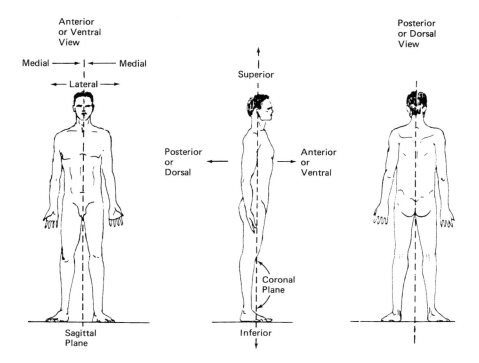

Figure 18.38.   **DIRECTIONAL TERMS.** (Courtesy of Virginia E. Thomas, Technicourse, Long Beach, California.)

4. *Posterior (dorsal):* Indicates the backside of the body. Hence, the heels are *posterior* or *dorsal.*

5. *Proximal:* Indicates nearer to a point of reference, usually the center of the body. Hence, the shoulder is *proximal* to the elbow.

6. *Distal:* Indicates farther away from the center of the body. Hence, the elbow is *distal* to the shoulder.

7. *Medial:* Indicates closer to the midline of the body. Hence, the little finger is *medial* in anatomical position.

8. *Lateral:* Indicates toward the side of the body or away from the midline. Hence, the thumb is *lateral* in anatomical position.

9. *Sagittal plane:* Is an imaginary line dividing the body into a right and left portion.

10. *Coronal plane:* Is an imaginary line dividing the body into a front and back portion.

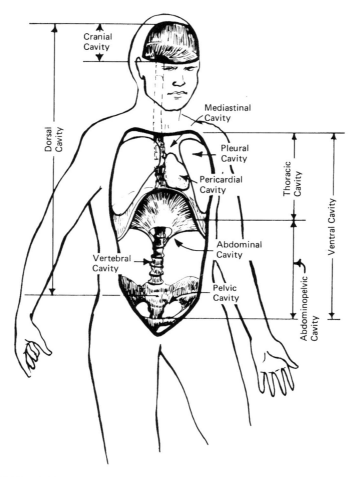

Figure 18.39.   **BODY CAVITIES.** (Courtesy of Virginia E. Thomas, Technicourse, Long Beach, California.)

Body Cavities

The body is divided into two large cavities called the *dorsal* (back) and *ventral* (front) cavities, which are then subdivided into smaller sections.

Dorsal Cavity

This cavity is subdivided into the *cranial* and *vertebral* cavities.

1. *Cranial cavity:* Is formed by the skull and contains the brain and the pituitary gland.
2. *Vertebral cavity:* Is contained within the vertebral column and houses the spinal cord.

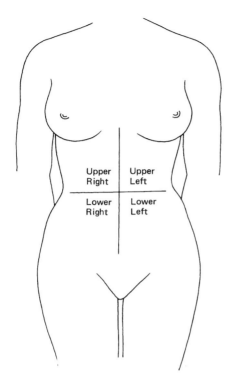

Figure 18.40.   **QUADRANTS.**

Ventral Cavity

This cavity is subdivided into two major sections, the *thoracic cavity* and the *abdominopelvic cavity*. These two sections are divided by the diaphragm. These two major sections are then subdivided into additional cavities as follows.

1. *Thoracic cavity:* This is the portion above the diaphragm and contains the following cavities.
   a. Two *pleural cavities:* These contain the two lungs.
   b. *Pericardial cavity:* This contains the heart.
   c. *Mediastinal* or *interpleural cavity:* This contains everything located in the thoracic cavity other than the heart and lungs. Includes the trachea, bronchi, esophagus, etc.
2. *Abdominopelvic cavity:* This is the portion below the diaphragm and contains two sections:
   a. *Abdominal cavity:* The upper portion of the abdominopelvic cavity. It contains the stomach, liver, gallbladder, spleen, pancreas, and most of the large and small intestines. The kidneys, ureters, and adrenal glands lie deep in the cavity.

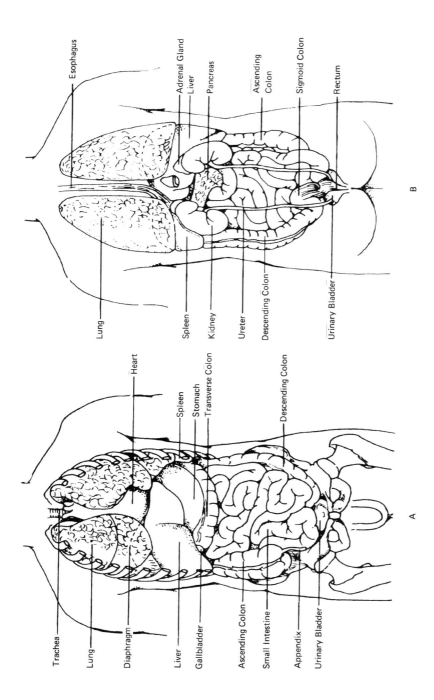

Figure 18.41.   Anterior and posterior views of the thoracic and abdominal pelvic cavities. (Courtesy of Virginia E. Thomas, Technicourse, Long Beach, California.)

b. *Pelvic cavity:* The lower portion of the abdominopelvic cavity, which begins roughly on a line with the iliac crests and ends at the inferior end of the abdominopelvic cavity. It contains the urinary bladder, the sex organs, and part of the small and large intestines.

Quadrants

There are additional points of reference to locate precisely the organs in the abdominopelvic cavity, because the cavity is both large and contains several organs. The medical description divides the cavity into four *quadrants.*

1. *Upper right quadrant:* Contains part of the small intestine, the descending duodenum, the upper ascending colon, most of the liver, gallbladder, and bile ducts, head of pancreas, right adrenal gland, right kidney, and upper part of right ureter.
2. *Lower right quadrant:* Contains the lower ascending colon, cecum, appendix, lower right ureter, terminal ileum, part of urinary bladder, and sex organs.
3. *Upper left quadrant:* Contains ascending part of duodenum, upper descending colon, left half of transverse colon, spleen, small part of liver, left adrenal gland, left kidney, and upper part of left ureter.
4. *Lower left quadrant:* Contains descending colon, small intestine (part of ileum), lower part of left ureter, part of urinary bladder, and sex organs.

The Skeletal System

The *skeletal system* consists of all of the bones in the body. The skeleton provides support, protects certain body organs beneath the bones, and serves as a system of connection for the muscles and ligaments. Practically speaking, it is not necessary for the homicide detective to understand the make-up, development, or detailed structure of the bones. However, the investigator should have some basic knowledge of the anatomical location of certain major bones in the human body, such as the *long bones* of the arms and legs, the *humerus, ulna, radius, femur, tibia,* and *fibula.* In addition, the location of the *clavicle, scapula, sternum, vertebral column, ribs, pelvis,* and *patella* may be useful in visualizing a specific portion of the body.

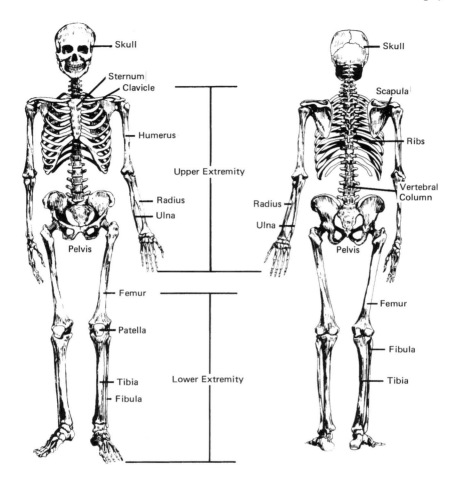

Figure 18.42.   **BONES OF THE SKELETON.** (Courtesy of Virginia E. Thomas, Technicourse, Long Beach, California.)

The Heart

The heart is basically a pump that maintains the circulation of blood throughout the human body. It is about the size of a man's fist and is located in the pericardial cavity between the lungs, posterior to the sternum, lying about two-thirds to the left of midline. The heart is divided into four chambers. The upper two chambers are called *atria* and the lower two chambers are called *ventricles*.

The heart is the major organ of the cardiovascular system. The pumping action maintains the circulation of blood to and from the heart through a series of blood vessels. These blood vessels are:

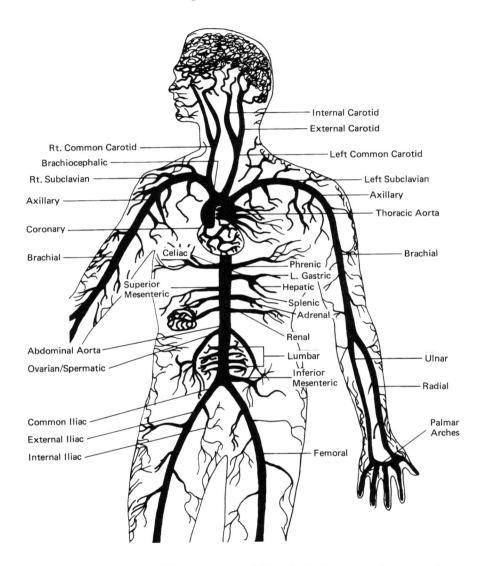

Figure 18.43. **THE ARTERIES.** (Courtesy of Virginia E. Thomas, Technicourse, Long Beach, California.)

1. *Arteries:* carry blood away from the heart.
2. *Veins:* carry blood to the heart.
3. *Capillaries:* connect arteries and veins.

The purpose of circulation is to bring the deoxygenated blood from various parts of the body through the veins to the lungs for purification.

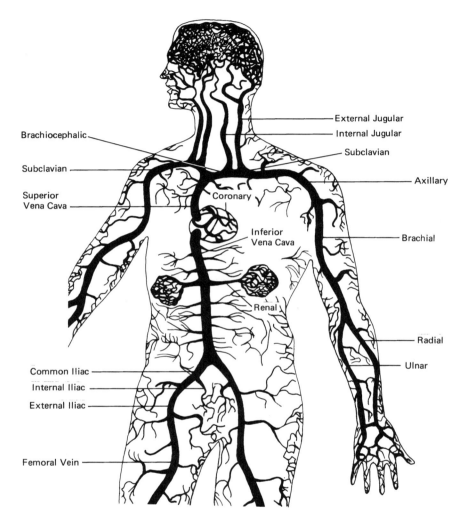

Figure 18.44.   **THE VEINS.** (Courtesy of Virginia E. Thomas, Technicourse, Long Beach, California.)

The oxygenated blood is then returned to the heart from the lungs for circulation to the body through the arteries.

It is not necessary for the investigator to have an in-depth knowledge of the workings of the heart and cardiovascular system. However, he or she may want to be familiar with the general location of the heart and the major veins and arteries in order to appreciate the trauma or damage which can be done to the body if one of these major blood vessels is injured. The following table lists the major arteries and veins for reference purposes.

ARTERIES		VEINS	
Carotid	Femoral	Jugular	Femoral
Subclavian	Brachial	Subclavian	Brachial
Aorta	Ulnar	Superior vena cava	Ulnar
Abdominal aorta	Radial	Inferior vena cava	Radial
Iliac		Iliac	

The author wishes to acknowledge the assistance and contributions of the following forensic pathologists who were instrumental in providing the technical data and information relative to the medicolegal autopsy. Dr. Dominick J. DiMaio, Former Chief Medical Examiner, City of New York. Doctor DiMaio has lectured at various forensic symposia and instructed various law enforcement agencies in the role of the medical examiner in homicide investigations. He is a professorial lecturer in pathology at Downstate Medical Center, State University of New York, and an Associate Professor of Forensic Medicine at New York University's Medical Center. Dr. Leslie I Lukash, Chief Medical Examiner of Nassau County, East Meadow, New York. Doctor Lukash is Professor of Forensic Pathology at Stony Brook University, Long Island, New York, and served as chairman of the committee on Standards for Inspection and Accreditation of Modern Medicolegal Systems of the National Association of Medical Examiners.

Finally, the author wishes to acknowledge the assistance of Virginia E. Thomas who also contributed to the illustrations herein.

Selected Reading

Adelson, Lester. *The Pathology of Homicide.* Springfield, Illinois: Charles C Thomas, 1974.

Fisher, Russell S. and Petty, Charles S. (Eds.). *Forensic Pathology: A Handbook for Pathologists.* Washington, D.C.: National Institute of Law Enforcement and Criminal Justice Law Enforcement Assistance Administration, U.S. Department of Justice, 1977.

Geberth, Vernon J. "Autopsy: The Medicolegal Investigation of Death," *Law and Order Magazine,* Vol. 30, No. 7, Illinois, July, 1982.

Gray, Henry F. R. S. *Gray's Anatomy.* Edited by T. Pickering. Philadelphia, Pennsylvania: Pick Running Press, 1974.

New York City Charter and Administrative Code Chapter 39 Chief Medical Examiner.

Snyder, LeMoyne. *Homicide Investigation,* 3rd ed. Springfield Illinois: Charles C Thomas, 1977.

Spitz, Werner U. and Fisher, Russell S. *Medicolegal Investigation of Death.* Springfield Illinois: Charles C Thomas, 1973.

Thomas, Virginia, *Life Sciences for Nursing and Health Technologies.* Long Beach, California: Technicourse, Inc., 1977.

The News Media in Homicide Investigations 19

The O.J. Simpson story, which captivated the nation, created news story coverage of a murder event without precedent. Consequently, there was a news media "feeding frenzy" for O.J. Simpson stories. It seemingly didn't matter what kind of story was published, as long as it had an O.J. Simpson angle. New stories about the evidence in the case, alleged statements of O.J. Simpson, police opinions, legal opinions, prosecutor's option of seeking the death penalty, the private lives of all concerned, etc. turned this particular event into a nationwide soap opera. In the opinion of the author, every rule in this book as well as the "Fair Trial Free Press Principles" were violated with the "news leaks," details, and revelations provided in the media regarding the People v. Simpson. I likened it to a large snowball careening down the side of a snow-filled mountain. As this snowball of information and misinformation gained in complexity, intensity, and speed, it became an avalanche. Anyone and everyone remotely attached to or involved in the O.J. Simpson debacle was crushed or had their reputations smashed in its wake. According to a Sunday *New York Daily News* article dated January 1, 1995, "In the 10 days before O.J. Simpson was picked up for questioning in the murder of his wife, Nicole Brown Simpson, and her friend Ron Goldman there were exactly eight references [to O.J. Simpson] ... In the 10 days after the murder, there were 1,769 references to Simpson in those same papers. ..." More than 30,000 articles and countless TV shows later, the opening statements haven't taken place." (p. 2, 3.)

It is not the author's intention to criticize nor to blame the media, the police, nor anyone else involved in this infamous case. However, I believe that the information in this chapter presents a more reasonable alternative then what we have been exposed to in the O.J. Simpson case.

A free press serves the public by supplying needed information, stimulating thought, and providing a medium for expression. An informed public is essential to the maintenance of a free society, and the public is entitled to be informed on topics of public interest. Crime, especially homicide, is always a subject for public concern and interest. Therefore, law enforcement officials can and should expect news media people to be present, make inquiries, and actively pursue the event.

The purpose of this chapter is to act as a guide in fostering better relations between the police investigative team and the news media in homicide investigations. To make better relations possible, I advocate mutual cooperation and understanding of each other's goals. The news media can be a tremendous asset in a homicide investigation or an equally staggering liability. Realistically, their impact usually falls between these two extremes.

Throughout the United States, law enforcement agencies and the news media are in daily contact. The days of "No comment" by the police to the media have been replaced by a more open and candid dialogue between the two. Therefore, there needs to be a thoughtful policy of police-media relationships which provides for the integrity of the investigation and the proper dissemination of information to the public.

Establishing a News Media Policy

Today, most large police departments and law enforcement agencies maintain a public information office staffed by designated public information officers or news media representatives to handle requests for information. These public information officers act as spokesmen for the department and maintain regular liaison with the media. In addition, most departments have established guidelines for the release of information by the members in the field to representatives of the media.

In homicide investigations, however, there must be a tighter control over the news release, justified by the legal considerations and the strategic aspects of the case. The public information officer should be kept advised of any such incidents and is responsible for notifying the media that police are investigating a homicide. However, all subsequent information and news releases from the department during the investigative stage should come from the detective supervisor or his equivalent in other agencies, who is in charge of the investigation at the scene.

Generally, local media will be more responsive than national to a request for cooperation because they are more sympathetic to local needs and sentiments. Likewise, representatives of major media organizations whom you have dealt with before will usually cooperate with you as long as they know they will be provided with information and given a statement from the investigator in charge. The trick is to engage in as much give-and-take as you can without compromising the case. However, as the newsworthiness of an event increases, out-of-town reporters or representatives of the wire services, radio, and television may become involved in gathering news, and this usually creates a strain.

The competitive nature of multimedia coverage usually presents law enforcement officers with problems they are ill-equipped to deal with. Too often there has been no previous thought given to how to handle a media-worthy situation. Suddenly, you're surrounded with an army of reporters seeking details of interest, ferreting out "new" information, interviewing witnesses, family, and anyone they feel might give them an edge over another news team. Photographers will be attempting to obtain photos of the body, the suspect, the scene of the crime, the investigators, and so on. Obviously, these media people will be "doing their own thing" without any consideration of the investigative needs of the case and the legal impact involved, not to mention consideration for the family. This is where planning comes into the picture. An intelligent news media policy will take into consideration the legal, strategic, and humanitarian aspects of the case and at the same time provide for the comprehensive release of news to the media.

Any policy instituted by a police department should provide guidelines for preserving the delicate balance between a free press and a fair trial when disseminating information. Most states and the federal government have provisions that are intended to promote accuracy and fairness in the release of information. The following "Fair Trial Free Press Principles and Guidelines for the State of New York" (reproduced in full here) are provided to the reader as a model.

"Fair Trial Free Press Principles"

Freedom of the press is guaranteed by the First Amendment of the Constitution of the United States. The right to a speedy and public trial by an impartial jury is guaranteed in criminal cases by the Sixth Amendment. The New York State bar, bench, law enforcement agencies, and news media, as represented by the organizations that have signed this document, recognize and uphold these guarantees and grant them equal validity.

They also recognize the right of the public in a democratic society to be informed about crime, law enforcement, and the administration of justice, and the right, in general, to have trials openly conducted.

While the news media recognize the responsibility of the judge to preserve order in the court and seek the ends of justice by all those means available to him, decisions about handling the news rest with the editors, who, in the exercise of news judgments should remember that:

1. An accused person is presumed innocent until proven guilty.
2. Accused persons and civil litigants are entitled to be judged in an atmosphere free from passion, prejudice, and sensationalism.
3. Readers, listeners, and viewers are potential jurors.
4. No one's reputation should be injured needlessly.

The proper administration of justice is the concern of the judiciary, bar, the prosecution, law enforcement personnel, news media, and the public. None should relinquish its share in that concern. None should condone injustices on the ground that they are infrequent.

1. When and after an arrest is made, the following information should be made available for publication:
   a. The accused's name, age, residence, employment, marital status, and similar background information.
   b. The substance or text of the charge such as a complaint indictment, information and, where appropriate, the identity of the complainant.
   c. The identity of the investigating and arresting agency and length of the investigation.
   d. The circumstances immediately surrounding the arrest, including the time and place of arrest, resistance, pursuit, possession and use of weapons, and description of items seized at the time of arrest.
2. The release of certain types of information by law enforcement personnel, the bench, and bar and the publication of this information by news media may tend to create dangers of prejudice without serving a significant law enforcement or public interest function. Therefore, all concerned should be aware of the dangers of prejudice in making pretrial disclosure of the following:

a. Statements as to the character or reputation of an accused person or prospective witness.

b. Admissions, confessions, or the contents of a statement or alibi attributable to an accused person.

c. The performance or results of tests or the refusal of the accused to take a test.

d. Statements concerning the credibility or anticipated testimony of prospective witnesses.

e. The possibility of a plea of guilty to the offense charged or to a lesser offense, or other disposition.

f. Opinions concerning evidence or argument in the case, whether or not it is anticipated that such evidence or argument will be used at trial.

3. Prior criminal charges and convictions are matters of public record and are available to the news media. Police, corrections, and other law enforcement agencies should make such information available to the news media on request. The public disclosure of this information by the news may be highly prejudicial without any significant addition to the public's need to be informed. The publication of such information should be carefully considered by the news media.

4. Law enforcement and court personnel should NOT prevent the photographing of defendants when they are in public places outside the courtroom. They should neither encourage nor discourage pictures or televising, but *they should not pose the accused.*

5. Photographs of a suspect may be released by law enforcement personnel provided a valid law enforcement function is served thereby. It is proper to disclose such information as may be necessary to enlist public assistance in apprehending fugitives from justice. Such disclosure may include photographs as well as records or prior arrests and convictions.

The preceding guidelines are those which address themselves to the law enforcement function. A separate set of guidelines is recommended for cases involving juveniles. Generally speaking, the following information should not be given to the press:

1. The names of children under 16 years of age who are charged with a crime or are complainants in a criminal proceeding; and

2. The identity of a victim of a sex crime.

In homicide cases, witnesses and others involved in the investigation should be cautioned not to speak to the press. However, it should be noted that the only persons whom police can effectively isolate from the media are suspects. It is utterly impossible to prevent others from speaking to reporters. If their disclosures present legal or other problems, you must be prepared to request cooperation from the media to withhold certain information in the interests of justice.

Remember, the best way to promote good media relations is through preparation and communication.

Know what you need to say to the media, and how to say it, in order to cooperate while still maintaining the integrity of the case.

Building a Relationship with the News Media

The relationship between the news media representative and the homicide spokesman usually starts off in a somewhat adversarial setting. The news reporter will be attempting to uncover facts of the investigation to obtain a better story, and the homicide spokespersons will be trying their best to keep certain strategic information out of the hands of the press.

How the police and the media deal with any given contact generally determines the ultimate associations, since a good relationship is usually the product of many individual contacts over a span of time. It is during these contacts that these persons get to know one another and learn to respect each other's professional position — for instance, I wouldn't expect a news representative to "kill" a story which was detrimental to the police, and likewise a news person shouldn't be insulted because an officer doesn't go along with an "off-the-record" request for information which might jeopardize the police investigation.

Professional homicide-news media relationships are usually built upon past experiences which have been mutually successful to both parties.

It also helps for each party to understand the other's pressures, particularly those relating to *time.* A murder investigation may take anywhere from a few hours to several days, weeks, or months. The news media representative, on the other hand, must complete his or her initial coverage of the event prior to a deadline which may amount to only hours or minutes. This is where a strain may set in between the two groups. A story which might rate front-page coverage prior to today's deadline, might tomorrow rate only a paragraph inside. A potential lead item on the "Eleven O'Clock News" that evening may not even be considered the following day. Time is of the essence to newspeople because other newsworthy events are taking place, deadlines must be met, and the space for newsprint and the time for broadcasts are tightly constrained. By the same token, time is of the essence to the homicide supervisor and detectives who are conducting the investigation. There is a tremendous amount of information generated in a very short period of time at the homicide crime scene. Furthermore, there are many investigative duties to perform and steps to be taken before valuable evidence is lost and suspects can be identified. The homicide spokesman cannot be expected to drop everything and engage in a news conference, nor should the reporter expect the police to prematurely disclose information in the early stages of the case so he or she can get a better story. In addition, news media people should resist the temptation to become part of the event. They should realize that their selection of news sources and the questions they ask may not only affect the story, but strain police-media relations by creating issues that jeopardize the homicide case. Practically speaking, a little flexibility and common sense in most cases will ultimately benefit both the news media and the police. Frictions can be minimized, issues put in proper perspective, and goals attained through mutual cooperation.

The homicide supervisor at the scene should be aware of media needs, and without neglecting investigative duties direct that a notification of the homicide be given to the public information officer along with some basic facts. In the event that there is no public information officer, the homicide supervisor can still encourage cooperation by providing for notifications to local media so that they may cover the story. This notification and subsequent release of information to the media will encourage cooperation and set the tone for future good relations.

Contacts between the homicide spokesman and the news media representatives are not limited to the formal news conference during a homicide investigation. Informal meetings reinforce relationships and encourage cooperation. It is usually during these informal exchanges that certain barriers to communication and misunderstandings can be discussed and eliminated. I have found from personal experience that the more frequent the meetings, the more candid the dialogue.

When reporters and police have been in daily contact over a period of time, they can come to a mutual understanding whereby both groups can benefit. This relationship, however, should never be abused, since any breach of trust on the part of either party may destroy in an instant a relationship which took years to develop.

News media people who handle crime stories pride themselves on their ability to develop sources of information within any given police agency. Similarly, homicide officials should also strive to develop sources and relationships within the media which are mutually beneficial and serve an intelligent investigative end. If the homicide spokesman has developed a good rapport with certain news media representatives, he or she may be able to obtain news coverage, which can benefit an investigation, for a case which ordinarily wouldn't be considered newsworthy enough.

Sometimes, a case which must be kept "under wraps" comes to the attention of the news media through other sources. If there has been an effective and cooperative relationship between the media and the agency, a request to withhold the story pending some investigative consideration will usually be granted. However, the agency cannot expect the news media to cover up an otherwise newsworthy event. Practically speaking, when you take the media into your confidence on a particularly sensitive case, you will have to rely on their good intentions and judgment not to compromise the investigation or prematurely release information to the public. However, by taking them into your confidence you have effectively made them part of the "team" and psychologically have set the tone for a cooperative venture.

I can recall many cases over the years which the media had access to and, upon conferring with the chief investigator, delayed release to give police the opportunity to perform a specific investigative step.

The key word in building relationships is *credibility* — the law enforcement representative and the news media person must be honest with each other if this relationship is to survive. If each can come to rely on the other's credibility, tested by time, there can evolve a compatible arrangement between the police and the press.

I remember reading about a particularly sensational murder case in which a news reporter purposely ignored a request by the police to withhold certain information. This official request was made when it had become apparent that the reporter had become aware of certain confidential information through a series of "leaks." In fact, the chief investigator had personally asked this reporter not to print this information. Instead, this reporter published a blow-by-blow description of every piece of physical evidence and detail of the murder investigation. This caused irreparable damage to the investigation, created additional legal problems, and embarrassed the police officials involved. Needless to say, such an obvious violation of trust destroyed not only this reporter's credibility with the agency concerned, but all future contacts between the news media and police officials in this jurisdiction. The agency subsequently changed its policy for dealing with the news media and has drastically curtailed the release of information to the press.

Hopefully, such situations as described above are the exception, not the rule. However, law enforcement personnel must be aware of such possibilities and take appropriate measures to prevent disclosures which may adversely affect the outcome of a case.

Homicide News Release Policy

The indiscriminate release of information in a homicide investigation is an invitation to disaster. An erroneous or improper statement can damage the confidentiality of the investigation, the future prosecution, the reputation of the department, the rights of the accused, or the sensibilities of the family of the victim. Therefore, I have provided the following guidelines for officers to follow in the dissemination of information to the news media:

1. During the investigative stage, all information from the police department should come from one person and one person only. Generally, this person should be the detective supervisor, the chief investigator, or some other ranking officer, so designated in advance. The reason for this restriction should be obvious. The person in charge of the investigation is familiar with all phases and will be aware of those items which can or cannot be released because of legal or investigative reasons.

2. Designating one person to handle news releases allows reporters an opportunity to obtain information about the case without interfering with operations at the scene. More importantly, however, it precludes the possibility of having conflicting information emanating from members of the same department. This tight control is necessary and all members of the department must abide by this rule if its purposes are not to be defeated.

3. Officers at the scene can and should expect news reporters to be present. It is a mistake to treat the news media rudely or shut them off entirely. Frequently, they can be exceedingly helpful in uncovering information which is valuable to the case. Officers on the scene or wherever any investigative activity is taking place may be approached and asked to comment on the investigation. All they need do is explain that the department will make information available to them through the person designated for this function "to assure equal treatment and accurate information."

The homicide investigator is expected to act as a professional and should handle each media contact in a manner which encourages cooperation.

4. The detective supervisor or designated police spokesman should confer with the medical examiner and the prosecutor in these early stages, so as to avoid any confusion or embarrassment from conflicting or inappropriate releases being issued by the various officers. During the preliminary activities only the police agency charged with the responsibility of conducting the homicide investigation should be making any official news-release statements. Later on, after the autopsy, the medical examiner and/or coroner may elect to make an appropriate statement as to cause of death. However, all initial statements as to investigative inquiry, discovery of a body, or arrest of suspected persons lies within the jurisdiction of the police. During the prosecutorial stage, beginning with the suspect's arraignment, all information about the case should come from the office of the prosecutor. Practically speaking, this thin line of jurisdictial prerogative can oftentimes result in conflict or embarrassment, particularly in sensational murder cases — the appropriate source to make the news release is determined by the expertise and authority of the agency concerned, whether investigatory, medical, or prosecutorial.

5. When releasing details of the homicide investigation, do not furnish the name of the deceased until there has been an acceptable identification and the next of kin have been notified. In some instances, the media will have been able to ascertain the identity from police radio transmissions, teletype alarms, bystanders, witnesses, etc. In these cases, a request should be made that they withhold this information pending official notification to the family. Generally such a request will be complied with. However, in keeping with the theme of mutual cooperation, the media should be advised when the police have notified next of kin so they may properly file their story.

6. In cases where the perpetrator has not been arrested and the investigation for suspects is continuing, it is imperative that certain information be withheld. During the course of a murder investigation, news items appearing in the press may be helpful or harmful depending on what *preparation* has been given to what is said. One of the classic means of establishing the veracity of a confession is to have the suspect give information which only the actual perpetrator could know. The more sensational

the case, the more the likelihood of persons coming forward with false information or even confessions. Obviously, it is always wise to withhold certain information from the media. This will preserve the integrity of the investigation.

7. When talking to the media, do not permit yourself to be maneuvered into a situation where you theorize or speculate, where you make predictions, or where you give personal opinions about the case. Statements such as "We expect to have the suspect in custody within the next 24 hours" have come back to haunt many an officer foolish enough to make that prediction. Such a personal observation can do nothing to assist the investigation and may, in fact, become a liability later on. The investigator is a fact finder, open to all possibilities. When asked, "Is it possible … Could he have … Have you ruled out …," the most practical approach is to merely state, "At this time, we are keeping all of our options open, and we would rather not speculate on any specific possibility."

8. Never pose for photographs, either at the scene or when transporting the suspect. Posed photographs can create the wrong impression with the public and can create legal problems during the prosecution. If the press is able to take photos outside the crime scene area of the investigators as they carry out their duties at the scene, there shouldn't be any problems. However, officers should be cognizant of their presence and maintain a professional demeanor.

9. If the news release is a taped interview, which will be aired on television or radio, the police spokesman should be aware that whatever he or she says will be recorded. It is best to prepare oneself by writing out, prior to the interview, a brief narrative account of the event, being careful to withhold information which might adversely affect the case. Prior to the actual taping, the news media people will usually go over your release and ask certain questions. This is done for their own benefit so that they can get a "feel" for the case. Practically speaking, this preliminary question-and-answer session can benefit both parties. The questions which are asked during this preliminary conference are basically the same questions which the reporter will be asking you on tape, so you will have an idea of the type of questions you will be responding to.

   If there is a particular question which you cannot answer, either for legal or strategic reasons, explain this to the news media people and set the ground rules. It is important to note that the entire interview will usually not be broadcast but will be edited to fit into an allotted amount of time. Therefore, to be sure that the interview gives the complete coverage you desire, stick to short and concise sentences.

Sometimes a reporter will try to force an issue by waiting for the television lights to go on and the camera to start rolling and then purposely ask a question which you had previously indicated you couldn't answer. At this point, without hesitation, look directly into the camera and state, "Excuse me, Mr. or Ms. So-and-So, I told you before we went on camera that it would be improper for me to respond to that question." I am pretty sure you will not be bothered by that kind of question again. However, more importantly, you will have maintained control over the interview and not compromised the investigation.

10. The news media provide an excellent vehicle for making appeals to the public for information. I have found that media personnel will usually make a special effort to assist law enforcement officials in requesting public assistance in a homicide investigation. For example, an unidentified body may be found whose physical qualities or possessions and clothing can be described. An appeal can be made through the media to ascertain if anyone recognizes the description with a request to call police with any information. A general appeal can also be made to anyone with information on a specifically heinous crime to obtain citizen involvement, thereby reaching persons not readily available through ordinary investigative means. It is usually a good idea to stress the fact that callers can remain anonymous, if they desire, and that the information will remain confidential.

The Offering of Rewards

A question often arises regarding rewards and what role the police should play. The offering of rewards usually results in additional unproductive investigative time as police check out vague tips which offer no help with the investigation. However, there is always the possibility that someone will come forward with useful information. It is usually better not to discourage the offer of a reward, even though it means more wasted effort. If the police reject the offer, they risk criticism for not doing everything possible to find the murderer. However, there should be two stipulations in connection with any reward offer: (1) no law enforcement officer is eligible to receive it; and (2) any information must be given directly to the police.

Handling the News Media at the Scene

News media people at the scene should be advised that any information will come from the homicide supervisor and not the officers who are actually working on the case. News media people usually learn about the homicide through police radio transmissions. All police press rooms monitor the police communications system, and most media organizations maintain mobile units which are similarly equipped that will respond to the scene. In some instances, these reporters will arrive before the investigators. First officers who are maintaining lines at the scene should tactfully explain to these media representatives that information will be made available to them as soon as possible by the homicide commander. Point out that it would be unfair to make information available to some members of the press which would not be equally available to all others. I have seen some police officers handle this situation quite tactfully, while others have embarrassed me by their ignorance or rudeness. In any event, most news media people who have dealt with the police before can appreciate the emergency nature of this preliminary phase of the homicide investigation, and they realize that any information must come from a ranking official. If there is a good, consistent homicide news-release policy, the media will usually cooperate.

It should be noted that members of the news media have a right to be present at the scene and perform their task of gathering information. However, this right to be present at the scene and gather news information does not include interfering with the police investigation, nor entering restricted areas such as the crime scene where valuable evidence may be lost or destroyed.

In homicide cases there are usually police lines established to prevent unauthorized persons from entering the scene. In most instances, news media people who are authorized to cross police lines to cover stories will be allowed entry. This entry is permissible as long as it does not interfere with police operations, jeopardize the integrity of the scene, or create a hazard. Witnesses or suspects who are being detained must be kept away from the media. However, the press should generally be permitted to report or photograph anything they observe while legally present at an emergency scene. Where publication of specific items would interfere with the investigation or place witnesses, suspects, or others in jeopardy, the homicide official in charge should advise the reporters and their editors of the consequences of publication and request their cooperation. If some member of the media is pushy or overzealous and threatens the security of the scene or interferes with the police operation, merely exercise intelligent police procedure and physically remove him or her from the crime scene just as you would any other unauthorized person.

In homicide cases, especially in the preliminary stages of the investigation at the scene, uniformed officers and detectives assigned to the case are usually in possession of information which must be withheld from the general public; for example, the identity of the deceased prior to notification of next of kin. News media people who have responded to the murder scene are anxious to obtain as much information as possible to "cover the story." Usually they will question bystanders and others at the scene in order to get a feel for the story, and probably will ask any officers present for information about the case. These officers must keep in mind that certain disclosures may harm the investigation, subvert justice, or infringe on individual rights to privacy. The professional response to such inquiry is simply to refer these reporters to the detective supervisor.

The more sensational murder cases and those involving well-known persons or celebrities result in a more aggressive style of reporting, as the various representatives from different news organizations strive to meet deadlines or outscoop each other. In situations like these, various pressures will escalate and strain relationships. The highest degree of cooperation between the police and the media will be necessary in order to reduce this pressure and neutralize these strains before they get out of hand.

There must be a policy as to what kind of information is given and who is to release it. Only one person should make the press release. If the release represents the formal position of the department, the public information officer should perform the duty. If the release is a news briefing of an active investigation, the homicide supervisor, who has been kept up to date on the investigation, is in the best position to determine what information can and cannot be released. This eliminates the possibility of two or more detectives independently releasing conflicting details or facts. News items given by others working on the case are usually a source of trouble, because jealousies can be created and information which embarrasses other phases of the investigation may result.

Generally, the chances for a successful outcome of the investigation are improved by being completely candid with the press. If the press is aware of what information should not be prematurely released and is kept informed of developments, they will be more receptive to investigative requests. If every minute detail of the crime appears in the local paper, it will be impossible to determine the truthfulness of some statement by the suspect later on.

Remember, always withhold certain details of the crime which only the murderer and the police can know about.

In connection with photographs, the police should neither discourage nor encourage reporters from taking pictures of a suspect.

Remember, prisoners should never be posed or allowed to make statements to the press.

However, if suspects or prisoners are in a public place, news media people are allowed to take pictures, just as they are allowed to take pictures of officers at the scene performing their duties. The identity of the suspect prior to arrest should not ordinarily be made public unless in the opinion of the homicide supervisor such information is necessary to assist in the apprehension of a suspect or warn the public of a possible danger. Photographs should likewise be released only if they serve a valid purpose such as identifying a victim or enlisting public assistance in finding a fugitive suspect.

From an investigative point of view, I would advise you to be very careful in making any predictions about solution or arrest, regardless of what your prospects appear to be at the moment. I remember one case which involved a shoot-out in a local social club. Although we had a double homicide on our hands, we had been able to determine within hours the identity of the shooter. I must admit it was very tempting to tell the press that we knew who did it and that we would be making an arrest imminently. The two victims had been innocent of any involvement in the shooting and were merely patrons in the club who had been caught in a cross-fire. The resultant community concern and subsequent media attention added to the pressure for immediate action. However, my gut feeling was based on knowledge of the "players," and so I merely indicated the basic facts — there were two dead, apparently the innocent victims of a shooting between two groups, and police were investigating to determine what person or persons were responsible. Later on, I was glad to have taken this route. The suspect wasn't apprehended for 3 months and then only after a tremendous amount of time and effort.

At-the-scene news releases can be just as effective as the formal news release if you maintain your composure and control.

> Remember, know what you are going to say and how you are going to say it.

Before you speak, consider the following:

1. Will the release cause the suspect to flee?
2. What information should be held for future interrogation?
3. Does the information you are releasing hinder the investigation?
4. Is the information released consistent with department policy?

Preparing the News Release

The news release in homicide investigations should either be personally prepared by the homicide supervisor or by the public information officer after consulting the homicide official. As mentioned earlier, the homicide commander is in the best position to know what can and cannot be released in any given case.

A basic principle to keep in mind is that the news release is an investigative tool which represents the official police position in the investigation. Therefore, any news release and subsequent news media coverage should be included in the official case folder because it is a public record and may ultimately affect the outcome of the investigation. The news release should be written in a clear and comprehensible manner and its organization and style should be simple and direct.

The acronym NEOTWY — when, where, who, what, how, and why should be considered when preparing the news release, and the following items should be included in the release.

1. The date and time of the homicide. (Avoid reference to military time and express the time in civilian hours; for example, 9:30 P.M. instead of 2130 hours.)
2. The exact location of the homicide.
3. The name of the deceased, if proper notification has been made to next of kin, and residence.
4. The type of homicide (gunshot, stabbing, etc.).
5. The facts of the preliminary investigation, including a summary of how the homicide occurred and the present status of the case.
6. The motive, if known.
7. If there are any arrests, the name, address, and age of the suspect(s) including nicknames and background information.

INVERTED PYRAMID

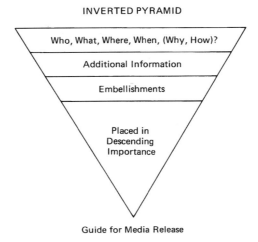

Guide for Media Release

Figure 19.1. **THE INVERTED PYRAMID.**

8. The exact charge or charges. (This refers to the charge under which the suspect was arrested. If there is a possibility of other charges, simply state, "additional charges pending.")
9. Place of the arrest and facts and circumstances surrounding it.
10. Officers involved in the investigation.

There are different methods for constructing the news release. One method which is recommended by journalists and students of communication is the "inverted pyramid." According to Charles W. Steinmetz, Instructor at the FBI Academy and an expert in the area of mass media and effective communication, the inverted pyramid is effective because it meets police requirements and can help avoid a distorted or rewritten story. Place the facts in a diminishing order of importance, with the most important facts at the top, or beginning, of the release, and the lesser facts placed in order of descending importance. This allows for shortening the article by a newspaper without changing the official facts of the release.

The length of the release depends on how much information the agency wishes to make available in any given homicide. I recommend that the spokesman first write out a narrative description of the event before making any official release. Then he or she can review the statement and eliminate information which might hinder the investigation. An example of a completed release is as follows:

I am (<u>name of official</u>) of (<u>name of agency</u>). On (<u>date and time</u>) the body of a (<u>male or female</u>) identified as (<u>name</u>) was found at (<u>location</u>). (He or She) had been (<u>shot, stabbed, etc.</u>). Investigation revealed that the deceased had been killed during (<u>robbery, etc.</u>). At this time the investigation (<u>is continuing, indicates, etc.</u>).

or

An arrest has been effected in connection with this investigation. The suspect is identified as (<u>name, age, address, nickname, etc.</u>). (He or She) was arrested at (<u>location</u>) and has been charged with (<u>charges</u>). (Relationship of victim to suspect optional.) The officers assigned to this investigation are (<u>names</u>).

Of course each department should design a format which suits its particular needs.

Handling Questions During News Conferences

If the murder case is a sensational type of homicide, or there is a considerable amount of public interest in the investigation, the agency will usually hold a news conference when they release the information. During these news conferences certain "loaded" questions may be asked by the media representative. The best course for the homicide spokesman to follow is to give straightforward and honest answers to such questions within the framework of his or her investigative priorities. The following suggestions are provided as a guide.

1. Repeat each question to the group. This will allow you to clear the question in your own mind, bide time, and allow the group to hear the question.
2. Avoid the original questioner, instead directing your response to the group.
3. Avoid a one-to-one exchange.
4. Keep your answers short and concise.
5. Rephrase unclear questions.
6. Have the question repeated if unclear.
7. Defuse and depersonalize antagonistic questions.
8. If you do not know the answer or cannot answer the question because of some legal or strategic reason, say so.
9. Do not allow yourself to theorize, speculate, or make predictions.

Conclusion

The homicide official who recognizes and understands the role of the news media and follows the principles and guidelines discussed in this chapter will better be able to deal with press inquiries and news releases as they relate to homicide investigations.

Sooner or later, every community will experience a murder case which arouses widespread attention. The results can be catastrophic if no thought has been given on how to deal with this situation. The subsequent pressure of the media blitz as reporters try to get the best story for their particular news agency mandates that there be a sensible news release policy. Although the police will not be able to manipulate the media, they can use the news release as a tool in performing certain functions. For instance, the release of certain information may stimulate the investigation, while withholding certain facts guarantees that only the police and the killer are aware of them. Good relations between the media and the police will keep pressures at a minimum.

Police agencies must strive to protect the rights of the victim's family, the rights of the accused, and the right to knowledge of society in general. Sometimes under the pressure of major media organizations this is not always possible. However, somewhere between the right of freedom of the press — as guaranteed in the First Amendment — and the rights of the accused — as specified in the Sixth Amendment — there exists a delicate balance. It can be maintained if there is cooperation and good faith between the news media and the law enforcement agency.

Selected Reading

Geberth, Vernon J. "The News Media in Homicide Investigation," *Law and Order Magazine,* Vol. 29, No. 7, Illinois, July, 1981.

Shaw, David. *Journalism Today — A Changing Press for a Changing America.* New York: Harper College Press, 1977.

Steinmetz, Charles W. "The News Release as a Tool." *Law and Order Magazine,* July 1980.

Steimetz, Charles W. "No Comment ... Law Enforcement and the Media." *F.B.I. Law Enforcement Bulletin,* July 1979.

Identification of Suspects 20

The purpose of this chapter is to familiarize homicide detectives with the availability of certain technical and psychological tools, which can be utilized in professional investigations. Practically speaking, these techniques may be limited to specific cases. However, they are viable adjuncts to the investigation and may provide additional facts, information, and identification of suspects. In order to acquaint detectives with these investigative methodologies, I have provided information, case histories, and recommendations for the following techniques:

Bite mark identification
Hypnosis
Latent prints on human skin
Polygraph
Psycholinguistics
Psychics
Munchausen Syndrome by Proxy (MSBP)
Stalkers
VI-CAP, State-Wide and Regional Information Systems

Bite-Mark Identification

The purpose of this section is to acquaint investigators with practical information and procedures which can be employed in the investigation of homicides involving bite-mark evidence. Bite marks are usually

Figure 20.1.   **HIGH-CONTRAST ENHANCEMENT OF BITE MARK.** From the Florida v. Bundy case. (Courtesy of Dr. Lowell J. Levine, Forensic Odontologist.)

Figure 20.2.   **BITE MARK.** Subtle bite mark on the cheek of a child assaulted and murdered by another child. (Courtesy of Dr. Lowell J. Levine, Forensic Odontologist.)

found in cases involving extremely emotional and violent episodes such as child abuse, felonious assault, sexual assault, and sex-related homicides. However, in order for investigators to utilize this evidence, they must first be able to recognize and discover the existence of this type of

Figure 20.3. **BITE MARKS FROM A SADISTIC BREAST ASSAULT.** Multiple bite marks were inflicted upon the breast of a victim, who survived an attack by a serial killer. (Courtesy of Lt. Frank P. Del Prete, Bergen County Prosecutor's Office, Bergen County, New Jersey.)

Figure 20.4. Photograph of bite-mark wound with ruler in place to show actual size. (Courtesy of Dr. Arthur D. Goldman, Forensic Odontologist.)

wound. I have included various photos of bite-marks herein to assist investigators in making this observation.

The homicide detective will obviously need the expertise of a forensic odontologist to interpret this type of evidence. Here we will look at certain basic steps which investigators must employ at the scene in order to assist the odontologist in his evaluations.

Forensic odontology has become a highly important and technically complex area, as a medicolegal investigation of bite-mark evidence has proved to be successful in many noteworthy cases which have occurred in recent years. The "Theodore Bundy" case in Florida is an example of the value of bite-mark evidence in homicide investigations. Bundy, who was convicted for murder, had inflicted bite marks on his victims during sexual assaults. These were examined by forensic odontologist who later testified with reasonable medical and dental certainty at the trial that the defendant had inflicted the bite marks.

The Bite Mark

Practically speaking, the bite mark should be viewed as an additional piece of evidence which may be utilized to identify a suspect. The teeth are actually used by people as "tools," and, in the simplest terms, tooth marks are tool marks. It has been well documented that owing to such factors as size, shape, wear, rotations, restorations, fillings, loss of certain teeth, and accidental characteristics such as breakage and injury, no two sets of teeth are exactly alike. The relative positions of the teeth, their width, and the distance between them together with ridges on the edges of the teeth and grooves on the back or front, vary for different individuals. These factors provide the forensic odontologist with specific and characteristic information about the person who has inflicted the bite mark and can be used to positively identify a suspect.

Generally, tooth marks come from the front teeth in the upper and lower jaws. The type of impression varies with the age of the individual. For example, children and young people have ridges on the lower edges of their front teeth, while persons over 20 years of age generally have front teeth which are smoother.

Bite mark identification is not limited to skin. Teeth leave impressions or scraping marks in the form of bite marks in chewing gum, cheese, fruit, chocolate, and similar materials. The discovery of a piece of discarded chewing gum at the scene of a homicide should certainly be considered a significant find. Its value is not only in its distinctive bite-mark impressions, but also in its ability to yield additional in-

Figure 20.5. **DEFENSIVE BITE ON A PERPETRATOR.** The victim, who was killed by her assailant managed to inflict her teeth marks on the perpetrator. (Courtesy of Dr. Arthur D. Goldman, Forensic Odontologist.)

Figure 20.6. **VICTIM'S TEETH.** Reconstruction of bite mark using a mold of the victim's teeth placed over the wound on the perpetrator. (Courtesy of Dr. Arthur D. Goldman, Forensic Odontologist.)

Figure 20.7.   **FRESH BITE WITHOUT DETAIL.** (Courtesy of Dr. Arthur D. Goldman, Forensic Odontologist.)

formation through a serological test to determine the blood grouping as well as DNA analysis of the suspect who chewed the gum.

According to Dr. Lowell Levine,[1] the markings found on the skin of a victim are more than just marks. The musculature of the lips, tongue, and cheeks, and the mental state of the biter, all seem to play a role in the infliction of the tooth-mark pattern on the skin. The skin itself contributes to the bite mark in that it is elastic, yielding, and variable from body area to body area and from body to body. Most bite marks

---

[1] Dr. Lowell J. Levine was President of the American Academy of Forensic Sciences. He is presently Consultant in Forensic Dentistry for the New York State Police.

Figure 20.8. **SAME BITE WITH TISSUE REFLECTED.** A subcutaneous view of the area shows capillary bleeding and detail of the bite mark. (Courtesy of Dr. Arthur D. Goldman, Forensic Odontologist.)

are found in the following types of homicides: (1) the homicide victim involved in sexual activity around the time of death; and (2) the battered-child homicide victim.

Sexually oriented homicides can be either homosexual or heterosexual and may involve voluntary sexual activity or forcible attack. Child victims may be either battered children or children murdered by other children in a single homicide assault. According to Dr. Levine, there are two types of bite-mark patterns:

1. Those which are inflicted slowly, almost sadistically, exhibiting a central *ecchymotic area* or "suck mark," and a radiating linear abrasion pattern surrounding the central area resembling a sunburst. This type is most often found in the sexually oriented homicide.
2. The second type more closely resembles a tooth-mark pattern. This is an attack or defense bite-mark and is seen most often in the battered-child type of homicide.

Figure 20.9.   **DOUBLE BITE WOUND.** Child abuse case. (Courtesy of Dr. Arthur D. Goldman, Forensic Odontologist.)

Collection of Bite-Mark Evidence at the Scene

The proper handling of bite-mark evidence begins at the scene of the crime where the homicide investigator must initiate procedures to insure that it is not destroyed or lost. The best course of action is to secure photographs of the bite-mark wounds. If the material is other than skin, consideration must be given to casting the object. Bite marks are usually found in materials which cannot be kept for long periods of time; once the materials have dried up or decomposed, the bite mark's appearance will change drastically and be of no value to the odontologist. It is therefore imperative to obtain photographs or casts of the bite mark before the material begins to change. Even if an object is to be cast, the bite mark should first be photographed in case the casting goes wrong. These first photographs are usually taken by the police photographer at the scene, followed by medical examiner photographs taken at autopsy. I recommend that the investigator take photos of any pattern of injury he or she observes on the body while at the scene, giving special attention to any ovoid-shaped wounds or marks which are less than 2 inches in diameter.

Figure 20.10.   Example of the type of ruler that should be used to photograph wound structures. (Courtesy of Dr. Arthur D. Goldman, Forensic Odontologist.)

The following procedures at the crime scene are recommended.

Photographs of the Bite-Mark Wound

1. The best type of camera to utilize is the Fingerprint type, which gives a 1 × 1 exposure or life-size photo of the wound.
2. Use a rule of measure in the photo to document size. The rule which is used should not be white in color because white is not conducive to enhancement (see example of ruler).
3. Use oblique lighting to enhance bite mark.
4. Provide for an anatomical landmark in photo.
5. Take photos in black-and-white and color.
6. Take an overall photo and a close-up of each wound.
7. Do not throw away any "bad" shots but save all negatives and photos. They are evidence.

Saliva Washings

1. Take a saliva washing of the bite-mark area for blood grouping and serological examination.
2. Washing should be done with distilled water and 100% cotton. Start at the periphery and work inward; use a separate swab for each bite mark. (If there is no distilled water available, use tap water, but take a control sample for examination.)
3. Air dry each swab.
4. Place each swab in a separate container, preferably a sterile test tube.
5. Take a saliva swab from victim for control.
6. Take a controlled swab from an area of the body other than bite mark.
7. Label each sample; keep items separate.

Remember, always keep track of the chain of custody.

Interpretation of the Bite-Mark Evidence

The interpretation of the bite mark requires the forensic odontologist to consider at least four factors:

1. The teeth of the biter.
2. Distortion.
3. The mental state of the biter at the time the bite was inflicted.
4. The portion of the body upon which the bite was inflicted.

Bite marks have been found almost everywhere on the body. However, certain patterns are most prominent in particular kinds of cases. For example, homosexual cases often involve bite marks of the back, arms, shoulders, axillae (armpits, face, and scrotum of the victim). Heterosexual cases usually involve the breasts and thighs. Battered children most often have randomly placed bite marks on the cheeks, back, and sides. However, bite marks on battered children have also been found on the abdomen, scrotum, and buttocks. In child cases, the biting seems to be done in a rapid, random, and enraged manner leaving tissue laceration, diffuse areas, and poor detail, as opposed to sexually associated bite marks, usually inflicted in a slow and sadistic manner and resulting in excellent detail.

Factors such as size and shape are helpful in establishing whether the bite mark was inflicted by a human being or an animal. If the bite mark is human, the time it was inflicted (antemortem or post-mortem), tissue reaction of the surrounding area, and position of the body when found are all taken into consideration by the odontologist.

Examination of the Bite Mark

The examination of the bite mark by a forensic odontologist can generally provide the investigator with sufficient information to rapidly include or exclude a suspect in a particular investigation. For instance, in a case involving a battered child, only a limited number of persons would have the opportunity to bite and murder the child. The suspect in such cases might include one or two adults (the mother and father) and siblings. On the basis of the size of the arch, the forensic odontologist can usually determine whether the attacker was an adult or a child. In addition, there may be enough individual characteristics (wear, missing teeth, dental restorations, rotations, arch form, etc.) to exclude all but the perpetrator of the bite.

The forensic examination includes the following procedures:

1. Saliva washings of the area for blood grouping (using 100% cotton dampened in distilled water).
2. Photographs of the bite mark:
   a. 1 × 1 camera fingerprint type model
   b. Black and white and color photographs
   c. Rule of measure
   d. Anatomical landmark
3. Examination of dental casts of possible suspects. Models of the teeth of all suspects which will subsequently be used for comparisons are taken only by informed consent or by court order. The models are made either by the forensic odontologist or another licensed dentist. This varies from case to case and from court order to court order. All models, however, are made according to accepted dental standards and labeled for evidentiary purposes.
4. Comparisons are made of the life-size photographs of the bite marks with bite marks made in wax either by the suspect or by models of the suspect's teeth.
5. A report is prepared indicating whether the bite marks are or are not consistent with the teeth of the suspect.

The Detection and Documentation of Trace Wound Patterns by Use of an Alternative Light Source

Alternate light source is more specifically the florescent light emitted by skin when illuminated by a 450-nanometer blue light. The enhancement or discovery of patterned injuries on the bodies of victims greatly enhanced the investigative process. The technique is possible because of the phenomenon of Stokes shift. This occurs when light strikes human skin. Some of the light is reflected and some is transmitted to deeper layers. Some is scattered and some is absorbed by molecules in the tissues known as chromophores. The molecules and atoms of the tissue that absorbs part of the energy of the light become excited, and the electrons within these atoms may move to higher energy orbits. Upon the return of these electrons to their normal, nonexcited states, they release energy which can be a photon (a quantum of light energy). In other words, they will glow or to use the scientific term, the "fluoresce."[2]

Alternate light sources have been used by law enforcement to scan bodies and crime scenes to obtain evidence such as fibers (with ultraviolet light), fingerprints, trace metals, and body fluids (blue light) not visible through other methods. A new method of detecting and photographing wound patterns on skin utilizes the fluorescent light emitted when skin is illuminated by ultraviolet or blue light. This technique is referred to as Narrow Band Imaging and is based on the fact that healthy tissue fluoresces and unhealthy, damaged, or diseased tissue does not. In this manner a wound pattern appears as a dark image against an illuminated screen of healthy tissue. The image can be viewed or photographed through UV- or blue-blocking filters and recorded on standard photographic film or video tape.

The author consulted with Dr. Russell E. Schneider, D.D.S., Dr. Carl Hagstrom, D.D.S., and Dr. Mary A. Cimrmancic D.D.S. of the Northern Illinois Forensic Odontologic Consultants Group[3] relative to this procedure. Figure 20.11 is a series of four photographs illustrating the value of Narrow Band Imaging.

---

[2] West, Michael, D.D.S.; Barsley, Robert E., D.D.S., J.D.; Hall, John, D.M.D.; Hayne, Steve, M.D.; and Cimrmancic, Mary A., D.D.S. "The Detection and Documentation of Trace Wound Patterns by Use of an Alternative Light Source." *Journal of Forensic Sciences*, November, 1992.

[3] Personal interview with Dr. Russel E. Schneider, D.D.S., relative to Alternate Light Source technology, May 30, 1995.

The photos show a wound pattern removed from the thigh of the female victim of an unsolved homicide. The wound was previously determined to be a bite mark and comparison of standard photos of the wound to the dentition of the prime suspect resulted in an "inconclusive" match. One year after the crime the investigation had stalled, the above odontologists were asked to evaluate the dental comparison. They proceeded to evaluate the specimen utilizing both standard and alternate photographic techniques. Figure 20.11.A shows the pattern as photographed in white light. There are clearly separate marks with underlying bruising in the pattern consistent with a bite mark. Figure B shows the pattern in reflective ultraviolet light. The pattern is similar but more defined because the UV light is reflected primarily from the skin surface, hence effectively eliminating the underlying bruising. Figure C demonstrates the fluorescence produced in skin by UV light as viewed through a W blocking filter. Again the photo provides crisp surface definition and minimizes the bruise. The image in Figure D utilizes the fluorescent light emitted by the skin when illuminated by a 450-nanometer blue light and viewed through a blue light blocking filter.

Figure D shows wound detail not seen in the other photos, and conclusively demonstrates that the wound is not a bite mark. Because the blue light penetrates 1.5 mm into the tissue, the fluorescent image is a record of the wound from that depth. Note that the surface of the skin presents as a diffuse blurry image when compared to the other photos, because blue light is not reflected from the surface but from below. Clearly, the pattern consists of a well-defined double line produced by a mechanism other than teeth.

Upon presentation of this information to the investigating agency, the case was re-opened but remains unsolved.

This case illustrates how all evidence of a wound pattern may not be gathered unless the technique of Narrow Band Illumination is incorporated. The result of not having all pertinent information or having misleading information can result in the thwarting of the investigative process.

Summary

The application of forensic odontology to bite-mark identification, and matching a serological group with a saliva washing of the suspected bite mark, are two viable investigative techniques which can provide the investigator with the necessary evidence to present a case for prosecution.

A

B

C

D

Figure 20.11.

Bite-mark identification has been recognized by the superior courts of several jurisdictions in noteworthy homicide trials. It is the opinion of the author that this excellent investigative technique should be utilized in every case of homicide involving bite marks. Even in cases where there has been a confession or other evidence linking the suspect to the crime, bite-mark evidence should still be obtained and submitted to the forensic odontologist. There is no such thing as "enough evidence" in homicide prosecution.

Remember, bite-mark identification represents individual characteristic evidence which can positively identify a suspect.

Hypnosis

The purpose of the section is to acquaint the homicide detective with the utilization of hypnosis in murder investigations.[4] In addition, there is a discussion of psychodynamics, the science pertaining to motives and other causative factors in mental life, and how these factors can affect the outcome of an investigation.

What is Hypnosis?

The word hypnosis is derived from the Greek word *hypnos* which means "sleep." However, the person under hypnosis is not really asleep but is aware of his or her surroundings. Hypnosis may be defined as "an altered state of consciousness involving focused attention, heightened awareness, and concentration."[5] The person in a hypnotic state can increase his or her capacity to restructure events by reorganizing his or her usual perceptions of things.

Psychodynamics

In order to comprehend how hypnosis works, it is useful to understand the systems of the mind referred to as the conscious, preconscious, and unconscious. The conscious consists of the thoughts, feelings, and actions we are aware of. The preconscious includes mental activity that we can be aware of if we attend to it. It will receive and remember those impressions that are classified as "safe," i.e., that have passed the screen-

---

[4] The technical data on hypnosis are based on materials and information provided by Sergeant Timothy P. Byrnes, former Commanding Officer of the New York City Police Department's Hypnosis Unit.

[5] Martin Raiser. *Handbook of Investigative Hypnosis.* Los Angeles, California: Lehi Publishing Co., 1980, p. 30.

ing of the ego's defenses. According to Sgt. Byrnes, these defenses ward off that which is dangerous and harmful to the ego. The unconscious contains all the rest of our memories, including the "unsafe" ones, which are not available for recall. This is why witnesses to very traumatic crime situations such as homicides are often unable to recall what they have seen. The investigator should be aware that this is not a deliberate effort on the part of these individuals to frustrate the investigation. They may very well not recall "seeing" the details of the incident in the trauma situation.

The unconscious consists of approximately seven-eighths of the brain. It not only receives repressed material that has been blocked by the defenses and classified as "harmful," but also stores impulses which were conscious and preconscious at one time. Furthermore, it is alert to responses on a 24-hour-a-day basis. It never sleeps. It records every stimulus regardless of the condition of the conscious of the individual. Thus, in spite of intoxication or trauma, accurate records are being received and recorded by the senses and stored in the subconscious.

Value to the Investigator

Hypnosis offers the homicide investigator a means of obtaining additional information, and its application in certain murder investigations has been very effective. Hypnosis has been used to enable people to recall names, places, or details including the actual verbalizations which took place during the crime. In addition, there are many cases in which persons under hypnosis have described vehicles including make, model, color, and complete license number.

When a person is hypnotized, the conscious mind is somewhat subdued. This allows the subconscious to become a little more active. When the hypnotist talks to the person under hypnosis, the subconscious mind is more acceptable to what it is told and governs the body accordingly. In other words, a person in a hypnotic state is prone to the suggestions of the hypnotist who acts as a guide. Thus, hypnosis and other related techniques designed to remove trauma may enable the subject to recall that which was stored in the subconscious and relate this information to the hypnotist in a clear and concise fashion.

Shortcomings of Hypnosis

There are some shortcomings of hypnosis which should be understood by the investigator prior to using this technique.

1. People can lie while under hypnosis. Although it is not policy to routinely explain this to the subject to be hypnotized, it should be noted that if the investigator seeks to know whether or not the subject is telling the truth, the polygraph should be employed. Hypnosis is not truth serum.
2. People see and remember things in various manners. Recollection may be colored by previous experience. Therefore, memory of numbers, letters, or phrases can be jumbled or mistakenly affiliated with previous associations.
3. The investigator must be vigilant about confabulation, whereby the mind fills in memory gaps with imagined or distorted information.

CASE HISTORY

The following case history is typical of those handled by the New York City Police Department's Hypnosis Unit.

An investigator called the unit and stated that he had reached a dead end in his investigation. He remarked that he only had one witness, who had looked out a window after the shooting. This witness was very quiet in nature but told police that the auto which the suspect had fled in was brown, and he was able to supply one number of the license plate.

At a prehypnosis introduction, Sgt. Byrnes noticed that the subject wore heavy, dark glasses that covered his eyes and part of his face. He spoke very little and nodded his yes-and-no answers, rather than saying them.

In conforming with legal parameters, the hypnotist was given limited information — only the subject's name, that he was a college graduate who lived alone, and that he had looked out the window after the shooting.

During the prehypnosis interview, the subject again only nodded when asked questions. Finally, when asked to relate the incident that he had witnessed, he replied slowly and with some difficulty. He suffered from a nervous condition of stammering, which was in fact totally out of character for this young educated individual. Apparently he was conscious of this condition and chose not to speak at length in order to avoid making the condition known to others.

Under hypnosis, Sgt. Byrnes asked him to remove his glasses, and thereby shed a defense mechanism. The subject did so and the session proceeded without incident until the discussion finally returned to the date and time in question. At that point, to the amazement of both Sgt. Byrnes and the investigator, the subject began to rapidly relate the details of the incident without even a trace of stammering. In addition, he provided the entire license plate number (explaining how he remembered the numbers in his own method of association), the type of vehicle, the conversation that he had heard immediately after the shooting, the description of the suspect, his route of travel, the fact that he had stopped and had a conversation with another person on a distant corner, and the fact that another person was present and had voiced his horror about the shooting (thereby supplying an additional witness to the crime).

As a direct result, the investigator was able to continue his investigation and eventually independently verify the veracity of the statements made by the subject under hypnosis. The result was an indictment for murder.

Sgt. Byrnes adds as a postscript that the subject of the hypnosis, immediately after the session, returned to his previous stammering condition.

Summary

Practically speaking, most law enforcement agencies using hypnosis have found this technique to be quite successful. It should be noted, however, that hypnosis is not the final answer. Any information obtained through this method must be independently corroborated by further investigation. From an investigative point of view, hypnosis may provide the police with additional facts and information and should be viewed as an additional investigative tool.

Latent Prints on Human Skin

There have been some recent advances in forensic science in the area of latent print development from human skin. The development of latent prints on human skin can be extremely valuable in homicide investigations and other crimes in which the perpetrator has touched the victim. Some of the methods used are simple and inexpensive, while other more advanced techniques require the use of a laser and other sophisticated equipment. The techniques presented in this section will be limited to those simple and practical methods which the average investigator can employ at the scene.

These methods are still in an experimental stage and may not be effective in all instances. However, their application should be encouraged, since fingerprints represent the ultimate piece of physical evidence in any criminal investigation. In homicide cases their presence takes on an added value because the victim, who is deceased, will never be able to "point the finger" at the suspect.

General Considerations

Experiments conducted in developing latent prints on human skin indicate that fingerprints on living skin seem to last for approximately

1 to $1^1/_2$ hours. In dead-body cases it is recommended that these procedures be employed as soon as possible. The state of the skin and atmospheric conditions will affect results. The ideal temperature is between 60 and 75°F.

Procedures

1. Kromekote lift technique or unexposed Polaroid film. This method involves the use of the following equipment:

   a. Fiberglass filament brush

   b. Black fingerprint powder

   c. Kromekote cards (15×7)[6]

   d. Unexposed Polaroid film can be substituted for Kromekote. The Kromekote card or unexposed Polaroid film is placed over the area of the skin where the suspected latent print is located, and pressure is applied to the card or film piece for approximately 3 seconds. The card or film is then carefully removed and dusted with the black fingerprint powder to develop the print which was transferred onto the card or film. The latent print obtained will be a mirror image of a normal print and can be reversed through photography.

2. Magna-Brush and powder direct to the skin: this method may be employed in the absence of Kromekote or unexposed Polaroid film, or in addition to the above procedure. The following equipment is necessary:

   a. Magna-Brush with magnetic powders

   b. Fiberglass filament brush with volcanic powders. The powder is applied directly to the skin. The use of volcanic or magnetic powders depends on the condition of the skin. When the skin is dry, you may obtain better results with the magnetic powder. If a print is developed, it should first be photographed using a 1×1 fingerprint camera. It is then lifted in conventional fashion, using cellophane "lifting" tape. Certain areas of the body will usually yield latent prints, because these areas are usually touched by the perpetrator, for example,

   i. Upper arms of the victim

   ii. Areas directly behind the ear and ear lobe

---

[6] The cards are similar to photographic paper, with a very high gloss. They are manufactured by various companies; however, unexposed Polaroid film can be used.

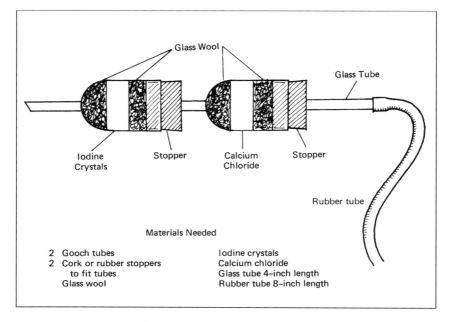

Figure 20.12.　**THE IODINE GUN.**

    iii. Inner thighs directly below the crotch area (sex cases)
    iv. Heels and skin around the ankles (body dragged)
    v. The neck area
    vi. Wrists

3. The Iodine-Silver Transfer Method.[7] The equipment needed for this procedure is as follows:

    a. Conventional iodine fuming gun

    b. A number of silver sheets approximately $2\leq$ square. These silver sheets should be between 0.005 and 0.010 inches thick in order to conform to the skin surface. These sheets can be cleaned with whiting or silver polish and may be reused.

    c. A strong light (photo floodlight is ideal).

There are four basic steps in this process, as follows.

---

[7] The following description is based on information in the FBI Police Instructor's Bulletin, Quantico, VA: Law Enforcement Training Division, 1976. The information compiled in this document was based on research by Robert J. Hazen and Clarence E. Phillips, both Supervising Fingerprint Specialists assigned to the FBI Training Division in Quantico, Virginia.

1. Fume the skin tissue with vapor from the iodine gun.
2. Press the silver plate directly onto the skin, covering the area where the latent prints are believed to be.
3. Remove the silver plate.
4. Expose the silver plate to the strong light.

It should be noted that the prints on the silver sheets are laterally inverted; i.e., the left side of the print on the silver sheet corresponds to the right side of the original print. In order to reproduce the position correctly, it will be necessary when preparing prints on the negative to place the glossy side of the negative next to the emulsion side of the printing paper.[8]

Fingerprint from Human Skin Using the Magna-Brush Technique

CASE HISTORY

On May 7, 1982, the Peel Regional Police Force Identification Bureau became involved in an extremely gruesome murder case. (See Chapter 21 for reference.)[9]

The victim had been badly battered, sexually assaulted, and otherwise perversely attacked. She was found on her back with clothing partially removed, exposing her upper and lower body. The police felt that she surely must have been handled by the offender and began an examination of the body at the scene with this in mind. Detective Sergeant Geoff Hancock, Inspector Mike Metcalf, and Inspector Frank Fernandes (now deceased) were the identification officers who conducted this portion of the investigation. Initial examination was performed at the scene using the Kromekote technique; however, a limited supply of Kromekote paper yielding negative results made it necessary to go on to another technique. At this point, the body was removed to the local morgue and prior to removal, the ambulance attendants and hospital pathologists were advised not to store the body in any refrigerated area and to ensure that none of the exposed skin areas were handled. An examination of the body for latent fingerprints was begun within an hour time at the morgue.

---

[8] Further information on this technique can be obtained by writing to the Law Enforcement Arts Research Unit, FBI Training Division, Quantico, Virginia 22135.

[9] The author acknowledges the Peel Regional Police Department, Brampton Ontario, Canada, specifically Inspector Rod Piukkala, for providing this information relative to the above procedures used to recover latent print evidence from a human body.

Figure 20.13. **CRIME SCENE PHOTO.** (Courtesy of Inspector Rod Piukkala. Photos taken by the Peel Regional Police Force, Brampton, Ontario, Canada.)

From this experience it can be recommended that a good quality portable light source be used to do this type of examination, using a large hand-held magnifying glass.

The officers had received information of a technique used success-fully by the police in Miami, Florida during their investigation of the "Spa Murders." They had also used the Kromekote technique and when this was unsuccessful, progressed to the Magna-Brush Powder Technique. The identification officers decided to implement the Magna-Brush Tech-nique, using MacDonnell Magna Jet Black Powder.

It appeared at the scene that the legs of the deceased had been forced apart. Her jeans had been pulled down around her ankles so the areas of the legs we felt would have been handled were the inner knee and thigh areas. When this area of skin was dusted with the Magna-Brush powder, two areas revealed evidence of ridge detail when examined using the large hand-held magnifying glass. They were both on the inner knee areas. The officers photographed this ridge detail so that a proper examination could be made. The photography of the ridge detail proved to be the most critical part of the fingerprint examination. A 120 camera was used, with a good quality, heavy tripod, initially using a Polaroid back, using Type 665 P/N film. The Polaroid film did not clearly reveal the ridge detail; however, it provided a good idea as to the best angle to position the lights,

Figure 20.14. **BODY AFTER MAGNA-BRUSHING.** Identification officers decided to implement the MAGNA-BRUSH Technique, using MacDonell Magna Jet Black Powder. (Courtesy of Inspector Rod Piukkala. Photos taken by the Peel Regional Police Force, Brampton, Ontario, Canada.)

in this case, a single head electronic flash unit. This angle was achieved only through trial and error. To ensure correct lighting, the recommendation is that perhaps several varied light angles be used.

During the subsequent photography the officers also used Kodak Tri-X black and white 120 film. However, they did not reveal the ridge detail as seen under magnification because of the lack of tonal separation. The black and white print tended to mask the ridge detail because of light reflecting on the natural skin creases. Kodak VPS 120 was also used as well as Kodak slide film in 35 mm format.

When the color proofs were completed a different story unfolded. The ridge detail originally seen at the morgue was quite visible on the color proofs because of the tonal separation. An identification was made shortly thereafter from the Kodak VPS 120 proofs. Although lacking a little in contrast and bearing a slight color cast, the ridge detail, which was from the area of the suspect's palm, was positively identified. The color slide photos also taken at the morgue revealed sufficient detail for examination as well. The color casts and low contrast can be corrected perhaps by attempting to print out the cast and to try Kodacolor 120 instead of the VPS 120 in order to increase contrast.

To briefly summarize the technique used, it should be noted again that the following steps be taken.

Figure 20.15. **PRINT EVIDENCE FROM SKIN.** Two areas revealed evidence of ridge detail when examined using the large hand-held magnifying glass. They were both on the inner knee areas. The officers photographed this ridge detail so that a proper examination could be made. (Courtesy of Inspector Rod Piukkala. Photos taken by the Peel Regional Police Force, Brampton, Ontario, Canada.)

1. Advise ambulance and hospital personnel not to handle any areas of exposed skin.
2. Do not refrigerate the body.
3. If any ridges appear as a result of applying the Magna-Brush powder, using a good light and magnifying glass, make sure that several angles of lighting are used to achieve optimum results. If possible, make an attempt to process the film prior to the start of the autopsy to ensure that you have the best lit photograph of the latent on the skin. If this is not possible, ensure that an adequate number of photographs are taken.
4. If possible, use Tungsten lighting when photographing the latent print. This should prove to be a more versatile light source than electronic flash. The latent print can be lighted and viewed directly through the ground glass on larger format cameras and should yield better results.
5. Use Kodak VPS film and also Kodacolor. If attempts are successful and a color cast is evident, attempt to print it out during the print processing to increase contrast.

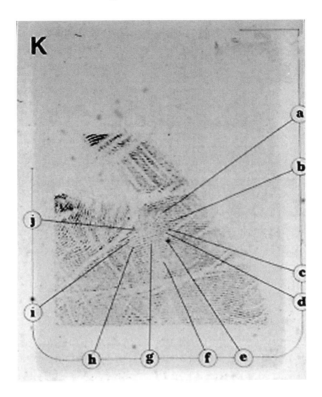

Figure 20.16.   **COMPARISON WITH AN INKED IMPRESSION.** An identification was made from the area of the suspect's palm. He was positively identified. (Courtesy of Inspector Rod Piukkala. Photos taken by the Peel Regional Police Force, Brampton, Ontario, Canada.)

This was the first time in the history of fingerprinting in Canada that the fingerprint of an accused on skin had been identified using this technique.

Polygraph Examinations

The purpose of this section is to familiarize the homicide investigator with the utilization of the *polygraph,* or, as it is more commonly referred to, the lie detector, in homicide investigations.[10]

Basically, the polygraph examination uses mechanical and electronic instrumentation to graphically record the physiological changes that take place in persons questioned under controlled conditions. Changes in cardiovascular activity, respiratory activity, and galvanic

---

[10] The information and technical data presented herein was provided by retired Detective Donald F. Sullivan of the New York City Police Department.

skin reflex are recorded on a moving chart as the examiner asks the subject specific questions. These charts are then evaluated to determine whether or not the person's answers were truthful, untruthful, or inconclusive.

Although polygraph results are generally inadmissible in a court of law unless an agreement and stipulation by counsel is obtained, the test can be very useful to the investigators during a homicide investigation. For example, during the early stages of the investigation when the number of suspects is large, the polygraph can be utilized to eliminate certain suspects so that investigative resources can be employed more productively.

The proper and intelligent utilization of the polygraph coupled with the ability and expertise of the polygraph examiner may be able to do what the deceased cannot; "point the investigation in the right direction."

The Examination

The polygraph is always a supplement to a good field investigation and never a substitute for it. Often the results of a polygraph examination will be only as good as the information developed by field investigation. The polygraphist should be consulted at the early stages of the investigation as to the feasibility of using the polygraph in the investigation; it should never be used as a last resort.

Polygraphs are conducted on a strictly voluntary basis. The subject cannot be forced into taking an examination, and the examination cannot be rushed. A properly conducted polygraph test lasts approximately 2 hours or more depending on the circumstances of the case.

There are four phases of a polygraph examination:

First phase — pretest interview. The polygraphist learns about the subject's medical history, physical condition, and psychological background. The pretest interview determines whether the subject is capable of taking the examination.

Second phase — explanation of how the polygraph works. During this phase the polygraphist discusses the crime with the subject, and he has the subject explain what he knows, if anything, about the crime. The polygraphist is looking for any changes in the subject's original statement given to the investigator.

Third phase — preparation of test questions. The subject is aware of the questions to be asked and there are no surprise questions. If the subject objects to one of the questions, the question is either changed or eliminated.

Fourth phase — the actual testing. After the examination, the polygraphist analyzes the charts and then renders one of three opinions: truthful, lying, or inconclusive. It must be noted that re-examinations are necessary in some cases.

Possible Subjects for Polygraph Examinations

The majority of examinations are conducted with suspects. If suspects are to be questioned, they should be advised of their rights prior to testing. If the suspect has an attorney, the polygraphist should have the attorney witness the waiver.

Informants may also be tested to ascertain that the information being supplied to the investigator is correct. Witnesses may be tested for the same reason, as well as to see if they are withholding any other details pertinent to the crime.

Subjects that cannot be Tested

Persons with physical disabilities, such as a serious heart condition (verified by a doctor), should not be tested, nor should pregnant women.

Investigator's Duties Prior to the Examination

The investigator should provide the polygraphist with correct and adequate case facts and not withhold anything from him or her. Remember, homicide investigation requires a teamwork approach. The polygraphist and the investigator must work together in order to be successful.

The polygraphist must know the subject's history. The investigator should provide the polygraphist with the following information:

1. Prior record, especially any arrests or investigations for a similar crime.
2. Possible motive for committing the crime.
3. Religion and how faithful.
4. Financial status.
5. Anything else the investigator can think of that might be of value to the polygraphist to get an insight into the subject.

The subject should be properly prepared for the examination. Like other physical evidence, he or she should be handled with care so that the examination can be done properly.

The investigator should find out why this person initially decided to take the test and the person's attitude toward it. The investigator should never assume the subject's truthfulness based solely on the fact that the subject agrees to take an examination. Any police polygraphist will show you cases of confirmed liars who are willing to take a polygraph examination.

Needless to say, certain information about the crime should always be withheld from all parties, including the news media, prior to the examination. The investigator should take the polygraphist into his or her confidence and inform the examiner of facts about the crime, which only the one who committed the crime or who was present when the crime was committed would know, for example, how the person was killed; where the entry was made; what weapon was used; what items were stolen or removed from the scene; or unusual facts about the crime, such as sex mutilation, tying up of the victim, etc.

Polygraph Procedures

The polygraphist usually has the final decision as to who can be tested, when the examination will begin, and whether or not the examination will continue.

Never use the polygraph as a bluff. The subject should only be asked if he is willing to take an examination when the investigator fully intends to have the subject examined.

The polygraphist is responsible for the issues to be covered in the examination. The exact wording of all test questions on the examination should be decided by the investigator and the polygraphist after conferral with each other regarding the facts of the case. Only one crime will be covered during the examination. If the subject is suspected of committing other crimes, then separate examinations should be conducted at later dates.

The polygraph examination should be conducted, if possible, first thing in the morning after the subject has had a night's sleep. On the day of the examination, the investigator should not interrogate the subject. When a person agrees to the polygraph, the investigators should cease all interrogation until after the completion of the examination.

Summary

The polygraph is an investigative aid and a supplement to a good field investigation. The homicide detective should be encouraged to use this tool and to discuss its capabilities with the polygraphist who will conduct the examination. The polygraph examination is not admissible in a court of law; however, statements made to a polygraphist are admissible. The polygraph represents an extremely valuable technique in homicide investigation when employed by a competent technician working as a member of the investigative team.

Psycholinguistics

The purpose of this section is to acquaint the investigator with psycholinguistic analysis and explain how this technique can be utilized to obtain information on the origin, background, and psychology of a homicide suspect who communicates with the authorities. The communication can either be verbal or written.[11]

What is Psycholinguistic Analysis?

Psycholinguistic analysis is a sophisticated method of examining the spoken or written communication for clues as to origins, background, and psychology of the speaker or writer. Every sentence, phrase, syllable, word, pause, and comma is automatically scanned by computer for what it can reveal about the person who has communicated the message. These messages can also establish the author's identity by comparison with other messages whose authors are known. Psycholinguistic analysis combines the two disciplines of psychology and linguistics to provide an understanding of the type of personality who has originated the communication as well as a strategy for dealing with such persons. Although the primary purpose of the program, initiated by Professor Miron, was to analyze threats in connection with terrorist activities, psycholinguistics can provide the homicide detective with an effective investigative tool to identify certain suspects who taunt police with verbal or written communications.

Methodology

Upon receipt of the message or communication, the psycholinguistic expert enters the information into a computer by means of a terminal keyboard. The computer then scans the message and assigns each word to a set of categories which research has identified as important in the characterization of a threat. In addition, the computer tabulates occur-

---

[11] The material presented herein is based on documents and information supplied by the FBI and on personal interviews with Dr. Murray S. Miron, a professor at Syracuse University, who has performed extensive research in the area of psycholinguistic analysis.

rences of such things as punctuation, speech hesitancies, misspellings, and sentence structure.

The computer used to analyze a wide range of threats over the years has established what is referred to as a "threat dictionary." This threat dictionary has continued to grow in size and comprehensiveness, composing more than 350 categories representing more than 250,000 words. These threats range from suicide notes to terrorist communications, including both hoaxes and threats which have actually been carried out. Furthermore, the computer stores over 15 million words gathered from analyses of ordinary spoken and written English. Any unusual usages or word occurrences which differ from this stored data are flagged by the computer for closer analysis. By weighing the vocabulary usages of an author or speaker against the usage employed by the average speaker, the psycholinguistic expert can derive a set of "signature" words which are unique to an individual and which can be expected to match across differing communications.

CASE HISTORY

The following case history represents the sort of information that psycholinguistic techniques can provide to law enforcement.[12]

Prepared from communications received from an unidentified subject (UNSUB) who threatened a flight from New York to Geneva, Switzerland, Dr. Miron drew several conclusions. On the basis of psycholinguistic analyses, he judged that the UNSUB was a German born male of at least 50 years of age who had immigrated to the United States as an adult and had resided in this country for at least 20 years. Further, the analyses indicated that the UNSUB had probably written previous messages to prominent officials in both the United States and Germany. Perhaps most revealing was the conclusion that the perpetrator's personality compelled him to leave clues as to his identity in the message itself. At the conclusion of the extortion message, there was a series of three-digit code numbers which seemed to correspond to the fictitious name of the group UNSUB claimed he directed. The following code appeared at the end of the message:

Sig: 604 247 945 305 734 430
915 837 907 Reciprocal Relief
Alliance for Peace, Justice and
Freedom Everywhere

---

[12] Reprinted from Murray S. Miron and John E. Douglas, "Threat Analysis — The Psycholinguistic Approach," FBI Law Enforcement Bulletin, September, 1979.

Each of the nine code groups appears to correspond to the nine words of the group name. No words are duplicated in the group name or in the three-digit code groups.

However, if the code groups are rearranged so that each group is written as a column of numbers, the code would look as follows:

$$6\ 2\ 9\ 3\quad 7\ 4\ 9\ 8\ 9$$
$$0\ 4\ 4\ 0\quad 3\ 3\ 1\ 3\ 0$$
$$4\ 7\ 5\ 5\quad 4\ 0\ 5\ 7\quad 7$$

When arranged in this way, the first three code numbers, 6 2 9, correspond to the alphabet letters of FBI. Using a standard coding device which employs a displacement key for the remaining text, the next code groups translate as "IM" followed by two initials repeated twice. Together the translation would read "FBI, I'm JK JK." A search of the names of the passengers on the flight revealed that one of the travelers matched the profile description and part of the initials of the deciphered code. Search of the records revealed that this passenger had written and signed his name to a series of similar messages written in 1969. Subsequent psycholinguistic comparisons established that these earlier messages were written by the same suspect. After this identification, the psycholinguistic tools where then used to suggest methods for conducting the interview with the suspect. Using the clues gleaned from the messages as to the personality of the suspect, specific stratagems for approaching him were devised. These involved predictions as to how the subject would react, and whether or not he might contemplate suicide or escape.

Psycholinguistics as an Investigative Tool

One of the more dramatic applications of psycholinguistic methods by Dr. Miron took place during the Patricia Hearst case. Soon after the first of the tape recordings sent by the Symbionese Liberation Army (SLA) had been received by the authorities, Dr. Miron prepared a series of reports for the FBI. He described the individual calling himself "Cinque" as one who fit the known background of Donald DeFreeze. Perhaps more important, these reports predicted that Patricia Hearst would join the SLA and commit some criminal acts with them. The analyses further indicated that DeFreeze and his followers were suicidal and that they would undoubtedly die in a final shootout with the authorities rather than surrender.

Practically speaking, the use of this technique in the investigation of homicide is limited to those occasions when the murderer chooses to communicate with or taunt the police with his messages. However, when such communications are received during a murder investigation, psycholinguistic analysis can be invaluable in providing authorities with an insight into the personality type of the suspect. The "Son of Sam" case in New York City is a good example of the type of homicide case in which psycholinguistics has been used.

In this particular investigation, the killer David Berkowitz, who called himself the "Son of Sam," roamed through the streets seeking out young couples and then gunning them down with a .44-caliber revolver. In a series of cryptic messages which he sent to a local newspaper, he claimed that he was acting under instructions communicated to him by a neighbor's dog.

The psycholinguistic method drew a profile of this killer early in the investigation which later turned out to closely fit the subject. Despite the fact that several eyewitness reports had indicated that the killer was in his mid-thirties (Berkowitz had a receding hairline), the psycholinguistic profile based on the written communications correctly placed the killer's age between 20 and 25. As an indication of just how detailed such a profile can be, even though based only upon what the perpetrator may choose to write or say, Dr. Miron's profile of Berkowitz included the information that the killer was of average height and overweight (he was both), that his mother was either dead or separated from the family (Berkowitz had been adopted and his adoptive mother had died when he was 14), that his father was ill or aged (he was retired), and that Berkowitz would continue to attack young attractive women until caught and when finally caught would surrender meekly to the authorities, as he eventually did.

According to Dr. Miron, a typical psycholinguistic profile consists of three sections. First, and most important from the standpoint of the homicide investigator, is a demographic profile of the author of the communication which attempts to identify the author's age, sex, birth place, and other details that can be gleaned from the communication. Second, the profile presents such aspects of the psychology of the author as his or her motivations, personality, and pathology, if any. Finally, the profile provides an assessment of the determination and capabilities of the writer to carry out the threatened or claimed actions.

Utilizing Psycholinguistic Analysis

Requests for psycholinguistic analysis should be made through the Technical Evaluation Unit (TEU) of the FBI. The request can be made through the local FBI field office covering the jurisdiction requesting this service, or can be sent direct to the following address:

Federal Bureau of Investigation H.Q.
Technical Evaluation Unit
FBI Laboratory Division
J. Edgar Hoover Building
10th and Pennsylvania Ave.
Washington, D.C. 20535

A request for psycholinguistic analysis should include reference to any previous communications or correspondence submitted to the laboratory in the case, and the facts concerning the violation insofar as they pertain to the specific laboratory examination. For further information, refer to Chapter 17.

Summary

This method of investigation is still considered to be in a developmental stage, and its adaptability to homicide investigation is limited to those cases in which there is some form of communication. The investigator should be aware of its limitations and not assume that psycholinguistics can replace traditional homicide investigation procedures. However, psycholinguistic analysis has proven to be a valuable investigative tool in those cases where it has been used. In homicide cases psycholinguistics has been used in just about every major investigation, from the Alphabet Bomber to the Zodiac and Zebra Killing.

Psychics

The professional homicide detective utilizes many tools in the investigation to assist in the retrieval of information, some of which may be inaccessible through ordinary methods. A somewhat sensational and often controversial practice is the use of psychics. The purpose of this section is to provide the investigator with information on the use of a psychic in homicide investigations.[13]

Practically speaking, police officers are naturally skeptical of psychics and psychic phenomena. However, from an investigative point of view, anything which has proven to be successful in one investigation should

---

[13] The information presented in this section is based on research of specific cases, personal interviews, and correspondence with several psychics including Ms. Noreen Renier, a psychic and recognized authority on the phenomena of extrasensory perception. Ms. Renier has worked with various police agencies including the FBI on homicide cases and other criminal investigations.

certainly be considered in other cases. It should be noted that information provided by the psychic may not always be accurate and in some instances may have no value to the investigation. However, this should not discourage authorities from using a psychic, especially in homicide cases where there is limited information. The use of a psychic can be considered as an additional investigative aid.

What is a Psychic?

A psychic is a person who is especially sensitive to nonphysical forces of life energy. According to Ms. Renier, being a psychic "involves getting rid of logic and rationale." A psychic is not someone with magical or mystical powers. Instead, the psychic is a person who learns to control a portion of the brain which is not generally used in order to see and feel things which the average person cannot experience.

How can the Police and Psychics Work Together?

The police and the psychic must understand each other's roles and respect each other's expertise before a proper working relationship can be developed. The credibility of the psychic will ultimately be tested by performance and results. However, the police have a responsibility to assure that the psychic is properly handled.

Before an agency decides to seek the assistance of a psychic, certain facts must be considered. The first consideration is that there is very limited information and knowledge on how psychics perform. Each psychic has his or her own distinctive method of operation. The second consideration is how to know whether or not the psychic is "legitimate." This is very difficult to ascertain, because even those scientists involved in the study of these phenomena cannot provide definitive guides for law enforcement. There is an abundance of exaggeration and sensationalism attached to psychic phenomena, yet there have been a number of instances where information provided by a psychic has been beneficial to authorities.

It should be noted that the police and not the psychic solve crime. Ideally, the psychic will be able to provide clues and information for the police to act on. The psychic should therefore be considered as an aid in developing clues that are not recognizable to the police. The police should then provide the necessary follow-up investigation in order to corroborate the information provided by the psychic.

In order to present the reader with an insight into how the police and psychic can work together, I have provided Ms. Renier's personal comments on her method of procedure and technique.

Ms. Renier states, "Because a psychic is usually called into an investigation as a last resort, when little or no clues to the identity of the criminal have been uncovered, there is often a lot of skepticism on the part of the police. First, because they do not understand psychic phenomena. The police deal in logic and hard facts and usually have never worked with a psychic. They have strong doubts. Secondly, a psychic is not a police officer and therefore is considered an outsider. I, as a psychic, have to contend with these areas of negativism before I even start to work on the crime. If the people I am working with are filled with doubts and animosity, I will pick up on these feelings and it will definitely hamper my work."

"I prefer murder cases, but will work on other crimes as well. I prefer not to know any details of the crime or personal background of the victim. I need only to know the first name of the victim and the type of case I am working on in order to use my talents. For example, Alice/Murder."

"I also like to hold an object that was on the victim at the time of the murder. I prefer metal objects, such as a ring or watch." This technique is called psychometry. Ms. Renier states that she is able to tune into impressions or vibrations left by the owner in or around metal objects. For example, the earring of a murder victim was sent to Ms. Renier by Michigan police. She was able, through psychometry, to reconstruct what the victim looked like, where she lived, what the house looked like, and how the victim was killed. In addition, she stated that she "saw" the murderer washing his hands and combing his hair. She even "saw" the tattoos on his arms. She was able to describe this person to the police, who later arrested their suspect based on physical evidence developed during the investigation.

"I try to see physically what the victim looks like. I then try to recreate the scene of the murder. I do these things for two reasons."

"First, to make sure that I am tuning into the correct case, and secondly, to give the police confidence in me as a psychic."

"Once the police start believing I'm real, and can do the things I say I can, we can continue."

"As I describe the victim and the scene of the crime, I insist on feedback. A simple 'Yes' or 'I understand' is sufficient. I do not need additional clues or information."

"After describing the victim and the scene of the crime, if it is a murder, I try to feel the way the person was murdered. I switch from psychic 'seeing' to psychic 'feeling.' During the session I will use all of my five senses to a degree which is beyond the average person. I have been 'shot,' 'stabbed,' and 'strangled' numerous times during this psychic 'feeling.' This usually is painful, since I can actually feel where the bullet or knife entered 'my' body. I often moan and groan. However, I can shake this feeling off instantly. The people who I am working with should understand this and not become upset for me. At this point, I have satisfied myself, and hopefully the police who are present, that I am 'tuned' into the case."

"I then like to describe the murderer. I explain to the police before we start the session how to question me. If they have not asked questions before, it is important that they do so now. I can see the murderer but the way I am questioned will help me see him or her more clearly. The police can then obtain the necessary information to help them apprehend this person. It is helpful to have a police or quick-sketch artist on hand to sketch the face I describe."

"Besides the murderer's appearance, I am able to go into his or her personality, mode of travel from the scene, etc. I can even switch back and become the victim again, whatever the police investigators request me to do."

"One thing which is vitally important, is how the police phrase the questions. They have to question me in a casual, gentle manner. I cannot be interrogated like a criminal, even when I am playing the part of the criminal. There should be no leading type questions, such as 'Is his hair black?' Instead, the question should be, 'What is the color of his hair?' Preferable, there should be *no* series of 'Yes' and 'No' questions, as sometimes I lose my train of thought. If it looks like I'm dying down, the question must be rephrased or I must be redirected. If an answer is unclear, it should be rephrased. If an answer doesn't sound right, instead of a negative, 'No, no you're all wrong,' I prefer, 'Let's go back to that later.' I may be slightly off in my interpretation of what I see, or maybe what I see is true, but totally unbelievable at the point. Sometimes, when we go back later, it will be clearer or 'fit in.' "

It should be noted that Ms. Renier does not claim to be 100% accurate in her interpretations, nor does she claim to be able to work on all cases equally well.

As far as the police working with the psychic, it has been determined that psychics respond better and are more accurate when the individuals working with them have a positive attitude. Practically speaking, if an officer feels that he or she cannot accept or work with the psychic, then this officer should not get involved in this segment of the investigation. Instead, someone who may be skeptical, but is able to put aside this personal prejudice, should be assigned to work with the psychic.

Charlatans and Frauds

The agency which decides to utilize the psychic in a particular investigation should first establish the authenticity of the psychic by routine inquiry. Generally speaking, the decision to use a psychic is based on a report of a successful investigation attributed to psychic phenomena. This report may appear in a local newspaper or come about by word of mouth. Official contact and interagency communication will usually indicate whether or not the psychic was of any investigative value.

It is important to note that charlatans and frauds exist in all professions. However, they flourish in the area of extrasensory perception. From an investigative point of view, the best way to avoid being taken in by a phony psychic is in the proper handling and control of this person. For example, many frauds merely "feed back" information to the police which is already a matter of public record, having read a newspaper account of the crime. Or a fraud may have access to information on the case through family members or "official leaks" which give the impression that he or she has some psychic knowledge of events.

It should be noted that the police should not be telling the psychic. The psychic should be telling the police. Once the agency decides to employ the services of the psychic, all information supplied about the case to the psychic, and all information provided by the psychic, should flow through one contact officer, in order to maintain proper control. In addition, certain facts should be purposely withheld from the psychic in order to maintain the integrity of the investigation and assure that the information provided by the psychic is genuine and not the result of the police investigation. All conversations relative to the psychic investigation should be taped. This is extremely important, since psychics can generate a tremendous amount of information in a short span of time. Also, this information is often in the form of disjointed impressions. An investigator cannot be expected to accurately take notes and intelligently formulate questions in the face of such voluminous information. Later on, the tape can be analyzed by other investigators for accuracy and follow-up, and additional questions can be formulated. Furthermore, the tape serves as a control and documentation of the information exchanged.

According to Ms. Renier, the reason for an abundance of phonies in the area of extrasensory perception is that the average person is ignorant about psychic phenomena. Wherever there is lack of knowledge, it is easy to trick and deceive people. The phonies like conditions they can control. They do a lot of key bending and blindfold tricks which are impressive. Their clarity and accuracy are usually overwhelming. Even individuals who have been involved in psychic phenomena for years are sometimes deceived by these frauds. Real psychics are human, and therefore are subject to error.

Conscious of the poor image the public has of psychics, Ms. Renier advocates strict licensing procedures by a recognized board. She states that if there were proper testing and licensing procedures, psychic ability could be proven and properly evaluated before official recognition. This would not only legitimize psychics in the eyes of the public, but could also serve as a referral system.

At present there are no plans for such a system, but there are groups involved in researching this phenomenon. If a law enforcement agency is interested in utilizing a psychic, a representative of the agency should contact one of these groups. Dr. Karlis Osis of the American Society for Psychical Research, which is a respected and conservative organization involved in the study of this phenomenon, can be contacted at 5 West 73rd Street, New York, NY 10023. The telephone number is (212)-799-5050.

Summary

Empirical research into psychic phenomena has been limited, and there just isn't any "hard" research data available to indicate an accurate percentage of cases materially aided by the use of psychic phenomena. However, investigatively speaking, there has been sufficient documentation of successes to merit the consideration of this technique on a case-by-case basis.

The police have much to learn about the relative value of psychic phenomena in criminal investigations. Furthermore, there is a definite need for an evaluation of the successes and failures of psychic phenomena as they relate to law enforcement before they can be recognized as a "legitimate" investigative tool. Perhaps in time, the psychic and homicide investigator may form the perfect partnership against crime. In any event, I neither encourage nor discourage the use of psychics in homicide investigations.

Munchausen Syndrome by Proxy (MSBP)

Introduction

The purpose of this section is to alert investigators to the phenomena of Munchausen Syndrome by Proxy (MSBP) which is a form of child abuse whereby the parent or adult care giver deliberately simulates or causes medical distress in a child in order to gain attention, praise, or the sympathy of others.

The result of this behavior on the part of the parent or care giver can be fatal to the child and there have been a number of documented cases of infanticide due to this behavior. The author is aware of a case in New York State, in which a woman killed eight of her nine children between 1972 and 1985, but most of the deaths were attributed to Sudden Infant Death Syndrome (SIDS). As each child died in what was perceived to be some unexplained illness she was afforded the sympathy of friends, neighbors, and the medical staff of the hospital. Today, the motivations in this case could have been attributed to *Munchausen Syndrome by Proxy.*

Actually, this disorder is similar to the diagnosis "Munchausen Syndrome" which is *self-inflicted.* The individual creates physical symptoms which result in multiple hospitalizations and medical testings. However, in the Munchausen Syndrome by Proxy (MSBP) scenario the physical symptomatology and medical disorders are either persistently fabricated or physically *induced in the child* by the perpetrating parent or care giver.

There are two distinct categories of MSBP. They are referred to as "simulation or mild form" and "production or severe form."

Simulation occurs when the offender fabricates a history for a non-existent illness or condition in a child. For example, the offender reports blood in her child's urine. However, the offender has pricked her finger and inserted her own blood into the sample. Or, the offender reports an undocumented history of fevers in the child. These alleged fevers are not witnessed by anyone. Or, the fevers may appear as notations on hospital charts, which have been entered on the chart by the offender (*there have been MSBP cases involving chart tampering*). In some cases, offenders may actually condition victims to believe that they are ill and they will act accordingly.

Production is the intentional inducement of injury to create signs and symptoms of an illness. There are documented cases of offenders who deliberately suffocate children to cause apnea and respiratory distress necessitating resuscitation. There are other offenders who administer non-authorized medications or poisons to produce symptoms which necessitate painful emergency procedures as well as a series of medical testings.

Current research indicates that this behavior provides the perpetrating parent with psychological and emotional benefits which range from a comforting, nurturing medical environment, and sympathy to feelings of power and control.

Munchausen Syndrome — History and Application

Munchausen Syndrome disorder is found in the *Diagnostic and Statistical Manual of Mental Disorders,* Fourth Edition (DSM-IV, 1994). It is listed within the "Factitious Disorder with Predominantly Physical Signs and symptoms" (300.19). It was named after Karl Fredich von Munchausen.

Munchausen was a German baron, who had fought with the Russian cavalry in the Russo-Turkish wars. Upon his return he amused and regaled his friends with preposterous and highly unlikely tales of his exploits. One of his associates published a collection of these outlandish tales which added to the baron's fame (*The Surprising Adventures of Baron Munchausen,* Raspe, R.E. (1944)).

"The baron's name and fame were rekindled in 1951 when an English physician, Dr. Richard Asher, described a psychiatric disorder whereby adults gave "dramatic and untruthful" physical histories along with the presentation of seemingly acute illnesses that were ultimately found to be false. Because of the completely factitious nature of these medical histories, the disorder, Munchausen syndrome, was named after the baron." (Mercer and Perdue, 1993, p. 74.)

Munchausen Syndrome by Proxy (MSBP) — History and Application

The newly revised *Diagnostic and Statistical Manual of Mental Disorders,* Fourth Edition (DSM-IV, 1994) references this disorder under "Factitious Disorder Not Otherwise Specified" (300.19). This category includes disorders with factitious symptoms that do not meet the criteria for Factitious Disorder. An example is factitious disorder by proxy. DSM-IV states, "The essential feature is the deliberate production or feigning of physical or psychological signs or symptoms in another person who is under the individual's care. Typically the victim is a young child and the perpetrator is the child's mother." (DSM-IV, p. 725.)

According to an article in the June, 1992 *FBI Law Enforcement Bulletin* written by Dr. Stephen J. Boros, M.D. and Special Agent Larry C. Brubaker, "The term *Munchausen Syndrome by Proxy" (MSBP)* was coined in a 1976 report describing four children who were so severely abused, they were dwarfed." (J. Money, "Munchausen's Syndrome by Proxy; Update," 1986.)

Dr. Stephen Boros and Special Agent Larry Brubaker, who are considered experts in MSBP, present a number of cases which they encountered in Minnesota. In these cases the perpetrators were both male and female, with the female parent most often involved.

According to an article in the January, 1993 *Social Work* magazine written by Susan O. Mercer and Jeanette Perdue, Dr. Roy Meadows was one of the first physicians to articulate this disorder as a diagnosis. In 1977, Dr. Roy Meadows described a case involving a 6-year-old girl who had recurrent bloody urine. The child was subjected to repeated tests and hospitalizations before the doctors realized that this condition had been produced by the child's mother. (Mercer and Perdue, 1993. p. 74.)

In each of the cases in which a diagnosis of Munchausen Syndrome by Proxy (MSBP) was made, the victim was a child and the perpetrator was a parent or parent substitute. The mother or female caretaker is reported as the perpetrator in almost all research and cases in literature (Jones et al., 1986; Meadow, 1989).

Susan O. Mercer and Jeanette D. Perdue state, "The mother or female caretaker is typically described as cooperative, pleasant to deal with, generally bright, appreciative of staff, involved in the child's care, and medically knowledgeable. The mother may even have a background of working in a health facility. Many of the mothers are reported to have features of Munchausen syndrome and in some cases their physical complaints are similar to those assigned to the child (Jones et al., 1986; Maker and Squier, 1990; Meadow, 1982)." (Mercer and Perdue, 1993. p. 77.)

I interviewed Detective Kathryn Artingstall of the Orlando, Florida Police Department, who is a recognized law enforcement authority on the subject of Munchausen Syndrome by Proxy (MSBP). She published one of the first law enforcement articles on this subject in the December, 1991 *FBI Law Enforcement Bulletin.* She states that even though most of the research and case histories indicate that the mother is the most likely perpetrator, the *offender profile* has now been expanded to fathers and other family members such as grandparents, aunts, uncles, and other siblings and even non-related individuals who are associated either directly or indirectly with the care of the victim. In fact, there are documented cases of babysitters, who have been praised for heroism for saving the life of a child. Subsequent incidents and/or investigation has revealed that the babysitter was actually the perpetrator of the emergency or distress in the child.

CASE HISTORY — EXAMPLES

On January 5, 1993, NBC aired a documentary on "Munchausen Syndrome by Proxy" on "Dateline NBC." The program focused on this relatively new form of child abuse and its lethal potentiality. The program featured a mother convicted of assault in connection with the asphyxiation of her son. The son had a reported history of 18 trips to emergency rooms of hospitals in three different states. In fact, the little boy's sister had died and was the reported victim of SIDS. She had also been to emergency rooms approximately 20 times and resuscitated before she was murdered. On the same program, viewers were shown a video tape of a mother suffocating her daughter. The woman, who was suspected of Munchausen Syndrome by Proxy by the medical staff, did not know that the hospital had placed a hidden camera in her child's hospital room. The mother is observed holding the child in her arms. She very carefully removes a plastic wrap from her pocketbook and places it over the face of her daughter. As she does this, she is looking towards the door to make sure no one sees her. The child is observed struggling for air for approximately 38 seconds and then falls unconscious. The mother then runs for the doctor to report that her child is not breathing.

The Investigative Response

In most instances the police will not be initially involved with the investigation. Mental health, social workers, and hospital personnel are usually in the best position to assess this behavior. However, when and if a child dies or authorities are brought in by child protective services, the police investigator should be aware of this phenomena and the necessity of a team-work approach to this event. This is best accomplished by having an awareness of the dynamics of Munchausen Syndrome by Proxy as explained within this article and the necessity for complete cooperation between the medical staff and law enforcement.

Team Approach

According to Detective Artingstall, "When law enforcement officials are contacted concerning suspected cases of (MSBP), it is critical to use a multidisciplinary approach to the case. Medical staff, child protection teams, social services personnel, and hospital administrators, as well as prosecutors and law enforcement personnel, should assist in the investigation." (*FBI Law Enforcement Bulletin,* December, 1991.)

There will be a need for an in-depth documentation and review of medical records, as well as a compilation of family social history, especially as it relates to any other deaths and/or injuries. Oftentimes, there is an extensive and confusing medical history, which extends across jurisdictions.

Collection of Evidence

Detective Artingstall states, "The most common method for securing evidence is by the suspect/victim seclusion test. Simply stated, the

Table 1.   Help for Investigators

Investigators assigned to work child abuse cases should investigate cases of MSBP as they do similar cases of abuse. In general, however, when confronted with possible cases of MSBP, investigators should:

- Review the victim's medical records to determine condition and illness
- Determine from contact with medical personnel the reporting parent's concerns and reactions to the child's medical treatment
- Compile a complete history of the family to determine previous involvement with law enforcement agencies, medical facilities, and social and child protection services
- Compile a detailed social history of the family, including deaths, injuries, and illnesses
- Interview family members, neighbors, and babysitters
- Use video surveillance in the hospital in accordance with State law
- Use a search warrant for the family's residence when collecting evidence of the assaults

Reprinted from the *FBI Law Enforcement Bulletin,* June 1992.

Table 2.   Munchausen Syndrome by Proxy Warning Signs

Illness which is unexplained, prolonged, and so extraordinary that experienced doctors state they have never seen anything like it before

Repeat hospitalizations and extensive medical tests without achieving a diagnosis

Symptoms and signs that do not make medical sense

Persistent failure of the victim to respond to therapy

Signs and symptoms that dissipate when the victim is removed from the suspected offender

Mothers who do not seem worried about their children's illnesses and are constantly at the child's side while in the hospital

Mothers who have an unusually close relationship with the medical staff

Families that have other children labeled as SIDS children

Mothers with previous medical or nursing experience that often give a history of the same type of illness as the child

A parent that welcomes medical test of the child, even if painful

Attempts to convince the staff that the child is still ill, when advised that the child will be released from the hospital

A "Model Family" that normally would be above suspicion

A caretaker with a previous history of Munchausen Syndrome

A caretaker that adamantly refuses to accept the suggestion that the diagnosis is non-medical

Adapted from Meadow (1982), Guandolo (1985), and Ophoven (1991).

suspected offender is secluded from the sole presence of the victim for a period of time. If the child's symptoms cease or dissipate when removed from the sole presence of the suspect and then reappear when again reunited, the inference of MSBP is significantly strengthened."

A particularly effective manner of obtaining evidence in these types of cases is the use of a concealed camera as depicted on the Dateline NBC documentary on "Munchausen Syndrome by Proxy."

Video surveillance has proven to be most effective in these cases especially when confronting the accused parent. However, this tactic may also increase the risk factor to the victim. Allowing the suspect access to the victim, even while under surveillance, does present the possibility of further harm to the victim.

In addition, placing video cameras in hospital rooms will not only require the cooperation and assistance of hospital administration and medical personnel, it may require the necessity for a court order. The early involvement of prosecutors is especially advantageous in MSBP cases when it comes to making the necessary legal determinations for covert video surveillance. In any event, investigators should consult their legal advisors to determine the appropriate applicable statutes in their particular jurisdiction. Application of this tactic requires medical safeguards to protect the child as well as sufficient personnel to properly document and preserve the legal aspects of the event.

Interviewing the Munchausen Syndrome-Related Offender

Persons who are known or suspected of participating in child abuse as defined within the MSBP or Munchausen Syndrome cases, may have different reactions to specific investigative questioning techniques employed for the purpose of truth determination. There are many factors including unknown components which influence the manner in which a person accused of perpetrating MSBP or Munchausen Syndrome may react. Although individual reactions to various direct and indirect questioning cannot be cemented into a specifically formatted protocol for offender interviews, commonalities in many of these interviews and empirical research provide a suggested guideline. This guideline must remain flexible as the interviewer attempts to enter the imaginary realm created by the offender.

In order to conduct these types of interviews, the detective must possess an understanding of human behavior and be able to anticipate the most common defense reactions of persons accused of child abuse through MSBP. This knowledge will provide the interviewer with the necessary skills to engage the offender in communication and dialogue that eventually overcomes the sophisticated explanations and the highly polished lying skills observed in MSBP offenders.

Historically, interviewers of known or suspected Munchausen Syndrome or MSBP have generally been unsuccessful in gaining admissions of guilt from offenders. It has been theorized that at times either the offender has been so immersed in the sequence of lies that lead to the interview that they have deemed their lies as reality and seemingly believe their deceptions as true or genuine in origin and/or they simply choose not to reveal the truth due to the magnitude of the crime or personal impact that such a disclosure would elicit. Subsequently, interviewers have been tasked with the responsibility of attempting to point out reality to an offender whose reality base may have been altered to accommodate the deception or find themselves interviewing pathological liars that refuse to admit truth and put an end to the deceptions.

Offenders of MSBP have exhibited intense emotions during interviews; e.g., crying or anger. The interviewer should expect these exhibitions by a person accused of perpetration of Munchausen Syndrome or MSBP. The exhibition of these emotions, while appearing genuine are actually calculated mechanisms to escape the exposure to reality which the interviewer is attempting to impose upon the offender. This evasive technique has been observed to be flowing as if regulated by a faucet switch which is turned off as quickly as it is turned on. In MSBP interviews it is common for an offender to appear to react with very intense emotions in the presence of the interviewer and then immediately become calm when the interviewer leaves the room, unless the offender knows or suspects he/she is being observed while alone.

The necessary skills possessed by the offender of Munchausen Syndrome or MSBP to further deceptive acts are generally well rehearsed. If the offender has never been approached by an interviewer regarding the possible existence of Munchausen Syndrome fabrication or MSBP abuse, then the abilities of the offender to refute accusations during the interview may be significantly lessened. Most cases, however, do not fit into this category and it is probable that the offender will have had time to prepare statements which may question the interviewer's hypothesis of Munchausen Syndrome-related acts. It is not uncommon for offenders to answer questions with questions and offer alternative reasoning for alleged acts. It could be expected for an offender to be versed in the area of Munchausen Syndrome or MSBP, to make open-ended statements which cannot be proven or disproved, and for the offender to verbalize this status to the interviewer. The manipulative skill which the offenders normally direct toward the professionals they encounter may be redirected toward the interviewer. The ability of the offender to maintain deception is oftentimes displayed in the interview forum.

The repetitiveness of Munchausen Syndrome-related actions may provide an avenue for the offender to "detach" him/herself from the actual abusive action inflicted upon the victim and hide the reality of the self-imposed role of "child abuser" (MSBP) or "victim" (Munchausen Syndrome) from his/herself deep within the offender's own mind. This mechanism of outward denial may be engaged to allow for the self-preservation of the offender. For example, the horribleness and shame caused by the deliberate infliction of harm onto one's own child would be a difficult reality to openly recognize and maintain a "normal" lifestyle above the suspicion of family members or health care professionals. Offenders deemed "great pretenders" may lie to themselves about parental worthiness and may subconsciously believe that they are not responsible for the MSBP abusive actions upon their children or upon themselves. With the detachment of responsibility may come the ability to hide from the reality of what is actually happening during each instance of MSBP infliction-aggravated child abuse and perpetuate the fantasy created. The determination of whether the offender subconsciously detaches from the Munchausen Syndrome actions or merely chooses not to disclose those actions of abuse, which are clearly remembered, may remain an unknown factor within the interview. In either hypothesis, if conscious acceptance of the offender's role in either self-vicitimization (Munchausen cases) or induced harm (MSBP cases) is not attained during the interview, then a confession and disclosure regarding offender responsibility may not be obtained.

When a Munchausen-related offender is confronted, the interviewer should recognize the dynamics of denial in the offender's mind. The key to obtaining an admission of guilt may rest with the ability of the offender to accept the reality of what he/she has done. When presented with overwhelming evidence of the abuse, which could be gathered via video surveillance and/or victim/offender separation tests, the offender is not likely to readily accept responsibility for the act. Reality may not be enough to persuade the offender to tell the truth regarding the MSBP offense. Lying is a way of life for the offender and it is unrealistic to expect explicitly truthful statements to readily flow without incentive.

When a MSBP or Munchausen Syndrome offender is confronted and realizes that he/she has been exposed, extreme elements of fear and shame may be present. These *combined elements* may serve to seal the offender's ability to "come clean" unless an "out" is presented. The stance which the interviewer takes is critical in the final outcome of the interview. If the interviewer is nonjudgmental and appears genuinely empathic to the offender, the avenue for dialogue should remain open. An effective interview tool is the offender's love for the MSBP child victim. Most offenders will not be able to explain why they committed acts of MSBP, especially with child victims, and will profess their genuine love for their child. By subtly suggesting that the offender has the opportunity to help the MSBP victim and quite possibly reverse permanent damage to the child by now telling the truth, the offender may see that the opportunity to redeem himself is present. Only the offender may know how the child was victimized; and by disclosing this information, the doctors may be able to correctly treat and save the victim. How the victim will view the offender in the future may very well be determined by the willingness of the offender to help the victim by disclosing the facts to the interviewer. If the love of the offender for the victim is strong enough, then the offender may find the strength to place the child before him/herself. In cases of self-inflicted injury commonly seen in Munchausen Syndrome cases, the strategy of the offender's family love, especially if children are accessible, may again provide the avenue to obtaining a confession.

Interviewers of Munchausen or MSBP offenders should be aware that Munchausen Syndrome-related tendencies may become multigenerational MSBP abuse. This possibility should be explained to the suspected offender of Munchausen Syndrome. The interviewer can then point out to the offender how this situation might provide an opportunity for both the offender and the interviewer to "work together" to intervene and halt the cycle of abuse which the offender has been "caught-up" in, thereby providing an "out" for the offender which may facilitate disclosure.

If a point is reached within the interview when the offender comes close to admitting the reality of the situation, and thereby the false allegation or MSBP act, the interviewer should expect the offender to attempt a retreat. This retreat may manifest itself in the direct refusal of the offender to answer any further questions or the offender threatening to end the interview if the current line of questioning does not stop. Although this manipulative technique may test the patience of the interviewer, it may be best to momentarily retreat from the current line of questioning and then revisit the issue(s) in another form later during the interview. This action would allow the offenders to feel that they are in control of the interview when in reality they are now being manipulated by the interviewer who will possess the ability to approach the issue in an alternate manner during a time chosen by the interviewer.

The offender's fear of losing the child should not be addressed during the interview because it appears to be one of the primary blocks to obtaining a confession in MSBP cases. The interviewer may choose to address the need of the offender to admit wrong doing before treatment could begin which could ultimately lead to a normalized relationship between the offender and the MSBP victim in the future. Care should be exercised to omit promissory statements of reunification since the likelihood that a child victim will be placed into protective custody is high. This almost certain separation of an offender from the child proxy should be minimized during the interview. If the offender chooses to make admissions regarding either MSBP or Munchausen Syndrome then in addition to losing the avenue of attention afforded during the Munchausen Syndrome-related incidents, the offender may realize that personal freedom or custody of the offender's children is an issue.

It appears that a Munchausen Syndrome offender's biological family network may play an intricate supportive role although the offender may deny that spouses are supportive. It appears that the offender's deception often includes their spouse, who may outwardly defend and/ or support the offender's allegation of victimization or the offender's lack of knowledge regarding the origin of a proxy's ailments. It appears that a large deviation in the amount of active supportive involvement in the care of a proxy target victim occurs between the offender and the offender's spouse. It is unknown if the offender's spouse may routinely have personal doubts about the allegations of either Munchausen Syndrome or MSBP victimization. This information may only be discovered if the spouse is interviewed in seclusion from the offender. Evidence alluding to the guilt of the offender and rationalization of the probable reality of the allegations may not be enough to convince the offender's spouse of guilt. Interviewers should remember that the offender's spouse has had the greatest personal access to the offender and therefore has probably been the most highly entrenched in the offender's twists of reality. It would be common for the offender's spouse to initially be in a state of denial followed by anger.

When a confession is elicited from the offender, it is important to recognize that the admission of responsibility for the Munchausen-related act may come as a shock to the offender because of the ingrained denial within the offender's mind. When the offender faces the reality of what he/she has done, suicidal tendencies may be prevalent once shock subsides. Interviewers should be aware of this tendency and take those measures necessary to protect the offender from his/herself once responsibility is assumed.

For the perpetrators of MSBP, it appears that the personal benefits of bestowed attention and oftentimes systems of rewards outweigh the natural instinct that most caretakers have ingrained in them to protect their children. The MSBP perpetrator can effectively push maternal or paternal feelings aside at will to allow themselves the ability to offend and then reinstate the masquerade of a doting parent whose life centers around an ill child apparently no one can properly heal.

Perpetrators of Munchausen Syndrome also seem to possess the chameleon ability to shift between self-abuser and alleged victim and continue an oftentimes long series of false allegations of various victimizations. For the offender of Munchausen Syndrome, it appears that the ability to grasp the focused attention afforded victims of crime outweighs the inconvenience or personal injury often associated with this form of factitious crime victimization.

Case reports of MSBP victimizations verify the belief that MSBP attacks are premeditated and carefully executed acts of covert child abuse performed with the precision of a professional. The production or simulation of MSBP are rarely caught first-hand by medical personnel without a carefully devised plan. The most common methods of detection have proven to be through video surveillance or suspect/victim separation documentation.

Cases of MSBP are difficult to understand because, unlike direct physical or sexual abuse of children, the abuse which the victim endures is not always clearly evident. The injury is frequently perpetrated through the actions of persons that are almost historically held above suspicion such as the mother. Medical professionals who act in good faith in the treatment of an apparently sick individual become unwilling instruments of medical abuse because of the direct actions of the MSBP offender. The mission of medical personnel is to search out the cause of a person's illness and relieve the problem. They unwittingly become the vehicle which the MSBP perpetrator uses to maximize the desired effect of attention and self-worth derived from the MSBP act or deception which they create within the victim. When an interviewer is confronted with the possibility of a MSBP case, he/she must search deeper and perhaps more diligently than in other types of child abuse cases in order to find the hidden abusive causes endemic in this form of child abuse. The root causes are normally masked in the separate world of hospitalization and medicine.

The interviewer must therefore re-evaluate his/her perhaps ingrained opinion of what constitutes abuse and be open-minded enough to explore the possibilities that exist strongly in these types of cases.

Remember, "Things are not always what they appear to be" and, *no one* is beyond suspicion.

In most cases of MSBP, there is a marked absence of other forms of abuse such as direct physical injury or sexual assault. The victims are not routinely brought to the attention of the authorities as in cases of physical or sexual abuse victims. Serial victimizations by known or suspected Munchausen Syndrome offenders requires that law enforcement become familiar with the dynamics of Munchausen Syndrome. The ability of an interviewer to elicit truthful responses ultimately rests with his/her knowledge, understanding, and experience with this phenomenon.

Conclusion

The potential for death as well as life-threatening physical damage make this particular disorder a genuine cause for concern for both the medical profession and law enforcement. From an investigative perspective, Munchausen Syndrome by Proxy (MSBP) should be considered as a possible motive in any questionable or unexplained death of a child especially when the death occurs under the circumstances presented in this section.

MSBP victims are commonly referred through intuitive medical personnel or citizens/family members that have been educated regarding MSBP as a form of child abuse. In some instances, the reporter may have a higher understanding of the MSBP concept than the agency to whom it is reported and become frustrated with a department's reaction to the allegation. It is imperative that law enforcement be aware of this variant form of child abuse (MSBP). The ever increasing numbers of cases reported and the public's education of MSBP, once thought to be rare, requires that law enforcement be prepared to confront this public health issue.

It should be noted that a failure to understand the dynamics of MSBP could very well allow previously committed homicides of children in a Munchausen Syndrome by Proxy environment to remain undetected.[14]

---

[14] The information on interviewing MSBP suspects provided by Artingstall, K.

Stalkers

Introduction

This section focuses on the phenomenon of stalking. The author presents specific types of stalkers and identifies experts and organizations which can assist in intervention strategies. In addition, the author will provide information on anti-stalker legislation which provides law enforcement with the necessary legal tools to protect society from the terror of this type of offender.

Stalkers

A stalker is someone who intentionally and repeatedly follows, attempts to contact, harasses, and/or intimidates another person. The author refers to such person as "The Target." A stalker usually follows the target to his or her home, school, place of employment, business, or any location. Stalkers often intimidate their victims through unsolicited and intrusive communications or by engaging in conduct which is threatening or indicates that the stalker intends to injure the person or property of the target. This includes sexual assault and/or bodily harm.

Stalking incidents indicate an obesssion on the part of the offender which is manifested through a persistent and intense preoccupation with the victim or target.

Historically, stalkers are usually males known to the victim and in most instances, involve former lovers, boyfriends, or spouses. However, it should be noted that there are also stalkers who are complete strangers to the target. These stalkers can be men or women who have a delusional fixation on the victim.

In either event, the stalker represents a significant law enforcement problem. The police may be keenly aware of the potentially lethal nature of the stalking activities, but are oftentimes prevented from taking any action or arresting the offender due to legal technicalities.

Orders of Protection

The traditional response of the criminal justice system to threats posed by stalking has been to issue "Orders of Protection" or "Restraining Orders." Court orders require that the respondent and/or defendant stay away from a person or premises, or refrain from verbal or physical abuse. If the person named on the order is proven to have violated the instructions, he or she can be held in contempt.

Figure 20.17. **STALKER VICTIM.** This victim was accosted in her sleep by an assailant who had been stalking her and her roommate. When her roommate left on "Spring Break," the killer gained access to the young woman's apartment. He blindfolded her eyes and secured her hands and arms with bindings. (Courtesy of Investigator Tom Jordan, State College Police Department, State College, Pennsylvania.)

In some instances, court orders may prove to be effective deterrents. Cases of this nature usually involve normal and rational respondents who remain away from the petitioners in order to avoid any further legal problems.

However, in most instances these court orders prove absolutely useless. The author has personally investigated hundreds of cases where women, who had obtained orders of protection, were beaten, knifed, sexually assaulted, and killed.

In one particular case the offender quite graphically indicated his contempt for both the Order of Protection and the criminal justice system. He had stabbed his wife to death after ripping-up the court order. When I arrived at the crime scene, I observed the woman's body lying on the floor with the shredded court order knifed into her chest.

In fact, at one point in my career, so many victims under orders of protection were being killed that we came to refer to the court orders as "Orders of Illusion." These documents gave the victim the illusion of being protected but were virtually unenforceable.

Figure 20.18. **STABBING INJURIES.** The victim was multiply stabbed in the chest and breast by her assailant, who became enraged when she defecated out of fear. His original intent was to rape her. He cleaned the blood off of her chest and then covered the stab wounds. The face of the victim was also covered with the bed cover, which had been removed when the body was found. (Courtesy of Investigator Tom Jordan, State College Police Department, State College, Pennsylvania.)

Anti-Stalker Legislation

Anti-stalker legislation appears to be a logical and workable solution. This type of legislation provides law enforcement authorities with the statutory tools they require to protect victims from inappropriate and unwanted contact. Anti-stalker laws are aimed at halting patterns of threats and harassment that often precede violent acts of assault, rape, and murder.

In 1990, the State of California passed the first anti-stalking law. This legislation was the direct result of the murder of five young women within a 6-week period. All but one had sought help in vain. Presently, more than 20 other states have enacted similar legislation.

The anti-stalker laws specifically define conduct which is considered threatening and intimidating and place the onus on the stalker to prove that he or she did not intend to harass or frighten the victim. The crime is elevated from misdemeanor to felony status based upon the issuance of an injunction or restraining order. In addition, the felony degree is also elevated based upon the seriousness of the violation or threat.

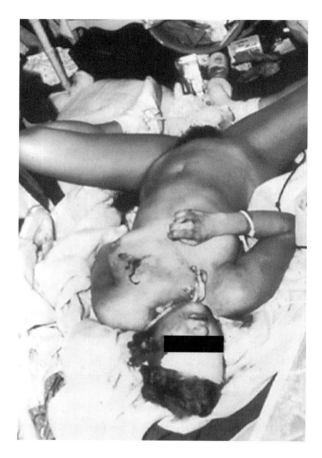

Figure 20.19. **THE VICTIM'S BODY POSED FOR VIEWING.** The killer then posed the
body spreading her legs open to expose the vaginal area. Police reconstruction indicated
that he had previously watched the victim from an empty apartment across from where the
victim lived. He then went back to this location to view the nude and sexually positioned
body of his victim. (Courtesy of Investigator Tom Jordan, State College Police Department,
State College, Pennsylvania.)

The overall effectiveness of anti-stalker laws, however, still remain
with the courts. In order for these laws to be effective, the judges must
take them seriously. Their legal responsibility must be guided primarily
by the nature of the act and the seriousness of the threat and they must
be willing to properly sentence and restrain offenders who stalk.

Types of Stalkers

Clinically speaking, stalkers can be divided into two specific types of
personalities. The psychopathic personality who is fully aware of the

Figure 20.20. **STALKING VICTIM (FOUND INSIDE HER APARTMENT).** The victim recognized her assailant at the front door and mistakenly had admitted him. He attacked her with a knife. The victim was then raped and sodomized. The investigation revealed that he had repeatedly attempted to make contact with her by leaving notes on her car and "showing-up" at her apartment. (Courtesy of Detective Alan Patton, Grand Prairie, Texas Police Department. Photo by Evidence Technician Don Swanz.)

criminality of his actions and the psychotic personality who may be suffering from a psychosis and/or has been diagnosed as having a specific disorder.

The motivations for stalking range from power and control scenarios to bizarre obsessive delusions including infatuation fantasies.

The Psychopathic Personality Stalker

This type of stalker is invariably a male offender and represents the largest population of stalkers. He comes from an abusive home and dysfunctional family where violence was the normal way to settle disputes. Both the offender and the offender's mother were themselves, subjects of domestic violence. They are basically control freaks who are easily stressed and frustrated and cannot take responsibility for their own actions.

This type of offender insists on male dominance. He will also exhibit a hypermacho exterior in order to hide feelings of inferiority.

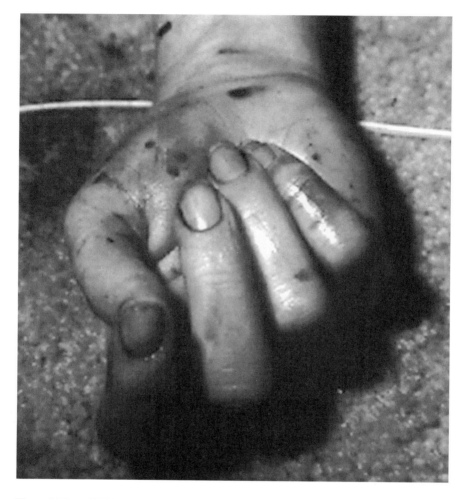

Figure 20.21. **DEFENSE WOUNDS.** Victim suffered multiple defense wounds as she tried to fight off her attacker. (Courtesy of Detective Alan Patton, Grand Prairie, Texas Police Department. Photo by Evidence Technician Don Swanz.)

They are abusive personalities who harbor hostility against women. However, if the woman attempts to separate or end this abusive relationship, this type of offender will respond with violence.

The stalker with the psychopathic personality is the most common type of stalker. This offender may have had a relationship terminated because of his abuse and then refuses to accept the termination.

Abusive men frequently wage psychological warfare against their victims in shrewd, untraceable ways. They destroy and vandalize property, send packages or deliveries, poison and kill pets, phone anonymous threats, and engage in various forms of harassment.

Figure 20.22. **BLOOD ON FEET.** Indicating that she had run through her own blood as she attempted to escape from the killer. (Courtesy of Detective Alan Patton, Grand Prairie, Texas Police Department. Photo by Evidence Technician Don Swanz.)

Figure 20.23. **MULTIPLE STABBING.** The victim had been stabbed 113 times into her chest and breast area. She also had numerous defense wounds on her hands and arms. The killer then manipulated her body to engage in sexual assault. Observe the blood dripping from her wounds indicating that the body has been turned over. This is a classic "lust murder." (Courtesy of Detective Alan Patton, Grand Prairie, Texas Police Department. Photo by Evidence Technician Don Swanz.)

The male abuser engages in stalking because he has lost his control over the target (a former girlfriend or wife). The stalking puts him back into control. He is motivated by the perverse psychology of "If I can't have you, then no one can have you!"

According to Ruth Micklem, co-director of Virginians Against Domestic Violence, "Nearly one third of all women killed in America are murdered by their husbands or boyfriends and as many as 90% of them have been stalked." (*Newsweek*, July 13, 1992.)

CASE HISTORY

April, a young woman who had divorced her abusive husband, secured a Family Court Order of Protection because the ex-husband, Anthony, continued to harass her. The police could not arrest Anthony when April reported that he had cut her phone lines and slashed her tires because there were no witnesses. Her ex-husband was finally arrested when police caught him breaking into his ex-wife's house.

However, the judge released Anthony on $25 bail and the harassment grew worse. The next incident was almost fatal. Anthony, who had managed to gain entry into April's house, ambushed April from a closet with a sawed-off .22 rifle and a knife. He repeatedly cut and stabbed her with the hunting knife rupturing her lung and liver. Anthony was arrested and charged with attempted murder. April remained hospitalized for over a month with her injuries.

Anthony was held on $25,000 bail despite pleas by the district attorney for higher bail and the seriousness of the charges; 8 months later, Anthony's family bailed him out. The police and district attorney feared for April's safety and installed a sophisticated intrusion alarm in her house. In addition, the police provided her with a hand-held electronic device to signal police in an emergency.

Within 2 months of his release, Anthony, who had been ordered to stay away from April, began to engage in further harassment. April informed the police and the District Attorney's Office. The district attorney tried to secure higher bail but the judge refused citing that the purpose of bail was only to secure the defendant's presence for trial.

The next incident was fatal. April was gunned down in front of her home by Anthony, who fled the scene and then committed suicide.

The Psychotic Personality Stalker

This type of stalker can be a male or female who becomes obsessed and/or preoccupied with one or more systematized delusions. Many of these stalkers do in fact have a diagnosable mental disorder, i.e., paranoia, schizophrenia, bipolar (affective disorder — manic-depressive), etc.

They suffer from a delusional fixation in that they become obsessed with the target. The target is usually a stranger. However, these types of stalkers have been known to target co-workers, neighbors, and even acquaintances. They attempt to contact the target thus making him or her aware of their existence or presence through a series of activities such as telephone calls, letters, gifts, visits, and surveillance.

A subtype of the psychotic personality stalker is found in the diagnosis of erotomania. In the erotomanic type, "the central theme of an erotic delusion is that one is loved by another." (DSM-IV 297.01, Delusional Disorder subtype, p. 297.)

In erotomania, the stalker, who can be male or female, is a stranger who believes that the victim, usually someone famous or rich, is in love with him or her. The targets are usually persons of higher social status than the stalker, i.e., actors, actresses, or other public figures.

CASE HISTORY — DELUSIONAL FIXATION

Kathleen began receiving telephone calls from a male, who identified himself as a classmate. The phone calls became quite strange. The next contact was made by following her and then threatening to kill her boyfriend. The offender was finally arrested in possession of a semi-automatic weapon, a knife, and handcuffs. He was given psychiatric evaluation and released.

Three months later, the same offender was caught surveilling Kathleen's parent's home. The police were notified and the offender was again arrested. Once again, he had a semi-automatic weapon and ammunition, a knife, a pair of handcuffs, and this time, a police scanner. He confessed that he was going to kidnap her and bring her into the mountains. This time the offender got a year in a mental hospital. Kathleen obtained a restraining order.

However, 3 years later, the offender again entered her life. While she was walking down the beach she saw him coming towards her with a .357 magnum. She managed to escape to her beach house where she called the police. The offender was able to elude the police. However, he called her house. The next day he was captured. However, since the gun didn't have a firing pin, he was charged only with a misdemeanor.

The offender received 60 days for violation of the restraining order and given 3 years probation. Two years later the same offender began to communicate with her. He staked-out her house, set off her alarm system, and made several phone calls to the frightened young woman. He was finally arrested for five counts of violation of a restraining order. The maximum sentence he could have received was 5 years; instead, he got 4 months.

Five months later, the offender confronted Kathleen in the kitchen of her home. He had a knife and a gun. She kept the offender talking.

While they were talking the phone rang. It was Kathleen's mother, who realized that something was wrong. Kathleen's mom called the police. The police were waiting when the offender exited the house with Kathleen.

The offender was charged with several counts including attempted kidnapping. His maximum sentence could have been 16 years. Instead, once again, the offender was able to plea bargain it down to 8 years.

At the sentencing, Kathleen told the judge that the experts had advised her that this offender's fixation was not curable and that when he is released he would be back. The offender nodded his head in agreement.

CASE HISTORY — DELUSIONAL FIXATION AND EROTOMANIA

In May of 1991, the family of a 10-year-old girl, who the author will refer to as Judy, began to experience an unsettling series of events. At first, these events seemed cute and harmless. The family was finding gifts and notes on their front porch addressed to Judy. The family at first thought that it might be some little boy from Judy's fourth-grade class. However, the messages and the gifts became more and more bizarre as the stalker pursued his delusion that he and the 10-year-old Judy were destined for one another.

The family called the police several times due to the series of strange events. In one note the writer stated "I saw you with the boy down the street, Judy you slut."

In another note, the writer referred to his fantasy of living on a desert island with Judy and that he had been watching Judy since she was 7 years old.

In October, 1991, the family left for a vacation in order to get away from these strange events. While they were gone someone broke into their house. When the family returned, they noticed that someone had gone through their telephone book and the page with the phone number of Judy's grandmother was open.

The next event involved a man calling the grandmother at 3:00 A.M. rambling on about how someday he and Judy would be in heaven together. The police were notified about the burglary and the phone calls. In addition, the family began to ask their neighbors for help. One of the neighbors recalled seeing a man staying at the home of a woman in the area. She recalled that the man had given her 12-year-old foster daughter a rosebush and when the man saw the girl playing with another neighborhood boy, he ripped the bush out of the ground.

The police were notified and questioned the woman that the man was staying with. She denied that there was a man living with her. The police obtained a search warrant and found a 24-year-old man hiding upstairs. He was arrested for burglary.

While he was in jail, Judy began receiving signed letters from the offender. The courts decided to release the suspect with a warning and have him sent to a different town where he would be set-up with a job. The family voiced their concern about the letters and their daughter's safety.

The court issued a restraining order against the defendant. His first day out, the family found a note from him on their front porch. The suspect was rearrested but continued to send both "love" and "hate" letters to Judy. He would write about waiting 10 years for Judy. He also wrote that he wanted her "pure" and that he wouldn't have sex with her until their honeymoon. This suspect has since been ordered by the courts to cease and desist.

However, the offender is due for release. In the words of the family, "He gains his freedom, we lose ours."

The important point to note in the above cases is that the offenders, despite the law enforcement intervention, continued to pursue their targets. This type of stalkers have a permanent and unshakable delusional system accompanied by a preservation of clear and orderly thinking. On the surface they present as "normal" or sane when not pursuing their target. Others may even keep their delusions a secret and hide their fixation from family, friends, or co-workers.

It is not enough to just arrest these type of offenders. They need to be vigorously prosecuted and jailed. New anti-stalker laws provide the basis for such prosecution.

Erotomania Involving Obsessed Fans and Stalkers

In 1989, actress Rebecca Shaeffer was killed by an obsessed fan named Robert Bardo. Subsequent investigation revealed that Bardo had been communicating and stalking Ms. Schaeffer for 2 years.

Bardo had fantasized and dreamed of someday marrying the former star of the short-lived "My Sister Sam" TV series. He actually believed that there was a relationship between him and Rebecca Shaeffer.

In 1982, actress Theresa Saldana survived a vicious knife attack by a stalker named Arthur Jackson, who believed that he had a "devine mission" to kill her and take her to heaven.

David Letterman, Johnny Carson, Michael J. Fox, and Olivia Newton-John are just a few of the famous celebrities who have been stalked by fanatical and obsessed fans.

According to the experts on celebrity stalking, there are literally thousands of dangerous and obsessed fans who stalk and are capable of violence.

Mr. Gavin deBecker of Los Angeles is the nation's acknowledged expert on star-stalking and the assessment of threats to public figures. His firm, Gavin deBecker, Inc. is located in Studio City, California

(818) 505-0177. The firm maintains an extensive library of threat communications and provides computer analysis, monitoring of potential stalkers, and protection services for a number of celebrities and V.I.P.s.

Gavin deBecker devised a computer program that analyzes "inappropriate communications" and rates the relative degree of hazard posed by their authors. The system focuses on what deBecker refers to as pre-incident indicators, or PINS. The MOSAIC system keeps track of these PINS, communications, and potential threats.

MOSAIC II, an updated version, has been adopted by the California State Police, who are responsibile for providing security for state government and elected officials. The contact person and liason for MOSAIC is available for consultation to other law enforcement agencies at 916-322-3337.

Law Enforcement Response to Stalker Incidents

Traditionally, law enforcement and the criminal justice system have been ill-equipped to deal with the stalker. The Orders of Protection and Restraining Orders meant to protect victims from unwanted contact have proven to be ineffective in stalker cases. In cases where stalkers communicate with their victims, the police are powerless to take any action unless the communications involve a threat.

Stalkers basically conduct a form of "psychological warfare" against their targets using methods which ordinarily do not, in and by themselves, necessitate or provide for police intervention. However, with many states now implementing anti-stalker legislation, the police and the criminal justice system have been provided with the legal ammunition and the tools necessary to thwart the stalker.

In California, the first state to pass such legislation, the City of Los Angeles Police Department established an anti-stalker squad, officially called a Threat Management Unit. The unit was established due to the increasing number of complaints and stalking incidents involving celebrities and other prominent people within the L.A. area.

According to their studies, the stalkers are placed into three categories; (1) 9.5% — erotomania: stalker falsely believes that the target, usually someone famous or rich, is in love with the stalker; (2) 43% — love obsession: stalker is a stranger to the target but is obsessed and mounts a campaign of harassment to make the target aware of the stalker's existence; and (3) 47% — simple obsession: stalker, usually a male, knows the target as an ex-spouse, ex-lover, or former boss, and begins a campaign of harassment.

Dr. Park Dietz, a forensic psychiatrist and nationally renowned consultant to law enforcement agencies, including the FBI, has conducted the only research and major study on the phenomenon of stalking. According to Dr. Dietz, "We have disproved the myth that only threats count. Nearly everyone makes the mistake of assuming that unless there is a threat, you can safely ignore 'nut mail,' 'kook calls,' and weird visitors. This false assumption is the source of more misguided policy and decision-making than any other error in this field."

Dr. Dietz states, "All threats should be recorded, reported, and assessed — and so should all other frightening, weird, or troublesome communications and visits, whether they contain threats or not."

Dr. Dietz is associated with Threat Assessment Group, Inc. located in southern Califronia. His organization can be accessed through telephone number (714) 644-3537.

This organization, under contract with the FBI, was created to analyze threat communications and provide consultation to law enforcement agencies, Fortune 500 companies, and media figures. This group also analyzes and assesses dangerousness of personnel and/or consumers in order to prevent workplace violence and cope with threatened tampering or sabotage.

The law enforcement response to these recommendations should be to encourage victims to make police reports of the incidents and have the victim document any harassment. These records can then serve as a basis for future actions by the police, prosecutors, courts, or psychiatrists who need such documentation to achieve maximum results from arrest or commitment.

Conclusion

Anti-stalker legislation provides law enforcement authorities with the statutory tools they need to protect victims from inappropriate and unwanted contact. However, laws alone will not protect victims from stalkers. The frightening reality of the stalker is in the complexity of their delusions, motivations, and objectives. Even the experts cannot agree on totally effective interventions.

The information provided in this section is intended to assist investigators by providing the psychopathology and symptomology of stalkers and their potential for violence as well as furnish information on viable resources available.

VI-CAP, State-Wide and Regional Information Systems

For many years police investigators working in different jurisdictions on similar cases have worked independently of one another. They did not have access to the information available elsewhere that could speed and enhance investigations in their own jurisdiction. For example, although investigators knew that similar crimes were being committed in jurisdictions across the country, they sometimes had difficulty finding out what types of victims had been singled out, what methods of operation had been repeatedly used, or which suspects were under investigation.

In addition to lack of information, some violent crimes are so unusual, bizarre, and vicious that they are only rarely encountered by detectives working in smaller agencies. Serial violent criminals often transcend boundaries as they travel from city to city and state to state. The crimes of these highly transient criminals are sometimes never linked together.

In 1981, a system designed to identify serial murderers was introduced by Pierce Brooks, a retired Chief of Police and former Homicide Commander of the Los Angeles Police Department. This system was called VI-CAP, an acronym for Violent Criminal Apprehension Program. It was designed to collect, collate, and analyze all aspects of an investigation using the latest computer and communications technology. This event represented an introduction to a new era.

In 1984, the National Center for the Analysis of Violent Crime was formally established by an interagency transfer of funds from the National Institute of Justice to the FBI. The VI-CAP concept of Pierce Brooks was conceptually merged within the National Center for the Analysis of Violent Crime (NCAVC) based at the FBI Academy in Quantico, Virginia.

The main concept of the system was to bring together the fragmented law enforcement efforts from around the country so that they could be consolidated into one national resource center. These services were to be available to the entire law enforcement community. The Brooks concept represented a down-to-earth practical method of accessing information on a nationwide basis, a system which would provide agencies across the United States with the necessary information to conduct investigations.

According to the December, 1986 *FBI Law Enforcement Bulletin,* "The goal of VICAP is to provide all law enforcement agencies reporting similar pattern violent crimes with the information necessary to initiate a coordinated multiagency investigation which will lead to the expeditious identification and apprehension of the offender responsible for the crimes."

However, the immediate problem from an investigative perspective was that, unlike the National Crime Information Center (NCIC), this program did not allow local law enforcement agencies to access the information being sent into the NCAVC files. Thus an excellent concept which originally provided for open access and good communication between agencies was encumbered with the addition of an FBI conduit of analysis and research.

This recognized problem was supposed to be addressed by VI-CAP, which would act as a resource center and a national clearinghouse with the result that law enforcement efforts would be conducted in a coordinated fashion. The National Center for the Analysis of Violent Crime (NCAVC) is capable of comparing and analyzing every VI-CAP report submitted in the United States as well as providing local law enforcement with the identity of the individual investigator and department conducting that inquiry. However, accessing this information continues to be a problem.

The Violent Criminal Apprehension Program — VI-CAP

This system to identify serial murders was introduced to the FBI by Pierce Brooks, a retired Chief of Police and former Homicide Commander of the Los Angeles Police Department.

This VI-CAP system, an acronym for Violent Criminal Apprehension Program, was designed to collect, collate, and analyze all aspects of an investigation using the latest computer and communications technology. It provides a national clearinghouse for unsolved violent crimes. A staff of VI-CAP analysts and investigative case specialists review unsolved violent crimes such as homicides, rapes, child molestations, and arsons which are submitted by law enforcement agencies on a VI-CAP form. The VI-CAP goal has been to centralize all active and unsolved homicide investigations wherein mutilation, dismemberment, torture, or violent sexual trauma was involved. Currently, cases which meet the following criterion are accepted by VI-CAP:

1. Solved or unsolved homicides or attempts, especially those that involve an abduction; are apparently random, motiveless, or sexually oriented; or are known or suspected to be part of a series

2. Missing persons, where the circumstances indicate a strong possibility of foul play and the victim is still missing
3. Unidentified dead bodies where the manner of death is known or suspected to be homicide

Profiling and Consultation Program

The NCAVC's Profiling and Consultation Program provides law enforcement agencies with consultation and opinion of experienced criminal personality profilers. It conducts careful and detailed analysis of violent crimes on a case-by-case basis in order to construct *Criminal Personality Profiles* of the unknown offenders. Consultation is furnished on serial and exceptional cases and also includes case planning strategies, developing probable cause for search warrants, personality assessments, interviewing techniques, coaching prosecutors of violent criminals, and "on-site" major case analysis, consultation and training, which falls under the Training division of NCAVC.

The overall goal of the National Center for the Analysis of Violent Crime is to develop a sophisticated and comprehensive knowledge-based computer system which will assist law enforcement. Eventually, detectives who are working on a murder, rape, arson, or sexual mutilation case, will be able to obtain assistance through a nationwide computer network. The expert-based computer system under development will allow the NCAVC to:

1. Eliminate useless investigative paths which historically have proven fruitless in profiling and identifying the offender
2. Preserve and recall knowledge of similar cases, criminal personality profiles, and research studies
3. Display the hierarchy of complex criminal network problems from the general to specific level
4. Develop and use decision rules which accelerate computation time, as well as allow the investigator to understand the problem better
5. Receive advice and consultation from the expert system on new and existing cases based upon prior knowledge captured by the system
6. Preserve information in an active form as a knowledge base, rather than a mere passive listing of facts and figures
7. Train novices to think as an experienced crime profiler would
8. Create and preserve in an active environment a system that is not subject to human failings, will respond to constant streams of data, and can generalize large bodies of knowledge

The Regional Organized Crime Information Center

The Regional Organized Crime Information Center is one of six projects called Regional Information Sharing Systems (RISS), which were formed to help local, state, and federal law enforcement agencies track and apprehend traveling criminals. ROCIC developed the *HUMP* system to serve as a foundation of a national clearinghouse on unsolved *Homicide/Unidentified body* and *Missing Person* cases, in which the suspect, known or unknown, may travel and operate multi-jurisdictionally.

The information is submitted to ROCIC on a HUMP card and the information is entered into a database. The ROCIC computer then analyzes and collates the information to identify any possible matches and trends on a national basis. Any case that shares certain key similarities with another case or cases in the database is further analyzed and each submitting agency is notified of the possible match so that their investigators can *compare notes and exchange information* about their respective cases.

Since its inception, the HUMP system has proven successful in identifying related and potentially related cases across the country and providing new leads and a direct line of communication between investigators.

The advantage of the HUMP system over the VI-CAP system is that it allows for immediate access by telephone and only requires a one-page report as opposed to a fifteen-page report for a VI-CAP analysis. In addition, ROCIC puts the inquiring investigator directly in touch with his counterpart on the related case (see HUMP card).

Submission of Cases

The investigator simply fills-out a HUMP card. In addition to the information on the card, ROCIC requests a short narrative on the back of the card or on a separate sheet of paper. ROCIC will accept telephone inquiries at 1-800-238-7985 or through FAX at 1-800-366-3658. Mail the card to:

Regional Organized Crime Information Center
545 Marriott Drive, Suite 850
Nashville, Tennessee 37214-5019

The Homicide Investigation and Tracking System (HITS)

Washington State's Homicide Investigation and Tracking System (HITS) system relies on law enforcement agencies to voluntarily submit information to HITS investigators on murders, attempted murders, missing persons cases in which foul play is suspected, unidentified persons believed to be murder victims, and predatory sex offenses.

Detectives conducting investigations need methods and tools that will help them do their jobs as effectively and efficiently as possible. Ready access to information about the crimes being investigated is one of their needs. This information is crucial in order to develop good leads and in turn to solve the case.

The Homicide Investigation and Tracking System (HITS) was developed by Robert D. Keppel who started the program in Washington State. HITS is helping investigators work better by allowing them *access* via computer to a wide range of information about serious crimes and to resources that can help solve them.

Basically, HITS is a murder and sexual assault investigation system that collects, collates, and analyzes the salient characteristics of all murders and predatory sexual offenses in the states of Washington and Oregon.

Ironically, it was the National Institute of Justice (NIJ), the research arm of the Department of Justice, which played a key role in the development of this project. This same organization encouraged Pierce Brooks in the 1970s to pursue VI-CAP, which was originally designed to provide local law enforcement access. Interestingly, HITS complements Federal research and programs against violent crime because the system generates a VI-CAP report which is sent to the National Center for the analysis of Violent Crime. VI-CAP staff can then determine if similar pattern characteristics exist among the individual cases in the VI-CAP system.

HITS provides three major services to law enforcement agencies. First, it supplies information related to a murder or predatory sexual assault case, including the following:

- Incidents with similar characteristics involving murder, attempted murder, suspected murder, or predatory sexual assault and persons missing as a result of suspected foul play
- Evidence, victimology, offender characteristics, offender's method of operation, associates, geographic location of the case, weapons, and vehicles
- Identification of known murderers and sex offenders living in a particular community

Second, HITS permits analysis of murder cases to identify:

- Factors that may help solve a particular murder case
- Possible links between a single victim, offender, or case and other incidents of violence

- Verification of statements provided by informants, offenders, or both, in which the information relating to an alleged murder is incomplete or questionable

Third, HITS provides investigators with the following resources:

- Names of experts who can assist with a murder or sexual assault investigation
- Advice and technical assistance on the various steps to be followed in a murder or sexual assault investigation

Prior to HITS' use in Washington State, the only way to obtain this type of crime information was through time-consuming, labor-intensive personal visits, interviews, telephone calls, teletypes, and letters. By filling out a simple form that takes less than 30 minutes, investigators save countless hours on the phone or on their feet searching for information that the HITS system locates for them. More importantly, HITS provides investigators with that important two-way communication.

HITS was founded on the premise that information plays a critical role in solving homicides. The key to solving crimes and making arrests is to understand *how much* and *what kind* of information is available and *how to organize* it to make it more accessible and useful. Because of the need to collect and collate violent crime information, HITS investigator/analysts work very closely with police detectives to provide assistance in their cases.

For further information on HITS, the reader is directed to contact HITS UNIT/Criminal Division, Washington State Attorney General's Office, 2000 Bank of California Center, 900 4th Avenue, Seattle, WA 98164 or call 1-800-345-2793.

In my opinion, as an expert in homicide investigations, the most viable alternative to VI-CAP is a series of state-wide or regional systems which compile all serious crimes such as rape, murder, and gang-related crime into integrated data bases that provide ready access to local law enforcement. In addition, any missing persons cases where the circumstances indicate that they are missing under suspicious circumstances as well as unidentified bodies where the manner of death is known or suspected to be homicidal in nature should be entered into the system.

The author wishes to acknowledge the assistance of Dr. Lowell J. Levine, D.D.S. and Dr. Arthur Goldman, D.D.S. for the technical information and for contributing the case histories in the section on bite marks. I also wish to acknowledge Dr. Russell E. Schneider, D.D.S., Dr. Carl Hagstrom, D.D.S., and Dr. Mary A. Cimrmancic, D.D.S. of the Northern Illinois Forensic Odontologic Consultants Group for their contribution on alternative light sources.

The author also wishes to acknowledge the contribution of Retired Sgt. Timothy Byrnes. He holds a B.S. Degree from St. John's University and an M.A. from John Jay College of Criminal Justice. He received his initial training in hypnosis at the Ethical Hypnosis Training Center in South Orange, New Jersey. In addition, Lt. Byrnes studied under Dr. Martin Reiser who was Director of Behavioral Science Services, Los Angeles Police Department and is Director of the Law Enforcement Hypnosis Institute, Inc. He is considered to be an expert in the field of hypnosis as used by law enforcement agencies.

The author acknowledges the Peel Regional Police Department, Brampton Ontario, Canada, specifically Inspector Rod Piukkala for providing this information relative to the above procedures used to recover latent print evidence from a human body.

The author wishes to acknowledge the contribution of retired Det. Donald Sullivan, who has conducted over 500 forensic polygraph examinations and participated in many homicide investigations. He is a graduate of the National Training Center of Polygraph Science, Vice President of the New York State Polygraph Association, Research Editor for the *Journal of Polygraph Science*, and lecturer and instructor in the field of polygraph examinations.

The author wishes to acknowledge the assistance and contribution of Det. Kathryn Artingstall, who is a recognized law enforcement authority on the subject of Munchausen Syndrome By Proxy. In addition, the author also wishes to acknowledge Supervisory Special Agent Larry C. Brubaker of the Minneapolis, Minnesota Office of the FBI, who provided his insights and expertise in the area of MSBP which is included in this section of the textbook.

Finally, the author wishes to acknowledge the assistance of Dr. Ronald Turco, a Forensic Psychiatrist, who assisted the author with an intepretation of behaviors as they apply to the dynamics of the stalker. Also, the author wishes to acknowledge the contribution of Dr. Park Elliott Dietz, a psychiatrist and medical doctor, who specializes in Threat Assessment and conducted the first survey into stalking. I also wish to acknowledge the contribution of Mr. Gavin deBecker, who is a recognized expert in the field, whose firm maintains an extensive library of threat communications and provides computer analysis, monitoring of potential stalkers, and protection services for a number of celebrities and V.I.P.s of stalking incidents.

Selected Reading

Bite Mark Identification

Levine, Lowell J. "Forensie Odontology Today — A New Forensie Science." *FBI Law Enforcement Bulletin*, August 1972.

Levine, Lowell J. "Bite Mark Evidence." Dental Clinics of North America 21 (1977).

Sperber, Norman D. "Bite Mark Evidence in Crimes Against Persons." *FBI Law Enforcement Bulletin,* July 1981.

West, Michael, D.D.S., Barsley, Robert E., D.D.S., J. D., Hall, John, D.M.D., Hayne, Steve, M.D., and Cimrmancic, Mary A., D.D.S. "The Detection and Documentation of Trace Wound Patterns by Use of an Alternative Light Source." *Journal of Forensic Sciences*, November, 1992.

Personal interview with Dr. Russel E. Schneider, D.D.S., relative to Alternate Light Source technology, May 30, 1995.

Hypnosis

Reiser, Martin I., (Ed.) *Handbook of Investigative Hypnosis.* Los Angeles, California. Lehi Publishing Co., 1980.

Latent Prints on Human Skin

Federal Bureau of Investigation. Police Instructor's Bulletin. Quantico, Virginia: Law Enforcement Training Division, 1976.

Svensson, Arne, Wendel, Otto, and Fisher, Barry A. J. *Techniques of Crime Scene Investigation,* 5th ed. New York: Elsevier Science Publishing Co., Inc., 1992.

Psycholinguistics

Foss, Donald J. and Hakes, David T. *Psycholinguistics.* Englewood Cliffs, New Jersey: Prentice-Hall, Inc., 1978.

Jakobovits, L. and Miron, Murray S. (Eds.), *Readings in the Psychology of Language.* Englewood Cliffs, New Jersey: Prentice-Hall, Inc., 1967.

Miron, Murray S. and Douglas, John E. "Threat Analysis — The Psycholinguistic Approach. *FBI Law Enforcement Bulletin*, September 1979.

Miron, Murray S. and Goldstein, A. P. *Hostage.* New York: Pergamon Press, 1979.

Miron, Murray S. and Pasquale, A. "Psycholinguistic Analyses of Coercion." *Journal of Psycholinguistic Research,* 2 (1978).

Munchausen Syndrome by Proxy

American Psychiatric Association. *Diagnostic and Statistical Manual of Mental Disorders,* (DSM-IV), 4th ed. Washington, D.C.: American Psychiatric Association, 1994.

Artingstall, K. "Officers Be Aware: Munchausens Syndrome by Proxy." January, 1994, in press.

Artingstall, Kathryn A. "Munchausen Syndrome By Proxy." *FBI Law Enforcement Bulletin*, August, 1995, pp. 5–10.

Artingstall, Kathryn A. and Brubaker, Larry. "Muchausen Syndrome-Related Offenses." *Law and Order Magazine*, Vol. 43, No. 10, October, 1995.

Artingstall Kathryn A. and Brubaker, Larry. "Interview Techniques for MSBP Related Investigations." *Law and Order Magazine*, Vol. 43, No. 10, October, 1995.

Asher, R. "Munchausen's Syndrome." *Lancet I*, 1951, 339–341.

Boros, S. M.D., Ophoven, J. M.D., Anderson, R., M.D., and Brubaker, L. "Munchausens Syndrome by Proxy: A Profile of Medical child Abuse." Children's Hospital of St. Paul, 1991.

Boros, Stephen, M.D. and Brubaker, Larry C. "Munchausen Syndrome by Proxy: Case Accounts." *FBI Law Enforcement Bulletin*, June, 1992, 16–20.

Dateline – NBC, documentary "Munchausen syndrome by Proxy" January 5, 1993.

DiMaio, D. J. M.D. and DiMaio, V.J. *Forensic Pathology*. Chapter 12 "Neonaticide, Infanticide, and Child Homicide" New York: Elsevier, 1989.

Geberth, Vernon J. "Munchausen Syndrome By Proxy (MSBP) — An Investigative Perspective." *Law and Order Magazine*, Vol. 42, No. 8, Illinois, August, 1994.

Guandolo, V. "Munchausen Syndrome by Proxy: An Outpatient Challenge," Pediatrics, Vol. 75 No. 3, March, 1985.

Hanon, K. "Child Abuse: "Munchausen's Syndrome by Proxy." *FBI Law Enforcement Bulletin*, December, 1991.

Jones, J. G., Butler, H. L., Hamilton, B., Perdue, J. D., Stern, H. P., and Woody, R. C. "Munchausen Syndrome by Proxy." *Child Abuse and Neglect*, October 1986, 33–40.

Meadow, R. "Munchausen Syndrome by Proxy: The Hinterland of Child Abuse." *Lancet II*. 1977, 343–345.

Meadow, R. Munchausen Syndrome by Proxy. *Archives of Diseases in Childhood*, Vol. 57, 1982.

Raspe, R. E. *The Surprising Adventures of Baron Munchausen*. New York: Peter Pauper, 1944.

Rosenberg, D. A. "Web of Deceit: a Literature Review of Munchausen Syndrome by Proxy." *Child Abuse and Neglect*, November, 1987, 561–563.

Stalkers

DeBecker, Gavin. Personal Interview, April 23, 1992.

Dietz, Park Elliot, M.D. Personal Interview, August 24, 1992.

Geberth, Vernon J. "Stalkers." *Law and Order Magazine*, Vol. 40, No. 10, Illinois, October, 1992.

Geberth, Vernon J. Author's Files.
Lane, John Lieutenant LAPD, Threat Management Unit, Personal Interview, August 18, 1992.
Newsweek, July 13, 1992, "Murderous Obsession." p. 60–62.
Turco, Ronald, M.D. Personal Interview, August 20, 1992.
U.S.A. Today, July 21, 1992, "Legislatures tackling the terror of stalking.", p. 9A.

VI-CAP, State-Wide and Regional Information Systems

Geberth, Vernon J. "State-Wide and Regional Information Systems." *Law and Order Magazine,* Vol. 42, No. 4, Illinois, April, 1994.
Geberth, V. J. *Practical Homicide Investigation: Tactics, Procedures, and Forensic Techniques,* 2nd ed. Florida, CRC Press, Inc., 1993.

Investigative Assessment: Criminal Personality Profiling 21

The purpose of this chapter is to provide the criminal investigator with practical information on the application of criminal personality profiling to the homicide investigation.

History of Profiling

Profiling is not an entirely new concept. During World War II, the Office of Strategic Services (OSS) employed a psychiatrist, William Langer, to profile Adolf Hitler.[1] Furthermore, as I will explain, such cases as the "Boston Strangler" and the "Mad Bomber" of New York City were similarly profiled by a psychiatrist in the 1950s and 1960s.

Traditionally, however, psychiatrists and psychologists only entered into an analysis of a crime after the suspect was in custody. Their evaluations were usually aimed at determining whether or not the suspect was "sane" at the time he or she committed the offense.

An exception to this traditional role took place during the late 1950s and early 1960s when Dr. James A. Brussel, a New York City psychiatrist, provided law enforcement authorities with valuable information on such sensational cases as the "Mad Bomber" of New York City, and the "Boston Strangler" of Boston, Massachusetts. There were other important investigations in which he "profiled" the suspect based on the psychodynamics of an event and the psychiatric "clues" he deduced from the crimes he examined.

In the Mad Bomber case, police authorities asked Dr. Brussel to provide them with his professional opinion. Dr. Brussel reviewed the huge case file, the photographs, and a number of letters that the suspect had mailed over a 16-year period. Without engaging in what best can be described as a lot of psychoanalytic double talk, he simply rendered the following opinion: "Look for a heavy man. Middle aged. Foreign born. Roman Catholic. Single. Lives with a brother or sister." He also added: "...when you find him, chances are he'll be wearing a double breasted suit. Buttoned."[2]

On January 20, 1957, police arrested George Metesky and charged him with being the infamous Mad Bomber. He was exactly as described by Dr. Brussel. When he was taken into custody he was even wearing a double breasted suit.

In April, 1964, Dr. Brussel was again invited into a major police investigation. A group of physicians and psychiatrists were brought together in Boston, Massachusetts in connection with the Boston Strangler cases, which had occurred between June 14, 1962 and January 4, 1964. The official name of the group was the Medical-Psychiatric Committee. There had been 11 sex-related murders in the Boston area (later this total would be amended to 13) and all investigative efforts to identify the person or persons responsible had failed. The circumstances of the deaths seemed to indicate that there were two stranglers involved. The Committee members based this opinion on the fact that the first group of stranglings involved older women, while the second group involved the stranglings of younger women. Also, the psychosexual activity in both sets of killings differed. Dr. Brussel, however, did not agree with the Committee. He maintained that one man was responsible. The killings mysteriously stopped and the Committee was eventually disbanded. However, in November, 1964 a man identified as Albert DeSalvo came to the attention of authorities. He was ultimately identified as the Boston Strangler. He "fit" the profile that Dr. Brussel had provided to the police.[3]

Dr. Brussel's ability to interpret bizarre behaviors and then translate this psychiatric knowledge into investigative realities proved to be an extremely effective tactic. He had his own unique method of applying psychiatric principles in reverse with a blend of science and intuition. Dr. Brussel also applied the results of studies by the late Ernst Kretschmer, a German psychiatrist who demonstrated that a person's physical build is often associated with a certain type of personality and in the event of psychiatric illness, with a particular disorder, e.g., 85% paranoiacs have an "athletic" body type.[4] A schizophrenic, according to Kreteschmer would most likely be asthenic in build, thin, small framed, angular,[5] while a paranoid schizophrenic with strong paranoid features would most likely have the well-proportioned build of a paranoiac.[6]

The "Son of Sam" case which occurred in New York City over a period of 13 months during 1976 to 1977 also enlisted the active involvement of both psychiatry and psychology into the investigation. The police were attempting to identify a "mad man" who shot young couples as they sat in parked autos at various locations within the city. The New York City Police Department sought the assistance of these forensic experts in an attempt to assess the personality of this serial killer. In addition, Dr. Murray S. Miron, a professor at Syracuse University, performed a *psycholinguistic* analysis of the communications sent by "Son of Sam" to local newspapers. This profile turned out to closely "fit" the suspect (see "Psycholinguistics," Chapter 20).

Professional investigators soon realized that the participation of psychiatrists and psychologists with the necessary experience and background to assist the police was a practical and logical procedure in specific criminal investigations. Use of profiles, however, remained sporadic until 1978, when the FBI established a *Psychological Profiling Program* within its Behavioral Science Unit in Quantico, Virginia.

Research which had been conducted within the Behavioral Science Unit revealed a serious deficiency in the number of credible and experienced forensic professionals available to assist law enforcement with psychological profiles. The Profiling Program attempted to fill this void by reviewing and researching specific types of cases, such as those previously described in this section and sexual homicides which yield much information about the mind and motivation of the killer.

The profilers worked closely with psychiatrists and psychologists who had the professional experience and background to assist authorities in the interpretation of crimes which demonstrated some sort of psychotic or psychopathic motivation on the part of the offender. These professionals were soon providing law enforcement agencies with strategic information in the form of psychological profiles. This program has proven to be beneficial to law enforcement and has provided homicide detectives with a viable investigative tool which has been successful in pinpointing potential suspects in certain types of murder cases.

In 1981, a system designed to identify serial murderers was introduced by Pierce Brooks, a retired Chief of Police and former Homicide Commander of the Los Angeles Police Department. This system was called VI-CAP, an acronym for Violent Criminal Apprehension Program. It was designed to collect, collate, and analyze all aspects of an investigation using the latest computer and communications technology.

The combined success of both the Psychological Profiling Program and the VI-CAP concept consequently produced Congressional legislation establishing a National Center for the Analysis of Violent Crime in July, 1984.[7]

The National Center for the Analysis of Violent Crime, based at the FBI Academy in Quantico, Virginia, functions as a subdivision of the Behavioral Science Unit and is composed of four sections: Research and Development, VI-CAP, Training, Criminal Personality Profiling and Consultation. In 1995, an additional unit was formulated within the National Center, known as the Child Abduction and Serial Killer Unit (CASKU). This unit is a rapid response component of the Bureau's Critical Incident Response Group (CIRG). The mission of CASKU is to assist law enforcement agencies in cases where a child's safety is believed at risk. It will also be responsive to cases of serial murder, which has been refined by the FBI to be two or more killings, or mass homicides linked to a single killer. Investigative support will be provided through violent crime analysis, investigative strategies, and technical and forensic resource coordination.

Law enforcement can submit investigations of mass, serial, and sensational homicides as well as sex crimes and other specified investigations, to a central location for analysis and identification of similar crime patterns which may exist in other jurisdictions and possibly be related.

In order to present the reader with a practical understanding of criminal personality profiling, the author with the cooperation of the FBI, researched this particular investigative technique by examining certain cases profiled by the Behavioral Science Unit. In addition, I have included personal interviews of Supervisory Special Agent William Hagmaier, now commander of CASKU and retired Supervisory Agent Robert K. Ressler, who was the Commander of the original profiling project. They provided the author with case history information along with the technical information, which has been enhanced with current publications, cited herein.

Criminal Personality Profile

A criminal personality profile is an educated attempt to provide investigative agencies with specific information as to the type of individual who would have committed a certain crime. It involves the preparation of a biographical sketch based upon information taken from the crime scene and victimology which is then integrated with known psychological theory. The profile can be a valuable tool in identifying and pinpointing suspects; however, it must be noted that the profile has its limitations. It should be utilized in conjunction with sound investigative techniques ordinarily employed at the scene of a homicide.

The Purpose of the Profile

The objective of criminal profiling is to provide the investigator with a personality composite of the unknown suspects that will aid apprehension. By studying the crime scene from a psychological standpoint, the criminal psychologist is able to identify and interpret certain items of evidence at the scene, which provide clues to the personality type of the individual or individuals who have committed the crime. Certain clues at a crime scene, by their very nature, do not lend themselves to ordinary collection techniques, such as the emotions of rage, hate, love, fear, and irrationality. According to professional profilers, there is nothing mystical about their work; the procedures they use are well founded in sociological and psychological roots.

When Profiling can be Productive

Criminal personality profiling is usually productive in crimes in which an unknown subject has demonstrated some form of psychopathology in his crime, for example: sadistic torture in sexual assault, evisceration, postmortem slashing and cutting, motiveless fire-setting, lust and mutilation murders, ritualistic crimes, and rapes.

Practically speaking, in any crime in which available evidence indicates a mental, emotional, or personality aberration by an unknown perpetrator, the criminal personality profile can be instrumental in providing the investigator with information that narrows down the leads. It is the behavioral characteristics of the perpetrator as evidenced in the crime scene and not the offense per se that determines the degree of suitability of the case for profiling.

According to Ressler, formerly of the FBI, "All people have personality traits that can be more or less identified. However, an abnormal person becomes more ritualized, displaying a distinct pattern to his behavior. Many times, the behavior and personality are reflected in the crime scene in the same manner that furnishings in a home reflect the character of the owner."[8]

In certain instances, agents of the Criminal Personality Profiling and Consultation section have been able to supply police with such details as approximate height, weight, body type, age, general occupation, and family environment of an unknown suspect. Such a description is based on their initial examination of the scene, using crime scene photos, and preliminary information concerning the crime provided by the requesting agency. *However, as an expert in homicide, I must caution the reader that viewing crime scene photographs without making a personal visit to the crime scene to get a "feel" for the area may prove to be very embarrassing. In addition, there may be other considerations not readily discernible to persons unfamiliar with the geographical areas, local customs, or unique patterns of behavior endemic to an area. Whenever I perform an investigative assessment of a case, I make it a point to visit the crime scene and conduct personal interviews with the assigned investigators, who many times have already "profiled" possible suspects, based on their expertise and knowledge of their jurisdiction.*

The following case history of a particularly bizarre series of homicides shows how criminal profiling can be of value in an investigation. This case, known as "The Vampire Killer" case, concerns an individual identified as Richard Trenton Chase. Chase, who may have also committed additional homicides, was conclusively linked to the murders of six individuals; five of whom were killed in one week. This case history information was provided by Lieutenant Ray Biondi, Commanding Officer of the Homicide Bureau of the Sacramento County, California Sheriff's Department.[9]

CASE HISTORY — DISORGANIZED OFFENDER

The first known murder occurred on December 29, 1977. A 51-year-old man, who had exited his house to retrieve groceries from his car in the driveway was shot once in the chest with a .22 caliber automatic. The man's wife, who was about to follow him out the door heard two shots. Neighbors also reported hearing shots as well as a car drive off. The authorities had no suspects nor motive for the murder. They did, however, have a comparable bullet from the victim's body as well as a shell casing found in the street. The police were perplexed by this murder, which was apparently random and motiveless and they certainly didn't have any suspects. Unbeknownst to police, an individual named Richard Chase was responsible for this crime.

On the morning of January 23, 1978, Chase was roaming around the same neighborhood looking for another victim. He attempted a burglary at one house but the woman, who was home, saw him and called the police. Richard left before they arrived. Less than a half-hour later, Richard was almost caught by another homeowner, who interrupted him as he was burglarizing the owner's home. The man chased the culprit but lost him in the neighborhood. However, he got a good description, which he provided to the police. Richard had stolen approximately $16, a pair of binoculars, and a dagger. In addition, while in the home, Richard urinated on an open drawer of undergarments and had defecated on a bed in the master bedroom.

Richard's next stop was a supermarket. He brought along his rubber gloves and his .22 caliber semi-automatic gun. He had gone home to change his clothes after the burglary. This time he wore his orange jacket.

Figure 21.1. **MULTILATED BODY BY THE VAMPIRE KILLER.** This eviscerated body is the female victim of Richard Trenton Chase, the "Vampire Killer," who was positively linked to six murders. He fit the category of a disorganized serial killer. (Courtesy of Lt. Ray Biondi, Commanding Officer Homicide Bureau, Sacramento, California Sheriff's Department.)

He ran into a woman he had known in high school. She at first didn't recognize him until he asked her if she had a friend named Kurt, who had been killed in a motorcycle accident. She was concerned by this man's appearance. He was unkempt, his hands were dirty, and there was yellow crust around his lips. She figured that this individual was either on drugs or crazy. She suddenly remembered that this stranger had been a classmate in high school and he was asking her about an incident that had occurred 10 years earlier when her boyfriend was killed. Richard tried to make conversation and even asked the young woman for a ride. She decided to try to get away from this individual by getting into line and making a purchase. However, he took an orange juice off the shelf and got in line right behind her. As soon she paid for her groceries, she ran from the store and jumped into her car. The stranger was running after her. She took off in her vehicle and left him standing in the parking lot. Shortly thereafter, Richard killed his next victim.

Figure 21.2. **EVIDENCE OF ANTHROPOPHAGY — RINGLETS OF BLOOD.** In this crime-scene photograph, you can see the ringlet of blood from the cup that the killer used to drink the victim's blood. (Courtesy of Lt. Ray Biondi, Commanding Officer Homicide Bureau, Sacramento, California Sheriff's Department.)

Later that same Monday, a man returned home from work, entered his home and discovered the body of his 22-year-old wife sprawled dead on the bedroom floor. She had been shot as she walked out her front door carrying some garbage bags. The killer then executed her by shooting her in the head. He then dragged her into the rear bedroom where he savagely mutilated her body. The victim's blouse had been pulled up over her chest, her pants forced down to her ankles, and fecal matter (later determined to be human) had been placed into her mouth. The killer, using steak knives taken from the kitchen, had opened up the midsection of his victim and removed her intestines. He then stabbed her through her left nipple. He smeared her blood over his own face and licked his fingers. He then smeared the blood along the inner thighs of the victim. In addition, the victim's blood had apparently been scooped out of her body cavity with a paper cup, which had been discarded at the scene. Investigators found various ringlets corresponding to the diameter of this cup on the floor next to the body. Later it was determined that the killer had drunk the woman's blood. Certain body parts were taken from the scene along with several steak knives.

The Sacramento Sheriff's detectives were completely baffled by this strange and vicious homicide and readily admitted to never having encountered such a bizarre crime. According to Ray Biondi, investigators recognized that this murder could be related to the homicide which had occurred a month earlier. There were some compelling reasons to believe that these two murders were linked. Primarily, the attacks had occurred in the same residential area. Both victims were attacked in "blitz-style" confrontations. Both victims had been shot with a .22 caliber automatic and similar shell casings had been recovered at both scenes. On the other hand, the activity in the most recent case was totally bizarre, compared to the "execution-type" attack on the male victim.

To add to this mystery, the next day within the same neighborhood a young store clerk was executed while on his knees in a cold storage box. Ballistics later indicated that the weapon used in this case was a .38 caliber. This case was eventually determined to be an unrelated event. However, one can imagine how this case complicated an already confusing series of events.

Sheriff's detectives relied heavily upon standard investigative techniques. The neighborhood was thoroughly canvassed for information. The investigators learned that there had been a burglary on the same block as the murder. The burglar had defecated on the bed in the master bedroom. According to Ray Biondi, "We were sure the burglary was related to the murder, we just could not establish the "why." Biondi and his fellow detectives began to look into some possible psychological motivations in an effort to establish the "why."

In the middle of that same week, sheriff's investigators learned that a Labrador puppy had been shot to death in the owner's back yard within this same neighborhood. Biondi arranged for an autopsy on the dog in order to recover the projectile.

Meanwhile, homicide investigators were performing the traditional routine "spade" work of interviewing the husband, who had discovered his wife's body, checking old boyfriends of the deceased, looking into friends and associates of the victim.

It was during this victimology phase that investigators were served another curve ball. A former girlfriend of the deceased's husband was extremely jealous of their marriage. When she had originally learned that the deceased had become pregnant, she had reportedly remarked to friends that she would like to kill the deceased and cut out the baby. Needless to say, this information certainly added to an already bizarre chain of events.

The investigation into Monday's murder had hardly begun when later that same week, five blocks away, another even more grisly discovery was made. On Friday, January 27, 1978 Sacramento Sheriff's deputies were called to a residence within the same general area on a report of a multiple murder. A woman, who had gone to visit her next-door neighbor, opened the door to her friend's house and discovered the whole family murdered. The dead woman, who was 36 years of age had been shot three times and had been eviscerated. Her 52-year-old boyfriend, who had been visiting, had died of gunshot wounds of the head, the woman's 6-year-old boy had been shot dead. A 22-month-old baby, who the woman was babysitting was missing from a bloodstained crib. Once again, the victim of the evisceration was female.

In this case there was evidence of anal sodomy and indications that the killer had stabbed at her rectum with one of the knives. The killer also cut one of her eyes out of the socket with a kitchen knife. This knife had been taken from the first crime scene and left behind by the killer. It had been used to mutilate this victim as in the first case; there was evidence of *anthropophagy* (consumption of the victim's flesh or blood). An examination of the woman's body revealed that certain body organs had been removed. In addition, a piece of rubber glove was found in the body cavity. (Later sheriff's detectives would learn that the killer wore these gloves because he believed he was performing surgery.) When the detectives searched the house, they discovered that the bathtub was filled with bloody water as well as brain matter, feces, and pieces of human entrails. The female victim's hair was soaking wet. Evidence at the scene indicated that she had probably just finished taking a bath when the offender confronted her and proceeded to execute everyone in the house.

When the killer did leave, he took the infant's body with him. He also took the male victim's wallet and car, which was found abandoned late Friday evening about a mile from the scene.

At this point in the investigation it was quite evident to investigators that these series of murders were being committed by a single individual, who was obviously quite disturbed. Ray Biondi was given the full resources of the Sacramento County Sheriff's Detective Division. Investigators assessed that the person responsible for these crimes came from within the geographical area of incident.

Sheriff's detectives "profiled" their suspect to be a white male, (the area was primarily white and the canvass had also indicated that there was a white male stranger in the area who had committed the burglary). The suspect would be in his twenties (males of this age commit most of the crimes). The suspect was probably schizophrenic (based upon the cutting, probing of the bodies in what detectives perceived to be curiosity). The suspect might have recently been released from a mental institution. (This was based on the fact that these bizarre crimes had suddenly occurred within a short span of time within one area.) The suspect seemed unconcerned about being apprehended based upon the daylight attacks, as well as the apparent lack of effort to hide the crimes or evidence. A loner type of individual; unmarried (based on who could live with a "wacko" like this). If the suspect did work, it would be a menial job at best. The suspect probably lived within the 1-mile circle due to the fact that the crimes were committed within the area as well as the fact that the stolen car was recovered in a parking lot of a building complex within the area.

According to Ray Biondi, "This profile generally suggested that investigators were looking for a psychotic individual who lived and/or worked in the neighborhood and was committing the crimes and murders on impulse or opportunity."

Ray Biondi and Sergeant Don Habecker established an investigative plan, which would focus the probe. Since all of the murders as well as the bizarre incidents had occurred within a 1-mile radius, a large circle encompassing this 1-mile radius was drawn on a map of the area. An extensive canvass operation was initiated. The entire investigative effort was effectively concentrated on these locations within the circle. In addition, detectives continued their inquiries at the present crime scene as well as the location where the stolen auto was later recovered. The stolen vehicle was put under 24-hour police surveillance Friday evening.

A supervisor was put in charge of the canvass, with explicit instructions to assure that each and every person within this circle be interviewed and asked whether or not they had observed any strangers or suspicious persons in the area.

The following day, Saturday, Biondi received information about a witness who had talked to an individual identified as Richard Chase. This civilian witness had seen Richard in a supermarket parking lot behind the residence of the first female victim on the day of the murder. Richard had asked this witness, whom he knew from high school, for a ride. The witness declined due to the fact that Richard was unkempt and acting really weird. Biondi assigned the Chase lead to three general assignment detectives for follow-up investigation. The three detectives, Ken Baker, Wayne Irey, and Bill Roberts contacted the building manager of the apartment complex where Chase lived. The manager told the detectives about dogs and cats missing from the buildings within the complex. The manager and the detectives went to Chase's apartment and knocked on the door. Unbeknownst to them, other detectives already had attempted to interview the occupant of this apartment with negative results. The manager opened the door to an unoccupied apartment next door. Through an interior wall Detective Baker could hear movement inside Chase's apartment. As Detective Roberts returned with the manager to his office and called Ray Biondi, detectives Baker and Irey staked out the suspect's apartment. The suspect suddenly came running out of the apartment carrying a box which contained bloody rags, fast-food containers with blood and other body parts enclosed, and other evidence of the crimes. When the detectives searched him, they found a gun in a shoulder holster. This was the same .22-caliber automatic he had used to kill his victims. The apartment revealed extensive evidence of the murders, including three blenders containing blood and human entrails. A diaper from the missing baby was also found in the apartment. (The baby's body was found 3 months later in a mummified condition. The body had been drained of blood and was beheaded.) There was dried blood caked on the suspect's mouth and hands, and additional evidence indicated that he had cooked, eaten, and drunk his victim's blood and body parts. In the refrigerator was a can containing brain matter. The remaining steak knives, which he had taken from the residence of the first victim, were found in the suspect's apartment.

According to the suspect, the reason for his vampire-like activity and grisly behavior was that flying saucers were drying up his blood through some sort of radiation and that in order to survive he had to replenish his supply. The suspect was eventually convicted. However, while awaiting appeal, he committed suicide or accidently overdosed himself trying to cure his imaginary illness on medication he had secreted in his cell.

According to Lt. Ray Biondi, this series of bizarre murders enabled the investigators to utilize some of the information they had received during an FBI Homicide School he had attended in 1976. The instructor was Special Agent Russell Vorpagle, who had presented a segment on the "Psychology of Murder." Ray Biondi stated, "The training that I and the other detectives in our Homicide Detail received from this school greatly influenced the tactics we took when the Chase murders were occurring."

Ray Biondi, who finally published his account of this case in the book "Dracula Killer," stated:

> "This case is often lectured about and documented in textbooks and other training material as a classic case in psychological profiling. Usually the facts are massaged or omitted to illustrate how the case was solved by the sole use of a psychological profile. I believe in any training that may provide another tool to the homicide detective. However, the practical use of this training is very limited. The danger in the belief of psychological profiling is that it may cause an investigation to focus away from the true killer. The intention of this book is to correct the misconception that complex murder cases are solved solely on the basis of a psychological profile."[10]

Factors that can be Determined by a Criminal Personality Profile

1. Age
2. Sex
3. Race
4. Marital status/adjustment
5. Intelligence
6. Scholastic achievement/adjustment

7. Life-style
8. Rearing environment
9. Social adjustment
10. Personality style/characteristics
11. Demeanor
12. Appearance and grooming
13. Emotional adjustment
14. Evidence of mental decompensation
15. Pathological behavioral characteristics
16. Employment/occupational history and adjustment
17. Work habits
18. Residency in relation to crime scene
19. Socioeconomic status
20. Sexual adjustment
21. Type of sexual perversion or disturbance (if applicable)
22. Motive

The Investigative Approach to Profiling

The criminal personality profile is based upon a good crime scene examination and adequate information supplied to the profiler. In order to facilitate this process there are certain investigative steps that must be taken at the scene by the detective.

1. The complete documentation of events. Photographs (both black and white and color) and/or videotape as well as crime scene sketches should be accomplished prior to any other police procedures at the scene.
2. A careful and complete search conducted for any forensic materials and other evidence that might provide a clue to the identity of the killer.

Furthermore, an extensive and thorough investigation of the victim's background must be undertaken in order for the profiler to appraise the type of suspect for which police should be looking. *Assessing the victimology of the deceased is standard operating procedure for any good homicide investigator. Many times the detective ends up learning more about the deceased than the victim knew about him or herself.* From the perspective of the profiler, however, the victim's background information takes on an added value as the profiler seeks a behavioral pattern or scenario upon which to build his or her hypothesis.

The following items are necessary to create a profile:

I. Photographs (the larger the photo the better, and the photos should focus on the depth and extent of the wounds.)
   A. Complete photographs of the crime scene.
   B. Color photos of the victim.
   C. Body positioning, different angles.
   D. If residence is involved, photos of other rooms, including a crime scene sketch which depicts the entire scene and floor plan of the residence.
   E. Photo of the area to include aerial shot to show relationship of body placement to the area. This is done so the profiler can get a feel for the area.
II. Neighborhood and complex
   A. Racial, ethnic, and social data.
III. Medical Examiner's report (autopsy protocol)
   A. Photos to show full extent of damage to body
      1. Stabs, cuts (number of)
      2. Gunshots
      3. Bruises
      4. Lividity
   B. Toxicology reports
      1. Drugs, alcohol
      2. Sperm present; sperm in anus; hair cut off, bits and pieces of hair, and oral swabs of mouth for semen
   C. Are wounds postmortem?
   D. Feelings of the medical examiner which are not committed to the report
IV. Map of the victim's travels prior to death
   A. Place employed
   B. Residence
   C. Where last seen
   D. Crime scene location
V. Complete investigation report of the incident
   A. Standard report of date, time, location, etc.
   B. Weapon used if known
   C. Investigative officer's reconstruction of the sequence of events
   D. Detailed interviews of witnesses

VI. Background of the victim
   A. Age
   B. Sex
   C. Race
   D. Physical description (including dress at time of incident)
   E. Marital status/adjustment
   F. Intelligence, scholastic achievement/adjustment
   G. Life style (recent changes)
   H. Personality style/characteristics
   I. Demeanor
   J. Residency (former and present) in relation to the crime scene
   K. Sexual adjustment
   L. Occupation (former and present)
   M. Reputation at home and work
   N. Medical history (physical and mental)
   O. Fears
   P. Personal habits
   Q. Use of alcohol or drugs/social habits
   R. Hobbies
   S. Friends and enemies
   T. Recent court action

In addition to providing a criminal personality profile of an unknown suspect based upon an analysis of the crime scene, the Behavioral Science Unit profilers of the National Center for the Analysis of Violent Crime (NCAVC) can also make an assessment of possible suspects based on an evaluation of certain background information on a specific suspect supplied by local police.

The following information should be obtained on the individual to be profiled:

1. Name
2. Age
3. Sex
4. Race
5. Height and weight
6. Marital status; ages and sex of children; recent births. Is wife pregnant?

7. Education level
8. Socioeconomic status
9. History (criminal record or psychiatric problems)
10. Physical abnormalities and/or defects (e.g., acne, speech impediment, obese, walks with a limp)
11. Residence (condition of, etc.)
12. Automobile (color, how maintained)
13. Behavior (describe any recent change)
14. Mannerisms and personality traits
15. Employment (recently laid off? skills associated with job)
16. Day or night person
17. User of drugs or alcohol (recent increase?)
18. Dress (sloppy or neat, type of clothing)
19. Known to carry, collect, or display weapons? (What type?)
20. Rigid vs. flexible personality
21. Prior military experience (branch of service)

Investigative Assessment — The Profiling Process

According to Ressler et. al. (1988), "The process used by the profiler is quite similar to that used by clinicians to make a diagnosis and treatment plan: data is collected, the situation reconstructed, hypotheses are formulated, a profile developed and tested, and the results reported back. The profilers combine brainstorming, intuition, and educated guesswork with prior experience in similar case scenarios to arrive at hypothetical formulations."[11]

Basically, a homicide detective follows these steps at the crime scene. The detective gathers information, attempts to reconstruct the incident, develops a theory about the incident, and then assesses this data to see whether or not the theory is consistent with the facts of the case. The investigators brainstorm the case during the investigative critique. They use their intuition, follow hunches, and make educated guesses based upon their extensive personal experience in homicide investigation.

In fact, an effective homicide detective is usually someone who has taken his experience and has enhanced it with knowledge, flexibility, and common sense.

Clinical Considerations and Descriptions of Behavior

The Psychopathic Personality

A person with a psychopathic personality is one whose behavior is largely amoral and asocial, who is characterized by irresponsibility, lack of remorse or shame, perverse or impulsive (oftentimes criminal) behavior, and other serious personality defects.[12]

Psychopathic characteristics include:

Complete disregard for community standards of behavior
Apparent absence of guilt feelings
Failure to learn by punishment
Desire for immediate satisfaction
Continuous sexual experimentation
Usually an extrovert
Can "go in" and "out" of feelings
Undue dependence on others[13]

Dr. Hervey Cleckley was one of the first clinicians to do an in-depth study of the psychopathic personality. In his textbook, *The Mask of Sanity,*[14] Dr. Cleckley describes the psychopath in terms of his actions and his apparent intentions. In fact, it is *The Mask of Sanity* that has influenced and provided the clinical framework for much of the scientific research on psychopathy. Cleckley lists the 16 characteristics of the psychopath as:

1. Superficial charm and good "intelligence"
2. Absence of delusions and other signs of irrational thinking
3. Absence of "nervousness" or psychoneurotic manifestations
4. Unreliability
5. Untruthfulness and insincerity
6. Lack of remorse or shame
7. Inadequately motivated antisocial behavior
8. Poor judgment and failure to learn by experience
9. Pathologic egocentricity and incapacity for love
10. General poverty in major affective reactions
11. Specific loss of insight
12. Unresponsiveness in general interpersonal relations
13. Fantastic and uninviting behavior with (alcoholic) drink and sometimes without
14. Suicide rarely carried out
15. Sex life impersonal, trivial, and poorly integrated
16. Failure to follow any life plan[15]

Dr. Robert D. Hare (1993), author of *Without Conscience: The Disturbing World of the Psychopaths Among Us,*[16] who devised *The*

Psychopathy Checklist, is the foremost expert in psychopathy. His *Psychopathy Checklist* is a complex clinical tool for professional interpretation of the actions and behaviors of the psychopath which have provided a measure of the assessment of dangerousness of individuals who meet the criteria of psychopath.

Key Symptoms of Psychopathy

Emotional/interpersonal

Glib and superficial
Egocentric and grandiose
Lack of remorse or guilt
Lack of empathy
Deceitful and manipulative
Shallow emotions[17]

Social Deviance

Impulsive
Poor behavior controls
Need for excitement
Lack of responsibility
Early behavior problems
Adult antisocial behavior

Dr. Hare describes psychopathy as a syndrome represented by a cluster of related symptoms. The cluster consists of both personality traits as well as socially deviant behaviors.[18] Sociopathy connotes that the syndrome is forged entirely from social forces and early childhood experiences. Antisocial personality disorder, as specified in DSM-IV refers primarily to a cluster of criminal and antisocial behaviors.

In the opinion of the author, the term psychopath as defined by Dr. Robert Hare, provides a more definitive description of the actions and personality of the organized offender.

Psychotic Personality (The Psychosis)

The psychotic personality suffers from a "psychosis" which is a major mental disorder in which the personality is very seriously *disorganized* and contact with reality is usually impaired.[19]

Psychotic characteristics

Loner-type personality
Generally remains isolated or secluded

Uncomfortable around people
Lacks interpersonal skills[20]

A psychosis is defined in DSM-IV as a "brief psychotic disorder" (DSM-IV 298.8). This disturbance involves the sudden onset of at least one of the following positive psychotic symptoms:

Delusions
Hallucinations
Disorganized speech (incoherence, fragmented speech)
Inappropriate response
Strange mannerisms[21]

This type of reaction is usually associated with a stressor of some intensity. Sex is certainly considered a stressor of significant magnitude. The *inadequate* individual experiencing such a stressor coupled with an engram (mind picture) of a particular sadistic fantasy is certainly capable of "acting-out" a bizarre sexual assault. The very nature of a sexual deviant engram is that it is substitutive for normal sexuality. It is oftentimes reinforced with masturbatory activities that become compulsive-patterned requiring repetition. The behavior and activities of this individual "acting-out" his fantasy during a sexual crime could very well be described as "psychotic."

From an investigative perspective, we would refer to such an event as "disorganized." The offender might possibly have a clinical diagnosis; however, the murder event could very well be the result of a temporary psychosis involving a sexual stressor. In any event, the crime scene presentation is significantly different than that of the "organized" offender.

Sexual Sadism (302.84 DSM-IV)

According to DSM-IV, sexual sadism is a paraphilia. Paraphilias are sexual deviations marked by persistent sexual arousal patterns in which unusual objects, rituals, or situations are required for sexual gratification. They are understood to reflect a psychosexual disorder in which the preferred or exclusive means of sexual gratification is deviant. The essential feature in sexual sadism is that the individual derives sexual excitement from the infliction of psychological or physical suffering (including humiliation) of the victim. Sadistic fantasies or acts may involve activities that indicate the dominance of the person over his victim (e.g., forcing the victim to crawl, or keeping the victim in a cage),

A

B

Figure 21.3.   **SADISTIC INJURIES INFLICTED ON VICTIMS BY A SERIAL KILLER.**
This serial killer engaged in sadistic sexual torture with his victims. In photos A, B, and C, the victim suffered breast assault with vice-grips and a paddling on the buttocks. The killer then pinched her nose closed with a pair of pliers. Photo D shows the third victim who had suffered a severe paddling. The killer also took the blade of his knife and inflicted the incised wounds on her buttocks and legs.

C

D

Figure 21.3. (continued)

or restraint, blindfolding, paddling, spanking, whipping, pinching, beating, burning, electrical shocks, rape, cutting or stabbing, strangulation, torture, mutilation, or killing.[22]

According to DSM-IV this is a chronic condition and a progressive disorder. "When Sexual Sadism is severe, and especially when it is associated with Antisocial Personality Disorder, individuals with Sexual Sadism may seriously injure or kill their victims."[23]

Among the number of paraphilias discussed in DeRiver's (1958) often cited work, *Crime and the Sexual Psychopath*, is lust murder.[24] DeRiver speaks of sadism as a compelling element in some lust murders; in others, arousal is not derived from the infliction of pain and suffering of the victim but rather from the act of killing itself. In this latter case, however, as with necrophiles, DeRiver recognizes that even though the offender may not witness any prolonged degree of suffering on the part of the victim, he is likely to "[call] upon his imagination and fancy to supply him with the necessary engrams to satisfy his craving for his depravity."[25] This is not unlike lust murderers who torture victims before killing them, and then recall "an after-image (engram) of the sensation produced by the physical torture and mutilation, extending beyond time and space."[26] The sadistic scenario is thus conjured in the imagination, be it a re-creation of the actual crime scene, or the product of fantasy. In each instance, lust murders are viewed as behaviors of sadistic sexual psychopaths. This is the type of offender who tortures and kills for sexual gratification and characterizes the *prototypical* serial killer, who we refer to as "organized."

However, it must be understood that "disorganized" offenders are also capable of similar behavior and also engage in sadistic activities with their victims as well.

Psychopathic Sexual Sadists

According to Vetter (1990),[27] serial murderers are almost routinely characterized in media accounts and much legal documentation as "psychopaths" or "sociopaths," which he notes are terms that were superseded by the diagnostic category "antisocial personality disorder" by the psychiatric community in its 1968 revision of the American Psychiatric Association's Diagnostic and Statistical Manual of Mental Disorders (DSM).

Cartel (1985)[28] outlines the crime patterns, biographies, detection, and case processing of 21 serial killings. He notes that in addition to the apparent lack of guilt or compassion for their victims, serial murderers claim to experience euphoria during their murders. These observations are consistent with the aforementioned aspects of antisocial personality disorder. The intense arousal derived from the torture and/or killing of victims which Lunde (1976) identifies as sexual sadism, "a deviation characterized by torture and/or killing and mutilation of other persons in order to achieve sexual gratification."[29] A reading of Brittain's (1970) work on the sadistic murderer reveals that such individuals are unconcerned with the moral implications of their brutality. They are excited by the sight of suffering and helplessness of their victims, whom they experience as objects. They usually kill by strangulation, apparently because of the total control over the victim that this method offers them.

Since it appears that a substantial proportion of male serial murderers violate their victims sexually, it is important to examine the role sexual behavior has in the killings. In the broader arena of sexual aggression — not limited to serial murder — clinical studies of sexually aggressive men have shown sadism as a dominant feature of their sexual arousal patterns. Dietz (1986), like Brittain before him, contends that the paraphilia most frequently associated with sex murders is sadism. In fact, of serial killers, Dietz states, "[w]hile every serial killer is mentally disordered, nearly all are psychopathic sexual sadists, and few, if any, are psychotic. Psychotic offenders rarely have the wherewithal repeatedly to escape apprehension."[30]

Meloy (1992) describes Theodore Bundy as "a contemporary sexual psychopath."[31] Moreover, he speaks of other sexually psychopathic serial murderers and entertains the contention by Lunde (1976), among others, that there is a temporal coupling of erotic stimulation and violence in the childhood histories of what they call sexually psychopathic serial murderers.

Crime Scene and Profile: Characteristics of Organized and Disorganized Murderers

The organized and disorganized dichotomy devised by the FBI's Behavioral Science Unit is a description of criminal offender typologies. The information presented herein as it relates to the phenomena of organized and disorganized offenders is based upon the studies and research of the FBI's Behavioral Science Unit, personal interviews with members of the Behavioral Science Unit, research in the field, and the author's personal experience with these types of cases. The terms "organized" and "disorganized" are excellent descriptions of human behaviors as they relate to the characteristics of sex-related murderers. It is important to note, however, that there may be a combination of both organized and disorganized behaviors evidenced in a crime scene, which in effect presents a "mixed" personality profile.

These are not clinical classifications but, they are based upon recognized psychological definitions and clinical diagnoses. The organized offender can be compared to the person suffering from an *antisocial personality disorder*. (However, the author uses the term psychopath and psychopathy because these terms are more meaningful in the descriptive characteristics of this specific type of offender.) The disorganized offender presents behaviors which may evince indications of a psychosis, such as schizophrenic disorders and/or paranoid diagnosis.

The following organized and disorganized profiles are an example of investigative assessment. These profiles, however, do not provide for local geography, demography, sociology, ethnic make-up, forensics, victimology, or special considerations which are unique to the local area.

The investigator is advised that these profiles are provided as a basic investigative tool for the purposes of focusing investigative resources on specific classifications of personality early-on in the investigation. (A more comprehensive criminal personality profile can be obtained through VI-CAP at the National Center for the Analysis of Violent Crime, Behavioral Science Unit, FBI Academy, Quantico, Virginia 22135.)

Note how Tables 1 and 2 compare with these clinical descriptions.[32] However, it should be noted that the organized/disorganized classifications go into much more investigative detail. The expertise of the criminal profiler rests in his or her ability to identify the clusters of information which demonstrate the psychopathology of the event and provide an insight into the behavioral make-up of the offender.

The Organized Offender

Age: This offender is approximately the same age as his victim. The mean or average age of this type of offenders is usually under 35 years old. This type of offenders, however, range in age from 18 to 45 years.

Sex: Male

Race: Usually the same race as the victim. However, the investigator should consider local ethnic make-up, victimology, geography, customs, culture, and other considerations unique to the area of the offense.

Marital status: Married or living with a partner. This type of offender is sexually competent and usually has a significant female in his relationship.

Education/intelligence level: This offender is of normal to superior intelligence. He is also street-wise. He has completed high school and may have some college experience. However, in school he was a disciplinary problem. He was known as a trouble maker due to his senseless and aggressive acts against others. He would be considered academically an underachiever.

Table 21.1 Profile Characteristics of Organized and Disorganized Murders

Organized	Disorganized
Average to above-average intelligence	Below average intelligence
Socially competent	Socially inadequate
Skilled work preferred	Unskilled work
Sexually competent	Sexually incompetent
High birth order status	Low birth order status
Father's work/stable	Father's work/unstable
Inconsistent childhood discipline	Harsh discipline as child
Controlled mood during crime	Anxious mood during crime
Use of alcohol with crime	Minimal use of alcohol
Precipitating situational stress	Minimal situational stress
Living with partner	Living alone
Mobility with car in good condition	Lives/works near crime scene
Follows crime in news media	Minimal interest in news media
May change jobs or leave town	Significant behavior change (drug/alcohol abuse, religiosity, etc.)

Reprinted from the *FBI Law Enforcement Bulletin.* August, 1985.

Table 21.2 Crime Scene Differences Between Organized and Disorganized Murders

Organized	Disorganized
Planned offense	Spontaneous offense
Victim a targeted stranger	Victim/location known
Personalizes victim	Depersonalizes victim
Controlled conversation	Minimal conversation
Crime scene reflects overall control	Crime scene random and sloppy
Demands submissive victim	Sudden violence to victim
Restraints used	Minimal use of restraints
Aggressive acts prior to death	Sexual acts after death
Body hidden	Body left in view
Weapon/evidence absent	Evidence/weapon often present
Transports victim or body	Body left at death scene

Reprinted from the *FBI Law Enforcement Bulletin,* August, 1985.

Socioeconomic level: Middle-class.

Mental health history: None.

Physical characteristics: Usually well-built. Tends to take good care of himself.

Residence: Lives some distance from the crime scene. (The exception to this is in the first offense. Many times the first offense is close to home.) Lives in a middle-class rental. Takes good care of his residence. Married or may be living with a significant female in his life.

Figure 21.4.   **SERIAL KILLING — ORGANIZED OFFENDER.** This female victim was sadistically tortured and killed. Note that the body is partially clothed, but has been arranged so as to expose the breasts and vagina. This homicide was the first in a series of killings by a sadistic sexual psychopath. The body has been purposefully displayed by the offender. (Courtesy of Delaware State Police.)

Figure 21.5.   **SERIAL KILLING — ORGANIZED OFFENDER.** This is the second victim of the same serial killer. This offense took place approximately 6 months later. She also has been sadistically tortured and killed. However, note the progression of the offense. Sexual sadism is recognized as a progressive disorder. The injuries to this victim were even more severe than those of the first victim. She is totally nude and there is evidence of severe breast assault as well as additional injuries of torture, including paddling. The body has been provocatively displayed in a public area by the killer for the purposes of "shock value." There were, in total, five victims. (Courtesy of Captain George O. Haggerty, New Castle County, Delaware, Department of Public Safety.) *Author's note:* These offenses, which occurred 6 months apart, took place under the jurisdiction of two separate law enforcement jurisdictions: New Castle County and the Delaware State Police. Early in the case, I was invited to review the investigation with the respective lead detectives, who had immediately recognized the murders as the work of a possible serial killer. Due to the cooperation and intelligent exchange of information among investigators and between the agencies involved, this case was effectively and successfully cleared.

Automobile: Middle-class vehicle. May be a sedan or possibly a station wagon. The auto may be dark in color and may resemble local police cars. This vehicle will be clean and well maintained. In the event you believe your offender to be young, in the early twenties, expect him to drive a red or black "muscle" or macho-type vehicle. If a pick-up truck is a masculine status symbol in the area of investigation, expect the offender to have a similarly colored vehicle.

Employment: This offender has the ability to handle almost any type of employment. However, he tends to seek jobs that project a "macho" image; for example, truck driver, bartender, construction worker, cowboy, security guard, police officer, fireman, paramedic, gunsmith, demolition worker, etc. or possibly a job which brings the offender into contact with bloodshed and death. His work record will be sporadic. He may have a reputation for walking off the job or being fired for unsatisfactory performance. His job is usually some distance from the crime scene; however, the crime scene may be along the route he takes to and from his place of employment.

Military history: Army or Marines. Volunteered. May have been discharged under other than honorable conditions. While in the service he was a disciplinary problem, AWOL, fights, etc.

Arrest record: Arrests for interpersonal violence, sex offenses. May have a poor driving record, DWI arrests as well as traffic violations including parking tickets, which have not been paid. The interpersonal violence arrests, if any, will involve sadistic acts, and/or beatings beyond the normal "fist-fight" which indicates an extreme cruelty and violence. He likes to "hurt" those he is angry with and probably planned his assaults with this objective in mind.

General Behavior Characteristics

1. This type of person fits well in society. Contemporary in style.
2. Gregarious, out-going person. Seemingly the type of person you might want to be friends with. However, you soon realize that this out-going person is actually a self-centered individual who cares only about himself. His social nature is actually a facade.
3. Good talker. Socially competent with good interpersonal skills. He uses these skills in a manipulative manner and usually "gets his way" with people.

4. Irresponsible, indifferent to the welfare of society, only cares about himself and doesn't think anything of hurting others.

5. Described as a ladies man. Known to frequent bars and lounges noted for large numbers of female patrons.

6. Dresses well, wears designer clothes, and is style conscious.

7. Dates frequently with many different women. Has multiple sex partners and is known to brag about his sexual conquests.

8. Methodical and cunning. He plans his crimes and selects his victims. He selects the site and is known to research his craft.

9. Travels frequently. Cruises seeking the right victim. Known for his mobility. Drives a car in good condition. Lives some distance from the actual crime scene. (Note exception to this is usually in the first incident, which oftentimes is close to offender's home or place of work.)

10. Acquaintances know him to have a violent temper and usually try to avoid becoming involved in any arguments with him out of fear or a desire to "keep the peace."

11. When insulted or threatened he will respond with violence, if not immediately, within a very short time. He externalizes his anger and is known to hold a grudge. *This person cannot accept criticism.*

12. He is a "Pathological Liar." Makes promises he has no intention of keeping and cannot be relied upon to "keep his word."

13. Does not meet his financial obligations.

14. He feels no guilt or remorse for his actions. He is an amoral person, who usually blames his troubles on others.

15. "Chameleon" personality, who leads a *compartmentalized life-style.*

16. He does not alter his behavior as a result of punishment. He fails to learn from his mistakes and will oftentimes repeat the same offense. When he gets caught, he will say he is sorry. However, what he really means is that he is sorry he got caught.

17. He is a consummate actor. He can play any role he desires. He has the ability to go in and out of feelings, cry real tears, evoke sympathy, and manipulate people's feelings.

18. Has a history of physical and/or sexual abuse by a female parent or parent figure. Important information for the structuring of any interviews of this type personality. (*This type may react to "cycle of abuse" syndrome to explain his crimes.*)

19. The triad are three significant components which form a pattern of behaviors among offenders involved in lust murders and serial killings. These activities include childhood cruelty to animals (for

Figure 21.6. **SERIAL KILLING — ORGANIZED OFFENDER.** This was the third victim of the serial killer. Her body was dumped into the Chesapeake-Delaware Canal. The killer became aware that the authorities had linked these series of killings through blue carpet fibers recovered from the bodies of the first two victims. An inappropriate news release by someone in the FBI alerted the suspect, who began dumping the bodies in water to eliminate the blue carpet fiber evidence.

this type of offender the severe cruelty which involves sadistic acts, i.e., disemboweling the family cat), childhood fire setting (for this type offender, arson that causes damage), and childhood bed wetting or enuresis. These three factors can be used to predict violent behavior, such as antisocial personality disorder.

20. High birth order status, may be first-born son.
21. Inconsistent childhood discipline.
22. Father's work known to be stable.
23. This offender may select a victim who resembles a significant female in his life, or choose victims of similar appearance, occupation, or life-style.
24. He selects victims he can *control* and *dominate*. This type of offender demands a submissive victim.
25. The crime scene will reflect controlled rage. Restraints will have been used. Items such as ropes, chains, tape, belts, pieces of the victim's clothing, gags, handcuffs, and/or blindfolds may be evident.
26. This type of offender will possess a "Murder-Kit," which will consist of weapons and/or restraints brought to and taken from the scene.

27. There will be evidence of torture, rape, and aggressive acts prior to death. This includes sexual experimentation with live victims.
28. This offender collects "trophies" of his victims as opposed to souvenirs, which are items taken by the *disorganized* type of offender. The trophies may be in the form of costume jewelry or other personal items of the deceased. The *organized* offender has been known to present such items to significant females in his life as a gift, which actually serves as a psychological remembrance of the event and provides the offender with a continuance of the fantasy.
29. Follows the news media. May keep news clippings of the event. Reads the daily newspapers, listens to the radio, and watches T.V. in order to judge the extent of the police investigation. This type of offender concentrates and focuses on police statements.
30. May communicate with authorities. Sometimes this type of offender likes to "bait" the police with information or he may communicate through the media. This type of activity on the part of the offender has as its objective the continuation of the fantasy. It also serves to reinforce the offender's feeling of superiority over the police. This type of offender is encouraged by the apparent inability of the police to solve the crime and takes great pleasure in designing his communications to frustrate and confuse the authorities.

It should be noted that this type of an offender can be stressed through the effective utilization of "proactive techniques." Any subsequent news release by the agency should be designed with this purpose in mind.

31. This type of offender may hang around establishments frequented by the police for the purposes of "overhearing" some shop talk about the crime. He is usually thought of as a police buff or friendly nuisance.
32. He is angry or depressed before the crime.
33. Precipitating situational stressors include problems with money, work, or women prior to the crime.
34. This type of offender may exhibit a fascination with firearms, guns, explosives, etc.
35. This type of offender will transport the victim or body.
36. This type of offender will usually conceal the body to hide it from authorities. The exception is the organized offender who wishes to "make a statement" by blatantly displaying the body for shock value.

37. This offender many times has a collection of S&M pornography, and shows an avid interest in torture, sadistic fantasies, and bondage materials. There is also research which indicates a propensity for "detective"-type magazines, which describe particularly brutal sex crimes and the police investigation techniques. In some instances, the crime scene and the activities engaged in by the offender will be similar to specific sadistic acts as portrayed in the pornographic materials collected by the offender. This is important investigative information, especially when considering the search warrant application.

38. This type of offender, who is focusing on the media as well as assessing the police investigation, may change jobs or leave town after a homicide if he feels threatened.

39. This type of offender has also been known to involve himself in the police investigation by providing information to authorities or participating in searches for the body.

Remember, the organized offender plans the crime, selects the site, stalks the victim, and researches his craft. He needs to be in control especially during the crime. Use this against him.[33]

The Disorganized Offender

Age: These offenders range in age from 16 to their late 30s. The age of the victim does not matter to the offender. The selected victim is simply a victim of opportunity who happens to be at the wrong place at the wrong time. Research indicates that many of these offenders experience their acting-out phase between the ages of 17 and 25.

Sex: Male.

Race: Usually the same race as the victim. However, the investigator should consider the local ethnic make-up of the area, victimology, geography, customs, culture, and other considerations unique to the area of offense.

Marital status: Single.

Education/intelligence level: High school drop-out. Possibly community college. Below average intelligence. Considered a marginal student.

Socioeconomic level: Lower to middle class.

Mental health history: This type of offender may have some history of mental disorders or have been treated for depression as an out-patient. If he did receive any professional help, he may have been classified as exhibiting schizoid behavior.

Physical characteristics: Thin, possibly with acne or some physical malady that contributes to an appearance that is different from the general population.

Residence: Close to the area of the crime scene. Usually lives alone in a rental property or with his parents or with a significantly older female relative.

Automobile: Generally does not own a vehicle. However, if he does own a vehicle it will be an older model that looks junky both inside and out. The investigator should consider his area of jurisdiction. If the area is rural expect the offender to have an older-type vehicle, messy interior, and not well maintained. If the area is within an urban setting, the offender will probably not own a car.

Employment: This type of offender may not be employed. If he is employed he will most likely seek out unskilled work. His job will be a simple or menial one, requiring little contact with the public. Dishwasher, busboy, janitor, maintenance man, stock boy, etc.

Military history: Probably none. If he was in the military, it was probably in the Army and he may have been discharged as unsuitable.

Arrest record: Arrests for voyeurism, fetish thefts, burglary, exhibitionism, and other nuisance offenses.

General Behavior Characteristics

1. Someone who has a societal aversion. He rejects society which he feels has rejected him and is considered socially inadequate.
2. A loner, he becomes secluded and isolated. He is quiet and withdrawn and might be considered a recluse.
3. An underachiever, he has a poor self-image, and his clothes are dirty and messy.
4. He has poor personal hygiene habits.
5. His acquaintances consider him weird or odd. He may have delusional ideas, and seems strange in appearance and behavior. He is the *"Little Johnny Weird"* of the neighborhood.
6. He internalizes hurt, anger, and fear.
7. He is sexually incompetent, and may never have had a sexual experience with someone of the opposite sex. He does not date; interpersonal relationships are difficult for this subject.

8. This offender is heavily into solo sex-related activities. (Substitute sex) voyeurism, exhibitionism, panty thefts, autoerotic activities, sadistic fantasies, pornography, and masturbation are used to compensate for his lack of interpersonal relationships.

9. Nocturnal, a night person.

10. He has no close personal friends.

11. This offender usually lives alone or with a significantly older female relative.

12. Low birth order status.

13. Father's work known to be unstable.

14. Harsh discipline as a child.

15. Anxious mood during crime.

16. Minimal use of alcohol.

17. Minimal interest in the news media.

18. This type of offender lacks the cunning of the organized offender.

19. He commits the crime in a frenzy,"blitz-style" of attack, attempts to quickly silence the victim, usually with blunt-force trauma. Sudden violence to the victim and death follows quickly.

20. His is a spontaneous offense. The crime scene is tightly clustered. The weapon is usually one of opportunity. There usually will be evidence found. The weapon may be present, and the body left at the location of assault.

21. The crime scene will be random and sloppy. There may be evidence of blood smearing on self, the victim, or upon surface areas at the scene, as well as uncontrolled stabbing or slashing.

22. There may be depersonalization of the victim, with extreme assault to the face.

23. Postmortem bite marks to breasts, buttocks, neck, thighs, and abdomen may be present.

24. Postmortem dissection of the body may be inflicted, which is exploratory in nature. Investigators may find mutilation of the body, and evidence of anthropophagy, the consumption of the victim's flesh and blood.

25. Sexual acts may be performed with the body; insertion of foreign objects into the anal or vaginal cavities; masturbation upon the victim or her clothing; ejaculation into stab wounds; and sexual experimentation. *Usually there is no penis penetration of the body by this type of offender.*

26. The crime scene may be isolated, but there is no real effort to hide or conceal the body. *The crime scene will be in proximity to the offender's residence or place of employment.*

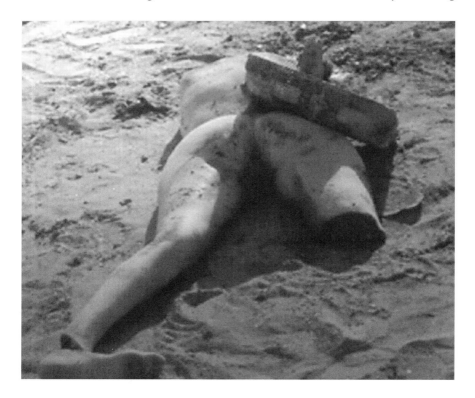

Figure 21.7.   **LUST MURDER — DISORGANIZED OFFENDER.** The victim of a "Blitz-Style" type attack by an offender as she was walking on the beach.

27. The body may be positioned by the offender for some symbolic purpose.
28. There may be evidence of ritualism. This type of offender may be expressing some sort of psychosexual need in the symbolic positioning of the body or in some ritualistic aspect of the crime scene. Since this type of offender is known to be extensively involved in pornography and solo sex-related activities, it would be good investigative technique to record this psychological aspect of the crime scene. Later on this information may serve as the basis for a search warrant of the suspect's home.
29. This type of offender may take a *souvenir*. The souvenir can be an object or article of clothing taken as a remembrance. Or, in some instances the souvenir may even be a body part. *This type of offender has been known to return souvenirs to either the gravesite or the crime scene.*

Figure 21.8. **POSTMORTEM MUTILATION — DISORGANIZED OFFENDER.** The offender eviscerated the woman and engaged in postmortem mutilation. He was removing organs from the woman's body and throwing them into the sea.

What is the Motive?	
PSYCHOPATHIC	PSYCHOTIC
Sadistic	Motiveless
Impulsive	Bizarre
Organized	*Disorganized*

Figure 21.9. WHAT IS THE MOTIVE?

30. This type of offender has been known to undergo a significant behavior change after the crime — drug and/or alcohol abuse, religiosity, etc.[34]

The above chart can be utilized by the investigator in making an assessment relative to the type of personality which may be involved in a particular investigation.

The following case history is presented to explain how the FBI Behavioral Science Unit evaluates information and requests for a criminal personality profile based upon crime scene analysis. This case involves a mix of both organized and disorganized behaviors. Supervisory Special Agent John E. Douglas prepared this profile based on information supplied by the requesting jurisdiction.[35]

CASE HISTORY — DISORGANIZED/ORGANIZED

According to police reports, the victim was apparently abducted at about 10:15 P.M. on the evening of her disappearance after she left a babysitting job in the area of her residence. Her nude mutilated body was discovered 3 days later in a local garbage dump. According to the autopsy report, the victim was probably murdered shortly after her abduction. Based on an analysis of the stomach contents, it was theorized she died about midnight that same evening. The cause of death was a massive head injury and the mutilation, according to the medical examiner, was postmortem.

The first questions, according to Douglas, are, "Why was the victim killed?", "Why was the victim mutilated?", and "Why was the victim's body placed at the garbage dump?".

The scene where the body was discovered was merely a disposal site, and had been placed there after being bled out elsewhere. Douglas stated that the body was probably placed at the garbage dump so it could be discovered. The deceased was discovered in a face-down position. She had been spread-eagled in a sexually provocative position, and there was evidence of mutilation to the buttocks and the left thigh. Furthermore, none of her clothing was found at the site, supporting the theory that she had been killed at another location. The victim's hair, which was in a long pony-tail style, had been cut from her head and hung on a nearby branch. When her body was rolled over, additional injuries were discovered. There was extensive trauma to the face, and both the jaw and nose bones had been broken. The deceased's throat had been cut and her breasts had been removed. Only one breast was found at the crime scene, and the other one was missing. In addition to this mutilation, there was a deep stab wound in the center of the stomach, and the offender had made an incision across the pelvic area of the deceased.

Douglas stated that based on his experience with these types of lust murders, the mutilation is usually performed after death. Also, the fact that one breast was missing provides additional information about the personality of the offender. In fact, based on just the circumstances described above, a definite type of offender can be profiled and zeroed in

Figure 21.10. **LUST MURDER — DISORGANIZED OFFENDER.** The deceased had been killed elsewhere and was placed in this position by the killer.

Figure 21.11. **POSTMORTEM MUTILATION.** This close-up of the same victim shows the effects of postmortem mutilation. The incised wound is open due to the cutting across the lines of cleavage. Note the lack of bleeding around the wounds.

Figure 21.12. **GROSS POSTMORTEM MUTILATION.** This turned-over body shows gross postmortem mutilation. The breasts have been removed (*defeminization*), and we observe evisceration and severe trauma to the head and facial area (*depersonalization*). These types of cases indicate certain traits in the murderer's make-up, which may provide police with additional investigative clues. An investigative assessment of this crime would indicate that the killer is a *disorganized personality*.

on. However, there was a circumstance in this case which didn't fit the profile. The autopsy report had indicated that there was seminal fluid in the deceased's vagina. Douglas said, "Generally the type of offender who removes breasts and mutilates his victim cannot complete a sexual act and usually engages in some sort of masturbatory activity at the scene. He may ejaculate on the victim's face or on the victim or her clothing, or he may masturbate with the victim's clothing. This case really threw us a curve".

In order to formulate a profile, it is important to get as much information as possible about the victim and the suspects so an accurate appraisal can be made. In this case, Douglas first examined the victimology of the deceased.

The victim was a white female, 22 years of age, 5 feet 5 inches tall, 120 pounds, with brown hair and blue eyes. A check into the victim's character and morals revealed that she was sexually promiscuous. She had both a lesbian relationship with a black female, and a heterosexual relationship with a white male. In addition, she was presently living with a white male, 26 years of age.

The local police submitted the names of six suspects to the FBI which included a suspect who had discovered the body, and the live-in boyfriend of the deceased. The first suspect, although initially thought to be a good prospect, didn't fit the profile of a person who would engage in the activity described. He was in his late twenties, married with children, an outdoors type, who had a few minor skirmishes with the law. He had been observed urinating at the location of the crime scene, and after being questioned by police secured an attorney. However, this suspect was quickly eliminated based on the FBI's profile, as were four others.

One suspect evaluated by Douglas was the live-in boyfriend of the deceased. He was described as a white male, 20 years of age, close to the victim, a loner, who according to his own admissions, had limited social and/or sexual relations — in other words, a socially retarded person.

The profile prepared by Douglas indicated that this suspect would probably be a high school drop-out — one who sat in the back of the room, was a slow learner with a reading disability, and by junior year had social problems. If he had gotten into the military service, primarily the army or marines, he wouldn't have lasted and probably would have been kicked out in a few months.

This profile along with additional information fit the suspect and also fit the pattern of the case with one exception, the sperm in the vagina. The Behavioral Science experts decided that there must be two suspects. According to John Douglas, the key ingredient in any profile is the intelligent gathering of information. The type of personality who mutilates his victims usually does not have normal social relationships and relies heavily upon fantasy. Douglas stated that the suspect would probably keep a scrapbook or diary, and he advised local police to try to locate these items in order to discover the suspect's innermost thoughts and secrets and maybe even recover additional evidence.

The information about the suspect's background and the FBI analysis indicated that the suspect was extremely influenced by his mother, who exercised an inordinate amount of control over his personal life. In fact, just before the incident, the suspect's mother had come to the house and asked the deceased when she was going to "put out sexually" for her son. The facts indicated that although the deceased was living with the suspect for 2 months, she had not engaged in any sexual relations with him. She had broken off a relationship with another male and would often boast to the suspect how great her other lovers were, including her lesbian girlfriend. When the deceased finally agreed to have sex with the suspect, she told him that he couldn't satisfy her. According to police reports, the deceased kept comparing the suspect with her other lovers and constantly reminded him how poorly he performed sexually. According to Douglas, this obviously distressed the subject and was an important factor to note, especially in the extreme facial damage and overkill of the victim. According to psychological studies, these types of injuries to the face of the victim usually indicate that the killer knew his victim and felt extreme rage. The sperm in the vagina, however, just didn't fit the suspect's profile. The police were requested to obtain additional information on the suspect's associates. It was the determination of the experts at the Behavioral Science Unit that although the primary suspect had probably done the mutilation, someone else had to have completed the sex act. This other person, it was reasoned, would be close to both the primary suspect and the deceased. This person would be the one who teamed up with the primary suspect, had the sexual relations, and supplied the vehicle. An individual like the primary suspect, according to Douglas, may possess a driver's license but generally does not own a vehicle and relies on public transportation.

Information about the brother of the primary suspect made the two-perpetrator theory more plausible. The primary suspect's brother had a history of assaultive behavior, was more explosive than the primary suspect, and had recently been hospitalized for this condition. The FBI began to look for certain "stressors" such as a recent marriage, a recent divorce, separation, a pregnant wife, etc. in the second suspect's background. The fact was that this subject was married and had a wife who was delivering a baby on the evening of the murder.

The profiles had been instrumental in identifying and pinpointing both suspects in the investigation.

The next question, according to Douglas, is, "How do you get the information from the suspects?" From extensive research with disorganized types of personality, certain actions on the part of these individuals can be forecasted.

Douglas felt that the primary suspect would be a nocturnal type and that he would probably go to the cemetery. It was suggested that the local police wire up the headstone when they staked out the cemetery.

The profile and information was correct. The primary suspect showed up at the grave site and openly conversed with the deceased. It had not been possible to wire up the headstone; however, the observation of the suspect at the site and his activities gave the police additional evidence. Later, when police went back to the crime scene, they found jewelry that belonged to the deceased. This scene had been thoroughly searched by police, and the only explanation was that the suspect had planted the items at the site. According to Douglas, this could possibly be an attempt to "enshrine" the victim.

The removal of the body from the place of death to the disposal site is also a factor to consider in these types of murders. In the "Yorkshire Ripper" case in England, the killer would often move his victim's bodies either to taunt the police or assist them in locating the victim. Douglas contended that the suspect in this case moved the body so it would be discovered and have a proper burial.

Apparently, the body had been preserved in some manner. This would be consistent with the suspect not wanting the body to decompose. In this case the suspect would probably attend the funeral; however, his actions and behavior would be inappropriate. For example, he would be smiling when he should be sad.

According to Douglas, the suspect might turn toward religion, alcohol, or drugs in order to repress unwanted memories or thoughts of the crime. Often this type of offender would move from the area in order to get away from the crime scene. This activity on the part of the subject is an attempt to cope. Douglas points out that this is where the investigator may be able to take advantage of a weakness. If this activity is identified in a suspect, he should be reminded of his act either through the media, or by being exposed to a high police profile. For example, allow him to observe police presence around him, but make no attempt to interview him.

The next question in this case was, "Who would be the best subject to interrogate?" One of the benefits of the profile is that it gives you an insight into how the suspect will react to any given circumstance. In this case, the brother of the primary suspect, who had raped the victim, would be the best one to approach. He had only raped the victim, as opposed to killing and mutilating her. The interrogation suggested by the FBI was to approach the suspect directly. He would be picked up and questioned on not whether or not he did it, but why. The assumption was correct, just as the profile had indicated. This suspect admitted his participation and made statements regarding the primary suspect's cutting and mutilation activities.

In the meantime, police had obtained a search warrant and found the suspect's diaries and scrapbooks, which according to the profile linked the suspect to the crime. Douglas suggested that the interview take place in the evening, since the primary suspect was nocturnal. In this case, it was suggested that the interrogation be indirect. Provide the suspect with a pencil and pad and allow him to write out his own statement. The suspect was allowed to continue at his own pace, and before long was describing things only the killer would know. He placed himself at the scene and then began talking in the third person, discussing someone else committing the crime. It was interesting to note that the brother of the primary suspect had stated that the primary suspect had taken the breast, which was never found, and had kept it in a container. This possibility was part of the initial criminal personality profile. In

Figure 21.13. **TED BUNDY SHORTLY BEFORE EXECUTION.** Ted Bundy (right) is giving a statement to Supervisory Special Agent William Hagmaier (left) of the FBI. This photo, taken on January 23, 1989, is one of the last photos taken of this infamous serial killer who was responsible for the deaths of over 30 young women. (See interview.) (Courtesy of Supervisory Special Agent William Hagmaier FBI.)

addition, it was learned that the primary suspect had kept the body wrapped in sheets in a cool area to preserve it. This also was significant to the original profile. This case was successfully concluded through the intelligent use of a criminal personality profile. The facts indicated that there were two different personalities, disorganized and organized involved in this crime.

Ted Bundy: Serial Killer — Offender Profile

On January 24, 1989, convicted murderer and serial killer Theodore Robert Bundy was finally executed in Florida's electric chair for the 1978 abduction and murder of 12-year old Kimberly Diane Leach, the last of his many victims.

Ted Bundy, who has been described as charming, charismatic, intelligent, and articulate was in fact a *classic organized offender*, who killed over 30 young women in various jurisdictions of the Northwest United States and Florida between 1973 and 1978. He was finally apprehended after a crude, murderous, and animal-like rampage in Florida where he killed two college coeds at the Chi Omega sorority house, left three others for dead, and 2 weeks later ravaged and killed young Kimberly Leach.

Clinically speaking, Ted Bundy was a sexual psychopath who enjoyed killing women in the context of expressing his sadistic sexual fantasies. Obsessed with the idea of total possession of his victims, Ted

Bundy killed with impunity until the end when he regressed into the classic disorganized offender.

In death, the activities and revelations of Ted Bundy will continue to be analyzed as psychiatrists, psychologists, and other behavioral scientists theorize about and attempt to explain the rationale behind this modern day horror.

A number of books and articles have been written about Ted Bundy, which provide interesting information about his life and his murderous activities.

The Only Living Witness (1989 updated version)[36] by Stephen Michaud and Hugh Aynesworth provides an excellent insight into the mind of Ted Bundy, the serial killer, as Bundy relates to the authors in the third person, how such an offender might think.

However, the most dramatic disclosures, which finally revealed the "entity" of Ted Bundy took place on death row in Florida State Prison during the final hours of Ted Bundy's life in January, 1989. The following information relative to Ted Bundy was provided to me during a personal interview with Supervisory Special Agent Bill Hagmaier on November 20, 1989 and updated in March, 1995.[37]

Offender Profile Program

William Hagmaier, a Supervisory Special Agent assigned to the FBI's Behavioral Science Unit at Quantico, Virginia first met Theodore Bundy as part of the FBI's efforts to gain a better understanding of serial killers and their crimes.

Supervisory Special Agent Hagmaier became Bundy's official contact with the FBI and maintained intermittent correspondence with the serial killer, who refused to admit any guilt but also never denied his involvement in the crimes.

Background

At 41 years of age at the time of the interview, Hagmaier was just a year younger than Ted Bundy. Over a period of some 4 years, Hagmaier visited Bundy at Florida State Prison on a number of occasions. They began to regularly exchange letters and greeting cards. As they got to know each other, they established a relationship based on mutual understanding and trust.

Bundy, according to Hagmaier, perceived himself as very intellectual. He liked to challenge the system and to play mind games. According to Hagmaier, "Bundy even told me that he had tested my motives.

However, I was totally honest with him. I even told him I thought he deserved the full penalty of the law for what he had done. I think it became clear to him after a while that I wasn't trying to judge him. I wasn't trying to get any new evidence on him, I wasn't writing a book or trying to profit from him. What I wanted from him was information on the thinking of serial killers."

Ted Bundy, in life became the subject of interest to many writers and clinicians as they attempted to recreate and present the motivations and machinations of such a sophisticated serial killer. It flattered his ego that so many psychiatrists, psychologists, reporters, and writers were interested in interviewing him. As he stated to Hagmaier, "It became almost like an acting role. The more the actor acts in a role, the better he becomes at it, the more he is apt to feel comfortable in it, to be able to do things spontaneously."

Eventually, Bundy began to communicate more freely with Hagmaier. Ted Bundy, a former law school student, apparently enjoyed sharing his insights into criminal investigations. In fact, according to Hagmaier, Bundy would provide him with his insights into other murders across the country. Hagmaier stated, "Those he chose to discuss were somewhat similar to his crimes and his insights were very good."

Bundy indicated to the FBI agent that he trusted him. He even told Hagmaier that if he ever decided to be totally candid about his activities he would ask for him to be there.

In the last few days before his execution Bundy, who had maintained his innocence throughout the appeals process, made a last ditch effort to prolong his life by offering to provide authorities with additional information and confessions on open homicide cases. At Bundy's request Agent Hagmaier was contacted and requested to participate in the negotiations.

In fact, Bill Hagmaier was the only law enforcement person that Ted Bundy would see alone, and he insisted that Hagmaier be present when he was interviewed by other investigators. It was during these last 4 days before execution that Bundy confessed to the murder of over 30 young women and girls.

Hagmaier sat through each of the confessions which consisted of 11 murders in Washington, 3 in Colorado, 8 in Utah, 3 in Florida, 2 in Idaho, 2 in Oregon, and 1 in California.

Supervisory Special Agent Bill Hagmaier was directly responsible for obtaining the confessions and facilitating the opportunity for law enforcement officials to meet with Ted Bundy during the week prior to his execution.

Investigative Analysis

According to Hagmaier, Bundy's attacks on women centered around control and total domination. Bundy wanted his victims to be totally submissive and in some instances Bundy performed necrophilia shortly after killing them. Hagmaier stated that most of the murders that Bundy told him about were planned with the exception of five or six which were committed impulsively. In fact, Bundy's first killing was an impulsive act of displaced aggression. Bundy's plans involved sadistic fantasies with a combination of sex and violence featuring a dominant male and a submissive and terrified female. All of his victims were raped, traumatized, and then killed.

The victim would be directed to act in a certain way or dress in a certain way thereby affording Bundy a firsthand "experience" of his fantasy.

In fact, some of Bundy's victims were discovered in clothes they had never worn and the bodies indicated that their hair had been washed and fresh fingernail polish had been applied to their fingernails. According to Hagmaier, Bundy admitted that he had his victims re-create the covers of detective magazines or scenes from "slasher" movies for him. Sometimes he took Polaroid snapshots of the young women during these sessions and kept them as souvenirs. "When you work hard to do something right," he confided to Hagmaier, "you don't want to forget it." Also, Bundy confirmed for Hagmaier a horror that other investigators had long suspected. On the day that he had kidnaped Janice Ott and Denise Naslund from Lake Sammamish, he kept both alive for awhile. One had to watch the other die.

According to Hagmaier, Bundy would first select a disposal site. He would then plan on targeting a specific type of victim, by age, physical appearance, dress, etc.

Hagmaier stated, "Bundy thought of himself as a predator. He liked the hunt as much as the kill and he selected what he called "worthy-prey," which he described as attractive, intelligent young women with good backgrounds." Hagmaier added, "It was the thrill of the hunt and the challenge. It was competitive for him in a heinous way."

Bundy would approach his victims and make verbal contact while faking an injury. He would have his arm in a sling or would be using crutches, while he asked for help. Ironically, Bundy had picked-up this technique while participating in a psychology course which was designed to examine whether people would be more trusting if a person asking for help appeared disabled, wearing a cast or using crutches. During his "official" mode, Bundy would pretend to be a police officer when approaching potential victims. In fact, he had tried to abduct a young woman named Carol DaRonch in Salt Lake City while posing as a plainclothes police officer.

Bundy told Hagmaier that he usually was drinking before his homicidal hunts. He would kill his victims by ligature strangulation as he was having sex with them and then later dispose of their bodies at the preselected burial site.

In his official confessions, Bundy told how he strangled his victims with lengths of rope, sometimes even as he raped them. After killing, he said, he beheaded at least a dozen of the corpses with hacksaws. Sometimes he cut off the hands as well.

Bundy told Hagmaier of the spiritual oneness he achieved with his victims. "You feel the last bit of breath leaving their body," Bundy said. "You're looking into their eyes. A person in that situation is God! You then possess them and they shall forever be a part of you. And the grounds where you kill them or leave them become sacred to you, and you will always be drawn back to them."

Hagmaier said, "Bundy could never understand why people couldn't accept the fact that he killed because he wanted to kill. He did it of his own volition. Although he chose the time, the place and method, people were always looking for some mysterious reason for his motivation."

Instead, Bundy had a conscious detailed plan to kill. He selected the burial site beforehand, he selected a location where he could act upon his fantasy, he stalked a specific type of victim, and then acted upon his sadistic fantasies dehumanizing the victim. This organized offender was able to consciously keep his heinous criminal behavior separate from his day-to-day "normal" life. According to Hagmaier, "Bundy had an uncanny ability to compartmentalize. He could actually disassociate himself from these brutal and sadistic crimes."

Post-Crime Behavior

According to Hagmaier, Bundy concentrated and focused upon police statements about the crimes and adjusted his activities accordingly. In fact, Bundy revealed that his success at avoiding apprehension was directly attributable to the inappropriate and revealing press releases made by certain police authorities during the investigation as well as the obvious failure of police agencies to cooperate with one another and share information relative to their cases. Bundy returned to certain burial sites, which were available to him, and was able to assess the police investigation as well as change the crime scene. This oftentimes was based upon the news media information which had been provided by the authorities. He engaged in dismemberment and decapitation to preclude identification of the bodies.

According to Hagmaier, Bundy also engaged in necrophilia with the corpses of some of his victims. The dissection of the bodies was for the purposes of transportation and/or making the crime appear to have a different modus operandi. In some instances, he carried the heads around with him for days. Bundy had told Hagmaier that he had as many as four heads of his victims at home with him at one time. Ted had even incinerated one of the heads of his victims in his girlfriend's fireplace. He buried some of his victims, placed others in the water, and spread the remains of his victims between burial sites.

Bundy was extremely conscious of the value of forensic evidence and took pains to assure that he had left no traces behind. He told Hagmaier that on one occasion he had steam cleaned his car three times to assure that there wouldn't be any evidence available for authorities. This included cleaning the car inside and out and even changing the upholstery in his car.

Ironically, one of the most crucial pieces of evidence introduced at Bundy's trial was forensic evidence in the form of bite marks upon one of the Chi Omega coeds. Ted Bundy, despite his clever attempts to avoid detection apparently was not aware of the then relatively new technique of forensic odontology. In fact, the Bundy case firmly established the use of forensic dentistry in future murder trials across the United States.

Conclusion

I have provided this section on Special Agent Hagmaier's interview of Ted Bundy because Bundy represented the epitome of the serial killer. He was an organized offender with a psychopathic personality that enabled him to manipulate people and systems right to the very end. In my professional opinion as an expert in homicide investigation, the information relative to the inappropriate news releases, as well as law enforcement's inability to cooperate with one another should be considered by law enforcement professionals as an investigative precaution.

Additional Information on Ted Bundy

In the Summer of 1995, Dr. Robert Kepple, Ph.D., who is now the Chief Criminal Investigator for the Washington State Attorney General's Office authored a book entitled: *The Riverman: Ted Bundy and I Hunt for the Green River Killer.*"[38] This book was based upon Bob Kepple's personal experiences with the original Ted Bundy killings in Washington State as well as a number of other serial murder cases which Kepple was requested to consult on. The focus of the book is on Ted Bundy, who offered to assist authorities in the infamous "Green River" serial murder case investigation and the subsequent conversations between Ted Bundy and Bob Kepple. This book provides the reader with a valuable resource of information about serial killers and the exploitive nature of a man like Ted Bundy, who attempted to manipulate an entire criminal justice system.

Some interesting points of reference within the book are listed briefly as follows:

- ☐ Ted Bundy was reading voraciously from detective magazines and books, gaining valuable information about how police investigators perform their duties. (p. 41)
- ☐ Bundy would move around the body parts of his victims in order to confuse authorities and escape detection. (p. 34)
- ☐ Disinformation is probably the best way to lure a serial killer out into the open, because serial killers carefully read the newspaper accounts of their crimes. (p. 84)
- ☐ Serial killers often change their M.O. during a series of killings for a variety of reasons, one of which is to throw investigators off track. (p. 149)
- ☐ In serial murder cases, usually the first and the last cases are most revealing about the suspect. (p. 171)
- ☐ Experience in serial murder cases has shown that the highest investigative priority must be given to isolating, as accurately as possible, the dates and times victims were last seen and to delineating their activity patterns up to the time of their disappearances. (p. 174)
- ☐ Ted Bundy revealed his expertise as a serial killer hunter by explaining to Kepple that Bundy's preferred strategy for catching the Green River Killer would be to put a newly discovered dump site under surveillance. Bundy explained that the "Riverman" as he referred to the Green River Killer would be someone who had a sensitivity to and knowledge of the "scene;" the life style, habits, movements, hangouts, and likes and dislikes of the women he was hunting from the time he started pursuing his victims. Bundy hinted that the Riverman would be part of that "scene." (p. 203)

☐ Bundy told Kepple that the Riverman had come to know his class of victims and their lifestyles in an intimate way that allowed him to manipulate and lure them to him. (p. 204)

☐ The serial killer doesn't want to get caught. So he's going to make changes in his behavior to stay ahead of you and avoid publicity. (p. 244)

☐ Leaving a victim nude is the best way to leave the least amount of evidence. No fibers, hairs, etc. (p. 301) The serial killer wants to make sure the authorities are deprived of any evidence. He has read enough detective magazines and newspapers to realize that clothing may provide the police with clues. (p. 320)

☐ Another way of disposing of the clothes according to Bundy was to simply throw items out of the car as he was driving along. His rationale was that there is trash picked along the highway all the time. He also suggested burning the clothes or burying them. (p. 321)

Regarding the interview of serial killers, Kepple's book indicates some of the following information:

☐ Bundy emphasized the urgency of immediately interviewing any suspected serial killer as soon as possible before his denial sets in. (p. 330)

Author's note: If the serial killer is caught in the act, such as Joel Rifkin, who was apprehended by New York State Troopers with a body in the back of his truck, he will usually be so overwhelmed that he will make statements. In the Rifkin case, authorities were provided with statements linking the suspect to 18 serial murders.

☐ The serial killer has the advantage in an interview situation because only he knows all the facts of the murder. Thus the savvy serial killer knows when the police are fishing for details and need him to make the case. (p. 331)

☐ Bundy suggested that the detective needs to display an active interest in or a fascination for murder. However, there are some crimes that he feels are so embarrassing that he can't even talk about them. Ted Bundy talked about how some murders are O.K. and others are too bad to talk about. He referred to these emotional attachments to victims as the killer's soft spots. (p. 336)

☐ The art of interviewing a serial killer was clearly interviewing without being judgmental. (p. 339)

☐ Ted Bundy explained why one category of serial killers were willing to confess. Their murdering careers are short in duration and they are called short-term serial killers. They had not had the time to strengthen their psychological framework in order to build up those barriers of denial and need for self-preservation, which takes years to accomplish. (p. 342)

☐ By interviewing someone and allowing them to respond in the third person, it may open lines of communication. (p. 350)

☐ During the hours immediately after the killing the serial killer is extremely vulnerable to detection. (p. 420)[39]

Criminal Personality Profiling — The Signature Aspect in Criminal Investigation

The signature aspect of a violent criminal offender is a unique and integral part of the offender's behavior. This signature component refers to the psychodynamics, which are the mental and emotional processes underlying human behavior and its motivations.[40]

Essentially, our human sexuality is established during our psychosexual development through conditioning and experience. Sexual behaviors, both healthy and unhealthy, are learned behaviors in which the individual develops a perception of what is sexually stimulating and satisfying.

Clinical Perspective

Clinically speaking, there is a behavioral distinctiveness in human sexuality. This unique aspect of our sexual arousal and response system accounts for why individuals differ in their sexual behaviors and engage in a specific series of behavioral patterns.

In sex-related criminal incidents the offender is oftentimes subconsciously "acting-out" a sexually significant behavioral pattern which reflects the underlying personality, lifestyle, and developmental experiences of the offender.

Dr. John Money (1986) refers to the "lovemap" as "a developmental representation or template in the mind and in the brain depicting the idealized lover and the idealized program of sexuoerotic activity projected in imagery or actually engaged in with that lover."[41] These are related to the natural human development of the individual and are influenced by both biological aspects as well as the environment; nature and nurture. According to Dr. Money, "Like a native language, a person's lovemap also bears the mark of his own unique individuality, or accent...it

Figure 21.14. **EXAMPLE OF PARAPHILIA MANIFESTED IN A CRIME SCENE.** This serial killer, who had a background of fetish burglaries and paraphiliac attraction to women's high heel shoes, propped his victim with these red shoes taken from her closet and then posed her in the crime scene. (Courtesy of Detective Dale Foote, Bellevue Police Department, Bellevue, Washington.)

is usually quite specific as to details of the physiognomy, build, race, color of the ideal lover, not to mention temperment, manner, and so on."[42] The lovemaps may be extremely detailed in specifying certain characteristics which take precedence over others, such as an attraction to thighs, buttocks, bosom, torso face, teeth, eye color, hair, skin, weight, height, and so on.[43]

Sexual deviation occurs when these "lovemap" patterns become derailed. Child molesters, rapists, deviant murderers, and others with peculiar erotic interests are an example of this phenomenon. The formulation of sexual deviance can usually be traced to aberrant erotic development. For example, strict anti-sexual upbringing, sexual abuse of a child by the primary care giver between the ages of 5 and 8, overexposure to sexually stimulating behaviors and/or inappropriate and pathological family dynamics.

According to Money (1983b), "Paraphilias are a mental template or lovemap that in response to neglect, suppression, or traumatization of its normophilic formation, has developed with distortions, namely ommisions, displacements, and inclusions that would otherwise have no place in it. A paraphilia permits sexuoerotic arousal, genital performance, and orgasm to take place, but only under the aegis, in fantasy or live performance, of the special substitute imagery of the paraphilia."[44] These derailed lovemaps are the precursor for sexual deviance and in the case of the serial killer, the "game-plan" for murder.

Human behavior, although unpredictable, is oftentimes repetitive. Research has indicated that certain actions engaged in at the homicide crime scene by certain types of personalities will repeat themselves in other homicide investigations. The homicide detective, who has enhanced his experience with a comprehension of the psychodynamics of human behavior will be able to develop a base of knowledge which can be applied to the review of similar cases.

Investigative Perspective

From an investigative perspective, it is important to note that an offender's M.O. or "method of doing things" is a learned behavior and tends to remain consistent. However, these types of behaviors are developed over time and change as offenders gain experience, build confidence, or become involved with the criminal justice system. The "signature" component may also change to some degree. However, the change usually involves a progression of violence and sexual mutilation, which is consistent with the paraphilia sexual sadism as seen in lust murders.

The modus operandi involves actions necessary to accomplish the activity while the "signature aspect" represents the underlying emotional "needs" of the offender. These "needs" or as Money (1986) would refer to them, "Lovemaps" usually present as behaviors and actions that go beyond those necessary to accomplish the crime. When dealing with an offender who is a sexual sadist, one can expect to see a progression of violence as the series evolves. Understanding and recognizing both the modus operandi and the signature aspect of the event can enable the professional investigator to "link" events in a series.

Linkage Blindness

Linkage blindness is defined as an investigative failure to recognize a pattern which "links" one crime with another crime in a series of cases through victimology, geographic region or area of events, the "signature" of the offender, similar M.O., and a review of autopsy protocols.[45]

LINKAGE BLINDNESS

A FAILURE TO RECOGNIZE A PATTERN WHICH "LINKS" ONE CRIME WITH ANOTHER CRIME IN A SERIES OF CASES.

- ⊙ **Victimology and/or background**
- ⊙ **Geographic region or area of events**
- ⊙ **Signature of Offender**
- ⊙ **Modus Operandi of Offender**
- ⊙ **Autopsy Protocols**

Figure 21.15. **LINE DRAWING OF LINKAGE BLINDNESS.**

Investigative Application of the "Signature" Aspect

When an offender displays behavior within the crime scene and engages in activities which go beyond those necessary to accomplish the act he is revealing his *signature*. These significant personality identifiers occur when an offender repeatedly engages in a specific order of sexual activity, uses a specific type of binding, injures and/or inflicts similar type injuries, displays the body for shock value, tortures and mutilates his victim, and engages in some form of ritualistic behavior.

In the "Vampire Killer" case, which appears earlier in the chapter, the killer was targeting young women whom he would eviscerate. Investigation revealed that the offender was removing blood and body parts from his victims. The sexual motivations were obvious in the mutilations. The other activities engaged in by the offender were so absurd and bizarre that authorities were immediately able to link the incidents. However, the motivation underlying these series of crimes appeared totally irrational. The offender, who was seemingly unconcerned about apprehension left an abundance of physical evidence at his crime scenes. The detectives properly focused their investigation on someone who would be described as a psychotic or *disorganized* individual.

One of the most common signatures is that of the psychopathic sexual sadist, who involves himself in complete domination of the

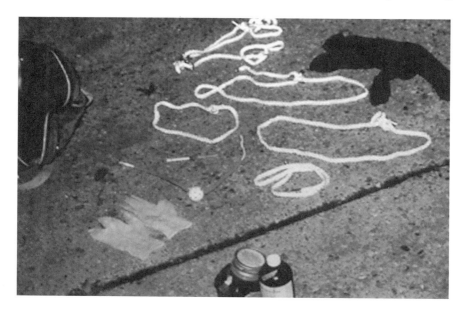

Figure 21.16.   **MURDER KIT.** This photograph depicts the typical contents of a Rape or Murder Kit. The masked offender had gained entry into the bedroom of a young woman while she was asleep. The contents of his "kit" were as follows: a camcorder with an x-rated porno tape, black nylon stockings and "fishnet" stockings, pair of gloves, a bottle of chloroform with mask, a syringe containing acepromozine (a horse tranquilizer), a bondage gag, two clothes pins, and a number of pre-tied ropes with slip knots. (Courtesy of Chief Thomas G. Witten, Sugarcreek Township, Ohio Police Department.)

victim. The author has reviewed and consulted on a number of serial murder cases that have revealed this signature aspect of the crime.

CASE HISTORY

Timothy Spencer, who was responsible for the sexual murders of four women, was a "cat burglar" and rapist who stalked his victims. (See Timothy Spencer case in Chapter 17 in DNA Section.) He was able to enter their homes while they were asleep. In fact, in the Chesterfield County case, he was able to access a 15-year-old victim while her parents were asleep in another part of the house. In the other three cases, he made sure that the victims, who were married or had a relationship, were home alone when he attacked. He exerted total control over these victims and spent considerable time in their homes. His behavior with the victims and his actions in the crime scene indicated that he was a classic sexual psychopath.

The prosecution of this offender was based upon the "Signature Crime Theory." In each of the incidents, the women had been raped and sodomized by their attacker after he had accosted them in their sleep.

Figure 21.17. **SIGNATURE ELEMENT IN A SERIES OF STRANGULATIONS.** This victim was found face down with her hands tied behind her back and a ligature around her neck. Four other female victims were found similarly bound and positioned face down in the crime scene. (Courtesy of Detective Joseph Horgas, Arlington Police Department, Arlington, Virginia.)

Each victim had been strangled to death with ligature. Each of the victims were found face down and had been similarly bound with their hands tied behind their backs.

CASE HISTORY

A series of murders occurred within Washington state in 1990. The murders began in Bellevue, Washington in June and ended within King County in September, 1990. Initially, authorities were not aware of the linkage of these cases, due to a delay in the analysis of pubic hair evidence retrieved from the first two crime scenes. In addition, the authorities were misdirected with the emergence of a more viable suspect in the second murder investigation. However, when the evidence analysis of the hair had been completed and the initial suspect in the second case was eliminated, the authorities were presented with a classic "signature-type" series of events.

It is important to note that in the real world of conducting an active homicide investigation, we don't have the luxury of "retrospective knowledge." Many alleged "experts," who criticize police investigations are "smart" after-the-fact, when *all* of the information is finally available for review. When you examine this case chronologically, and assess the information that authorities had at the time they were conducting their inquiry, one can understand how these cases were not initially linked.

CASE NUMBER 1

The first victim was a 27-year-old, white female, whose nude body had been discovered in the parking lot of a restaurant. Her body was found face-up, lying on her back with her legs crossed at the ankles. Her face was partially covered with a lid from a plastic cup, which covered blunt-force injuries to her head. There was also evidence that her necklace had been used as a ligature along with scratch marks on the side of her neck. In addition, there were postmortem drag marks on the high points of her body, indicating that she had been dragged. The assailant had posed the victim's body with the victim's hands crossed on her chest with a pine cone beneath her fingers. The police recovered foreign pubic hairs on and near the body. The medical examination revealed that she had been vaginally raped and anally sodomized with an unknown object.

Her clothing was missing along with any identification. As a result, her identity remained unknown until June 27, 1990 when she was identified as a "missing person" from Redmond, Washington. She had last been seen in the early morning hours of June 20th at a popular bar and restaurant. Her car was later located in the parking lot of the establishment where her pocketbook was discovered in the restaurant's lost and found.[46]

Signature Aspect

The body of a nude female, who had been sexually assaulted (raped and anally sodomized with an object), was posed with a prop (the pine cone) beneath her hands. The body had been positioned so that the victim was lying on her back, face up, thereby exposing her breasts and genitalia. Semen and sperm were recovered along with unknown foreign pubic hairs. This pointed towards an organized offender, who was able to "con" the victim away from a safe area. She was raped at one location and then deposed of at another location. Her body was displayed for shock value and her clothing was taken to hinder identification.

Figure 21.18. **SIGNATURE ASPECT — VICTIM NUMBER 1.** This victim who had been raped and anally sodomized with a foreign object was posed and propped by the killer for the purposes of "shock value." This murder was the first in a series of brutal sex-related homicides that escalated in violence as the killer progressed. (Courtesy of Detective Marv Skeen, formerly with the Bellevue Police Department in Bellevue, Washington now with the State Attorney General's Office in Washington State.)

CASE NUMBER 2

The next case also occurred within the City of Bellevue. On August 9, 1990, the body of a 32-year-old white female was discovered in her bedroom by her 13-year-old daughter.

The victim's nude body had been displayed on the bed with a pillow over her head. The barrel of a shotgun had been inserted into the victim's vagina. The body was totally nude except for a pair of red high heel shoes, which had been placed upon her feet by the offender. The body had been positioned so that whoever walked into the room would be confronted with this grotesque sight. There was evidence of blunt-force trauma to the head and manual strangulation. Although there wasn't any evidence of vaginal rape or sodomy, there were foreign pubic hairs found on the mattress and the rug in the victim's bedroom. Two expensive rings were missing from the hands of the victim.[47]

Figure 21.19. **SIGNATURE ASPECT — VICTIM NUMBER 2.** This victim was found in the bedroom of her home with a shotgun placed into her vagina. She also had been posed and propped for "shock value." The injuries on this victim were much more extensive than victim number 1 and there was evidence that the offender had spent an inordinate amount of time with the victim. (Courtesy of Detective Dale Foote, Bellevue Police Department, Bellevue, Washington.)

Signature Aspect

The body of a nude female, who had been sexually assaulted (the victim was nude, object inserted into vagina, foreign pubic hairs), was found in her residence. There wasn't any evidence of forced entry. The body had been displayed and then posed with props (insertion of the shotgun into the vagina and the red high heel shoes on her feet). Foreign pubic hairs were retrieved from the crime scene. The offender had managed to enter her home, assault and kill her, and then spend a considerable amount of time in the crime scene as he engaged in unknown conduct with the body. The body was face-up exposing her breasts and genitalia and posed for shock value. The injuries to this woman's head were more extensive and the posing more degrading than victim number 1. Two expensive rings were stolen from the victim's hand.

However, in this case the police had good reason to suspect a former boyfriend, who made an excellent suspect due to his activities prior to the murder. In addition, when the police attempted to question him, he hired an attorney, who refused to even discuss the case with the

Figure 21.20. **SIGNATURE ASPECT — VICTIM NUMBER 3.** This victim was also found in the bedroom of her residence. She also had been posed and propped for "shock value." The injuries were much more extensive than victims number 1 and 2 and there was evidence that the offender had spent an inordinate amount of time with the victim. In addition to the extensive head injuries, the killer engaged in "piquerism" with the victim's body inflicting approximately 241 postmortem stab wounds throughout her body which indicated a progression of violence. (Courtesy of Detective Larry Petersen, King County Police Department, Seattle, Washington.)

authorities. The pubic hair from the first case as well as the present case was not analyzed until September. In fact, this case, as presented to authorities, appeared to be a classic interpersonal violence-oriented type dispute and assault.

CASE NUMBER 3

The next case took place within King County. The body of the 24-year-old, white female victim was discovered in her bedroom on September 3, 1990. Her nude body had been positioned under the bed covers with a pillow covering her face. There was a vibrator placed in the victim's mouth and next to her head was a book entitled *More of the Joys of Sex*. There was also evidence of blunt-force trauma to the victim's head. When the police removed the bed covers, they saw that the body had been placed spread-eagled on her back, with a series of postmortem slashings and stabbings. The victim's body was face-up thereby exposing her breasts and genitalia. Crime scene technicians recovered a foreign pubic hair, which was adherent to one of her stab wounds. There was evidence that the offender had spent considerable time in the crime scene. The cause of death was blunt-force trauma to her head. However,

Figure 21.21. **PIQUERISM.** Postmortem stab wounds throughout the body. Sexual inclinations to stab, pierce, or cut. Obtaining a sexual gratification from the shedding of blood, tearing of flesh, and/or observing such pain and suffering of a victim who is being subjected to this activity. (Courtesy of Detective Larry Petersen, King County Police Department, Seattle, Washington.)

the offender felt the need to inflict over 240 postmortem stab wounds throughout the victim's body. There were frontal wounds into the side of the victim's neck, into her chest, breasts and abdomen, and upper thighs. There were a series of dorsal wounds into the back and buttocks, and along both legs. Even the bottom of the victim's feet bore evidence of this piquerism. An expensive ring was missing from the victim's finger.[48]

Signature Aspect

The body of a nude female, who had been sexually assaulted (the victim was nude, piquerism, foreign pubic hairs), was found in her residence. There wasn't any evidence of forced entry. The body had been sexually displayed and then posed with props (insertion of the vibrator in the victim's mouth and the book, *More of the Joys of Sex* placed next to her head). A foreign pubic hair was recovered from her body. The offender had managed to enter her home, assault and kill her, and then spend a considerable amount of time at the crime scene. The infliction of over 240 postmortem wounds throughout the body took a considerable amount of time. The offender had degraded the victim in death and had posed the body for shock value. The injuries to this woman's head were much more extensive and the posing, with the vibrator in her mouth, more degrading then victim number 2. A ring was stolen from the victim's hand.

The Suspect

The suspect was a 33-year-old black male. He was a known burglar who as an adolescent had a history of fetish burglaries and other nuisance offenses. He was developed as a suspect when he was found in possession of a gun which had been taken from a residence nearby to the last homicide. The pubic hairs recovered from each of the crime scenes were Negroid in origin and were found to match the suspect. The subject, who was a police buff, was fascinated with police work. He had police scanners, and told people he worked for the police and the FBI. He was also fascinated with serial murder cases and reportedly was well read on the Ted Bundy and Green River cases. He followed the news stories very closely and had cut out the news stories as well as the photographs of the victims. He would compare them to each other and ridicule the police techniques. He had stated to a friend, "that the only way the police will catch the killer is with trace evidence."

Evidence

Each of the bodies had Negroid hairs on or near their bodies. The semen and sperm found on the first victim was matched to the suspect through DNA. The police located a vehicle used to transport the first victim and discovered blood in the front seat cushion. This blood matched the blood of the first victim through DNA analysis. Police located a witness who identified one of the rings stolen from the second victim. The suspect had tried to sell the ring to the witness. The ring stolen from the last victim was traced back to the suspect.

Signature Aspect of the Crimes

Each murder was sexually motivated. Each of the victims were discovered totally nude. Each victim's body had been positioned face-up to expose the breasts and genitalia. Each victim had been posed and/or positioned after death with props and/or objects inserted near or placed on their bodies. It was apparent that the killer spent a considerable amount of time with each of the victims and engaged in activities, which went well beyond those necessary to kill the victims. In fact, there was a classic progression of violence inflicted on each new victim. The cause of death for each of the victims was blunt-force trauma. In each case, trophies had been taken from the victims, i.e., clothing, rings, jewelry. Each crime scene revealed Negroid pubic hairs, suggesting a black offender.

Conclusion

The homicide detective who has enhanced his experience with a comprehension of the psychodynamics of human behavior will be able to develop a base of knowledge which can be applied to the review of similar cases. The ability to "read" the crime scene and recognize the "signature" of an offender can be extremely instrumental in the investigative process.

Geographic Profiling

Geographic profiling is a sociological concept which scrutinizes and analyzes an offender's activity within a specific geographic area. This application of theory was first promulgated by Rossmo (1994a).[49] The concept is based on the fact that, *We as human beings are creatures of habit.* We repeat those actions and things that are familiar and comfortable to us. Rossmo refers to what he defines as "mental maps" which are a cognitive image of our spacial surroundings based upon our daily activities and experiences. These activities occur in areas around our home, workplace, recreation sites, shopping districts, etc., causing those neighborhoods to become known and familiar. Connecting these centers of activity are various routes which we choose in our daily travel. According to Rossmo, these familiar sites, areas, paths, and routes influence our mental maps.

Consider the first time you took an automobile trip on your vacation. I'm sure that you probably planned the trip taking a map showing you the best course as well as the identification of certain locations that you could stay along the route. Perhaps you enjoyed the location and decided to go back the following year. I am sure that you still made preparations and planned-out the trip. However, this second time you probably knew where you would stay and you probably chose the same location because it was familiar. Also, you probably used the same rest stops and gas stations along the way. In addition, you really didn't need to refer to the map as often as the first time.

If you returned the following year, you probably didn't even need the map because your route of travel had became memorized, landmarks were easily recognized, and this led to your comfort and reassurance. Basically, you developed a mental map of this scenario which provided you with a feeling of comfort.

Offenders behave in a similar fashion as they cruise for victims or search for places to dispose of bodies. The direct and alternative routes that offenders select reflect their "mental maps."

The areas of home, work, shopping, and recreation comprise comfort zones which allow predatory offenders to cruise and commit their crimes under a psychological blanket of protection. The same psychological reassurance that you experienced in your repeat travels also applies to the criminal and his travels.

The predator has a zone of behavioral activity. These zones contain activity sites, offense locations, and the connecting paths between them.

Dayton Leroy Rogers, who was responsible for the murders of eight women in the Portland, Oregon area was a prime example of this type of offender; a predator who operated within a specific zone of behavioral activity.

Rogers would cruise the streets of Portland's "Red Light" district looking for prey. He would solicit the women for sex and entice them into his pick-up truck. He would then drive along pre-selected and secluded routes out of town towards the mountains and the Molalla Forest in Oregon. Once he had gotten his victims into the truck, which was a comfort zone, he would demonstrate his power over them in a series of sexual bondage and torture scenarios. His victims would be killed in a brutal and horrific manner. He would then dispose of their nude and mutilated bodies within the confines of the Molalla Forest. In fact, authorities eventually found the remains of seven young women in the Molalla Forest. The offender had been familiar with the Molalla Forest for years and had grown comfortable within this location. The Molalla Forest represented his *primary* comfort zone. This was a location where he could dispose of his victim's bodies and return again and again. He could not only dump new victims, but he could also savor his conquests. The Molalla Forest became a "totem place," a location that afforded him the opportunity to relive the events and fantasize about his earlier kills. The routes to and from the Molalla Forest as well as the streets of Portland, where he picked up his potential victims, represented his geographical comfort zones.[50]

Geography plays an important role in the offender's selection of "suitable victims." Suitability depends on the "rightness" of the place. Is the area appropriate for predation? Is it familiar? Does it possess a feeling of comfort? Does it contain sufficient and suitable victims? Is the risk of apprehension low? Are there sufficient escape routes?

Investigative Elements to Consider in Geographic Profiling

- Crime location type
- Arterial roads and highways
- Physical and psychological boundaries
- Land use (residential, commercial, industrial, parkland)
- Neighborhood demographics
- Routine activities of victims
- Displacement[51]

Investigative Elements in the Criminal Case Assessment Process

- Crime scene similarities
- Traditional investigative techniques
- Linkage analysis
- Psychological profiling
- Geographic profiling
- New investigative strategies[52]

Types of Crime Locations

- Encounter location
- Attack location
- Crime location
- Victim disposal location
- Vehicle dump location[53]

The author refers the reader to the text *Profiling Violent Crime,* 2nd Edition (1996), by Holmes for further information on geographic profiling.[54]

CASE HISTORY — ORGANIZED OFFENDER

The following case history concerns a serial killer who operated within New York City and Bergen County, New Jersey. He is a classic organized offender, who could be clinically defined as a psychopathic sexual sadist. In addition, the "signature" element of these events ultimately linked these crimes. This case history includes information from a personal interview of Lt. Frank Del Prete, Bergen County Prosecutor's Office.[55]

Figure 21.22. **MID-TOWN TORSO CASE — SERIAL KILLINGS.** In these figures you see the mutilated bodies of two women found in a midtown hotel. Both women had been sadistically tortured over a period of days. Note that the heads as well as the hands have been severed from the bodies. The mutilation in this particular circumstance was purposeful and performed by the killer so as to prevent authorities from identifying the victims. The killer then set the room on fire before leaving the hotel. Note the linear torture marks on the body in the bottom figure.

Figure 21.23. **VICTIM OF SERIAL MURDERER.** Female victim a serial killer was found beneath a bed in a New Jersey motel. This victim had been tortured and sexually abused. There is breast assault as well as bondage activity (handcuffs) in the crime scene. Note the linear lines of torture on the body. (Courtesy of Lt. Francis P. Del Prete, Bergen County Prosecutor's Office.)

New York City homicide detectives first became involved in this serial murder investigation when the bodies of two women were discovered in the Travelodge Motor Inn on West 42nd Street. The Fire Department had responded to this location to extinguish a fire in one of the motel rooms. In the room were the nude and mutilated bodies of the two young women. Their heads and hands had been removed almost surgically, according to the pathologist, who confirmed that both women had been sexually abused and physically tortured.

This investigation became known as the "Mid-Town Torso Case." It was believed that both women were prostitutes who had somehow been lured to the room. A check of the hotel register indicated that this room had been occupied for 3 days by an unknown male, white, who gave a fictitious address in New Jersey. Radiological tests on the bones of the victims revealed one woman to be in her early 20s and the other was estimated to be approximately 16 years of age. The newspapers printed everything they could lay their hands on including how the police were attempting to identify the young women by dressing mannequins with the clothing recovered at the murder scene.

There were stories on the progress of the investigation including stories on "Johns," who had been arrested for abusing prostitutes. The newspapers also reported on the efforts by the police in the area to come

Figure 21.24. **SERIAL KILLER VICTIM.** In this photo we see the victim of the same serial killer found in a New York City hotel. This victim had also been tortured and sexually abused. The offender had removed the breasts of the victim and placed them on the bed board to shock the police. He did attempt to change his modus operandi, however, and set the room on fire. New York City authorities immediately linked this killing to the midtown case. He was finally caught on his next attempt in New Jersey.

up with information. Approximately 1 month later the body of one of the victims was identified as a high-priced prostitute who worked the Atlantic City-New York City set. Despite this break, the investigation was still going nowhere.

Four months later, in Hasbrouck Heights in Bergen County, New Jersey the nude body of a 19-year old woman would be found in the Quality Inn Motel by a maid, who was cleaning the room. This victim was identified through fingerprints as a prostitute who was originally from Miami, Florida but was now working the streets of New York City. She had been tortured and sexually abused. In fact, the killer had left behind a pair of handcuffs, which had been used to bind the victim. Her body bore evidence of bondage-type injuries, nipple and breast assault, as well as superficial torture-type cuttings to the skin.

The Bergen County Prosecutor's Office took over this investigation. They got their first break when a partial latent fingerprint was discovered on the handcuffs that the killer had left on the body. Although the New Jersey authorities conducted interviews in New York City and conferred with New York City Police, this case was not considered related to the Mid-Town Torso case because of the different M.O. and crime scene information.

Eleven days after the Bergen County homicide, New York City Police were once again summoned to a hotel room fire by the Fire Department, which discovered a nude and mutilated body. New York City homicide detectives immediately linked this death to the Mid-Town Torso case. However, this time the killer did not remove the victim's head and hands. Instead, the killer removed both of the woman's breasts, which he left on the headboard of the bed. Once again there was evidence of bondage and torture. This victim, like the one who had been identified in the Mid-Town case, was a high-class prostitute, who ordinarily wouldn't be operating out of this type of premises. This time there wasn't any clothing left behind for police to analyze. Had the killer been focusing on the news reports? The New York City Police still had no viable leads.

One week after the New York City case, and approximately 3 weeks since the discovery of the body at the Quality Inn Motel in Hasbrouck Heights, police once again were called to the motel. This time, Hasbrouck Heights Police were responding to cries for help coming from one of the rooms.

A male, white, 33 years of age identified as Richard Cottingham, was arrested by police as he attempted to flee from the motel. An 18-year-old prostitute from New York City was found in the room. She had been bound with handcuffs and sadistically tortured by Cottingham. Her screams for help had been heard by the motel staff, who immediately called police. Cottingham tried to talk his way out of the assault by stating he had "paid for this service from a prostitute" and that he wasn't trying to kill her. He feigned cooperation readily admitting to sadomasochistic activities with the prostitute but steadfastly denied any involvement with the 3-week-old murder investigation. However, Bergen County detectives were convinced that they had just apprehended a killer. The New Jersey officials secured a search warrant for Cottingham's house in Lodi, New Jersey.

Police were shocked to discover that Cottingham maintained his own private room that even his wife was not allowed to enter. It became known as the "Trophy Room." Cottingham would take souvenirs from his victims, which are referred to as trophies. In this room would be the crucial evidence linking Cottingham to both the New Jersey and New York City homicides. In addition to the murders, Cottingham also became the primary suspect in a series of abductions and rapes of New York City prostitutes, who had been drugged and then brought to New Jersey motels, where he would torture and sexually abuse them.

The latent print on the handcuffs was matched to Richard Cottingham. The evidence recovered in the Trophy Room became the basis of the New York City investigation and the victims of the abductions and sex-torture were able to identify Cottingham in the subsequent line-ups conducted by Bergen County Prosecutor's detectives.

Bergen County detectives were convinced that Cottingham had killed before in New Jersey. In fact, 3 years earlier, the body of a beautiful

27-year-old nurse had been found in the parking lot of the Quality Inn Motel in Hasbrouck Heights. She had died of asphyxiation from a gag, as she was being abducted. Ironically, this victim had been a neighbor of Cottingham when he lived in Little Ferry, New Jersey.

Her body bore some similar wounds, like those of the other victims. There were enough similarities to convince the prosecutor, Dennis Calo, to seek an additional murder charge against Richard Cottingham. This case subsequently became known as the "Signature Case," when Dennis Calo was able to convince the court that the modus operandi in respect to the cases was so unique and so novel as to be personal to Richard Cottingham. Cottingham was eventually convicted of the New Jersey murders and rapes and is currently serving several lifetime prison sentences in Trenton State Prison.

Cottingham displayed the following traits, which are considered classic Organized Offender. His behavior and the activities with his victims are consistent with DSM-IV criteria found in the clinical definition of Antisocial Personality Disorder and Sexual Sadism. He is a classic *psychopathic sexual sadist.*

He selected each of his victims for the purpose of sexual and psychosexual gratification. He became sexually excited by the suffering of his victims.

He was methodical and cunning and planned his offense. He had his "murder-kit" and props, which he used on his victims.

He maintained control over his victims — handcuffs, restraints, tape across mouths, etc.

He was excited by the cruelty of the acts.

He had an extensive collection of S&M pornography, which displayed his avid interest in sadistic fantasies, torture, and bondage paraphanalia.

He demanded submission from his victims, engaged in sexual experimentation, and degraded his victims.

He engaged in mutilation for the purposes of hindering identification in the Mid-Town Torso case. He removed the breasts of the other victim for "shock-value."

There was a distinctive lack of evidence at most of his crime scenes. He used fire to destroy evidence in two of the cases.

He followed the news media accounts; changed his M.O. accordingly, and changed his location.

He took souvenirs from his victims. In the case of Organized Offenders these become "trophies" of his conquests.

He lived some distance from his crime scenes and his victims were targeted strangers, except in the nurse killing, which may have been his first murder.

He led a compartmentalized life-style. He was married with three children and had a home in New Jersey. He worked in Manhattan and maintained a separate life-style in New York City. He had two girlfriends in the city, each of whom was unaware of the other. He was involved with prostitutes, whom he would date, or abduct and rape. And, he was also torturing and killing certain prostitutes in between his other activities.

CASE HISTORY — MIXED PERSONALITY

An interesting illustration of the classic "mixed" personality was provided to the author from the Peel Regional Police Force in Brampton, Ontario, Canada. I had the opportunity to interview Inspector Rod Piukkala, who provided the following case information on a particularly brutal "Lust Murder."[56]

This case, which presented the authorities with both an "organized" and "disorganized" scenario provides an exquisite example of why we in law enforcement must be cautious in our assessments of typology in the application of psychology to the crime.

The suspect, who was 17 years of age at the time of the offense, worked as a shipping clerk in a local factory. His victim was a 16-year-old high school student. She had just left her boyfriend's house and was waiting for a bus when the suspect pulled up and offered her a ride. The victim accepted the ride after the suspect got out of his vehicle and opened the rear door for her. He was able to verbalize her into his vehicle and take her to an isolated location, where he sodomized and raped her. This type of activity is appropriately described as *organized*. However, what followed were the activities of a classic *lust murder* committed by a *disorganized offender*.

The suspect provided police with the following confession. He stated that he had pulled into the back of the 600 Group (a factory) and then put the car into park. He stated, "I then lunged at her over the front seat real quick. I was beside her and I started to grab her tit. I reached over and put my hands under her knees and pulled them up onto the seat so she was laying on the seat. I told her to take her pants down and she did. I spread her legs and licked her vagina. Then I took my pants down and got up on her and screwed her. After I ejaculated I said that's it and she asked if she could sit up in the front seat. I said sure and then said hold on a second and I grabbed her belt loop so she wouldn't run away...While we were walking I said I had a present for her...I reached into the car through the open window and grabbed a brick from the floor. I looked at her and then hit her with the brick over the left eye. She screamed "oh no" just before I hit her with the brick and then sort of screamed in pain. I hit her one or two more times on the side of the head and then she fell down. Then I saw a bigger brick, so I put the small one down and then picked up the bigger one and hit her in the head about seven times. Then she screamed and said, "Don't strangle me." Then I looked over and seen the board and picked it up and put it on her throat and applied pressure. I released it

Figure 21.25. **LUST MURDER.** These photographs depict the condition of the body when it was discovered by the police. The body had been posed after death in a manner to degrade the victim. The offender who had raped and killed the young girl then engaged in deviant postmortem activities with the corpse. (Courtesy of Inspector Rod Piukkala. Photos taken by the Peel Regional Police Force, Brampton, Ontario, Canada.)

after about a minute and she sucked some air in and she was still breathing so I saw another board that was longer so I got it and held the end against her throat and stood up and leaned my weight on it. I did this for about 2 or 3 minutes. Then I let up and threw the board away and I grabbed her by the feet and dragged her over to the field.

I was dragging her by her pant leg and when I got over there I noticed her clothes were pulled up around her shoulders. Her breasts were exposed and I could see her lighter and a safety pin. I leaned over and bit her right nipple then I got the lighter and I pulled her jeans off to her ankles and I ripped her panties off and just tossed them aside. I used the lighter and singed her pubic hair. Then I picked up the safety pin and put it through her left nipple. Then put the lighter to her right breast. I spotted a piece of wood with a nail in it and I put the board with the nail in it on her chest and hit it with my hand and drove the nail into her chest. I did this between five and seven times. Then I saw this big brick about 3 feet away and I picked it up and dropped it on her chest. I did this probably seven or eight times. She was still quivering at this time so I put the board with the nail under her neck with the nail up and pushed her head on it. Then I pulled the lumber jacket over her head and I got the big brick beside her head and then flipped it over her head. I stood up and urinated on her and then I left. Oh, I forgot one thing, I remember the moon shining on her necklace which was around her neck but was broken. I took it off and put it in my pocket and the lighter too. I walked over to the car and picked up the small brick and put it on the floor of the front seat. I got in the car and drove home. I got home about 12:20 (midnight) and I went right to sleep.

The next day I got up about 6:00 A.M. and went to work between 7 and 7:30. On my way to work I drove (past the location where the murder was committed to get the name of the company). When I got to work I phoned information and got the name of the company. I wrote it down on a piece of paper. I wrote out this piece of paper (indicating the evidence on the desk) as soon as I got to work. At 10:20 I phoned the 600 Group and spoke to a secretary and told her there's a body out back, she's been killed, call the proper authorities. I told her my name was Fred Baker. I called back to see if the police had got there yet. I said 'this is Fred, have the police arrived yet?' The third time I called a man answered and I hung up. I called back again and said, 'The future's uncertain, the end is always near. And you're gonna die too.' I hung up the phone then. I made another call a little bit later and I was trying to scare them, I had seen it in the movies. I said three sticks of dynamite set for 3 minutes I think I said a couple of doors up. Then I hung up and called back about a minute and a half later and said, 'Minute and a half to go.' Then I called up *Mississauga News* and the receptionist put me through to (name of the reporter). I told him the girl's name was Darlene, that she was 17 to

19...At lunch time I walked down the road and noticed the police cars at 600 Group. I asked one of the reporters what happened and he said there's a murder but there's not much information. I turned around and went back to work."

The suspect's statement included information that he had gotten the victim's name from the newspapers and placed calls to the victim's relatives. He also called her school to inquire about the funeral. In addition, he called the cemetery and got the location of the plot. He also wrote a four-page letter to the police in which he graphically described the murder and events leading up to the death of the young victim.

The letter which taunted the police and warned of other murders was delivered along with the victim's necklace and her cigarette lighter to a library with instructions to phone the police.

I refer the reader to Tables 21.1 and 21.2 in this chapter. Note that there are a number of both organized and disorganized characteristics in combination with one another, which represent the suspect as well as the activities at the crime scene.

The Police Investigation

Peel Regional Police Homicide Inspectors Rod Piukkala and D'Arcy Honer were assigned to investigate the case. Detective Sergeant Geoff Hancock, Inspector Mike Metcalf, and Inspector Frank Fernandes (now deceased) were assigned the identification duties in connection with this case (see Chapter 20 "Latent Prints on Human Skin").

The deceased's head was covered with a 66-pound block. Her sweater and bra were pulled up, fully exposing her breasts. Her jeans were rolled down to her ankles exposing her genitalia and her legs were positioned in a spread-eagled manner. The officers observed a safety pin inserted into her left nipple as well as several scratches and bite marks on her breast. They also observed burn marks on her breast and pubic area. There were several puncture marks on her neck and chest along with deep lacerations on the top and sides of her skull. The board with the nail protruding was located beneath her skull. The crime scene search revealed a number of bloodstains and drag marks leading towards the body along with a smaller bloody building block. The identification officers were able to "lift" palm prints from the inner thigh of the deceased, which later matched the suspect Dobson (see "Latent Prints from Human Skin," Chapter 20). In addition, a forensic odontologist was able to match the suspects dentition to the bite marks inflicted on the victim's breast.

A

Figure 21.26.   **POSTMORTEM ACTIVITIES.** (A) The offender engaged in deviant activities with the corpse. There were bite marks on the victim's breasts, nail punctures of her neck and chest, deep lacerations on the top and sides of her skull, as well as burn marks to the breast and pubis. The offender also urinated on the corpse. (B) Shows a safety pin which the offender used to pierce the victim's left nipple. (Courtesy of Inspector Rod Piukkala. Photos taken by the Peel Regional Police Force, Brampton, Ontario, Canada.)

The suspect, David Dobson, was identified early on as a result of the telephone calls to the 600 Group. The authorities had requested Bell Canada to install tracing equipment on the company's line. As a result the calls were traced to another factory about a block away. The authorities also learned that someone, who was later discovered to be the suspect, had made two additional calls to the *Mississauga News*. The owner of the factory where the calls originated was requested by police

B

Figure 21.26. (continued)

to listen to a tape recording of the suspect. The owner identified David Dobson. Court-approved audio and video surveillance was immediately commenced on the subject. Tape recordings of the subject were also played for the secretaries of the 600 Group and the *Mississauga News* as well as the reporter.

The following day an employee at the plant where Dobson worked located a piece of paper with the telephone numbers of the 600 Group and the *Mississauga News* on Dobson's desk. A further search of the plant by Detective Sergeant Hancock and and Inspectors Piukkala and Honer revealed a piece of paper with the phrase "The future's uncertain, the end is always near" taped to the wall above Dobson's work bench. The phone numbers for the 600 Group and the *Mississauga News* were again observed on another piece of paper.

On Monday, the subject was shown a newspaper account of the murder by a fellow employee, who was acting under the direction of investigators. He immediately opened the paper to the appropriate page and began to read aloud to the other employees. The subject then proceeded to cut both stories from the paper and place them in his wallet. Upon his arrest these articles were still in his wallet.

The subject was also monitored making telephone calls to people listed in the telephone book with the same last name as the deceased. In addition, authorities were able to document him calling the deceased's school requesting information about the funeral. The authorities then recorded him calling the cemetery requesting the location of the plot.

Later that same day the surveillance officers observed him delivering a package to the Mississauga Library. This package was a four-page letter addressed to Inspector (now deputy chief) Wingate detailing what had transpired on May 6th, and included several taunting messages to the police. In the envelope was the victim's necklace and her cigarette lighter.

On May 12th the subject was arrested by Inspectors Honer and Piukkala. Dobson subsequently provided the officers with a complete verbal and written account of the murder. He also provided handwriting, voice, dental impressions, and physical specimen samples which were matched to the crime. His palm prints were matched to the latent prints taken from the victim's legs. The bloody brick that he used to strike the victim in the face was found on the front floor of his car.

David Dobson was convicted of first degree murder and is serving life in prison with a minimum of 25 years ordered by the court before he will be eligible for parole application.

A Psychology of Evil

The behaviors of these subjects who are referenced within this chapter can appropriately be described as psychopathic sexual sadism.[57] For the purposes of discussion, I have defined this behavior as a "psychology of evil."[58]

Human evil is too complex to be studied from a single framework of reference. In an attempt to understand the psychopathology of evil behavior, scientists use specific models. The medical model remains one of the most useful vehicles for understanding mental illness. Oftentimes, scientists must embrace multiple models in order to gain a clearer understanding.

In psychology there are the biological model, the psychological model, the sociological or environmental model, the sociobiological model, the Freudian model, the behavioral model, the existential model, and so on. In the study of sexual homicide, the motivational model (Ressler, et.al. 1988) provides an excellent vehicle for the analysis of serial murder behaviors.

A Model for a Psychology of Evil

Dr. M. Scott Peck, author of *People of the Lie*,[59] considered various possible factors in the genesis of human evil. He based his study on clinical histories and focused his hypothesis on the general population.

According to Peck (1983), "Although we do not yet have a body of scientific knowledge about human evil worthy of being dignified by the term "psychology," behavioral scientists have laid a foundation that makes development of such a psychology possible...[60] Peck goes on to describe the contributions of Sigmund Freud and Carl Gustave Jung.

He suggested that "...a psychology of evil must be a religious psychology."[61] and recommended a theological model for analyzing and studying evil.

Peck discusses evil and sin, which are obviously not referenced in clinical literature. Yet, his integration of the clinical with the theological encompassing the concept of free will and narcissism provide an excellent example of the psychopathology of evil, which may contribute to law enforcement's understanding of the phenomenon of serial murder.

According to Peck, Erich Fromm was the first and only scientist to clearly identify an evil personality type.

Erich Fromm, who wrote the book *The Heart of Man: Its Genius for Good and Evil*[62] saw the genesis of evil as a developmental process; "We are not created evil or forced to be evil, but we become evil slowly over a period of time through a long series of choices."[63]

According to Peck, however, Fromm's analysis of evil does not seem to take into account the tremendous forces that tend to shape the being during early developmental processes. However, it should also be noted that not everyone who is subjected to a dysfunctional environment becomes evil and this is because we have free will.

If we apply free will and freedom of choice to the serial killer's murderous and sadistic activities we are suddenly confronted by the reality of an evil human predator. An evil entity, who has made a conscious decision to kill. Someone, who as Fromm suggests has made a choice between good and evil.

Peck, in his hypothesis of evil, presents a particular pathologic variant that Erich Fromm called "malignant narcissism."

> "Malignant narcissism is characterized by an unsubmitted will. All adults who are mentally healthy submit themselves one way or another to something higher than themselves, be it God or truth or love or some other ideal...In summary, to a greater or lesser degree, all mentally healthy individuals submit themselves to the demands of their own conscience. Not so the evil, however. In the conflict between their guilt and their will, it is the guilt that must go and the will that must win.[64]

The serial murderer is extremely selfish and narcissistic. His goal is power and sexual gratification. An evil person is characteristically hedonistic and feels superior to other human beings. Despite any intrapsychic conflict between guilt and his ability to exercise his free will, the serial murderer opts for free will and chooses to do evil. I therefore propose that serial murder is representative of a *psychology of evil.*

What is important from an investigative perspective is that when you are dealing with someone who is a psychopathic sexual sadist, you are in effect dealing with a "psychology of evil." This is certainly not a clinical definition, but should serve to alert the professional investigator to the thinking patterns and the potential of such an individual.

If we apply the Freudian concepts of the id, the ego, and the super-ego to the serial murderer, we gain some additional psychological insight into the psyche of the offender. Sigmund Freud proposed that the "id" was the source of instinctual drives which are both constructive and destructive. "The id is completely selfish and concerned only with immediate gratification of instinctual needs without reference to reality or moral considerations. The id operates on what is called the *pleasure principle.* The id however, cannot undertake the actions needed to meet instinctual demands. The id needs the ego, which mediates between the demands of the id and the realities of the external world. The basic function of the ego is to meet id demands, but in such a way as to ensure the well-being and survival of the individual. This requires reason and other intellectual resources in dealing with the external world, as well as the exercise of control over id demands and is referred to as the reality principle. Freud viewed id demands, especially sexual and aggressive strivings, as inherently in conflict with rules and prohibitions imposed by society.

The superego is an outgrowth of learning the taboos and moral values of society. The superego is essentially what we refer to as *conscience* and is *concerned with right and wrong.* As the superego develops, it becomes an additional inner control system that copes with the uninhibited desires of the id."[65]

In the case of a serial murderer, his inner police officer or conscience is either absent or off-duty. The serial murderer kills in order to satisfy his lust or id impulses. However, he is also quite devious and clever. He is aware of the criminality of his actions and will not commit a murder when there is an external police officer watching because his ego will work to assure his well-being in what has been described as the reality principle.

According to Markman (1989), the primary ingredient missing from the sociopath's psyche is conscience.

"That is perhaps, the most significant characteristic of a sociopath, because it allows full and violent expression without significant hesitation, guilt, shame, or remorse. Sociopaths are unable to learn from experience or punishment, and they frequently get in trouble with the law....Sociopaths are hedonistic, emotionally immature, selfish, impulsive, and devious. Their goals are often primitive, and usually are centered on power and pleasure. Sociopaths tend to consider other people only as objects to be exploited, avoided, or neutralized."[66]

Psychopathy, sociopathy, and antisocial personality disorder are not generally classified as a mental illness per se, but rather as a disorder of character. From Markman,

> "A sociopath knows right from wrong — he simply doesn't care. He lacks the internal prohibitions, or conscience, that keep most of us from giving full expression to our most primitive and sometimes violent impulses. He will be self-indulgent, narcissistic, and not concerned about the rights and feelings of other people, who will be treated as objects to be manipulated, exploited, avoided or destroyed." (p. 274)[67]

"When sexual sadism is severe, and especially when it is associated with Antisocial Personality Disorder, individuals with Sexual Sadism may seriously injure or kill their victims.[68]

This type of killer never stops killing. In my opinion, as an expert in homicide investigation, "There is no cure for the psychopathic sexual sadist except life in prison or death".

Murders committed by serial killers who are psychopathic sexual sadists transcend human understanding. The subhuman aspects of these killings coupled with the atrocities visited upon the victims manifest an appetite for violence and sexual mutilation that have people referring to the killers as animals. Yet, animals do not rape, sodomize, torture, and mutilate their prey. They kill for biological survival. Serial murderers, on the other hand, are evil predators who kill for pleasure and their own vile sexual perversion. They are able to operate in an emotionally detached manner because they totally lack any empathy for their victims. In my opinion, the definitions of conduct provided in the clinical diagnoses of Antisocial Personality Disorder and Sexual Sadism are insufficient to define such behaviors. The enormity of such malevolence exceeds these and remains incomprehensible without a concept of a *psychology of evil.*[69]

Interview Strategy

Each criminal interrogation or interview situation is distinctively unique. The success in obtaining statements which inculpate an offender are based upon the individual investigator's knowledge, experience, expertise, and patience.

I recommend that detectives who plan to interrogate the serial murderer consider that the person sitting opposite him or her in an interrogation setting is in fact functioning with a *psychology of evil*. If you appreciate and understand the nature of this type of offender's thinking, you might be able to design an interview strategy which appeals to the serial murderer's own self-interests and facilitate dialogue.

A psychology of evil provides the serial murderer with a unique ability to withstand ordinary investigative interview techniques which focus on guilt, admission, and disclosure. Remember, in a psychology of evil, the fundamental machinery of conscience, responsibility, and feeling or empathy for other human beings is totally lacking. For instance, attempting to invoke sympathy for the victims or surviving families or appealing to the subject's conscience will probably be a waste of time. An offender who evinces a psychology of evil doesn't care about anyone except himself because he is evil. An evil person is clever, devious, selfish, and extremely narcissistic.

Therefore, the investigator should prepare himself for a lengthy session because the suspect will be playing "mind games" in an attempt to gain control of the interview or elicit information about the case.

Evil people like to control and dominate. Therefore, this element should be taken away from the offender as soon as possible. This is accomplished by strict and professional adherence to rules and protocol which put the detective in control of the interview setting. Let the subject know, in an authoritative manner, that the investigator is completely aware of the offender's criminal activities as well as his chargeability.

However, do not attempt any fabrication relative to evidence. Don't forget that the offender has spent a good amount of time planning his murders and taking into account any subsequent police reaction. The suspect knows exactly what he has done and what evidence is available to the police.

An effective interrogation technique to employ with these types of offenders is for the investigator to explain to the offender why he is suspect and "lay-out" the facts of the case in a confident and professional manner.

This is accomplished by displaying knowledge; not only about the crimes, but of the psychodynamics as well as the psychopathology of other offenders who have been involved in similar events. Many serial killers are students of serial murder and have exhibited an avid interest in reading and hearing about the exploits of other serial murderers.

The one glaring defect in a psychology of evil is ego. Their narcissism provides them with a grandiose sense of self importance and a total lack of empathy for anyone else. The interrogator should focus on convincing the suspect that his situation is in fact unique and can only be understood by a specially trained detective with knowledge of these types of crimes. Hedonistically, the offender may attempt to impress the investigator by disclosing details of the murders which indicate how smart and clever he was. This behavior can then be encouraged by generously complimenting the offender on his cleverness and intelligence. In fact, once the detective engages this type of offender in conversation, which feeds his ego, the suspect will want to further impress the officer in search for additional compliments and recognition of his abilities.

Offenders with a psychology of evil possess an extremely sadistic nature and are fascinated by violence, injury, and torture. They most probably will enjoy disclosing certain particularly outrageous and cruel aspects of the crime. They do this not only to shock the investigator but also to psychically relive the event in a selfish and perverse manner of continuing their own sadistic fantasies. It is imperative that the investigator, throughout the interview, maintain an unemotional and professional detachment and not display any personal feelings about the crime or the serial killer. Likewise, it is imperative to avoid any criticism of this type of an offender because he will probably react negatively and terminate further discussion.

It is important to note that interviewing offenders who have perpetrated the unspeakable is an extremely stressful undertaking. Needless to say, in order to comprehend such evil, one must possess a strong belief in a higher order and implement appropriate individual coping mechanisms.

Conclusion

Criminal profiling can be a valuable investigative tool in identifying and pinpointing potential suspects in certain types of murder cases. The VI-CAP Program as well as the additional knowledge-based systems being developed offer law enforcement exciting new capabilities. However, criminal personality profiling cannot replace sound investigative techniques, nor eliminate the need for *experienced homicide investigators.* It should be noted that knowledge-based systems, as well as criminal profiles, are *only* investigative tools.

Practically speaking, these tools are meaningless unless the primary and basic investigative function of information gathering, through crime scene process, interviews, and interrogation, and the medicolegal autopsy are effectively accomplished .

I would like to close this section with an investigative precaution which I came across in my research;

> "Investigators...should gain enough insight into scientific psychology to see how unreliable and unsuitable psychological evidence from character is in criminal detection, and how rarely and cautiously it should be used".[70]

My years of personal homicide investigation experience in the field have taught me a valuable lesson. The theories and strategies involved in the application of criminal profiling techniques to a homicide investigation are subject to the realities of human behavior, which is at best an unpredictable commodity. Although I am an advocate of profiling, I also personally advise against, "Putting all your *investigative eggs* into a "psychological basket".

References

1. Richard L. Ault and James T. Reese. "A Psychological Assessment of Crime Profiling". *Law Enforcement Bulletin*, March 1980, p. 23.
2. James A. Brussel. *Casebook of a Crime Psychiatrist.* New York: Bernard Geis Publishing Company, 1968, p. 47.
3. Ibid., p. 136–162.
4. Ibid., p. 33.
5. Ibid., p. 101
6. Ibid., p. 117.
7. Vernon J. Geberth. "Mass, Serial and Sensational Homicides: The Investigative Perspective". *Bulletin of the New York Academy of Medicine,* June 1986, Vol. 62. No. 5. p. 495.
8. Robert K. Ressler, Ann W. Burgess, Roger L. Depue, John E. Douglas, Robert R. Hazelwood, Kenneth V. Lanning, et. al.: "Crime Scene and Profile Characteristics of Organized and Disorganized Murderers." *FBI Law Enforcement Bulletin*, August, 1985. (LEB)
9. Lt. Ray Biondi, Commanding Officer Homicide Bureau Sacramento County, California Sheriff's Department. Personal interview with Lt. Ray Biondi, December 19, 1989.
10. R. Biondi and W. Hecox. *The Dracula Killer.* New York: Pocket Books, 1992.
11. Robert K. Ressler, Ann W. Burgess, and John E. Douglas, *Sexual Homicide: Patterns and Motives.* Massachusetts: D.C. Heath & Company, 1988, p. 135.

12. *Webster's New World Dictionary.* Editor in Chief David B. Guralnik. New York: Simon & Schuster, 1982, p. 1147.

13. James C. Coleman, James N. Butcher, and Robert C. Carson. *Abnormal Psychology and Modern Life.* 7th ed. Texas: Scott, Foresman & Co., 1984, pp. 247–50.

14. Dr. Hervey Cleckley, M.D. *The Mask of Sanity.* 5th Edition. Augusta, GA: Emily S. Cleckley, 1988.

15. Ibid., pp. 337–8.

16. Dr. Robert D. Hare, M.D. *Without Conscience: The Disturbing World of the Psychopaths Among Us.* New York: Pocket Books, 1993.

17. Ibid., p. 34.

18. Ibid., p. 25.

19. Webster's, op. cit., p. 1147.

20. Coleman, et.al. op. cit., pp. 237–9.

21. American Psychiatric Association. (1994). *Diagnostic and Statistical Manual of Mental Disorders,* 4th ed., rev. Washington, D.C.: American Psychiatric Association, p. 302.

22. Ibid., p. 530.

23. Ibid., p. 530

24. J. Paul DeRiver. *Crime and the Sexual Psychopath.* Springfield, Illinois: Charles C Thomas & Co., Inc. 1958.

25. Ibid., p. 41.

26. Ibid., p. 276.

27. H. Vetter. Dissociation, Psychopathy and the Serial Murderer. In S. Egger (Ed.), *Serial Murder: An Elusive Phenomenon.* New York: Praeger, 1990.

28. M. Cartel. *Disguise of Sanity — Serial Mass Murderers.* North Hollywood, CA. Pepperbox Publishing Co.,1985.

29. D. T. Lunde. *Murder and Madness.* New York: W.W. Norton & Company, 1976, p. 48.

30. P. E. Dietz. Mass, Serial and Sensational Homicides. *Bulletin of the New York Academy of Medicine,* 62(5), 1986, p. 483.

31. J. R. Meloy. *The Psychopathic Mind: Origins, Dynamics, and Treatment.* Northvale, NJ: Jason Aronson, Inc.,1992.

32. R. K., Ressler. et. al. *FBI (LEB),* 1985, p. 19.

33. Vernon J. Geberth. Profile "A" Prepared for I.P.A.C C.A.P. Program. *Computer Assisted Profiling,* 1989.

34. Vernon J. Geberth. Profile "B" Prepared for I.P.A.C. C.A.P. Program. Computer Assisted Profiling, 1989.

35. John E. Douglas. This case history was described in a personal interview with Douglas, March, 1981.

36. S. Michaud, and H. Aynesworth. The Only Living Witness. New York: Penguin Books, 1989.

37. William Hagmaier. This information was provided in a personal interview with Hagmaier, November 20, 1989 and updated in March, 1995.

38. Robert Kepple. *The Riverman: Ted Bundy and I Hunt or The Green River Killer.* New York: Pocket Books, 1995.
39. Robert Kepple. Personal interview, August, 1995.
40. Vernon J. Geberth. The Signature Aspect In Criminal Investigations. *Law and Order Magazine.*Vol. 43, No. 11, Nov., 1995.
41. John Money, Ph.D. *Lovemaps: Clinical Concepts of Sexual/Erotic Health and Pathology, Paraphilia, and Gender Transposition in Childhood, Adolescense, and Maturity.* New York: Irvington Publishers, Inc., 1986 and 1993, p. 290.
42. Ibid., p. 19.
43. Ibid., p. 68.
44. Ibid., p. 39.
45. Geberth, op. cit., p. (Vol. 43, No. 11, 1995).
46. Marv Skeen. Personal interview and communications with Detective Skeen. May 15, 1991 and April 20, 1993.
47. Dale Foote. Personal interviews and communications with Detective Foote. April 26, 1991 and April 20, 1993.
48. Larry Petersen. Personal interviews and communication with Detective Petersen. November 4, 1991 and April 26, 1994.
49. D. K. Rossmo. Investigative Geographic profiling: Validity, Reliability, and Utility. (Paper) Presented at the meeting of the Academy of Criminal Justice Sciences, Chicago, IL. March (1994a).
50. Gary C. King. *Blood Lust.* New York: Onyx, 1992.
51. D. K. Rossmo, Targeting Victims: Serial Killers and the Urban Environment. In T. O'Reilly-Fleming (Ed.), Serial and Mass Murder: Theory, Research and Policy. Toronto: University of Toronto Press, 1994a.
52. Ibid.
53. Ibid.
54. Ronald Holmes. *Profiling Violent Crime,* Second Edition. California: Sage Press, Inc., 1996.
55. Frank Del Prete. Pesonal interview with Lieutenant Del Prete, Bergen County Prosecutor's Office, January, 1984.
56. Rod Piukkala. Personal interview and communication with Inspector Piukkala, January 17,1991, March 11, 1994, and May 15, 1995.
57. Vernon J. Geberth. Thesis. "Antisocial Personality Disorder, Sexual Sadism, and Serial Murder." California Coast University, December, 1994.
58. Vernon J. Geberth. "A Psychology of Evil." *Law and Order Magazine.* Vol. 40, No. 5, May, 1992.
59. M. Scott Peck, M.D. *People of the Lie: The Hope for Healing Human Evil.* New York: Simon & Schuster, 1983.
60. Ibid., p. 46.
61. Ibid., p. 45.
62. Erich Fromm. *The Heart of Man: Its Genius for Good and Evil.* New York: Harper & Row, 1964.
63. Peck, op. cit., p. 82.
64. Ibid., p. 78.

65. Coleman, et. al. op. cit., p. 63.

66. Ronald Markman, M.D. and Dominick Bosco, D. *Alone with the Devil: Famous Cases of a Courtroom Psychiatrist.* New York: Bantam Books, 1989, p. 91.

67. Ibid., p. 274.

68. American Psychiatric Association, op. cit., p. 530.

69. Geberth, op. cit., 1992.

70. Theodore Reik. The Compulsion to Confess. Toronto, Canada: Papers written by Dr. Theodore Reik 1926–1928. Ambassador Books, Ltd., 1959, pp. 34–35.

Selected Reading

American Psychiatric Association. *Diagnostic and Statistical Manual of Mental Disorders,* (DSM-IV) 4th. ed. Washington, D.C.: American Psychiatric Association, 1994.

Ault, Richard L. and Reese, James T. "A Psychological Assessment of Crime Profiling." *FBI Law Enforcement Bulletin,* March, 1980.

Biondi, R. and Hecox, W. *All His Father's Sins — Inside the Gerald Gallegro Sex-Slave Murders.* California: Prima Publishing, 1988.

Biondi, R. and Hecox, W. *The Dracula Killer.* New York: Pocket Books, 1992.

Brussel, James A. *Casebook of a Crime Psychiatrist.* New York: Bernard Geis Publishing Company, 1968.

Burgess, Ann Wolbert, Ressler, Robert K., and Douglas, John E. "Offender Profiles — A Multidisciplinary Approach." *FBI Law Enforcement Bulletin*, September, 1980.

Cartel, M. *Disguise of Sanity — Serial Mass Murderers.* North Hollywood, CA. Pepperbox Publishing Co.,1985.

Coleman, James C., Butcher, James N., Carson, Robert C. *Abnormal Psychology and Modern Life.* 7th. ed. Texas: Scott, Foresman and Company, 1984.

Cleckley, Hervey, M.D. *The Mask of Sanity.* 5th Edition. Augusta, GA: Emily S. Cleckley, 1988.

DeRiver, J. Paul. *Crime and the Sexual Psychopath.* Springfield, Illinois: Charles C Thomas and Co., Inc., 1958.

Dietz, P.E., "Mass, Serial and Sensational Homicides." *Bulletin of the New York Academy of Medicine,* 62(5), 1986, pp. 477–490.

Fromm, Erich. *The Heart of Man: Its Genius for Good and Evil.* New York: Harper & Row, 1964.

Geberth, Vernon J. "Mass, Serial and Sensational Homicides: The Investigative Perspective." *Bulletin of the New York Academy of Medicine*, 62(5), 1986, pp. 492–496.

Geberth, Vernon J. "The Serial Killer — The Revelations of Ted Bundy." Illinois: *Law and Order Magazine.* Vol. 38, No. 5, May, 1990, pp 72–77.

Geberth, Vernon J. "The Investigation of Sex Related Homicides." Illinois: *Law and Order Magazine*, Vol. 34, No.7., July, 1986, pp. 40–47

Geberth, Vernon J. "A Psychology of Evil." Illinois: *Law and Order Magazine.* Vol. 40, No. 5, May, 1992, pp. 107–110.

Geberth, Vernon J. "Psychopathic Sexual Sadists: The Psychology and Psychodynamics of Serial Killers." Illinois: *Law and Order Magazine*. Vol. 43, No. 4, 1995, pp. 82–86.

Geberth, Vernon J. "The Signature Aspect In Criminal Investigations." Illinois: *Law and Order Magazine* (in press, 1995).

Geberth, Vernon J. "Antisocial Personality Disorder, Sexual Sadism, and Serial Murder." Thesis. California Coast University, December, 1994.

Hare, Robert D., M.D. *Without Conscience: The Disturbing World of the Psychopaths Among Us*. New York: Pocket Books, 1993.

Holmes, Ronald. *Profiling Violent Crime*, Second Edition. California: Sage Press, Inc., 1996.

Kepple, Robert D. *Serial Murder: Future Implications for Police Investigations*. Cincinnati, Ohio: Anderson Publishing Company, 1989.

Kepple, Robert D. *The Riverman: Ted Bundy and I Hunt for the Green River Killer*. New York: Pocket Books, Inc., 1995.

Lunde, D. T. *Murder and Madness*. New York: W.W. Norton and Company, 1976.

Lunde, D. T. and Morgan, J. *The Die Song: A Journey into the Mind of a Mass Murderer*. New York: W.W. Norton & Company, 1976.

Markman, Ronald and Bosco, Dominick. *Alone with the Devil: Famous Cases of a Courtroom Psychiatrist*. New York: Bantam Books, 1989.

Meloy, J. R. *The Psychopathic Mind: Origins, Dynamics, and Treatment*. Northvale, NJ: Jason Aronson, Inc.,1992.

Michaud, Stephen G. and Aynesworth, Hugh. *The Only Living Witness*. New York: Simon & Schuster, 1983 and 1989.

Michaud, Stephen G. and Aynesworth, Hugh. *Ted Bundy: Conversations with a Killer*. New York: Signet Book, 1989.

Money, John, Ph.D. *Lovemaps: Clinical Concepts of Sexual/Erotic Health and Pathology, Paraphilia, and Gender Transposition in Childhood, Adolescense, and Maturity*. New York: Irvington Publishers, Inc., 1986 and 1993.

Peck, M. Scott, M.D. *People of the Lie: The Hope for Healing Human Evil*. New York: Simon & Schuster, 1983.

Reik, Theodore. *The Compulsion to Confess*. Toronto, Canada: Ambassador Books, Ltd., 1959.

Ressler, Robert K., Burgess, Ann W., and Douglas, John E. *Sexual Homicide: Patterns and Motives*. Lexington, Massachusetts: D.C. Heath and Company, 1988.

Ressler, Robert K., Burgess, Ann W., Douglas, John E., Hartman, Carol R., and D'Agostino, Ralph B. "Sexual Killers and Their Victims: Identifying Patterns Through Crime Scene Analysis." *Journal of Interpersonal Violence*, Vol. 1 No. 3, September, 1986, pp. 288–308.

Ressler, Robert K. Burgess, Ann W., Douglas, John E., et. al. "Crime Scene and Profile Characteristics of Organized and Disorganized Murderers." *FBI Law Enforcement Bulletin*, Vol. 54, No. 8, August, 1985.

Rossmo, D. K. "Targeting Victims: Serial Killers and the Urban Environment." In T. O'Reilly-Flemming (Ed.), *Serial and Mass Murder: Theory, Research and Policy*. Toronto: University of Toronto Press, 1994a.

Rossmo, D. K. Investigative Geographic Profiling: Validity, Reliability, and Utility. Paper presented at the meeting of the Academy of Criminal Justice Sciences, Chicago, IL., March 1994a.

Rossmo, D. K. Target Patterns of Serial Murderers: A Methodological Model. *American Journal of Criminal Justice* (in press).

Teten, Howard D. "Offender Profiling." In *The Encyclopedia of Police Science,* edited by William G. Bailey. New York: Garland Publishing, Inc., 1989, pp. 365–367.

Vetter, H. "Dissociation, Psychopathy and the Serial Murderer." In *Serial Murder: An Elusive Phenomenon,* S. Egger (Ed.). New York: Praeger, 1990.

Practical Homicide Investigation: Supervision and Management of the Homicide Investigation

22

The purpose of this chapter is to provide the homicide supervisor with practical and specific considerations for formulating management objectives in the investigation of homicide. Practically speaking, the administrative policies and procedures employed by police agencies are usually determined on a jurisdiction-to-jurisdiction basis. Therefore, the author cannot and will not attempt to present an all-inclusive management technique applicable to all law enforcement agencies. However, it should be noted that certain basic principles of homicide investigation, along with interagency responsibility, can be proceduralized into police department guidelines that contribute to the proper and intelligent handling of murder cases.

Management Policy

Two basic principles of homicide investigation are documentation and preservation. In order to ensure that these principles are accomplished, there must be an established management policy that gives direction to the investigative unit. Management is necessary to assure that the preliminary investigation and initial actions taken at the scene, as well as the total investigative effort, have been properly documented, and that any evidence recovered has been properly handled and preserved.

The effective and professional investigation of homicide is the responsibility of the entire police organization and not just the individual investigator assigned to the case. Hence, there is a need for an efficient coordination of activities and procedures critical to the processing of the case. Some of these activities are the collection of evidence, procedural tactics, duties of patrol officers at the scene, preparation of official forms and required reports, overtime allowance, case-officer responsibility, confidential informant funds, allocation of police department equipment, supervisor's duties, and notifications. These activities must be properly managed in order to bring the entire organization into play to effect the successful conclusion of the case.

> However, the intelligent management of homicide investigations must provide for flexibility and common sense. Therefore, any system that is implemented to direct and manage murder cases should be realistic and allow for policy variations at the point of execution.

All members of the police department can contribute to the process of crime-solving. Whether it be the operator in the communication division who initially takes the call and elicits additional information from the person reporting the crime, or the officer in the patrol car who responds to the scene and detains a key witness or suspect, the fact remains that patrol officers and investigators must be willing to work together toward a common goal — solving the homicide.

> Therefore, the duties of detectives and the activities of patrol officers must be integrated to complement one another, and the management policy should stress the principle of teamwork.

Police Department Policy

Each police department must establish guidelines and procedures that will allow their organization to function efficiently within their jurisdictional purview. Homicide investigations, however, present additional management considerations because two distinctively unique operational divisions are involved. For example, the investigation of homicide is usually initiated by the patrol division, which operates under patrol guidelines. The patrol division, in turn, notifies the investigative division, which operates under investigative guidelines. Investigators, upon their arrival, assume responsibility of the case and take over the investigation from patrol officers, possibly directing uniformed officers and additional police units at the scene as required by the investigation.

> Police department policy must provide for the efficient coordination of these various units by either the investigator assigned to the case or the detective supervisor, if present, in order to maintain control over the homicide investigation.

In addition, any policy established by the police department must meet the legal requirements of, and be compatible with, the responsibilities of other agencies. For example, the offices of the district attorney, state's attorney, or solicitor have a specific responsibility for the ultimate prosecution of the case, and the medical examiner or coroner's office has the legal responsibility for determination of the cause of death. As each of these organizations is required by law to conduct independent investigations into the facts and circumstances of death, police department policy will have to make a provision for mutual cooperation and exchange of information.

Criminal Investigation Management

The structure of the department and how it is organized to perform investigative functions includes selection and training of personnel for investigative assignment, management of investigative personnel, and the designated units which are responsible for conducting criminal investigations.

How are members selected for assignment to investigations?

Is someone within the police department's hierarchy trying to create some sort of "Rainbow Coalition" that fails to recognize the need for qualified personnel without regard to sex, race, creed, or color? This is unacceptable in staffing a professional homicide unit.

What type and quality of training is afforded the members?

Is the training level provided to members sufficient for the assignment or does the department allow the new investigator to "just feel his or her way" around the assignment? Are outside sources utilized for more advanced in-service training? Are members encouraged to attend training sessions both within and without the agency?

Is specialization, generalization, or rotation assignment utilized?

In the opinion of the author, specialization for Homicide assignment is the ideal situation if the agency can justify specialists for the workload. Even in agencies where the workload is not sufficient for full-time homicide specialists, a select few are generally chosen to investigate the homicide cases. Medical professionals specialize due to the enormous amount of knowledge and information required to practice specific medical techniques. Likewise, in homicide investigation where the practitioner is required to be knowledgeable in law enforcement, medicolegal procedures and wound structures, human behavior, evidence collection and preservation, interview and interrogation techniques, crime scene processing, management of resources, photography, court testimony, inter-agency cooperation, and a number of other more subtle considerations, one can readily understand the need for specialization and continuing education in this type assignment. Generalization is certainly acceptable for smaller departments that do not have a substantial case load. However, specialized training in homicide investigation should be implemented within the investigative division to assure that members are provided with the necessary skills to perform their inquiries.

Rotation, however, has proven to be "asinine." It was designed and created by officials with absolutely no understanding, nor appreciation, of the investigative mission. It is demoralizing for officers who are transferred out of a preferred assignment; it does not allow for career growth; and actually frustrates professional ambition. Practically speaking, it takes at least 1 year for an officer to become somewhat familiar with investigations work and 2 years before the officer begins to make a contribution to the assignment. Needless to say, periodically transferring experienced detectives back to patrol is not only demoralizing to the members of the agency but is counterproductive to the professional investigative process. Not only are investigations disrupted but oftentimes these cases remain unresolved.

How are supervisors selected for investigative assignment?

Are qualified members from within the department's investigative units selected for assignment as supervisors or commanding officers within detective commands? Or, does the policy of your department erroneously dictate that when an investigator is promoted he or she must first go back to a uniform assignment for some sort of "cleaning." This policy has also proven to be a failure that has adversely effected the overall success of the investigations sections.

The inexperienced supervisor fails to properly delegate routine matters and involves him or herself in operations rather than the supervision of operations. Time and time again, I have observed the transfers of Internal Affairs or Office of Professional Standard types being assigned to command investigative units. Obviously, such assignments have been designed to enhance their respective careers and usually prove to be disastrous. In reality, these types of personalities are anally retentive and ill-equipped to deal with the unpredictable nature of investigations work and cannot properly supervise detectives. They have difficulty making critical decisions and a tendency to micromanage operations. They do not have an understanding of the mission of the homicide investigator and are oftentimes too arrogant to ask anyone for advice.

Their usual response as to whether they are capable to run a homicide squad is, "Our department provides training to allow us to go into any assignment just as in Corporate America." Ironically, they wouldn't last "5" minutes in Corporate America because they would be judged by the "bottom line" or the ultimate results of their supervision.

Case management relates directly to the processes involved in monitoring the progress of an investigation. This begins with the initial report or officer-initiated police action, and continues through all phases of the investigation until the case is closed.

> **What administrative procedures have been implemented to provide for the proper documentation of the case and preservation of evidence?**

The official police report as well as the major case folder are extremely important instruments. The documentation of events as well as the official police response to the investigation form the basis for the prosecution. The path from arrest to conviction is fraught with technical and legal "booby traps." Hence, there is a need for intelligent case management, which takes into account the reality of discovery vs. documentation.

Investigatively speaking, proper case management should require pertinent official documentation of the facts of the case and not police administrative matters, i.e., supervisory reviews, case recommendations, meal times, travel to and from, roll call assignments, and DARs (daily activity reports). This type of information does not belong in the major case folder. However, rest assured, some individual who has never been involved in a major case criminal trial or investigation will attempt to "enhance" the operation with some administrative obstacle.

My personal advice is to assure him that he will be receiving a subpoena later on requiring him to testify in court if his procedure is implemented. That should be sufficient to correct the situation.

Major Pitfalls to Practical Homicide Case Management

1. *Inappropriate departmental policy and/or procedures regarding investigative strategies.* Usually based upon bureaucratic, political, and/or personal considerations not related to the primary objective which should be solving the case.

2. *Inappropriate interference by high-ranking officials.* Police commissioners, chiefs of police, sheriffs, majors, and/or colonels are supposed to be police administrators, not detectives or squad commanders. The immediate mission of the detective supervisor is to provide coordination to investigative personnel. High ranking officials are supposed to communicate their orders and directions through the squad commander. This is referred to as the "chain of command." The chain of command is necessary to maintain order and responsibility. Therefore, high-ranking officials should not be communicating orders directly to officers, and definitely should not be involved in operational processes such as interrogating suspects and other tactical procedures best left to the detectives. Too many times, I have seen chiefs of police and others in command positions interfere in an investigation by interjecting themselves or their personal opinions into an investigation.

3. *Interagency rivalry.* Practically speaking, a working relationship must be established among police, prosecutors, and medical examiner/coroners based upon cooperation, trust, and respect. The police and the prosecution should complement one another, and both should feel at ease in giving and receiving advice from each other during the investigation.

There is no room for interagency rivalry in professional homicide investigation. Law enforcement agencies with dual responsibility for the investigation of sudden and unexplained deaths must reach an accord as to ultimate case *responsibility* among the state, county, and local jurisdictions involved.

The best way to accomplish this cooperative venture is through continued personal contact and understanding of each other's roles and duties. Each of these three official agencies of inquiry has specific responsibilities and duties that may at times overlap. This overlap is where a misunderstanding can sometimes take place, especially in the more sensational murder cases where there is an inordinate amount of pressure, with requests for day-to-day progress reports, coupled with requests by the news media for a story.

Professionally speaking, the duties of each agency involved in the investigation of homicide will be determined by both tradition and law. However, policies should be instituted within each organization that transcend individual positions and address the common goal or objective. Courtesy and tact are always helpful in inter-agency dealings. Basically, the duties of each agency are as follows:

1. The ultimate responsibility for the investigation of crime rests with the law enforcement agency. The chief law enforcement official within any community is the chief of police, the sheriff, or the police commissioner and his or her designated representatives.
2. The district attorney, state's attorney, or solicitor, in turn, is responsible for the ultimate prosecution of the crime, and as such should be kept aware of all developments of the police investigations. He is responsible for all legal investigative operations such as search warrants, arrest warrants, and grand jury presentations.
3. The medical examiner/coroner is responsible for the determination of cause, manner, and mode of death, and as such should be apprised of all developments of the police investigation.

Practically speaking, a little flexibility and common sense by the representatives of each of these agencies will ultimately benefit all concerned and eliminate any misunderstanding.

Procedures for Effective Management and Supervision of Homicide Investigation

Practically speaking, the management and supervision of the homicide investigation can be separated into five specific segments listed below. The case preparation for court and prosecution as well as any subsequent case analysis are separate prosecutorial and administrative functions which do not apply to the following practical homicide investigation supervision techniques. The first three segments are presented as a checklist, whereas the remaining segment follows the list in an expanded form.

1. Supervising the preliminary investigation at the scene
2. Directing specific investigative duties
3. Supervising the homicide crime scene search
4. Providing for the effective documentation of events
5. Conducting the investigative critique

Supervisor's Homicide Checklist

Supervising the Preliminary Investigation at the Scene

☐ Initial receipt of information. It is imperative that the Supervisor, upon being notified that detectives are requested to respond to a possible homicide, record the following information:

☐ Date and time received.
☐ How initial report was received.
☐ Name of person making report (this includes police officers).
☐ Complete details.

At this point the homicide supervisor either responds directly with investigators in their unit, or responds in his or her own unit. I recommend that the supervisor take his or her own unit to the scene.

☐ Assign a member to maintain communications within the command. This member's responsibility will be to make follow-up notifications, record checks, requests for special services, as well as take requests from the command post at the crime scene. This assignment becomes critical in major case investigations when overhead commands attempt to assess the investigation.
☐ Duties upon arrival at the scene.
  ☐ Record the exact time of arrival.
  ☐ Record the exact address.
  ☐ Record police units present.
  ☐ Confer with detectives at the scene. Ascertain that there is an investigator assigned to the case. If an investigator has not been officially assigned as *case officer,* do so immediately.
  ☐ Confer with uniform supervisor and establish cooperation.
  ☐ Confer with first officer — obtain a quick briefing.
  ☐ Make a visual inspection of the crime scene and victim. Have the first officer or detective escort you in order to get a feel for the case and establish perimeters.
  ☐ Solicit any opinions and/or theories from police personnel at the scene. Evaluate these with your own observations.
  ☐ Determine any investigative needs — make assignments as necessary. Establish your authority by providing any manpower and equipment.
  ☐ Implement an assignment sheet. Record assignments, know who is performing what assignment to assist in the coordination effort.

The supervisor's notebook becomes a log detailing exactly who has what assignment. This enables the supervisor to properly assign members and record exactly what has transpired at the crime scene. As members report back, the supervisor jots down a brief paragraph detailing their activities. Later, this notebook can be utilized to conduct the investigative critique and designate responsibility for the subsequent written reports.

☐ Initiate an investigative canvass. The investigative canvass is simply a door-to-door inquiry or road-block operation in order to obtain information and/or locate witnesses.

The supervisor should assign a sufficient number of officers to effectively cover the area to be canvassed. I recommend assigning a supervisor to coordinate the canvass and instruct members to use canvass questionnaires and canvass control sheets for effective follow-up surveys.

☐ Victim removed to hospital. If the victim has been removed to a hospital, assign either a patrol unit or detective to respond to the hospital to assure proper evidence-collection procedures (re: clothing, ID papers, etc.) are undertaken. In addition, there may be an opportunity to obtain a dying declaration.

☐ Transmittal of alarms. Ascertain what alarms have been transmitted. Review alarms for appropriate information and consider updating them based upon information developed at the scene.

☐ Dissemination of information. Provide for the dissemination of information to all units and personnel involved in the investigation. Keep the command post and investigators informed of all relative and current information as it becomes available.

☐ Handling curious onlookers. Utilize patrol officers to maintain lines and instruct detectives to use courtesy and tact in dealing with people at the scene.

   ☐ Assign members in street clothes to "work-the-crowd" to obtain any overhears and direct bilingual officers to mingle with bystanders, etc. (depending upon circumstances).

   ☐ Direct that photos be taken of crowd.

☐ Interview of ambulance personnel. Direct that ambulance or EMS personnel be interviewed if they arrived before police relative to their activities at the scene as well as any persons they may have seen or things they may have overheard.

Directing Specific Investigative Duties

- [ ] The suspect in custody.
  - [ ] Establish the probable cause for arrest.
  - [ ] Determine the scope of the preliminary investigation.
  - [ ] Ascertain the location of any evidence.
  - [ ] Advise detectives to instruct patrol officers to document their observations (re: any overhears, statements, and any information provided by informants and/or witnesses).
- [ ] Interview and interrogation of suspect in custody.
  - [ ] Direct investigators to document their Miranda warnings.
  - [ ] If the suspect is cooperative, have detectives take a preliminary statement at the scene, which can be used to assist in the recovery of any evidence, etc.
- [ ] Formal interrogation. This is best undertaken at the station house.
  - [ ] Direct that no one interfere with an investigator who is in the process of taking a statement from a suspect.

The cardinal rule of interrogation — Never intrude on an interview of a suspect. This includes supervisors as well.

- [ ] Examination of a suspect for evidence.
  - [ ] Advise investigators to document by both photography and sketch any scratches, bruises, injuries, etc., observed on suspect.
  - [ ] Advise transporting officers to be aware of evidential considerations. (Do *not* allow suspect to wash.)
- [ ] Dying declarations. Anytime you have a seriously injured victim, a consideration should be made to obtain a dying declaration.
  - [ ] Direct investigators to respond to the hospital, obtain a witness if possible, and attempt to obtain a statement from the injured victim.

Actually, there are no set guidelines for the exact sequence of questions. Basically, you want to establish that the victim is competent, lucid, and does believe that he or she is about to die.

- [ ] Evaluation of a suspect's demeanor and/or mental capacity.

☐ Direct detectives to document the suspect's demeanor and/or mental capacity from the time of arrest to arraignment. This procedure is necessary to prepare against a possible *diminished capacity defense.*

Supervising Homicide Crime Scene Search

Supervision of the investigation conducted at the scene is a *separate* and *distinct* function. Ideally, there should be a Crime Scene Investigator or Evidence Technician assigned to conduct the search. I recommend that departments select and train a sufficient number of investigators for this extremely important function.

> People have come to expect that evidence of a crime will be found and retrieved by police investigators at the scenes of crimes. *This may not be true in all instances.* Often agencies do not put enough emphasis on this phase of the investigation, opting, instead, for something less time-consuming, e.g., a confession. Make sure you do a proper search.

The purpose of the crime scene search is to obtain evidence. The function of the supervisor is to document and preserve the event. Practically speaking, if there is any possibility that any evidence you are about to seize for use in a homicide prosecution requires a search warrant, it's your job as the *supervisor* to assure that this warrant is obtained. Supervisors should also be aware of the warrant exceptions: emergency, plain view, consent, and search of persons after arrest.

Practically any method of search can be used, depending on the size, location, and complexity of the scene, as long as the search is *systematic* and *complete.*

The scope of the search is usually determined by a theory or hypothesis arrived at by the detective supervisor and investigators based upon their initial observations of the scene. This *theory,* which is provisional, is based upon simple assumptions of how and why the homicide occurred.

> Remember, anything and everything can be evidence.

The primary responsibility is the isolation and protection of the crime scene. The objective is to establish the *corpus deliciti* and the identity of the criminal.

☐ Preliminary steps.
  ☐ Upon arrival, ascertain boundaries. Do not move blindly into an area (confer before moving).
  ☐ Decide how to approach the crime scene. Paths of entry and exit (confer with first officer, etc.).
  ☐ The initial survey (escort by first officer). Use this opportunity to develop a mental image.
  ☐ Ascertain whether or not any fragile evidence is present (assure collection).
  ☐ Prior to any crime scene search, direct the photographs and crime scene sketches be made.
☐ The supervisory hypothesis. The supervisory hypothesis is as follows. You ask yourself what happened. You keep an open mind; don't be influenced by the original report, the police call, or initial statements. Note all the information. Make your own determination based upon the total information available. Was the death caused by homicide, suicide, accident, or natural causes? The answer to this question is based upon the facts, crime scene, statements, and physical evidence supporting this explanation.

Remember, things are not always as they appear to be. Don't be afraid to change your mind. Any hypothesis is only provisional at best.

☐ Examination of the body at the scene.
  ☐ Direct that all photographs and sketches be completed before examining the body.
  ☐ Direct that a complete description of the body as well as clothing be obtained.
  ☐ Portions of the body which were not accessible prior to the photos can now be examined and photographed.
  ☐ Direct a complete examination of the body, note wounds, and direct that this information be recorded.
☐ Release of the body. This decision is critical. Once the body is released from the scene *no additional* procedures can be undertaken, i.e., photos, etc.
  ☐ Direct that the body be wrapped in a clean white sheet before being placed in a body bag.
☐ Examining an outdoor crime scene.

☐ Direct the following:
  ☐ Rope off the largest area.
  ☐ Establish a path of entry and exit.
  ☐ Conduct examination as soon as possible (before losing daylight or experiencing weather changes).
  ☐ Direct that surrounding area be searched.
  ☐ If weather changes suddenly — order that evidence be collected immediately.
☐ Examining an outdoor scene at night. Under ordinary circumstances, an outdoor scene should not be searched during nighttime hours — this is common sense.
  ☐ Direct the following:
    ☐ Safeguard and secure the area.
    ☐ Direct that photographs be taken before body is moved.
    ☐ Safeguard body against additional damage in transport.

The search should be postponed until daylight because it is utterly impossible to discover or detect minute traces of evidence under nighttime conditions. Weather changes the rule. *Under no circumstances should the crime scene and/or body be left unguarded and unprotected until daylight hours.* Assign sufficient coverage for the purposes of "chain of custody."

☐ Release of the crime scene. This decision is also critical. Practically speaking, the authorities should hold onto the scene as long as possible. There may be a need for additional photos, or information may reveal the need to collect additional materials, an additional search may be necessary, etc.

Before releasing the crime scene, consider: A good defense attorney will visit the crime scene to judge the extent of the police investigation. He or she will be alert to areas that were or were not processed.

☐ Recommended procedure.
  ☐ Direct that all materials used to process scene be placed in a receptacle that can be taken from the scene when the police leave.
  ☐ Direct members to make sure that all police equipment has been secured and removed from premises before release.

Providing for the Effective Documentation of Events

Case Management

Practically speaking, case management is the official documentation of events and should be an extension of good investigative techniques. Investigatively speaking, the most perturbing problem in relation to management is that all too often the "designers" of case management have no conception of what constitutes the proper and intelligent documentation of a criminal investigation. It is quite apparent to the experienced detective and supervisor that these "designers" have never investigated a case in their careers and/or certainly never had to testify in court. Otherwise, they wouldn't perpetrate some of the nonsense I have seen mandated in various investigative units. Some tips on the intelligent documentation process in a criminal investigation follows.

Documentation

Notekeeping

Practically speaking, no one, no matter how many homicides he or she has investigated, can know for sure at the beginning just what witness, suspect, feature, or piece of physical or trace evidence will be important. Therefore, notetaking is of the utmost importance in homicide investigations. The investigator's notebook will eventually accumulate vast amounts of information, which may later be instrumental in proving or disproving a specific point or fact in question.

Because notekeeping is essential to any good homicide investigation, it is imperative that investigative notes be comprehensive, accurate, and reflective of a proper chronological time frame. In fact, on each separate notation, the investigator should record the time and date of the event. These notes must be preserved for later review and/or admission into evidence.

Official Reports

The official police report is the tool used by the criminal investigator to document the findings of his investigative actions. It is the principal source used by the courts, the defense, the district attorney's office, and the police department to evaluate the thoroughness of an investigation and the ability of the reporting detective. A thorough field investigation, accompanied by an accurate and readable report, reflects profes-

Figure 22.1. **THE AUTHOR TAKES NOTES WHILE HE IS BRIEFED BY ONE OF HIS DETECTIVES AT THE SCENE OF A MULTIPLE DRUG-RELATED HOMICIDE IN THE SOUTH BRONX.** Detective First Grade Andrew Lugo from Bronx Homicide is pointing out the rear of the location from which shots were heard by a possible witness. This briefing will determine the focus of the subsequent neighborhood canvass. Throughout the early stages of a homicide investigation the supervisor engages in a number of these on-scene briefings from the detectives "working" the case in order to properly assess and manage the investigation.

sionalism and underlies success. A good report starts with an organized approach to the investigation. A new steno pad should be used for each homicide case, and the information available at the start of the homicide investigation should be immediately recorded. There are three basic steps involved: (1) collecting the information; (2) collating the information and organizing the notes; and (3) writing the report.

1. *Collecting the information.* A good report requires a good field investigation. No amount of rhetoric or literary expertise can disguise the fact that an investigator has failed to conduct a thorough investigation. In fact, even a good investigation may look haphazard if the report is not properly prepared or written. The investigator should:

   a. Gather and record as much information as possible while conducting the investigation, e.g., time of initial report, who notified you, condition of the body when you arrived, who was present, etc.

b. Record the facts in a clear and logical order. Remember that your notes are subject to subpoena during trial, therefore you should be able to read and interpret them at a later date.

c. When collecting the information, make a clear distinction between hearsay, opinions, and facts.

d. Keep your notes on file with the case folder. If you are transferred or otherwise unavailable, the detective who is assigned to your case will be aware of your investigative efforts.

2. *Collating the information and organizing the notes:*

a. Review completely the information obtained during the investigation, including any information that was obtained by other investigators at the scene, such as interviews, names, and canvass results. The value of this procedure is twofold:

1. It enables the investigator to prepare a better report.
2. It highlights what future steps may be required in the investigation.

b. As all the information gathered during the investigation cannot possibly be put in the report, the detective must decide what is appropriate and needs to be included. The official report must be a complete and true account of what has transpired, whether favorable or not to the suspect, victim, or witness. Hence, the investigator should attempt to include all the facts necessary to present a candid account to the reader.

c. Organize the material in a logical order so that it can be understood by anyone who reads it.

d. Include all the investigative steps that were taken, with their results, both positive and negative.

e. Occasionally, it helps to compose a rough draft on scrap paper first, in order to get an idea how the finished report will look and read.

3. *Writing the report.* If you have collected and organized your material as discussed, the actual writing of the report is relatively simple.

COMPLAINT: Homicide   METHOD: Shotgun   DATE: 5/4/90

VICTIM: Mary Smith F/B 18   HOMICIDE: 1/22/90

SUBJECT: Response to the scene

1. On the above date at 2205 hours, the undersigned officer was informed by Police Officer Moffett 48th Pct. that there was a homicide at 637 Jefferson Place, 4th Fl. landing.

2. Lt. Commander Geberth and Detective Lugo 7th Homicide Zone responded and arrived at 2215 hours.

3. The deceased identified as MARY SMITH F/B 18 yrs. address 1392 Crotona Park No. apt. 6D Tele. # 998-   was lying face-up on the 4th. floor landing, dressed in a brown coat, blue sweater, blue shirt, gray pants, rust colored boots, and a type of blue kerchief on her head. It appeared that she was shot in the right chest area.

4. Attendant O'Grady #1721 Jacobi Hospital Ambulance #237 pronounced the victim DOA at 2230 hours.

5. The deceased's cousin Sarah Brown 1679 Franklin Avenue apt. 3B Tele. # 783- present and identified the body.

Figure 22.2. **THE RESPONSE REPORT.**

a. The information must be accurate and complete.
b. The language should be clear and concise.
c. The entire report should be as brief as possible, yet still contain the necessary information.

Below is an example of an official report referred to as a "response report." This report is required by the New York City Police Department's Detective Bureau to show receipt of the homicide investigation:

COMPLAINT: Homicide   METHOD: gun   DATE: 5/4/90
VICTIM: Mary Smith F/B/18   HOMICIDE: 1/22/90
SUBJECT: Response to the scene

1. On the above date at 2205 hours, the undersigned Officer was informed by Police Officer Moffett 48th Pct. that there was a homicide at 637 Jefferson Place. 4th floor landing.

2. Lieutenant Commander Geberth and Detective Lugo 7th Homicide Zone responded and arrived at 2215 hours.
3. The deceased identified as Mary Smith F/B/18 yrs. old, address 1392 Crotona Park No. Apt. 6D Tel#998-0000 was lying face up on the 4th floor landing, dressed in brown coat, blue sweater, blue shirt, gray pants, rust-colored boots, and a type of blue kerchief on her head. It appeared that she was shot in the right chest area.
4. Attendant O'Grady #1721 Jacobi Hospital Ambulance #237 pronounced the victim DOA at 2230 hours.
5. The deceased's cousin Sarah Brown 1679 Franklin Avenue Apt. 3B Tel#783-000 was present and identified the body.

The structure and process of homicide report writing is flexible and usually varies with the length of the investigation and the number of investigators who are involved. If, for example, the perpetrator has been arrested on the scene, or shortly after the commission of the crime or discovery of the body, the assigned detective will be able to assemble all the facts from his notes and type them into a unified, complete, and well-structured report. Usually this can be accomplished shortly after the initial chaos that is characteristic at homicide crime scenes. In these cases, the report itself serves primarily as a record of details of the crime, the subsequent investigation, and the apprehension. Normally, such rapidly cleared cases present no major problems; however, the investigator must be careful that he does not leave out any significant facts, or treat the report too lightly.

On the other hand, in a large-scale continuing investigation, involving a relatively large number of investigators, reports must be filed on a daily basis to expedite the indexing of the vast amount of information being gathered, thereby making the information available to the various investigators when needed. Some of the investigators may be from different units. This varied mass of reports can create a problem in terms of format, structure, and readability of the whole report when finally collated. The prosecutor, and possibly some other investigator who may be assigned to the investigation at some future time, will have to decipher these reports (which are, in effect, reports of numerous separate investigations into distinct phases of the case) and be able to relate them to the entire case.

In order to clarify these voluminous reports and provide for uniformity, the report filed for each new facet of an investigation should begin with an assignment paragraph which sets forth:

1. The date and time of the assignment.
2. The rank, name, shield number, if any, and the command of the person who made the assignment.
3. Full details as to the source and nature of the lead, if there is such.
4. The objective of the investigation, if it arises in the normal course of investigative routine, or because of the particular needs of the investigation.

Without these explanatory "pegs," a long report can possibly degenerate into a meaningless mass of disjointed interviews. An example of a proper format would be as follows:

ASSIGNMENT: At 2115 hours, Thursday, August 18, 1995, the undersigned and Detective Andrew Lugo were assigned by Lieutenant Commander Geberth Bronx Homicide Squad, to investigate a lead that was received by P. O. Henion, shield #2107 Communications Division. Henion, on duty at Communications Division on Thursday, August 18, 1995, at 2040 hours received a call as follows: "The man you are looking for in the cop killing works as a bag packer at the Triple A Supermarket on Jerome Avenue." The voice appeared to be that of a male, Hispanic. There was no further conversation and no other identifying information. Triple A Supermarket: The undersigned and Det. Lugo present at...

The report will now continue with the results of the investigation in chronological order, until that particular avenue of inquiry is exhausted or abandoned due to more pressing priorities. Where the investigation of one lead produces another, the report of the investigation should continue in a chronological fashion. If for some reason in the future abandoned lines of inquiry are resumed, the assignment paragraph should clearly reflect that fact and refer to the earlier reports. Each new line of inquiry or new phase of an investigation should begin on a new page. This will ease the grouping of similar leads and investigative processes so that the final report will have a logical arrangement.

When the final report is correlated, it should be arranged with the main portion of the investigation appearing first, followed by a grouping of reports on the results of neighborhood canvassing, grouping of leads checked under appropriate subtitles, and so on. The final report, whether short or long, should begin with a resume or summary of the case. This summary will enable the reader to relate to the overall picture as he or she goes through the case.

ASSIGNMENT: At 1815 hours, Thursday, August 18, 1995 the undersigned and Detective

Lugo were assigned by Lt.Cmdr. Geberth, Bronx Homicide Squad, to investigate a

lead that was received by Police Officer Henion, shield #2801 Communications Division. P. O.

Henion, on duty at Communications Division on Thursday August 18, 1995, at 1740 hours

received a call as follows: "The man you are looking for in the Mendex homicide case worked at

the E/Z Car Wash on Washington Avenue." The voice appeared to be that of a male, Hispanic.

There was no further conversation and no other identifying information. E/Z CAR WASH: The

undersigned and Det. Scroope present at etc.

Figure 22.3. AN EXAMPLE OF REPORT WRITING WHICH INVOLVES EXPLANATORY "PEGS."

In a large-scale investigation, investigators are generally too busy the first day to type any formal reports, with the exception of brief official reports, such as "the response report." At this stage, investigators should take copious notes, while orally keeping the chief investigator informed of developments. This should be a two-way communications, so the investigators can better evaluate any information they receive. The chief investigator at this phase of the investigation should appoint someone to act as recorder, who will list any assignments that are given out with the names and commands of the investigators assigned, to fix responsibility for each report and prevent duplication of effort. I recommend a logbook as a running chronological record. The first entries in this log can be taken from the assignment sheets used at the scene of the crime. At this stage of the investigation, the command post should be moved to the station house and all activities in connection with the case should originate and be directed from this central location. The command post at the crime scene or place of occurrence is temporary and used only initially during emergency operations. Once the emergency or crime scene work is complete, the operations center should be at a police facility where the necessary equipment and resources are available within a secure building. If by the second day an arrest has not been made or perpetrators identified, and the department has involved numerous investigators, formal typed records should be filed at the conclusion of each investigator's tour. Needless to say, this will require typewriters, supplies, and space to accommodate the number of personnel involved. It helps to avoid confusion if the newly assigned and regular investigators are thoroughly briefed on what is required from them.

First Day of Investigation

Supervisor checklist

- ☐ Implement assignment sheet and assign a recorder to the command post.
  - ☐ List all assignments of personnel at the scene.
  - ☐ Indicate individual assignments by name, rank, and command.
- ☐ Chief investigator keeps track of various assignments in his notebook. Usually a brief paragraph relating to results obtained, facts of interviews, results of canvass, evidence recovered, etc.
- ☐ Implement major case forms (delegate recorder to issue as members arrive at crime scene): checklists, assignment sheets, canvass questionnaires, interview reports, investigative plans, witness forms, canvass control sheets, and lead sheets.

Indexing the Homicide Investigation

As the volume of daily reports grows, the amount of information becomes unmanageable without an effective indexing procedure.

Index cards should be prepared for names of all persons that arise in an investigation, locations or premises mentioned, vehicles, license plate numbers, or other such categories as may be required in a particular investigation. An investigator should be assigned to type and file the index cards that will be required, according to the following procedure.

Daily reports should be reviewed and signed by the supervising officer or chief investigator. They should be prepared in duplicate. The original is handled per department requirements; the duplicate is given to the index officer for processing. The officer who prepares the report will underline in red, on the case folder copies of the report, all names, addresses, vehicles, plate numbers, phone numbers, and any other information that the chief investigator decides is necessary. The case folder copies of the reports are filed chronologically and numbered consecutively with the response report as number 1.

The index officer then prepares an index card for each name, address, etc. The name cards will be filed alphabetically by last name. If only a first name or nickname appears, it will be filed according to the single name. Name cards will be cross-referenced with location cards, vehicle cards, etc., when applicable.

Each card will list the case number, a brief summary of the information, and a reference to the original report by listing the consecutive

Homicide #192

VICTIM _John W. Doe   M/W/38Yrs. old_

TIME _2230 Hrs._ DATE _December 14, 19_

PLACE OF OCCURRENCE _3335 Webster Avenue_

METHOD _Gunshot_

COMPLAINT NO. _7881_ PCT. _52_

DET. ASSIGNED _Det_

DET. ASSISTING _Det. Andrew Lugo_

FIRST OFFICER _Police Officer_

PHOTO _Det. Charles Carway_

FORENSIC _Det. Arne Roussine_

LAB. _Dr. Shaler_

BALLISTICS _Det. Sgt. Scaringe_

M.E. _Di Maio_

A.D.A. _Kelly_

CASE NO. _192_ COMPLAINT NO. _7881_ PCT. _52_ DATE OF OCC. _12/14/_ DATE OPENED _Same_

Figure 22.4.   **THE CASE FOLDER.**

number from the case folder copy. Below is an example of such an index card:

JONES, HOWARD A.   HOMICIDE #78/89
1368 Bathgate Avenue
Apt. 3D Bronx   Report #37
Name found in wallet of deceased

A quick glance at the index card indicates that the name Howard Jones was in the deceased's wallet. As other information relative to Jones surfaces, it can be added to the card with a reference to the original report. If further information is required, the investigator can refer back to the report by number.

The location cards can be filed according to any plan, i.e., alphabetically by name of the street, then in numerical house number order. When necessary, a category can be prepared for different towns or communities, or by borough or county.

The vehicle cards can be filed alphabetically by make, year, etc., and license plates can be filed alphabetically or numerically.

Before the index officer prepares an index card for any red-lined name, location, etc., he will first consult the existing file to determine if any such information has previously appeared. Where a card already exists, that information should be brought to the attention of the chief investigator and other investigators concerned. The index officer then adds the new information to the existing card, with the number of the corresponding report from the case folder. This system of calling "hits" to the attention of the investigators minimizes the possibility of important information being lost or delayed in a mass of uncatalogued information. Although a computerized system is much more effective, this system is still recommended as a back-up.

The index officer becomes a valuable aid in the investigation, especially when he becomes meticulously aware of each phase of the case. He or she should attend all conferences and freely contribute to all discussions of the case. Even when there is insufficient typing and filing to keep the index officer busy, he or she should remain with the investigation until it is cleared, if possible. The index officer can be used to fill in on teams where a partner may be sick or in court, can be assigned to investigations that can be handled by one man on a part-time basis, and can use his remaining time to attend to typing and filing.

News Clipping File

Investigators should maintain a file of news clippings relating to the crime. These clippings may prove important later if a suspect admits to an intimate knowledge of the crime which he or she claims to have perpetrated. A news file on the case will assist the police in determining the veracity of any statements. In addition, investigators should be aware of what information has been released by the press so that they can make proper investigative decisions. The index officer can also be

INVESTIGATIVE PLAN   PART 1

Assigned Supervisor _____   Date Received _____

Supervisor _____   Complaint # _____ Precinct _____

                                        Case # _____ Command _____

ACTIVITY CHECKLIST   REMARKS

Weapon Used   ☐   _____

Vehicle Used   ☐   _____

Injury Involved   ☐   _____

Canvass Conducted   ☐   _____

Crime Scene Searched   ☐   _____

Evidence Obtained   ☐   _____

Print Kit Used   ☐   _____

Polaroid Camera Used   ☐   _____

Forensic Notified   ☐   _____

Reporting P. O. Interviewed ☐   _____

Alarm Transmitted   ☐   Date _____

Wanted Card Forwarded   ☐   Date _____

Visit to B.C.I.   ☐   Date _____

View Photos at Command   ☐   Date _____

Additional Activity and/or comments:

Figure 22.5.   **THE INVESTIGATIVE PLAN.**

INDEX SHEET

ITEM NO.	DATE	ITEM

ALL COMPLAINT FOLLOW–UPS will be consecutively numbered on this sheet. All other items submitted (Photographs, Laboratory Reports, Property Vouchers, etc.) will also be included on the sheet, but will not be numbered.

FIGURE 22.6. **THE INDEX SHEET.** All reports are chronologically numbered on this sheet and placed into the case folder.

7th HOMICIDE ZONE

COMPLAINT # _____

CASE # _____

NAME OF DECEASED   DATE & TIME OF OCCURRENCE   PLACE OF OCCURRENCE

DATE	DET. ASSIGNED	ASSIGNMENT	REPORTS	FOLLOW UP

FIGURE 22.7. **ASSIGNMENT SHEET.** All assignments are recorded on this running sheet in order to "fix" responsibility for certain "jobs."

INTERVIEW REPORT

Case # _____

Date: _____ Day: _____ Time Start: _____ Time Finished _____

Location and Room # of Interview: _____

Name of Person Interviewed: _____

Address: _____ Date of Birth: _____

B # _____ Marital Status: _____ Wife/Husband Name: _____

Address of Wife/Husband: _____

Where Employed: _____ Employer: _____ Position: _____

Telephone: _____ Ext.: _____

Children's Names _____ Age _____ School _____

Previous Arrests: Date   Jurisdiction   Charge   Disposition

Present at Interview: _____

A.D.A.: _____ Bureau: _____

Investigator: _____ Command: _____ Shield # _____

Name of Attorney: _____ Address: _____

Others Present at Interview: _____

_____

Advised of Rights: Yes/No   N/A   By: _____

Interview:

FIGURE 22.8. **INTERVIEW REPORT.** This form is used as a preliminary interview form at the scene. A more extensive report appears in Chapter 4.

assigned to clip and file all newspaper clippings about the case. This file can also be expanded to include recordings of any television newscasts on videotape using a VCR. In larger departments, with a more sophisticated taping system, a number of news stations can be monitored at the same time and the newscasts videotaped for the investigative unit's library. I have been involved in a number of major cases during the past few years that received an inordinate amount of news coverage. It was to our advantage to have copies of the TV coverage, both during the investigation as well as later for court purposes.

Good press-relations policy can come in handy. If the agency and the news media are cooperating, the news media people will make available to the law enforcement agency any publications relating to the case. This will eliminate the possibility of missing any printed item in the local papers. (See Chapter 19 "The News Media in Homicide Investigations.")

I remember one case in which we had requested the local newspapers to print a story on a gang-style execution in an attempt to identify the deceased. As the story was carried in a number of different newspapers, we had missed one of the articles for the file. Later, we developed two suspects who had claimed to have read of the death in a certain paper. This was approximately 3 weeks after the original story. Because the paper involved and the news person were generally cooperative with the police, and the police cooperative with them, the reporter had someone research the files and find the particular article involved. We were then able to properly evaluate the alibi.

Conducting the Investigative Conference

The investigative conference is one of the most important phases of any well-run homicide investigation. The conference need not be a formal gathering back at the station house. In fact, the investigative conference takes place during and after each of the other four phases. The conference is directed by the chief investigator at each critical point of the investigation. The object is to assess the investigation by gaining an overall synopsis. Each member and/or team relate their progress and ideas; everyone is kept abreast of all developments, and there is a general discussion. The daily investigative conference, which is somewhat different and usually takes place at the station house, attempts to assess the entire investigation on a daily basis.

In my professional opinion, the investigative critique should be used as a guide by the experienced members to conduct the homicide investigation.

The Investigation of Police-Related Shootings

Law enforcement officers, in their capacity as the guardians of law, are authorized to be armed with a firearm to protect themselves and others against the immediate threat of death or serious bodily injury. This authority is also extended to apprehend a fleeing felon who has committed a violent crime, i.e., an armed robbery, murder, or serious felonious assault, and whose escape presents a substantial risk of death or serious bodily injury to others.

The necessary and appropriate use of this authority is an awesome responsibility. The decision to use deadly force is based on the circumstances as presented at the time of incident. The final determination of justification, however, is based on law.

Police administrators must establish fair and appropriate guidelines within their respective departments for the use of deadly physical force, which instill public confidence by assuring official accountability. Commensurate with this formulation of policy relative to the justifiable use of force, however, should be a mandate not to unduly place the law enforcement officer in an unnecessary position of any danger or harm. The justification for the use of deadly physical force is usually decided on a case-by-case basis within the context of the law and interests of society. Therefore, it is not the intent of the author to argue the necessity for the use of deadly physical force by police officials, for the protection of others and the general public, or the legal basis of any justification defense. Instead, the purpose of this section is to provide practical guidelines to the investigator who is charged with the responsibility of conducting an official investigation in connection with a police-related shooting that results in death.

Police-related shooting incidents involve the discharge of a firearm by a sworn officer in the performance of duty, which results in injury or death. The investigation of these matters can have far-reaching consequences for all parties involved. The outcome may involve criminal as well as civil litigation, not to mention the psychological trauma inherent on the part of the officer. I know because I have been there.

The official police investigation usually concentrates on the issue of whether or not the officer acted within the agency guidelines. The determination is based upon the law as it relates to the "Justifiable Use of Force," ethics, good judgment, and departmental policies established within the agency. The author acknowledges that there may be variances in the law, and that case management and/or investigative techniques are usually determined on a jurisdiction-to-jurisdiction basis.

However, in situations where a death has occurred in connection with a police-related shooting incident, I personally recommend that a homicide investigation take precedence over any type of internal investigations inquiry. An internal investigation can always be conducted after the homicide probe.

Pierce R. Brooks recommends that an Incident Case Book be prepared for each fatal shooting incident. The initial Officer Involved Shooting report and the information added as addendum become the *Incident Case Book.* The addendum includes:

All scene diagrams
Other related reports
Supplemental reports
Transcribed or lengthy statements
Medical examiner's protocol
EMT/hospital treatment reports
Lab reports
Evidence reports
Suspect's criminal record
Photos
News clips
Review Board decision
Other pertinent information

I have provided the following checklist format, which has been designed to assure that a complete, factual, and unbiased report can be generated.

Police-Related Shooting Report

Opening paragraph

- ☐ Summarize the basic incident in concise terms.
- ☐ Time and date.
- ☐ Location (exact address, intersection, etc.).
- ☐ Name of officer(s).
- ☐ ID numbers: badge number and/or shield number.
- ☐ Agency/command and/or assignment.
- ☐ Number of shots fired.

☐ At whom (identify suspects, etc.).
☐ State the reason for the shooting (i.e., attempted robbery, assault, effecting an arrest, narcotics buy operation, etc.).

Paragraph two

☐ Identity of department and/or other agency investigators preparing the report.

Paragraph three

☐ Explanation of the event: when, where, who, what, how, and why.
   ☐ Explain the events leading up to, during, and following the incident.
   ☐ Use descriptive matter as necessary to clarify the *facts* and/or *support conclusion.*
   ☐ Document officer's duty status.
      ☐ On or off duty.
      ☐ Last tour of duty performed.
      ☐ Next tour of duty.
      ☐ Where was officer going to or coming from?
☐ Detail the following information in appropriate format, covering the areas listed below.
   ☐ Detail the extent of the investigation conducted.
   ☐ Identify all persons involved.
   ☐ Provide a complete list of all notifications made during the investigation.
☐ Crime scene search.
   ☐ Identity of searchers.
   ☐ Description of area searched.
   ☐ Time of search.
   ☐ Results of search.
   ☐ Property damage (if any).
   ☐ Spent bullets recovered.
   ☐ Weapons found, etc.
   ☐ Complete crime scene sketch.
      ☐ Accurate measurements.

☐ Positions of law enforcement officers as well as others involved in the event.

☐ Identity of sketcher.

☐ Injuries and/or wounds.

☐ List injuries and/or wounds; identify victim with injury and/or wounds.

☐ Name of hospital.

☐ Admitting or attending physician.

☐ Medical examiner's report and appropriate photographs.

☐ ME photographs.

☐ Investigation photographs taken at crime scene.

☐ Statements.

☐ Insure that all statements from law enforcement persons are complete and exact.

☐ What did civilian witnesses see and/or hear relative to the discharge?

☐ Document attempts to locate witnesses.

☐ By whom.

☐ Submit list of witnesses; document names and addresses.

☐ Perpetrator's pedigree.

☐ Description of suspect (pedigree, age, DOB, address, etc.).

☐ Clothing.

☐ Criminal record.

☐ Officer's pedigree.

☐ Describe officer's pedigree (age, DOB, assignment, etc.; personal information omitted from pedigree).

☐ Uniform or plainclothes.

☐ Examination of firearm.

☐ Who examined firearm.

☐ Is the firearm authorized? Listed with agency?

☐ Was the ammunition authorized?

☐ Statement of the above inspection.

☐ Ballistics.

☐ Notify the ballistics section.

☐ Have the firearm examined by ballistics.

☐ Obtain ballistics report.

Final paragraph

☐ Make appropriate recommendation. The recommendation is based upon the results of the investigation as well as interviews of all parties concerned. The report should indicate within this final paragraph whether or not the shooting incident was within agency guidelines.

Apprehension of Homicide Fugitives

When I was the Commander of Bronx Homicide, I initiated an Apprehension Unit within the command that focused on known perpetrators who had become fugitives. The members of this unit were selected based on their expertise in conducting covert surveillance as well as their contacts and abilities to access information from various agencies and different confidential sources. The investigative strategy in having a specialized apprehension team within the Homicide Squad was that pursuing known fugitives was a full time, 24-hour-a-day job, which required the assigned members to be available on short notice to make apprehensions.

The members of this unit developed extensive background information on their subjects. They knew their subjects, the girlfriends and wives of their subjects, the known associates of their fugitives as well as their haunts and habits. This was important information which not only facilitated apprehensions but minimized some of the hazards in connection with fugitive arrest situations.

This consistently effective operation was disrupted when an arrogant chief, who reportedly didn't appreciate detective expertise, refused to allow a specific fugitive case to be assigned to the Apprehension Team under my command. This suspect had been identified as the perpetrator of a quadruple homicide and should have been assigned to our Apprehension Unit. The chief's rationale was that homicide detectives considered themselves elitists. He felt that the local detective squad should handle the apprehension even though they didn't have the resources. Needless to say, the results were devastating. Six New York City Police Officers were shot in an abortive attempt to apprehend this fugitive, who managed to escape. Thank God these officers weren't killed as a result of this pompous blunder.

In any event, I ultimately had the pleasure of leading my detectives on a subsequent raid which resulted in the apprehension of this murder suspect and would-be cop killer.

Incidentally, the subject was located and apprehended using the very same tactics and procedures which had been employed on all of the other cases handled by our Apprehension Team.

Detective Second Grade John Tierney, who was one of my top investigators in the Apprehension Team provided the following information within this section on apprehending fugitives.

Use of Wanted Posters

The strategic placement of wanted posters at locations that are frequented by prisoners and informants, who come into the police station has proven to be successful. Wanted Posters displayed at Prisoner processing areas, fingerprint board locations, and outside holding cells in police stations are seen by persons who may have information and are looking to exchange that information for consideration on their own case. Likewise, these posters can also be displayed at court houses, parole and probation offices, debriefing rooms, and any other place where someone who might be interested in "striking a deal" might be tempted to come forth with information on the whereabouts of the wanted fugitive.

Distribution of Photographs and Information Flyers to Patrol

Patrol officers represent the eyes and ears of the police department. They are out there 24-hours-a-day 7-days-a-week. Most patrol officers are eager to apprehend a wanted felon, especially a homicide fugitive. By distributing color photographs of wanted subjects along with informational flyers on the subject's known locations and activities, the patrol force becomes an additional resource to be employed in apprehensions.

Cellular Phones

Pocket cell phones are an important tool for apprehension teams who are actively pursuing a fugitive. According to Detective Tierney, "It's always better to have the 'Bad guy' come out the door then to have the 'Good guys' go through the door and put themselves at risk. Detective Tierney recommends a telephone "ruse" be employed to assist in the apprehension of the fugitive.

When the arrest team is in position with a view of the subject's door there are two tactics that have proven to be successful:

1. Have someone call (preferably a female) and ask for the subject to determine if he is at home. This tactic isn't foolproof, but it minimizes the chance of blowing the operation by alerting the fugitive or someone else at the location that you know where he lives. If he isn't home you can always return at a later time or another day when the subject is home and answers the phone.
2. When you are sure that the wanted subject is in the location, have someone call from the cellular phone using "street talk" stating; "The Cops are coming. Get out now while you can." According to Tierney, "nine out of ten times the subject will come running out the door."

Beepers

Many times investigators will discover that the wanted subjects have beepers, which they use to conduct business and remain a few steps ahead of the police. According to Detective Tierney, you can request subscriber information but many of the subjects don't use their real names or provide fictitious information to the company. Tierney recommends the following tactics using a police "undercover phone:"

1. When you obtain the wanted subject's Pager number, *beep* him to the *undercover phone number* at your office, which should be equipped with "Caller I.D." This will give you the number he used to call you. If the Bad guy has a "Block" on his phone, which most bad guys do, go to Step #2.
2. Page the bad guy to the *undercover phone number*. When he calls back there is a code you can hit, e.g., *57 (you need to check with your local phone company to ascertain the proper code in your area). After speaking to him and telling him you didn't page him, punch in the code. You will get a recording from the phone company stating that your call has been successfully trapped and the number to call for further information. In most situations the phone company will provide you with the location that the call was made from. It is good practice to have an Assistant District Attorney on stand-by for a subpoena to be faxed. (*The author recommends that the reader confer with their local prosecutor or State's Attorney since certain States have different legislation regarding telephone number interceptions.*)

3. If you have an indication of the area where the subject is calling from, have surveillance units available in that area ready to respond to the location when the phone company provides you with the address.

Planning the Apprehension

Assessment of Physical Hazards

The purpose of this section is to stress the importance of safety and eliminate risk hazards to members of the apprehension team. Carefully consider whether the hazard factor may be above the acceptable level before proceeding with any tactical plan.

- ☐ Consider:
    - ☐ Time of the day or night
    - ☐ Type of location (highrise, private house, multiple dwelling, drug location, schools in area, type of neighborhood, traffic conditions)
    - ☐ Firearms involved
    - ☐ Vehicle pursuits — consideration
    - ☐ Request assistance of other specialized units

The Tactical Plan

- ☐ **Research your subject:** Develop extensive background information on your subject. Know the fugitives, associates as well as their haunts and habits. Know your subject's history, the areas they frequent, their social activities, past criminal activity, driving, and summons activity.
- ☐ **Conduct reconnaissance of the subject's location:** Know the physical layout of the subject's location. (locked front doors, rear exits, fire-escapes, rear yards, security, alarms, dog, etc. Conduct roof-top surveys.
- ☐ Consider the best method of approach to location to minimize hazards and provide an alement of surprise.

The Tactical Operation

Notification to Central Communications by Land Line.

- ☐ Prior to enforcement action, the city-wide or local police communications division should be advised by telephone of the planned raid in the event that someone calls 9-1-1 to report activities. *Do not use the radio to alert communications. Subjects are known to monitor police frequencies.*

Hospital

☐ Designate a hospital and a route for *emergency* response.

Personnel

☐ Whenever practical in enforcement operations, members should wear recognizable *Police identification, i.e., police jackets, uniforms, etc.*

☐ Ample personnel should be assigned.

☐ All members of the Apprehension Team (uniform and plain clothes) should familiarize themselves with other assigned members.

☐ Bullet-proof vests should be worn at *all* times.

Briefing

☐ **Work as a team:** All members should be apprised of *all* information about the subject. Keeping information about the subject private can result in the escape of the subject or injury to your fellow officers.

☐ Prior to enforcement operations, conduct a meeting with *all* members assigned to the operation to discuss:

    ☐ Personnel assigned and each specific duty

    ☐ Equipment

    ☐ Set-up locations

    ☐ Targeted locations

    ☐ Execution tactics

    ☐ Potential hazards

Equipment

☐ Determine the type of equipment necessary for the operation. *Type of weapons to be utilized, tear gas, percussion grenades.*

☐ Insure that *all* portable radios are charged and have extra charged batteries. Handcuffs should be carried by *all* members of the team. Flashlights should also be available during enforcement operation. *All* vehicles should have full tanks of gas prior to the start of the operation.

☐ Cellular phones

Conclusion

The management and supervision of a homicide investigation is unique in its comparison to other police management operations. The management of day-to-day patrol operations and administrative functions can be proceduralized because of their routine and repetitive nature. In fact, management and supervision of many police operations are interchangeable and allow for supervisory reassignment and career growth within the organization. The supervisor's experience with the function is not considered a prerequisite for assignment.

This rationale is based on the theories of police administrators, whom I refer to as "the police intelligentsia." They believe that "police managers" should not participate operationally in the function. Instead, these managers should be taught to rely strictly upon the written rules and procedures of the organization. This, the "police intelligentsia" believe, will assure operational uniformity.

Generally speaking, this strict and rigid bureaucratic control does not allow for on-site common sense and the flexibility necessary in a practical homicide investigation. These administratively oriented rules eventually become insulative and effectively relieve the "manager" of the on-line supervisory responsibility commensurate with the direction of operations.

Investigatively speaking, the intelligent management and supervision of homicide investigations requires a different approach that takes into account the unpredictable aspects of a murder investigation. There are rules, procedures, and established policies that give direction and coordination to the function, as well as guidelines implemented for specific investigative actions.

In homicide investigation, the on-scene supervisor directs and coordinates a team effort based upon established policies. However, as a manager, he or she is given the authority to allow for variations of the guidelines to occur when needed at the point of execution. This flexibility is based upon necessity and common sense.

The supervision and management function requires the supervisor to actively participate in the investigation. This does not mean "playing detective" and/or jumping into the operational aspects, such as interrogation of suspects, searching the crime scene, collecting and/or handling evidence, interviewing prospective witnesses, etc.

Active participation means sharing an interest in the investigation intelligently directing activities and utilizing the investigative critiques to establish priorities properly. In addition, active participation enables the supervisor to assess the case and provide the necessary resources to his people so that they may effectively investigate the case.

The supervisor of homicide should ideally have a homicide or an investigative background as experience is a prime asset. This does not mean that a supervisor who lacks a homicide or investigative background cannot effectively supervise investigations. However, it does suggest that there is a need for learning the investigative processes involved. Even for the experienced supervisor, managing investigations is an on-going educational process. And remember, you're never too smart to learn.

Epilogue

As far as homicide detectives are concerned, there are two types of homicide: one in which the suspect is caught quickly, and the unsolved homicide. In New York City, the former are referred to as "ground balls," and the latter are appropriately called "mysteries." Mystery or ground-ball, the fact remains that you are dealing with the ultimate crime — murder. Whether you have the killer-in-cuffs or it's a who-done-it-and-ran, the investigation should remain the same. Each case must be properly managed and the investigation must be thorough and complete. This is what professional homicide investigation is all about.

Homicide investigation is a profound duty. As an officer entrusted with such a duty, it is incumbent upon you to develop an understanding of the dynamics and principles of professional homicide investigation.

Practical homicide investigation suggests that "things be done right the first time," and "knowledge is power" — knowledge that has been enhanced with experience, flexibility, and common sense.

Practitioners must be prepared to use tactics, procedures, and forensic techniques in their pursuit of the truth, and then to follow the course of events and the facts as they are developed to their ultimate conclusion.

Death investigation constitutes a heavy responsibility and as such let no person deter you from the truth and your own personal commitment to see that justice is done — not only for the deceased, but for the surviving family as well. And remember, "You're working for God."

Glossary

Abdomen — Portion of the body between the thorax (chest area) and pelvic area.

Abdominal cavity — Contains the stomach, liver, gallbladder, spleen, pancreas, and most of the large and small intestines. The kidneys, ureters, and adrenal glands lie deep in the cavity.

Abdomino-pelvic cavity — This is the portion of the ventral cavity below the diaphragm, consisting of the abdominal cavity and the pelvic cavity.

Abortion — Uterus empties itself prematurely. Criminal abortion is a willful production of a miscarriage of a woman who is pregnant by drugs, instruments, or any other means not authorized by law.

Abrasion — An injury to the skin in which there is a removal of the superficial epithelial layer of the skin (the epidermis) due to friction against a rough surface with resultant scraping away of the superficial portions of the epidermis. (Wearing away of the skin in small shreds by friction.)

Abrasion collar — The circular perforation and blackening effect on the edges of the skin as the bullet passes through the skin.

Accident — An unforeseen occurrence, especially one of an injurious character.

Acid phosphatase — An enzyme found in the kidneys, serum, semen, and prostate gland. Acid phosphatase is found in high concentrations in semen. It is most useful as an indicator of recent sexual intercourse.

Acute — Sharp or severe.

Adhesions — Places where the tissues adhere to the skin, normally found at previous operation scars.

Adipocere — Waxy soap-like substance formed during the decomposition of animal bodies buried in moist places. It consists principally of insoluble salts of fatty acids. Also called "grave wax." Composed of oleic, palmitic, and stearic acids.

Adrenals — Either of two secretory organs perched atop the kidneys. Each consists of two parts; the cortex and the medulla which secret hormones.

AIDS — Acquired Immune Deficiency Syndrome (HTLV-3). A disease involving a defect in cell-mediated immunity. Usually transmitted through sexual contact or exposure to contaminated blood.

Allele — Alternative forms of a gene; e.g., an allele for blue eyes.

Amnesia — Lack of or loss of memory, especially for past experiences.

Anal intercourse — Insertion of one partner's penis into another partner's rectum.

Anatomy — Study of the structure of the human body.

Anemia — Insufficient oxygen-carrying capacity of the blood.

Anesthetics — A group of drugs capable of producing either localized or general loss of sensation. Examples: (1) chloroform, a heavy, colorless liquid with a characteristic odor and taste; and (2) ether, a colorless volatile liquid with penetrating odor.

Aneurysm — A sac formed by the dilation of the walls of an artery or a vein and filled with blood.

Angina — Spasmodic pain.

Angina pectoris — Spasmodic pain in chest caused by sudden decrease of blood supply to the heart muscle.

Anoxia — Total oxygen deprivation

Antemortem — Before death.

Anterior — (Ventral.) The Front. Indicates the front or belly side of the body. Hence, the toes are anterior or ventral.

Antitoxin — A substance found in the blood serum and in other body fluids which is specifically antagonistic to some particular toxin.

Anus — The distal end and outlet of the alimentary canal.

Aorta — The great trunk artery which carries blood from the heart to be distributed by branch arteries throughout the body.

Arachnoid membrane — Thin covering of the brain and spinal cord.

Areola — The pigmented ring around the nipple of the breast.

Arrhythmia — Any deviation from the normal pattern of the heartbeat.

Arsenic — A medicinal and poisonous element; a brittle, lustrous, graying solid, with garlic odor.

Artery — Any one of the vessels through which the blood passes from the heart to the various parts of the body.

A.S.H.D. (Arteriosclerotic heart disease) — Hardening of the arteries, frequent in old age and resulting from the accumulation of fat in the arteries.

Asphyxia — The end stage of significant interference with the exchange of oxygen and carbon dioxide, as in suffocation.

Aspiration — Breathing or drawing in of a substance into the respiratory tract, blocking same.

Aspiration of vomitus — Breathing or drawing vomitus into the respiratory tract, blocking same.

Asthma — Wheezing and coughing, usually caused by allergies affecting the bronchi or air passages to the lungs.

Auto — A combining form meaning self.

Autoeroticism — Arousal and satisfaction of sexual emotion within or by oneself through fantasy and/or genital stimulation.

Autolysis — The breakdown of cells and organs from the aseptic chemical process caused by intracellular enzymes.

Autopsy — The internal examination of the body after death.

Autoradiograph — The autoradiograph or AUTORAD is the final product in a DNA probe. The nylon membrane, which has been probed by the radioactive marker, is placed against a piece of x-ray film and exposed for several days. Black bands appear where the radioactive probes stuck to the fragments.

Autosadism — Sexual gratification through self-inflicted pain.

Avulsion — The separation, by tearing, of any part of the body from the whole.

Barbiturates — Depressant medicines prescribed by doctors; common in suicide by overdose.

Bases — The chemical units (adenine, thymine, guanine, and cytosine, (in humans) whose order in DNA molecules governs the genetic code.

Bestiality — Use of animals for sexual arousal (includes intercourse with animals as well as training the animal to lick or rub the human partner). This sexual disorder is clinically referenced in DSM-IV as *zoophilia*.

Biliary tract — Of or pertaining to bile or gall bladder and its ducts, which transport bile.

Bitch — In prison slang, a feminine-looking woman who is used sexually, as "insertee," by tougher females. In gay male slang, a general term of abuse for a gay male.

Bondage — A masochistic involvement with ligatures, restraints, blindfolds, gags, hood, or restrictive containers. In autoerotic episodes, these restraints may vary from the very simple to very complex and bizarre.

Bottom man — The homosexual male, who receives the fist of the "top man" during a "**fisting.**" Or, the insertee (passive partner) in anal intercourse.

Bradycardia — Abnormally slow heartbeat. Cardiac output is decreased causing faintness, dizziness, and chest pains.

Bruise — Bluish swelling of blood beneath the skin.

Bull — In prison slang, a tough female who plays the dominant sexual role.

Bull dyke — A lesbian who adopts masculine manners as well as wears men's clothing.

Butch — A homosexual male or female, who is masculine in looks and manner.

Bullet track — Is the path of the bullet or projectile as it passes through the body.

Burking — Mechanical asphyxia plus smothering that is homicidal in nature. Murder by suffocating so as to leave the body unmarked. (William Burke executed in Edinburgh 1829. He and another would supply bodies for anatomical dissection. They would get an individual intoxicated and Burke would sit on the victim's chest while the mouth and nose were covered.)

Cadaveric spasm — Stiffening and rigidity of a single group of muscles occurring immediately after death.

Carbon dioxide — A heavy, colorless gas. Forms in tissues during respiration and eliminated by the lungs.

Carbon monoxide (CO) — A colorless, odorless, very toxic gas, formed by burning carbon or organic fuels.

Carcinoma — Cancer. This will usually be defined by the organ or body affected.

Cardio- — A combining form denoting relationship to the heart.

Cardiovascular system — The network of structures, including the heart and the blood vessels, that pump and convey the blood throughout the body.

Carotid — Arteries of the neck.

Cartilage — The gristle or white elastic substance attached to articular bone surfaces and forming certain parts of the skeleton.

Castration — Removal of the gonads (primary sex organs).

Cause of death — Any injury or disease that produces a physiological derangement in the body that results in the individual dying.

Cavity — A hollow place or space.

Cell — The basic unit of all living organisms, including humans, animals, insects, and plants. The cell consists of a nucleus and cytoplasm. The human body has more than 10 trillion cells.

Cerebral — Pertaining to the cerebrum, which is the main portion of the brain occupying the upper part of the cranium.

Cerebrospinal fluid (CSF) — The fluids about the brain and spinal cord.

Cerebro-vascular accident (CVA) — A stroke; severe injury to the brain resulting from spontaneous hemorrhage or thrombosis.

Cervical — Pertaining to the neck.

Chicken — In pedophile slang, a young boy who is used sexually by an adult homosexual.

Chickenhawk — An adult homosexual male, who seeks children or young teenagers for sexual activities.

Choking — Asphyxia caused by obstruction within the air passages.

Chop wounds — Wounds caused by a heavy object which has an edge, e.g., an axe, machete, or a meat cleaver.

Chromosome — A structure in the cell nucleus composed mainly of DNA and other proteins, which stores and transmits genetic information.

Chronic — Of long duration (said of sickness).

Circulation — Movement in a regular course, as the circulation of the blood.

Cirrhosis — A disease of the liver marked by progressive destruction of liver cells.

Clustered crime scene — Involves a situation where most of the activities take place at one location; the confrontation, the attack, the assault, and sexual activity, etc.

Coagulate — To become clotted.

Colon — The part of the large intestine that extends from the cecum to the rectum.

Comatose — Unconscious and unresponsive to stimuli. Note that a comatose person is not dead.

Congenital — Existing at or dating from birth.

Conjunctiva — Delicate membrane lining of the eyelid.

Contact wound — Occurs when the firearm is pressed against the head or body. Consequently, gases from the explosion expand between the skin and the bone producing a bursting effect and ragged wound.

Contrecoup — Injury to a part of the body (usually the brain) caused by a blow to the opposite side. Occurs frequently in falls.

Contrecoup contusions — These occur in the brain directly opposite to the point of impact. They are seen most commonly in the frontal and temporal lobes. Contrecoup contusions are classically associated with falls.

Contusion — An area of hemorrhage into soft tissue due to the rupture of blood vessels caused by blunt trauma.

Convulsion — A violent, involuntary contraction or series of contractions of the voluntary muscles.

Coprophilia — A sexual attraction to feces.

Coprolangia — A sexual desire to consume feces.

Coronary — Of or pertaining to the heart.

Corpse — The dead body of a human being.

Corpus delicti — The body of the crime. The facts constituting or proving a crime; material substance or foundation of a crime. The corpus delicti in a murder case is not just the body of the victim, but the fact that he has been murdered.

Crack — Concentrated form of cocaine which is used in vapor form. It is smoked or inhaled through "crack pipes." It is a highly addictive drug that causes psychotic behavior which is often times violent.

Craniotomy — The opening of the skull, as for brain surgery.

Cranium — The skull or brain pan.

Cremains — Human remains which have been cremated.

Cricoid — A ring-shaped cartilage connected to the thyroid cartilage.

Criminal Investigative Analysis — The current term utilized by the FBI Behavioral Sciences Unit at Quantico to define their Psychological Profile and Criminal Personality Profiles of Offenders.

Cruising — In homosexual slang, to go looking for a homosexual pickup or partner for a brief sexual encounter.

Culpable — Meriting condemnation or blame.

Cunnilingus — The act of kissing and licking a female's vagina and stimulating them with the tongue.

Cutaneous — Pertaining to the skin.

Cyanosis — Blueness of the skin, often due to cardiac malformation resulting in insufficient oxygenation of the blood.

Decomposition — The separation of compound bodies into their constituent principles; postmortem degeneration of the body. It involves two principles: autolysis and putrefaction.

Defecation — Elimination of solid waste matter from the intestines.

Defeminize — To remove a woman's breast as in defeminization.

Defense wounds — Cuts, abrasions, and contusions on the hands wrists, forearms, and arms which occur during a violent struggle as the victim attempts to ward-off his or her attacker.

Degeneration — Deterioration.

Delirium — A mental disorder marked by illusions, hallucinations, physical restlessness, and incoherence.

Depersonalization — The actions taken by a murderer to obscure the personal identity of the victim. Face may be beaten beyond recognition, or the face of the victim may be covered.

Depraved — Corrupt or perverted.

Deteriorate — To become worse.

Deviant — Gay slang to describe homosexual activities that are particularly strange or bizarre, e.g., S&M, sex with a child, fisting, urophilia, coprophilia, etc.

Diagnosis — The art of distinguishing one disease from another.

Diaphragm — The musculomembranous partition that separates the abdomen from the thorax.

Diesel dyke — A particularly masculine or tough lesbian.

Dildo — An artificial penis-like sex toy.

Disarticulation — Amputation or separation at a joint.

Disease — Any departure from a state of health; illness or sickness.

Disembowel — To take out the bowels or entrails. Eviscerate.

Disinterment — Digging up a body after burial.

Distal — Indicates farther away from the center of the body. Hence, the elbow is distal to the shoulder.

DNA (Deoxyribonucleic acid) — This molecule is housed in every nucleated cell of the body. Often described as the body's blueprints since they carry the genetic codes that govern the structure and function of every component of the body.

Dorsal — Pertaining to the back.

Dorsal cavity — Subdivided into the cranial and vertebral cavities.

Double homicide — Two victims killed during one event and at one location.

Drag — Wearing the clothing of the opposite sex; especially when a male wears female attire.

Drag queen — A gay male, who dresses as a woman in a spirit of playacting. (Not to be confused with transvestism.)

Drowning — Asphyxiation because of submersion in a liquid. Sequence of events are breath holding, involuntary inspiration and gasping for air at the breaking point, loss of consciousness, and death.

Duodenum — The first portion of the small intestine.

Dura mater — Outermost and toughest membrane covering the brain.

Dyke — A street term used to describe a lesbian.

Dysentery — A term given to a number of disorders marked by inflammation of the intestines, and attended pain in the abdomen and frequent stools containing blood and mucus.

Dyspnea — Difficult or labored breathing.

Ecchymosis — Swelling from a bruise caused by bleeding beneath the skin.

Eczema — An inflammatory skin disease.

Edema — Collection of abnormal amounts of fluid in tissue, as in lungs, limbs, etc.

E.E.G. (Electroencephalogram) — A tracing of the electrical activity of the brain allowing diagnosis of disease of the brain.

Ejaculate — To discharge.

E.K.G.; E.C.G. (Electrocardiogram) — A tracing on a strip of paper showing the electrical activity of the heart and allowing diagnosis of heart disease.

Electrophoresis — A technique for separating biological molecules by size by exposing them to an electrical charge.

Embalming — The treatment of the dead body to prevent putrefaction.

Embolus — A thrombus which breaks away from where it formed and travels to another area of the body.

Embryo — The fetus in its earlier stages of development.

Emphysema — Lung disease. The area of the lungs are reduced by this disease causing wheezing and difficult breathing.

Engram — (In psychology "A mind picture.") Attributed to early sexual psychic trauma. Paraphilic in nature. A typical "engram" might be a sadistic fantasy or specific sexual *scenario*. The sadistic scenario is thus conjured in the imagination, be it a re-creation of the actual crime or the product of fantasy.

Entomology — Branch of science which deals with the study of insects. For example, in making a determination of "time-of-death" a forensic entomologist evaluates the structures and habits of certain necropagous insects collected from the carrion, which provide cycle time frames for the species.

Entrails — The inner organs of humans and animals. Specifically, the intestines.

Enzyme — Proteins that initiate specific biochemical reactions.

Epidermis — The outermost layer of the skin.

Epiglottis — Lid-like structures covering the entrance to the larynx.

Erotic — Arousing sexual desire.

Eroticism — Sexual or erotic quality or character of something.

Evisceration — Removal of the viscera from the abdominal cavity; disembowelment.

Exhibitionism — Exposing the genitals to an unsuspecting stranger for the purposes of obtaining sexual excitement.

Exsanguination — Loss of blood.

Exhume — The disinterring or removal of a body from the grave.

Fag, faggot — A street-term used to describe an effeminate homosexual man.

Fag bashers — A street-term used to describe "straight" men who beat up gay men.

Fag workers — A street-term used to describe offenders who setup and rob homosexual men.

Fantasy — An imaginative sequence in which one's desires are fulfilled.

Fatal injury — An injury resulting in death.

Feces — Excrement discharged from the intestines.

Fellatio — The act of kissing and mouthing a sex partner's penis. A sexual activity involving oral contact with the male genitals.

Femme — A street-term used to describe a feminine-looking lesbian.

Fetish — Any object or nongenital part of the body that causes a habitual erotic response or fixation.

Fetishism — Compulsive use of nonliving objects for sexual arousal (usually female undergarments (e.g., panties), shoes, etc.).

Fetus — The unborn offspring of a human or an animal.

Fibrillation — Fluttering of the heart not controlled by motor nerves.

Filicide — The act of murdering one's child.

Fisting — A deviant sexual act which is practiced among homosexual males. The human hand is inserted into the anal cavity of the other participant during sadomasochistic sex.

Fistula — An abnormal passage leading from an abscess to the body surface.

Flaccid — Soft, limp.

Flaming faggot — A street-term used to describe a flamboyantly effeminate homosexual man.

Floater — A dead body in the water, which comes to the surface due to decompositional gases.

Fratricide — The act of killing one's brother or sister.

Frotteurism — A sexual attraction to touching or rubbing against a nonconsenting person. Rubbing his genitals against the body of another.

Frye rule — A legal standard of admissibility used by a number of jurisdictions which requires that scientific evidence to be introduced into court must have gained general acceptance by the scientific community. Based on Supreme Court decision Frye v. U.S., F 1013 at 1014 (D.C. Cir. 1923). A number of these Frye rulings have occurred as a result of DNA technology. Most courts have upheld DNA.

Gangrene — Death of tissue, characterized by anoxia and marked inflammation.

Gastric — Relating to the stomach.

Gastrointestinal tract — Of or pertaining to the organs of the GI tract, from mouth to anus. Specifically of the stomach and intestines.

Gastroscopy — Looking in the stomach with a metal instrument, a gastroscope.

Gay — Homosexual

Gay bashing — The politically correct reference to "fag bashing."

Gene — A segment of DNA that codes for the production of a specific protein.

Genitalia (Genitals) — The sexual organs. In males, the testes and penis; in females, the vulva and vagina.

Girl — In prison slang, a male who is used sexually by other males. An "insertee."

Glycoprotein (P30) — A semen-specific glycoprotein (P30) of prostatic origin discovered in 1978. This substance is only present in semen and has essentially replaced analysis for acid phosphatase in rape investigations except for rapid screening tests.

Gorilla — In prison slang, a tough male who plays the insertor role sexually.

Helix — A double-spiral of deoxyribonucleic acid in the shape of a twisted ladder, i.e., DNA as a double-stranded helix.

Hematoma — A large focal collection of blood in an area of contusion. Or, local swelling filled with effused blood.

Hemolysis — Breakdown of red blood cells and the release of hemoglobin.

Hemophilia — Condition in which blood is slow to clot or does not clot, allowing a person to bleed to death.

Hemorrhage — Heavy bleeding. A loss of a large amount of blood in a short period of time, either externally or internally. May be arterial, venous, or capillary.

Hemothorax — An accumulation of blood and fluid in the pleural cavity, between the parietal and visceral pleural; usually the result of trauma.

Hepatic — Relating to the liver.

Heterophobia — A fear or hatred of heterosexuality. An irrational and/or paranoid fear or animosity of heterosexuals because of one's affinity toward homosexuality. An example would be the need to *overtly demonstrate* homosexual proclivities in order to affront heterosexual ideals, mores, and/or values because of the *perceived threat* of attack by heterosexuals.

Homeostasis — A relative constancy in the internal environment of the body, naturally maintained by adaptive responses that promote healthy survival. An example of some functions controlled by homeostatic mechanisms are the heartbeat, blood pressure, and respiration.

Homophobia — Fear or hatred of homosexuals. Irrational fears of homosexuality in others, the fear of homosexual feelings within oneself, or self-loathing because of one's homosexuality. (Weinberg, 1973.)

Histology — The science dealing with the microscopic identification of cells and tissues; the structure of organ tissues, including the composition of cells and their organization into various body tissues.

Histotoxic — Poisonous to tissue or tissues.

Histotoxin — Any substance that is poisonous to the body tissues. It is usually generated within the body rather than introduction externally.

HLA (Human leukocyte antigen) — A polymorphic protein system commonly identified for paternity testing.

Homicidomania — Impulsive desire to commit murder.

Homosexual — A person who is attracted to and obtains sexual gratification from acts performed with a person of the same sex.

Homosexual handkerchief codes — The color-coded handkerchief signals employed by certain homosexual subcultures to indicate their sexual proclivities and/or preferences.

Hustler — In homosexual terminology, a male prostitute, especially a young male who takes pay to let himself be felatted.

Hybridization — Probes, usually tagged with a radioactive marker, are applied to the nylon membrane (see *Southern blotting*). These probes are designed to "seek-out" a predetermined chromosomal locus containing a polymorphic region of DNA.

Hydrophobia — The usual common name for rabies in man.

Hyoid bone — Small U-shaped bone at base of tongue.

Hypertension — High blood pressure.

Hyperthermia — A much higher than normal body temperature.

Hypothermia — An abnormal and dangerous condition in which the body is below 95°F. Usually caused by prolonged exposure to cold.

Hypoxia — Partial deprivation of oxygen.

Incision — A wound inflicted by an instrument with a sharp cutting edge.

Incised wound — Caused by a sharp instrument or weapon. A wound which is longer than deep, with minimum bruising, no bridging of skin, and bleeds freely.

Infanticide — The act of killing an infant soon after birth.

Infarct — An area of necrosis (death of a cell or group of cells) in a tissue, produced by sudden arrest or circulation in vessel.

Inferior — Indicates direction further away from the head end of the body or towards the lower part of the body.

Infibulation — Self-infliction of pain on the genitals.

Inguinal — Of the groin.

Inhalation — The drawing of air or other vapor into the lungs.

Insertee — In homosexual terminology, a homosexual male who receives the partner's penis in his mouth or anus; a homosexual female who receives the partner's tongue in her vagina. (See also "*Bottom man.*")

Insertor — In homosexual terminology, a homosexual male who puts his penis in the partner's mouth or anus; a homosexual female who performs cunnilingus on her partner. (See also "*Top man.*")

Intestine — The membranous tube that extends from the stomach to the anus.

Intra — Prefix meaning within.

Jaundice — Yellow pigmentation of skin most commonly resulting from liver failure.

Klismaphilia — A sexual attraction to the giving or receiving of enemas.

Laceration — A split or tear of the skin, usually produced by blunt force (shearing or crushing type injuries from blunt objects, falls, or impact from vehicles). These injuries tend to be irregular with abraded contused margins. Internal organs can also have lacerations.

Laryngeal prominence — The bulge at the front of the neck produced by the thyroid cartilage of the larynx (Adam's Apple).

Larynx — The voice box, located between the root of the tongue and the trachea.

Lateral — Pertaining to a side.

Leather freak — In homosexual terminology, a homosexual, usually a male, who dresses in leather and acts tough and masculine. Street-term which also means someone who practices S & M. (See Sadomasochism.)

Lesbian — A female homosexual.

Leukemia — Cancer of the blood cells.

Ligament — Any fibrous, tough band which connects bones or supports viscera.

Ligature — Anything which binds or ties.

Linkage blindness — An investigative failure to recognize a pattern which "links" one crime with another crime in a series of cases through victimology, geographic region or area of events, the "signature" of the offender, similar M.O., and a review of autopsy protocols.

Liver — The largest glandular organ situated in the upper part of the abdomen on the right side, usually of a dark red color.

Lividity or livor mortis — Postmortem discoloration due to the gravitation of blood into the dependent capillaries and veins.

Locus — The specific position occupied by a particular gene or allele on a chromosome.

Lumbar — Pertaining to or near the lower region of the back.

Mandible — The large bone constituting the lower jaw.

Manic depressive — A psychosis characterized by alternating periods of mania and mental depression.

Manner of death — Explains how the cause of death came about. Medicolegal manners of death are: homicide, suicide, accident, natural, and undetermined.

Marbling — Produced by hemolysis of blood vessels with reaction of hemoglobin and hydrogen sulfide and development of greenish black coloration along the vessels.

Masochism — Sexual perversion in which the individual takes delight in being subject to degrading, humiliating, or cruel treatment such as flogging or choking.

Mass murder — A homicide involving the killing of four or more victims during a single event at one location. *Classic* — Involves a single individual, who kills more than four persons at one location during a period of time (minutes, hours, or days). *Family-member murder* — More than three family members are killed and the perpetrator takes his own life is a mass murder/ suicide. *Family killing* — Four or more family members killed by a family member who does not commit suicide.

Master — In S & M sex; the dominent, active, insertor partner.

Masturbation — Manual manipulation of the genitals resulting in sexual excitement.

Maxilla — One of a pair of large bones that form the upper jaw.

Mechanical asphyxia — Asphyxia created by pressure on the outside of body, which prevents respiration. Examples are: traumatic asphyxia, positional asphyxia, and riot crush or "human pile" deaths.

Mechanism of death — The physiological derangement produced by the cause of death that results in death, i.e., hemorrhage, septicemia, cardiac arrhythmia.

Medial — Pertaining to the middle. Indicates closer to the midline of the body.

Membrane — A thin layer of tissue which covers a surface or divides a space or organ.

Meningitis — Inflammation of the meninges (thin membranous covering of the brain).

Midline — The center of the head, chest, and abdomen.

Miscarriage — The premature emptying of a uterus prior to 28 weeks of gestation.

Misdemeanor murders — A "Geberthism" which suggests that when two "shit-birds" (less than productive citizens) kill each other in some sort of drug-related homicide that the crime might actually be considered a less than felony offense. The author obviously uses the term in a facetious manner.

Modus Operandi — "Mode of operation or way of doing things." The M.O. is a learned behavior that changes as offenders gain experience, build confidence, or become involved with the criminal justice system.

Monomania — Insanity on a single subject or class of subjects.

Mummification — The complete drying up of the body as the result of burial in a dry place, or by exposure to dry atmosphere.

Munchausen Syndrome By Proxy (MSBP) — A form of child abuse whereby the parent or adult care giver deliberately simulates or causes medical distress in a child in order to gain attention, praise, or the sympathy of others.

Musculoskeletal system — All of the muscles, bones, joints, and related structures, as the tendons and connective tissue, that function in the movement of the parts and organs of the body.

Myocardial infarction (MI) — An occlusion of a coronary artery, caused by atherosclerosis or an embolus resulting from a necrotic area in the vasculature myocardium.

Myocardium — The heart muscle.

Mysophilia — A sexual attraction to filth.

Narcomania — An insane desire for narcotics or alcohol.

Natal — Pertaining to birth.

Nausea — Tendency to vomit; sickness at the stomach.

Necrophagia — The eating of dead bodies or feeding off a carrion, e.g., necrophagous insects such as flies and beetles can provide entomological evidence in death investigations.

Necrophilism — Morbid attraction to corpes; sexual intercourse with a dead body.

Necrosis — Death of tissue.

Neonaticide — The killing of a child within 24 hours of its birth.

NCAVC (National Center for the Analysis of Violent Crime) — A subdivision of the FBI's Behavioral Science Unit located in Quantico, Virginia. Composed of four sections: Research and Development, VI-CAP, Criminal Personality Profiling Program, and Consultation Program.

Necrophilia — A sexual attraction to dead bodies. Having sexual intercourse with a dead body.

Necrosis — Localized tissue death that occurs in groups of cells in response to disease or injury.

Nitroglycerine — Medicine to treat heart patients; a pill taken under the tongue.

Non compos mentis — Not sound of mind; insane.

Nucleus — The part of the cell which contains the chromosomes, which are composed of DNA and associated proteins — the genetic program.

Occlusion — (In anatomy) a blockage in a canal, vessel, or passage of the body.

Organized crime "hit" — A murder of a known or recognized member of an organized criminal enterprise.

Ossification — Formation of bone or a bony substance.

Osteitis — Inflammation of bone caused by pyogenic organism.

Osteomyelitis — Inflammation of bone caused by pyogenic organism.

Overlay — Mechanical asphyxia combined with smothering. An example would be an infant in bed with one of the parents, who inadvertently rolls on top of the child, thus compressing the chest and occluding the nose and mouth with the bedding or the body.

Padding — Material placed between a body portion and the ligature or device used to alter the physiological state of the victim.

Pancreas — A large elongated gland located behind the stomach.

Papillary — Pertaining to or resembling a nipple, ridges, or grooves.

Paralysis — The loss of power of voluntary motion.

Paranoia — A mental disorder characterized by systematized delusions, as of grandeur or especially those of persecution, often except in a schizophrenic state, with an otherwise intact personality.

Parenticide — The act of killing one's own parents.

Parietal — Of or pertaining to the outer wall of a cavity or organ.

Pathognomonic — Of a sign or symptom. Specific to a disease or condition.

Pedophilia — Engaging in sexual activity with prepubertal children. *Pedophile* — A person who engages in pedophilia.

Pelvic cavity — Contains the urinary bladder, the sex organs, and part of the small and large intestines.

Peritoneum — An extensive serous membrane that covers the entire abdominal wall of the body and is reflected over the contained viscera.

Peritonitis — An inflammation of the peritoneum produced by bacteria or irritating substances introduced into the abdominal cavity by a penetrating wound or perforation of an organ.

Permeation — The spreading through a tissue or organ of a disease process.

Petechial hemorrhages — Minute (pin-like) hemorrhages that occur at points beneath the skin. Usually observed in conjunctiva (the mucous membrane lining the inner surface of the eyelids and anterior part of the sclera).

Phalanx — Any bone of a finger or toe.

Physiological mechanism — The ligature or device used to alter the physiological state of the victim.

Phlebitis — Inflammation of veins.

Piquerism — Sexual inclinations to stab, pierce, or cut. Obtaining a sexual gratification from the shedding of blood, tearing of flesh, and/or observing such pain and suffering of a victim who is being subjected to this activity.

Pleural — The chest cavity about the lungs.

Pleuritis — "Pleurisy," inflammation in the chest cavity.

Pneumatic — Pertaining to air or respiration.

Pneumothorax — Air in the chest cavity.

Polymorphism — A naturally occurring or induced variation in the sequence of bases on a segment of DNA.

Positional asphyxia — Asphyxia which occurs as a result of body position, which restricts respiration.

Posterior — (Dorsal.) Indicates the backside of the body. Hence, the heels are posterior or dorsal.

Postmortem — After death.

Postpartum — Pertaining to the period following childbirth.

Probe — In genetic engineering, a fragment of DNA carrying the complementary code for a specific base sequence. Probes can be used to detect variations in base sequence that establish individual identity.

Probable cause — Reasonable grounds to believe that a person has committed a crime.

Protein — A molecule consisting of linked amino acids. Proteins serve as the "building blocks" of body structures or as the enzymes that initiate specific biochemical reactions.

Proximal — Indicates nearer to a point of reference, usually the center of the body. Hence, the shoulder is proximal to the elbow.

Psychiatry — Branch of medicine concerned with the study, treatment, and prevention of disorders of the mind, including psychoses, neuroses, etc.

Psychodynamics — The study of the mental and emotional processes underlying human behavior and its motivation.

Psycholinguistic analysis — A sophisticated method of examining the spoken or written communication as to origin, background, and psychology of the speaker or writer.

Psychology — The science dealing with the mind and with the mental and emotional processes; the science of human and animal behavior.

Psychological autopsy — A collaborative procedure involving law enforcement and mental health experts, who attempt to determine the state of a person's mind prior to a sudden death.

Psychopathic personality — A person whose behavior is largely amoral and asocial and who is characterized by irresponsibility, lack of remorse or shame, perverse or impulsive (often criminal) behavior, and other serious personality defects, generally without psychotic attacks or symptoms.

Psychopathic killer — A person who kills for pleasure.

Psychopathic sexual sadist — A person who inflicts pain, either physical or psychological on another for the purposes of causing suffering, submission, humiliation, fear, and terror on another. The suffering of the victim is sexually arousing for the offender.

Psychopathology — The science dealing with the causes and development of mental disorders. Psychological malfunctioning, as in mental disorder.

Psychosis — A major mental disorder in which the personality is very seriously disorganized and contact with reality is impaired.

Psychosomatic — Pertaining to the mind-body relationship.

Psychotic — Of or having the nature of a psychosis; having a psychosis — a person who has a psychosis.

Psychotic killer — A person, whose psychosis drives him to kill.

Pubic — Pertaining to the pubes (anterior pelvic bones).

Pugilistic attitude — Position the body assumes in fire deaths. Coagulation of the muscle due to heat causes contraction of muscle fibers with resultant flexion of the limbs.

Pulmonary — Pertaining to the lungs.

Pulmonary embolism — The closure of the pulmonary artery or one of its branches by an embolus.

Pulmonary infarction — An area of necrosis in lung tissue, produced by sudden arrest of circulation in a vessel.

Purge fluid — Decomposition fluid which drains from the mouth or nose. Sometimes mistaken as blood and head trauma.

Purines — Basic chemicals of life. As in DNA molecule. Adenine (A) and guanine (G).

Putrefaction — Decomposition of soft tissues by bacteria and fermentation and enzymes. After death, the bacterial flora of the gastrointestinal tract invades the vascular system, spreading throughout the body, producing putrefaction.

Pyrimidines — Basic chemicals of life. As in DNA molecule. Thymine (T) and cytosine (C).

Queen — Gay slang. A term used to describe effeminate or queer male homosexuals. Usually combined with other words such as "drag queen," etc.

Queer — A homosexual, usually refers to a male.

Queer queers — In gay slang, deviants.

Quickie — In gay slang, a hasty sex act between strangers.

Rancid — Having a musty, rank taste or smell.

Renal — Relating to the kidneys.

Reproductive system — The male and female gonads, associated ducts and glands, and the external genitalia that function in the procreation of offspring. In women these include the ovaries, fallopian tubes, uterus, vagina, clitoris, and vulva. In men these include the testes, epididymis, vas deferens, seminal vesicles, ejaculatory duct, prostate, and penis.

Respiration — The act or function of breathing.

Respiratory tract — The complex of organs and structures that performs the pulmonary ventilation of the body and the exchange of oxygen and carbon dioxide between the ambient air and the blood circulating through the lungs.

Restriction endonuclease — Enzyme that "cuts" the DNA molecules at specific locations.

Resuscitation — To revive, as in drownings or electrical shock.

rDNA — Recombinant DNA. rDNA technology in which a molecule of DNA is cloned or synthesized.

Retardation — Delay or hindrance.

RFLP — Restriction Fragment Length Polymorphisms.

Rigor mortis — A rigidity or stiffening of the muscular tissue and joints of the body after death due to the disappearance of adenosine triphosphate (ATP) from muscle.

Ritual — Any practice or pattern of behavior repeated in a precise manner.

Ritualism — Adherence to or insistence on ritual.

Rough trade — In gay slang, extra tough, masculine type males, who pretend to be straight but play the insertor role in homosexual sex.

Sacro- — Combining form denoting relationship to the sacrum, the large, triangular bone at the dorsal part of the pelvis.

Sadism — Getting sexual pleasure from dominating, mistreating, or hurting one's partner. Obtaining sexual gratification from inflicting physical or psychological pain on another.

Sadomasochistic acts — Sexual relations in which one partner purposely hurts the other physically, or abuses and humiliates the other, or both, with both partners becoming sexually aroused by these activities. Example: a sexual sadist, who dominates and abuses a consenting sexual masochist.

Safe sex — Sexual acts that avoid an exchange of or contact with the partner's sperm, vaginal fluid, saliva, or blood.

Sarcoma — Malignant tumor; cancer.

Schizophrenia — A major mental disorder of unknown cause typically characterized by separation between thought processes and the emotions; a distortion of reality accompanied by delusions and hallucinations; a fragmentation of the personality, motor disturbances, bizarre behavior, etc. often with no loss of basic intellectual functions.

Schizophrenic — Of or having schizophrenia; a person who is schizophrenic.

Sclera — The white of the eye, a tough membrane.

Sclerosis — Induration or hardening of tissue.

Self-rescue mechanism — The object (knife, key) or method (pressure point change) utilized by the victim to alleviate the effects of the physiological mechanism.

Semen — Thick, whitish secretion of the reproductive organs in the male.

Senile — Pertaining to or characteristic of old age, i.e., the physical or mental deterioration.

Septicemia — Systematic infection in which pathogens (microorganisms capable of producing disease) are present in the bloodstream having spread from an infection in any part of the body.

Serial murder — Three or more separate murders with an emotional cooling-off period, which may consist of days, weeks, or months, between the homicides. *Note:* This was the FBI's definition in *Crime Classification Manual* and *Sexual Homicide Patterns and Motives.*

Serial murder — Two or more separate murders where an individual, acting alone or with another, commits two or more homicides over a period of time, with time breaks between each murder event. *Note:* Author's definition which reflects a homicide detective's perception of serial murder events.

Serology — The science dealing with the properties and actions of serums, e.g., blood analysis.

Sexual masochism — Getting pleasure from being humiliated, bound, beaten, or otherwise made to suffer for sexual arousal. (Considered chronic.)

Sexual sadism — The infliction of physical or psychological pain on another person in order to achieve sexual excitement. (Considered a chronic and progressive disorder.)

Shrimping — Shrimping is a disgusting action in which one homosexual, who has engaged in anal intercourse with another then "sucks out" the ejaculate from the recipients anal cavity.

SIDS (Sudden Infant Death Syndrome) — Crib death as characterized by the sudden, unexpected death of an apparently healthy infant.

Signature — The signature aspect of a violent criminal offender is a unique and integral part of the offender's *behavior*. This signature component refers to the psychodynamics, which are the mental and emotional processes underlying human behavior and its motivations.

Signature — (legal definition) "Where evidence of a separate crime is used to establish the identity of the accused; more is required than merely proving the repeated commission of crimes of the same class. Generally, the device used to commit the crime, or the manner in which the crime was committed, must be so distinctive as to indicate a modus operandi or to act as a signature of the accused.

Slave — In S & M sex. The submissive, passive, or insertee partner.

Smothering — Asphyxia due to mechanical obstruction or occlusion of the external airways, e.g., mouth and nose.

Sororicide — The act of murdering one's own sister.

Southern blotting — Process by which the DNA fragments separated during electrophoresis are transferred from the wobbly surface of the agarose gel onto a sheet of nylon membrane.

Spasm — Sudden, violent, involuntary contraction of a muscle or group of muscles.

Sperm — A combining form meaning seed. The male germ cell (spermatozoon) found in semen, which penetrates the ovum, or egg of the female.

Spree murder — The murder of more than one person at two or more locations during a single event without any cooling-off period.

Sputum — Matter ejected from the mouth; saliva and mucus. This substance contains DNA.

Stab wounds — Caused by relatively sharp pointed instruments such as knives, screwdrivers, ice picks, daggers, scissors, or pieces of glass. These wounds are deeper than they are wide, with possible damage to vital organs beneath the skin and bone, and internal bleeding with little or no external blood.

Staging — Staging a scene occurs when the perpetrator purposely alters the crime scene to mislead the authorities or redirect the investigation.

Sternum — The breastbone.

Still birth — A fetus at least 28 weeks old, born dead.

Stippling — Also referred to as Tattooing, which are pinpoint hemorrhages due to the discharge of burning powder against the skin.

Strangulation — Any abnormal constriction of the throat, causing a suspension of breathing.

Straight — In gay slang, a heterosexual person.

Stroke — (Cerebrovascular accident.) A sudden or severe attack, with rupture of the blood vessels of the brain.

Subdural — Under the dura matter, or between the dura and arachnoid membranes covering the brain, as in subdural hematoma.

Subdural hematoma — The most common lethal injury associated with head trauma. Bleeding, almost always from injury, between the inside of the skull and the dura which covers the brain. This accumulation of blood produces pressure on the brain.

Suffocation — The failure of oxygen to reach the blood. This can occur through entrapment, smothering, choking, mechanical asphyxia combined with smothering, or through suffocating gases.

Superior — Indicates direction toward the head end or upper part of the body. Hence, the lungs are superior to the liver.

Suspension point — That location from which the victim has suspended himself.

Survival interval — The period of time between the infliction of injury and the actual death.

Tache noire — It is an artifact of the drying eye after death, consisting of a brown to black band of discolored sclera where the eyes are partly open and exposed to the air.

Tachycardia — An abnormally fast heartbeat.

Tarsus — The instep proper of the foot with its seven bones.

Tea room — In gay slang; a public place, usually a toilet, where homosexual males meet for "quickie" sex, generally fellatio.

Tea room trade — Those who take part in sex acts in tea rooms.

Telephone scatologia — A sexual attraction to making obscene telephone calls (lewdness).

Tetanus — An acute potentially fatal infection of the central nervous system caused by bacteria which release a powerful toxin.

Thermo- — Combining form denoting relationship to heat.

Thoracic cavity — This is the portion of the ventral cavity above the diaphragm which contains two pleural cavities that contain the two lungs; the pericardial cavity, which contains the heart; and the mediastinal or interpleural cavity, which contains everything located in the thoracic cavity other than the heart and lungs, e.g., trachea, bronchi, esophagus, etc.

Thorax — Chest. A bony-cartilaginous cage containing and protecting the heart, the lungs, and their major blood vessels.

Thrombo- — Combining form denoting relationship to clot.

Thrombosis — Blood clotting inside the blood vessels often in leg veins.

Tibia — The inner and large bone of the leg below the knee.

Tissue — An aggregation of cells united in the performance of a particular function.

Top man — The "fister" who inserts his hand into the anal cavity of the "bottom" man.

Torso — The trunk of the body without the head or extremities.

Toxic — Poisonous.

Toxicologist — An expert in the knowledge and detection of poisons.

Toxicology — The scientific study of poisons, their detection, their effects, and methods of treatment for conditions they produce.

Trachea — Commonly referred to as the windpipe. It is a nearly cylindric tube of cartilage and membrane that extends from the larynx to the bronchi. It conveys air to the lungs.

Tracheotomy — An incision into the trachea, below the larynx to gain access to the airway below the point of blockage.

Transvestism — Cross dressing by heterosexual males for the purpose of sexual excitement. (Ranges from solitary wearing of female clothes to extensive involvement in a transvestitic subculture.)

Trauma — A physical injury caused by violent or disruptive action, or by the introduction into the body of a toxic substance.

Traumatic asphyxia — Occurs when a large weight falls onto or presses down on an individual's chest or upper abdomen, making respiration impossible.

Tremor — An involuntary trembling or quivering.

Triage — *Military medicine* — A classification of casualties of war and other disasters according to the gravity of injuries, urgency of treatment, and place for treatment. A process in which a group of patients is sorted according to their need for care, the kind of illness or injury, the severity of the problem, and the facilities available govern the process. *Disaster Medicine* — A process in which a large number of patients is sorted so that care can be concentrated on those who are likely to survive.

Tricking — In gay slang, cruising; seeking quickie sex with strangers.

Triple homicide — The murder of three victims during one event at one location.

Umbilical — Pertaining to the umbilicus (navel).

Unconscious — Being unaware of the surrounding environment; unresponsive to any stimuli; comatose.

Uremia — Presence of urinary materials in the blood. Could indicate renal failure.

Urinary tract — All organs and ducts involved in the secretion and elimination of urine from the body. These include the kidneys, ureters, and bladder.

Urophilia — A sexual attraction to urine.

Urolangia — A sexual desire to consume urine.

Vagina — The part of the female genitalia that forms a canal from the orifice through the vestibule to the uterine cervix.

Vascular — Pertaining to a blood vessel.

Vein — A vessel which conveys the blood to or towards the heart.

Vena cava — Superior main vein draining the abdominal and pelvic viscera and the lower extremities.

Ventricle — One of the two lower cavities of the heart.

Viscera — The internal organs enclosed within a body cavity, primarily the abdominal organs.

Visceral peritoneum — One of two portions of the largest serous membrane in the body. The free surface of the visceral peritoneum is a smooth layer of mesothelium exuding a serous fluid that lubricates the viscera and allows them to glide freely against the wall of the abdominal cavity or over each other. The attached surface of the membrane is connected to the viscera and the abdominal wall by subserous fascia.

Vulva — The external genitalia of the woman. It includes the mons pubis, the labia majora, the labia minora, the vestibule of the vagina, and the vestibular glands.

VI-CAP (Violent Criminal Apprehension Program) — A system designed to collect, collate, and analyze all aspects of an investigation.

Victimology — Pedigree such as sex, age, height, weight, etc. The essential information about the victim, such as family, friends, and acquaintances, education, employment, residence, neighborhood, etc. This also includes the background information on the lifestyle of the victim. Was this person a low, moderate, or high risk victim?

VNTRs (Variable Number of Tandem Repeats) — Polymorphic DNA regions known to repeat themselves over and over which are unique to an individual.

Voyeurism — Repetitive looking at unsuspecting people, who are either naked, in the act of disrobing, or engaging in sexual activity. "The Peeping Tom."

Water sports — In gay slang, urination by one sex partner on the other.

Zoophilia — Use of animals for sexual arousal. (Includes intercourse with animals as well as training the animal to lick or rub the human partner.) This sexual disorder is also commonly referred to as *bestiality*.

Index